the Indian Mind

Essentials of Indian Philosophy and Culture

Charles A. Moore, editor
With the assistance of Aldyth V. Morris

AN EAST-WEST CENTER BOOK
Published for the East-West Center
by The University Press of Hawaii

FIRST EDITION 1967, 1968
PAPERBACK 1968, 1978

ISBN 0-8248-0076-1
LIBRARY OF CONGRESS CATALOG CARD NUMBER 66-24012
MANUFACTURED IN THE UNITED STATES OF AMERICA

Gavean

THE INDIAN MIND:
ESSENTIALS OF INDIAN PHILOSOPHY AND CULTURE

how the outsider learns p. 9
w. feeling of superiority pp 9-10
p 139 the scientist as of
YOGA view of
scientist p. 137
their over scientific 139-140

THE EAST-WEST CENTER—officially known as the Center for Cultural and Technical Interchange Between East and West—is a national educational institution established in Hawaii by the U.S. Congress in 1960 to promote better relations and understanding between the United States and the nations of Asia and the Pacific through cooperative study, training, and research. The Center is administered by a public, nonprofit corporation whose international Board of Governors consists of distinguished scholars, business leaders, and public servants.

Each year more than 1,500 men and women from many nations and cultures participate in Center programs that seek cooperative solutions to problems of mutual consequence to East and West. Working with the Center's multidisciplinary and multicultural staff, participants include visiting scholars and researchers; leaders and professionals from the academic, government, and business communities; and graduate degree students, most of whom are enrolled at the University of Hawaii. For each Center participant from the United States, two participants are sought from the Asian and Pacific area.

Center programs are conducted by institutes addressing problems of communication, culture learning, environment and policy, population, and resource systems. A limited number of "open" grants are available to degree scholars and research fellows whose academic interests are not encompassed by institute programs.

The U.S. Congress provides basic funding for Center programs and a variety of awards to participants. Because of the cooperative nature of Center programs, financial support and cost-sharing are also provided by Asian and Pacific governments, regional agencies, private enterprise and foundations. The Center is on land adjacent to and provided by the University of Hawaii.

East-West Center Books are published by The University Press of Hawaii to further the Center's aims and programs.

CHARLES A. MOORE, for many years senior professor of philosophy at the University of Hawaii, died in April, 1967, before his work on this volume was completed. Long an advocate of the promotion of greater tolerance between people of the East and West, Professor Moore was known internationally as the innovator and driving force behind the East-West Philosophers' Conferences, held in Honolulu in 1939, 1949, 1959, and 1964, which brought together some of the leading thinkers of the Orient and the Occident to exchange ideas and to enhance their understanding of other traditions. His career as teacher, conference director, editor, and author was distinguished in its breadth and effectiveness in achieving East-West rapport.

Every effort has been made by those involved in finishing this book to maintain the high standards set by Professor Moore. A special recognition is owing to Professors S. K. Saksena, Walter H. Maurer, and Kenneth K. Inada for their help in preparing this posthumous work.

WINFIELD E. NAGLEY
University of Hawaii
Department of Philosophy
Chairman

Preface

THIS VOLUME presents a middle-of-the-road explanation of the fundamentals of the Indian mind as expressed in its great philosophies, religions, and social thought and practices. The essays which comprise this symposium, since they are technical in themselves and written by experts in their special areas, will meet the needs of the technical scholar. But they will also meet the needs of the educated reader generally, as well as the technical expert, because over-technical considerations have not been stressed except where necessary to avoid the sacrifice of fundamental accuracy and technical integrity.

The chapters in this volume are papers presented at the four East-West Philosophers' Conferences held at the University of Hawaii in 1939, 1949, 1959, and 1964.* Not all of the papers presented at these conferences are included here because of technical and publication limitations; among the papers not presented are a few of the extremely technical papers in specialized areas.

While this is essentially a reprint volume in the sense that all the papers have already been published, they have been re-edited by the editor and by the authors of the papers, except in the case of the paper by Professor Takakusu, who died in 1945.

* These volumes are: *Philosophy—East and West* (Princeton: Princeton University Press, 1944); *Essays in East-West Philosophy* (Honolulu: University of Hawaii Press, 1951); *Philosophy and Culture—East and West* (Honolulu: University of Hawaii Press, 1962); *The Status of the Individual in East and West* (Honolulu: University of Hawaii Press, 1967).

The order in which the papers are published herein does not correspond with the order of their presentation at the conferences, but has been determined in a more systematic manner regardless of the date of the original presentation. Following this Preface, there will be a more technical and yet general introductory treatment of the Indian view of the status and nature of philosophy as such. This is followed by papers dealing, in succession, with metaphysical matters; epistemological concerns; problems within the areas of ethical and social philosophy; special and particular problems in more restricted areas, such as religion, legal and political philosophy, etc.; and, finally, the status of the individual in Indian thought and culture. This last section of the book is a concentrated examination of this particular problem, which has always been of major importance in philosophy, in both East and West, but is of special importance in the contemporary world and therefore requires full and detailed consideration—partly also because it is the basis of so much misunderstanding all around.

One of the basic principles of the conferences at which these papers were presented was that the descriptions (and evaluations) of the various philosophical and cultural traditions of East and West should be entrusted to representatives of those traditions, so that listeners and readers could most closely approach the ideal of understanding other traditions as the people of those traditions understand themselves. This principle has been followed in this volume—as in the volume on China, and will be followed in the volume on Japan in this series—but, for special reasons, there are two exceptions here.

In order to do full justice to the very complicated developments of Buddhist philosophy, which originated in India, despite its less significant status there than the various systems and thinkers within the Hindu tradition, it was considered highly advisable to include here a paper which deals essentially with early Buddhism—the paper by Dr. G. P. Malalasekera—and a paper which deals with the more technical developments of Buddhist philosophy and with Buddhism in its specific relationship to the Hindu systems—the paper by Dr. Junjirō Takakusu. These authors are not Indians, to be sure, but the subject-matter with which their chapters deal is of basic importance in an over-all consideration of Indian philosophy, and it is felt that their chapters add materially to the soundness of the volume as a whole.

It is possible that this generally wise policy of having each

Asian tradition described by personal representatives rather than by "outside" scholars has led to somewhat more idealized presentations than might have been given by more "objective" Western experts. On the other hand, there is the thought that it is really more accurate to see a people—or even an individual person—in its best light, in terms of its ideals, because these do essentially constitute the mind of the given tradition. (The law of the land as written out in somewhat ideal form in constitutions and formal statute law, for example, is often said to constitute or express the real mind or character of a people or nation, but that does not mean that there are no lawbreakers.) There is also the thought that "outside" experts are sometimes even more biased—one way or the other—than the representatives who, as the ones here do, combine personal knowledge of the tradition and sound scholarship.

Partly because of the technicalities of the subject-matter and the languages involved, and partly because the volume is a symposium to which outstanding scholars have contributed, the matter of detailed editing has been somewhat more difficult than it would have been in a different kind of volume. While general consistency and uniformity of basic style have been achieved, there are some variations in several aspects of style, because of the occasional adoption of common usage rather than of complete technical accuracy and also because some of the authors themselves strongly preferred different styles—and the editor respected these preferences.

For the careful—and possibly critical—reader it may be helpful to call attention to a few of the perhaps unusual styles involved, and some of the variations.

In general, hyphenation has been used abundantly, the purpose being to provide greater ease of reading on the part of the non-Indian reader who is not familiar with the technical and sometimes very long words, expressions, titles, etc., in Sanskrit and Pali (Pāli). This may irritate the technical expert, but it will unquestionably help the uninitiated and the general reader. At times, with admitted inconsistency, some expressions and titles are not hyphenated—because they are so well known.

Capitalization is always a problem in articles and books written by Asian authors, because most of them strongly prefer a much greater use of capitals than Westerners would in the same situation. In general, capitalization has been kept to something of a minimum, but not always, and in these latter cases the retention of capitals was out of respect for the wishes of the author or because of fear of distortion of technical meanings that might have resulted from "outside" editing. (Reference is made especially to Professor Takakusu's chapter.) The matter of capitalization of some technical terms is of genuine significance. Generally speaking, in these cases the capital is used to refer to ultimates or metaphysical principles or realities, whereas the lower case is used for the empirical aspect referred to by the same term—as especially illustrated by *Nīrvaṇa* and *nīrvaṇa*—sometimes very difficult to distinguish—and *Ātman* and *ātman.*

Common usage is occasionally employed, usually involving the inconsistent use of the stem form and the nominative case—as, e.g., *karma* (not *karman*), *ātman* (not *ātma*), and *parva* (not *parvan*). Among other cases of following common usage are Ārya Samāj for Ārya Samāja and Brāhmo Samāj for Brāhma Samāja and *sannyāsin* for *saṁnyāsin.* In some cases, technically accurate terms are used rather than those in common Western usage: e.g., *brāhmaṇa,* not *brāhmin; yogī,* not *yogi.* The words "*buddha*hood" and "*buddha*-nature" have been used because they are technically more accurate than the capitalized form.

Different authors not only sometimes strongly prefer different styles of editing, but also frequently prefer different translations of technical terms, and it would be presumptuous, even dangerous, for any editor to force such a learned group of authors into any single pattern of English equivalents. This policy seemed the better part of wisdom. Sometimes authors have used different styles of documentation—at no sacrifice of clarity.

In all the editing, clarity and ease of reading were the goals sought, provided that this attempt did not sacrifice technical accuracy. This seemed to be the only feasible guiding principle to follow.

One of the discrepancies in some of the papers is that between the use of Sanskrit terms and Pāli (and, in fact, of "Pāli" and "Pali") terms—sometimes almost indiscriminately. Some changes have been made, but, again, because of the editor's deferring to the wishes of the authors there are still some discrepencies in this area. A few specific examples should probably be mentioned: Brāhmaṇas, to refer to the texts, which are parts of the Vedas; Brāhmaṇism, to refer to the philosophy or religion which is based upon those texts; and *brāhmaṇa,* to refer to the highest order in society, the priest or teacher. Both *yogī* (Hindi) and *yogin* (Sanskrit) are used rather indiscriminately.

For the convenience of Western readers, plurals have been formed by simply adding a terminal "s" to words in Sanskrit, although this practice is not followed in the chapter by Dr. Malalasekera, where most of the terms are in Pāli. (The reader is referred to an editor's note at the beginning of that chapter which will explain the special style used there and the reason for that style.)

Appreciation is hereby expressed by the editor to Professor Kenneth K. Inada, Professor Walter H. Maurer, and Professor S. K. Saksena for their significant assistance in connection with the editing of these papers, and in connection with the transliteration of Sanskrit and Pāli terminology. Appreciation is also expressed to Princeton University Press for permission to re-publish, not completely but in large part, the paper by Professor Junjirō Takakusu, which was originally included in *Philosophy—East and West,* published by Princeton University Press in 1944.

Charles A. Moore

Honolulu
April 29, 1966

Contents

Charles A. Moore	Introduction: The Comprehensive Indian Mind 1
S. K. Saksena	Relation of Philosophical Theories to the Practical Affairs of Men 19
P. T. Raju	Metaphysical Theories in Indian Philosophy 41
Gunapala Piyasena Malalasekera	Some Aspects of Reality as Taught by Theravāda Buddhism 66
Junjirō Takakusu	Buddhism as a Philosophy of "Thusness" 86
Dhirendra Mohan Datta	Epistemological Methods in Indian Philosophy 118
Swami Nikhilananda	Concentration and Meditation as Methods in Indian Philosophy 136
T. M. P. Mahadevan	Social, Ethical, and Spiritual Values in Indian Philosophy 152
S. Radhakrishnan	The Indian Approach to the Religious Problem 173
P. T. Raju	Religion and Spiritual Values in Indian Thought 183

Contents (continued)

Swami Nikhilananda	The Realistic Aspect of Indian Spirituality 216
C. P. Ramaswami Aiyar	The Philosophical Basis of Indian Legal and Social Systems 248
Dhirendra Mohan Datta	Some Philosophical Aspects of Indian Political, Legal, and Economic Thought 267
Kalidas Bhattacharyya	The Status of the Individual in Indian Metaphysics 299
T. R. V. Murti	The World and the Individual in Indian Religious Thought 320
Surama Dasgupta	The Individual in Indian Ethics 341
S. K. Saksena	The Individual in Social Thought and Practice in India 359
Tara Chand	The Individual in the Legal and Political Thought and Institutions of India 374
P. T. Raju	Extracted from "Indian Epistemology and the World and the Individual" 394
	Who's Who 397
	Index 405

THE INDIAN MIND:
ESSENTIALS OF INDIAN PHILOSOPHY AND CULTURE

CHARLES A. MOORE

Introduction: The Comprehensive Indian Mind

THERE ARE two vital reasons for studying—and understanding—Indian philosophy: first (for the general reader), in order to understand the country and its people, which is impossible in the case of India without understanding its basic philosophies because the intimacy of philosophy and life in India is so fundamental to the whole Indian point of view; and, second (for those concerned with philosophy), in order to enlarge the scope of philosophy and to broaden the horizons of philosophers by attending seriously to the important contributions that Indian philosophy and philosophers have made to the totality of philosophical knowledge and wisdom —or at least can make if the rest of the world will attend seriously to those contributions. Intense and comprehensive study and fundamental knowledge are necessary for the realization of these two goals, or, in fact, for the realization of either of them.

Fact and fancy, truth and error, understanding and misunderstandings, truths and half-truths, a tendency toward extremes and exaggerations, admiration and ridicule, devotion and what seems at times to be malicious distortion—all these abound, and frequently in a very confusing mixture, whenever one thinks of the great subcontinent of India with its 450 million people, its recent unbelievable plight in terms of starvation, disease, and ignorance, and the plethora of ideas and practices that seem to isolate her from all other peoples and thought-traditions of the world, East and West. Confusion, misunderstanding and misrepresentation, bewilderment, and almost universal neglect—especially by Western thinkers—have been much in evidence for centuries with reference to this greatest democratic nation in the Eastern world. We are not thinking here of those Westerners (and some Easterners) who have seen in India the source of fulfillment of their own selfish search for power and riches. These people have not known India; they have merely used her—mis-used her. Not only that, but they have apparently attempted to destroy the spirit and even the "mind" of this great people. But that spirit has refused to die, and now, at long last, is reasserting itself. India is determined, now that she has survived almost unendurable tragedies by maintaining her indomitable spirit, to revive its proud tradition and heritage and to take the place among the great peoples of the world which it once held—in culture, in learning, in religion, and in philosophy.

It should not be necessary today even to remind the peoples of the West—and, in fact, some of the people of Asia as well—that India must be understood—correctly and profoundly. Superficial knowledge will not do. Looking for the exotic will not do. Finding in her mind and spirit either the antithesis, or merely the complementary, to the West will not do. These will not do because they prevent genuine understanding and lead only to distortion and falsification—and mystification.

We must concern ourselves—and we are concerned here—with the mind of India in its richness, its variety, its profundity, its depth and its heights in the broad area of philosophy, and with the powerful molding force which the philosophies of the Indian tradition have exerted on the many-sided culture of the Indian people throughout the ages—with great difficulty during the dark era of foreign domination, to be sure, but even then. The philosophies, the religions, and the basic cultural patterns of India have been so deeply engrained in the minds and lives of the Indian people that not even virtual slavery—politically and economically—could prevail against them. It is these deep-seated ideas and ideals that are the mind of India, and it is these that we must understand in their fullest significance—both in themselves and, in many cases, for the world at large.

Understanding is a very complicated matter. Genuine understanding must be comprehensive, and comprehensive understanding must include a knowledge of all the fundamental aspects of the mind of the people in question. Philosophy is the major medium of understanding, both because it is concerned deliberately and perhaps uniquely with the fundamental ideas, ideals, and attitudes of a people, and also because philosophy alone attempts to see the total picture and thus includes in its purview all the major aspects of the life of a people.

But there is still more to understanding and to the search for understanding, and here we face attitudes which the authors of the learned essays in this volume cannot provide but can only encourage. Reference is made to the indispensable need, on the part of the "outsider," for a genuine desire to understand. Open-mindedness, cordiality to alien ideas and ideals, and actual determination are necessary ingredients of the attempt to understand an alien people, if that attempt is to be successful. One must at least attempt to see the other people as those people see themselves—and the chapters in this volume are in accord with this maxim. We cannot truly understand as long as we merely stand outside and look at; we must try to think and feel with. Above all, we cannot understand another people if we look through biased eyes, with the conviction of superiority, or with the assumption that what is different from our own must therefore be worthless. These are difficulties that attend any attempt to understand any "other" people, but they call for special notice here since they probably apply to India with unusual force because of the many wrong impressions and distortions that are such a part of the Western "understanding" of India. It is going to be especially difficult to rid our minds of these strong misconceptions—but it must be done. There is no other way.

One final point: understanding does not involve approval or acceptance: it may lead to exactly the opposite. However, we must understand each other in any case, and, in the case now at hand, India, the conviction is here expressed that genuine understanding will promote genuine friendship and harmony and a much greater meeting of the minds than ever seemed possible. In philosophy, India is more like the West, basically, than is any other Asian tradition, and India is more like the West than it is like any other Asian tradition, at least in one man's opinion. Furthermore, there is nothing inscrutable or non-understandable in or about Indian philosophy, either because of the substance of Indian philosophy itself or because of the allegedly "totally different" bias of Western philosophy and the Western mind. But these points of similarity—and the writings in which they can be found—are almost completely ignored or very largely overshadowed by the excessive attention given to the early, to the religious, and to the "different" aspects of the Indian tradition as a whole. This is tragic, but true, and it perpetuates clichés, oversimplifications, and actual distortions. And these, in turn, prevent genuine understanding and also prevent the West's taking Indian philosophy seriously. That is why it is tragic.

It is not easy to understand such a complex mind, civilization, culture, tradition as India presents. There are probably some common denominators of mind and practice which may be said to constitute the essence of the Indian mind in certain respects. But there is such great complexity and variety in practically every field —even in the languages which are causing so much practical difficulty for the government at the present time—that we must not even seek simplicity or even attempt to determine fundamental ideas and ideals without realizing from the start that these fundamentals express themselves in a great variety of ways and have changed greatly over the long span of some 4,000 years of a high level of thought and civilization. While we must seek out the basic pattern of thought and culture, we must realize, too, that the Indian mind is made up of more varieties of religion, more philosophies, and a greater complex of cultural practices than most any other major civilization in the world.

Philosophy is our business in this volume, and it may be well to quote an outstanding authority on Indian philosophy, Professor Mysore Hiriyanna, who says, "A striking characteristic of Indian thought is its richness and variety. There is practically no shade of speculation which it does not include."[1] The longer one studies Indian philosophy, the more one realizes the accuracy of that observation.

It may be appropriate to offer literal and factual justification and clarification of this contention concerning the richness and variety of Indian thought. Let us look, then, if ever so briefly, at the major movements and periods of Indian philosophy—in its broad meaning—and at the major systems and some of the subsystems which constitute the Indian philosophical tradition—and realize, too, that there is ever so much more to the Indian thought-tradition as a whole, including a vast literature of strictly religious thought as such which is not to be—but has long been—confused with the philosophical thought with which we are concerned here.

There is, first, the Vedic period—usually dated approximately between 2500 and 6000 B.C. This is the period in which the foundations of Indian philosophy were established, in which the two fundamental aspects of Indian thought and life, the two *dharmas*, the active and the contemplative, were developed and formulated, in the Vedas and Upaniṣads, respectively. To some, these may not be strictly philosophical—by others, they are mistakenly accepted as the whole or the essence of Indian philosophy—but, in any case, they do establish many of the basic ideas to which much of Indian philosophy conforms, and they contain a degree of authoritativeness, to such an extent that orthodox Hindu philosophy is defined in terms of its acceptance of the Veda—in the fuller sense of the word, including the Vedas and Upaniṣads. True, one would have some difficulty recognizing the ideas of the Vedas and the Upaniṣads in most of the technical philosophies of India, but this authoritativeness prevails even today as a basic part of the tradition. In the Vedas, we start with a very multitudinous polytheism, with all its appendages, and develop gradually to monotheism and, finally, to what might be called a strictly philosophical monism resulting unquestionably from the innate intellectual curiosity of the Indian mind[2]—but the activism of this part of the Indian tradition is never sacrificed. In the Upaniṣads, the usual interpretation calls for either a complete break with the Vedas, certainly in the sense of a replacement of activism by contemplation and inner searching for the real, or what might be called a speculative continuation of the problem of the One which the Vedas speculatively envisaged at its final stage, as it were. But, now—in the Upaniṣads—this speculation takes place primarily in terms of the experiences of the great mystical seers, and their basic method is mystical experience or intuition, with the minimizing of the role of reason as the, or even a, final method of reaching the ultimate truth.

The second period is the Epic period, dated approximately from 500 or 600 B.C. to A.D. 200. This is often considered either not a strictly philosophical period at all or, at most, a semi-philosophical era, because much of its product is primarily descriptive of the social customs and practices of the Hindu people, and the laying down of laws for life in accord with the Hindu philosophical and religious convictions. This is the period of the two great epics, the *Mahābhārata* and the *Rāmāyaṇa*, which are a combination of history, mythology, and religio-philosophical thought. It is the period of the Dharma-śāstras, the treatises on social philosophy and law, with their emphasis on social welfare, on the three basic values of morality, pleasure, and material welfare—with little or no real concern for ultimate emancipation (*mokṣa*)—and on social stability in line with the caste system. During this period are developed the several and various political philosophies of India, including the very realistic *Artha-śāstra* of Kauṭilya, which would vie well with the most realistic political philosophies the world has ever known. It is the period that produces the *Bhagavad-gītā,* what has been called the living bible of Hinduism to this day. In other words, this is the period in which the basic ideas of original Hinduism are applied to life in its many facets, thus, as it were, completing the picture of Hinduism and giving it complete control over the mind and the actions of the Indian people.

But this period is much more than that. It is probably the most productive, the most creative, the most open-minded, and the richest period of Indian thought in terms of the great variety of specific ideas and theories developed, and also in terms of the rise of actual major philosophical systems, and many minor systems or viewpoints (skepticism, irrationalism, etc.), which were later crowded out of significant existence. These major systems are the non-Hindu, the heterodox, but still Indian, systems of Cārvāka materialism, Jaina realism, dualism, pluralism, and relativism, and the four (or more) major schools of Buddhism, which embrace, *depending greatly upon interpretation:* pluralism *and* monism; realism, relativism, "nihilism," idealism, *and,* according to some, even Absolutism, *but,* to others, intrinsic anti-Absolutism; unmetaphysical (or even anti-metaphysical "ethicism" *and* transcendental metaphysics; the scientific method and empiricism *and* even "analysis" *and* faith *and* mysticism; intuitionism *and* rational and logical methods and methodology—and perhaps *especially* the denial of all "labels" or "isms," or schools or specific viewpoints.[3] All of these arose in opposition to the Hindu tradition in their basic philosophies, though they retain some of the traditional manners of living and, except for Cārvāka, something of the same ultimate goal of life, ultimate emancipation from the sufferings and evils of life itself.

As S. Radhakrishnan, the great contemporary Indian philosopher and statesman, has said:

> . . . it [the Epic period] was an age keenly alive to intellectual interest, a period of immense philosophic activity and many-sided development. We cannot adequately describe the complex inspiration of the times. The people were labouring with the contradictions felt in the things without and the mind within. It was an age full of strange anomalies and contrasts. With the intellectual fervour and moral seriousness were also found united

a lack of mental balance and restraint of passion. It was the era of th Cārvākas as well as the Buddhists. Sorcery and science, scepticism and faith, license and asceticism were found commingled. When the surging energies of life assert their rights, it is not unnatural that many yield to unbridled imagination. Despite all this, the very complexity of thought and tendency helped to enlarge life. By its emphasis on the right of free inquiry the intellectual stir of the age weakened the power of traditional authority and promoted the cause of truth. Doubt was no longer looked upon as dangerous.[4]

The third period is the Sūtra period. This begins, according to some interpreters, one or two or three centuries before the Christian era and lasts into the early centuries of the Christian era. During this period the great Six Systems of Hindu philosophy were formulated, systematized, and written in terms of the original basic texts of these great—and greatly varying—schools of philosophy. The tendency among contemporary Hindus is to synthesize these systems as six aspects of one unified point of view or perspective, but the basic differences among them, the sometimes vigorous arguments between the competing systems, and the fact that each system continued for centuries in its philosophical identity would tend to question that interpretation. Here are represented, in these major systems, the logical realism and pluralism and theism of the Nyāya (the School of Logic); the atomic realism and theism of the Vaiśeṣika; the evolutionary dualism—and pluralism—of non-theistic Sāṁkhya; the meditative method—and dualism and pluralism—of theistic (?) Yoga; the practical and ethical—and what might be called linguistic—emphases of the realistic, pluralistic, and anti-theistic Mīmāṁsā, which is the systematization and rationalization of the Vedas; and the systematization and rationalization—of several varieties—of the Absolutism and monism of the Upaniṣads in the Vedānta. There is no philosophical uniformity among these systems except their alleged acceptance of the authoritativeness of the Vedas and the literal, but somewhat questionable, unanimous search for *mokṣa,* emancipation. These systems vary in practically all philosophical essentials except for their common agreement in the belief in the soul—as well as matter, by the way, except in the Vedānta, and in later periods even there.

This basic period is followed by what has been called the Scholastic period or the period of commentaries or commentators. This period endures even to today. It consists of an almost unbe-

uity of development of all the systems, heterodox and ot the Cārvāka. But it also produces, in the guise of ries, a wide variety of points of view—at times, tems—that reveal the originality and creativity of possessed by these commentators, many of whom only in what might be called the polite sense of . Many of the major problems of philosophy are originated and developed during this period, sometimes on the basis of development of the ideas suggested in the Sūtras, sometimes going far beyond anything even suggested there. Also, among these commentators one finds, even within the same school, a sometimes unbelievable variety of points of view, as even in the Vedānta, where the range reaches from realistic pluralism to illusionistic monism and practically all varieties in between, and yet all are called Vedānta. Vedānta is decidedly not to be identified with Śaṁkara, as is usually the case, especially in the West.

Thus, in the vast changes that took place from the rise of religio-philosophical thought in the Vedas to the present day—with the omission of a dark age when Indian philosophy suffered practical oblivion while India was dominated by outsiders—Professor Hiriyanna's contention that "practically no shade of speculation" is not included in Indian philosophy and that a striking characteristic of of Indian thought is its richness and variety is amply justified and "documented."

Most of India's philosophical systems and her most significant ideals and concepts originated centuries ago, and they suffered a dark age far darker than the alleged dark age of the West. However, this does not mean that our concern is merely of antiquarian interest. Instead, we are concerned with India's philosophies because they still provide the guiding principles of the life of the people and also because there are very significant ideas and concepts there—no matter how old they are—to which the rest of the world may well turn for new insights and perhaps deeper wisdom.

Nor is it true that the philosophies of India, the great systems and the important concepts, have little relevance for the India of today. It is a major mistake to think that the philosophies of India belong to the past and that the "new India" is simply the India of today or a wholly different India molded by contemporary, chiefly Western, influences. The striking developments and changes that are taking place in contemporary India are not out of accord with the Indian tradition—though they are out of accord with some of the distortions and excesses of that tradition which arose primarily under the stress and pressure of unfortunate events and almost unbearable circumstances. The apparent incompatibility of traditional India and contemporary India is basically only that—apparent. Long-range, comprehensive, and deep understanding will correct such an impression. There are changes, yes, but changes within the essential context of the many-sided and inclusive tradition that is India.

To illustrate this: India's strong contemporary interest in raising the standard of living—and its emphasis on practical activities and on practical idealism—is as intrinsic to the Indian mind and culture and tradition as it could be to any people on earth. Let it be said, too, as will be explained in one of the chapters of this volume, that the deep spirituality which is so dominant in India, both in thought and in life, is not so otherworldly, or escapist, or pessimistic, or negative that it finds violation of the spiritual in the abundant life. There is no incompatibility here.

As said before, philosophy is our concern here. But philosophy is not merely an (or *the*) indispensable medium of understanding and of knowing a people or a culture. Philosophy is also—and more basically, of course—the search for knowledge, for truth, for wisdom. In this respect, India provides the basis for a potential philosophical renaissance, if only the rest of the world, especially the West, will search out the new insights, the new intuitions, the new attitudes and methods which might well at least supplement if not replace or correct—and at least enlarge—the restricted perspective of the Western mind. As Professor George P. Conger has said, ". . . the question here is not so much whether Indian can contribute, as whether the West is ready to receive."[5] As in the case of understanding, so in the case of learning *from* another people, some remarkable attitudes and attributes are indispensable—and very difficult to adopt. Perhaps it is even more important in learning from than in learning about another people that the "outsider" must come with the spirit of humility, with open-mindedness and cordiality, and with both willingness and determination to learn—or learning will be impossible, or superficial, or possibly self-defeating.

Of course, every tradition is biased in its own favor—and India is not free of this limitation, either. The West, however, generally speaking, suffers not only from such a conviction of the superiority of its own attitudes and methods in the sphere of philosophy (and all learning)—not to mention the influence here of certain basic Indian ideas which "make no sense" to the Western mind—but has the additional disadvantage, at least as of now, of being largely ignorant of the tremendous riches of the almost inexhaustible Indian philosophical mind. What the West knows about India (and China, too, in fact) is largely only one aspect (and frequently a misleading aspect) of the very complex total picture. In India's case (as well as in China's), it is a knowledge which is historically, philosophically, and even simply intelligently so one-sided as to make genuine and comprehensive understanding impossible, and also to deny even the existence, let alone the significance, of many of the greatest philosophical concepts the mind of India has discovered. Oversimplification and distortion are the inevitable results of such partial and historically false—early—and consequently significantly superficial knowledge of the great philosophical panorama of the Indian intellect, as well as of the Indian spirit. The Vedas, the Upaniṣads, and the *Bhagavad-gītā,* along with one extreme Vedāntin, Śaṁkara, have dominated the Western "picture" of Indian philosophy, but they do not constitute anything like the whole or the essence or even, as so often contended, the basic spirit of the almost infinite variety of philosophical concepts, methods, and attitudes that make up the Indian philosophical tradition. Instead, if these are taken as the whole or the essence—as, to be sure, even many Indians would have us believe—there would be a narrowness and a limitation of significant philosophy that would well warrant the neglect that Western philosophers have shown toward that tradition. But they are not the whole.

The all but utterly ignored rational and logical, the systematic and analytical, character of the Indian philosophical tradition—for all its intuition and mysticism and Absolutism—is just one, but a vital, illustration in this connection, and is an undeniable fact, one which makes India much closer to the West in its philosophizing than any other philosophical tradition in the whole of Asia. And, yet, this is almost completely ignored by the West and is frequently played down by those who are so seriously concerned with bringing the great spirituality of India to the allegedly unspiritual West. Another significant illustration of this same general point is the very much greater emphasis on theism rather than Absolutism in the Indian spiritual tradition as a whole. Another is the tendency to emphasize the spiritual alone and in its purity, in isolation from all relationships with the non-spiritual, although this is an extreme interpretation, and is not by any means unanimously held either by the major systems and thinkers or by modern interpreters. For example, Sri Aurobindo says, ". . . spirituality itself does not flourish on earth in a vacuum,"[6] and many would agree with him as reflecting the transcendent and immanent character of the spiritual, as in the West. This is not to deny the significance of intuition and spiritual realization in Indian thought—and religious zeal in Indian life—but it is to deny their exclusive significance and to emphasize, as strongly as possible, the keen and profound intellectual and logical attitudes which are of the essence of Indian philosophy as such, as sharply contrasted with China and Japan. There are many such affinities, many compatibilities, many actually common or shared ideas, ideals, and attitudes—as well as methods. On this latter point, by the way, reference is made to the fact that the use of intuition in India is not a source of incompatibility with Western philosophy when one recognizes the actual use and significance of intuition in Western philosophy, and the fact that intuition is actually of strictly limited use in Indian philosophy.

However, there are many differing approaches to reality, to life, to truth, and to philosophy itself in the Indian tradition which, at least in emphasis or relatively speaking, are or should be of exciting significance for the inquiring mind of the Western philosopher. They should also be of profound significance to any philosopher who is seeking the traditional and basic—and unique—goal of philosophy. That goal is the total truth about reality as a whole, and that goal, and our attempt to achieve it, which *is* the true work of philosophy, requires, as Professor B.A.G. Fuller said a long time ago, "an observation and study of the data presented by all . . . aspects [of life, experience, and the universe itself]."[7] This means that philosophers need, indeed must have, the insights, the suggestions, the experiences, and the different approaches of all philosophers everywhere. Otherwise, as is so commonly the case in the West, philosophers will be limited to their own narrow perspective, to their own biased methods, and, believe it or not, to most of the traditional Western ideas, ideals, attitudes, and methods. And to be so limited is not to be a philosopher.

It might be in order to cite some specific philosophical concepts, attitudes, and methods which are widely considered to constitute the philosophical mind of India or its essence. These points might well serve at least as guidelines. It might also be valuable to suggest a list of specific "new" ideas that India offers to the philosophical world out of its unique experiences, ideas which, possibly, are different only in emphasis but at least in that respect and to that extent. But, since any such attempt is sure to be questionable, in that no such list can be compiled with complete accuracy and comprehensiveness without so many exceptions as to make it almost meaningless (and certainly not *characteristic*), it could be wiser, rather, to suggest that the reader judge for himself from the various—and varying—presentations to follow what he considers to be the essence of the Indian philosophical perspective and of the Indian mind and also what he considers to be—to repeat—"new" or "different" ideas, ideals, attitudes, and methods which might well be worthy of serious and unbiased consideration in the interest of philosophy and truth itself.

However, although it is dangerous and questionable to do so, it is deemed justifiable and even helpful to cite here those philosophical principles, attitudes, and methods which are, by rather common agreement, considered characteristic of Indian philosophy as a whole. Prior to this listing, however, it is advisable to repeat the caveat to the effect that a substantial case could be made against every one of these characterizations as genuinely characteristic of Indian philosophy and certainly as characteristic of it in its entirety, since every one violates or ignores the multiplicity and complexity of the Indian mind in these specific areas. (In the list that follows, some of the doubtful aspects of these "characteristics" will be cited so as to offset the danger of oversimplification of the complex Indian attitudes.) Be that as it may, it is usually contended—by Indians—that the following are the important principles of Indian thought.

1) A universal and primary concern for, and almost a preoccupation with, matters of spiritual significance—in practically every sense of the word, in all its many ramifications, and perhaps especially with reference to the ultimate spiritual goal of man. (There is not *too much* of an argument against this "characteristic"—except for the entire extensive literature of the Dharma-śāstras and the Artha-śāstras, in which social welfare is the primary concern and man's ultimate destiny is of little or no serious concern—and the possibility that *mokṣa,* emancipation, may not in fact be of supreme or even genuinely significant concern to the authors of at least four of the Darśanas.)

1a) Belief in a soul or self or spiritual principle—except in materialistic Cārvāka and, some contend, except, too, in Buddhism, with its doctrine of *an-ātman,* no self, but this latter contention is clearly a too literal and unacceptable interpretation.
1b) Belief—throughout all of Hinduism, Buddhism, and Jainism—in the doctrine of *karma* (the principle of ethical cause and effect, or justice) and rebirth.
1c) Monism and/or Absolutism—well-known but extremely questionable *characterizations* unless we indulge in extreme and excessive limitation of view and ignore very much, if not most, of the comprehensive philosophical literature that demands inclusion. (There is no Absolutism or monism in any of the Six Systems of Hinduism except the Vedānta, in any school of Buddhism, in Jainism, or in the Cārvāka.)
1d) Basic concern with ultimates—the metaphysical perspective, or the "sense for the infinite," as it has been called—and only secondary concern for the empirical perspective.

2) An emphasis upon the close relationship of philosophy and life, in the sense that, as Radhakrishnan says, "Every doctrine has been turned into a passionate conviction, stirring the hearts of man and quickening his breath and completely transforming his nature,"[8] and also in the sense that philosophy and its activities are not to be undertaken as an "intellectual exercise," or motivated by a desire for truth for its own sake, but must be lived, such that, in common agreement, the truth must not only be known but also *"realized."* As Professor W. H. Sheldon once said—in paraphrase—in the West we want to *know* the truth, in India they want to *be* the truth.[9] Even this could be challenged in most of the six systems.

3) The recognition of the validity and necessity of intuition (and also the wisdom of certain authoritative texts) to supplement the rational and intellectual pursuit of truth—and the corollary, or preliminary conviction, that reason is distinctly limited in scope and finality, although it is the basic method of philosophy in India as elsewhere. (Intuition, authority, and criticisms of reason are all overemphasized both in Indian and in Western descriptions, generally.)

4) Another interesting corollary of this perspective is the view that truth is achieved by the whole man, not by his intellect alone—in sharp contrast with the Western perspective and accepted procedure. Dr. S. K. Saksena, in his paper here, states the case succinctly:

What, then, should be the source of philosophical knowledge? It is neither sense, nor reason, nor intuition, but the whole of the man. Philosophy is the reaction of the whole of man to the whole of reality. Man is a spirit, an integral whole, consisting of his body, mind, intellect, passion, and will, and his reason alone can no more exhaust him than his animality can encompass his reason. Reason or rational thought is only a part of his being. Purely rational knowledge, therefore, militates against and contradicts the affirmations of the rest of a man's being and receives acceptance only by a corner of his self.[10]

(This view is not followed unanimously among Indian philosophers, however.)

5) The synthetic attitude in both philosophy and religion, such that practically all views are deemed partly true or true from their particular points of view, and such that the ultimate truth is a synthesis of the many partial truths discovered by different approaches to truth and reality. (An aspect or application of this synthetic point of view is in a sense violated in this volume and in the volumes for which the papers were originally written.) In India—at least, this is the general contention—metaphysics, religion, ethics, social philosophy, political philosophy, psychology, and methodology and epistemology are all parts of one substantial and total problem; they are all therefore essentially interrelated. They are not to be isolated or separated even for the sake of specialized study, for that violates their unity in life and in reality. Yet, here we find these problems, in the large, treated separately. The style followed at the conferences and in the volumes in this series was chosen deliberately, however, for the sake of clarity for non-Indian students and readers—and also to avoid too general presentations and the consequent overlapping of material and the repetition that would be practically inevitable. (Even this synthetic interpretation might be an exaggeration, because there are several distinctly separate areas of philosophical literature dealing with different aspects of the total problem—such as, for example, Dharma-śāstras, Artha-śāstras, Mokṣa-śāstras, etc.)

6) Consequent upon this synthetic perspective—whether we apply it to reality, to truth, to the pursuit of truth, to the approaches to spiritual fulfillment (religions or ways of living[11]), or in one's perspective toward the values of life, India is proud of her over-all attitude of intellectual, philosophical,[12] religious, ethical, and practical tolerance (although, as said earlier, there is reason to question

the degree of tolerance among the great systems and thinkers in the long and complex Indian philosophical tradition).

7) Deep concern with the inner man and with the introspective approach to truth, as contrasted with outer things and values, such that, generally speaking, the transformation of the inner self is primary, while concern with changing or controlling the outer world is distinctly secondary, if significant at all. Put another way: to be, not to do, is of supreme importance.

8) An emphasis upon—and great achievements in—the area of psychology in its broadest and most comprehensive sense. India seems to be characterized by the conviction that the mind (and even what the West calls "soul") is transcended by the "self" and that the ranges of man's psychic capacities are "infinitely" greater than in any other philosophical tradition, both in its highest reaches and in its subtlest potentialities.

9) Allegedly, although there are strong arguments against it in its exclusive accuracy and especially in metaphysics, there is a general consensus among Indians that their tradition is characterized by idealism in one sense or another, and certainly in the areas of ethics, political thought, and social thought and practices. (*In fact,* the Indian attitude is really a synthesis of idealism and realism, of spirituality and cultural, intellectual, and worldly values.)

10) Ethics, though considered of absolute importance in life, is, nevertheless, considered to be subordinate to spiritual realization, as only a means thereto, and to be completely transcended once the ultimate goal of spiritual fulfillment or emancipation has been achieved.

11) There are certain common ethical principles that seem to dominate the life of India, essentially non-hurt (sometimes called non-violence), restraint and self-control, non-attachment, and what, for lack of a better word, may be called charity.[13]

12) While the values of social life—morality, pleasure, and material welfare, in general—are accepted as significant in the empirical realm, these are all subordinate to and, at most, instrumental toward the ultimate spiritual goal of emancipation (*mokṣa*), or spiritual realization.

13) A common social philosophy, including the three empirical values previously mentioned—morality, pleasure, and material wel-

fare—and, in its proper sense, some form of classification of the members of society in the interest of the welfare of society as a whole and as a means of spiritual progress through the performance of one's social and moral duties.

14) The need for moral purification as a necessary preliminary to the process of knowledge—fitting the Upaniṣadic (and Vedāntic) teaching that without moral purity one cannot even enter upon the search for spiritual truth.[14]

15) An interesting somewhat related "theory" is that, once one has entered upon the search for knowledge, the process consists of three steps, namely, hearing it from a teacher (or reading it in an authoritative text), reasoning about it, and then meditating upon the conclusions so reached until those conclusions become, not mere academic knowledge, but the kind of soul-stirring convictions mentioned before which alone are capable of transforming one's nature in accordance with truth.[15]

16) Some—though not all—Indians point to the belief in what is called "initial pessimism"—life is suffering—and "ultimate optimism" consisting essentially in the achievability of spiritual emancipation from the sufferings and spiritual inadequacies of life.[16]

17) *Yoga,* in one or more of its many forms, is considered essential to the pursuit of spiritual truth and the freedom of the spirit, since it provides the mental concentration necessary for freedom from all distractions which encourage or even produce ignorance and prevent the achievement of spiritual purity, truth, and fulfillment.

These major principles and attitudes may or may not be characteristic of Indian thought as a whole in any essential and exclusive sense, but, as emphases, (1) they must be understood if we would understand the Indian people, whose life and thought they guide, and (2) they are unquestionably at least basic tendencies in Indian philosophy and life—and, consequently, it is within these areas of emphasis in which India is the "expert" that she can contribute most to the total picture which is philosophy. And they may serve as useful guidelines for study—cordial or critical—of the many interesting and exciting, sometimes difficult, sometimes disturbing, ideas presented in the informative and provocative chapters to follow.

Notes

1. *Outlines of Indian Philosophy* (New York: The Macmillan Co., 1932), p. 16.
2. *Ṛg-veda,* X.129.
3. This is the major point of the Mādhyamika system, and the Buddha also denied adherence to any one doctrine. (*Majjhima-nikāya,* 1.483–488.)
4. *Indian Philosophy* (London: George Allen & Unwin Ltd.; rev. ed.; New York: The Macmillan Co., 1929), Vol. I, p. 272.
5. "An Outline of Indian Philosophy," in Charles A. Moore, ed., *Philosophy—East and West* (Princeton: Princeton University Press, 1944), p. 23.
6. Sri Aurobindo, *The Renaissance in India* (3rd ed.; Calcutta: Arya Publishing House, 1946), p. 11.
7. The full quotation is "a reflective and reasoned attempt to infer the character and content of the universe, taken in its entirety and as a single whole, from an observation and study of the data presented by all its aspects." *A History of Philosophy* (rev. ed.; New York: Henry Holt and Co., 1945), p. 1.
8. See S. Radhakrishnan and Charles A. Moore, eds., *A Source Book in Indian Philosophy* (Princeton: Princeton University Press, 1957), pages xxiii–xxiv. See also S. Radhakrishnan, *Indian Philosophy, op. cit.,* pp. 26–27.
9. See "Main Contrasts Between Eastern and Western Philosophy," in Charles A. Moore, ed., *Essays in East-West Philosophy* (Honolulu: University of Hawaii Press, 1951), pp. 288–297.
10. See his chapter here, "Relation of Philosophical Theories to the Practical Affairs of Men," at p. 25.
11. See examples: *Ṛg-veda,* I.164.46; *Bhagavad-gītā,* IV.11; IX.23; VII.21.
12. A. B. Dhruva, "Presidential Address," in *Proceedings of the Second Session of the Indian Philosophical Congress* (Benares: Philosophical Association, 1926), pp. 1–26; also S. Radhakrishnan, in S. Radhakrishnan and Charles A. Moore, eds., *A Source Book in Indian Philosophy,* p. xxv. See also S. Radhakrishnan *The Heart of Hindusthan* (Madras: G. A. Natesan and Co., n.d.), pp. 135–137.
13. In this connection it might be good to cite Surendranath Dasgupta, who says that the fundamental points of agreement among Indian systems, excepting the Cārvāka, are: the theory of *karma* and re-birth, the doctrine of *mukti* or emancipation, the doctrine of the existence of the soul—Buddhism excepted—a pessimistic attitude toward the world and an optimistic faith in the end and certain general principles of ethical conduct such as control of passions, non-injury, etc. See *A*

History of Indian Philosophy (Cambridge: Cambridge University Press, 1922), Vol. I, pp. 71–77.

14. *Taittirīya Upaniṣad,* II. vii; *Bṛhadāraṇyaka-upaniṣad,* IV.iv. 23; *Kaṭha upaniṣad,* II.24; and *Brahma-sūtra-bhāṣya,* I.i.1.
15. *Bṛhadāraṇyaka-upaniṣad,* II.iv.5.
16. Satischandra Chatterjee and Dhirendra Mohan Datta, *An Introduction to Indian Philosophy* (3rd ed. rev.; Calcutta: University of Calcutta, 1948), p. 16.

S. K. SAKSENA

Relation of Philosophical Theories to the Practical Affairs of Men

I. *Practical Affairs and Religious and Scientific Beliefs*

BEFORE WE inquire into the relation which philosophical theories as a class may have with the practical affairs of men, it may be worth while to ask what it is which generally guides and determines our conduct. The answer would probably be that it is by our beliefs, religious or secular, that we generally live and act. As the *Gītā* says, "Man is of the nature of his faith: what his faith is, that, verily, he is."[1] These beliefs may or may not be true, but, in the last analysis, it is these true or false beliefs which determine our conduct. While beliefs may be acquired in different ways, their chief sources are either the religious experiences of mankind, transmitted through theological knowledge, or the scientific knowledge of the day. These two sources of our beliefs cover almost the entire range of man's activities.

1. INADEQUACY OF SCIENTIFIC AND RELIGIOUS BELIEFS

While the above two sources of our beliefs, religious and scientific, are practically the originators and modifiers of our conduct, there is a philosophical unsatisfactoriness about each of them. Scientific beliefs, which have the merit of objective validity, have, nevertheless, a grave defect inasmuch as they do not refer to man's deepest questions regarding the meaning and purpose of life, nor do they deal with questions of valuation and worth. Scientific knowledge, which deals with the true, ignores the good, and theological beliefs, which have the opposite merit of being practically useful by virtue of their relevance to the practical aspirations of man, have the great defect of lacking objective validity and rational appeal. In other words, while theological beliefs are practical without being always true, scientific beliefs are true without being practical in the sense that, while they ascertain for us the relationship of ends and means, they do not tell us anything of the ends to be pursued by us. The realization that scientific knowledge and beliefs are not adequate since they do not touch even the fringe of man's problems of life and that the religious beliefs of one individual are of no use to another unless they percolate through his own rational thinking leaves the thoughtful man with a sense of vacuity and despair in the matter of the proper guidance of his life. While some have made their peace with science or religion, a large number are unable to do so. Nor is the mental vacuum thus created intellectually tolerable. The question, therefore, is: Can we find in philosophy grounds for satisfactory belief-formations and, if so, with what success and how?

2. CONTEMPORARY SKEPTICISM ABOUT PHILOSOPHICAL KNOWLEDGE

It is obvious that the task of philosophy is more difficult than that of science or religion; for, while philosophy is unable to accept the unproven beliefs of theology, it is not aided by science in its quest for the good and the valuable. Nevertheless, philosophical knowledge, if it is to fill the gap, must combine the virtues of both science and theology without the defects of either. It must furnish us with beliefs about the real nature of the world and the meaning and the purpose of our lives which will not only possess the subjective certainty of the religious consciousness but also the objective validity of the sciences.

A glance at the balance sheet of contemporary philosophical performance with special reference to its practical utility will no doubt show that philosophy has drifted far away from life and that men no longer look to it for guidance in their daily lives. Deprived of both the subjective certainty of theological knowledge and of the objective certainty of the sciences, philosophical knowledge today seems to have surrendered its role of providing men with a fundamental or basic system of beliefs to live by, leaving men to be guided in their practical affairs by such beliefs as they may chance to have or not have. Russell, in this respect the most pessimistic of modern philosophers, says, "To teach how to live without certainty . . . is perhaps the chief thing that philosophy, in our age, can still do for those who study it."[2] This opinion of philosophy and philosophical knowledge by one of the greatest philosophers of the age reveals the extent to which the modern mind has despaired of philosophical knowledge. One hopes, however, that things are not as bad as that, and that Russell himself will admit that he is not without at least the belief that he should continue to behave and conduct himself according to his reason and conscience and be free to propagate his views irrespective of their consequences to himself and to his reputation. This itself is a rational belief which has not only guided Russell but also influenced a large number of his admirers and followers in this age of philosophic uncertainty. It may be true that our philosophers have so far made only a negative contribution to our systems of beliefs, yet our philosophical beliefs or our lack of them is all that we as rational human beings have to depend upon and live by. In being contemptuous of the role of philosophy in the determination of our beliefs we should not forget that the contempt applies, not to philosophical knowledge as such, but only to particular varieties of it which, by and large, may deserve the condemnation.

But there is no denying the fact that philosophy has today stepped down from its high calling and has been progressively withdrawing itself from the practical problems of life and straying into both a rarified realm and a stultifying method in which, by the very nature of the case, no conviction or faith is either possible or even desired. To quote Russell again, "The philosophy, therefore, which is to be genuinely inspired by the scientific spirit must deal with somewhat dry and abstract matters, and must not hope to find an answer to the practical problems of life."[3] It appears that philosophy, now by ridiculing religion, now by imitating science, and in turn being ridiculed by both, has itself become ridiculous without being able to correct the faults of either. From ancient times to modern and from modern times to contemporary, the journey of philosophical reflection in the West has been, broadly speaking, from the "practical" to the "useless" and from the "useless" to the "nonsensical." This may appear as too unsympathetic an oversimplification, but the element of truth in it cannot be denied. There is little relation today between philosophical theories and the practical affairs of our lives, and such little relation as might seem to exist between political or economic theories, which have practical results, and their philosophical background is due more to the demands of respectability and propaganda than to any logical relation between them and their philosophical counterpart.

3. NEED OF PHILOSOPHICAL KNOWLEDGE IN THE FORMATION OF BELIEFS

That philosophy should have come to such a predicament in the matter of providing certainties and conviction for the guidance of our daily life is regrettable and is certainly not in keeping with its best traditions throughout its history of more than twenty-five centuries. Philosophical reflection throughout the world was the earliest and has been the boldest effort of man's reason and thought to face the mystery and complexity of life and existence without passion or attachment to any particular creed or dogma. So long as man has an awakened mind whose energies and function exceed his biological and economic needs, there is no relinquishing of philosophical pursuit, which by nature must seek the real behind the apparent and not rest until man has attained to the highest truth and the destiny of his being. Man was, thus, never without a metaphysics or a philosophy about the world, or without some ideals for his life. The choice, for man, as Bradley said, has never been between metaphysics and no metaphysics but only between a good metaphysics and a bad metaphysics. He must have a metaphysics of life, of right and wrong, and must, from time to time, undertake a revision of this conceptual or ideal framework with which he necessarily thinks about the world. This drawing or the re-drawing, in the world of his thought, of the map of total reality and integrating it with his life, this ideational framework of the highest possible generality, which constitutes his metaphysics, is inevitable for him, for a thoughtful life is not possible without it. This is not to say that philosophical theories are merely inevitable and do not have their uses. The metaphysics of Hegel had a great effect on historical studies in the nineteenth century, and the philosophical ideas of the Renaissance were responsible for the political and social revolutions of the eighteenth century. Nor have scientific discoveries and religious faiths been without inspiration from metaphysical insights and presuppositions, as is evident from the lives of a number of scientists and saints. If the purpose and function of philosophy are understood properly, there is no reason philosophical theories and knowledge should lack conviction and fail to supply men with a rational and comprehensive system of beliefs for a better guidance of their lives. In decrying philosophy and philosophical knowledge we are prone to forget that we are criticizing thought by thought. If it is through our philosophical reasoning that we are critical of either theological or scientific knowledge, the same philosophical reasoning should also provide us with positive beliefs for the guidance of our lives. The alternative to philosophical beliefs is either to allow the practical affairs of our lives to be governed by the haphazard uncertainties of a skeptical age or to surrender our minds to men who have "power without knowledge" (the politicians), "faith without truth" (the theologians), or "knowledge without purpose" (the scientists). This would be a sign more of our mental regression than of our intellectual advancement.

There is still another reason philosophy should not only step in but also be specially fitted for the task of belief-formation for the guidance of life. Looking at the map of world thought today, we find that the unity of man and his being is torn into numerous separate, disintegrated, and autonomous fields of reason and passion, persuasion and coercion, simultaneously pulling him in mutually contradictory directions without at the same time supplying him with any integrated view of life or of the ends to be pursued. While knowledge in these separate fields is constantly expanding, man's belief and conviction are progressively receding, because truth and knowledge gained in one direction are negated and contradicted by knowledge acquired in another. Lack of unified knowledge weakens belief, and it is philosophical knowledge alone which can stand for comprehensive and unified knowledge. The need of a synoptic vision was never so imperative and urgent as it is today, for, if, in these days of increasing multiplicity of fields of narrower and narrower specialization, philosophy also is to succumb to the temptation of specialization, all hope of a unitary knowledge is lost. Philosophy or philosophical reflection, which is distinctive of man's nature, should, therefore, be resurrected from its present plight and helped to undertake and perform its proper function.

4. CAUSES OF GENERAL SKEPTICISM ABOUT PHILOSOPHICAL KNOWLEDGE

What is wrong with philosophy and philosophical knowledge today? Why does it fail to supply us with a system of beliefs to live by?

a. Lack of a Synoptic Outlook

The first cause of skepticism about our philosophical pursuit is that philosophy, in its subject-matter, has tended toward an increasing alienation from life. To be a philosopher is no longer to know anything about the business of life. It is always the other fellow, the non-philosopher, who is the expert in the art of living and who must take care of the philosopher's own problems of life. Knowing and living have become two separate compartments of life, so that a philosopher can live in a world of ideas and knowledge, while others inhabit a world of life quite unknown to the philosopher. Philosophy no longer means a philosophy of life but only analysis and clarification of terms and propositions which have no reference to beliefs or conduct. Its outlook is no longer either practical or synoptic. The tragedy of the theoretical or the abstract philosopher is that the end sought by him is often lost in the activity itself. Seeking itself comes to occupy the place of finding. His aim is no longer truth but knowing. This is a paradoxical situation but not quite unlike an abstract philosophic search. Little wonder, therefore, that philosophical pursuit should be devoid of conviction and should inspire philosophers like the Buddha to declare: "The Tathāgata, O Vaccha, is free from all theories."[4] Knowledge for the sake of knowledge has never been the proper function of the philosophical pursuit. As the *Gītā* says, "Insight into the *end* of the knowledge of Truth—this is declared to be true knowledge, and all that is different from it is non-knowledge."[5] The true philosophical endeavor is not just one theoretical discipline among others but one supreme quest for the whole of truth, which is both known and lived in the soul of man. A philosophy which is not of life and practiced in life is barren. How can our philosophical theories inspire us to belief and action when we find philosophers who have made great intellectual strides in their theoretical fields suffer in their own daily lives from almost all the failings of common man? Philosophy should be no more divorced from life by reason of its rational approach than religion should be bereft of philosophical truth by virtue of its insistence on the life of realization.

b. Lack of an Integralist Epistemology

The other and more important reason which makes philosophical knowledge and theories unconvincing is what Charles Morris[6] has called its intellectual excessiveness and what I should prefer to call its intellectual exclusiveness. Here I refer to a fundamental defect in the epistemological belief of philosophy itself. It has been too long assumed by philosophers that man has one or more cognitive faculties, such as sense, reason, and intuition, each of which separately and appropriate to its own nature and function reveals to him knowledge of the outside and the inside world. He has senses for external objects, reason for objects not to be grasped by the senses, and intuition for the reality not to be grasped by either. The common assumption about philosophical knowledge has been that reason alone is its cognitive apparatus and that whatever belongs to or comes through the realm of the heart, feeling, will, or vision is an unphilosophical blend. This analytic view of man and his epistemological tools is a great blunder, for, in reality, the integral cognitive-affective-conative man is never so completely abstracted as to be all sense without reason, or all reason without feeling. Even if he were so abstracted for a moment, we have no reason for thinking that the truth or the reality revealed to him by any one of his absolutely pure and exclusive apertures is for that reason more reliable. In fact, it should be less trustworthy. While the atomistic view of the faculties of man stands condemned by modern psychology, it is not a little surprising that this analytic division of man still persists in philosophical discussions. What, then, should be the source of philosophical knowledge? It is neither sense, nor reason, nor intuition, but the whole of the man. Philosophy is the reaction of the whole of man to the whole of reality. Man is a spirit, an integral whole, consisting of his body, mind, intellect, passion, and will, and his reason alone can no more exhaust him than his animality can encompass his reason. Reason or rational thought is only a part of his being. Purely rational knowledge, therefore, militates against and contradicts the affirmations of the rest of a man's being and receives acceptance only by a corner of his self.

Moreover, to know is to believe in what one knows. It does not make sense to say that one knows something but does not believe in what one knows. What one believes in may not be true, but what one knows has to be believed in so long as that knowledge lasts. That seems to be true of all knowledge except philosophical knowledge. The question should therefore be asked as to why is it that, of all kinds of knowledge, only philosophical knowledge should lack conviction in what is thus known. Is it because of the object of philosophical knowledge or because of the method of philosophical knowledge or because of both? To a certain extent, it can be said that, since philosophical knowledge concerns itself with the ultimate origin and end of the whole of reality and wants to grasp it with man's finite mind, an ultimate skepticism about it is involved in the very nature of the rational situation. This may be so, but still there is no reason to suppose that in the ultimate scheme of things this rational skepticism is not overcome in an integral vision (*darśana*) within the philosophical endeavor itself, an integral vision such as was attempted by the earlier philosophies of India and the West.

The real misfortune of philosophy seems to have been that philosophers themselves have misunderstood the function and the purpose of philosophy. They have generally agreed in calling it a rational and intellectual search, and, today, when the results of this rational quest are before us in the form of philosophical skepticism and lack of any reliable system of philosophical beliefs, it is time for us to re-examine our premises and presuppositions and begin anew. As Montague says, "The problem of validating belief is intimately associated with the problem of ascertaining the sources of belief."[7] Philosophy, therefore, should not be conceived of as merely a rational or intellectual quest, but a spiritual endeavor of the whole of a man's being. It is only of a knowledge born in the whole of a man's being that we can say that to know is to believe. In this way alone does a man acquire the additional authority and power to speak with the language of reality and fact. As the Yoga says: "Truth-bearing is, then, knowledge."[8] In the last analysis, it is this psychologically integral quality of Indian epistemology which gives it an intuitive (or, technically, the "*sākṣāt-kāra*") attitude, which Northrop calls an aesthetic sense and which it has never lost. According to Northrop, this integralist standpoint, or the necessity of a unified epistemic correlation between the subjective and the objective, has remained a characteristic, not only of the Hindu, the Buddhist, and the Jaina theories of philosophy and knowledge, but also of all Western philosophies which have not been purely speculative or concerned with abstractions alone.[9]

Closely related to the integralist theory of knowledge is the question of the immediacy of knowledge. When philosophical knowledge is not grounded in the direct experience of the whole of a man's being, it lacks a necessary union of the knower and the known. The distance that is thus produced by the separation of the two and the inevitable mediation of thought which thinks out the things are also not conducive to conviction and belief. In revealed or self-discovered knowledge the knower feels an identity with what he knows as true without any shadow of doubt. The case of scientific knowledge is similar. I do not think anyone will seriously maintain that scientific knowledge is either mediate knowledge or purely deduction. If scientific knowledge is a blend of many elements such as imagination, hypothesis, generalization, verification, and perception, it is at least the most integrated knowledge that we know of in which the knower is so related to what is known that knowledge is equal to faith in what is thus known. And theological and scientific knowledge, which are responsible for our beliefs, have this characteristic in common: they both carry instant conviction. This may also be due to the fact that, in both cases, there is neither mediation between the knowing subject and the known reality nor any dialectics of thought making doubt possible. In this they both differ from philosophical knowledge, in which what is thus known can be doubted at the very moment of knowing and the truth of knowledge depends either on another knowledge or on something outside of knowledge, and hence fails to carry conviction. Knowledge as we understand it today can hardly yield conviction or certainty about what is thus known unless a state of identity of the subjective and the objective is reached at some stage of our endeavor in knowing. As Bradley admits, "Ideal or perfect knowledge would not be anything like what we mean by knowledge, it would be more like feeling, in that the distinction between the knower and the known would have disappeared altogether, and knowledge would no longer be mediated through the forms of language or through our limited categories of thought. It would be direct and intuitive, an identification of mind with reality. . . . For this reason . . . the use of these mystical phrases is the necessary consequence of following an entirely rational line of argument, as a kind of last chapter, of metaphysical systems."[10] Purely rational and mediate theories of knowledge have lacked conviction, and hence only such philosophical theories as have been based on some form of the unitary theory of knowledge, such as that of the mystic, the *ṣūfī*, and the Upaniṣads, have carried conviction and certainty and have been successful in influencing conduct. Also, pure thought, by its very nature, works in dialectics: it creates and develops its own antithesis. It is one of the characteristics of rational and discursive thinking that it is at the same time aware of the other side also, and therefore an element of doubt is always there in the thinker's mind. No stable convictions can be built on mere dialectics. No true philosopher would ever be sure that there could not be another viewpoint or argument which has escaped him. It is of this kind of partial and unconvincing knowledge that the *Īśa-upaniṣad* speaks:

> *Into blind darkness enter they*
> *That worship ignorance;*
> *Into darkness greater than that, as it were, they*
> *That delight in knowledge.*[11]

It would thus appear that whatever is immediately or intuitively known is believed in, at least for the moment, and, the more the mind of man takes to a discursive, an inferential, and a mediate way of knowing, the more there is skepticism or lack of conviction in what is thus known even at the time of knowing. Belief or conviction and an immediate theory of knowledge seem somehow to be related to each other, as also mediate theories of knowledge and skepticism seem necessarily to go together. For philosophical theories and knowledge to be practical, it is necessary that they should be believed in, and, in order to be believed in, they should have a basis in some form of immediacy.

Knowledge, therefore, before it can lead to action, must be accompanied by a conviction about its truth: knowledge without conviction is practically useless, and man without faith, as the *Gītā* says, perishes: "But the man who is ignorant, who has no faith, who is of a doubting nature, perishes. For the doubting soul [*ātman*] there is neither this world nor the world beyond, nor any happiness."[12]

In addition to the fact that philosophy has not adopted an integralist theory of knowledge, it has barred valid sources of knowledge other than reason or perception, as, for example, the testimony of a reliable person, which exclusion is not justifiable, especially from the point of view of its role of belief-formation. Indian philosophy, besides admitting the two kinds of perceptual knowledge, sensory and non-sensory, acknowledges testimony also as a means of true knowledge. It also subordinates other valid means of knowledge, such as inference, analogy, and others, to the two primary ones of perception and testimony, and perhaps much can be said in support of their being included within the purview of legitimate epistemological sources for philosophical knowledge. Of course, it is possible to say for that reason it is not philosophy, but the point is that to the extent it relies on immediate knowledge philosophy influences man's conduct, and, if this is not to be thought of as philosophy, then whatever is philosophy can neither produce beliefs nor be practical.

Philosophical knowledge and theories will assuredly achieve all that they can—namely, critical acumen, sharpening of wit, even occasional insight—but will ever lack conviction so long as they confine themselves to inferential and ratiocinative knowledge as the only valid knowledge. In other words, philosophy, before it can affect men's conduct, must revise its ideas about the exclusive validity of its accepted sources of knowledge and include once again what it excluded when it became contemporary and purely scientific.

What has been said above about philosophical knowledge does not apply to the validity or the truth of that knowledge but only to its quality of being psychologically believed. What is maintained here is that philosophical knowledge and theories will carry conviction and give man a system of beliefs to live by only when philosophical knowledge stands for knowledge acquired by the whole of a man's self and by no single part of him. The truth-quality of such philosophical knowledge will depend upon the all-round perfection of the integrated being of the knowing self. It follows that, if philosophical knowledge is the result of the whole of the integrated personality of a man, the more perfect the soul of the knower, the purer his mind, senses, reason, and heart, the greater will be the philosophical truth revealed to him. No man will claim to have true knowledge in any sphere if he believes his instruments of cognition to be defective. Similarly, no philosopher can hope to attain the truth except in proportion to the perfection of his soul. Ultimately, therefore, it is the intellectual, the moral, and the spiritual perfection of the man which reveals the perfect truth. The ideal philosopher, therefore, will be the *yogin* (or *yogī*), in the sense of the most integrated and spiritually the most perfected individual.

I have been at pains in this section to clarify two separate but related points, the recognition of both of which is considered important if philosophical knowledge is to be both convincing and true. The first refers to the standpoint and the second to the conviction-value of philosophic knowledge, i.e., a synoptic outlook and an integralist epistemology for the philosophic quest. One reason philosophical knowledge has been open to doubt is found in its too narrow and exclusive epistemology—in its acceptance of only perception and reason (and that, too, in its too obvious and superficial meaning), to the exclusion of other parts of a man's being. It is suggested that sound sources of knowledge other than reason should also be admitted by philosophy in its integral search for total reality. This relates only to the valid sources of knowledge and not to their validity.

The second point deals with the criterion and validity of knowledge. Here it is suggested that the criterion of philosophical knowledge cannot be merely cognitive. For philosophical truths to be valid, the cognized material should have come through perfect receptacles. Philosophy does not seem to recognize the necessity of any moral or spiritual development on the part of its seekers after truth and seems to think that a developed intellect or reason is competent by itself to achieve its objectives. This is open to doubt: an integralist epistemology for the sources of knowledge and an ethical or spiritual perfection for the validity of knowledge seem to be two neglected requirements of the philosophical pursuit without which philosophical knowledge will neither produce conviction nor be true.

II. Relation of Indian Philosophical Theories to Practical Affairs

Indian thinkers of the past left behind some fundamental philosophical beliefs which have not only governed the lives of the Indian people for ages but have not lost much of their hold on men even today. But, before we pass on to these beliefs and see their intimate relation to conduct, we might look at the origin itself of the Indian philosophic endeavor. This is rooted in the indubitable experience of suffering in the affair of living itself as contrasted with the origin of philosophy in the West, which lies in the intellectual possibility of doubting the nature and the existence of anything whatever. This reaction of the whole of a man's being to the experience of suffering is common to almost all the schools of philosophy in India. Philosophical endeavor in India thus began with a practical aim and purpose, which was not merely understanding the why and the wherefore of suffering but an absolute and final elimination of the curse of it all, and of the bondage of the causal chain of desire, and of the attainment of a state of liberation from even the possibility of suffering in this life as well as hereafter. This concept of liberation (*mokṣa*) of men from suffering from all bonds and fears whatever is not only a common *Summum Bonum* of all the different systems of Hindu philosophy, Buddhism, and Jainism, but is also a philosophical concept which is not to be dismissed as merely a theological or religious dogma. The Upaniṣadic philosophers, who were at the same time sages, arrived at this concept by their reflection on the nature of the one and the many, and founded their doctrine of freedom from pain and death—to be more precise, from fear as such (of any sort whatever)—on the truth of the oneness of reality to be realized within their own and irrefutable direct experience. The systems of the Nyāya-Vaiśeṣika, the Sāṁkhya-Yoga, and the various forms of the Vedānta have been led to the same goal of liberation by not being able to accept philosophically the conditioned and empirical existence of man as his true state, which is declared to be that of a state of freedom from all limitations. These systems have differed among themselves by emphasizing one or the other of the three ways for the attainment of *mokṣa*—knowledge, devotion, or action. They also differed concerning the exact nature of the liberated state in terms of its positive or negative character. But what is of significance for us to note here is that all the different schools and systems of philosophy have been occupied with this practical problem of man and with the practical means for its resolution. With all of them, it has not been merely the problem of knowing or of solving an intellectual puzzle but of finding a more satisfactory way of living. Even if all of Indian philosophy had given different answers to the questions of the true nature of man and of the means to its realization, it would have been entitled to the claim of a practical philosophy by virtue of its adherence to the practical problems of man and his life on earth.

It is also significant that, among the different systems of Indian philosophy, tradition should have given the highest place to the Yoga. Patañjali's Yoga, and his school, is through and through a system of psychological discipline, and its being a necessary practical counterpart of the theoretical philosophy of the Sāṁkhya has never been doubted. We do not know of any system of philosophical reflection in which a course of conduct has been classified under philosophy. This shows how theory and practice, or knowledge and conviction, went hand in hand and influenced men's conduct in the past. As Huston Smith has pointed out, India's specialization has been in psychological wisdom as against the natural and the social emphasis of the West and the Chinese, respectively.[13] The Vedānta has quite another kind of peculiarity in this respect but with an identical result. Here, what is primarily claimed is not that any practical discipline is required for the attainment of the highest but that the attainment of true knowledge or the annulment of obstinate and inborn nescience itself constitutes the miracle of the attainment of the highest; for, in reality, nothing is to be attained or approximated except the lifting of the veil of *māyā,* or partial knowledge, something like the claim of modern psychoanalysis in the attainment of freedom from neurosis.[14] Here again, knowledge and action are not separated or even distinguished. The Vedānta came to this conclusion of the unity of theory and practice, knowledge and action, through criticism and analysis of the process of knowledge itself. All knowledge at the empirical level is conceived of as a mixture of true and false knowledge, which is the cause of all striving and activity at that level. Complete and pure knowledge was found to be all there is. Thus, while the Yoga is practical in the psychological sense of the term, the Vedānta is so in a metaphysical sense. By its insistence on the absolute reality of pure and absolute knowledge alone, it reduces all activity to the removal of nescience, or the lack of true knowledge.

The philosophical distinction between the partial reality of this world and the absolute reality of quite another kind of world has had perhaps the most profound and most durable influence on the conduct of men in India. While in all philosophizing a distinction has always been made between the sensory and the ideational, the empirical and the transcendental, or, at least, between appearance and reality, and, while all the scientists and philosophers in all parts of the world have had to start from a distinction of a "this" world and a "that," the distinction has remained practically a dead letter in the conduct of our daily lives. In spite of Plato's "world of ideas," Hegel's "Absolute," Kant's "Transcendental Ego," Husserl's or Hartmann's "Essences," and, even in spite of the "original" or the "neutral stuff" of the realists and their distinction between the primary and the secondary qualities of matter, the practical affairs of men have proceeded as if these theories did not exist. But, in India, it would not be correct to say that this distinction is altogether erased from the daily conduct of men, even today, when philosophy, traditional or living, is not playing the dominant role it played in the past.

That the theory of *māyā* is believed to have altered the outlook and the life of its believers in India is clear from the reproach Indian thought has received from the Western world. That the cause of India's present backwardness, political and economic, should have been put on the shoulders of the philosophical theory of *māyā* is an evidence of the fact that the theory was believed to have been followed in life. The point here is not whether a particular philosophical theory is correct, but only whether it is believed in and guides conduct. We are concerned only with the question as to whether philosophical theories are believed and acted upon and, if so, how?

Again, that the philosophical pursuit was not conceived of as merely an intellectual excellence but was meant to be integrally related to the personality and the life of the philosopher is shown from the Indian doctrine of *adhikāra,* or of the merit and qualifications of the aspirant to philosophical wisdom. One of the repeated strains of Indian philosophical thought is that true knowledge and wisdom can be acquired only by the pure in heart, by one who has already attained the requisite moral virtues and is free from the psychologically and morally undesirable traits of personality and character. He must have controlled certain ignoble emotions and must be free from unworthy motives and desires. Mere mental gifts or intellectual abilities are not enough for the attainment of the highest truth.

> *Not he who has not ceased from bad conduct,*
> *Not he who is not tranquil, not he who is not composed,*
> *Not he who is not of peaceful mind*
> *Can obtain Him by intelligence.*[15]

Indian philosophical literature abounds in its repeated emphasis on this fourfold discipline (*sādhana-catuṣṭaya*) for aspirants to philosophical wisdom.[16]

This blend of virtue and knowledge, of thought and moral practice, may seem to be a distasteful superfluity to the modern mind, which cannot understand the reason things clearly separate could not be treated as separate. But the view that philosophical wisdom should be ethically conditioned should cause no surprise to anyone today, when it is being increasingly realized that the intellectual and the moral cannot be separated in any ideal system of instruction and learning. If this is true of everyday knowledge, how much more true it would seem to hold that, for the realization of the highest truth of reality, adequate moral and spiritual preparation is necessary. After all, what is it to be intelligent or rational? Is it really possible to be intelligent or rational without being moral? If we analyze the behavior of a truly rational man, we are sure to find a number of qualities in him which will prove to be moral. To be rational, for instance, is not to be partisan, or to have prejudices, or to be swayed by passions or self-interest, or to falsify truth, or to have double standards, but it is to stand for truth under all conditions, etc. These are moral qualities. In fact, to be rational is to be moral, and to be completely rational is to be completely moral. The moral and spiritual qualification of a philosopher is, therefore, a condition of his philosophizing properly. Passion or ethical failings cannot but distort the vision of even a philosopher. In fact, what is called intuition is not so much an independent faculty as a purity of the moral being of the knower which itself constitutes enlightenment. As the Upaniṣad says, "Therefore let a *brāhmaṇa* become disgusted with learning and desire to live as a child."[17] It is one of the merits of Indian philosophical thought to have insisted on virtue for knowledge, for it is only thus that knowledge leading to belief and action can be acquired.

The Indian doctrine of *karma,* which is the extension of the universal principle of causation to the realm of the inward as well as the outward life of man, also illustrates the application of philosophical theory to life. The belief that there is no escape from the welcome or the unwelcome effects of our minutest thoughts and deeds has had the most profound effect upon the practical affairs of men in India. It has saved men from temptations and has provided great consolation in their hour of misfortune. Related to this doctrine of *karma,* which provides an Indian with a practical and ready reckoner of the deeds of his life, is the corresponding theory of non-attached living (*niṣkāma-karma*), which is believed to undo what the law of *karma* does. The law of *niṣkāma-karma* is a philosophical antidote to the evil of bondage to the law of *karma.* While the Law of *Karma* binds the doer to the fruits of his deeds, the practice of *niṣkāma-karma* frees him from this thraldom. As is said,

Thus on thee—not otherwise than this is it—
The deed adheres not on the man.[18]

It is one of the characteristics of Indian philosophical thought that corresponding to every law that binds man it discovers a law that liberates him. In the realm of action, if our deeds bind us through their fruits, we can so act as to free ourselves from that chain of causal action and reaction by acting in disregard of that chain. We can act and yet not be attached to any thought of our act's consequences. In *niṣkāma-karma,* action having been started unilaterally and with no thought of its consequences, the fangs, as it were, of the law of action and reaction to touch or hurt us are removed. The non-attached man, who performs actions only because he considers it his duty and not because he has bargained for results, has liberated himself from the chain of action and consequences to himself. It may be interesting to recall here that the same psychology applies to the practice of non-violence, in which it is the violence of the other party which is to be disregarded. The idea is coming to be gradually appreciated in the West, especially through its psychological and sociological studies of the types of personality and leadership, if not in strictly philosophical fields. It is not merely a moral ideal but a philosophical theory arrived at by deep reflection on the psychology of desiring or striving and its effect on the reasoning purity of the knowing mind. The theory of *niṣkāma-karma* is the counterpart in the sphere of action to the theory of the non-attached mind (*niṣkāma-citta*) in the realm of knowledge. A *kāmya* (end-seeking or purposeful) mind, a mind that is infected and tarnished by low personal desires and aspirations, can with difficulty see the truth as it is. The *niṣkāma-karma* can flow only from a *niṣkāma* mind, which appears to be a necessary qualification of an ideal philosopher, whose task is to perceive the truth about reality with undefective and clean instruments of reason and heart. While, for all practical purposes, the analogous moral theory of Kant's conscientious living and action is only of historical interest in the West, the theory of *niṣkāma-karma* is still significant in India because it is a philosophy of action which lays down an ethical determinant to the epistemological validity of knowledge as well. As referred to above, a philosopher who is not otherwise ideal or perfect, i.e., in his practical outlook and action, is, by the very nature of his psychological situation, not entitled to true knowledge or to any reliability of his cognitive theories. Just as Kant deduces his theory from the principle of the pure reason in man, the theory of non-attachment in India is the outcome, not only of a philosophical theory of the true nature of the pure or non-attached *puruṣa* or *ātman* (person or self), but also of a theory of the relationship of knowledge to personality. And, though in the Buddhist theory of *anātma-vāda* there is no corresponding non-attached *puruṣa* or *ātman,* it is philosophically interesting to note that this absence makes little difference to the mechanism and the framework of the possibility of the attainment of philosophical enlightenment as the outcome of freedom from attachment in both Buddhism and Hinduism. The non-attached *yogin or sannyāsin* (*saṁnyāsin*), in whom the ideal of *niṣkāma-karma* is exemplified, is not only a perfect or ideal man but is also more truly a philosopher, having attained true philosophical knowledge (*prajñā*), because in his life is typified the completest identity of philosophical knowledge and practice.

The above reflections should have shown how Indian philosophical theories of suffering, ultimate freedom, non-attachment, the unreality of the apparent, and of moral requirements for intellectual attainments have produced convictions and beliefs which have not only altered the outlook of their believers, but have also given a different turn to their style of living. This could be attained because these philosophic theories not only originated by reflection on the practical affairs of life but were also founded on the direct experience of the whole of the being of man and were not based on any single sensory, rational, or intuitive part of his being.

Through sages and saints these philosophical systems of belief came to be so crystallized into the common heritage of India that today it does not require a philosopher in India to proclaim that the world is but another name for the unceasing changes of creation and dissolution, the rise and fall of civilizations and cultures, or of birth and death, health and disease, richness and poverty—which is believed to be the very nature of the world and is picturesquely characterized as the wheel of life and death (*saṁsāra-cakra*), in which man is caught. Further, it takes ages of tireless effort for the individual to emerge unscarred, as it were, by the ravages of the wheel. The fact that these beliefs came to Indians through their sages and saints, not only does not make them less philosophic, but is actually the reason for their being believed, showing once more the integral and unitary character of knowledge and action. Even today, when these traditional philosophical beliefs have dimmed in the stress and strife of modern life, it is difficult to say that an Indian goes through his daily life of birth, marriage, and death unimpressed and unaffected by these beliefs, the truth of which he seems to feel in his very bones.

How is it that these philosophical truths in India have permeated the entire population irrespective of the mental caliber or intellectual status of its people, while elsewhere philosophical truths are supposed to be the mental furnishings only of the intellectually gifted and informed minds? The answer is that these truths not only had their roots in the total experience of man but have, at the same time, served as the foundation of their religious beliefs as well. Ultimately, philosophical truths and religious institutions are arrived at by the same integral, direct, ethical, and psychological process. These are the same truths arrived at philosophically by the learned which have filtered down to the unlettered masses through their religious beliefs. That is perhaps the only way we know in which philosophical knowledge and beliefs can influence and guide the practical affairs of men, i.e., by being philosophic and religious at the same time.

Many a scholar interested in Indian and comparative philosophies has complained of the dimness of the borderline between Indian philosophical truths and Indian religious beliefs. They have been puzzled to find that there is very little distinction between the two, and have wished it were not so. This is symptomatic of the modern analytical trends of breaking up the unity of man into separate and autonomous compartments of reason and faith. The chief merit of Indian philosophical thought lies in its unitary vision of man and life, in its intimate relation to religious beliefs, which gives it its practical character. Philosophy and religion are aspects of the same human activity. Philosophy is the theory of religion, as religion is the realization of that theory in practice. A philosophy which is not lived is as barren a pastime as a religion that is not founded on valid truths is a meaningless ritual. Where theory is divorced from life, reason from conduct, what expectation may one have that such theories can or will influence the practical affairs of men?

III. Distinction in the Meaning of the "Practical" in India and the West

Incidentally, the above remarks about the practicality of Indian philosophy also show that the term "practical" itself has been understood in India in a sense not quite the same as that which it carries in the West, at least in the modern period. In the West, the term "practical" has referred to man's relation with his environment and to changes and alterations in it. It has not been so in India, where the term has referred to just the opposite meaning of effecting change and alteration within one's own self, where the entire effort has been concentrated on transforming the empirical ego into the pure self, or egoity itself into non-egoity or mere "thusness." In short, the emphasis on the practical in India has been with reference to the inner transformation of man rather than to any socialized transformation in his style of living. The world of objective Nature is to be used only as the material for this inner change. The need to become his true self rather than to conquer outer Nature has been his deepest aspiration. His practicality has consisted in a constant effort toward self-discovery, self-discipline, and self-development.

It is heartening to note that one of the great American sociological thinkers, Lewis Mumford, while commenting upon the exclusively horizontal socialization of our present civilization, which equates life with property and power, comes to a similar conclusion about the need of richness and depth in the individual's own personality rather than in externals. "The progressive exchange of his natural, biological, and psychological self to his truly human self is what man alone can effect and create and he is human only in so far as this has been effected by him in his own person."[19] The more a man becomes externally socialized, the less is his depth within himself. This value attributed to the inward depth of the individual in Indian thought continues up to the present time, as is evident from the response of the people to the philosophies of Tagore, Gandhi, and Aurobindo, in which all practical programs of action in political, social, and economic fields are to conform to the belief that no achievement in any sphere is in itself worth while unless it leads at the same time to a desired transformation in the psychological quality of the inner nature of man, the individual.

IV. The Present Situation

Though India is free politically, its best minds are occupied in an attempt to catch up with economic targets in national living. *Pari passu,* there is to be noticed a general revival of the arts, literature, and other cultural activities—about which it is too early to form any opinion as to what it will achieve and in which direction. But indications are not lacking to show that it will be in the direction of a synthesis of the best in the West and the best in the Indian cultural tradition. So far as philosophy is concerned, there is evidence, not only of an increased awareness of the philosophical knowledge of India's own past, but also of contemporary trends in Western philosophical thought. From the philosophical writings of Indians today one gains the impression that Indian thinkers are either critical or unenthusiastic about the modern Western philosophical trends of logical positivism, existentialism, and the philosophy of mere analysis. Whether this is due to traditional bias or to genuine philosophical insight is hard to determine. In recent times, the only philosophers of fame have been Aurobindo Ghosh and Radhakrishnan, whose philosophies are both integral and practical. For the rest, there has been no philosophical reflection or theory which has yet crystallized into being properly called the contemporary Indian philosophical theory. The place of philosophy and philosophical thought in India consists at present of the ideas and ideals which are in general the products of its spiritual and moral leaders, such as Ramakrishna, Tagore, and Gandhi. What India still retains today of its past philosophical tradition, after centuries of inactivity, is not any development or modification of its earlier philosophy or philosophical theories, but perhaps a philosophical attitude and outlook which is more critical than creative. If philosophy is a product of the general climate of ideas (as it certainly is), it seems safe to predict that India's future philosophical activity will be in the direction of a philosophy of the co-existence of the ideas of the West and the East and of the old and the new, and in the discovery of the largest measure of agreement and compatibility between the two. It would be a pity if Indian philosophers, too, adopt the view of an autonomous realm of philosophical pursuit divorced from the practical problems of life. Any approach toward life and the universe which is not integral, synoptic, or unitary, but divides and cuts life and its problems into compartments which tend to be autonomous, is likely to be skeptical. If India can retain an integral attitude, something of value may well result from its re-emergence in the arena of creative thought.

QUESTION: I do not see any logical connection between intellectual attainments and ethical perfection. Consequently I do not see why a perfect philosopher has to be ethically perfect—or a *yogin*, etc.

ANSWER: It is psychologically a fact and quite obvious that a man's desires, emotions, passions, ambitions, etc., affect his logical thinking and that a would-be philosopher is not immune from this danger—as anyone can look around and see for himself. What I meant was only an extension of this same psychological fact to a philosopher's thinking.

Notes

1. *Bhagavad-gītā,* XVII.3, in S. Radhakrishnan and Charles A. Moore, eds., *A Source Book in Indian Philosophy* (Princeton: Princeton University Press, 1957), p. 155. All quotations cited from Indian sources are taken from this volume, hereafter referred to as *Source Book.*
2. Bertrand Russell, *A History of Western Philosophy* (New York: Simon and Schuster, 1945), p. xiv.
3. Bertrand Russell, *Our Knowledge of the External World* (Chicago and London: The Open Court Publishing Company, 1929), p. 31.
4. *Majjhima-nikāya,* I. 483–488. *Source Book,* p. 290.
5. *Bhagavad-gītā,* XIII.11. *Source Book,* p. 146. (Italics mine.)
6. Charles Morris, *The Open Self* (New York: Prentice-Hall, Inc., 1948).
7. W. P. Montague, *The Ways of Knowing* (London: George Allen & Unwin Ltd., 1928), p. 34.
8. *Yoga-sūtra,* I.48. *Source Book,* p. 461.
9. F. S. C. Northrop, *The Meeting of East and West* (New York: The Macmillan Co., 1946).
10. D. F. Pearce, ed., *The Nature of Metaphysics* (London: Macmillan and Co., Ltd., 1957), p. 32.
11. *Īśa-upaniṣad,* IX. *Source Book,* p. 40.
12. *Bhagavad-gītā,* IV.40. *Source Book,* p. 119.
13. Huston Smith, "Accents of the World's Philosophies," *Philosophy East and West,* VII, Nos. 1–2 (April–July, 1957), 16.
14. *Brahma-sūtra,* III.iv.1. *Source Book,* p. 539.
15. *Kaṭha-upaniṣad,* II.24. *Source Book,* p. 46.
16. *Ibid.,* I.20–24. *Source Book,* pp. 45–46. See also *Bhagavad-gītā,* II, III.
17. *Bṛhadāraṇyaka-upaniṣad,* III.v. *Source Book,* p. 83.
18. *Īśa-upaniṣad, II. Source Book,* p. 40. See also *Bhagavad-gītā,* II.47–48. *Source Book,* p. 110.
19. L. Mumford, *The Transformations of Man* (New York: Harper & Brothers, 1956), p. 24. (Italics mine.)

P. T. RAJU

Metaphysical Theories in Indian Philosophy

I

FOR THE PRESENT DISCUSSION, we shall take a metaphysical theory to be a theory of reality, being, or existence. The question, What is real? cannot be separated from the question, How is it known to be real? If a person says that X is real, we naturally ask, "How do you know it is real?" The problem of reality cannot be detached from the problem of knowledge.

Thus, reality is what is known to be real and is an object of knowledge. But, if reality remains an "other" to knowledge, the problem of truth becomes insoluble. None of the theories of correspondence, coherence, and pragmatism is self-sufficient to solve the problem for us. Nor do they together constitute a criterion adequate to prove beyond theoretical doubt that a cognition is true or an object real. So, if self-sufficiency or self-validation is needed somewhere, if we are to get it in some cognition, then why not acknowledge it in every cognition? That is, the truth of every judgment must be self-revealing, and reality or existence must be self-revealing. But what would be the nature of a reality that is self-revealing? It cannot be anything but Self. Hence the Upaniṣadic utterances: "All this is the *Ātman*,"[1] and "All this is from the *Ātman*."[2] The *Brahma-sūtra* says that the ultimate reality is known and realized within us as the Self,[3] and this work is treated as an authority by all Vedāntic schools, monistic and pluralistic. The Vedānta is regarded as the essence of Indian philosophy, and, of the Vedāntic schools, the Advaita of Śaṁkara, for which truth is self-revealing and therefore of the nature of Self, is regarded as belonging to the orthodox tradition.

What the Upaniṣads mean by the word *Ātman* (Self) is not the finite mind but something deeper and higher. Yet, it should not be imagined that it is a mere transcendental entity, disconnected from us and existing elsewhere. It is our own self existing everywhere dividing itself into subject and object, matter and form, and "I" and "thou."

Further, it should be noted that not all schools accept the view that Self is the only reality. And even those that deny reality to everything other than the Self accord the former a lower reality that is ultimately to be sublated or transformed into the highest, which is the Self. Then, do all schools follow the Upaniṣadic tradition? Even the Buddhist and Jaina schools, averse as they are to accepting the Vedas and the Upaniṣads as the final authority, belong to the spiritual tradition started by the Upaniṣads.

II

The early Aryans of India were nature worshippers. They were children of Nature and did not think very much about ultimate problems. Yet, we find in the *Ṛg-veda* a hymn giving painful expression to the deep doubt as to whether the world comes from being (*sat*) or non-being (*asat*).[4] But, on the whole, the Ṛg-vedic Aryans cared more for the pleasures of this life than for salvation. Natural forces themselves were at first their gods, but later the conception of a deity dwelling in each force took shape. These gods were conceived of as controlling the destinies of mankind and as amenable to prayer, gifts, and sacrifice. Still later, the spiritual element, the idea that the ultimate reality is within us and not without, that the fullest satisfaction of life can be had by realizing it and not by appealing to external deities, entered their philosophy of life and finally dominated it. The idea took definite shape by the time of the *Bṛhadāraṇyaka-upaniṣad,* that is, the ninth century B.C., according to many scholars. Further, the idea developed into that of the Self as being everything, as being prior to everything, as being identical with the *Brahman,*[*][5] and as being that upon the knowing of which everything else becomes known.[6]

One would rather be tempted to ask how we are to reconcile the view that the *Ātman* or the *Brahman* is the prior, final, and only

[*] In the two papers by Dr. Raju "the *Brahman*" is used, at his request, instead of omitting the article, as is customary.

ultimate reality with the dualism of the Sāṁkhya and the Yoga and the pluralism of the Nyāya and the Vaiśeṣika, all of which claim to be Upaniṣadic. To answer this question, let me bring to your notice the references made in the life stories of the Buddha and Mahāvīra, who belonged to about the sixth century B.C., to ascetics such as Maskarin Gośāla and Sañjaya[7] and to others who were independent seekers of ultimate truth, not caring to follow the way prescribed by the orthodox tradition. These ascetics are an indication of the existence of independent thinkers and seekers after the ultimate truth and after a way that would lead man to the realization of the highest aim of life. Many such thinkers came to the conclusion that the highest truth lay deep within man. Evidently some of them, e.g., the Buddha and Mahāvīra, did not care to pay obeisance to the Vedas. But others, like Gautama, Kaṇāda, Kapila, and Patañjali, did not cut themselves off from the Vedic tradition. Nevertheless, they found it practically impossible to fit their ideas into the Upaniṣadic theory, and so could not furnish commentaries on the *Brahma-sūtra,* which was written by Bādarāyaṇa for the purpose of giving a connected interpretation of the Upaniṣads. Vijñānabhikṣu, of the fifteenth century A.D., practically gave up the dualism of the Sāṁkhya in the attempt to write a Commentary from the standpoint of that school. There has never been a Commentary from the side of the Nyāya or the Vaiśeṣika.

It is interesting to note that the *Śvetāśvatara-upaniṣad* refers to several views: that the world is to be explained in terms of time (*kāla*), the nature of things (*sva-bhāva*), fate (*niyati*), chance (*yadṛcchā*), elements (*bhūtāni*), womb (*yoni*), and person (*puruṣa*), which shows that at that time, a little later than the *Bṛhadāraṇyaka-upaniṣad,* several philosophical views were accepted by men independently of the general Vedic tradition. But, whether the particular school developed out of the Vedic tradition or grew independently at first and later was assimilated by its followers, into the Vedic tradition, whether it was orthodox or unorthodox by accepting or rejecting, respectively, the authority of the Vedas and the Upaniṣads, its guiding motive was invariably the discovery of the nature of man in relation to the universe and of the highest aim of life on earth. It was not the mere satisfaction of intellectual curiosity. However, the questionings of intellect were to be answered, because the questioners were anxious that the aim of life which they set before themselves should not be a false aim, but an aim which was in accord with the nature of man and the universe. The discord between Nature and morality, or the indifference of the former to the latter, which was so painfully felt by the time of Kant and particularly in the nineteenth century in the history of Western philosophy, did not offer a serious problem to the Indian thinkers of the time.[8] The highest aim of man was not merely the improvement of the life of man as a member of society but the realization of a state of existence which, in terms of the whole of the universe, was the purest and the best. Morality was valued, not merely for morality's sake, but as leading up to, and sustaining, the spiritual ideal, in the realization of which it finds its own completion.

Historically, the Buddhists seem to have been the first great synthesizers in philosophy. The Prajñā-pāramitās, which formed the basis of all the Mahāyāna schools, belong to the first century B.C. or A.D. It is now generally accepted that Buddhism is an offshoot of the Upaniṣads.[9] The Buddha's object in leaving his home was not different from the aim of life extolled by the Upaniṣads. And, though early Buddhism tried to cut itself off from the Upaniṣadic tradition, Mahāyāna, or later, Buddhism staged a significant return to the philosophy of the Upaniṣads, if not to the texts, at least to the main doctrines. The Mahāyāna schools took shape in the first four centuries after Christ, by which time the orthodox schools of Hindu philosophy also had come to be systematized: the Nyāya by Gautama, the Vaiśeṣika by Kaṇāda, the Yoga by Patañjali, the Sāṁkhya by Kapila, the Mīmāṁsā by Jaimini, and the Vedānta by Bādarāyaṇa. The Jainas, the followers of Mahāvīra, did not at first care to build up a metaphysical system to support their way of life, but had to construct one following their rival schools.

CĀRVĀKA

The Cārvākas were a school of materialists who accepted the reality of only four elements—earth, air, water, and fire—and the validity of perception alone, and not even inference. But in some of the later references to, and expositions of, this school, we find that a few of its followers accepted inference and a few rejected even perception as a valid source of knowledge. This school had few followers and no developed system of philosophy. But its ideas were worked out as hypothetical anticipatory objections by the followers of orthodox schools, some of whom indulged in a display of logical powers by writing books on behalf of the Cārvākas. The *Tattvo-*

paplavasiṁha, for instance, seems to be a book of that kind, written by an orthodox *brāhmaṇa.* It is important to note that, according to the traditional belief, the school was founded by Bṛhaspati, the priest of the gods, in order to mislead the demons by giving them a false philosophy of life, supporting a low type of Epicureanism.

JAINISM

The Jainas accepted the Upaniṣadic ideal of the realization of the pure state of the *ātman* as the highest aim of life. But to the end they remained naïve realists, and we find no evolution of metaphysical theories in their writings. One peculiarity of this school is that, like most schools of Buddhism, the Sāṁkhya, and the extreme forms of the Advaita, they admitted no God and believed that salvation lies in the liberation of the soul from the bondage in which it finds itself and which is due to accidental impurities entering it. The Jaina metaphysics is an out-and-out metaphysics of substance (*dravya*), for even what we generally regard as unsubstantial, e.g., time (*kāla*), is a substance for them. Substance is every entity to which we can assign an attribute, and time therefore comes in this class. Substance is of two kinds, the extended (*asti-kāya*) and the non-extended (*an-asti-kāya*). Time falls in the second class. The extended is of two kinds: the soul (*jīva*) and the non-soul (*ajīva*). The soul can be either the liberated (*mukta*) or the unliberated (*baddha*). The non-soul is of four kinds: the principle of movement (*dharma*), the principle of rest (*adharma*), space (*ākāśa*), and body (*pudgala*). The three peculiar doctrines of this school are: first, action (*karma*) and its effects are regarded as consisting of material particles which enter the soul and bind it down, a theory which appears to be a very naïve form of the philosophy of substance; second, the soul is of indefinite magnitude and assumes the size of the body it enters; and third, *dharma* and *adharma* mean motion and rest, meanings not given to the terms by any other school.[10]

BUDDHISM

Like Jainism, Buddhism started in revolt against the Vedic ritual and sacrifices, and at first occupied itself exclusively with the practical method of attaining salvation by analyzing all the accumulated overgrowth on our deeper and purer being—an overgrowth which it discovered to be ultimately due to ignorance and which concealed the pure truth from vision. But later Buddhists felt the need for a theory justifying their practice and slowly developed system after system in consequence of controversies among themselves and with rival schools. The history of Buddhist philosophy offers a vast panorama of various types of realism and idealism, pluralism and monism, starting with naïve realism and culminating in certain types of high idealism. Buddhism showed the greatest amount of open-mindedness, not only in matters of religious practice, but also in matters of philosophical speculation.

The Buddha refused to answer the question as to whether or not the self existed after death, as both the term "self" and his answer were subject to conflicting interpretations and misinterpretations. We can best appreciate his silence when we remember that even the Mīmāṁsakas, followers of Jaimini, and the Vedāntins, followers of Bādarāyaṇa, understood it differently, the former contending that the purpose of the Vedic teaching could not be the discovery of such an obviously simple entity as the *ātman,* which was the same as the ego (*aham*) of each person, and the latter claiming that it was something more than the simple empirical ego. However, the Buddhist sought to discover the substratum, by whatever name it was to be called, underlying our worldly being, which they thought was an aggregate of aggregates (*skandhas*). Personality (*pudgala*) consists of five aggregates: the aggregates of matter (*rūpa-skandha*), of feeling (*vedanā-skandha*), of ideas (*saṁjñā-skandha*), of instincts, propensities, and impressions (*saṁskāra-skandha*), and of consciousness (*vijñāna-skandha*). The aggregates are all subject to momentary (*kṣaṇika*) change. *Nirvāṇa,* or salvation, which is above change, results from analyzing away the aggregates and reaching their substratum. This analysis is a hard self-analysis involving discrimination of elements within oneself.

All the Buddhist schools accept Four Noble Truths (*ārya-satyas*): all is pain; pain has a cause; it has cessation; and there is a way leading to its cessation. If pain is to be removed, its cause should be analytically understood; and therefore the second and the third of the Four Noble Truths were later developed into the twelve-linked chain of causation (*pratītya-samutpāda*). These twelve links are: ignorance, instincts and propensities, consciousness, mind and matter (*nāma-rūpa*), sense, sense-contact, feeling, craving, grasping, becoming, birth, and old-age-and-death. Of these, each is a condition of the next following.

Another classification of truths is: everything is pain, everything is momentary, and everything is *śūnya* (void).

As indicated already, there are so many Buddhist schools that it is possible to find several types of metaphysical theory among them. The Hīnayāna (Theravāda) schools on the whole tend to be realistic and pluralistic, and the Mahāyāna schools to be idealistic and monistic. But there is a sense in which it can be said that all Buddhist schools are idealistic, because the analysis of the world by which the underlying *nirvāṇa* is to be realized is an analysis of personality, and vice versa. The doctrine of the aggregates has already been mentioned. Reference may also be made to the doctrine of fields (*āyatanas*). They are the bases or fields for the growth and working of personality. They are twelve in number: the five fields of the senses (eye, ear, tongue, nose, and touch), the five fields of their corresponding objects, mind (*manas*), and law (*dharma*). It is obvious that this analysis takes the individual and the world together: the world ceases with the cessation of personality, and so must have taken form with the formation of personality.

The Buddhists hesitate to characterize the underlying *Nirvāṇa* as either being or non-being, for they contend that in this world there is no being without non-being and no non-being without being. And as *Nirvāṇa* is beyond this world, though forming its substratum and pervading it, it can be neither being nor non-being. The Mādhyamikas develop this idea further and maintain that it is neither being nor non-being, nor both, nor neither. They therefore call it *śūnya,* void, or indeterminate. It is still identical with the world, because it is the essential truth of the world;[11] and yet it is different from the world, because it is above the flux of becoming. To be more exact, they say that *Śūnya,* or *Nirvāṇa,* is neither identical with, nor different from, the world.

The Vijñānavādins, however, say that its nature is *vijñāna,* consciousness, at the same time acknowledging that even to call it by the name *vijñāna* is to assign an attribute to that which lies beyond attributes. Reference may be made here to the pluralistic idealism of Śāntarakṣita and Kamalaśīla, according to which these *vijñānas* are many.

The Vijñānavādins on the whole distinguish between a receptacle-consciousness (*ālaya-vijñāna*), which is the potential state of the world, and a kinetic consciousness (*pravṛtti-vijñāna*), which is the world in the process of becoming. Yamakami speaks of a higher *vijñāna* than the former, called *alaya-vijñāna* (with a short a), the unperishing consciousness.[12]

THE NYĀYA AND THE VAIŚEṢIKA SYSTEMS

The Nyāya and Vaiśeṣika systems are generally treated together because of the great similarity of their metaphysical theories. Both of them are pluralistic. They postulate seven categories: substance, quality, activity, universal, particular, inherence, and negation. All these categories are familiar to Western philosophy except inherence, which means the eternal relation obtaining, for instance, between substance and quality. The relation of the quality red to the rose is not a relation of contact like that between a pen and a table. It should be noted, however, that, though the Naiyāyikas regard all these entities as belonging to reality, most of them attribute existence only to the first three and not to the rest.

Substance is of nine kinds: earth, water, fire, air, ether, time, space, soul, and mind. The peculiarity to note here is that time, space, and soul are treated as substances. The first five substances are to be understood, not merely as hard, soft, subtle, etc., but as ground causes of the properties of smell, taste, color, touch, and sound. Both schools accept the atomic theory of the first four substances and mind and regard the visible world as due to the grouping of atoms.[13] The *ātman* (soul), though infinite, is by nature unconscious and remains so after salvation. Both schools, again, accept God, who is just one of the *ātmans* and is as eternal as the other substances, but is somehow able to control the processes of creation and dissolution. But they do not explain how. They reject *śakti,* or the energy of God, as a category, which, it is interesting to note, is employed to solve the problem by the Vedāntic and non-Vedāntic monistic systems, for which plurality is the expression of God's energy (*śakti*). And every man naturally has control over his own power.

In these two schools, salvation is a return to the original unconscious state of the *ātman.* It involves, further, the severing of all contact with the world, a retreat into an eternal state of blind unconscious existence, devoid of pain, of course, but also equally devoid of pleasure.

THE SĀṀKHYA AND THE YOGA

Like the Nyāya and the Vaiśeṣika, the Sāṁkhya and the Yoga are usually taken together, the only difference between them being that, while the Yoga accepts God, the Sāṁkhya rejects him. According to both, the two fundamental categories of reality are spirit (*puruṣa*) and Nature (*prakṛti*). Nature has three attributes (*guṇas*), which are really factors as well. They are transparence (*sattva*), activity (*rajas*), and inactivity (*tamas*). When *prakṛti* is left to itself, the three *guṇas* are in a state of equilibrium, and there is no world. But, when it comes into contact with *puruṣa,* their equilibrium is destroyed, and the creation of the world begins. In this creation, the *guṇas* do not become separated from each other, but each tries to dominate the others. The contact of *puruṣa* and *prakṛti* results in the latter's receiving the reflection of the former; and, in the consequent disturbance of the three *guṇas,* when the *sattva* is predominant, *prakṛti* transforms itself into *mahat* or *buddhi* (intelligence). This intelligence is not the intelligence of any particular individual, but has a cosmic aspect and is therefore called *mahat,* 'the great."

The transformation (*pariṇāma*) of *prakṛti* is regarded by these two schools as the actualization of the potential. It is like pressing oil out of the sesame seed. The effect is therefore existent (*sat*), though only in a potential state, in the cause. This is called the theory of existent effect (*sat-kārya-vāda*) in Indian thought. This theory is not accepted by the Nyāya and the Vaiśeṣika schools, according to which the effect is non-existent before it comes into being. This is called the theory of non-existent effect (*asat-kārya-vāda*).

Out of *mahat,* the next lower category, ego (*ahaṁkāra*), is born; and out of the ego are born mind (*manas*), the five sense-organs, the five organs of action (hands, feet, speech, the generating organ, and the anus), and the five subtle elements (*tan-mātras*), which are actually the subtle forms of the physical elements out of which the gross elements issue forth. Western readers should be careful not to identify mind with ego, and the two, again, with intelligence (*buddhi*). Further, the ego is not the same as the subject, which is generally the correlate of the object in Western philosophy, but is the matrix of the correlates of the sense-organs and their objects; so that what the Sāṁkhya calls the ego is not merely the correlate of the body but of the body as well as the objects that are concerned with it. The human body is just a gross object among gross objects, made up of gross elements that issue out of the ego. Yet, it is a privileged object for the ego and is a special instrument for the enjoyment of other objects.

When the bond between *prakṛti* and *puruṣa* is severed, the former regains its original equilibrium, and *puruṣa* is liberated. We should note here one important point of similarity between the early Buddhist method of liberation and that of the Sāṁkhya. For both, liberation consists in reaching a level beyond Nature, not in transforming Nature into something sublime.[14]

THE PŪRVA MĪMĀṀSĀ

The school of Mīmāṁsā, also called Pūrva Mīmāṁsā, or the Prior Mīmāṁsā, started, not as a philosophical system, but as an attempt to explain the nature of right action (*dharma*), which according to them consisted in obeying the Vedic injunctions and prohibitions. The Vedas enjoined different kinds of sacrifices in order to obtain pleasures in this world and the next. Consequently, questions arose about the nature of actions, how they could produce effects in this and the other world after a lapse of time, and how the effectuality of the sacrifices could be guaranteed. These questions led the Mīmāṁsakas into speculation about the nature of self, God, action (*karma*), etc. We get a rounded-out activist system of metaphysics in this school, and its followers made very significant contributions to individual problems.

The Mīmāṁsakas believe in the reality of this world and the next; and they remain to the end fairly consistent realists. Kumārila and Prabhākara were the important followers of this school who tackled metaphysical and epistemological problems. The categories of this school are, with some additions and omissions, very nearly the same as those of the Nyāya-Vaiśeṣika. Prabhākara accepts eight categories: substance, quality, action, universal, inherence (*samavāya*), force (*śakti*), similarity (*sādṛśya*), and number. Kumārila divides all categories into the positive and the negative. The positive categories are four: substance, quality, action, and generality. Force and similarity are brought under substance, and number under quality.

The nature of the self is said to be consciousness but not bliss. Here the Mīmāṁsā and the Sāṁkhya are in agreement.

A most interesting doctrine of the school is that of *apūrva*. The performance of sacrifice leads to heaven; but it does not lead one there immediately in this body. *Karma*, as sacrifice, then, becomes an unseen force, which Jaimini, the founder of this school, calls by the name *apūrva* (generally, unseen, imperceptible), and which remains in a latent form until the time comes for producing the effect.

The Mīmāṁsakas did not at first accept God. But the question arose as to how the fruition of *karma* could be guaranteed, and they had to include God as the preserver of the principle of *karma*. The ultimate reality of the world is, on the whole, looked upon as the constant principle of *karma*, and God is the principle of duty or law (*dharma*), the contents of which are embodied in the Vedas. As Professor Radhakrishnan says, the emphasis of this school is on the ethical side.[15]

THE VEDĀNTA, OR THE UTTARA MĪMĀṀSĀ

The Vedānta, also called the Uttara Mīmāṁsā, or the Posterior Mīmāṁsā, is the philosophy of the Upaniṣads. There are several Vedāntic systems, each system being the result of the attempt of a school to systematize the teachings of the Upaniṣads and give its own interpretation to them. This attempt was made by realists and idealists, monists and pluralists alike. We have, therefore, several varieties of Vedāntic systems, three of which, namely, those of Śaṁkara, Rāmānuja, and Madhva, are well known. But there are several others, the most important of which are those of Bhāskara, Nimbārka, Śrīkaṇṭha, Śrīpati, Baladeva, Vallabha, and Śuka.[16] All of them maintained, in accordance with the Upaniṣads, that the *Brahman* is the highest reality. All of them were avowedly absolutistic, for, in one form or another, they had to reckon with and accommodate the dominant monistic and absolutist trend of the Upaniṣads. But, if the *Brahman* is the only reality, what becomes of the world of individuals (*jīvas*) and Nature? To Śaṁkara, individuals and Nature were neither real nor unreal, nor both, nor neither; some, like Madhva, were prone to treat them as real and separate from the *Brahman;* but Bhāskara was satisfied with treating Nature only as real and separate from the *Brahman,* for he thought that the finite individual could be derived by bringing the *Brahman* into relation with Nature, which was the "finitizing" principle. Others, like Rāmānuja and Śrīkaṇṭha, wanted to treat the *Brahman* as the sole reality, while regarding the individuals and Nature as real, though not separate from the *Brahman,* but forming its body; others, again, following Nimbārka and Śrīpati, thought that the individuals and Nature were both identical with, and different from, the *Brahman.*

Further questions, such as whether this identity or difference is of form only, or of being only, or of both, were raised, Nimbārka maintaining that identity was of both kinds while difference was only of being, and Śrīpati contending that both were of both kinds.

It is important to note that Rāmānuja did not accept the view that the relation between the *Brahman* and the phenomenal world could be both identity and difference, as the two are contradictories, but viewed it as that between body and soul; while those who accepted the relation of identity-and-difference rejected the body-soul relation since it involves mutual interaction and therefore the affectability of the *Brahman* by the actions of the individuals. Śuka, like some Advaitins, believed that there is only one individual (*jīva*), who assumes the forms of many.

While the self, according to the Nyāya and the Vaiśeṣika, has only being and no consciousness, and, according to the Sāṁkhya and the Yoga, both being and consciousness, according to the Vedāntic schools, it possesses bliss also as a part of its essential nature.

In spite of so many differences, whether the soul is ultimately identical with the *Brahman* or different from it, all Vedāntic schools maintain that the *Brahman* is to be realized as one's own soul. That is, the Absolute is within us; in searching for it, we have to look inward and not outward. Bādarāyaṇa, to whom all Vedāntic schools owe allegiance, says in his *Brahma-sūtra*[17] that the *Brahman* is known and grasped as one's soul. For one who views the Vedāntic or Upaniṣadic tradition as a whole, in order to adjudge it in comparison with other traditions, this is the most important aphorism; and the views of causality, etc., depend on how this aphorism is interpreted by the particular school. Rāmānuja says that the Absolute is realized as the soul of one's soul; Śaṁkara says that it is just one's soul; but Madhva says that it is the controller of one's soul from within.

The problem of how God could control the world if the world had an independent existence did not escape the notice of the Vedāntins. This question has greater force against the philosophical dualism of Madhva than against the systems of the rest, for he emphasized the relation of difference between the *Brahman* and the individual more strongly than any other. But, curiously enough, he rounded out his system by saying that these independent individuals and Nature were only expressions of God's *śakti* (power, potentiality). And, as we have control over our own power, God has control over his. This peculiar absolutist trend of the Vedāntic schools was overshadowed by controversies over the reality and unreality of *māyā;* and even modern interpreters have missed its importance, as they have followed the fashion of the epistemological approach set by modern Western philosophy. Consequently, the importance of the role which the concept of *śakti*, or energy, played in the Vedānta has so far been ignored. It is with the help of this concept that the dualistic systems, e.g., the Sāṁkhya, and the pluralistic systems, e.g., the Nyāya, have been incorporated into the Vedānta and rounded out into varieties of absolutism.[18] Thus, in the Vedāntic tradition, we shall not be wrong if we say that the distinctions between realism and idealism, and between pluralism, dualism, and monism, hold good within absolutism. The Sāṁkhya was content with the dualism of *prakṛti* and *puruṣa;* but the gap between the two was bridged by Vijñānabhikṣu in his Commentary on the *Brahma-sūtra* by making *prakṛti* the *śakti* (power) of the *Brahman.*[19] Similarly, Madhva adopted a large number of categories apparently independent of each other, but ultimately made them all expressions of God's power (*śakti*).[20] Herein was a way for the Nyāya pluralism to rise above itself; but what prevented it from doing so was its rejection of *śakti* as a category. Even Śaṁkara admitted *śakti;* he explicitly called *māyā* by the name *māyā-śakti.* But he was not prepared to accord it reality. He maintained that the rays of the sun have no existence independent of the sun but are expressions of its energy. But some would say that they have an independent reality, some that they are both identical with and different from the sun. It is more appropriate, therefore, to say that the Vedāntic systems, except that of Vallabha, differ from each other in metaphysics by understanding the nature of *śakti* differently. But all accept the view that *śakti* is logically inexplicable: why and how it works in the way it does we cannot understand. To this Śaṁkara adds that it is inexplicable ontologically also: we cannot prove that it is real or unreal, or both, or neither.

Rāmānuja, Nimbārka, and others, who accept the ontological validity of the *śakti* of God, maintain that God creates the world by allowing his *śakti* to undergo transformation (*pariṇāma*), while he himself remains unaffected by the process. But Śaṁkara says that this is impossible, like slicing half the hen for cooking and leaving the other half to lay eggs, for, if God's *śakti* undergoes transformation, he also changes. Therefore, Śaṁkara postulates a *śakti* that is neither real nor unreal, and makes it responsible for the creation of the world. It is interesting to note that, in spite of being neither real nor unreal, its details are as seriously worked out by the later Advaitins as if it were real. Now, if the *Brahman* does not produce the world by transforming its own *śakti,* how can the Upaniṣads declare it to be the cause of the world? Śaṁkara here formulates a new concept of cause called *vivarta-kāraṇa.* It is difficult to translate the word into English, but it means essentially a cause that produces the effect without itself undergoing any transformation. Thus the cause of the world can be the *Brahman* itself.[21]

THE PĀŚUPATA, THE ŚĀKTA, AND THE PĀÑCARĀTRA SYSTEMS

Reference should be made here to the Pāśupata, the Śākta, and the Pāñcarātra systems, from which all the commentators except Śaṁkara and Bhāskara obtained their philosophical inspiration before they approached the *Brahma-sūtra* to write their Commentaries in order to gain prestige and recognition as Vedāntins. The Pāśupata, the Śākta, and the Pāñcarātra Āgamas (sacred works) are sectarian as opposed to the Vedas, and are accepted by the Śaiva, the Śākta, and the Vaiṣṇava sects, respectively, as their final authorities.[22] The most interesting feature of these works is the way they synthesize pluralism, dualism, and the Buddhist doctrine of *śūnya,* and erect a monism which is at once sublime and constructive. While the Sāṁkhya and the Advaita Vedānta could not find a place for entities like time, these systems gave it a distinct place, of course, as a manifestation of either Śiva's or Viṣṇu's *śakti,* identifying Śiva or Viṣṇu with the *Brahman* of the Upaniṣads. Some of them, particularly the followers of the Kashmir school of Śaivism, such as Vasugupta and Abhinavagupta, who were definitely influenced by Śaṁkara, accepted his non-dualism intact, with the proviso that *māyā,* as the incomprehensible power of the *Brahman,* was real. And now and then for argument's sake, they even admitted Śaṁkara's position, thereby implying that this kind of formulation is of secondary importance when we accept the fact that *māyā* is a *śakti* of ultimate reality and is identical with it. Śaṁkara's reluctance to concede reality to *māyā,* while maintaining identity of existence between it and the *Brahman,* is due to his feeling that people would identify them in form also. Herein lies the answer to the charge of pantheism often brought against him; the world is not identical with the *Brahman* in form but only in being.

These systems hold that *śūnya* is the state in which the subject-object distinction disappears, and yet the final state of their thoroughly mediated immediacy, in which the *puruṣa* and *prakṛti* become absolutely identical in both being and form and transparent to each other, is not reached. This is a state in which the *puruṣa* is shrouded and does not shine in its full glory. The highest stage is still above. The Buddhist schools, indeed, would not accept this interpretation, which gives only a subordinate position to their highest concept. However, this shows how eagerly and systematically the orthodox schools incorporated the metaphysical discoveries of Buddhism, in spite of the severe criticisms they leveled against them.

Among contemporary metaphysical thinkers such as Radhakrishnan, Bhagavan Das, Aurobindo Ghosh, and Tagore, the tendency to regard *māyā* as an element of the Absolute is very strong. Though Radhakrishnan is a follower of Śaṁkara, we do not find in him that negative attitude to the world which a few extremists among the Advaitins adopted. The others make *māyā* definitely an element of the Absolute.

III

A paper like the present one can hardly present all the metaphysical theories. But Indian philosophy has a rich variety of them; and the extreme form of the Advaita is only one of them. In spite of several important differences, the systems strove hard to preserve the unity of the Indian philosophical tradition, which is spiritual or, we may say, Upaniṣadic. In spite of their heterodoxy, several Buddhist and Jaina scholars openly trace their origins to the Vedas and the Upaniṣads. The only system that is completely independent of them is the Cārvāka, which is a purely materialistic school, and according to which there is an end to our existence after death and we should make the most of our life here.

It might have been noticed by now that, while, for Jainism, early Buddhism, the Nyāya, the Vaiśeṣika, the Sāṁkhya, and the Yoga, salvation lay in becoming something, whatever be its name, that is detached from the rest of being, in the Vedāntic systems it lies in the realization that everything is the ultimate being. Even Śaṁkara makes no secret of this: the *Brahman* is everything, and the world is the *Brahman.* Viewed *sub specie temporis,* the world is the world of finitude around us; but, viewed *sub specie aeternitatis,* it is the *Brahman.* The Mahāyāna schools also proclaim the same truth. *Śūnya* is *Nirvāṇa: Nirvāṇa* is this world, and this world is *Nirvāṇa.*[23] Yet, the two are not the same. This may sound paradoxical; but the paradox disappears when we introduce the distinction between viewing the world *sub specie temporis* and *sub specie aeternitatis.* It amounts to this: Salvation lies in transforming what appears to be the material world around us into something spiritual; it is not an escape from the world but a spiritual conquest of the world—not a retreat after defeat but assimilation after conquest.

An important question that arises while discussing the value of Indian metaphysics is: Have the Indian philosophers given a metaphysics of morality? We should consider carefully the significance of the fact that the first great philosophical work written in the West was the *Republic* of Plato and in India the *Bṛhadāraṇyaka-upaniṣad.* These two works are mainly responsible for the respective traditions. The main interest of the *Republic* is the discovery of the true nature of man in society in order to build a stable society upon earth. But this interest is conspicuously lacking in the *Bṛhadāraṇyaka.* It would be wrong to conclude from this fact that the Indian society of the time was in a chaotic state. To have no metaphysics of ethics is not the same as to be unethical. One might conclude that a metaphysics of ethics was necessitated by social and ethical instability in Greece at that time and that conditions in India were such as not to make its thinkers feel this need. But the safest conclusion to draw would be that the thinkers of ancient India were not motivated by the aims of Plato's *Republic.* Thus, while the Indian philosopher tried to discover within himself the ultimate truth, which was an eternally accomplished fact, the Platonic philosophy was intent upon discovering eternal laws of man and society, in order to remold them accordingly. The only metaphysical work of importance with some reference to society is the *Bhagavad-gītā.* But it should be mentioned that this is part of the *Mahābhārata,* which is an epic. Writers such as Manu and Yājñavalkya, who gave India her ethical codes (Dharma-śāstras), did not push their inquiries to their metaphysical foundations, nor did the metaphysicians develop the social implications of their systematized technique of spiritual self-control. It was not impossible to do either. The material was there, but the attempt was not made.

It would be wrong to say, with Hegel, that in Indian philosophy the concept was merged with existence, while for Western thought Socrates liberated it from existence, for the reason that Indian philosophy has had a variety of theories about the universal. Yet, there is some meaning in this statement, in that the practical motive of Plato was to apply the concept to man and society, whereas the motive of Indian philosophy included no notion of such application. I am therefore much in sympathy with Mr. Northrop's distinction between the general characteristics of Indian and Western philosophy, but should add that the terminology he uses should bring out more clearly the distinction between spiritual immediacy and an immediacy at the sensory level. Indian philosophers would accept the former but not the latter. So far as the higher categories are concerned, they are conceptual constructions in Western philosophy, postulates of thought made to meet the demands of logical explanation. The question of treating those concepts as realizable in experience is ignored except by a few mystics, with whom most logical thinkers will have little to do. But, in Indian philosophy on the whole, the categories of existence (*tattvas*), to whatever level they belong, are meant for realization in experience. These categories include our deepest levels of being, the deepest category being the *Brahman,* which forms the basic spiritual principle pervading and sustaining everything. Furthermore, the word "continuum" is not suitable here, as it suggests extension. At the sensory and mental levels there is interruption of continuity, as the separateness consequent upon the formation of the individuals begins to be felt. But the categories of existence, as they are derived or evolved from our deepest being, always have the quality of immediacy to us, viewed, we should note, from within, not from without. If ultimate reality is inclusive of both subject and object, then we should look for the center of that reality, not within the subject, but between the subject and the object, and view its circumference as including both the subject and object. We have already seen how, in the Sāṁkhya, mind and its objects are included in, and derived from, the ego. Our natural tendency is to look for the ego within the body; we should, on the contrary, look upon the physical body as within the ego. All the Vedāntic systems, particularly those inspired by the Pāśupata and the Pāñcarātra Āgamas, may rightly be regarded as the developed and integrated forms of the Sāṁkhya, and they thoroughly exemplify the inwardness[24] of the categories (*tattvas*).

What would Indian metaphysicians say regarding categories of material and social existence? Ultimately these categories would be inward and, therefore, immediate. But, at our level, they belong to conceptual mediacy until they are applied to the realms of matter and society and are made to embody themselves in existence. To say that the concepts of matter and society do not belong to existence in Western thought would be wrong; but to say that they are considered in detachment from existence, manipulated, combined, and reconstructed, and then applied to matter and society in order to make the two conform to the built-up concepts would be right. Indian philosophy, in the narrower sense of the well-known systems, did consider the concepts in logical detachment from existence, but did not manipulate, combine, and reconstruct them for further application, for the reason that such an application was out of place and impossible in the realization of the deepest truths, which are eternally accomplished facts. The difference between the two traditions is due to the difference between the levels of being in which they have been primarily interested, the interests giving peculiar color to the respective traditions. If Indian thought had directed its attention to social and material sciences, it might have set up a different philosophical tradition. It would perhaps have found concepts at the social level that fall short of concepts of ideal society and need combination, modification, and reconstruction for final application, and concepts at the material level needing the same process for molding matter to serve man's ends. The need for detaching concepts from existence comes only with reference to realms in which the actual falls short of the ideal but not where the two are one. The realm with which Indian philosophy mainly deals, namely, the inward spirit, is of the latter kind.

Judged with the standards of modern philosophy, Indian thought can be said to have reached the highest speculative heights; but it lacks the breadth which Western philosophy has attained, for the reason that it did not think it necessary to be broad. The sense of self-sufficiency long suited India. But times have changed. The West has built up philosophical structures to support newly discovered, formulated, or revived values, which are demanding recognition from the East as well. It is here that Indian philosophy should incorporate elements from Western philosophy in order to make up for its one-sided preoccupation with the realm of spirit.[25] Thereby it would not only include all the realms of being with which man's life is concerned but would make its logic and metaphysics richer and lay the foundation of a social philosophy that could supply a plan for at once meeting the spiritual needs of man's inner spirit and the material and social needs of his mortal existence. The West also might find it worth while to supplement what it has achieved in philosophy with the deeper elements of Indian thought. Western philosophers might find it useful to understand man, not only as a product of material atoms, as the materialists do, or as a product of society as, for instance, Mead and Dewey do, but also as the product of the Great Spirit, as a spiritual being far transcending his relations to matter and society. The integration of the three perspectives without doing injustice to any, not merely to satisfy our intellectual demands, but also to furnish a plan of life for working out our life's aim that would aid in the realization of all our potentialities, should be the aim of East-West philosophical synthesis. The cosmopolitan and universal outlook which philosophy had from Greek and Roman times changed, as Ruggiero says, into the national outlook by the eighteenth century, so that until very recently each nation was supposed to have a philosophy of its own as a systematic articulation of its own culture.[26] The emphasis is now shifting from nations to cultural groups; but simultaneously the idea that we can have a synthesis of cultures, an integration of values framed and fostered by different cultures during centuries of their history, is dawning upon the minds of men of thought. The new culture, which would contain all the highest values for which peoples have lived and died, would not appear alien to any group and, when adopted by all, would lessen the possibility of conflict at least at the cultural level. The philosophy representing such a culture would be a world philosophy. It would be difficult to maintain that it would be one system of philosophy; there would be several systems, but all of them would be expressive of the same new outlook in its broader aspects, integrating all the highest values, each in its own way.

What significance do the peculiar spiritual point and aim of the Indian metaphysical tradition have for the metaphysical tendencies that have become strong in the West? Professor Radhakrishnan, India's leading contemporary philosopher, has very significantly named one of his books *Eastern Religions and Western Thought.* The thought of the East, except for Confucianism in China, has tended to give one-sided importance to the spiritual viewpoint, delved deeply into our being, transformed what to the West is a matter of faith into ideas of reason, which it carried to its very bounds, until it found its completion and rest, and was transformed into self-conscious spiritual immediacy, in which the provoking strangeness of an "other" was annulled. The thought of the West, on the other hand, has been content on the whole to remain conceptual; it has conceptualized matter and on the whole has succeeded in rebuilding the idea of matter in terms of pure conceptual formulas representing the ultimate constituents—ultimate in consequence of their being further unanalyzable in terms of the method it has adopted—of even unperceivable atoms. It is attempting to conceptualize life, mind, man, society, and spirit, and to reconstruct their meanings in terms of the ultimate concepts it has postulated and successfully used in explaining matter. Against this attempt, it received vigorous protests from the sciences of life, mind, man, society, and spirit. The biological revolt succeeded in freeing its science from the domination of the concept of mechanism, and the concept of organism compelled men of thought to recognize its autonomy. Matter is instrumental to life, and so is mechanism to organism. Still, this instrumentality is not recognized as such: philosophers speak of life as a quality emerging out of a structural pattern of material particles, which in their turn are, according to some philosophers, repetitive patterns or events. But this way of understanding life leaves out the idea of the organism as an agent acting on its own mechanism. Life seems to be equated with this structural pattern. What is more than the pattern is reduced to the status of a quality of the pattern. Quality might be interpreted as an active agent, but then we would be doing so much violence to the concept of quality as to destroy it. There is a priori no mistake in using the concept of evolution in understanding the relationship between matter and life. But that which evolves is not a mere quality of matter, but an agent that tries to rule matter. Similarly, the higher and higher forms of being rule the lower and lower ones—the significance of which fact has not been fully recognized by some philosophers.

Mind, and especially the unconscious mind, obtained adequate recognition only after World War I. Its processes defied explanation in terms of matter or life. These protests and refusals are a sufficient indication that a conceptual reconstruction of the world, in which we can get a complete correlation of mediacy (concepts) and immediacy (being), is bound to be a failure even at the lower levels of being, and, as a practical consequence, may result in the destruction of being if pressed into what we treat as the mediated concept. Moral disaster is sure to follow, if, at the level of man and society, we are too sure of the adequacy of our mediated concepts and press being into their forms. Our mediated concepts may be our favorite concepts, results of an ideological bias, partially true and partially untrue. But, when a part is made to do the work of the whole, the other parts suffer and the whole is destroyed. And destruction at the level of man and society is a moral disaster. At the level of matter we are in an advantageous position. Though the principle that no amount of conceptual analysis can exhaust the nature of the individual is true at all levels, still our analysis of matter, with the practical mechanistic motive in view, has given us conceptual constituents with which we can rebuild the concept of matter, which, for practical purposes, is equivalent to matter in the realm of reality. We have the further advantage that we are more agreed as to what matter is than what life or mind is; and we are much less agreed as to what man or spirit is. To put the same point in an extreme form, many generally agree that matter is, but fewer will agree that mind is. At higher and higher levels we have greater and greater difficulties in building up adequate concepts, because the forms of being are less and less tangible to sense perception, and verification of our conceptual formulation by reference to the forms of being is more and more difficult. At the purely biological level, the moral and spiritual implications of the process do not bother us very much. But at the higher levels, particularly of man, society, and spirit, it is the historical process of centuries that verifies our concepts and brings to light their inadequacy. It is here that the total truth or falsity of our cultures and ideologies is made manifest to us, but made manifest, unfortunately, through political, moral, and spiritual catastrophes, involving misery for millions. Our obvious conclusion would be that the philosophical foundations of these cultures and ideologies contain an inadequate formulation of the concept of man and that, when man is pressed into that conceptual mold, he suffers "destruction." At the level of man and society, our conceptual formulations are likely to move in a vacuum.

Here, therefore, we seem to have an a priori insoluble problem. We require a verification of the concept of man, but we are in doubt as to what man is. Experimental verification is not impossible. But it is experiment with a moral being and involves moral catastrophes, very often on a vast scale. Even the concept of man as a mere moral agent, which Fichte and some German idealists formulated, failed because it was an incomplete concept. Morality implies, not only that man is confronted by an alien "other," which is to be forced to conform to the dictates of his reason, but also that he can so force it. It is easy to confuse the moral dignity and prestige of man in facing an "other" and making it bend to his will with the necessity for arrogance and aggresiveness involving moral violence to the "other," which must be man and not matter. Here is the need for what we may call a spiritual ethics, a standard of conduct that involves self-surrender to a universal will within, the laws of which we can imperfectly comprehend. Such an ethics will counteract our tendency to impose our own selfish will, which we can easily mistake for the universal will, upon the other. Here is the true role of religion as reason with spiritual orientation, which is distinct from what we usually call ethics, which is reason with social orientation, between which, of course, no clear-cut distinction can be drawn, since each passes into the other. And here is the need for a metaphysics that is consistently spiritual in outlook and aim.

It would be wrong to say that India did not produce conceptual reconstructions of the world, but we do not find in Indian philosophy that tenacity and stubborn resolve to analyze and reconstruct the world conceptually at all levels, starting with the lowest concepts at the material level and gradually building up the concepts at the higher levels. We have seen that the inherent failure of the Western attempt is due to not recognizing the instrumentality of the lower to the higher and to treating the higher as merely a qualitative emergence. What emerges should be a new substantiality—if we are to use the concept of emergence at least for argument's sake—and not a quality. The higher should be the substance, turning the lower into its own quality, as it were. Correspondingly, what Indian metaphysics lacks is the systematic working out of the necessity of the lower as an instrument of the higher. This underemphasis can do violence to man as a social unit, while allowing an overemphasis on man as a spiritual being. The lower as a quality cannot exhaust the nature of the higher as the substance. But substance cannot exist without qualities. At the spiritual level, if man is engrossed in the spiritual and is indifferent to the values of the world, he may neglect his lower nature. But, at the purely ethical level, this attitude does violence to man as such and to society. Just as at the biological level inanimate material particles become transformed into living particles, so at the spiritual level the ethical becomes transformed into the spiritual, and the spiritual should be looked upon therefore as the transformation of the ethical. Just as life has an independence of its own from matter, however imperfect that independence may be, so the spiritual also can have an independence of its own from the human and the ethical. Further, like any bit of matter which is connected at the material level with every other bit of matter, no human being at the human and the ethical levels should regard himself as independent and isolated from other human beings. Social orientation cannot be lost sight of by man at the human level. What Indian philosophy needs is the recognition of the necessity of a social ethics as an indispensable instrument of social life. Just as life suffers if it is equated to a structural pattern of material elements, so spiritual life suffers if equated to ethical life, and man suffers if equated to a social unit. But, again, ethical life and therefore man as a social unit suffer if man is equated only to spirit. So long as he remains man, his nature as a socially ethical being should not be ignored. And this idea should be made an essential part of our metaphysics and should be worked out accordingly. Thereby naturalism, empiricism, and realism, on the one hand, and spiritualism, rationalism, and idealism, on the other, can unite and furnish man with a balanced view of life.

Taking into consideration the Confucian humanism of China and certain philosophical trends of India, it would be truer to say that by the above method we bring together different trends of thought and modes of approach dominant in both the East and the West more than trends in East and West, respectively. Neither is the East completely devoid of science and humanism nor is the West devoid of spirituality. Moreover, there has been no development of thought in India since the fifteenth century, because of constant communal and political unrest, and it is only since the British advent that India has been having some respite for reflection. Thus men of thought in both the East and the West may object to being classified into two distinct groups; and we shall be on safer ground if we make the dominant trends and philosophical outlooks of the world bear on each other for reconciliation and synthesis. We should not ignore the Indo-European kinship in metaphysical thought and the Sino-European kinship in humanism. Again, Islam, which has its origins in the Near East, has a humanism of its own kind, however communal it may be. The Oriental influence, however subtle, on Plato and Neo-Platonism and on Christian mysticism and German idealism was not unimportant. The influence of the Upaniṣadic ideas on the Schlegels, Schelling, and Schopenhauer and, through them, on German idealism and Christian theology has not completely escaped the notice of scholars. The East-West philosophical, religious, and other cultural contacts from a time before the invasions of Alexander the Great will create serious difficulties if, in philosophy, we distinguish the East and the West too sharply. But certain interests became all-engrossing in certain cultures in both the East and the West and gave rise to differences of outlook, and the analytical classification of the world's philosophies would therefore be more advantageous than one based on East-West differences. We need not assume that the two hemispheres must have their differentia philosophically also. Further, the common features of the East as distinct from those of the West and the common features of the West as distinct from those of the East may not be so important as the dominant trends of thought that obtain in the world, including the East and the West.

Notes

1. *Chāndogya Upaniṣad,* VII.xxv.2
2. *Ibid.*, VII.xxvi.1.
3. IV.i.3.
4. "Nāsadīya-sūkta," *Ṛg-veda,* X.129.
5. *Bṛhadāraṇyaka-upaniṣad,* I.iv.1 and 10.
6. *Ibid.*, II.iv.5.
7. B. M. Barua, *A History of Pre-Buddhistic Indian Philosophy* (Calcutta: University of Calcutta, 1921).
8. W. R. Sorley paraphrases T. H. Huxley's views thus: "The cosmic order has nothing to say to the moral order, except that, somehow or other, it has given it birth; the moral order has nothing to say to the cosmic order, except that it is certainly bad." *Recent Tendencies in Ethics,* p. 47. Quoted in J. T. Merz, *History of European Thought in the Nineteenth Century* (Edinburgh and London: W. Blackwood and Sons, 1914–1930), Vol. IV, p. 232.
9. See E. J. Thomas, *The Life of Buddha* (London: Kegan Paul, Trench, Trübner and Co., Ltd., 1927; New York: Alfred A. Knopf, 1927), pp. 201–203; also E. J. Thomas, *History of Buddhist Thought* (London: Kegan Paul, Trench, Trübner and Co., Ltd., 1933; New York: Alfred A. Knopf, 1933).
10. There is further classification. See Umāsvāti, *Tattvārthādhigama-sūtra,* J. L. Jaini, trans., Sacred Books of the Jainas, Vol. II (Arrah: The Central Jaina Publishing House, 1920). For a condensed account, see Mādhava Ācārya, *Sarvadarśana-saṁgraha,* E. B. Cowell and A. E. Gough, trans. (4th ed.; London: Kegan Paul, Trench, Trübner and Co., Ltd., 1904).
11. *Mādhyamika-kārikā,* XXV.19; see also S. Yamakami (Yamakami Sōgen), *Systems of Buddhistic Thought* (Calcutta: University of Calcutta, 1912), p. 258.
12. *Ibid.*
13. See A. B. Keith, *Indian Logic and Atomism* (Oxford: The Clarendon Press, 1921); also Gautama, *Nyāya-sūtra,* S. C. Vidyābhūṣaṇa, trans., Sacred Books of the Hindus, Vol. VIII (Allahabad: The Panini Office, 1930); also Kaṇāda, *Vaiśeṣika-sūtra,* Nandalal Sinha, trans.,

Sacred Books of the Hindus, Vol. VI (Allahabad: The Panini Office, 1923).

14. See *Sāṅkhya-tattva-kaumudī,* Ganganatha Jha, trans. (Poona: The Oriental Book Agency, 1934); also Patañjali, *Yoga-sūtra,* J. H. Woods, trans., *The Yoga System of Patañjali,* Harvard Oriental Series, Vol. XVII (Cambridge: Harvard University Press, 1927).
15. S. Radhakrishnan, *Indian Philosophy* (London: George Allen & Unwin Ltd., 1923–1927), Vol. II, p. 427. For an account of this school, see Jaimini, *Mīmāṁsā-sūtra,* Ganganatha Jha, trans., *The Pūrva Mīmāṁsā Sūtras of Jaimini,* Sacred Books of the Hindus, Vol. X (Allahabad: The Panini Office, 1925).
16. See P. N. Srinivasachari, *The Philosophy of Bhedābheda* (Madras: S. Varadachari and Co., 1934).
17. IV.i.3.
18. One is here reminded of the Islamic conception that matter is the habit of Allāh.
19. Vijñānabhikṣu, Commentary on the *Brahma-sūtra.*
20. H. N. Raghavendrachar, *The Dvaita Philosophy and Its Place in the Vedānta* (Mysore: University of Mysore, 1941).
21. There are several differences of view on this point among the Advaitins themselves. See the *Siddhānta-leśa-saṁgraha.*
22. F. O. Schrader, *Introduction to the Pāñcharātra* (Adyar, Madras: Adyar Library, 1916); J. G. Woodroffe, *The Serpent Power* (Madras: Ganesh and Co., 1924).
23. *Mādhyamika-kārikā,* XXV.
24. See the writer's article, "The Western and the Indian Philosophical Traditions," *The Philosophical Review,* LVI (March, 1927), 127–155.
25. It should not be inferred from this that all Indians are preoccupied with the realm of the spirit, taking no interest in the world, though the Indian would understand by philosophy the subject dealing with spiritual life.
26. G. de Ruggiero, *Modern Philosophy* (London: George Allen & Unwin Ltd., 1921), p. 16: "The philosophy of this new era in history is thus a national philosophy. Criticising the anti-historical and impersonal tendency of naturalism, it springs from the traditional thought of each separate people and thus represents in its spontaneity and originality of its growth the theoretical and self-conscious aspect of this historical movement towards the differentiation of nationalities."

GUNAPALA PIYASENA MALALASEKERA

Some Aspects of Reality as Taught by Theravāda Buddhism[*]

IN REGARD TO THE QUESTION "What is ultimate reality?" the different schools of philosophy or systems of thought seem to fall into two main divisions. Some of them say that the ultimate reality is *one:* they believe in a permanent unity behind all the variety and change of the world. They are the monists, theists, animists, eternalists, traditionalists, fideists, dogmatists, ontologists, realists, idealists, and energists. All these schools, though distinct among themselves and even opposed to each other on many points, nevertheless have this in common: they accept an ultimate reality as an entity in the metaphysical sense, whether that entity be called substance, or soul, or God, or force, or categorical necessity, or whatever other name may yet be invented. They may be said to follow a subjective method, molding reality on concepts; hence theirs is mostly a

[*] This paper deals with Theravāda, or early, Buddhism. The basic texts of this aspect of Buddhist philosophy are written in Pāli, not in Sanskrit. Consequently, most of the words, expressions, titles, etc., in the body and in the notes of this chapter are in that language. There are differences between Pāli and Sanskrit which can be very confusing, but, despite effort, the editor has been unable to find any system of editing which would provide unquestioned clarity. Transliteration of Pāli words has been left as written by the author, although it would have been possible, by editing, to make it parallel with that used for Sanskrit elsewhere in the volume.

Confusion occurs occasionally because of the fact that "ā" is used to indicate the plural, but it is also the normal ending of some words. The (technically) incorrect but useful addition of "s" to indicate plurals of Sanskrit terms therefore cannot be used in this case. The terms are consequently left as they were in the paper as written by the author. It is hoped that the context will provide clarity.

method of conjecture. The other schools say, some of them not very explicitly but still implicitly in their doctrines, that the ultimate reality is *plural:* they follow an objective method, molding their conceptions on observations. They generally deny a unity behind or within Nature's plurality. These are the dualists, pluralists, atheists, nominalists, relativists, rationalists, positivists, phenomenalists, annihilationists, occasionalists, transformists, progressivists, materialists, and so on. Here, again, all these schools, though differing among themselves on many points, have this in common: they reject a metaphysical entity.

Now, what is the place of Buddhism among these different "isms"? The answer is that it does not belong to either group. The ultimate reality of the phenomena in the universe—the chief phenomenon around which all others center being the "I," the self—is, according to Buddhism, neither plural, nor one, but *none.* In religion and philosophy, as well as in metaphysics, the words "real" and "reality" express more than one aspect of things: the actual as opposed to the fictitious; the essential as opposed to the accidental; the absolute or unconditioned as opposed to the relative or conditioned; the objectively valid as opposed to the ideal or the imagined; that which ultimately and irreducibly is as opposed to that which by means of various names signifies the mind's stock of knowledge. It must be admitted that in the *Suttas,* or Discourses, attributed to the Buddha we do not find any terms exactly corresponding to "real" and "reality," but all the above antitheses do occur and find expression in a variety of ways. The Buddha's teachings are more deeply and directly concerned with truth and the pragmatic importance of things, more with what might be called "spiritual health," than with theories. There are certain facts regarding spiritual health, however, about which it is necessary to have right views in order that action may be taken accordingly. These are the actualities; other things are of very much less value. The true is, therefore, the actual, that which *is;* it is expressed by the Pali word *sacca* (Sanskrit, *satya*), which means "the fact" or "the existent."

It must always be borne in mind that Buddhism is primarily a way of life and, therefore, that it is with the human personality that it is almost wholly concerned. Various metaphors are used to describe the essential nature of the personality;[1] they are meant not so much to indicate the ontological unreality of objects and sense-impressions (like the *māyā,* or illusion, which we come across in the

Vedānta) as to express a repudiation of permanence, a sense of happy security, a superphenomenal substance or soul underlying them. They are also meant as a depreciation of any genuine, satisfying value in spiritual life to be found either in "the pride of life" or in the lust of the world.

At the time of the Buddha (563–483 B.C.) there were in India views similar both to those of the Parmenidean school of Greater Greece—that the universe is a plenum of fixed, permanent existents—and to that other extreme held by Gorgias and the Sophists, that nothing is. In all things, the Buddha's teachings represent what he terms the Middle Way (*majjhimā-paṭipadā*), and here, too, he formulated the doctrine of the Golden Mean, the theory of conditioned or causal becoming, the most succinct statement of which is to be found in the *Saṁyutta-nikāya*.[2] "Everything is: this, O Kaccāyana, is one extreme; everything is not: this, O Kaccāyana, is the second extreme." The Tathāgata (that being the term which the Buddha used when speaking of himself), not accepting these two extremes, preaches his doctrine of the Middle Way.

The followers of the first extreme were known to the Buddha as eternalists (*sassata-vādino*). Some of them stuck to the old sacrificial religion, which promised blissful existence in heaven after death. Others favored a monistic view of the universe and believed in the attainment of a supreme bliss which consisted in the dissolution of personality in an impersonal, all-embracing Absolute. There were others who held the idea of an eternal, individual soul, which, after many existences, would return to its genuine condition of free spirit as a result of accumulated merit. These various views are described in the Brahmajāla-sutta of the *Dīgha-nikāya*.[3] It is interesting to note from these descriptions that the various schools of idealism, which later appeared in the West, had their counterpart in the India of the Buddha, e.g., subjective idealism, which holds that it is the "I" alone which exists, all the rest being a modification of my mind; or the objective idealism which holds that all, including the "I," are mere manifestations of the Absolute; or, again, the absolute idealism of Hegel, which informs us that only the relation between the subject and the object is real.

All these varieties of idealism the Buddha held to be "painful, ignoble, and leading to no good, because of their being intent upon self-mortification."[4] Idealism, according to the Buddha, has but one reality, that of thought, and strives for but one end, the liberation of the thinking self. Addiction to self-mortification is merely the practical side of the speculations of idealism, in which the "self" is sublimated, with the natural consequence that the "self" must be liberated from matter; the "soul" must be freed from the bonds of the body. The passions of the body must be subdued even by force; body becomes the eternal enemy of the spirit, to be overcome by prayer and fasting and other austerities.

The followers of the second extreme, who denied any survival of the individual after death or any retribution for moral and immoral deeds, the Buddha called annihilationists (*uccheda-vādino*). The annihilationists, too, or, as they came to be called later, the materialists, had many varieties of belief in ancient India. Some, like the Epicureans, denied any external agency as the cause of matter and maintained that the highest good was pleasure. Others, very much in the manner of Hobbes or Comte or John Stuart Mill, held that only the sensuous could be an object of knowledge. But all of them saw only one origin, matter, and strove only for one end, material well-being. Increase of comfort, said the Buddha, leads only to desire for still more, and the desire for more leads and will always lead to conflict and conquest. He therefore condemned materialism as "despicable, vulgar, ordinary, base, and leading to no good."[5]

In the Buddha's view, both idealism and materialism, though theoretically opposed, converge both in their starting point and in their goal, for "self is their beginning and satisfaction their end." Between these two extremes of materialistic self-indulgence and idealistic self-denial, not as a compromise, but "avoiding both," the Buddha formulated the Middle Way, " the way of knowledge and wisdom," not in the wavering of speculation, or in the excitement of discussion, but "in tranquillity of mind and penetrative insight, leading to enlightenment and deliverance, enlightenment with regard to the real nature of things and deliverance from suffering and its cause."[6]

In following the middle course the Buddha borrowed from the eternalists their doctrine of the gradual accumulation of spiritual merit in a series of existences, but rejected their doctrine of an eternal spiritual principle. He saw contradiction in assuming an eternal, pure, spiritual principle which for incomprehensible reasons became polluted with the filth of mundane existence only to revert later to original purity. With the annihilationists he denied every permanent principle. The Buddha's originality consisted in denying substantiality altogether and converting the world process into a progression of discrete, evanescent elements. His position was not an easy one, because he had also to find a theoretical basis to establish morality. He was faced with the contradiction of a Moral Law without a personality on whom the law was binding, salvation with nobody to reach the goal. How he solved the problem will appear in the sequel.

The shortest statement of the Buddha's doctrine is contained in a formula which has come to be regarded as the Buddhist credo: "Whatsoever things proceed from a cause, the Tathāgata [i.e., the Buddha] has declared the cause thereof; he has explained their cessation also. This is the doctrine of the Great Recluse." It declares, in other words, that the Buddha has discovered the elements of existence, their causal connection, and a method to suppress forever their active efficiency and secure their quiescence.

The Buddha claimed that his was a practical teaching; its object was to show a way of escape from the ever-revolving round of birth-and-death, which constitutes *saṁsāra* and which is considered a condition of degradation and suffering (*dukkha*). This way of escape was meant primarily for human beings. True to this central conception, therefore, as stated above, the Buddha started with a minute analysis—using "analysis" in its strictest sense of "dissolution"—of the human being into the elements of which his being is composed. Analysis has always played a very important part in Buddhist teaching; in fact, one of its names is the doctrine of analysis (*vibhajja-vāda*).

In this analysis, the human being was found to consist of two parts, *nāma* and *rūpa*, loosely translated as mind and matter, *rūpa* representing the physical elements and *nāma* the mental ones. Matter is composed of the four elementary qualities of extension, cohesion, caloricity (*tejo*), and vibration. The relative qualities of hardness and softness and the occupation of space are due to the elementary quality of extension (*paṭhavī*). It is the element of cohesion (*āpo*) which makes the many parts adhere intrinsically and to one another, and this prevents an aimless scattering about or disintegration, thus giving rise to the idea of a "body." Caloricity depends on vibration (*vāyo*), for by increased vibration the temperature rises and when the temperature is lowered the speed of vibration is reduced; thus do gases liquefy and solids solidfy.[7]

The mental elements are similarly divided into four groups: feelings or "receptions" (*vedanā*), ideas or "perceptions" (*saññā*), variously translated as "mental activities" or "complexes" (*saṅ-*

khārā), and cognition or "conception" (*viññāṇa*). *Rūpa* (matter) and these four divisions of *nāma* (mind) are called *khandhā* (aggregates or groups). The whole, in brief, is an analysis of the "I" or "personality" (*sakkāya*). The apparently unitary "I" is broken up into a number of layers, somewhat as in a burning flame a number of layers of color can be distinguished. But the layers of color in a flame are not parts laid out after the fashion of pieces in a mosaic, alongside one another; so also is it with the five *khandhā,* or groups. They are a continuous, unbroken process of action, of which it is expressly said that they are a "burning."[8] In all of them an arising and a passing away are to be cognized; they are not parts of a whole but forms of *action,* a process of mental-corporeal "nutrition" or "sustenance," in which the corporeal as well as the mental forms of grasping (*upādāna*)[9] fall together into one conceptual unity. They are the different modes in which the "I" enters into relation with the external world, lays hold of it, "seizes" it. The relationship is not an immediate relation with the external world in which a metaphysical "I" is endowed a priori with the power of cognizing, nor is it the mediate relation of a purely physical process in which the "I" only builds itself up a posteriori on the basis of continued experiences.

The external world with which the human being comes into relationship is also analyzed into its component elements. This relationship is one of cognition, and in discussing how this cognition is established mention is made of cognitive faculties (*indriya*) and their objects (*visaya*). There are thus six cognitive faculties, or senses—the senses of vision, audition, smell, taste, and touch, and the faculty of intellect or consciousness.[10] Corresponding to these as objects of cognition are, respectively, color and shape, sound, odor, savors, tangibles, and non-sensuous objects. These twelve factors, the cognitive faculties and their objects, are called *āyatanāni,* or bases of cognition. The term "*āyatana*" means place, sphere, entrance, or point of support, and is used to cover both organ of sense (internal, or *ajjhattāni-āyatanāni*) and sense-object (external, or *bāhirāni āyatanāni*), the meeting of which constitutes cognition (*viññāṇa*). This cognition, which results from the meeting, can be divided into six classes, according to the cognitive faculty concerned and the sense-object, such as eye-cognition (*cakkhu-viññāṇa*), and so on. In the case of the sixth cognitive faculty (*manas,* or *mano*), consciousness itself, i.e., its preceding moment, acts as a faculty for apprehending non-sensuous objects. The three constituents that comprise a cognition—sense-faculty, sense-object, and resultant consciousness—are classified under the name *dhātu* (element). We thus get eighteen *dhātu*—the six sense-faculties, their six sense-objects, and the six varieties of resultant consciousness. This consciousness is the experience of the unity between concept and object; it is not something that *is*, but something that *becomes*. It is not an object of knowing, but *knowing* itself, an ever-repeated new becoming, new upspringing, out of its antecedent conditions. As such, it resembles what the physicist calls living-force, vital energy. It is formed, enfleshed, in *nāma-rūpa*, (mind-form, i.e., mind and body). Mind-form is the antecedent condition of consciousness, on the basis of which the next new upspringing of consciousness will assume new individual value. Consciousness is actuality as action, which means something that is not, but which, in order to be present, first must ever spring up anew. Between mind-form and consciousness exists the same ceaseless, quivering, leaping play which exists among the ever-repeated, new moments of combustion of a flame and its external shape. Without sufficient cause (*aññatra-paccayā*) no consciousness can arise.[11] Just as for consciousness to be present it must ever and again spring up anew, so the antecedent conditions upon the basis of which it springs up must also be present. It is from the friction of the living contact of senses with things that consciousness is born. It is thus a process of nutrition, of grasping, which embraces itself in its grasping, a process of growth, in which one moment is neither the same as the next, nor yet another, but in which every moment becomes another, passes into that other, just as one moment of a flame is neither the same as the next nor yet another, but becomes the next.

The human personality and the external world with which it enters into relationship are thus divided into *khandha*, *āyatana*, and *dhātu*. The generic name for all three of them is *dhamma* (plural *dhammā*), which is translated as "element of existence." *In Buddhism these* dhammā *are the only ultimate reality*. Broadly speaking, the *dhammā* are divided into two classes, *saṅkhata* (conditioned, i.e., subject to various conditions) and *asaṅkhata* (unconditioned). *Ākāśa* (generally, but unsatisfactorily, translated as space) and *nibbāna* (Sanskrit: *nirvāṇa*) are *asaṅkhata dhammā;* all other *dhammā* are *saṅkhata* (conditioned). The *saṅkhata* (conditioned *dhammā*) have four salient characteristics: they are non-substantial (*anatta*), evanescent (*anicca*), in a beginningless state of commotion (*dukkha*), and have quiescence only in a final cessation (*nirodha*).

It must always be recalled that the basic idea of this analysis is a moral one. Buddhism is defined as a religion which teaches defilement and its purification (*saṅkilesa* and *vodāna*). Purification or salvation lies in *nibbāna,* or *nirodha,* which is cessation from *saṁsāra.* Thus, when the elements of being are analyzed, they are divided into purifying and defiling elements, good and bad (*sāsava* and *anāsava*), propitious to salvation and averse to it (*kusala* and *akusala*). Purifying, good, and propitious factors are those elements, those moral factors, that lead to *nibbāna;* their opposites lead to or encourage *saṁsāra.*

This analysis was part of the Buddha's attempt to find answers to the great, primary questions which lie at the root of every religious system, which form the seed of religious development, upon the answer to which depends the nature of any religious philosophy —such questions as: Whence am I? Whither do I go? What happens to me after death? How do I know myself? How does this world enter into me, into my consciousness? To the Buddha's way of thinking, all these questions have one great fallacy, that of begging the question, *petitio principii.* His view was that there should be another question prior to all these inquiries upon which depends the very possibility of further questioning, namely, Is there anything at all which deserves the designation "I"? Here was a problem which the Buddha felt could not be solved by argument or mere logic (*atakkāvacara*), for in logic one has to presuppose the reality of the thinking subject as standing outside the process of thinking, as a witness or, rather, as a judge. The concept cannot sit in judgment where it itself is the judge. Only one kind of logic, he said, could help here: the logic of events, because it is beyond sophistry; actuality can be understood not by argument but by analysis (*yoniso-manasikāra*).[12]

As a result of such analysis, the Buddha discovered that the individual, conventionally called "I" or the "self," is a mass of physical and psychical elements without any permanent entity behind them to keep them together, without any "soul" inhering in them, the elements themselves being a mere flux (*santāna*), a continuity of changes. In postulating a mythical, unchanging entity as the possessor of changing qualities, one merely assumes, he said, the existence of that which has to be proved. The conviction that men hold that, though thought and actions change, the thinker and the doer remain the same is a delusion, for it is exactly by thought that we change our minds, by actions that we change our lives. Actions cannot exist apart from the doer, cannot exist freely as such. If the action changes, the so-called actor must change at the same instant. Thus, the "I" must be identified with action. It is only the "I" which can walk and sit and think and eat and sleep. But that "I" is not a permanent, unchanging entity; it is identified with the action and is the action itself, and thus changes with the action. "I" cannot stay at home while "I" go out for a walk. It is conventional language (*sammuti*) which has spoiled the purity of conception (*paramattha*—ultimate sense, the supreme-thing-meant), though, in some cases, language does remain pure enough, as when we say, "It rains." Who rains? What rains? Simply, it rains, meaning, there is rain. Likewise, the concept should not be: "I think," but "There is thinking." This is the teaching which came to be known as the doctrine of *anattā*.

In this doctrine, the Buddha went counter to the three main systems of philosophy that were current in India in his day: the teachings of the Upaniṣads, of the Jainas, and of the Sāṁkhya. Briefly stated, the Upaniṣadic teaching is a kind of monism, in which a real being, *Brahman*, is assumed to be something eternal, without beginning, change, or end, and man's soul (*ātman*) is assumed to be an integral part of that Being, *Ātman* and *Brahman* being one. The Jainas had a highly developed theory of moral defilement and purification and a theory of spiritual existence extending even to plants and inanimate, non-organic things, which are also supposed to possess souls. The Sāṁkhya taught the existence of a plurality of souls, on the one hand, and of a unique, eternal, pervasive, substantial matter, on the other. Buddhism is opposed to all three systems. Forsaking the monism of the Upaniṣads, it declares that there is no real unity at all in the world. Everything is discrete, separate, split up into an infinity of minute, impermanent elements, without any abiding stuff. It agrees with Jainism in opposing the monism of the Upaniṣads and in maintaining that being is joined to production, continuation, and destruction, but disagrees with the Jaina doctrine which ascribes a physical nature to *kamma*. To the dualism of the Sāṅkhya the Buddha opposes the most radical pluralism, converting the world process into an appearance of evanescent elements, and calls the eternal pervasive matter, which is imagined as their support or substratum, a mere fiction.

The term "*anattā*" (Sanskrit, *anātman*) is usually translated as "no-soul," but, strictly speaking, *attā* is here synonymous only with a *permanent,* enduring, entity, ego, self, conscious agent, etc. It is the permanence that is denied in *anattā.* The underlying idea is that, whatever may be designated by these names, it is *not* a *real, ultimate* fact; it is a mere name for a multitude of interconnected facts which Buddhist philosophy attempts to analyze by reducing them to real elements (*dhammā*). Buddhism does not deny the existence of a personality or a "soul" in the empirical sense. What it does deny is that such a "soul" is an ultimate reality, a *dhamma.* The Buddhist teaching of *anattā* does not proclaim the absence of an individuality or self; it says only that there is no permanent individuality, no unchanging self. Personality or individuality is, according to Buddhism, not an entity but a process of arising and passing away, a process of nutrition, of combustion, of grasping. A man's personality is conceded as being something real, a fact (*sacca*) to him at any given moment, though the word "personality" is only a popular label and does not correspond to any fixed entity in man. In the ultimate constituents of conditioned things, physical and mental, Buddhism has never held that the real is necessarily the permanent. Unaware of this anticipation, modern philosophers such as Bertrand Russell are asking modern philosophy to concede no less.

The Buddhist term for an individual, a term which is intended to suggest the Buddhist view as opposed to other theories, is "*santāna*" (stream), viz., the stream of interconnected facts. It includes the mental elements as well as the physical, the elements (*dhammā*) of one's own body and those of external objects, as far as they constitute the experience of a given personality. The representatives of the eighteen classes of *dhātu* mentioned earlier combine to produce the interconnected stream. Every combination of these elements represents a nominal, not an ultimate, reality. The number of psychical elements at any given moment is variable. It may be very considerable, because undeveloped, dormant faculties are also reckoned as actually present. Some *dhammā* are constant, present at every moment, others only under certain conditions. Elements which combine at any moment vary both in number and in intensity. In any individual, at a given moment, a certain element may predominate. All mind at every moment is an assemblage of mental faculties (*saṅkhārā*) or elements. Two elements which are constantly present are most precious: *samādhi* (power of concentration) and *paññā* (insight). If they become predominant, they change the character of the individual and his moral value. The predominant element in ordinary men is ignorance (*avijjā*), which is the reverse of *paññā* and not merely its absence. It is a separate element, present at the same time with dormant *paññā*. But it is not constant, and can be cast out of the mental stream.

There is a special force of *kamma,* sometimes called *patti* (Sanskrit, *prāpti*), that holds these elements in combination. It operates only within the limits of a single stream and not beyond. The stream of elements kept together is not limited to the present life but has its source in past existences and its continuation in future ones. This is the Buddhist counterpart of the soul or self in other systems.

From the denial of substance follows the denial of every difference between the categories of substance and quality. There is no "inherence" of qualities in substance; in this respect all real elements (*dhammā*) are equally independent. As separate entities they then become "substances" *sui generis.* All sense-data are also substances in the sense that there is no stuff they belong to. We cannot say that matter has extension, cohesion, temperature, and vibration, but that matter is extension, etc., and that without these qualities there is nothing called matter. Matter is thus reduced to mere qualities and forces which are in a constant state of flux, in which there is no entity to support the qualities or to be the possessor of attributes or, as substance, to stand under them all, to uphold them all, and to unite all the phenomena associated with it. Independent of attributes, there is no substance, no substratum, not even the idea, because the idea is dependent on certain conditions. When science bends more and more to the view that all matter is merely a form of energy, a grouping and re-grouping of forces, as advocated by scientific materialism, or as some would prefer to call it, energism, it is only admitting in different words the unsubstantiality of matter, which the Buddha declared more than two thousand years ago.

The same principle applies to the mental sphere. Mind is not an *entity* but a *function;* consciousness is thought, and it arises when certain conditions are present. Thought does not arise as the action of a "thinking subject," but is conditioned by, originates from, is dependent on, other states. As such, it will again be the condition, the origin, the *raison d'être,* of further *states.* When it ceases to be it passes on its momentum, thus giving the impulse to new arising. Yet, the individuality of consciousness is not a mere physical process, either. It is a process of grasping and will last only as long as grasping lasts. Just as a fire can only burn as long as it lays hold of new fuel, so the process of individuality is a constant arising, an ever-renewed laying hold of the objects of its craving that causes the friction between sense-objects and sense-organs, and from that friction leaps forth the flame of new *kamma* which, because of *avijjā* (ignorance), will not be extinguished, but in grasping lays hold of fresh material, thus keeping alive the process of burning.

Thus the universe, with all that is in it, represents an infinite number of discrete, evanescent elements, in a state of ceaseless activity or commotion. They are only momentary flashes of efficient energy, without anything perdurable or stable, not in a condition of static *being*, but in a state of perpetual *becoming*. Not only are entities such as God, soul, and matter denied reality, but even the simple stability of empirical objects is regarded as something constituted by our imagination. The empirical thing becomes a thing constructed by a process of synthesis on the basis of sensations. Reality does not consist of extended, perdurable bodies, but of point-instants (*khaṇa*) picked up in momentary sensations and constituting a string of events. Our intellect, then, by a process of synthesis, so to speak, puts them together and produces an integral image, which has nothing but an imagined mental computation.

A single moment of existence is thus something unique, unrepresentable and unutterable. In itself, set loose from all imagination, it is qualityless, timeless, and spaceless (indivisible), timeless not in the sense of an eternal being, spaceless not in the sense of being ubiquitous, motionless not in the sense of an all-embracing whole, but all these in the sense, respectively, of having no duration, no extension, and no movement. It is a mathematical instant, the moment of an action's efficiency. A representation and a name always correspond to a synthetic unity, embracing a variety of time, place, and quality, but this unity is a constructed unity, constituted by an operation of the mind, a chain of moments cognized as a construction on the basis of some sensation. Actions take place in time and space, space as the expression of the pure simultaneousness of things and time as the pure successiveness of the processes, but there is no space or time apart from their being correlatives of the concept.[13]

There are thus two kinds of reality: the one, ultimate or pure reality (*paramattha-sacca*), consisting of bare point-instants (*khaṇa*), without definite position in time or space and with no sensible qualities; and the other, empirical reality (*sammuti-sacca*), consisting of objectivized images, endowed by us with a position in time and space and with all the variety of sensible and abstract qualities.

How, then, is the illusion of a stable, material world and of perdurable personalities living in it produced? It is in order to explain this that the Buddha put forward the doctrine of dependent origination (*paṭicca-samuppāda*). Just as the Four Noble Truths—of Suffering, its Cause, its Cessation, and the Way thereto—form the heart of the Buddha's teaching, so does the doctrine of *paṭicca-samuppāda* constitute its backbone. According to this doctrine, although the separate elements (*dhammā*) are not connected with each other either by a pervading stuff in space or by duration in time, there is, nevertheless, a connection among them. It is this: their manifestations are subject of definite laws, the laws of causation (*hetu-paccaya*). The flow of evanescent elements is not a haphazard process (*adhicca-samuppanna*). Every element, though appearing only for a single moment, is a "dependently-originating-element," i.e., it depends for its origin on some other preceding element or elements. Thus, existence becomes dependent existence (*paṭicca-samuppāda*), and this is expressed by the formula, "If there is this, there comes to be that" (*asmiṃ sati, idaṃ bhavati*). Every momentary entity springs into existence or flashes up in co-ordination with other moments. Strictly speaking, there is no causality at all, but only functional interdependence, no question of one thing's producing another, since one momentary entity, disappearing as it does at once, cannot produce any other entity. The relation is one of "consecution," in which there is no destruction of one thing and no creation of another, no influx of one substance into another, but only a constant, uninterrupted, infinitely graduated change.

Thus, the formula, "If there is this, there comes to be that," came to be supplemented by another formula, "Not from itself, not from something else, nor from a combination of both, nor by chance, does an entity spring up."[14] It is *co-ordinated,* not actually produced. There is neither *causa materialis* (continuing substance) nor *causa efficiens.* This view of causality, that the law of causality is, rather, the law of co-ordination between point-instants (*khaṇā*), is not strange to modern science and philosophy. The world of Buddhism is like the world of the mathematician; the world dies and is born afresh at every instant; it is evidently the world that Descartes was thinking of when he spoke of "continuous creation."

The fact that the Buddha declared the *khandhā* (*nāma* and *rūpa,* i.e., mind and matter) to be completely free from any unchanging, undying essence does not mean that Buddhism taught annihilation of body and mind at death. For, besides the doctrines of transience (*anicca*) and soullessness (*anattā*), there is also the doctrine of *kamma,* or the transmitted force of the act, bodily and mental. A living being is a *khandha*-complex, ever changing, but ever determined by its antecedent character, and that is ruled by *kamma.* The long-drawn-out line of life is but a fluctuating curve of evolving experience. Man, even in this life, is never the same, yet ever the result of his pre-existing self. Action, which is another word for *kamma,* will be present as long as there is existence, because existence is not something static but a process. A process must proceed, and this is done by activity, the activity of the senses. Just as a flame cannot exist without consuming, its very nature being combustion, so also the senses cannot exist without activity. But this is not the same as the psychological determinism of Leibniz and Herbart, for *kamma* is not fatalism. "If anyone says," declares the Buddha, "that a man must necessarily reap according to all his deeds, in that case no religious striving is possible, nor is there an opportunity to end sorrow."[15]

How is the doctrine of rebirth to be reconciled with that of *anattā?* The question "What is reborn?" is based on ignorance of the selfless process of *kamma. Kamma* is not an entity that goes from life to life, like a visitor going from house to house. It is life itself, insofar as life is the product (*vipāka*) of *kamma.* In each step we take now in full-grown age lie also the feeble attempts of our babyhood. The present actuality, which expresses itself as the result of all the preceding processes, carries in its very action all the efforts which went into the making of the previous actions. When a seed becomes a sprout this is done by the last moment in the seed, not by those moments when it lay placidly in the granary. Yet, it is also true, in a sense, that all the preceding moments of the seed are the indirect causes of the sprout. Every moment in the phenomenal world has its own totality of causes and conditions owing to which it exists. What we regard as a break in the continuity is nothing but the appearance of an outstanding or dissimilar moment. Death is but one such moment.

When a man dies, the component elements of his new life are

present from its very inception, though in an undeveloped condition. The first moment of the (apparently) new life is called conventionally *viññāṇa,* "conception." Its antecedents are *kammā,* which in the formula of the doctrine of dependent origination (*paṭicca-samuppāda*) are designated *saṅkhārā* (pre-natal forces). These *saṅkhārā,* which through conception (*viññāṇa*) find continuity in the new life, contain latent in them the *anusayā,* which is the name for the resultant of all the impressions made on the particular flux (*santāna*) of elements in the whole course of its faring (*saṁsāra*). It is these latent factors that the psychoanalyst, for instance, finds as so much refuse and slag in a man's mind when he penetrates into it. They are his heritage of action (*kammadāyāda*), brought down through countless lives and not inherited by him, as is sometimes stated, as the heritage solely from the past of his race. Life is kinetic; rebirth in Buddhism is nothing but a continuity of impulse, *kamma-santati.*

It is sometimes said that the doctrine of *anattā* takes away moral responsibility and that with it goes overboard the whole fabric of social morality. But it will be seen from what has already been stated that there is no contradiction at all between the denial of an unchanging entity and the fact that former deeds engender a capacity for having a consequence. In fact, the doctrine of *anattā* enhances the idea of responsibility, for there is here no Savior or Redeemer to intercept the unfailing consequence of one's actions. Likewise, the statement that the doctrine of *anattā* is inconsistent with free will is also due to a misconception. If nothing arises without a cause, if everything is of "dependent origination," can there be free will? That is the question. There is a tradition that the doctrine of dependent origination (*paṭicca-samuppāda*) itself was established by the Buddha in defense of free will and against a theory of wholesale determinism. The Buddha singled out for special animadversion the doctrine of his contemporary, Makkhali Gosāla, who maintained that all things are unalterably fixed and that nothing can be changed. The Buddha called this the "most pernicious" of doctrines.[16] On the other hand, the Buddha declared himself to be an upholder of "free action" (*kiriyā-vādī*). The law according to which a moral or immoral deed must have its fruition is the Law of *Kamma,* but in order to have a consequence the action must be produced by an effort of the will. The Buddha declared, "Will alone is *kamma*" (*cetānahaṃ bhikkhave kammoṃ vadāmi*).[17] It must also be remembered that free will really means "strong will," for the possibility of choosing shows the presence of two or more opposites. If there were no attraction or motive, equilibrium would have been established already and no choice would be necessary. When inducement or coercion is not absent, it is a contradiction to speak of free will. Will is thus only a milder term for craving, and craving exists only in dependence upon feeling. Our real freedom lies, therefore, not in the will, but in being without will.

How is the cessation of this round of birth and death, which is transient, sorrow-fraught, and "soulless," brought about? By following the path laid down by the Buddha. There are two factors that help a man to get started on the path: the one is right reflection (*yoniso-manasikāra*) and the other is friendship with the good (*kalyānamittatā*). The Buddha is man's best friend; that is why the appearance of a Buddha in the world is an event of such significance. The cessation of suffering is called *nirodha,* or *nibbāna. Nibbāna* has so often been discussed that there is no need to say much here.

Only when the grossly wrong views regarding personality are disposed of is the path entered upon which leads to final deliverance. *Nibbāna* consists of two stages. When, by treading the Noble Eightfold Path, the process of the arising of craving has come to a stop, the grasping of the "aggregates" (*khandhā*), which form the individual, will cease also. When the lust for life has ceased, no further rebirth will take place, and the highest state, that of a saint (*arhant*) is attained. But, when the lust for life has ceased, life itself will not disappear simultaneously. Just as the heat in an oven, produced by fire, will remain for some time even after the fire is extinct, so the result of the craving which produces rebirth may remain a while even though the fire of the passions be extinct. In this state of sainthood or *arhant*-ship which is called *nibbāna* with residue (*sa-upādisesa-nibbāna*), neither act nor thought can be regarded as moral or immoral. The *arhant's* apperception is ineffective. His actions are not influenced by craving and do not, therefore, produce *kamma.* They are free from tendencies, from likes and dislikes. Where no new *kamma* is produced no results follow. But, when the result of previous *kamma* is exhausted and the *arhant's* life comes to an end, this state is called *nibbāna* without residue (*an-upādisesa-nibbāna*).

In this final emancipation, all suffering (*dukkha*) ceases. *Nibbāna* is where lust, ill-will, and delusion are not. In Buddhism life is a process which has its sufficient cause neither in something metaphysical, like God, nor in something physical, e.g., parents. It is a process which is destined to come to an end and awaits the moment of coming to an end. Ignorance (*avijjā*), i.e., ignorance about life itself, is the beginningless starting point from which life ever and again springs forth, as from some hidden source that never dries up *as long as it remains undiscovered.* Life is begotten of ignorance; what keeps it going is grasping or clinging, which is prompted by craving (*taṇhā*). In life, grasping is the only activity, and there is only one actual object of this grasping, that which is conventionally called personality. Personality is *the* object in dependence upon which grasping exists, and, at the same time, is that which exists in dependence upon grasping. It is grasping that gives life its nutrition (*āhāra*). Through this nutrition, through the power of maintaining itself, life proves itself to be life. But to say this is not to say that grasping is the cause of life; that would be like saying that the cause of a flame is the fuel there present. Fuel creates no flame; it only maintains the flame. To understand this, to realize this, to live it out—that, in the deepest sense, is Buddhism.

Ignorance is destroyed by knowledge, by insight. The first step is insight into the real nature of conditioned things (*samma-sana-ñāṇa*) as having the three characteristics of impermanence, suffering, and soullessness. He who perceives suffering only, but not the transiency thereof, has only sorrow, but, when the unreality of life is understood, the unreality of suffering will also be perceived. From this understanding will ensue insight into the nature of all things as processes (*udayab-baya-ñāṇa*), the knowledge that there is nothing but a process of becoming. The next step is insight that becoming is ceasing (*bhaṅga-ñāṇa*). Becoming and ceasing will be seen as two aspects of one process. This is followed by knowledge of the dangers that have to be feared (*bhaya-ñāṇa*) and the understanding of the perils inherent in clinging (*ādīnava-ñāṇa*), together with the reasons for being disgusted with such an empty show (*nibbidā-ñāṇa*). Thereupon arise the desire to be set free and the knowledge thereof (*muñcitukamyatā-ñāṇa*) which will grow into recontemplation (*paṭisaṅkhāna-ñāṇa*), that is, contemplation of the characteristics of transiency, sorrow, and soullessness, but with increased insight as seen from a higher plane. This will be followed by even-mindedness regarding the activities of life, which is due not to lack of interest but lack of self-interest. The climax of discernment is reached with the insight of adaptation (*anuloma-ñāṇa*), which is the gateway to emancipation (*vimokkha-mukha*), where the mind is qualified for final deliverance.

The basis of all this is renunciation. Renunciation cannot be learned; it must grow, like the dawn. When it is night we can admire the millions of stars, but all their beauty and the glory of the moon, too, fade with the first rays of the sun. Renunciation begins when one learns to distinguish between the value a thing has because one wants it and the value it has apart from one's desire. The value of a thing is regulated by one's desire for it; if one wants to know its real value one must give up one's desire for it, but then it will be seen at once that it has lost all value. To be carefree—that is the secret of happiness—but not to be careless. This freedom from care is the result of forgetting the self, the result of self-renunciation. When pleasures vanish of their own accord, they end in keen anguish of the mind; when relinquished by one's own will, they produce infinite happiness, proceeding from tranquillity. Just as darkness can be experienced only when all light is extinguished, so, also, *nibbāna* can be realized only when all attachment has been destroyed.

The realization of this truth is attained by the threefold practice of *sīla, samādhi,* and *paññā. Sīla* is discipline of both body and mind, whereby the defilements that cloud wisdom are removed. But mere morality is not enough; it must be accompanied by mental development. All morality which strives to perpetuate the self is a subtle kind of selfishness. The more subtle and sublimated it is, the more rationalized and idealized, the more dangerous. *Samādhi* is the stilling of thought, the perfect equilibrium of mind, which is attained by the *jhāna* (Sanskrit, *dhyāna*), the so-called "trances," perhaps better translated as "musings." They constitute the first taste of the happiness of *nibbāna.* It is the joy of having found a possibility of escape from the round of birth, suffering, and death. The increase of this joy becomes sheer delight, which then gives place to a serene tranquillity, and then to a sense of security and equilibrium, the bliss of well-being (*sukha*), which is the very opposite of insecurity and unbalanced striving. In that state of tranquillity, not disturbed by likes and dislikes, not made turbid by passions, not hazed by ignorance, like sunlight that penetrates a placid lake of clear water, there arises the supreme insight (*paññā*) that "all birth and death have ceased; the noble life has been lived; what had to be done has been accomplished, and beyond this there is no more." This is the supreme moment of illumination when the saint (*arhant*) sees the whole universe with the vividness of a living reality. It is described as a double moment, a moment of feeling as well as a moment of knowledge. In sixteen consecutive thought-instants, the *arhant* has seen through the whole universe and has seen it in the four stages of its evolution toward quiescence. This supreme moment of illumination is the central point of the teaching regarding the path to salvation.

Such is *nibbāna,* where the insight of non-self has taken the place of delusion and ignorance; where being is seen as a mere process of becoming, and becoming as ceasing; where the spell that has kept us in bondage is broken; where the dream-state will vanish into reality, and reality will be realized. This reality is not the eternalization of a self but escape therefrom, not the deliverance or the salvation *of* the self but the deliverance and salvation *from* the self, from the misconceived "I." And, with this, the last word has been said. Where craving has ceased, the process of becoming, which is grasping, has ceased also. Where there is no more becoming, there is no more birth, with all its concomitants of sorrow, decay, and death.

Is *nibbāna* annihilation? Yes and no. Yes, because it is the annihilation of the lust for life, of the passions, of craving and grasping, and of all the things that result therefrom. But, on the other hand, where there is nothing to be annihilated, there can be no annihilation. That which constantly arises and in arising is nothing but a process of change and in changing also constantly ceases—that cannot be said to be destroyed; it merely does not arise again. *Nibbāna* is thus best described as deliverance, surpassing all understanding, above all emotion, beyond all striving, the non-created, the non-conditioned, the non-destructible, which all may attain through insight and realization. It is the culmination of the Buddha's teaching: "Just as, O monks, the ocean has but one taste, the taste of salt, so the doctrine and the discipline have but one taste, the taste of deliverance."[18]

"Hard is the infinite to see; truth is not easy to see; craving is pierced by him who knows; for him who sees naught remains."[19]

Notes

1. *E.g.*, "To regard the body as something of worth would be like taking frescoes to be real persons." Or, again, "As one would view a bubble, as one would view a mirage, so should the world be looked at."

(*Dhammapada*, 170.) "The world is like a dream." (*Saṁyutta-nikāya*, III, 141.)

2. *Saṁyutta-nikāya*, II, 17. With an Introduction by Mrs. Rhys Davids, F. L. Woodward, trans., *Kindred Sayings* (London: Oxford University Press, 1926), Vol. IV, p. 13.
3. The first discourse of the *Dīgha-nikāya*. See T. W. Rhys Davids, trans., *Dialogues of the Buddha* (London: Oxford University Press, 1901), Vol. I.
4. *Majjhima-nikāya*, Dhammacakkappavattana-sutta. See Lord Chalmers, trans., *Further Dialogues of the Buddha* (London: Oxford University Press, 1926).
5. *Ibid.*
6. *Ibid.*
7. For a very good exposition of this and what follows, see Th. Stcherbatsky, *The Central Conception of Buddhism* (London: Royal Asiatic Society, 1923).
8. "*Saṅkhārā*" is a very difficult term to translate, since it means various things in various contexts. Etymologically, it means "what is put together as a composite thing." See T. W. Rhys Davids and W. Stede, *Pali-English Dictionary* (Chipstead, England: Pali Text Society), s.v.
9. "The Form, O monks, is a burning" (*rūpaṁ bhikkhave ādittaṁ*)—and so on with the other *khandhā*. *Saṁyutta-nikāya*, Khandha Saṁyutta, 61. See F. L. Woodward, trans., *Kindred Sayings* V.
10. For an excellent exposition of this point, see Paul Dahlke, *Buddhism* (London: Macmillan and Company, 1927), pp. 129 ff.
11. See the *Majjhima-nikāya* (*Further Dialogues of the Buddha*) (London: Oxford University Press, 1926–), Mahā-taṇhā-sāṅkhya-sutta, 38.
12. For an explanation of this very significant word, see *Pali-English Dictionary*, s.v.
13. The Buddhist conception of time and space is given in *Saṁyutta-nikāya*. See Mrs. Rhys Davids, trans., *Kindred Sayings*, Vol. I.
14. See *Majjhima-nikāya*, Mūlapariyāya-sutta, 1.
15. *Aṅguttara-nikāya*, I.237. F. L. Woodward, trans., *Gradual Sayings* (London: Oxford University Press, 1932), Vol. I.
16. *Ibid.*, I.33.
17. *Aṅguttara-nikāya*, III.415.
18. *Ibid.*, IV.201.
19. *Udāna*, VIII.2. See F. L. Woodward, trans., *The Minor Anthologies of the Pali Canon*, Pt. II (London: Humphrey Milford, Oxford University Press, 1935).

JUNJIRŌ TAKAKUSU

*Buddhism as a Philosophy of "Thusness"**

A Preliminary Remark

BRAHMAṆISM, as it was represented in the Upaniṣads, was a philosophy of "Thatness" (*Tattva*) and was based on the theory of the reality of Being. The chief concern was, therefore, the immortality of *ātman* (self) as an individual principle and the eternity of *Brahman,* which was also conceived as *Mahātman* (Great Self), as the universal principle. The highest principle, *Brahman,* which words were inadequate to describe, was rarely defined. Sometimes, no definition would be admitted, as exemplified in the famous words of Yājñavalkya, *"neti, neti"* ("not this, not this"). At other times

* There is much in this chapter which is strange and difficult for the Western reader. Some preliminary and general knowledge of Buddhism is almost imperative. The difficulty is due in part to the condensation of so much basic material into the short space available. This presentation treats only of the fundamental principles, and not of the more well-known and popular phases, of Buddhist philosophy. However, as G. P. Conger has said, "If we are to understand the Buddhist systems, we must not be deterred by ordinary difficulties."

The original chapter is somewhat abbreviated by eliminating material that applies specifically to Far Eastern developments. The reader is referred to Professor Takakusu's book *The Essentials of Buddhist Philosophy,* which provides a much more extensive treatment of the basic ideas of this chapter and detailed expositions of the major schools as they developed in China and Japan. That volume is edited by Wing-tsit Chan and Charles A. Moore, and is published in its third American edition by Office Appliance Company, of Honolulu, and by the Asia Publishing House, of Bombay. It was first published by the University of Hawaii in 1947.

The author's preferred style, especially his abundant use of capitalization—except in cases in which a possibly presumptuous and perhaps sometimes controversial attempt has been made by the editor to distinguish between *nirvāṇa* as a state of emancipation and *Nirvāṇa* in its metaphysical sense—is, for the most part, retained.—Editor's note.

some appropriate definitions, such as *saccidānandam*, to which we shall return soon, were given and seriously discussed.

Buddhism, on the other hand, was a philosophy of "Thusness" (*Tathātā*)—things as they actually are—and started with the theory of becoming, admitting no *ātman*, individual or universal, and no eternalism whatever. The staying reality of Being is, according to Buddhism, only for one instant. Things come into being and pass on; nothing remains the same for two consecutive moments. The universe is thus a never-ceasing conflux of life-waves (*Saṁsāra* [*Saṅsāra*]). Even in Buddhist realism, a reality is conceived in momentary existence or in the continuum of transitoriness.

The fundamental principles of Buddhism were summed up by the Buddha in the three items of negation: 1. All elements have no self (*sarva-dharma-anātmatā*). 2. All component things are impermanent (*sarva-saṁskāra-anityatā*). 3. All is suffering (*sarvam duḥkham*), or, to use Stcherbatsky's wording, no substance, no duration and no bliss.

Even the ultimate principle, *Nirvāṇa,* which was said to be Bliss, was literally the "state of fire blown out," i.e., the state in which life-conditions were negated, a non-created state.

Buddhism was thus from the outset based on the theory of negation, by which the principle of "Thusness" was established. Accordingly, all the Buddhist schools which rested chiefly on some dialectic arguments can be designated as those of negative Rationalism, the static nature of "Thusness" being only negatively arrived at as the remainder.

Before we proceed to see the far-reaching contrast of Buddhism with Brāhmaṇism we must note that within the sphere of Buddhism one finds no story of Creation, no Creator, no God, no First Cause, no monotheistic idea. Nor do we have any trace of materialism, hedonism, or extreme asceticism.

SACCIDĀNANDA (BRAHMAN)

The indefinable "*Brahman*" (n.) was "defined" in the Upaniṣads as *saccidānanda.* The name "*Brahman*" was not without a meaning. The word $\sqrt{Bṛh}$ means "to grow," "to increase." Probably the source of strength in matter and mind was the purport. Whatever it was, it was the name of the "highest principle" (n.), and the "manifested God" (m.), and sometimes it meant "prayer." It existed from the beginning, one without a second, the real, the true. Its attribute was *saccidānandam.*

sat	*cit*	*ānandam*
Being	Thinking	Joy
Existence	Thought	Bliss
self-existent	all-knowing	Blissful
the real	the intellectual	the valuable

In the Upaniṣads a pantheistic idea was already ripe and the universal principle was conceived also to be immanent in an individual. The Self (*Ātman*) gradually became the individual principle. The Supreme God which the Upaniṣadic philosophers objectively sought and found was now discovered subjectively in their own person. It was an Intellectual Reality, the Lord of Cognition, the Internal Guide, the Light of Mind, the True Light, the Highest Splendor. Where there is no sun, no moon, no star, no lamp, *Ātman* alone shines in darkness, from whom all beings partake of the light. It was finally identified with the universal Self, which was also called *Mahā-puruṣa* (Great Person) or *Mahātman* (Great Self). Finally, the mysticism of identity was realized: *"Tat tvam asi"* (Thou art that), and *"Aham Brahman asmi"* (I am *Brahman*).

The theory of "Thatness" was thus completed; it was the conclusion of the Upaniṣadic philosophy. Now we come to the "Six Systems" of Hinduism. The trend of thought seems to have been divided into two, though they were always interdependent.

For convenience, let us suppose that Buddhism arose along with those six schools of Indian philosophy, although in reality those schools were all *systematized* after Buddhism. Some primary forms of the schools, at least special tenets of each, must have existed at the Buddha's time.

The Buddha denied the existence of the universal principle and the individual principle (*ātman*) of the Vedānta and proposed selflessness (*an-ātman*). In contrast to the Mīmāṁsā, the Buddha rejected the eternity not only of voice, but of everything else, and proposed impermanence (*anitya*). In this way the idea of *sat* was removed. Then *cit* was denied, too, and the theory of ignorance (*avidyā*) was set forth. Not only was *sat-cit* removed, but also *ānandam* (joy), and the proposal of the theory that all is suffering (*duḥkha*) was brought forward.

Besides, the authority of the Vedas was denied, and the sacrifice of animals was denounced. The charms and sorceries of the *Atharva-veda* was strictly forbidden. The caste system, based

SIX INDIAN SYSTEMS OF PHILOSOPHY IN RELATION TO BUDDHISM

Sat (Being)		*Cit* (Knowledge)
Action section (*Karma-kanda*) (Realistic)	Buddha 566–486 B.C.	Knowledge section (*Jñāna-kāṇḍa*) (Idealistic)
I *Mīmāṁsā school* (Ritualistic Realism) Theory of eternity of voice Six sources of knowledge Five-membered syllogism		IV *Vedānta school* (Idealistic, Pantheistic Monism) Theory of reality and identity of *Ātman* and *Brahmaa,* the individual and universal principles
II *Vaiśeṣika school* (Atomic Pluralism) Indivisibility and eternity of atom Polarity and neutrality of atom Theory of effect not inherent in cause Six categories (later 7 or 10) of reality (substance, attribute, function, sameness, variousness, unity)	Buddhism 500 years of its metaphysical and dialectical development	V *Sāṁkhya school* (Evolutional Dualism) Immortality of *ātman* and eternity of *prakṛti,* the natural principle Threefold suffering Theory of effect inherent in cause Theory of the world's periodic destruction Three sources of knowledge
III *Nyāya school* (Logical Realism) Theory of non-eternity of voice Sixteen categories of argument Four sources of knowledge Five- or three-membered syllogism Fifty-four fallacies or causes of defeat	Nāgārjuna *ca.* 125 Four methods of argument Two truths Eight negations	VI *Yoga school* (Dualistic meditative Intuitionism) Eight methods of restraint in meditation Three sources of knowledge Four immeasurable meditations
Dignāga (Dinnāga) (*ca.* 500) Buddhist Logic Two sources of knowledge Three-membered syllogism Thirty-three fallacies	Mādhyamika school	Asaṅga-Vasubandhu (*ca.* 410–500) Buddhist Yogācāra meditation Three sources of knowledge Four immeasurable meditations
Hsüan-tsang and Chi (*ca.* 650) in China		Bodhidharma and Hui-k'o in China (*ca.* 530) Foundation of Zen
Last Systematization of Logic		

Figure 1

on racial distinction, was rejected in his community. He called it the "community of one caste" (*saṅgha*), and the "*saṅgha* of the noble" (*āryas*), notwithstanding the fact that the *Ārya* and the *an-ārya* (non-*Ārya*) races came together. He often protested, saying, "It is not races altogether, but of persons individually, that we can speak as the noble (*ārya*) or ignoble (*an-ārya*) because there will be some ignobles among the *āryas* or some nobles among the *an-āryas*." The highest stage of cultivation in Buddhism was an "*ārya-pudgala*," a noble person.

The Buddha's rejection of the Brāhmaṇistic principles was thus complete. All the fundamental Brāhmaṇistic elements were wiped out and completely eliminated from Buddhism. The Buddha was not antagonistic toward the other systems, however. With the Sāṁkhya he shared the theory of periodic destruction of the world-system (*kalpa*) and the prohibition of animal sacrifice; with the Yoga, the meditative doctrine of immeasurability (*apramāṇa*) and other rules of concentration; and with the Vaiśeṣika and the Nyāya, the pluralistic ideas and the logical method of argument.

The Buddha's system was the philosophy of self-creation. The Buddha's view of human existence was very peculiar. According to his idea, the generation-move of beings was different from the intellection-move. The generation-move was again the *sat*-move, i.e., the real particles moving on, while the intellection-move was *cit*-move, i.e., the active energy moving on. These two motions when combined form our life-flux.

One's intellection way will be different from that of father and mother. Every man is created by himself and is creating himself, each taking his own way and completing the wave length of his generation-move. "Intellection-move" means that, even when we are born in an hereditary life and inherit our father's and mother's particles, we have our own accumulation of intellection energy latent in us. In Buddhism, this is called innate intellect or a priori knowledge. It is something like "subconscious intellect." All intellect that can be acquired after our birth is called postnatal intellect or a posteriori knowledge. According to Buddhism, education ought to be carried on so as to draw out and not distort the prenatal intellect. To perfect one's personality means to perfect one's intellect, i.e., to attain Perfect Enlightenment.

Buddhism is personal and individual to the end. One holds fast to one's own personality until one's final beatitude is attained. One does not come down from a highest principle, for such does not exist. One will attain his own highest principle. That is *Nirvāṇa*, "perfect freedom," totally non-conditional and non-determinant. One is perfectly free, even to condition and to determine. Even one's realm is not definite or conditioned. It is the *Nirvāṇa* of No-Abode.

Fundamental Principles of Buddhist Philosophy

The following are the general principles which are to be regarded as a common denominator of all the schools of Buddhism. At present I shall bring out six such basic principles:

(1) The Principle of Causation.
(2) The Principle of True Reality (Thusness).
(3) The Principle of Totalism.
(4) The Principle of Indetermination.
(5) The Principle of Reciprocal Identification.
(6) The Principle of Perfect Freedom, *Nirvāṇa*.

THE PRINCIPLE OF CAUSATION

According to Buddhist thought, human beings and all living things are self-created or self-creating. The universe is not homocentric; it is a co-creation of all beings. Even if the universe is not homocentric, as long as all beings have common purposes, it is natural that there should be groups of similar types of beings. Buddhism does not believe that all things came out of one cause, but holds that everything is inevitably created out of two or more causes.

The creations, or becomings, out of antecedent causes continue in series in point of time—past, present, and future—like a chain. This chain is divided into twelve divisions, called the Twelve Stages* of Causations and Becomings. And, since these stages are interdependent on one another, they are called Dependent Production or Chain of Causation.

The formula of this theory is as follows: From the existence of *this, that* becomes; from the happening of *this, that* happens. From the non-existence of *this, that* does not become; from the non-happening of *this, that* does not happen.

a. Causation by Action-influence

There is law and order in the progress of cause and effect. This is the theory of Causal Sequence.

* Dr. Takakusu's original word, "Cycles," was changed in the interest of greater clarity.

In the Twelve Stages of Causations and Becomings, it is impossible to point out which one is the first cause, because the twelve make a continuous circle which we call the "Wheel of Life." It is customary to represent the Wheel of Life in the following manner:

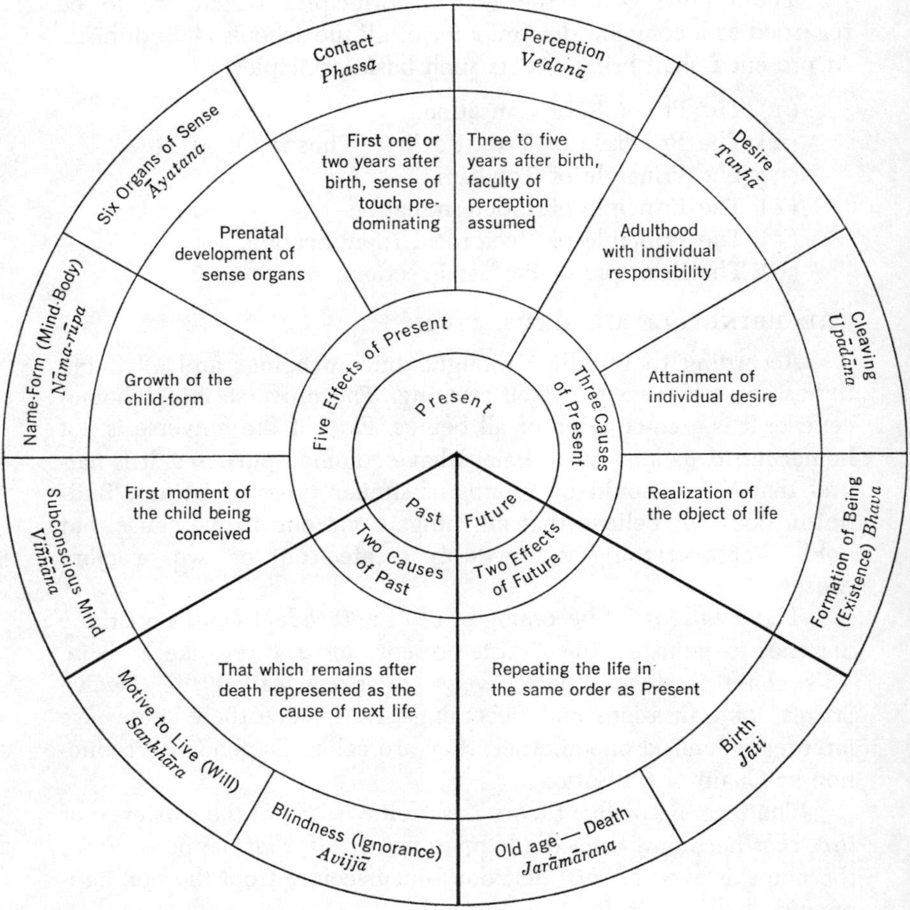

Figure 2*

* Terms in Figure 2 are in Pāli, rather than Sanskrit, because the earliest texts of Buddhism are in that language.—Editor's note.

Modern people generally regard time as progressing in a straight line from the infinite past through present to infinite future. In Buddhism, however, time is regarded as a circle with no beginning or end. Time is relative.

The death of a living being is not the end; at once another life begins to go through a similar process of birth and death, and thus to repeat the round of life over and over again. Thus a living being, when regarded in relation to time, forms an endless continuum.

It is impossible to define what a living being is, for it is always changing and progressing through the stages of life. The whole series of stages must be taken in its entirety as representing the one individual being. So, a living being, when regarded in relation to space, forms a complex in the shape of a ring. The Wheel of Life—in the diagram—is an ingenious representation of the Buddhist conception of a living being in relation to both space and time.

The Wheel of Life is a circle with no beginning, but it is customary to begin its exposition at Blindness: Blindness is only a continuation of Death. At death the body is abandoned, but the Blindness remains as the crystallization of the effects of the actions performed during the preceding life. This Blindness is often termed Ignorance, but this Ignorance ought not to be thought of as the antonym of knowing; it must include in its meaning both knowing and not knowing—Blindness or blind mind.

Blindness produces blind activity. The "energy," or the effect of this blind activity, is the next stage, Motive to Live, or Will. This Motive to Live is not the kind of will which is used in the term "free will" ; it is, rather, a blind motive toward life or the blind desire to live.

Blindness and Motive to Live are called the Two Causes of the Past. They are causes when regarded subjectively from the present, but, regarded objectively, the life in the past is a whole life just as much as the life of the present is.

In the life of the present, the first stage is Subconscious Mind. This is the first stage of an individual existence and corresponds, in the actual life, to the first moment of the conception of a child. There is no consciousness yet; there is only the subconscious mind or the blind motive toward life. When this Subconscious Mind advances one step and takes on a form, we have the second stage of the present, "Name-form." The Name is the mind, because mind is something we know by name and cannot grasp. Name-form is the stage of prenatal growth, when the mind and body are combined.

In the third stage, a more complex form is assumed, and the six organs of sense are recognized. They are the eyes, ears, nose, tongue, body, and mind.

The fourth stage corresponds to the first one or two years after the birth of the child. The six organs of sense reach the state of activity, but the sense of touch predominates. The living being begins to come into contact with the outside world.

Now that the living being is able to manifest its consciousness, it begins to take in the phenomena of the outside world consciously. This is the fifth stage—Perception, representing the period of growth of a child three to five years old. Here the individuality of the living being is definitely recognized; in other words, the status of the present life has been achieved.

The above five stages are called the Five Effects of the Present. In these stages the individual is formed, but the individual is not entirely responsible for its own formation, because the causes of the past have pushed the development of these stages. From here on, the individual begins to create causes on his own responsibility, or, in other words, enters the true sphere of self-creation.

The first of the Three Causes of the Present is Desire. Through Perception the individual experiences sorrow, pleasure, suffering, enjoyment, or neutral feeling. When the experience is sorrow, suffering, or neutral feeling, nothing much will happen. But when it is pleasure or enjoyment, the individual will endeavor to make it his own. This effort is Desire. It produces attachment. The first step of this attachment is the next stage. Cleaving, the effort to retain the object of Desire. The last state of this attachment is Formation of Being. The term "Existence" is often used for this stage, but, since it is a link between the present and future, and the preliminary step for Birth, "Formation of Being" is a more fitting term.

Desire, Cleaving, and Formation of Being represent the three stages of the activities of an adult, and together they constitute the Three Causes of the Present. While an individual is enjoying the effects of the past, he is forming the causes for the future. While the plum fruit is ripening on the tree, the core in the fruit is being formed. By the time the fruit is ripe and falls to the ground, the core, too, is ready to bring forth a new tree of its own to bear more fruit in the future.

In the Future two stages are listed—Birth and Old-age-Death, or, in short, Birth and Death. When viewed from the Three Causes of the Present, Birth and Death may be termed the effects. But, when viewed in the light of the continuous Wheel of Life, we may regard the future as the time when the causes of the present open out and close. Also, the Effects of the Future contain in themselves causes for the life still further in the future.

The present is one whole life, and so is the future. Past, Present and Future are each an independent whole life. Past, Present, and Future are relative terms, however. Objectively, there is no Future or Past. There is Present only. A living being does nothing but repeat the life in the Present.

It is clear that the Causation Theory of Buddhism is not like the Theory of Causality of modern physical science, for the latter is a fixed theory. In Buddhism every stage is a cause when viewed from its effect. When viewed from the antecedent cause, it is an effect. Also, it may be said that there is a cause in the effect, and an effect in the cause. There is nothing fixed in this theory. The Theory of Causality of physical science may be disproved, but the Causation Theory of Buddhism is never to be disproved.

Blindness, which remains after the death of a living being, is the crystallization of the actions (*karma*) which the living being performed during its life, or, using other words, the "energy" or influence of the actions that remain. Action—the most suitable translation of *karma*—is the dynamic manifestation of mental and physical energy. The crystallized or stilled form of this energy may be called Action-influence or potential energy. Action-influence remains after the action ceases, and this is what makes the Wheel of Life move. As long as there is energy it has to work, and the stages of causation and becoming will inevitably—blindly—go on forever.

In other words, a living being determines its own nature and existence by its own actions. Therefore, we may say it is self-created. The act of self-creation has continued in the past for thousands and millions of lives, and the living being has gone around the circle of Twelve Stages over and over again. And, according to the nature of the preceding Action, the next Wheel of Life may be of a higher order or of a lower order. That is, a living being may assume any form of life—human form, *Deva's* form, or animal form. The incessant transformation of life is called undulation of life (*saṁsāra*).

Often *Saṁsāra* (Constant flow) is translated as "Transmigration of soul," but that is a very misleading translation, for the idea is not that a soul lives after the death of the body and moves into another body. *Saṁsāra* means the creation of a new life by the influence of the actions of the former living being. In the first place, Buddhism denies the existence of soul. Life is like the waves on the water; the vibration of one particle causes the vibration of the next particle, and thus the waves are transmitted a long distance. One wave is one life, and the series of lives is *Saṁsāra.* In the Buddhist theory, the series of lives does not go on infinitely as in a straight line. They turn in a circle and repeat the circle over and over again. The Wheel of Life is a small circle of one life, while the great circle (the series of the Wheel of Life in its totality) is *Saṁsāra.*

Since this self-creation is regulated by the Action of the individual being, it does not depend upon the authority of another—for instance, a God. Nor is it affected by the Action-influence of different individuals. "Self-acted, self-rewarded," and "For a good cause, a good result; for an evil cause, an evil result"—these are the rules.

In Action-influence, there are Individual Action-influence and Common Action-influence. Individual Action-influence creates the individual being. Common Action-influence creates universality and the worlds where living beings exist. In this connection the expressions "Individual Effect" and "Common Effect" are used.

From another point of view, Action may be classified into three kinds: Good Action, Evil Action, and Neutral Action. Also, according to the way its retribution is received, Action may be classified into four kinds: Action to receive retribution immediately, Action to receive retribution in the present life, Action to receive retribution in the life to come, and Action to receive retribution in one of the lives following the next.

There are two ways of viewing the process of becoming. The order of cause and effect is usually regarded as arising in sequence in relation to time. However, when all the factors of the Twelve Stages of Causation are considered as belonging to one being, it possesses all at the same time. (For example, one does not abandon the Six Organs of Sense to gain Contact.) Therefore, all factors are mutually dependent, none being purely a cause nor purely an effect, but all developing simultaneously.

Buddhism regards all things in the universe as "existence depending upon series of causes." Only when there is cause is there existence. Without cause there can be no existence. No existence is permanent or conclusive. In Buddhist terminology, such an existence is called "Conditional Existence." Such a way of regarding all things is called "Knowing and perceiving reality *as such.*" To regard all things in the universe as dynamic becoming is the characteristic of Buddhism.

Delusion is the illness of the mind, while Action is its physical manifestation, and the result is Suffering. For instance: one may be angry in mind and act accordingly, striking or killing, and later suffer retribution. From this suffering of retribution one will acquire more delusions and consequent actions and suffering, thus repeating the same wandering ever and anon. Such is the Chain of Causation by Action.

Who or what is responsible for the progression of the Chain of Causation by Action? To explain this question clearly we must study the theory of Causation by the "Ideation-store."

b. Causation by the Ideation-store (Ālaya-vijñāna)

Actions (*karma*) are divided into three groups, i.e., those of the body, those of speech, and those of volition. When one makes up one's mind to do something, one is responsible for it and is liable to retribution, because the volition is a mind-action even if it is not expressed in speech or manifested in physical action. But the mind being the inmost recess of all actions, the causation ought to be attributed to the mind-store or Ideation-store.

The Buddhist Ideation Theory divides the mind into eight faculties: the eye-sense, the ear-sense, the tongue-sense, the nose-sense, the body-sense, the sense-center (the sixth, *mano-vijñāna*), the individualizing center of egotism (the seventh, *manas*), and the storing center of ideation (the eighth, *ālaya-vijñāna*—Ideation-store or mass).

Of these eight faculties, the seventh and eighth require some explanation. The individualizing Center of Egotism is the center where all selfish ideas, egotistic opinions, arrogance, self-love, and illusions are fermented and is the source of all delusions. The Storing Center of Ideation is the center where the seeds of all manifestations (i.e., ideas behind all actions) are deposited. Buddhism holds that the origin of all things is the effect of ideation. Let it suffice at present to say that the Storing Center of Ideation is the "seedbed" of all that exists. Every seed (i.e., every idea or mental impression) lies in the Storing Center, and when it sprouts out into the object-world (as an action), a reflection returns as a new seed (idea or impression upon the mind). That is, the mind reaches out into the outer world and, perceiving objects, puts new ideas into the mind-store. And, again, this new seed sprouts out to reflect a still newer seed. Thus the seeds accumulate and all are stored there together. When they are latent, they are called seeds, but, when they are active, they are called manifestations. The old seeds, the manifestations, and the new seeds are mutually dependent, forming a ring which forever repeats the same process. This is called the "Chain of Causation by Ideation."

That which makes the seeds sprout out is the manifestation of the seed itself. That is, the motive force which makes the chain of causation move is nothing but the ideation. It is easy to see from this theory of Causation by Ideation that Delusion, Action, and Suffering originate from mind-action, or ideation.

The Storing Center of Ideation is carried across rebirth to determine what the next form of life shall be. This Storing Center may be regarded somewhat as the soul is looked upon in other philosophies and religions. According to the Buddhist idea, however, what is reborn is not the soul, but is simply the result (in the form of ideational effects) of the actions performed in the preceding life. In Buddhism the existence of soul is denied.

One should ask where this Storing Center of Ideation comes from. To explain that we must study the theory of Causation by "Thusness."

c. Causation by Thusness (Tathātā *or* Tathāgata-garbha)

"Thusness," or "Suchness," is the only term that can be used to express the ultimate indefinable, the unnamable reality. It is otherwise called the "Matrix of Thus-come."

"Thus-come" is a designation of the Buddha employed by himself instead of "I" or "we," but not without a special meaning. After he had attained Enlightenment, he met the five ascetics with whom he formerly shared his forest life. These five ascetics addressed him saying, "Friend, Gautama." The Buddha admonished them, saying that they ought not to treat the Thus-come as their friend and their equal, because he was now the Enlightened One, the Victorious, All-wise One. When he had "thus come" in his present capacity as the instructor of all men and even of *devas,* they should treat him as the Blessed One, not as an old friend.

Again, when the Buddha went back to Kapilavastu, his former home, he did not go to the palace of his father, but lived in the banyan grove outside the town, and as usual went out for daily begging. Śuddhodana, his King-father, could not bear the idea of his own son, the prince, begging on the streets of Kapilavastu. So he visited the Buddha in the grove and entreated him to return to the palace. The Buddha answered in the following words: "If I were still your heir, I should return to the palace to share your comfort with you, but my lineage has changed. I am now a successor to the Buddhas of the past, all of whom have 'thus gone' as I am doing at present, living in the woods and begging. Accordingly, your majesty must excuse me." The king understood the words perfectly and became a pupil of the Buddha at once.

Now, "Thusness" or the matrix of "Thus Come" or "Thus Gone" means *the true state of all things in the universe,* the source of an enlightened one, *the basis of enlightenment.* When static, it is enlightenment itself (with no relation to time or space), but, when dynamic, it is in human form assuming an ordinary way and feature of life. "Thusness" and the "Matrix of Thus Come" are practically one and the same—the ultimate truth. In the Mahāyāna, the ultimate truth is called "Thusness."

Now we are in position to explain the "Causation Theory of Thusness." Thusness in its static sense is spaceless, timeless, undifferentiated, without beginning or end, formless, and colorless, because Thusness itself without its manifestation cannot be sensed or described. Thusness in its dynamic sense can assume any form. When driven by a pure cause it takes a lofty form; when driven by a tainted cause it takes a depraved form. Thusness, therefore, is of two states. The one is Thusness itself, the other is its manifestation, its state of Life and Death.

There are, therefore, three series of causations to be considered: (a) Causation by Action-influence as depicted in the Wheel of Life; (b) The origin of action, Causation by Ideation-store; (c) The origin of the Ideation-store, Causation by Thusness. One must not ask where Thusness, or the Matrix of Thus-come, originates, because it is the ultimate Thusness.

d. Causation by the Universal Principle (Dharma-dhātu)

We have thoroughly examined the origin of causation, but it is still necessary to consider the mutual relationships of the becomings of all things, and, therefore, we pass on to the principle of universal causation.

The Universe, or all things, is the dynamic manifestation of

Thusness. All things are mutually dependent, mutually permeating without any hindrance to one another.

"*Dharma-dhātu*" means "the element of the principle," and has two aspects: (1) the state of "Thusness," or noumenon, and (2) the world of phenomenal manifestation. In this Causation Theory it is usually used in the latter sense, but, in speaking of the ideal world as realized, the former sense is to be applied.

Buddhism holds that nothing was created singly or individually. All things in the universe—matter and mind—arose simultaneously, all things in it depending upon one another, the influence of all mutually permeating each, thereby making a universal symphony of spiritual totality. One item lacking, the universe is not complete; without the rest, one item cannot be.

When the whole cosmos arrives at a harmony of perfection, it is called the "Universe One and True," or the "Lotus Store" ("wreath"). In this ideal universe all beings will be in perfect harmony, each finding no obstruction in the existence and activity of another.

Although the idea of the interdependence and the simultaneous rise of all things is called the Theory of Universal Causation, the nature of the rise being universal, it is a philosophy of the Totality of All Existence rather than a philosophy of Origination.

According to this theory, four states of the universe can be conceived: (1) the real, or the world of actual life; (2) the ideal, or the world of principle; (3) the ideal realized, or the world in which the principle is applied in actual life, or the fact and the principle harmonized; (4) the real harmonized, or the world in which the actuality attains harmony in itself.

The first, second, and third states are easily understood, for those are the ideas often discussed by thinking men. But the fourth may be somewhat difficult to understand, because in these individualistic modern times it is usually thought that one individual is inevitably opposed to another, that classes in a society are opposed among themselves, that a business concern is in competition with another. A similar thought is often held in physical science also—no more than one object can occupy one position, and, therefore, all objects are opposed among themselves. Even in the world of learning, philosophy, for instance, stands by itself; so do religion and politics. According to some, even art should have an independent existence—art for art's sake. Such independent existence of all the branches of learning is in fact a dissolution of civilization. But the unification of the divergent branches will be a difficult task, for dissolution is the natural outcome in a world of individualistic tendencies.

The Principle of Totality, on the other hand, demonstrates that all things in the real world ought to have harmony among themselves, and it advances the following reasons: (1) Because of the simultaneous rise of all things; (2) Because of the mutual permeation of the influence of all things; (3) Because of the necessity of mutual identification between all beings (mutual self-negation to agree with each other) for the realization of harmony; (4) Because of the necessity of unity, or harmony, between the leaders and the followers for the attainment of a purpose; (5) Because all things have their origin in ideation—therefore a similar ideal ought to be expected of all; (6) Because all things are the result of causation and, therefore, are mutually dependent; (7) Because all things are indeterminate and mutually complementary—therefore harmony should be established among all things without hindrance; (8) Because of the fact that all beings have the nature of a *buddha* (or *buddha*-nature, i.e., the potential of enlightenment) dormant in themselves; (9) Because of the fact that all beings, from the highest to the lowest are parts of one and the same *maṇḍala* (circle, or knowledge of reality expressed in the form or figure of a circle); (10) Because of the mutual reflection of all activities—as in a room surrounded by mirrors, the movement of one image causes the movement of the thousand reflections. Buddhist writers enumerate twenty reasons, but for our purpose these ten will be quite sufficient.

THE PRINCIPLE OF TRUE REALITY (TATHĀTĀ)

Many of the problems concerning "Thus-come," "Thus-gone," "Thusness," or "Suchness" have just been studied in connection with the Causation theory. Thusness, however, is the ultimate foundation of Buddhist thought concerning the real state of all that exists, and, therefore, deserves further treatment in itself.

It is natural for people, first, to seek the innermost essence among the outward appearances of all things or to seek an unchanging fact among changing things. Failing in this, people try to distinguish the unknowable from the knowable, the real from the apparent, or the thing-in-itself from the thing-for-us. This effort, too, ends in failure, for what they select as the real or the thing-in-itself is utterly beyond human knowledge. Such efforts may be called the search for the world-principle or for the life-principle. The method of search is also various. Some are monistic or pantheistic, while others are dualistic or pluralistic.

Against all these views Buddhism stands aloof by itself. Buddhism is atheistic—there is no doubt about it. When questioned about the first cause or principle, the Buddha always remained reticent. The Buddha was, after all, a man, but a man with perfect enlightenment. As a man he taught men to become men like himself. Though people are apt to regard him as a superman, he did not regard himself as such. He was simply a perfected man. The Buddha did not deny the existence of gods (*devas*), but he considered them only as the higher grade of living beings, also to be taught by him.

As to the life-principle, he denied the existence of ego or soul or any kind of thing which one may call the real self—as we have seen before. To see the true nature or the true state of all things is not to find one in many or one before many, nor is it to distinguish unity from diversity or static from dynamic. The true state, or the true reality, is the state without any specific characteristic. It is very difficult for the human mind to understand this idea of a reality in which there is no "sub-stance" at all.

The idea of an abiding substance with changing qualities is very deeply rooted in our habits of thought. Buddhist schools, no matter what they are, Theravāda or Mahāyāna, realistic or idealistic, are utterly free from such a habit of thought, and all maintain the theory of pure change without substratum. So, when *any* Buddhist speaks of the true state of reality he means the state without a specific nature. The state without any specific characteristic or special condition is *nirvāṇa,* according to the general views of the Theravāda schools, because *nirvāṇa* as the goal is the state of perfect freedom from bondage. The Realistic school (the Sarvāstivāda), belonging to the Theravāda, goes a step further and assumes that selflessness, impermanence, and flamelessness are the true state of all things. The Nihilistic school (the Satya-siddhi, the completion of truth) holds that all things, matter and mind, are void or unreal and that nothing exists even in *nirvāṇa.*

The Mahāyāna school teaches, on the one hand, that the truth can be discovered only by negative views of becoming (the school of negativism, the Mādhyamika, the middle doctrine), and, on the other hand, it holds that true perfection can be realized negatively by denial of the illusory and causal nature of existence (the school of idealism, the Vijñaptimātra). The "Wreath" school (the school of totalism, the Avataṁsaka) of the Mahāyāna thinks that the ideal world, or the "World One and True," is without any independent individuals. The "Lotus" school (the phenomenological school, the Saddharma-puṇḍarīka) considers the manifested state to be the true entity immanent in Nature.

On the whole, to see only the fact that a flower is falling is, after all, a one-sided view, according to the theory of impermanence. We ought to see that immanent in the fact of a flower's falling there lies the fact of a flower's blooming, also that immanent in the blooming of the flower there is the fact of its falling. Thus, the antithesis of falling (extinction) and blooming (becoming) being synthesized, we form the view of mutual identification which is an unbiased view of the mean, the Middle Path.

We have to admit the saying that in any color or smell of a flower we see the manifestation of the true mean. This amounts to saying that we see inaction in action and action in inaction, immotion in motion and motion in immotion, calm in wave and wave in calm. We thus arrive at the true state of all things: i.e., the Middle Path. And this is Thusness or Suchness. This view of the true state of things is somewhat like the phenomenological view, which holds that noumenon can be seen only through phenomenon.

When the view is negatively expressed, it is the true negation or void, because any special state of things is denied altogether. Such is considered to be the ultimate basis of Buddhist thought. When the ultimate principle is viewed from the universal point of view it is called "the principle- or law-element" (*Dharma-dhātu*), but, when it is viewed from the personal point of view, it is named "the Matrix of Thus-come or Thus-gone" (*Tathāgata-garbha*), the Nature of Principle, *buddha*-nature, and the spiritual or Law-body. These are all practically synonymous. Without knowing the principle of Thusness, or the Void, in the highest sense of the word, one can in no way understand the Mahāyāna doctrine. The word "void" in its highest sense does not indicate "nothingness"; it means "devoid of special conditions," "unconditioned," "indeterminate."

As a summary: The ultimate indefinable, when defined, the nameless, when named, can be expressed only in a word like "Thusness." It is *Dharma*-nature in things in general and is *buddha*-nature in living beings. It is *nirvāṇa* (Perfect Freedom) as the ultimate principle of life, when all earthly conditions have been blown out. Strictly as the Buddha's personality, it is *Dharma-kāya* (ideal body), but when "Thusness" refers to the universe, it is *Dharma-dhātu* (principle- or law-element). Another name for "Thusness" is the "Matrix of the Thus-come" (*Tathāgata-garbha*). These synonyms are all intuitively given names and are to be considered as interpretations of the indeterminateness of *Nirvāṇa.*

THE PRINCIPLE OF TOTALISM (DHARMA-DHĀTU)

This principle—which has been discussed somewhat more fully above—is based upon the universal causation of *Dharma-dhātu* (element of law or principle) which we may regard as the self-creation of the universe itself. One ought not to forget that it is nothing but a causation by the common Action-influence of all beings, and that the principle is also based upon a synthesis of two conflicting ideas, self and selflessness, i.e., the world of one-all.

THE PRINCIPLE OF INDETERMINATION

Buddhism has nothing to do with fatalism, for it does not admit the existence of anything like destiny or the decree of fate. According to Buddhist doctrine, all living beings have assumed their present life as the result of self-creation, and they are, even at present, in the midst of creating themselves, or, in other words, every being is a stage of dynamic becoming. Though the grade and form of life vary in each birth, one ought not to think of the strict distinction of time as past or future. In truth, there is present only. That is to say, we have a long continuity of existence, birth and death being simply the rise and fall of the waves in the ocean of life. Birth and death are not the predestined fate of a living being, but a "corollary of action (*karma*)," as it was called by some. One who acts must sooner or later reap the effect; while enjoying an effect, one is sowing seeds anew, thus causing the next wave of life to be high or low according to circumstances. There is no idea of the transmigration of soul in the ordinary sense of the term.

Now, by way of contrast, let us examine other Eastern schools of thought. Confucianism is a determinism in the sense that Heaven is considered the basic principle of human life. The same is true of Taoism, as it holds *Tao,* or the vivifying principle, to be the source of the universe. With Brāhmaṇism in India, too, *Brahman* is made the creative principle or a personified god. Very similar ideas of determinism can be found among many Western schools of thought.

Buddhism, on the other hand, has quite a different method of approach. While practically all other schools of thought begin with a static first principle, Buddhism begins with the actual, dynamic world, and on the basis of the principle of self-cultivation strives to realize the ideal. *Saṁsāra* (the Rise and Fall of Life) is not an onward flow, but a waving circle, each wave being a cycle of life appearing on the great orbit of *Saṁsāra.* It has no beginning or end; one cannot point out the beginning of a circle. There is, therefore, no place in Buddhism for the idea of a first cause or creation. In the first verse of the *Dhammapada* (Book of Religious Verse, literally, Works of the *Dhamma*) the idea is described as follows: "All that we are is the result of what we have thought; it is founded on our thoughts; it is made up of our thoughts." We must remember, however, that though the volition is free or undetermined in the human world, it may appear as abstract energy-instinct or animal desire among the beasts and lower forms of life which are the lesser waves in the continuity of self-creation.

It is the motion of the mind-action which defines the form of an individual life. All things, matter and mind, have no substratum, no soul, no reality, no such thing as absolute self or ego. What appears to be real is a temporary existence, a causal sequence, one ripple in the long line of waves, the effect of two or more causes combined.

As long as you do not insist on the existence of a central principle or absolute ego, you may define yourself in any way you please. Generally speaking, it is satisfactory to say that you exist and to describe yourself. But in minutely definite and exact language, it is impossible to define your own self or to describe yourself. However, there is no danger of losing yourself, for no one can extinguish the influence of your action or latent energy. A particular manifestation of that energy in human form is yourself and the whole of you.

By virtue of your own action you will get your next life and so on along the continuous line of lives. Having no permanent center, a living being changes itself as time goes on, sometimes for better, sometimes for worse. Your self does not exist apart from the changing manifestations, but the cycle of the changing manifestations as a whole *is* yourself. There is, therefore, no possibility of the disappearance of your identity.

The idea of indetermination in the world of differentiation is expressed by many terms: "having no special nature" or "having no definite nature"; "all things are emptiness" or "having no special state"; "all are of temporary existence" or "all are existent by combination of causes." "No substance, no duration" is the root idea of Buddhism.

A real and permanent thing and a real and permanent self do not exist in the world of becoming. "Without change no life," as Bergson asserts. Buddhism has been teaching the Principle of Indetermination of matter and mind for over 2,500 years, but no anxiety or inconvenience has been caused by it as some modern physicists fear over the spread of the idea of the Uncertainty Principle of physical science.

THE PRINCIPLE OF RECIPROCAL IDENTIFICATION

Identification here means synthetic unification. An identification may be found in the union of two different materials, just as two different metals mixed make an alloy. Another kind of identification may be assumed when the same entity appears different according to viewpoint. The statement "Ignorant will is identical with perfect enlightenment" sounds very strange, but it is the same mind or person, tied down by ignorant will in illusion, who becomes enlightened when his wisdom is perfected. Still another identification is established in the case of the whole entity's being one and the same thing, like water and wave. If one does not understand the principle of reciprocal identification one cannot understand Mahāyāna Buddhism.

The Theravāda school is generally satisfied with analysis and is rarely inclined to synthesis. The Mahāyāna school, on the other hand, is generally inclined to synthetic identification of two conflicting ideas. If one party adheres to its own idea while the other party insists on its own, a separation will be the natural result. And this is what happens in the Theravāda school. The Mahāyāna school teaches that one ought to put one's own idea aside for a moment and identify oneself with the position of the other party, thus mutually synthesizing the opposed positions. Then both parties will find themselves perfectly united. This is really a process of self-denial and is minutely taught in the dialectic method of the school of Negativism.

This mutual identification by mutual self-negation, when realized, has a great practical value in smoothing out conflicting opinions or in creating a sympathy among opposing parties. In this way diversity can be brought to unity, the world is identified with a paradise, and illusory existence is synthesized with the enlightened life. Such ideas as seeing noumenon in phenomenon, regarding motion as calm or calm as motion, identifying action and inaction, purity and impurity, perfection and imperfection, one and many, the particular and the general, permanence and impermanence, all are attainable on this theory. It is one of the most important ideas of the Mahāyāna and it is indispensable to a clear understanding of the Buddhist doctrine as taught in this school.

THE PRINCIPLE OF PERFECT FREEDOM (NIRVĀṆA)

The year 486 B.C. or thereabouts saw the conclusion of the Buddha's activity as teacher in India. The death of the Buddha is called, as is well known, *nirvāṇa*—literally, "the state of a fire blown out." When a fire is blown out, nothing remains to be seen. So, the Buddha was considered to have entered into an invisible state which can in no way be depicted in word or in form.

In spite of thoughtful instructions by the Buddha, some of his disciples expressed a dissenting ideal on the subject of *nirvāṇa* even before his funeral. There were some who had an idealistic and free-thinking tendency. This free-thinking group, the forerunners of the Mahāyāna school, took great liberty in their interpretation of *nirvāṇa*, because the Buddha did not speak much of it during his lifetime. Whenever he was asked by a questioner whether he was to live after death or what sort of world he was to enter after he had achieved *nirvāṇa*, he always remained silent. But we cannot say that, because of his silence, he denied the existence of the *nirvāṇa* world. Whenever the Buddha remained silent to a question requiring an answer of "yes" or "no," his silence meant a unique kind of assent. His silence to the question concerning *nirvāṇa* was due to the fact that his listeners could not understand the profound philosophy involved. The Buddha advised people to become his disciples without wasting time on problems which were too profound to be understood by an ordinary man—probably after a long cultivation as a disciple of the Buddha, they might come to understand. It is quite natural, therefore, that, after his departure, all the metaphysical discussions and speculations should center around the subject of *nirvāṇa*.

The main problem of Buddhism, either formalistic or idealistic, concerned the extinction of human passion, because this distorted state of mind is considered to be the source of all the evils of human life. Human passion can be extinguished even during one's lifetime.

Therefore, liberation from disorder of mind is the chief object of Buddhist culture; and the extinction of passion, of desire, of sense, of mind, and even of individual consciousness are also mentioned.

Nirvāṇa did not involve any idea of deification of the Buddha. It simply meant the eternal continuation of his personality in the highest sense of the word. It meant returning to his original state of *buddha*-nature, which is his *Dharma*-body but not his scripture-body as the formalists take it to be. *Dharma* means the "ideal" itself which the Buddha conceived in his perfect Enlightenment. The idealists hold that the Buddha has the *Dharma*-body, the body identical with that ideal, i.e., the spiritual body. The ideal was expressed in the Buddha's teachings, but those teachings were always restricted by the language and the occasion and the listeners. Therefore the idealists hold that the scripture is not the Buddha's ideal itself. This ideal body without any restricting conditions whatever is *Nirvāṇa*.

The formalists, on the other hand, hold that the scripture is the perfect representation of the ideal of the Buddha. Hence their opinion is that the Buddha lives forever in the scripture-body, *nirvāṇa* being entire annihilation and extinction.

Now, let me illustrate the principle of *Nirvāṇa* in the light of space and time. It was an illusion on the part of philosophers, especially some of the other Indian philosophers, to believe that space and time were infinite. Buddhism, however, has never treated space and time as infinite, for Buddhism takes them to be physical matters. Space is one of the five elements—earth, water, fire, air, and space—and it is sometimes represented to be of round shape as if to anticipate the modern theory of the curvature of space. The atoms are said to be so fine that they are almost empty. Time is treated as real in some schools while in other schools it is treated as unreal. But it is to be particularly noted that time has never been considered to exist apart from space. Space and time are always correlative.

The theory that space is curved, set forth by modern physicists, has considerably facilitated the elucidation of the doctrine of *Nirvāṇa*. The universe, or the *Dharma-dhātu* (principle-element) as it is technically called, is the region which is occupied by space and time, and where all the waves of existences are controlled. So, in practice, the space-time world is the ocean of the waves of life and death. It is the sphere of *Saṁsāra* (Flowing cycles of life), the world of creation, of energy, of action, of causation and ideation, of self-creation, and of dynamic becoming. It is the sphere of desire, form, and mind.

In opposition to such a world we can presume theoretically that there must be a sphere spaceless and timeless, of no creation, with no causation, and not disturbed by the waves of life and death.* There will be no *Dharma-dhātu* (principle-element) in the dynamic sense of the word, i.e., the world of manifestation. But there will be the *Dharma-dhātu* in the static sense of the word: i.e., as it is in itself, namely, Thusness or Suchness, the ultimate state of *Nirvāṇa.*

. . . .

The Mahāyāna text of the *Mahā-parinirvāṇa-sūtra,* not being satisfied with negative elucidations, explains *Nirvāṇa* in affirmative words such as: permanency (in contrast to worldly impermanence), as bliss (against human suffering), as self (against the selflessness of all beings), and as purity (against the pollution of human life). As they are all transcendental qualities of the Buddha, these terms ought not to be taken in the ordinary sense of the words. For instance, one must not picture to oneself a special location, a world of *Nirvāṇa,* where the Buddha lives in peace and joy, for the Buddha's *Nirvāṇa,* is the *Nirvāṇa*-of-No-Abode, the state of Perfect Freedom.

An ordinary *Arhat* (Saint) will cut off all obstructions caused by passion or desire, thereby attaining his purpose of annihilation. He finds a satisfaction in the destruction of his intellectual life, because he thinks that the source of distinction, opposition, or differentiation in things lies in consciousness. He thinks his state of annihilation is the ideal *nirvāṇa.* In truth, however, he has returned to the original blindness (*avidyā*—ignorance) in leaving the obstruction of intellect. He may be thinking that he has done away with the blindness, too, but blindness is the basic principle of existence which cannot be simply cut off, just as darkness cannot be destroyed without a light. The only way to eliminate darkness is to bring a light into the room. By virtue of enlightenment the darkness that bars intellect will be destroyed.

Technically, the extinction of human passion is called the "*nirvāṇa* with the condition of 'being' still remaining" or, in a more literal expression, "the *nirvāṇa* with the *upādhi* remnant," *upādhi* being the material and immaterial condition of being. Plainly, this

* This does not mean, as in Hinduism, that there is a static World of Being beyond the world of change, but that *Saṁsāra* and *Nirvāṇa* are identical.—Editor's note.

means becoming a person without passion while yet alive. It can be termed "conditional *nirvāṇa.*"

Then the next question will be: What is the *nirvāṇa* without this *upādhi* remnant? It is the total extinction of the conditions of being as well as passion, or one may call it the annihilation of being. This is the *nirvāṇa* exemplified by "Perfect Quiescence."

The formalistic view of the Buddha here comes to an end with the annihilation of being. But the speculative views of the idealistic standpoint have a fresh start with the passing of the visible Buddha into the invisible state. Even in his lifetime the Buddha had perfect freedom in intellectual activity, and, while he was a person, he had been superpersonally enlightened. How much more free must he have been when he passed into the thoroughly unconditioned state of *Nirvāṇa!* He had now returned to his "Spiritual" body, i.e., Ideal-body. It is called the Body of His Own Nature, "self-natured Body," in contradistinction to the "Body Manifested for All Beings" ("Body for Things or Beings"). All the incarnation theories entertained later have their origin in this interpretation of *Nirvāṇa.*

The Buddha in *nirvāṇa* has perfect freedom to live anywhere he pleases; he can act in whatever way he wishes, and on that account he has no fixed abode and his *nirvāṇa* is called the "*nirvāṇa*-of-No-Abode." The Blessed One may reappear in this world when he feels the necessity of saving all beings as Śākaymuni did. Therefore the Buddha, according to the idealistic view, does not live in the world of life and death, since he is not bound by causation. However, at the same time he does not rest at ease in *nirvāṇa,* because he is the sufferer of others' suffering.

Methods of Attaining the State of Perfect Freedom (Nirvāṇa)

To reach that state of perfect freedom Buddhism sets forth two methods. One is by a dialectical ladder, the other by an introspective (meditative) plan. Which to choose is a matter of taste but it depends on one's preparation.

METHOD OF DIALECTIC

The spiritual inheritance of the Buddha, handed down to the present world, was threefold: the way-of-life-view (*darśana-mārga*), the way-of-life-culture (*bhāvana-mārga*), and the way-of-life-ideal (*aśaikṣa-mārga*). The last, negatively expressed as "the way of no more learning," is most significant.

The Buddha regarded the world as the emanation of ignorance. With the Buddha ignorance is the cause of all of the dynamic becomings of life. To begin with, ignorance covers the blind motive to live, the conscious ignorance of childhood, illusory ideas or earthly desires of manhood, erroneous assertions, false doctrines, superstitions, hallucinations, epistemological mistakes, and the incapability of escaping from a perplexed life. It is, in fact, the ignorant activity of will. However, there is no definite entity called ignorance, because it is merely the state of being without knowledge. Buddhism aims at the undoing of ignorance. It is foolish to think of getting light by destroying darkness. Bring a light, then darkness will cease to be. Buddhism, therefore, begins with the search for knowledge.

People who join the Buddhist community are first taught the "threefold learning": higher conduct, higher thought or meditation, and higher wisdom. "Knowledge and views resulting from deliverance from ignorance" and "knowledge and views according to truth as it ought to be" are results of the "threefold learning." In case one is well prepared for progress, the way-of-life-view is carefully taught. The central principle is the Eightfold Path. At length, when the noble aspirant attains the position of a *Bodhi-sattva* (one whose essence is perfect wisdom), he is further trained in the Six Perfections, of which the "perfection of knowledge and wisdom" is considered most important. The completion of knowledge and wisdom is Perfect Enlightenment (*Bodhi*). It follows naturally that the perfection of knowledge and wisdom is perfection of personality. Such a personage is called a "*buddha*," or "enlightened one." And one who has become perfectly enlightened is one who has the power of enlightening all others.

(1) *The Theory of the Double Truth: Common-sense Truth and Higher-sense Truth*

Now, let us see how the Buddhist philosophers applied the original principle of knowledge and wisdom to the problem of life in order to clarify or illumine the world of ignorance.

It was Nāgārjuna, one of the greatest and foremost philosophers India has ever produced, who solved the problem successfully. He was a talented thinker of the Nāga tribe of south India, and flourished about A.D. 125 at the time of King Kaniṣka. He first proposed the theory of double truth: common-sense truth (*saṁvṛti-satya*) and higher-sense truth (*paramārtha-satya*). On one side, he would admit a popular common-sense argument as a truth, but, at the same time, would lead the people to a higher truth based on, say, a scientific investigation. Gradually, the common-sense truth would absorb that higher truth. The formerly conflicting truths, being united, would now become a new common-sense truth. This common-sense truth would confront another still higher truth based on a thorough investigation. Both would be admitted as truths. Now—to use modern terminology—the people would all begin to live on the basis of scientific results. Science would become a common-sense truth. However, a still more advanced scientist would come forth and declare the assumption of old scientists untenable. If modern scientists go hand in hand with philosophers, there will perhaps be a time when philosophers will represent the common-sense truth of the world. An illustration would be:

A	common-sense truth
B	higher truth
AB	common-sense truth
C	higher truth
ABC	Common-sense truth
D	higher truth

and so on until we reach the highest truth, that of "Thusness," negatively, by denying all special, one-sided, or biased common-sense truths.

During Nāgārjuna's time the problem was that of *ens* or *non-ens*. The Buddha once said, "All exists." At other times he said, "All is void," "Nothing exists." Self was denied, individual self (*ātman*) and universal self (*Brahman*). "No substance, no soul, no permanence, no duration" was the Buddha's idea. Therefore, a nihilistic as well as a realistic tendency of thought might have existed side by side even during the Buddha's time.

After the Buddha's *nirvāṇa*, there was a period of great confusion in Buddhist thought for some centuries. Sarvāsti-vāda (all-exists school), the Realistic school, seems to have been the first to systematize its ideas. These thinkers compiled a great literature of the *Abhi-dharmaka* (higher *dharma*) philosophy. This Realistic school was called *Vaibhāṣika*. Against this Realism, Harivarman's (A.D. 250) Nihilistic school was systematized. When the realistic *ens* (*sat*) is common-sense truth, the nihilistic *non-ens* (*a-sat*) is higher-sense truth. When, however, both together become common-sense truth, the negation of both will be the higher-sense truth. This is Nāgārjuna's philosophy of "middle view" (*mādhyamika*). The theory of repeatedly leaving behind the common truth involves the assumption of a highest truth and is at the same time a gradual denial of common truth ever enriched intensively.

(2) *The Eightfold Negation of Becoming*

Nāgārjuna then proposed another wholesale denial of the world of phenomena: neither birth nor death, neither permanence nor extinction, neither unity nor diversity, neither coming nor going. This Eightfold Negation (in four pairs) is the basis of his negativistic philosophy. This theory of Eightfold Negation is the extensive denial of all dynamic becomings. The denial of phenomena means that the state of being is not real but that it is a causal wave, a relative existence, only temporary, transitory, and nominal. The thought that phenomena exist is illusory and erroneous. If you hold to one view or the other, either to *ens* or to *non-ens,* or to a conditional *ens* or to a conditional *non-ens,* you get only a biased idea, a one-sided view, and the real Middle Path can never be realized. The theory of Middle-Path-Ideal can be reached only by the wholesale denial of both *ens* and *non-ens*. Negation is the only way to attain the highest truth. The "Middle-Path-Ideal" of Nāgārjuna is identical with the highest truth.

(3) *The Fourfold Basis of Dialectic Argument*

The third theory of Nāgārjuna is the establishment of Four Bases of Argument. The fourfold argument, e.g., as to cause, are: 1. self-caused (as self-existent); 2. caused by another; 3. caused by both together; and 4. caused by neither (e.g., in the materialistic school which admits no cause). These are all negated: "not caused by self," "not caused by another," "not caused by both together," "not caused by neither." These negations seem to have been directed against some tenets then prevalent. But when the fourfold method of argument was made applicable to any problem expecting an answer of "yes" or "no," we have: 1. "yes"; 2. "no"; 3. either "yes" or "no" depending upon conditions; 4. neither "yes" nor "no." Thus we get *ens, non-ens,* either *ens* or *non-ens* (conditional), and neither *ens* nor *non-ens*. An argument cannot have any form other than these four. Without investigation of these four aspects no problem can be satisfactorily solved. People often judge from the opposite points of "yes" or "no," and do not think of the case of "either yes or no, according to conditions offered." The fourth point, "neither 'yes' nor 'no,'" may have a double meaning. It may mean "the question has nothing to do with me" or "I stand over and above 'yes' and 'no.'" From the standpoint of the fourth argument, Nāgārjuna denied reality in the four manifestations as explained in the Eightfold Negation. Life-wave is void; that is, all elements are void because they become devoid of all specific features. This is the all-transcending truth, the ultimate principle, because all pluralistic ideas are done away with. This is the Middle Path, the Golden Mean, because all inclinations one way or the other and all one-sided views are eliminated. It is the absolute *Śūnyatā* (Void). Thus we are led to the highest ideal, that of the Middle Path. "Thusness" is hereby arrived at negatively as the remainder.

(4) *The Theory of the Middle-Path-Ideal*

The highest truth—or you may call it the true Real—is the Middle Path, the Golden Mean. With Nāgārjuna, the Middle Path is simply the middle view (*mādhyamika*) and it is synonymous with the "Highest Truth," "the view that has no inclination, no bias, no attachment and no specific feature." Now let us call this Middle Path the Ideal. The Ideal of the *ens* school (realism) is the middle path between hedonistic inclination and pessimistic tendency. The Ideal of the *non-ens* school (nihilism) is the middle path, that is, the truth attainable by admission of the non-reality of all things and beings: no self, no permanence, non-reality of all elements (*dharma*) and non-conditioned *Nirvāṇa* (extinction). The Ideal of the either-*ens*-or-*non-ens* school (idealism) is the middle path between *ens* and *non-ens,* but it is, in one way, the school of conditional neither-*ens*-nor-*non-ens.* It is "neither *ens,*" because the *ens* of the outer world (matter and form) is entirely denied, and it is also "nor *non-ens,*" because the *non-ens* of the inner world (mind) is negated. That is, the *ens* of the mind-world is affirmed. The idealists, therefore, call their Ideal the middle path of neither-*ens*-nor-*non-ens.* As a matter of fact, however, the Mādhyamika is really the school of neither-*ens*-nor-*non-ens,* for it denies both *ens* and *non-ens.*

(5) *The Theory of the Reciprocal Identification of Any Two Opposed Ideas*

Another phase of the method of dialectic is the theory of a Reciprocal Identification of any two opposed ideas, but this has been treated above.

METHOD OF MEDITATION

All the basic principles of Buddhism at once melt into the way-of-life-culture which, in reality, is the application of the life-view to the practical life. As to the realization of the life-ideal, the theory of perfect freedom (*nirvāṇa*) speaks for itself. It is a state, spaceless, timeless, of no condition, of no abode, of no limitation whatever. Negatively, *nirvāṇa* is "extinction," "total negation," "undifferentiated indetermination"; but, positively, it is perfect freedom. It is identical with Perfect Enlightenment (*Bodhi*). *Nirvāṇa* may be attained by meditation and contemplation, if the negation theory of the method of dialectic still proves unsatisfactory to anyone. Buddhism is pansophism.

If Buddhism as rationalism is negative and as intuitionism is passive, it may seem to some to have nothing to do with actual life. On the contrary it is a philosophy of self-creation and teaches the way-of-life-view, the way-of-life-culture, and the way of realization of the life-ideal. Since Buddhism takes the integration of consciousness seriously, its method ought to be exhaustive and negative to wipe out all possibilities of errors and perplexities. If the fullness of insight, that is, the perfection of knowledge and wisdom, is aimed at, one should not linger in the world of transitoriness or be entangled in the wire of attachment. For without self-discipline there will be no equipoised mental activities; without poise, no insight. The Buddha, therefore, teaches the threefold learning: higher discipline, higher thought or meditation, and higher insight. These three are inseparable. The ideal of the *Bodhi-sattva* is the Sixfold Perfection: charity (for others), discipline (for oneself), resignation (in toil), bravery (in effort), contemplation (meditation), and wisdom (insight). Insight cannot be attained without the preceding five, especially meditation.

The Buddha contemplated under the *bodhi* tree on the twelve stages of causation, first in order, then in reverse, "this is, therefore that is; this is not, therefore that is not," all being interdependent. When he became perfectly enlightened, and was about to teach his ideal, he further meditated forty-nine days as to how, where, and whom to teach his ideal. When he began to teach, he taught about the actual life of suffering which was easy to demonstrate or intuit. "Aging, ailing, and dying are suffering. Birth is not joy, because it ends in death; union is not joy, if it ends in separation." When people began to realize the hardship of life, he taught them not to be deceived by the guise of joy but to face the suffering as suffering.

His Four Noble Truths to be believed by the noble are: 1. Suffering; 2. Cause of suffering; 3. Extinction of suffering; 4. The way to the extinction of suffering. Truths 1 and 2 are real, and 3 and 4 are ideal. What these are should be known by the first round of learning (investigation) according to the way-of-life-view. Next, the Truth of suffering should be fully realized. The cause of suffering should be cut off. The extinction of suffering fully experienced (or intuited) and the way leading to extinction of suffering should be cultivated (or practiced). These should be pursued by the second round of learning (realization) according to the way-of-life-culture. Thirdly, the Truth of suffering has been known, the cause has been cut off, the extinction has been attained, and the way leading to the extinction of suffering has been cultivated. These constitute the third round of learning (perfection), the stage of no-more-learning.

The way to extinction of suffering is the well-known Eightfold Path of the noble (*ārya*), i.e., right view; right thought; right speech; right action; right remembrance; right effort; right livelihood; right contemplation. These are principles of ethics, but at the same time a religion by which perfection of personality is attained and self-creation is fulfilled.

Though the highest principle is reached chiefly and ultimately by meditation, we must realize that Buddhists use other methods of self-culture in order to attain the ideal end. The Buddhist schools which use chiefly the method of meditation (*dhyāna*) can be called the schools of intuitionism, in which Thusness is intuited in differentiations, noumenon and phenomenon being inseparable.

. . . .

Conclusion

In Buddhist systems, investigation by oneself and argument with others, meditation by oneself and teaching to others, all go together. When the life-view is formed it is at once applied to life-culture, aiming at a realization of the life-ideal. Accordingly, it is philosophy, but it is at the same time religion; there is, in fact, no distinction between the two. One ought not to think that these two are not as yet differentiated in Buddhism, because Buddhism holds that these two should not be divided. Otherwise, it will end either in philosophical amusement or superstitious belief. Some Buddhist ideas may seem to be purely theoretical, but no Buddhist theory, however negative or passive, will be without an application to actual life—and this is the essence of religion.

So, with Buddhism, philosophy will be at once an ethics. For example, the theory of selflessness will at once melt into the denial of all egocentric ideas; one will become non-individualistic, not thinking of self-interest, unselfish, non-egoistic. A negation of all such becoming in the real world may appear dreadful at first sight, but, when it is applied to actual life, it becomes self-denial, a negation of all biased ideas, or of all one-sided views, a wiping-out of all attachments, a preparedness for the final fullness of insight, the state of *nirvāṇa,* perfect freedom, an unconditioned, non-determinate Thusness. In this way no negative principle or passive view will remain negative or passive when it is applied to life-culture. All tends toward the realization of the life-ideal.

DHIRENDRA MOHAN DATTA

Epistemological Methods in Indian Philosophy

THE SUBJECT OF THIS PAPER raises two questions which are very closely connected but are not identical. They are: (1) What, according to Indian philosophy, are the methods or sources through which men in general acquire knowledge? (2) What are the methods which Indian philosophers employ for solving their problems and acquiring knowledge? I shall discuss the subject in its first aspect (i.e., general epistemology) in some detail, and in its second aspect very briefly.

Knowledge and Its Sources

In Sanskrit the word for cognition in general is "*jñāna.*" The word for valid cognition is "*pramā,*" and that for the source of valid knowledge is "*pramāṇa.*" The problems of *pramā* and *pramāṇa* are discussed threadbare by the different schools of philosophy, because nearly all of them believe that human suffering is rooted in ignorance, the removal of which is the chief object of philosophy, and also because they believe that without a critical discussion of the theory of knowledge truth cannot be attained.[1]

As Indian philosophy has developed from the days of the Vedas in the midst of a series of changing racial, social, political, and religious influences over a period of at least five thousand years, there have arisen innumerable schools of thought, and consequently there has also been a large variety of epistemological theories. So, while in Western philosophy we are generally told of two sources of knowledge, perception and inference, which are treated as synonymous with immediate and mediate knowledge, respectively, Indian philosophy, in its different major schools, recognizes up to six sources of knowledge, and some minor schools even add two or three more. Elaborate arguments are adduced to show the necessity of recognizing each as a separate source.[2]

THE MANY SOURCES OF KNOWLEDGE

The Cārvāka materialist admits perception as the only source of knowledge. Kaṇāda (the founder of the Vaiśeṣika school) and the Buddhist admit two, perception and inference. The Sāṁkhya admits three, perception, inference, and authority. Gautama (the founder of the Nyāya school) admits *upamāna* (knowledge by similarity), in addition to these three. The Prabhākara school of the Mīmāṁsā admits five, the four sources mentioned before and *arthāpatti* (postulation). The Bhāṭṭa school of the Mīmāṁsā and Śaṁkara's monistic (*advaita*) school of the Vedānta admit also a sixth source, namely, non-cognition, in addition to these five. Some others recognize instinctive or intuitive knowledge (*pratibhā*); some, unbroken tradition (*itiha*); and some, possible inclusion (*sambhava*) as other kinds of knowledge—but these three are not recognized by the major schools. Before we discuss these different sources of knowledge it will be useful to note a few important things about knowledge and validity in general.

VALIDITY

Valid cognition, which is obtained by any of these methods, is generally regarded as cognition which is free from doubt (*saṁśaya*), indefiniteness (*anadhyavasāya*), and error (*bhrama*), and which, therefore, reveals things as they are (*yathārtha*), furnishes the basis of successful activity (*saṁvādi-pravṛtty-anukūla*), and is not contradicted (*abādhita*) by any other experience. Nyāya-Vaiśeṣika realists regard agreement with reality as the essence of truth. Bauddha (Buddhist) thinkers, e.g., Dharmakīrti, regard practical efficiency as the distinguishing mark that differentiates a valid cognition from an invalid one,[3] whereas the Advaitins (non-dualistic Vedāntins) emphasize more the uncontradicted nature of valid cognition.

Most thinkers hold that novelty should also be regarded as a necessary character of knowledge worthy of the name. So, memory (which is a reproduction of knowledge acquired in the past through perception or any other source) is not regarded as a separate kind of valid cognition. Some others point out, however, that memory should be regarded as a substantive source of knowledge at least insofar as it yields valuable information about the pastness of an experience or its object—information which could not be obtained from any other source without its aid.

Two other important questions[4] regarding validity are: (1) Whether conditions that generate the validity of a perception or any other knowledge are intrinsic to the conditions that generate that knowledge, and (2) Whether the validity of that knowledge is known by the knowledge itself. Opinions are sharply divided on these matters. Roughly speaking, the Mīmāṁsā and the Vedānta hold that validity should be regarded as the natural or normal character of knowledge and invalidity as an exceptional phenomenon which arises when there are some accidental vitiating factors. So, they hold that the conditions of validity lie within the very conditions that generate the knowledge, and they also hold that the validity of knowledge is known from the knowledge itself, as it arises. For example, if the relation of the visual sense to the object is regarded as the condition of visual perception, then the validity of this cognition is also due to this very condition; and, moreover, as soon as such a perception arises we believe it to be true, and, therefore, we act upon it without hesitation and without waiting for its confirmation by any other knowledge. This position regarding the two questions of validity is called the theory of self-validity (*svataḥ-prāmāṇya-vāda*).

The Nyāya-Vaiśeṣika thinkers hold the opposite view, namely, that of external validity (*parataḥ-prāmāṇya-vāda*). They believe that there are some special conditions (other than those of the knowledge itself) which generate its validity. For example, whereas the mere sense-object relation may be said to generate visual perception in general, the soundness of the visual organ, sufficiency of light, etc., may be regarded as the special conditions generating its validity (the absence of which may cause perceptual error). Again, the validity of this knowledge is not self-manifest. It is inferred from these special conditions or from some other data.

From this brief discussion it would appear that, whereas the attitude of some Indian thinkers toward knowledge is one of belief, that of others is one of neutrality or open-mindedness. But in addition to these two attitudes there is also a third, that of disbelief, held by the skeptical Buddhists, according to whom invalidity is the self-manifest character of every cognition, and validity (which is nothing other than the practical efficiency of it) can be established only indirectly (by its successful practical consequences).

Regarding the knowledge of knowledge itself there are also different views. The Sāṁkhya, the Vedānta, Prabhākara, and the Jaina hold that knowledge is self-manifest; the Nyāya holds that it is known as an object of subsequent introspection (*anuvyavasāya*). But Bhāṭṭas hold that knowledge is known by inference from the knownness of its object.

OBJECTS

In Indian epistemology, we also have different views regarding the status of the object of knowledge. Within the same system of Buddhism, for example, we have what may be called, in terms of modern Western epistemology, direct realism (held by the Vaibhāṣikas), critical realism (held by the Sautrāntikas), subjective idealism (held by the Yogācāras), and a fourth variety, which has no Western analogue, indeterminism (*śūnya-vāda,* held by the Mādhyamikas), according to which the object of knowledge (as well as any other thing) is not describable either as "is" or as "is not" or as "both is and is not" or as "neither is nor is not." Here is an example of subtle distinctions—even much subtler in some respects than most up-to-date Western epistemology—and a complete scheme of possible epistemological positions which evolved in India at least a thousand years ago. Except for Buddhism, most of the schools are realistic. The Sāṁkhya, which holds that all objects are the products of intellect, can also be called realistic, if it is admitted that this intellect is cosmic and not personal. Though there are among the later followers of Śaṁkara some extreme subjectivists who hold the theory that creation is only perception (*dṛṣṭi-sṛṣṭi-vāda*), yet Śaṁkara, in spite of his metaphysical idealism, was an epistemological realist, as is clear from his emphatic refutation of the subjective idealism of the Yogācāra Buddhists. It is interesting to note that even an illusory perception is regarded by most Advaitins as having a corresponding object momentarily created.

But, though Sāṁkhya, Vedānta, and Jaina thinkers believe, like realists, in the presence of objects independent of knowledge, they do not think that consciousness is the product of the relation of the object to the knower. They hold that the knower is the self, which is intrinsically conscious, and that knowledge of objects is like the illumination of objects by the pre-existing light of a lamp. Consciousness, in itself, is eternal and original, but its relation to a particular object is conditional and accidental. But ranged against this position there is a group of influential thinkers of the Nyāya, the Vaiśeṣika, and the Mīmāṁsā schools who, like Locke, think that the self is primarily unconscious and that consciousness arises in it when it is properly related to objects. With this general idea about knowledge, let us have a bird's-eye view of its different sources.

PERCEPTION (PRATYAKṢA)

Perception is generally described as knowledge arising from the relation of the object to some sense. Five external senses (namely, those of hearing, sight, touch, taste, and smell) and at least one internal sense (*manas*, mind) are commonly postulated for explaining external perception and internal perception (of pleasure, pain, etc.). A peculiarity of Indian thought worth notice here is that a distinction is made between mind as knower and mind as the internal sense and organ of attention—the first being called *ātman* or *puruṣa* and the second *manas* or *antaḥ-karaṇa*. These two are considered to be two different substances by the Nyāya-Vaiśeṣika school. To perceive an object the self must attend to the object through its *manas*, and be related to it through the appropriate sense.

Is any immediate knowledge possible without the help of sense? This question is variously answered. The Nyāya-Vaiśeṣika[5] thinks that immediate knowledge ordinarily involves the direct relation of the object, so known, to some sense. But it recognizes certain exceptions which may be classed under two categories. First, there are those cases in which the sense is related indirectly to the object, yet the object can be said to be immediately known. For example, when the table is directly related to the skin of the hand, not only the table is perceived, but also the quality of touch, which is in the table, the hardness which inheres in the touch, the absence of an inkpot which characterizes the table—all these are immediately perceptible, though these latter cannot be said to be directly related to the sense, but only indirectly through the substance in which they are. The second class of exceptional cases includes those in which even no such indirect relation can be traced between the object and sense, and yet the object is felt to be immediately known. These cases are called extra-ordinary perception (*alaukika-pratyakṣa*) and are of three kinds. When we *see* a piece of sandal as fragrant (or cotton as soft, or stone as hard), the smell and touch are felt as immediate though really we cannot trace the relation of these to the sense of smell or touch. Erroneous perception of a rope as a snake, of heated air in the desert as water, etc., also belong to this class. In all such cases, some memory-idea vividly aroused by similarity, etc., functions like a sense relation and causes immediate perception. Whether such immediate perception is true or false depends on whether it represents the object as it is or not. There is a second kind of extra-ordinary perception in which an entire class of objects can be said to be immediately known when a particular member of it is immediately known. When a man sees his first tiger, and *sees* in it the general character of tigerhood, he can be said to see thereby all tigers, not, of course, as possessed of their respective individual properties, but as possessed of the general character of tigerhood, because, except tigerhood, there is no other attribute of tigers as a class which remains to be perceived. Such knowledge of a class helps induction. The third kind of extra-ordinary perception, admitted on the basis of the experience of the *yogins,* is perception through successful complete mental concentration on any object too small, too far away, or too much concealed to be related to sense.

It may be remarked in this connection that as the Sāṁkhya, the Yoga, the Nyāya, the Vaiśeṣika, and the Advaita Vedānta believe the self to be really infinite, the question of the possibility of the relation of the self to the rest of the universe without the medium of sense or body does not raise any theoretical difficulty. On the contrary, the fettering of the soul to the body is, for them, the reason for its limited knowledge. Even the Jainas, who do not admit the infinity of self (*jīva*), but admit only its power of expansion, hold that the self can the more directly know other minds and other things unconnected with sense, the more it can free itself from the forces of attachment that fetter it to the body. So, they hold that knowledge through sense, being through some medium, cannot be called truly immediate. Only the liberated saint can obtain full and immediate knowledge directly without the help of any sense. Patañjali, the founder of the Yoga system,[6] holds that one can know the mind of another person and also imperceptible objects by complete concentration of the mind on them. The Advaitins view immediacy as the basic character of the Absolute Consciousness, of which the knower, the known, and the process or mechanism of knowledge are apparent differentiations due to ignorance. So, for them, immediacy is not generated by the knowing process. The self's knowledge of an external object is empirically describable, of course, in terms of the function of the mind, or internal organ, and the sense concerned. In the light of this, the Advaitins say that in every perception the mind flows out to the object through the sense and assumes the form of the object and establishes thereby a sort of identity between the mind and the object. But this process does not generate consciousness or immediacy. It only destroys the imagined barrier between the knower (which is nothing but the basic consciousness delimited by the mind) and the object (which is also the same consciousness delimited by the objective form) by a kind of identity established between the two delimiting and differentiating factors.[7]

So, for the Advaitin, every sense-perception is really the restoration of the basic identity between the knower and the known, and the allowing of the basic reality, i.e., consciousness, to reveal itself immediately. But such immediate knowledge is an extremely limited expression of the basic consciousness. When a person can altogether overcome his sense of identification with the body (mind, senses, vitality, and other individuating conditions) by realizing his identity with the basic consciousness, there is revelation of this self-shining basic existence. This is pure and absolute immediate consciousness.

DIRECT REALIZATION OF PHILOSOPHICAL TRUTHS

In this connection we may briefly mention the characteristic Indian notion of the direct realization (*sākṣāt-kāra*) of truth. This is common to all the schools, except the materialist, though truth or truths are differently conceived. The process of realization (*sādhana*), though differing in detail from school to school, has also a common pattern. This consists in learning the truth (from authoritative texts, preceptors, or other sources), reasoning critically about its pros and cons, and, if thus found acceptable, meditating on it intensely and repeatedly. This vigorous intellectual culture must be accompanied by moral reformation, that is, reorganization of all emotion and behavior by changing all old habits based on previous ignorance or misconception of the truth.

But how can such intellectual and moral exercise lead to direct or immediate knowledge? The matter is not so mysterious as it may seem to be. By repeated thought and behavior based thereon, we feel that we directly see a material body existing in all dimensions though only a color-patch forming a part of its front surface is present to sense. We see time on looking at the dial of a watch; on receipt of a piece of paper called a bank note we feel that we are receiving real money; we see danger in a frown or a red signal; we see thoughts in printed letters. Similarly, I directly feel as though I am the body and separated from the rest of the world by my outer skin, limited and helpless. I feel that I am a man, a teacher, a Hindu, and so on. The objects of my ordinary desire—food, dress, house, and money—all directly appear as values, relatively stable and worth while.

Is it not possible to think, that by a similar but more consciously, rationally, and intently initiated process of repeated thinking, willing, and feeling, truths about the self, the world, and its values, different from these ordinarily accepted ones, can also be felt and realized at least as directly as these are in life?

In such realization the intellect rather than sense experience takes the lead, and reinterprets and re-evaluates the latter. It is the "theoretic component" which rules here over the "aesthetic" and even reveals itself through the latter.

INFERENCE (ANUMĀNA)

Inference[8] is generally regarded by Indian thinkers as knowledge from a sign (say, smoke) to the signified (say, fire) on the basis of previous knowledge of invariable concomitance (*vyāpti*) between the two. Though all systems discuss inference, the Nyāya treats it very elaborately. According to the Nyāya, a universal relation or induction is based on repeated observation in the light of the method of agreement in presence (*anvaya*, e.g., "All cases of smoke are cases of fire") and also (where possible) the method of agreement in absence (*vyatireka*, e.g., "Where there is no fire, there is no smoke"). Induction may be vitiated by non-observation of hidden essential conditions (*upādhis*) responsible for the apparent invariability between the two phenomena. Such a defect can be removed only by repeated and varied observation (*bhūyo-darśana*). The truth of an inductive generalization may also be deductively tested by indirect hypothetical argument (*tarka*) leading to a *reductio ad absurdum*, e.g., "If smoke were not accompanied by fire, then it would be without a cause, which is absurd." But, if the doubt is still raised, "What if events are without a cause?" it is silenced by the contradiction (*vyāghāta*) it would have with practical behavior, where we always seek a cause for producing an effect.

The Buddhists employ the method of five steps (*pañca-kāraṇī*) in order to discover a causal connection, and thereby an invariable relation, between phenomena: (1) non-observation of the cause as well as the effect; (2) observation of the cause; (3) observation of the effect; (4) observation of the disappearance of the cause; and

(5) observation of the disappearance of the effect. Thus, with the help of this double method of difference (as Dr. Seal calls it), a causal connection may be established between fire and smoke. Buddhists also lay down identity of essence (*tādātmya*) as another ground on which a universal proposition (e.g., "All oaks are trees") can be based.

But the Nyāya says of the first method that it cannot be applied when other circumstances vary and the suspicion of a plurality of causes cannot be removed. Moreover, there are many cases of non-causal uniformity (established by the Nyāya methods previously described), e.g., "All animals having horns have tails," on which inference also can be based. Regarding the second method, identity of essence, the Nyāya points out that it is not really a ground of inference. To say, "This is a tree, because it is an oak" is really no inference at all if an oak is already known to be identical with a tree.

An important distinction is made between the psychological process of inference (not necessarily expressed in language), which takes place in the mind of one who infers for his own self (*svārthānumāna*), and the demonstrative form of inference, which is used for convincing others (*parārthānumāna*). In the former, one argues: "This hill has smoke; whatever has smoke has fire; so, the hill has fire." But the demonstrative form, as Gautama conceives it, must have five steps:

(1) Clear enunciation of the proposition to be proved—This hill has fire.
(2) Statement of reason—This hill has smoke.
(3) Statement of universal relation, supported by concrete instances—Whatever has smoke has fire, e.g., the fireplace. Whatever has no fire has no smoke, e.g., the lake.
(4) Application of the universal relation to the present case—The hill has such smoke (which is invariably accompanied by fire).
(5) Conclusion—Therefore, the hill has fire.

There are some important points to note about this five-membered argument (*pañcāvayava-nyāya*).

First, it is the form in which debate and discussion should be conducted for the ascertainment of truth and establishment of theories. In order that there may be no ambiguity, digression, and shifting of ground, there is an explicit statement of the *probandum* and the checking of it by its restatement at the end—as in Euclid's geometrical proof.

Second, we do not have here a mere formal syllogism, but also an attempt to establish its material validity by the citation of concrete instances supporting the universal major premise. It is, as Dr. Seal says, an inductive-deductive, formal-material process.

Third, (because of this) it does not always assume the form of finality. Sometimes (to start a discussion and invite criticism) it lays down a tentative proposition with a provisional induction, supported by an example, waiting to see what the opponent can say against it. It then becomes a process of tentative discovery and provisional proof.

The fallacies which may vitiate the conclusion of such a process are mentioned by Gautama and treated by his followers very elaborately. The more important of these arise from (1) assigning a reason (middle term) which has no invariable relation to what is to be proved (major term), e.g., "The hill has smoke, because it has fire"; (2) assigning a reason which has no relation to (and, therefore, contradicts) what is sought to be proved, e.g., "Sound is eternal, because it is produced"; (3) assigning a reason which is not really present in the case in hand, e.g., "Sound is eternal, because it is not produced"; (4) assigning a reason which leads to a conclusion that is contradicted by an opposite and stronger inference, e.g., "Sound is eternal, because it is invisible, like the atoms" (this is contradictable by the valid counter-inference, "Sound is non-eternal, because it is produced, as is a pot"); and (5) assigning a reason which leads to a conclusion contradicted by direct perception, e.g., "Fire is cold, because it is a substance, like water."

KNOWLEDGE BY SIMILARITY (UPAMĀNA)

This is differently conceived by different schools and writers. The earlier version, that of Gautama,[9] describes it as knowledge of something, previously unknown, on the basis of its similarity to a familiar thing, e.g., "The *gavaya* (a wild deer) is like the cow." In later Nyāya it is more explicitly defined as the process by which we know the denotation of a new word on the basis of its similarity to a familiar object. In the same example, a man knows from an authority that a *gavaya* is a wild animal like the cow; then he happens to see that animal in the forest and comes to know, from that knowledge of similarity, that an animal of that kind is a *gavaya*.

The claim of this process to a status different from perception and inference is that the relationship between the name and the object is not perceived, nor is it inferred, because no invariable concomitance (a universal premise) is used for reaching the knowledge.

Śabara,[10] the commentator on the *Mīmāṁsā-sūtra,* describes this knowledge as a kind of analogical argument, as would appear from his example that we know the existence of souls in other bodies on the analogy of our knowledge of our own bodies' having souls.

But later Mīmāṁsā and the Advaita Vedānta conceive *upamāna* in a different way. About the Nyāya conception, they point out that it is a mixture of knowledge from authority and an inference based on it. According to them, *upamāna* is a process like this: When a man perceives a cow, and afterward perceives a *gavaya,* he judges, "This *gavaya* is like that cow." From this knowledge of similarity he passes to the knowledge "That cow (perceived in the past) is like the *gavaya.*" This last knowledge[11] is peculiar. It is not perceptual, for the subject "cow" is not now present, and when it was perceived in the past it was not known to be similar to the *gavaya* (which was not known then). It is not an inference, since no universal premise is used to reach the conclusion. So, it is classed apart and called knowledge from similarity (*upamāna*).

TESTIMONY (ŚABDA)

Words of an authority (a reliable person or book) are recognized as a source of knowledge. The Vaiśeṣika holds that this is inferential knowledge based on the reliability of the authority. But against this the Nyāya points out that even though this is admitted it only shows that the truth of the knowledge is established by inference, but not the content of the knowledge. If a patient says that he has a headache and you accept his statement because he is truthful, you first know about the headache from his words and then know the truth of his statement by inference from his truthfulness. The Mīmāṁsā and the Advaita Vedānta, which believe that the validity of every knowledge is inherent in it, go a step further to hold that as soon as you learn from the person about his headache you know and believe his statement. It is only in exceptional circumstances when there are reasons for doubt that you use inference to remove the doubt. Inference thus does only the negative work of removing obstacles to knowledge, and, as soon as this is done, knowledge arises and claims self-evident validity.

Moreover, it is pointed out by all the supporters of authority that the conditions that generate such knowledge are very different from those which are necessary for inference. Such knowledge arises from the synthetic understanding of the meanings of the different words of a sentence. Four conditions are needed for this. The meaning of each word must raise a sense of incompleteness; this must be removed by the meanings of the other words which must be compatible with it; the words must be sufficiently close together so that they may be construed together; and, lastly, the purpose of the speaker (or the universe of discourse) must be understood. The knowledge of a command, or a request, from an imperative sentence more clearly supports this view.

POSTULATION (ARTHĀPATTI)

This fifth source of knowledge admitted by the Mīmāṁsā and the Advaita Vedānta is illustrated by the following stock examples: A man is known to fast during the day and yet grow fat. To explain this it is postulated that he must be eating during the night. Again, seeing that a man who is believed to be alive is not at home, it is known that he is outside his home. Similarly, finding that in the sentence "The chair ruled" the literal meaning of "chair" does not suit, we take the figurative meaning, "chairman." In all such cases we explain given conflicting phenomena by supposing the only thing that can resolve the conflict. It looks like an explanatory hypothesis, but it is not provisional and uncertain like a hypothesis. The Nyāya and other schools try to reduce it to inference drawn from a negative major. The first example is reduced thus: No one who does not eat at night while fasting during the day grows fat. This man grows fat. So, he is not such as does not eat at night, etc., i.e., he eats at night. Against this explanation it is pointed out that the very knowledge put in the major premise is not obtainable without a postulation. So, the explanation really begs the very question. Moreover, if we consult introspection (*anu-vyavasāya*), we find that we do not feel here like inferring from any premise, but, rather, like *supposing* or postulating something unknown which alone can resolve a conflict.

NON-COGNITION (AN-UPALABDHI)

Non-cognition is the source of our primary knowledge of non-existence. It is generally believed that we can perceive non-existence just as we can existence. For, looking at the table, we can say that there is no cat there, just as we can say that there is a book there. But the Bhāṭṭa school of the Mīmāṁsā and the Advaita Vedānta point out that perception requires the relation of sense to its objects; but how can the sense be thought to be related to non-existence? The Nyāya says that sense is related to the positive locus of non-existence (in this case, the table) and through that to the non-existence which is a character of the locus. But this explanation is not accepted, because any and every character that is in something is not perceived by the relation of the thing to sense. (Seeing the table, we do not know its weight.) The character itself must be perceptible. But how can non-existence be perceptible? Thus, we come back to the old problem.

To explain this difficulty Bhāṭṭa Mīmāṁsakas hold that non-existence is known through non-cognition, just as existence is known through positive cognition. Of course, only appropriate non-cognition can yield such knowledge. If a thing should have been known under some circumstances had it been existing there, then the want of knowledge under those circumstances becomes the source of the knowledge of its non-existence.

THEORIES OF ERROR

Like knowledge, error also has been discussed threadbare by the different schools. Seven chief theories have been held and mutually criticized. We can give only the gist of them here. The nihilistic Buddhists hold that error is the appearance of the unreal as real (*asat-khyāti*). The idealistic Buddhists hold that the illusory object is nothing but the external appearance of what is really a subjective idea (*ātma-khyāti*). The Sāṁkhya holds that the illusory appearance is a mixture of the appearance of the real and the unreal (*sat-asat-khyāti*)—an unreal character attributed to a real substratum. The Advaita Vedānta holds that erroneous appearance is the temporary creation of ignorance, of a temporary object which can be described neither as wholly real nor as wholly unreal (*anirvacanīya-khyāti*). The Nyāya and Bhāṭṭa realists hold that an illusion occurs by the dislocated appearance of a real object (perceived in the past) in another place and time (*anyathā-khyāti*). Rāmānuja (Vedāntin) holds that the so-called illusory object is really not unreal; it is the appearance of the real element (*sat-khyāti*) which is common to the present reality and what it is apprehended as. The Prabhākara school of the Mīmāṁsā, like Rāmānuja, holds that all knowledge is valid (*akhyāti*), and that what is called an illusion is really a mixture of two valid mental states, the perception of the presented reality and the vividly revived memory of a similar thing perceived in the past.

We see here again the wide variety of standpoints and theories ranging from extreme nihilism to extreme realism.

The Methods of Philosophy

We shall now try to give a very brief idea of the different methods adopted by Indian thinkers for reaching philosophical truths.

The earliest philosophical treatises of India are the Upaniṣads, which are many in number. The earliest of them go back to about two thousand years before Christ. Some of these are written in verse and contain inspired utterances of truths which come with the force of direct realization and, therefore, are not supported by any reasoning. But some are written in prose and in the form of dialogues between the student and the teacher. We find in them the beginnings of attempts at removing doubts by examples and arguments. But still the art of reasoning with mere words (called in the *Chāndogya Upaniṣad vākovākya*), without the backing of spiritual insight and experience, was not at all encouraged. But later on in the *Mahābhārata,* in Kauṭilya's *Artha-śāstra* (*Treatise on Political Economy*), and in the *Manu-saṁhitā* we find much appreciation of the science of reasoning (variously referred to as *ānvīkṣikī, hetu-vidyā,* etc.).

In Gautama's *Nyāya-sūtra* we find an elaborate treatment of the methods which should be adopted for carrying on arguments and establishing philosophical theories. There is also an elaborate account of the many defects and errors which should be avoided. Vātsyāyaṇa, the commentator on the *Nyāya-sūtra,* gives a hint that Gautama is not the first propounder of this branch of knowledge, and the detailed nature of the treatise also strongly suggests that the work must have been preceded by long discussion, analysis, and practice of the art of debate, the results of which were available to Gautama. The followers of Gautama develop this branch, particularly the theory of inference, in the course of about two thousand years. The Nyāya method and the technical language for carrying on arguments came to be adopted to a large extent by all the other schools, with occasional addition and alteration. So, we should briefly discuss this method in the light of Gautama's *Nyāya-sūtra.*

Doubt (*saṁśaya*) is regarded by Gautama as the chief incentive to philosophical inquiry. For the removal of doubt one must consider carefully the pros and cons (*pakṣa-pratipakṣa*) and ascertain the true nature of things. For this purpose one is advised to take the help of all valid sources of knowledge, use (and avoid conflict with) previously established theories (*siddhānta*), use examples (*dṛṣṭānta*) which are acceptable to all, employ the five-step method of discovery and proof (*pañcāvayava-nyāya*), use the indirect hypothetical or postulational method of strengthening the conclusion (*tarka*), and also take care to avoid five kinds of material fallacies (*hetvābhāsa*), three kinds of quibbles (*chala*), twenty-four kinds of false analogies (*jāti*), and twenty-two kinds of self-stultifying steps which would cause defeat in debates. This elaborate method of critical inquiry was regarded as the light for all branches of knowledge, as the means of all (*rational*) activity, and as the basis of all virtues (*dharmas*).

It is only when such a rigorous method is employed that the solution of any problem can claim to be a *vāda,* that is, a full-fledged theory.

In further clarification of this standard method, let us observe a few important points from Gautama, Vātsyāyana, and other general writers. Every philosophical discussion starts with an explicit statement of its utility (*prayojana*) for human good (*puruṣārtha*).

The ultimate purpose of philosophical knowledge is the avoidance of evil, pursuit of desirable ends, and remaining indifferent to other things. Philosophical discussion arises from the desire to know (*jijñāsā*) and from doubt (*saṁśaya*). It aims at the elimination of doubt. It is based on the assumption that argument and the arguer have the capacity of attaining truth.[12] Though doubt is necessary for philosophy, it must be given up when it leads to contradiction.[13]

The material basis of philosophical discussion is the individual's own direct experience (*pratīti* or *anubhava*), including introspection and knowledge obtained from other valid sources. Not only normal waking experience, but also sleep, dream, and other kinds of experience should be explained and utilized. Current linguistic usage (*vyavahāra*), implying socially accepted experience, is often taken as the material basis of philosophical theories (cf. Socrates). Knowledge of previously established theories (*siddhānta*) is a source of new theories and helps one also to avoid errors. Distinction must be made, however, among (1) universally accepted theories, (2) sectarian theories, (3) implied theories, and (4) theories admitted for argument's sake.[14]

Philosophical discussion should proceed by accurate definition of terms (*lakṣaṇa*) and indication of their denotation (*uddeśa*).

One should not believe that what cannot be perceived does not exist. For, failure to perceive may be due to the object's being too distant, too near, too subtle, too much mixed up with other things, to the senses' being damaged, or to lack of concentration.[15] Knowledge of the unperceived may be obtained from inference based on analogy and general observation or from postulation (i.e., necessary supposition), or, in some cases, from reliable authority possessed of superior knowledge of the unperceived.

One of the important criteria of a good supposition adopted by all is its lightness (*lāghava*), that is, simplicity, as opposed to its undue heaviness (*gaurava*), i.e., redundance (cf. Occam's razor). Again, so long as the perceived is sufficient, nothing unperceived should be supposed.[16] The supposition of an unperceived cause is justified only if it can explain the perceived effect. When many alternative suppositions are possible, either (1) the acceptable alterative is retained by the method of residues (*pāriśeṣya*) by eliminating the defective ones, or (2) all the alternatives may be examined and found defective, and nothing can be ascertained. In the latter case the very basic presupposition underlying the many alternatives is shown to be wrong.

The validity of a theory is also indirectly established by *tarka*, which consists in showing that the supposition of its contradictory leads to undesirable consequences. These latter are enumerated by Gautama as the defects of (1) self-dependence (*ātmāśraya*), (2) mutual dependence (*anyonyāśraya*), (3) circular reasoning (*cakraka*), and (4) infinite regress (*anavasthā*)—all these errors may be either in respect of origination or existence or knowledge of the thing or things about which discussion is held. In addition to these four, there is a residual class of general defects, the chief of which is contradiction (*virodha*), i.e., conflict with either itself (*svavirodha*) or with other established facts, ideas, and theories. Noncontradiction (*a-bādhitatva*), coherence (*saṁvāda*), agreement with facts (*yāthārthya*), practical utility (*arthakriyā-kāritva*), self-evidence (*sva-prakāśatva*), etc., are recognized by different thinkers as the criteria of truth. The laws of contradiction and excluded middle are explicitly formulated by Udayana in the following way: If two terms are contradictory, they cannot be identical, nor can there be any other alternative besides these.[17]

Conclusion

It is hoped that even this very meager account of Indian epistemology will not fail to point out the following important facts. In epistemology, as elsewhere, the Indian mind has regarded philosophical discussion as a means to a better life, and consequently great emphasis is laid on living and realizing in life the truths obtained in philosophy. Not in spite of this, but because of this, there is a rigorous and sincere attempt to ascertain all possible avenues to knowledge and to evolve the different rational methods of checking and correcting knowledge and ascertaining truth in such a way that unsound philosophy may not ruin life. Reason and argument, therefore, find their full place here as in Western philosophy. If there are differences between certain Indian and Western ideas and beliefs, we have only to bear in mind that there have been greater differences between Indians and Indians, as well as Westerners and Westerners. So, these differences may not be all racial but mostly individual. On the other hand, there is ample similarity and identity of thought as well between the Indian and the Westerner. This is no wonder, but is what it should be if man is human and reason is his chief instrument for understanding things and convincing his fellow creatures.

Notes

1. See Vātsyāyana, Commentary on Gautama's *Nyāya-sūtra.* See S. C. Vidyābhūṣaṇa, ed. and trans., Sacred Books of the Hindus, Vol. VIII (Allahabad: The Panini Office, 1913), I.i.1.
2. For an elaborate discussion, see D. M. Datta, *The Six Ways of Knowing* (2nd ed.; Calcutta: University of Calcutta, 1960).
3. See Dharmakīrti, *Nyāya-bindu,* with Commentary of Dharmottarācharya, P. Peterson, ed. (Calcutta: Asiatic Society of Bengal, 1929), chap. I.
4. For a detailed discussion, see D. M. Datta, *The Six Ways of Knowing,* chap. VI.
5. See S. C. Chatterjee, *The Nyāya Theory of Knowledge* (Calcutta: University of Calcutta, 1939), chaps. IX–X.
6. Patañjali, *Yoga-sūtra,* Ram Prasad, ed. and trans., Sacred Books of

the Hindus, Vol. IV (Allahabad: The Panini Office, 1912), III.19.25 ff., *et passim.*

7. See *Vedānta-paribhāṣā* (Calcutta: University of Calcutta, 1930), and D. M. Datta, *The Six Ways of Knowing,* on perception.
8. For an excellent account of scientific methods, see B. N. Seal, *The Positive Sciences of the Ancient Hindus* (London: Longmans, Green, and Co., 1915).
9. *Nyāya-sūtra,* I.i.6.
10. Jaimini, *Mīmāṁsā-sūtra,* M. L. Sandal, ed. and trans., Sacred Books of the Hindus, Vol. XXVIII (Allahabad: The Panini Office, 1923), I.i.5.
11. The word "knowledge" seems peculiar in this and the following paragraphs, but Mr. Datta has requested that no change be made. His explanation is as follows: "I understand it [the word 'knowledge'] is not usually used in this sense, but that is because European philosophy does not recognize more than two kinds of knowledge (perception and inference). Indian philosophy makes a strong case for the extension of this limited view and hence the strain put on 'knowledge.' I would, therefore, keep it, for want of a better substitute. Moreover, a change here would require many other changes in other parts of the paper." [Editor's note.]
12. See Vātsyāyana, Commentary on *Nyāya-sūtra,* I.i.32.
13. Udayana, *Kusumāñjali,* E. B. Cowell, ed. and trans. (Calcutta: Baptist Mission Press, 1864), III.7. See also Ravi Tirtha, trans. (Madras: Adyar Library, 1946), Vol. I, Bks. I, II.
14. *Nyāya-sūtra,* I.i.26–31.
15. Īśvarakṛṣṇa, *Sāṁkhya-kārikā,* Suryanarayana Sastri, ed. and trans. (Madras: Madras University, 1935), pp. 7–8.
16. "*Dṛṣṭe tu na adṛṣṭam,*" Puruṣārthānuśāsanam.
17. *Kusumāñjali,* III.8: "*Paraspara-virodhe hi na prakārāntara-sthitiḥ/ Naikatāpi viruddhānām ukti-mātra-virodhataḥ.*"

SWAMI NIKHILANANDA

Concentration and Meditation as Methods in Indian Philosophy

I PROPOSE TO DISCUSS the subject of concentration and meditation from three standpoints of Hindu philosophical thought, namely, *rāja-yoga, bhakti-yoga,* and *jñāna-yoga.* The word "*yoga,*" much misunderstood in the West, really means union with ultimate reality and also the disciplines necessary to realize that union.

Rāja-yoga, the "kingly *yoga,*" was systematized by the ancient Hindu seer Patañjali. It deals mostly with concentration as a means to the attainment of the knowledge of the self. *Bhakti-yoga,* the path of religious devotion, and *jñāna-yoga,* the path of philosophical discrimination, both regard concentration as an effective discipline for the realization, respectively, of God and of the identity of the individual self and the universal Self.

According to Hindu philosophy, a genuine philosopher must have direct knowledge of reality. Ultimate reality, or the first principle, differs from scientific reality. It belongs to a supramental realm and is known through direct and immediate experience. The knowledge acquired through the senses is colored by the condition of the sense-organs and the mind. But ultimate reality belongs to the universal experience of humanity. It is not confined to any person or time.

I

Rāja-yoga is a discipline by which the direct experience of ultimate reality is made possible. It is a practical and rational method, tested time and again by Indian philosophers. Every science—physics, chemistry, and botany, for instance—has formulated its own discipline. No man can be called a true philosopher if he only believes in a theory but has not directly experienced the object of knowledge. Untested philosophical beliefs are no more trustworthy than untested scientific hypotheses.

All knowledge is based upon the observation of facts. First, a generalization is made from these facts, and then a final conclusion is arrived at. It is much easier to observe the facts of the outer world than to understand such states of the mind[1] as passion, love, and hate. In the latter instance the observer, the object, and the instrument are all different states of the mind itself. The mind must be directed toward itself. The powers of the mind, scattered in the average man, become, when concentrated, a powerful searchlight to illumine its different states. To use another illustration, through concentration the mind acquires the quality of a lens and can penetrate deeply into any object, external or internal. But this is an extremely difficult task, for most of us have been trained from childhood to observe and analyze only the outer world and not the inner world of the mind. In the West, the systematic study of physics and astronomy began much earlier than that of psychology, embodying the study of the emotions and passions.

Concentration is the sole method by which to learn the secrets both of the outer and of the inner world. Chemists, physicists, and astronomers direct their attention to the objects of their inquiry. But the mere observation of facts does not constitute the scientific method. Before one can arrive at scientific truth, these facts must be properly studied. The falling of apples had been observed since the beginning of creation, but the reflection of Sir Isaac Newton on this fact resulted in the formulation of the law of gravitation. So it is with the observer of mental states. All creative scientists must cultivate concentration to succeed in their research.

Yoga develops the innate powers of the mind through concentration, focuses them on the mind itself, and then analyzes its true nature. One can be a *yogī* (one who practices *yoga*) whether or not one accepts any form of religious belief. By means of *yoga* an atheist, no less than a Christian, a Hindu, or a Jew, can discover the ultimate nature of things. Again, through *yoga* it can be demonstrated that genuine religious experiences are as valid as scientific truths.

Yoga has been defined by Patañjali as "restraining the mind from taking various forms (*vṛttis*)." How does one perceive an object? The sense-organs carry the impressions to the brain-centers and present them to the mind, which, through its different aspects, functions in different ways. One aspect of the mind creates doubt regarding the object it is observing; a second, called intellect (*buddhi*), comes to a conclusion by comparing the impression with the stored-up impressions of the past; a third part, called ego (*aham*), flashes I-consciousness. Thus it is that one says: "I perceive a cow." But according to *rāja-yoga* the entire mind is a subtle material substance and cannot function unless activated by intelligence or consciousness. This consciousness, called *ātman,* acts also like the screen in a cinema, which enables the spectator to obtain a coherent story from the separate pictures of the film. With the help of consciousness, the separate impressions or suggestions coming from the outside world are formed into mental states. These mental states constitute our everyday universe.

The nature of these mental states is influenced by certain characteristics of the mind. According to Hindu psychologists, matter, like a twisted rope, consists of three elements, called *guṇas.* These elements are present in all material objects, gross and subtle. The mind, being a subtle form of matter, is also made up of the three elements, which are called *tamas, rajas,* and *sattva. Tamas* is the darkening element, whose chief characteristic is inertia and indolence, and is generally found in animals and men of undeveloped mind. *Rajas,* which functions in the energetic man, is the active element, whose chief characteristics are love of power and enjoyment. *Sattva* is found among highly developed souls and is characterized by calmness and a balance between extremes. The impressions of the outer world presented to the mind are influenced by *sattva, rajas,* and *tamas.* Thus the same object creates different emotions in different minds. A beautiful woman, for instance, is regarded by her disappointed lover with bitter pain, by her successful suitor with great joy, and by a saint with complete indifference.

The surface of the mind is constantly agitated by impressions from the outside world. Hence one does not see what lies beyond the mind. If the water of a lake is muddy or disturbed, one does not see the bottom. But when the mud settles and the ripples subside, an object lying on the bottom can be clearly seen. As water is clear by nature, mud being extraneous to it, so the mind itself is translucent and capable of revealing the true nature of things. But the uncontrolled sense-organs constantly draw the mind outward and create waves. It is the aim of *yoga* to detach the mind from the sense-organs and check its outward tendency. Only then can it reflect the true nature of any object it contemplates.

The ordinary mind is "darkened" or "scattered." The darkened mind is characterized by dullness and passivity. The scattered mind is restless. In neither of these states is it capable of higher perceptions. Through the disciplines of *yoga* the darkened or scattered mind can be "gathered" and made "one-pointed." When this has been accomplished, it attains total absorption (*samādhi*), in which a man realizes the true nature of his self. When the waves cease and the lake quiets down, one sees the bottom. But an unillumined person identifies himself with one or another of the states of the mind, and thus experiences grief, fear, or happiness.

Rāja-yoga declares that by practice and non-attachment the mental states may be controlled. Practice means an unceasing struggle to keep the mental states perfectly restrained. It becomes easy through protracted effort accompanied by intense longing for the goal. Non-attachment means the control of yearning for any object unrelated to the goal one has set out to realize. For a *yogī,* who aspires to realize supramental reality, non-attachment means the repression of yearning for all material objects, either tangible or intangible. The intangible objects are those which, it is said, can be enjoyed in the heavenly world. But these are as impermanent as tangible objects, because they, too, like the latter, are subject to the laws of time, space, and causation. A non-attached person renounces the desire for everything that belongs to Nature, or matter, including mind. He is as detached from exclusive love as from earthly possessions.

There are different kinds of concentration. One can concentrate on the external, gross elements and thus learn their true nature. Certain *yogīs,* by means of such concentration, acquire psychic, or so-called "occult," knowledge, which is really a kind of subtle knowledge of material objects. Knowledge is power. Through this knowledge these *yogīs* acquire what is generally known as supernatural power. The concentration practiced by scientists may be said to belong to this category. Without deep concentration they could not have understood the inner nature of the atom and released the energy locked in it. According to Patañjali, the power acquired through such concentration enables one to obtain mastery over material objects and enjoy material happiness. But such mastery over Nature, unless controlled by ethical and spiritual laws, can produce evil results. Therefore, before taking up concentration, every *yogī* is required to eradicate evil tendencies by the practice of ethical disciplines. Further, the happiness obtained from impermanent, material objects is transitory; it ultimately brings suffering.

Other forms of concentration, directed toward different material objects, produce corresponding results; but they do not give one knowledge of reality, which alone makes one free.

In the higher concentration, the mind concentrates on itself. Every thought that appears is struck down. The mind is made a vacuum. But there is danger in this form of concentration. Without proper discipline and guidance, it may make the mind negative or morbid. Rightly practiced, however, it enables the mind to become "seedless," which means that all the latent tendencies of the mind are destroyed. No more is it disturbed by the outer world or by impressions from the past. Thus one attains knowledge of one's true nature and achieves freedom from the bondage of matter.

Patañjali suggests various methods of concentration, success depending upon the intensity of the seeker's desire. One of these is devotion to the personal God. God is conceived of as omniscient and all-powerful. In him knowledge, which in others is found only as a germ, reaches perfection. Every minimum must have its maximum. God is unconditioned by time and is the transmitter of spiritual knowledge through human teachers. Patañjali suggests the mystic word "*Om*" as an effective symbol of God, both personal and impersonal. Through repetition of this word and meditation on its meaning, the mind acquires the power of introspection and at the same time frees itself from many obstacles. Some of these obstacles are as follows: disease, mental laziness, doubt, lethargy, clinging to sense enjoyment, and non-retention of concentration once it has been acquired. Without proper guidance, the aspirant, while practicing concentration, experiences grief, mental distress, tremor of the body, and irregular breathing. Meditation on a fixed object removes these obstacles.

Other disciplines are prescribed by Patañjali to quiet the mind. For instance, one should cultivate an attitude of friendship toward those who are happy, mercy toward those who are unhappy, gladness toward the good, and indifference toward the evil. (But a *yogī* is not a social reformer.) The regulation of breathing, through certain definite exercises, is also a method. Again, one can concentrate on light or on a pleasant dream or on any delectable object.

With the help of such concentration the mind acquires the power to contemplate all objects, whether as minute as an atom or as huge as the sun. It can then function either like a heavy scale in a warehouse or like a delicate balance in a chemical laboratory.

When the *yogī* becomes proficient in concentration, he can withdraw his mind from all extraneous things and identify himself solely with the object of his thought. His mind then becomes like a crystal. When a crystal is placed near a flower, the crystal identifies itself, as it were, with the flower. The mind has now acquired one-pointedness and can penetrate deeply into the nature of things. Thus it can obtain knowledge which is far more profound than that acquired through the senses, inference, or the testimony of others. This is what is meant by direct experience. Scientists, philosophers, artists, statesmen, and all creative thinkers should find the practice of yogic concentration an invaluable help in their various fields of work.

The greatest of the obstacles to concentration is the distraction caused by latent tendencies of the mind. Every action leaves behind it a subtle impression. These impressions remain hidden in the deeper layers of the mind. Ordinarily a man is hardly aware of them. But, as he tries to concentrate his mind, they come to the surface and cause distraction. Like waves on the surface of a lake, concealing an object lying on the bottom, they hide a man's true nature. But if, with undaunted mind, one practices concentration, they gradually become attenuated. Intense concentration on one object creates a strong wave which gradually swallows up, as it were, the other waves created by past impressions. Finally, by a supreme act of will, the last wave also is destroyed, and the mind becomes free of all impressions. Then a man's true and complete nature is revealed. He realizes the soul to be non-material, completely separate from the body and mind, and untouched by time, space, and causation. It is the essence of consciousness, immortal and indestructible. This state of realization is called *kaivalya,* isolation, when the *yogī* realizes his utter non-attachment to material objects, which include, as has already been noted, the various states of the mind—such as doubt, intellect, and the ego—and all possessions and possessiveness.

Rāja-yoga consists of eight "limbs," or parts. The first two are called *yama* and *niyama.* Both denote, in a general way, control or restraint. *Niyama,* which refers to lesser vows, is not as obligatory as *yama.* It includes internal and external purification, contentment, mortification, study, and the worship of God. According to Patañjali, *yama* includes non-killing, truthfulness, non-stealing, continence, and non-receiving of gifts. These are great vows and should be undertaken by *yogīs* irrespective of time, place, or caste rules. Morality is the steel-frame foundation of the spiritual life. Without it the practice of concentration can bring harmful results, not only to the seeker but also to others. The power released by concentration may be used for destructive purposes. A Sanskrit proverb says: "To feed a cobra with milk without first taking out its poison fangs is only to increase its venom."

The third limb of *yoga* is posture (*āsana*). The *yogī* sits in the posture that comes easiest to him. Eighty-four postures are described in *yoga*. But the general principle is to hold free the spinal column, through which nerve-currents rise in the course of meditation. The *yogī* sits erect, holding his back, neck, and head in a straight line. The whole weight of the upper body rests on the ribs. With the chest out, he finds it easy to relax and think high thoughts.

The fourth limb is control of the breath (*prāṇāyama*). According to *rāja-yoga*, our breathing is part of the cosmic energy. The breath is like the fly-wheel of a machine. In a large engine, first the fly-wheel moves, and then that motion is conveyed to the finer parts of the machine, until the most delicate mechanism is set in motion. The breath is the fly-wheel supplying motive power to all parts of the body. When breathing is regulated, the whole physical system functions rhythmically.

The fifth limb of *yoga* (*pratyāhāra*) consists in training the mind to detach itself, at will, from a particular sense-organ. The perception of an object arises only when the mind joins itself to a sense-organ. Through the practice of this discipline the *yogī* can check the outward inclination of the mind and free it from the thraldom of the senses. At the beginning of this discipline the *yogī* relaxes his mind and lets it move in any way it likes. He does not interfere with his thoughts or try to suppress them. He remains their witness. Gradually, as the mind grows tired, the thoughts become fewer. At last, the mind comes completely under his control. The mind of the average person may be compared to a monkey. Both are restless by nature. The monkey has taken a deep draft of liquor. Its restlessness is aggravated. Likewise, the mind, after a deep dose of worldly pleasures, becomes intensely restless. And, finally, the intoxicated monkey is bitten by a scorpion. The worldly man is also bitten by the scorpion of egotism, jealousy, etc. How is one to calm the monkey? Allow it to jump about. At last it will become tired. Likewise, allow the mind to indulge in its fancies. Do not try to suppress them or it will be stubborn. Be a witness to its restless movements. At last, when the mind becomes tired, you can bring it under control by the power of will.

The sixth limb of *yoga* (*dhāraṇā,* concentration) consists in holding the mind to a certain point in the body. It is trained to feel that part only, to the exclusion of all others. For instance, the *yogī* may remain aware only of the hand or the tip of the nose, not feeling the existence of any other part. This concentration is uninterrupted.

The seventh limb is called *dhyāna,* meditation. In this stage the mind acquires the power to think of an object uninterruptedly. The flow of the *yogī's* mind to the object on which he is meditating is unbroken, like the flow of oil when it is poured from one vessel to another.

The eighth and last limb is called *samādhi,* a state of mind in which the *yogī* rejects the external part—the name and the form—of the object of meditation, and contemplates only its essence. He thus comes face to face with the true nature of the object, which ordinarily remains hidden behind the outer form. He is no longer deceived by appearances. He knows the reality that lies behind the body and the senses. *Samādhi* can be attained by all human beings. Each one of the steps leading to it has been reasoned out and scientifically tested. When properly practiced, under a competent guide, these steps lead the seeker to the desired end, namely, the realization of his utter isolation from and independence of matter and mental states, which are, by their very nature, transitory.

II

Concentration is discussed in the *Bhagavad-gītā* from the standpoint of the personal God, who is defined as the possessor of infinite blessed attributes.[2] It is he who is the object of meditation. In this process of meditation, love of God plays an important part. It enables the mind to become one-pointed. The follower of this path is also a *yogī.* He must practice certain disciplines before he can achieve success in meditation.

As his spiritual discipline, the aspirant performs his daily obligatory duties toward others, regarding himself as an instrument in God's hands and renouncing the results of his actions. Thus he cultivates inner serenity, remaining unruffled by pain and pleasure, success and failure, and the other pairs of opposites. Further, he practices non-attachment to sense objects and thus brings the turbulent mind under control. An unbounded faith in himself is necessary: "Let a man be lifted up by his own self, and let him not lower himself; for he himself is his friend and he himself is his enemy."[3] He who has brought the body, the senses, and the mind under control is his own friend. But he who has no such control does injury to himself, like an external enemy. The aspirant maintains an attitude of sameness toward friends and foes, the righteous and the sinful. While practicing concentration, he remains serene and fearless. Observing chastity of body and thought, he renounces "all desires born of the mind," draws back the senses from every direction by strength of will, and subdues the turbulent passions. He follows the middle path, avoiding extremes in matters of food, sleep, play, and work.

The aspirant concentrates his mind on God, regarding him as the supreme goal of life and the embodiment of peace, blessedness, and freedom. God is to him, not only the power that creates and sustains the universe, but also the one who dwells in all beings as their inner controller. He is both transcendent and immanent. Love of God, if genuine, leads to love for all human beings, because all human beings, in essence, are God. As the aspirant's contemplation deepens, he realizes greater and greater tranquillity. At last he sees God in his own self and himself in God. He experiences the boundless joy that comes from the knowledge of reality and thereafter remains unmoved by the heaviest of sorrows. His mind remains fixed in the Lord alone, like a "lamp, which, when kept in a windless place, does not flicker." Every time the mind, by nature fickle and unquiet, wanders away from the goal, he brings it back under his control.

As the culmination of his contemplation, the *yogī* on the path of devotion comes to view all things alike, beholding himself in all beings and all beings in himself. He sees God in all things, and all things in God. Established in this oneness, he worships God, who dwells in all beings. He devotes his life to the service of humanity; for he now regards the pleasure and pain of all beings as he regards them in himself. Infinite compassion flows from his heart, and infinite love from his soul. This is the fruit of the concentration attained through devotion to the personal God.

III

Finally, we shall consider, in brief, concentration from the standpoint of the non-dualistic (*advaita*) Vedānta philosophy. The essence of non-dualism is that *Brahman* alone is the ultimate reality; the phenomenal universe is unreal; and the individual creature is none other than *Brahman* itself. The goal of the non-dualist is to realize, in the depths of meditation, the unity of existence. This is a supersensuous and supramental experience in which the illusory notions of name and form, and subject and object, completely disappear.

According to non-dualistic Vedānta, it is through *māyā*, metaphysical ignorance, inscrutable to the finite mind, that the infinite *Brahman* appears as the finite universe. The Vedānta states, further, that there are two orders of experience. From the transcendental standpoint, the illumined soul experiences unity, which includes his own self. From the empirical standpoint, the ordinary man experiences multiplicity and sees himself as its perceiver. No relationship exists between the Infinite and the finite, the One and the many, because they belong to two entirely different levels of experience. If anyone seeks to establish such a relationship, the Vedāntist calls it the result of *māyā*. One can find a relationship between two things perceived to exist at the same time. But when the One alone is perceived to exist, the many are non-existent, and vice versa. According to non-dualistic Vedānta, it is the One that appears as the many, the Absolute that appears as the relative. And this is *māyā*. The doctrine of *māyā* is simply a statement of fact regarding the phenomenal universe. *Māyā* cannot be explained by reason. But this is not an admission of the defeat of intellect, but the realization of the fact that there dwells a great mystery in the heart of reality which makes it possible for the One to appear as many, the Absolute as the phenomenal world.

There are two powers of *māyā*. First, through its veiling power, reality is concealed. Second, through its projecting power, the manifold universe comes into existence. Individuality is also a product of *māyā*. Under the spell of metaphysical ignorance, man forgets the knowledge of his identity with the Absolute and superimposes upon himself the illusory notions of mind and body, caste and sex, color and social position. Though the innate nature of his true self is not affected in the slightest degree by *māyā*, yet he regards the illusory superimposition as real. A mirage is regarded by an ignorant person as real, though even then the true nature of the desert remains unaffected. According to the Vedānta, man has hypnotized himself into the belief that he is a finite being subject to time, space, and causation. It is this self-forgetfulness, followed by the perception of multiplicity, that creates friction and fear and becomes the cause of suffering. The goal of the Vedānta is to de-hypnotize man and help him to rediscover his eternal but hidden spiritual nature. In the achieving of this goal, concentration and meditation play an important part.

The follower of the Vedānta practices a number of definite disciplines. He cultivates discrimination between what is real and what is unreal. He renounces the unreal. He feels an unwavering zeal to realize the absolute truth. Like the follower of *rāja-yoga* and of *bhakti-yoga,* he practices all the moral virtues, for these form the basis of any higher life. Special emphasis is given to chastity of body and thought, austerity, and self-control. As the mind becomes purified, the spiritual nature of the soul reveals itself to the seeker, and the knowledge of his identity with *Brahman,* or ultimate reality, becomes clear.

Students of self-knowledge, while practicing concentration, meet with four obstacles. The first is a sleep-like state, when the mind, detached from worldly objects and unable to rest on the ideal, falls into a state of passivity. The way to overcome this obstacle is to stimulate the mind by healthy spiritual exercises, such as music or the reading of an inspirational book. The second obstacle, often experienced, is called "distractions"—the "little imbecilities of the mind," as they have been aptly described. These are caused by the student's vain talk or actions in the past, whose latent impressions rise to the surface of the mind at the time of concentration. Such distractions are to be overcome by forcibly fixing the mind on the ideal. The third obstacle is the sudden awakening of a deep-seated attachment to a material object experienced long before but meanwhile suppressed. The way to overcome it is to exercise discrimination and realize the transitory and painful nature of all material attachments. The last obstacle, known as the "taste of bliss," is caused by the acquisition of various supernatural powers during the different stages of concentration. It also includes the enjoyment of ecstasy resulting from communion with the personal God. This is the final obstacle in the path of the realization of the unity of existence and can be overcome by the austere discrimination of the aspirant. The student should remove all these obstacles with iron will, directing his mind to the realization of the ultimate oneness of God, the soul, and the universe.

The treatises of the Vedānta emphasize that the qualified student should be instructed by an illumined teacher, to whom the utmost reverence must be shown. The teacher instructs him regarding the oneness of the individual self and *Brahman*. Next, the student constantly contemplates *Brahman* and strengthens his conviction by means of careful reasoning. In this way his illusory notions regarding the self are removed. Finally, he meditates on *Brahman* with one-pointed attention.

Meditation is defined, in the Vedānta philosophy, as the direction of attention on a stream of ideas consonant with the non-dual *Brahman,* to the exclusion of such foreign ideas as body, senses, mind, and ego. Meditation practiced uninterruptedly, for a long time, with intense devotion to the ideal, and with unflagging determination, leads to the knowledge of the seeker's complete identity with *Brahman.*

The teacher instructs the student on the precise meaning of the Vedic dictum: "That thou art." The word "That," he teaches, refers to pure consciousness, which, in association with *māyā,* is associated with omnipotence and omniscience and becomes the creator and preserver of the universe. The word "thou" refers to the same pure consciousness, which, through *māyā,* appears also to have become the finite created being, endowed with limited power and limited knowledge. Then, by a subtle process of dialectics, the Vedāntic philosopher eliminates the extraneous ideas superimposed, through *māyā,* upon "That" and "thou," and points out that the Vedic dictum actually refers to pure and indivisible consciousness, unaffected by time, space, and causation. As the student meditates on this consciousness, or *Brahman,* there arises in his mind a *state* which makes him feel that he is *Brahman,* pure by nature, eternal, self-illumined, free, infinite, supremely blissful, and non-dual. This mental state, illumined by pure consciousness, destroys his ignorance with regard to his identity with *Brahman.* But even now the idea of *Brahman* is only a state, or wave, of the mind. With the destruction of the student's ignorance, its effect, namely, the various mental states, is also destroyed—just as when a cloth is burned, the warp and woof are also burned. When the mental states are destroyed, there remains only pure consciousness, which now becomes overpowered, as it were, by the effulgence of *Brahman* itself. Thus the subject and the object, the perceiving consciousness and the pure consciousness, become one, and there remains only the supreme *Brahman,* one and without a second. This experience cannot be described in words; it is known only to him who has attained it. The experiencer becomes a new being, the Absolute *Brahman.* The illusion of name and form is destroyed. The knower is no longer a victim of the false expectation and false fear that plague the life of an unillumined person at every step.

A person endowed with the knowledge of *Brahman* is called a *jīvan-mukta,* one who enjoys freedom though still living in a human body.[4] To become free while living on earth is the goal of the Vedāntist. He demonstrates by his life and action the reality of *Brahman* and the illusoriness of the relative world. It is such men who keep true philosophy and religion alive, and not merely erudite scholars or subtle theologians. Whether absorbed in the ecstasy of communion or engaged in action in the outer world, the free soul's knowledge is steady and his joy constant. Though sometimes he appears to act like an unillumined person in respect to hunger, thirst, or sleep, he is never oblivious of his true nature. Though outwardly active, yet he is free from the notion of being a doer. He does not dwell on the experiences of the past, takes no thought for the future, and is indifferent to the present. Aware of his identity with all beings, he feels through all hearts, walks with all feet, eats through all mouths, and thinks through all minds. Physical death and birth have no meaning for him, a change of body appearing to him like a change of garments or like passing from one room to another.

Though a free soul lives in a world of diversity, yet he is unaffected by the pairs of opposites. Whether tormented by the wicked or worshipped by the good, he remains undisturbed. The outside world cannot produce any change in his self, just as the rivers flowing into the ocean cannot disturb its bottomless depths. He regards all things without prejudice or passion. His charity for others is without bounds.

An illumined person transcends the scriptures and the conventions of society. He is beyond the imperatives of ethics; yet he cannot do anything that is not conducive to the welfare of others. He is free but not whimsical, spontaneous but not given to license. The great ethical virtues—compassion, humility, unselfishness, chastity, fellow feeling—which, prior to the attainment of knowledge, he practiced assiduously as spiritual disciplines, now adorn him like so many jewels. He no longer seeks them. They cling to him.

Though without riches, yet he is ever content; though helpless, yet endowed with exceeding power; though detached from sense objects, yet always satisfied; though active, yet immersed in inner peace; though possessed of a body, yet unidentified with it; though apparently limited by time and space, yet omnipresent and omniscient. He neither directs the senses to their objects nor withdraws them from them, but looks on everything as an unconcerned spectator. While dwelling in the physical body he may experience disease, old age, and decay, which are characteristics of all material forms. He may be blind, or deaf, or deformed in other ways. Or he may feel hunger and thirst, or may appear to be a victim of grief and fear. Nevertheless, though experiencing all these momentarily—the characteristics of the body, the senses, and the mind—he is never overwhelmed by them. Having once realized their unsubstantiality, he never imagines them to be real.

One who witnesses the performance of a magician, and who knows that what he is seeing is magic, does not take it to be real. He is not deceived by appearances. Yet, he enjoys the performance to his heart's content. Accordingly, it is said: "He who sees nothing in the waking state, even as in dreamless sleep; who, though seeing duality, does not really see it, since he beholds only the Absolute; who, though engaged in work, is really inactive—he, and no other, is the knower of the Self."[5]

A free soul, while in the body, devotes himself to the spiritual welfare of others working under the spell of the soul's eternity, immortality, and non-duality. But he is not altogether indifferent to their physical welfare, if it gives the receiver spiritual uplift, or creates conviction in the efficacy of *yoga*. With the exhaustion of the momentum of his past actions, which are responsible for his present embodiment and which sustain his body, the illumined soul is ready to depart from the world. His death is not like the death of others. The Upaniṣad declares that he comes out of the body purer and brighter, like a snake that has cast off its slough. His soul does not go out to be reborn, but is absorbed into *Brahman*, leaving behind no trace of its separate existence. As milk poured into milk becomes one with the milk, as water poured into water becomes one with the water, as oil poured into oil becomes one with the oil—

so the illumined soul, absorbed into *Brahman,* becomes one with *Brahman.* As, when dwelling in the body, the illumined person does not lose the knowledge of his identity with *Brahman,* so also, after discarding it, he attains supreme freedom in *Brahman* and merges in light, peace, knowledge, and reality.

Thus did the ancient Indo-Aryan philosophers of various schools, by means of detachment, self-control, and concentration, seek to solve the riddle of the universe and of the self, leaving the legacy of their thought for the enrichment of human culture.

Notes

1. *Rāja-yoga* is concerned mainly with analysis, control, and concentration of the mind. Hence, it will be helpful to obtain a general idea of the mind according to Hindu philosophers and psychologists. The five elements of matter, as originally evolved, were in a subtle and rudimentary state. They combined with one another to form the gross elements, which constitute the visible universe. The mind (*manas*) is made of subtle elements. There are two organs of perception, namely, the inner and the outer. By means of the outer organs such as ears, eyes, nose, tongue, and skin, one perceives external objects. The mind is the inner organ, by which one analyzes sense data and also perceives inner states, such as doubt, passion, anger, hate, happiness, and unhappiness. The *Bṛhadāraṇyaka-upaniṣad* (I.v.3) gives the following functions of the mind: desire (*kāma*), cognition of the individuality of objects (*saṁkalpa*), doubt (*vicikitsā*), faith (*śraddhā*), disbelief (*aśraddhā*), fortitude (*dhṛti*), unsteadiness (*adhṛti*), intelligence (*dhī*), and fear (*bhī*). According to Hindu psychologists, the ego, the mind, and the intellect are not different from external material objects, such as trees or stones, as far as their essential nature is concerned. Endowed with a beginning and an end, they are objects of consciousness or *ātman. Ātman* is the unrelated witness of the activity of the senses and the mind during the waking and dream states and of their non-activity in deep sleep. Consciousness, which is the very stuff of *ātman,* can never be non-existent.
2. According to the Vedānta, the ultimate reality is *Brahman,* or pure consciousness. Its highest manifestation in time and space is *Saguṇa Brahman, Brahman* endowed with attributes. According to its different functions, it is the creator, the preserver, and the redeemer or savior. When personified, *Saguṇa Brahman* is regarded as the personal God of different religions, and is worshipped as the Father in heaven, Jehovah, Allāh, Śiva, Viṣṇu, and Kālī. Another manifestation is the divine incarnation, such as Christ, the Buddha, and Kṛṣṇa. Whenever

virtue declines and vice prevails in the world, *Saguṇa Brahman,* is incarnated for the protection of the righteous and the destruction of the wicked. God becomes man so that man may become God. A third manifestation is the inner guide (*antar-yāmin*), who dwells in the hearts of all living beings and controls their activities from within.

3. *Bhagavad-gītā,* VI.5.
4. This description of liberation applies to illumined persons who have attained perfection following the discipline of any path.
5. Śaṁkarācārya, *Upadeśa-sāhasrī,* II.x.13.

T. M. P. MAHADEVAN

Social, Ethical, and Spiritual Values in Indian Philosophy

INDIAN PHILOSOPHY is essentially a philosophy of values. Facts as such do not fascinate the Indian philosopher except as revealers of value. The discovery of facts and of the laws that govern them is the business of science and not of philosophy. It is true that the discoveries of science are often put to some use for mankind; but such use is a *consequence* and not the *end* of science; and the use may in no sense be construed as a value which is pertinent to philosophy. Philosophical inquiry, on the contrary, must, according to the Indian view, lead to the apprehension of value. Any metaphysical investigation which does not so lead is generally compared to such futile occupations as examining the teeth of a crow. Logic is a useful instrument of catharsis by means of which the philosopher rescues his intellect from obscure and conflicting conceptions, and from unreflective modes of thinking. It is of negative help insofar as it may clear away impossible ideas about the nature of reality, self-contradictory notions, and uncritical dogmas. By employing the canons of logic, one may know, at any rate, what reality is not. It is the purified intellect that is said to become the instrument of intuition. But when logic degenerates into logic-chopping, reveling in a mere display of fine-spun theories, it is worse than useless to the philosopher, because it does not then aid in the process of discovering and realizing the supreme value. So it is that the Upaniṣads declare that wisdom is not obtained by intellectual acrobatics.[1] A philosophy is to be judged by its fruits; and the final fruit of philosophy is the experience of value.

A well-known episode in the *Chāndogya Upaniṣad* is illustrative of the typically Indian philosophical outlook. Nārada, a versatile genius, master of many arts and sciences, secular as well as sacerdotal, finds himself sorrow-stricken in spite of all his learning. He approaches a preceptor, Sanatkumāra by name, confesses that he knows only the texts and not the Self, and implores the teacher to impart to him the knowledge of the Self, which alone would ensure the attainment of sorrowlessness.[2] The plight of Nārada, the problem he faces, and the way he goes about solving it are typical of the manner in which reflective thought begins and functions in India. The attainment of sorrowlessness is the common goal of all the schools of Indian philosophy. The Sāṁkhya, for instance, which sets out to distinguish spirit from matter and trace the various stages in the evolution of the universe, prefaces its inquiry with the statement that its ultimate aim is to help man achieve complete freedom from all misery. The Nyāya, which is the school par excellence of logic, regards the investigation into the categories of knowledge as the means to the attainment of liberation (*niḥśreyasa*). It was the observation of cases of sorrow and pain that made Gautama, the Prince of Kapilavastu, leave a sheltered life of ease and pleasure and wed the strenuous life of inward seeking, which led to his enlightenment (*bodhi*). "Just as the great ocean has one taste only, the taste of salt," says the Buddha, "just so have this doctrine and description but one flavor only, the flavor of emancipation."[3] The critical student of Indian thought often wonders why the school of materialism known as the Cārvāka came to be counted as a system of philosophy at all. The reason is that the Cārvāka does not stop with advocating a philosophical view, but aligns itself with the rest of the systems insofar as it professes to show a way of life as well, however crude and short-sighted that way may be. Thus, one of the fundamental features of Indian philosophy as a whole is that it goes beyond logic, and becomes an affair of one's life—not sound and fury signifying nothing, but a thing of utmost significance for man's entire being.

The Scheme of Values

The Indian scheme of values recognizes four human ends (*puruṣārthas*). They are: wealth (*artha*), pleasure (*kāma*), righteousness (*dharma*), and perfection or spiritual freedom (*mokṣa*). Not all these, however, are really ends. The first of these, wealth, is never an end in itself except for the miser in his moments of miserliness. In the *Bṛhadāraṇyaka-upaniṣad,* a wise lady, Maitreyī, puts this question to her husband, Yājñavalkya: "If this entire earth filled with wealth were mine, would I become immortal by that?" The reply which Yājñavalkya gives is, "No; just as is the life of men of means, so will your life be. There is no hope of immortality through wealth."[4] The Cārvāka, in conformity with its positivist-materialist outlook, recognizes only one intelligible human end, pleasure, the second of the values listed above. Quite apart from the Cārvāka view of reality, its view of the human end is unacceptable because it is not only the pleasure of the moment, sense-pleasure, or the greatest amount of pleasure in this life that we desire, but everlasting happiness. Indulging the senses does not seem to be the way to attain happiness. Desire grows by what it feeds on. "Never are one's desires satisfied with their indulgence," says the *Mahābhārata,* "but they flare up like fire with clarified butter poured into it."[5] The *Kaṭha-upaniṣad* declares: "The good (*śreyas*) and the pleasing (*preyas*) come to man. One who is wise considers the two comprehensively and discriminates between them. He chooses the good in preference to the pleasing. One who is stupid chooses the pleasing for the sake of acquisition and prosperity."[6]

While it is true that wealth and pleasure are not intrinsic values, they have their own place in the scheme of things. Man has to live before he can live spiritually. His physical body is the location of all his endeavor, including that which relates to morality and the higher life. A certain measure of economic security is essential, therefore, to keep body and soul together. There is no virtue in poverty. The example is often cited in India of King Janaka, who lived in the world, shared a large measure of its burdens, and yet pursued the path of spiritual discipline and wisdom. Anyone who is acquainted with the history of India will testify to the fact that the arts and the sciences, the systems of philosophy, and the great religions flourished most when the country was prosperous and the people contented. There is a maxim in the Tamil language that one must cross even the high seas in quest of wealth. But, at the same time, it must be remembered that the Indian view of property is that it must be held as a trust. Kālidāsa, the great poet, speaks of acquiring wealth in order to give it away.[7] Earning is not for hoarding, but for sharing. Almsgiving is one of the essential virtues enjoined on the householder, though in degenerate days this led to the encouragement of laziness and parasitism on the part of a section of Indian society.

Elaborate and detailed instructions are to be found in the scriptures as to how, under what circumstances, and to whom gifts are to be made. The economic factor, then, has its value; and the value consists precisely in the use made of it. As for the question as to whether one can attain everlasting happiness (*mokṣa*) through wealth, the reply has been indicated. One can understand and appreciate the statement of Jesus that it is easier for a camel to pass through the eye of a needle than for the rich man to enter the Kingdom of God. The Sanskrit term for wealth, *artha,* means what is sought after as good. But it is a misnomer, since not infrequently wealth is the source of what is evil. As Śaṁkara says *artha* is *an-artha.*

The normal man has his desires, and he seeks pleasure in the objects of sense. The passions are an integral part of his nature, and there must be channels through which they may flow. The world would be a dull affair without its dance and music, sport and recreation, connubial love and filial affection. Indian thought does not attempt to suppress the desires and emotions that well up from the human heart. On the contrary, its purpose is to let them flow within bounds and so canalize them that through them one may reach higher levels of experience. Marriage and the founding of a family are helpful in that they make the individual less egocentric and assist in the process of sublimating his desires. Kṛṣṇa in the *Bhagavad-gītā* says: "I am pleasure (*kāma*) that is not opposed to goodness (*dharma*)."[8] But here, again, one should not be so purblind as to believe that outside of life in a family there is no happiness. The number of broken homes is legion; and this shows, among other things, that to regard domestic happiness as the goal of human life is to court disappointment and spiritual desolation. It it not unusual for worldly men to look upon those who are unworldly with pity and say: "They do not know what they are missing," little realizing that there may be much more that they themselves miss by not making their vision extend beyond the limited and the finite. According to the Indian view, the stage of the householder is but a stage in life's journey, and not the stopping place. As a householder, the individual has to earn and spend and take his pleasures without serious transgressions. But there is a stage when he has also the duty to renounce and mount the higher reaches in the path to his goal. In order to gain an insight into the nature of Hindu ethics, one must understand the character of the classes into which society is divided and of the stages in an individual's life. This is usually referred to by the expression *varṇāśrama-dharma.* But, before I proceed to deal with that, let me complete my account of the human goals (*puruṣārthas*).

One of the most difficult terms to translate into any other language is *dharma*. It is derived from the root *dhṛ*, which means "to uphold, to sustain, to nourish." The concept itself may be traced to the *Ṛta* of the *Ṛg-veda*, which means both the order of Nature and the moral order. The advocates of the Mīmāṁsā define *dharma* as obedience to the commands of scripture. The more general meaning is righteousness or moral goodness. Man's life, individual as well as collective, would be impossible but for a certain measure of morality. In this sense, *dharma* is man's inner nature. The greater the approximation to the moral standard, the more truly does man realize his own nature. Each man's *dharma*—what the *Bhagavad-gītā* calls *sva-dharma*—is to perform the duties that pertain to his station in life. But how is one to know what one's duties are? So long as one is immature, one has to depend on an external authority. In what may be regarded as the oldest convocation or graduation address on record, the teacher in the *Taittirīya Upaniṣad* gives the following advice to his pupil: "Should there be any doubt regarding conduct, you should conduct yourself after the manner of those wise men who may be living in your vicinity—those who are competent to judge, dedicated to good deeds, not led by others, not cruel, and lovers of virtue."[9] The persons who are already perfect need not obey any commands. Neither prohibitions nor prescriptions apply to them. They are good by their own nature. The majority of men, however, have to take into cognizance (1) the declarations of scripture, (2) the tradition and practice of those who are learned in scripture, (3) the conduct of virtuous men, and (4) their own conscience. There are several modes in which the rule of *dharma* is presented. One of them, and the most comprehensive of all, is that one should look upon others as upon oneself. "What is harmful to oneself, one should not do to others. This is the quintessence of *dharma*. Behavior which is contrary to this is born of selfish desire."[10]

It is an oft-repeated charge leveled against Indian philosophy by Western scholars that it is unethical, or that, at any rate, it does not give to morality its proper place. Such a verdict, however, is based on an acquaintance with the Upaniṣads and the philosophical works inspired by them, without a corresponding appreciation of all that they imply. It is the function of the Dharma-śāstras (treatises on *dharma*) to deal exhaustively with questions of ethics.

The Upaniṣads generally assume an intensive ethical discipline before a student can even hope to understand what they teach. The *Kaṭha-upaniṣad* says, "Not he who has not ceased from bad conduct, not he who is not tranquil, not he who is not composed, not he whose mind is turbulent can obtain him (i.e., *Brahman*) by intelligence."[11] Śaṁkara prescribes cultivation of the cardinal virtues as an essential prerequisite for the study of the Vedānta. Since the Upaniṣads presuppose ethical excellence on the part of the prospective student of philosophy, they do not discuss elaborately the principles of ethics. But, even so, they do contain, here and there, teachings about morals. The *Taittirīya-upaniṣad,* for instance, gives detailed instructions as regards the most ordinary rules of conduct. In the *Bṛhadāraṇyaka-upaniṣad,* a whole ethical philosophy is summarized in the three words, *dāmyata, datta, dayadhvam,* which mean, "Cultivate self-control; be generous; and have compassion."[12]

It is true, however, that the aim of Indian philosophy is to yield an experience which is supra-moral, as it is supra-mental. The realm of morality with its claims and counterclaims, rights and obligations, necessarily involves imperfection. Though the goal of moral life is perfection, one cannot attain the goal so long as one remains merely moral. The difference between the level of moral experience and that which goes beyond can best be explained with the help of the doctrine of sheaths as it is taught in the *Taittirīya-upaniṣad.*[13] The soul or spirit is said to be enclosed by five sheaths—the sheaths of matter, life, mind, reason, and bliss. Each of these sheaths is pictured in the form of a bird, and the parts of each are mentioned. For our present purpose we need to consider only the last three of these sheaths. The sheath of mind and the sheath of reason correspond roughly to what Kant would call pure and practical reason, respectively. The parts of the sheath of mind, as enumerated by the Upaniṣad, are the different Vedas, the books of knowledge. The parts of the sheath of reason are the moral values. "Faith is its head; righteousness, the right wing; truth, the left wing; contemplation, the body; greatness, the tail, the foundation." Beyond the sheath of reason, which represents the level of morality, is the sheath of bliss. Describing the parts of this sheath, the Upaniṣad says, "Love is its head; delight, the right wing; great delight, the left wing; bliss, the body; *Brahman,* the tail, the foundation." This represents the experience of *Brahman,* which transcends even the realm of morality.

We now come to the last of the human goals, which is described as the supreme end, viz., *mokṣa,* spiritual freedom. In the Indian philosophical schools, *mokṣa* is variously conceived. According to some, it is a negative state of absence of sorrow. According to others, it is a positive experience of unexcellable bliss. To the former group belong the Sāṁkhya and the Nyāya-Vaiśeṣika systems, and to the latter the schools of the Vedānta.[14] The Sāṁkhya conception of the final goal is the spirit's realization of its complete difference from the prius of evolution, called *prakṛti* in the system. The spirit no longer identifies itself with *prakṛti* and its evolutes; it remains as a witness, alone and uncontaminated. This state is known as *kaivalya,* aloneness. According to the Nyāya-Vaiśeṣika view, the soul, when it attains freedom (*apavarga*), is stripped of all qualities, including consciousness. The reason the state of release is conceived in these views to be a state of absence of sorrow and not a positive experience of happiness seems to be that, since it is not possible to have pleasure without pain, one must get rid of pleasure also in order to be free from pain. The schools of the Vedānta, however, regard the state of release as involving, not only the utter absence of sorrow, but also the realization of plenary happiness or bliss. As to what this happiness consists in, the various schools differ greatly. It may be the presence of or participation in God, who is the home of all auspicious attributes. Or, it may be the realization of identity with the Absolute, which is of the nature of bliss (*ānanda*). But in all the schools of the Vedānta, by the happiness which is characteristic of release is meant, not pleasure as opposed to pain, but an experience of fullness and peace which transcends both. The term for release which is most frequently used in Buddhist teachings is *nirvāṇa,* which literally means "blowing out" or "becoming cool." Opinion is divided as to what the Buddha meant by *nirvāṇa,* whether he meant a negative state of ceasing to be or the positive experience of bliss. Is *nirvāṇa* "only the sleep eternal in an eternal night," or is it "life eternal?" The classical schools of Buddhism and the critics thereof seem to think that the Buddha meant by *nirvāṇa* "really nothing." Others, especially some Vedāntic interpreters of Buddhism, take *nirvāṇa* to mean "*as if* nothing" or "nothing, *as it were.*" "It does not mean complete extinction or annihilation," says Radhakrishnan, "but the extinction of the fire of the passions and the bliss of union with the whole."[15]

Though the schools of Indian thought differ among themselves in their views regarding the content of *mokṣa,* all of them are agreed that *mokṣa* is release from the wheel of life and death, which is termed *saṁsāra*. Like the worms that are hurried from one whirlpool to another in the rapids of a swift current, the souls are tossed from one birth to another and are thus caught up in a cycle of repeated births. *Mokṣa,* or release, consists in an ultimate withdrawal from this cycle, in non-return to birth, or, phrased differently, it is no-more-death.

Metempsychosis and Karma

Regarding the duration of the soul, three views are possible: (1) that the life of the soul is coeval with the existence of the body; (2) that the soul is born with the body, but does not perish with it; and (3) that the soul has neither beginning nor end. The systems of Indian philosophy, with the exception of the Cārvāka, adopt the third of these views. The soul is timeless. Somehow, on account of metaphysical ignorance (*avidyā, ajñāna*), it gets involved in the time-process. It goes from birth to death, and from death to birth. The expressions "birth" and "death" refer to the soul's "entry into" and "departure from" a physical body. The vehicle which carries the soul, as it were, from one body to another, and from one location to another, is the mind-stuff, which attaches itself to the soul, with all its accumulated impressions (*saṁskāras*) of previous states of existence. The law or principle which governs the nature of the successive births, their respective endowments, and the types of experience is *karma.*

Karma means "deed" and "the result of deed." The Law of *Karma* applies to the realm of morality the principle of cause and a regulated course of things. According to this law, there is nothing chaotic or capricious in the moral world. As we sow, so we reap. What we are and what circumstances we find ourselves in are dependent on what we were and what we did; similarly, what we shall be and how we shall be circumscribed will depend on what we are and what we do. Nothing is lost which has been earned by work; and nothing comes in which is not deserved. Every action has a double effect: it produces its appropriate reward and it also affects character. The reward may be reaped either here or in a hereafter, either in this life or in a later one. The determination of character is in the form of residual impressions (*saṁskāras*) left on the mind by one's deeds. These are responsible for the repetition or avoidance of similar deeds. Thus, the chain revolves, character informing conduct, and conduct in turn molding character. "A man becomes good by good deeds," says the Upaniṣad, "and bad by bad deeds."[16]

If the Law of *Karma* is the counterpart in the moral sphere of the mechanical law of causation, where, then, it may be asked, is the scope for freedom, without which morality would be meaningless? In reply to this question, I should like to point out that modern science no longer believes in an unalterable and absolutely determined mechanical process. On the contrary, it admits that there is a certain measure of indeterminacy or uncertainty in Nature. The past, no doubt, is determined and can be calculated. But the future is uncertain, not merely because of our ignorance, but also because of the very nature of things. The causal law is not absolute and cannot explain all things. Even where it applies, the plurality of causes imports an element of uncertainty. Scientists used to characterize the doctrine of plurality of causes as a popular myth. But now they seem to be convinced that it is a genuine defect of the causal concept. If there is uncertainty and incalculability even in the realm of physical Nature, there must certainly be a greater degree of freedom in human nature. *Karma* does not bind man completely. The cycle of *saṁsāra* has not the inevitability of fate. Man has the freedom to get out of the vicious circle; and, if he has the will, *karma* will help and not hinder his progress. There is a certain amount of determination; but it is not to the exclusion of all freedom. In the words of Radhakrishnan, "The cards in the game of life are given to us. We do not select them. They are traced to our past *karma*, but we can call them as we please, lead what suit we will, and, as we play, we gain or lose. And there is freedom."[17] It is important to remember that the goal of man is not to continue perpetually in the process of *saṁsāra*, and be governed by the rule of *karma*, but to break through both and become eternally free. *Mokṣa* is the final end, not longevity. For, as the boy Naciketas in the *Kaṭha-upaniṣad* pertinently asks his teacher, Yama, "Who would revel in mere length of life?"[18] "There are people," remarks Emerson, "who cannot dispose of a day; an hour hangs heavy on their hands, and you offer them rolling ages without end."[19]

The Class System

Having explained the Indian scheme of values, and incidentally the doctrines of metempsychosis and *karma*, let me proceed to give a brief account of the institution of classes in society and the scheme of stages in individual life.

No effort is made here to defend the extremely complicated social texture of castes and subcastes as it has been in vogue for the last several centuries in India. Due to historical circumstances, the classes became castes with numerous subdivisions, and a cold rigidity made them freeze, as it were, thus preventing the growth and progress of Hindu society. Fortunately, in recent times, the inflexibility of caste has been under the sledge-hammer blows of a revival of interest in the original teachings of Hinduism, the rise of national consciousness, and a zeal for reform and purification. The old lawgivers of India repeatedly said that social institutions were not ends in themselves, but only means to the social good, and might be reconstituted or even discarded to suit the changing conditions of each age.

The four classes in Hindu society are those of priest-teachers (*brāhmaṇas*), warrior-kings (*kṣatriyas*), trader-craftsmen (*vaiśyas*), and manual laborers (*śūdras*). These, to start with, should have been professional groups based on the principle of division of labor. They were meant to be complementary classes, each fulfilling certain specific social needs. The "Puruṣa-sūkta,"[20] in which the earliest reference to the division of Hindu society into the four classes is to be found, describes the classes as having come out of the different limbs of the body of the Primeval Being, and thus shows the organic relationships among the classes. If the hands quarrel with the stomach or the head, it is not the stomach or the head alone that suffers but the entire organism, including the hands. The head, again, cannot claim superiority over the feet simply because it extends in the air while the latter tread the dust; the feet are as essential to the organism as the head. It is the principle of integration and co-ordination, then, that must have weighed with the builders of the class system. "It is a law of spiritual economics," says Mahatma Gandhi. "It has nothing to do with superiority or inferiority."[21]

"*Varṇa*," which is the Sanskrit term for class or caste, means color. Originally, the term may have referred to the color of the skin. India has had to deal with the problems of race in its acutest form. Even at the dawn of her history, she had as her inhabitants the dark aboriginal tribes, the sturdy Dasyus, the yellow-pigmented Mongols, and the fair-skinned Aryans. Very soon she developed trade relations with the Persians, the Greeks, and the Scythians, some of whom settled in India. Then there was a succession of invaders through the northwestern passes of the Himalayas—the

Bactrian Greeks, the Parthians, the Śakas, the Kuṣaṇas, and the Huns. These alien races mingled with the native groups, and the result was a medley of cultures and civilizations. India tackled this problem in her own characteristic way. Not elimination but assimilation was her watchword. The various racial groups were absorbed into the Hindu fold; and with the progress of time the contrast between colors was toned down by all sorts of permutations and combinations. The result was a composite Hindu society; and the term *varṇa* assumed a new meaning—no longer the color of the skin, but the color of one's character.

According to the Sāṁkhya theory, which may be traced back to the Upaniṣads, there are three fundamental types of nature, called *guṇas*. Out of these all things are made, both bodies and minds. The three *guṇas* are purity (*sattva*), virility (*rajas*), and dullness (*tamas*), represented symbolically by the three colors, white, red, and black, respectively.[22] No individual in the universe is made exclusively of any one of these *guṇas*. What we have in each case is a mixture in different proportions. The social classes, like everything else phenomenal, represent varying groupings of the *guṇas*. The *brāhmaṇas* are those in whom *sattva* is predominant; they are men of thought. The *kṣatriyas* are those in whom *rajas* is the dominant trait; they are men of action. The *vaiśyas* are those in whom *tamas* predominates; they are men of feeling. The *śūdras* are those in whom none of these traits is highly developed. As the aptitudes of these classes differ, so do their professions. These two, then, viz., character (*guṇa*) and kind of work (*karma*), determine the class to which a person belongs.[23] Looked at from the point of view of society, all the classes are equally important, since each fulfills a set of definite social functions. Viewed from the standpoint of the individual, each person is a mixture of these character types and has to evolve from *tamas,* through *rajas,* to *sattva,* and beyond; for the goal of spiritual evolution is transcendence of the *guṇas*.

The classes as social groups probably started as professional guilds; but soon they became hereditary in character. It is difficult to examine each individual, determine what his aptitudes are, and then fix his calling. And so, heredity is made to serve as a working principle. Normally, the son inherits the trade of his father since he shares in some of his traits. But this principle was never intended to be applied like an iron rod, inflexible and inviolate. Manu, one of the codifiers of law, expressly says, "The *brāhmaṇa* who, not having studied the Vedas, labors elsewhere, becomes a *śūdra* in that very life along with his descendants."[24] And again: "A *śūdra* becomes a *brāhmaṇa,* and a *brāhmaṇa* a *śūdra* [by conduct]. Know the same [rule to apply] to him who is born of a *kṣatriya* or of a *vaiśya.*"[25] In the *Mahābhārata,* Yudhiṣṭhira gives the same teaching: "Truth, charity, fortitude, good conduct, gentleness, austerity, and compassion—he in whom these are observed is a *brāhmaṇa.* If these marks exist in a *śūdra* and are not found in a twice-born, the *śūdra* is not a *śūdra,* nor the *brāhmaṇa* a *brāhmaṇa.*"[26] According to the *Bhāgavata,* "One becomes a *brāhmaṇa* by his deeds and not by family or birth."[27] Thus, class is primarily a question of character. Conduct counts and not lineage. An interesting incident is recorded in the *Chāndogya Upaniṣad.*[28] Satyakāma, a young lad, desired to lead the life of a student. Before he could approach a preceptor for this purpose, he had to know his lineage. He had only his mother to enlighten him on this matter. But she could not throw any light on it. She told him, "I do not know to what lineage you belong, my son. In my youth when I was moving about as maid-servant, I conceived you. So, I do not know to what line you belong. I am Jābālā by name; and you are Satyakāma. Therefore, you may call yourself Satyakāma Jābāla." Then the boy went to a preceptor, Gautama, and announced himself in the manner in which his mother had instructed him. The preceptor was pleased with the boy's outspokenness and concluded that he must be a *brāhmaṇa* because he had spoken the truth. Thus, in Satyakāma's case it was character and not birth that determined his class.

The duties of the classes are these: The *brāhmaṇa* is the custodian of the spiritual culture of the race. His first duty is to specialize in spiritual ideas and disseminate them. He is the friend, philosopher, and guide of humanity. He is not to burden himself with worldly goods, and society has the obligation of keeping him above want. He is the leader (*purohita*) of the community. He leads not by virtue of physical might, but by the strength of spiritual power. His counsel is sought by all, from the king to the commoner. Serenity, self-control, austerity, purity, forbearance, uprightness, knowledge, insight, and faith—these are his virtues, according to the *Gītā.* The *kṣatriya* is the guardian of society, its protector and preserver. He is the soldier, who fights for the freedom of the race, and the prefect, who keeps the peace of the land. He has to save the social polity from alien domination and internal dissensions. His duties are deeds of heroism, vigor, firmness, resourcefulness, dauntlessness in battle, generosity, and majesty. The *vaiśya* is the expert in economics. His is the duty of arranging for the production and distribution of wealth. The *Gītā* enumerates three of the important professions of the *vaiśya:* agriculture, tending cattle, and trade. The *śūdra* is the worker.[29] His place in society is no less important than that of the other three classes, and he is to receive no less honor. By his manual labor he places the entire community under a debt of gratitude. The weal of society depends upon his welfare. No nation can rise higher than the level of its proletariat. With a fluid and functional class system based on the principle of bearing the burdens and not of sharing the spoils, there is no reason why a community should not live in harmony and peace, and progress toward the ideal of perfection.

The Indian mind is characterized by its critic as being individualistic. That such a characterization is unfair will be evident to those who take the care to study the class system. Not rights but obligations are said to be the foundation of the system. The state, in the abstract, is, no doubt, a means to the individual's realization of his ends. But the individual cannot realize his ends without the help of society. His dependence on the community for realizing ends like economic security, pleasure, and even moral goodness is obvious. His pursuit of *mokṣa,* spiritual freedom, too, redounds to the benefit of society, since the Self that is sought to be realized is not the empirical ego but the supreme Spirit, which is the substrate of all beings. The *Mahābhārata* declares: "One individual may be forsaken for the sake of protecting a family; one family may be forsaken for the sake of protecting a village-community; one village-community may be forsaken for the sake of preserving society; and for the sake of [realizing] the Self even the earth may be forsaken."[30]

The Four Stages in Life

Turning from society to the individual, we notice that, according to the teachings of Indian thinkers, each individual has to go through four stages in his life's journey. These stages are called *āśramas,* a term which means rest-places as well as training-grounds. The four *āśramas* are: *brahmacarya,* the period of studentship; *gārhastha,* the stage of a householder; *vānaprastha,* the stage of a forest-dweller or ascetic; and *sannyāsa* (*saṁnyāsa*), the life of renunciation.

The first stage is the period of study and discipline. The student is required to stay in the house of his teacher and learn the sciences and the arts. The preceptors in ancient India usually lived in hermitages not far from towns. These forest-hermitages were centers of common and equal living. The student has to regard the teacher as his spiritual parent and render unto him unstinted service. He has to eschew distracting pleasures and refrain from active participation in the affairs of the world. Secular as well as sacred knowledge is imparted to him. He learns, not only through word of mouth, but also through communion with nature. At the conclusion of his formal education, he returns to his home.

The second stage in life is that of the householder. Normally, when the period of studentship is over, one should marry and shoulder the responsibilities of life. Marriage is to be regarded as a sacrament which launches two companions on a career of righteous living. The status of the householder is all-important in the body politic. According to Manu, just as air is essential to the life of all creatures, so is the householder necessary for the support of those who belong to the other three orders. His duty is to acquire wealth and dispose of it in the proper way. He may court pleasures; but he should not overstep the bounds of the moral law. Through the opportunities afforded by the institution of the family he has to outgrow his innate egocentrism.

The next stage is that of the *vānaprastha.* Manu says: "When the householder sees wrinkles [in his skin], greyness [in his hair], and the son of his son, let him retire to the forest."[31] Married life is not an end in itself. It is a home of trial and a school for sublimation. When a man has passed through it, he must relinquish the responsibilities of restricted life and seek conditions which will accelerate his spiritual progress. As a *vānaprastha* he undergoes the second period of probation which prepares him for the final stage, that of *sannyāsa.*

The *sannyāsin* (i.e., one who has renounced the world) is the ideal man. He renounces all worldly cares in order that he may attain the supreme goal (*mokṣa*). As has been aptly remarked, "The last part of life's road has to be walked in single file."[32] The *sannyāsin* spends his days in contemplation, ponders over the mysteries of life, and wanders far and wide as the spiritual sentinel of the human race. His very striving for perfection, and his experience of it when he attains it, are a great blessing to the world. If he scorns worldliness, it is because he desires to place the world above scorn. He is the free man of the spirit, who has broken through the narrow confines of clan and country. Praise and blame, success and failure, make no difference to him. He has no private ambitions or personal desires. He has nothing to accomplish for himself either in this world or in the next. When he has achieved the supreme human goal, what need has he for the trinkets of the world? He beckons all —though only a few listen to the call—to share in the infinite happiness which has become his.

The four *āśramas* are intended to lead man to perfection by successive stages. In exceptional cases, some of the stages may be skipped. But, whether the progress be quick or slow, by grades or by leaps, the goal that one should keep in view is the same, viz., spiritual perfection and freedom.

The Paths to Perfection

Of the paths to perfection outlined in Indian thought, especially in the Vedānta, three are the main ones: *karma-yoga, bhakti-yoga,* and *jñāna-yoga.* The term *"yoga,"* which is cognate with the English *yoke,* means union with the ultimate reality, as also the way thereto. *Karma-yoga* is the path of selfless work, dedicated service. *Bhakti-yoga* is the method of unwavering devotion to God. And *jñāna-yoga* is the way of self-knowledge.

Work ordinarily binds the individual to finitude. He works in order to enjoy, and enjoys in order to work. Each of his deeds is intended to yield a particular end. These ends, which are by nature perishing, do not afford him lasting happiness. There is toil in getting a thing; and, after getting it, there is anxiety in keeping it and the fear of losing it. This, then, is the round of desire, work, enjoyment, and more desire. The method of *karma-yoga* consists in working without desiring the reward of work. Whatever be the action one has to perform, let it be performed without a selfish motive. But, is action without desire possible? Is not desire the spring of action? The answer to this is: It is true that action without an end is like a road without a destination. What the doctrine of *karma-yoga* teaches is that, instead of each action's having its own particular, finite end, the sole end of all action should be God-realization or Self-realization—these being the theistic and absolutistic ways, respectively, of expressing the same goal.

Bhakti-yoga is the method of sublimating one's emotions by turning them toward God. This is what a Vaiṣṇava saint of South India says: "The emotional feeling which, in the case of the ignorant, flows toward sense-objects, is called *bhakti* when directed to God."

Love for things that are transient is the cause of misery. Love for God, who is the eternal source of all things, makes for everlasting happiness. *Bhakti* takes several forms, and is of different grades. The highest of them transcends all convention. What is ordinarily called mystic experience is the soul's direct experience of God. Nārada, the author of the *Bhakti-sūtra*, says, "It is as if a dumb man who has tasted delicious food could not speak about it. It is an experience pure and selfless, subtle, unbroken, and ever-expanding. A man who has once experienced God-love will see that alone, hear that alone, and speak of that alone, for he ever thinks of that alone."[33]

Jñāna-yoga is the path of knowledge. According to the Advaita Vedānta, knowledge (*jñāna*) is the principal means to release (*mokṣa*). Ignorance (*ajñāna*) is the root of all the imperfections and ills of the world; and it can be removed only by its opposite, which is knowledge. On account of ignorance, the individual thinks that he is a finite center—an agent and an experient. The truth is that the Absolute Spirit is non-dual and the so-called individual is non-different (*abheda*) from it. When the individual realizes this truth, he is freed from finitude. The knowledge that liberates, however, is not mere intellectual understanding, but intuitive insight. The difference between mediate knowledge and immediate experience is sometimes explained thus: Once a group of travelers, ten in number, crossed a swollen river. After crossing, they began counting themselves to be sure that all had safely arrived. But, each time, the one who counted forgot to include himself in the counting, and so, according to the reckonings, there were only nine. A passerby detected the mistake, and addressing the man who had counted for the last time said, "There is the tenth man," and then added, "You are the tenth." The first of these statements gave to each of the travelers the mediate knowledge of the tenth man; the second revealed the immediate identity of each person with the one whom each thought had been lost in the river. Similarly, the *Knowledge* that there is the non-dual *Brahman* is but mediate. The further immediate *experience* of *Brahman* as non-different from the soul is necessary for effecting release. This is to be accomplished by the removal of obstructions that block the way to knowledge—obstructions such as identification of the self with the body, mind, etc.

There are two stages in the discipline to be undergone before the intuition of *Brahman* can be gained. The first is the stage of moral, intellectual, and emotional preparation. It consists of discrimination between the eternal and the non-eternal, detachment from all selfish pursuits, cultivation of the cardinal virtues, and intense longing for release. The second stage consists of three steps: study (*śravaṇa*), reflective thinking (*manana*), and meditative contemplation (*nididhyāsana*). The process is not unlike the one pursued by the scientist in his field of inquiry. But there is this difference: while the object of the scientist's inquiry remains at all stages external to him, the object of the Vedānta is the deeper reality of the inquirer himself—a reality which he realizes to be the ground of all things.

Metaphysical Basis of the Value Scheme

The metaphysical basis for the Indian theory of values is to be found in the Upaniṣadic conception of *Brahman.* The term "*Brahman*" probably meant at first "prayer" or "speech," from the root "*bṛh,*" "to burst forth" or "to grow." In the Upaniṣads, it comes to mean the ground of the universe or the source of all existence, that which has burst forth into the universe, or that from which the universe has grown. From an analysis of the cosmos, the ancient thinkers seem to have arrived at the truth that there is a common ground of all things, which is of the nature of spirit or self. By a parallel process of inquiry into the reality of the subject, they discovered that what lay as the substrate of the soul (*Ātman*) is the same *Brahman* which is the ground of the universe. Thus, the grand doctrine of identity or non-difference was formulated: *Brahman* = *Ātman.*

What is the nature of this reality? From the standpoint of the Absolute (*paramārtha*), if standpoint it may be called, there is no plurality, not even the least distinction. But from our standpoint, the standpoint of empirical usage (*vyavahāra*), the supreme reality is the ground of the pluralistic universe. Reality-in-itself is the *Nirguṇa Brahman* (the Absolute without attributes). Reality-in-relation-to-the-world is the *Saguṇa Brahman* (God with infinite attributes).[34] While the latter may be designated and described, the former admits of no such designation and description. The *Nirguṇa Brahman* is that from which mind and speech return, being unable to comprehend or express it.[35] The best that one can do is to indicate what it is *via negativa* by saying what it is not (*neti, neti*—not this, not this). Even such a statement requires careful understanding. In truth, there is nothing other than *Brahman*. But *somehow* there seems to be an other, *as it were*, the world of plurality. To questions like "How did the pluralistic universe arise out of the non-dual *Brahman*?" one can only say, "It is *māyā*." *Māyā* may be interpreted from three different levels. From the level of worldliness, *māyā* is real. From the standpoint of the inquiring mind, *māyā* is a puzzle. The world of *māyā* is neither real, nor unreal, nor both. It is not real, because it comes to be sublated at the dawn of self-knowledge. It is not unreal, because it appears to us so long as we are in it. It is not both real and unreal, because contradictory predications cannot be made of one and the same thing. So, from the standpoint of inquiry, *māyā* is indeterminable. There is a higher standpoint, viz., that of self-realization or wisdom, at which there is no problem to be solved. And, here, *māyā* is a name for that which is not.

When the plenary experience is realized, there is no speech and no discourse. All philosophizing is necessarily from the middle standpoint, that of the inquiring mind. The highest conception of reality that one may obtain from this vantage point is that *Brahman* is attributeless; for, even to say that *Brahman* is without attributes is to indulge in a conception. This negative conception, however, is not that of a blank or a void. While *Brahman* is indeterminable, it is not indeterminate. While it is devoid of characteristics, it is not characterless. It is as a corrective to a barely negative interpretation of the negative texts that *Brahman* is indicated by such terms as "being" (*sat*), "consciousness" (*cit*), and "bliss" (*ānanda*). These expressions, however, should not be understood as importing either the distinction of substance and attribute or a plurality of attributes into *Brahman*. It is not that *Brahman* is existent, conscious, and blissful, but that *Brahman is* existence-consciousness-bliss.[36]

This is expressed in axiological terms in the *Bṛhadāraṇyaka-upaniṣad* in the famous text:

> *From the unreal lead me to the Real;*
> *From darkness lead me to Light;*
> *From death lead me to Immortality!*[37]

Unreality, darkness, and death constitute the world of *māyā*, which, when viewed by itself, is disvalue. Reality, the light of intelligence, and the bliss immortal, are value expressions indicative of the nature of *Brahman*. Thus, *Brahman* is the supreme reality and value; it is the final end (*paramārtha*), the fulfillment of all aspiration, the goal of all endeavor.

World Philosophy (Viśva-Darśana)

It is interesting to note that Orientals, in the main, play the role of analytical exponents of their respective views, while Occidentals generally attempt syntheses of the philosophies of East and West. And yet, strangely enough, the Oriental approach to problems of life and reality is said to be synthetic, and the Occidental approach analytic. The truth is that analysis and synthesis are aspects of the same process, though the emphasis may shift from the one to the other at different times and under different conditions. The problem of synthesis, as it has emerged from our discussions, seems to relate, not only to the philosophical views of East and West, but also to the differing doctrines of each hemisphere and each country.

Now, in what sense can we achieve "a world philosophy through a synthesis of the ideas and ideals of the East and the West?" The Sanskrit expression for cosmic philosophy is *viśva-darśana.* In the eleventh chapter of the *Bhagavad-gītā* there is a beautiful allegory which may be pressed into service for our present purpose. Kṛṣṇa confers a blessing on Arjuna by offering to reveal to him his cosmic form (*viśva-rūpa*). But, before revealing it, he says to his disciple: "With these eyes of yours you cannot see me; I shall bestow upon you the eye divine, with which you shall behold my lordly power." The cosmic philosophy, or more strictly the all-view or total perspective, would require for its comprehension the eye divine. So long as there is plurality, the synoptic vision is only a remote possibility. But we can approximate it through our different perspectives, which we are wont to call systems of philosophy. A world understanding through appreciation of one another's point of view is not only possible but also what the world urgently needs today. In order to promote such understanding, the following, it seems to me, would be necessary:

(1) Each philosophical view or perspective should be, as far as possible, self-consistent.
(2) It should contain within itself seeds of self-correction.
(3) It should not be so narrow as to prevent it from realizing that there may be truth in other views also.

(4) It should be such that it is integrated with life as a whole. Philosophy, instead of being a fraction of life, should aim to become the whole of life.

(5) It should not stop with edifying the mind; it should also exalt life—exalt it in such a way that we are drawn closer to the highest value.

If our different perspectives strive to satisfy these conditions, then we shall be able to appreciate the truth of what an early teacher of the Advaita, Gauḍapāda, said regarding those who considered themselves to be his philosophical adversaries:

We do not dispute with them.
Realize the truth of non-dispute.[38]

Notes

1. *Kaṭha-upaniṣad,* II.ix.
2. *Chāndogya Upaniṣad,* VIII.i.
3. *Culla-vagga,* IX.i.4.
4. II.iv.2. See T. M. P. Mahadevan, *The Upaniṣads* (Selections) (3rd ed.; Madras: G. A. Natesan & Co., 1945), p. 219.
5. I.lxxv.49; see also *Manu-smṛti,* II.94.
6. II.2; see T. M. P. Mahadevan, *op. cit.,* p. 31.
7. *Raghuvaṁśa,* IV.86.
8. VII.11.
9. I.xi.2.
10. *Mahābhārata,* XIII.cxviii.8; see also *Manu-smṛti,* XII.91.
11. II.24.
12. V.ii.3.
13. II.
14. No attempt is made here and in similar contexts to enumerate and classify exhaustively all the schools of Indian philosophy. Only some of them are chosen as examples.
15. S. Radhakrishnan, "Gautama the Buddha," *Proceedings of the British Academy,* Vol. XXXIV (London: Oxford University Press, 1938), pp. 181–182; see also p. 183: "*Nirvāṇa,* the fruit of the noble path, the freedom from passions, the rest that knows no break, the life that even the gods are said to covet, the goal of all striving, is not nothingness."
16. *Bṛhadāraṇyaka-upaniṣad,* IV.iv.5.
17. S. Radhakrishnan, *The Hindu View of Life* (London: George Allen & Unwin Ltd., 1927), p. 75.
18. I.28.

19. Quoted by A. Seth Pringle-Pattison in *The Idea of Immortality* (Oxford: Oxford University Press, 1922), p. 205.
20. *Ṛg-veda,* X.90.
21. *Young India,* Sept. 22, 1927.
22. See *Śvetāśvatara-upaniṣad,* IV.5.
23. *Bhagavad-gītā,* IV.13.
24. *Manu-smṛti,* II.168.
25. *Ibid.*, X.65.
26. *Mahābhārata,* III.clxxx.21 and 25.
27. See VII.ix.10.
28. IV.iv.1–5.
29. *Bhagavad-gītā,* XVIII.41–44.
30. I.cxv.36.
31. *Manu-smṛti,* VI.2.
32. S. Radhakrishnan, *The Hindu View of Life,* p. 90.
33. Pp. 52–55.
34. According to systems less absolutistic than Advaita Vedānta, this is the highest reality.
35. *Taittirīya-upaniṣad,* II.ix.
36. According to philosophers such as Rāmānuja, however, the former mode of expression would be the truth.
37. I.iii.28.
38. *Māṇḍūkya-kārikā,* IV.5.

S. RADHAKRISHNAN

The Indian Approach to the Religious Problem

I. East and West

THERE IS NO REASON to believe that there are fundamental differences between the East and the West. Human beings are everywhere human and hold the same deepest values. The differences which are, no doubt, significant are related to external, temporary social conditions and are alterable with them.

East and West are relative terms. They are geographical expressions and not cultural types. The differences among countries like China, Japan, and India are quite as significant as those among European or American countries. Specific cultural patterns with distinctive beliefs and habits developed in different regions in relative isolation from one another. There were periods when China and India were pre-eminent in cultural affairs, others when Western nations became dominant. For the last four centuries Western nations, aided by scientific development, have dominated the East.

The world has now reached a stage of intercommunication. All societies are fast becoming industrialized, and new sets of values are springing up. We are called upon to participate in the painful birth of a new civilization. If we are to live together in peace we must develop international co-operation and understanding.

It is for the political leaders to determine the practical steps by which the sources of power and communication now available to us can be used for closer co-operation and friendliness among the peoples of the world. No political understanding can be made permanent without understanding at the cultural level. Apart from its intrinsic importance, such understanding contributes to the enrichment of human experience. Facile generalizations which are highly misleading are made by philosophers of history. Hegel in his *Lectures on the Philosophy of History* says that "Persia is the land of light; Greece the land of grace; India the land of dream; Rome the land of Empire."[1]

If we glance at the long history of India covering nearly five millenniums, we are struck by the contrasts of extreme situations, summits and chasms. The country rises, wavers, falls, shrinks into herself, tears herself to shreds and pieces, and again endeavors to regain her greatness. She passes through different moods of pride, resignation, shame, detachment, excitement, and adventure. Yet, all through runs an idea which she is attempting to realize, a kind of equilibrium, a wholeness of human nature, which events and vicissitudes inseparable from all forms of life shake but do not shatter. The country is mobile on the surface but constant in the depths. India is a complex equilibrium with an extremely rich diversity. The country is not defined by any dominant race or religious doctrine or economic circumstances. She has a remarkable mixture of ethnic elements, but the great tradition which has affected all her people is the work of human hands.

In a conference of East-West philosophers, it will be useful to consider briefly the metaphysical presuppositions which are the formative forces of any civilization. Metaphysics is not an esoteric pursuit. It has an important place in the life of every reflecting person.

Philosophy is a wide term including logic, ethics, aesthetics, social philosophy, and metaphysics. The last is concerned with the ultimate nature of things. The search for metaphysical certainty has been the source of much that is profound and significant in the history of thought. Metaphysics comprises two main fields: ontology, derived from the Greek word for "being"—what is the reality which exists in its own right and is not dependent on anything else?—and epistemology, which is derived from the Greek word for knowledge." What can the human mind know with certainty? How does opinion differ from knowledge? What is real? What can be known? These are the problems with which metaphysics deals.

In Indian philosophical circles, a ferment has been caused by the impact of Western thought on the traditional doctrines. Generally speaking, this has not resulted in any major changes of outlook though the methods of approach have been affected. There are a few who have abandoned the Indian tradition and adopted the ideas of some Western thinkers, but, unfortunately, they have not made any deep impression either on Indian thought or on Western philosophy. The most effective development is in the presentation of India's fundamental thought in the idiom of our age and its development in new directions. One may indicate the Indian approach to the problem of religion by a reference to the first four aphorisms of the *Brahma-sūtra,* which is said to give the main purport of the Upaniṣads, which are a part of the Vedas. The four *sūtras* deal with (1) the need for knowledge of ultimate reality, (2) a rational approach to it, (3) the experience of reality, and (4) the reconciliation of seemingly conflicting formulations of the nature of ultimate reality.

II. Desire for Knowledge of Reality

The theme of the first *sūtra* is *brahma-jijñāsā.* It indicates man's desire to know the real. There is dissatisfaction with the world. History—astronomical, geological, pre-human, and human—appears to be an aimless process of creations and perishings from which no meaning for the individual human existence can be derived. We discern no principle in the whole chain of being which demands man's meaningful participation in the adventure of time. The world seems to be meaningless, vain, and futile. It is *anitya,* transitory, and *asukha,* painful. Animals are subject to disease and decay but are not capable of distress. The Buddha bases his way of life on the fact of suffering. St. Augustine speaks of "the ceaseless unrest which marks the temporal life of the individual." The consciousness of death is the cause of anxiety. Confucius says (*Shih chi* [Historical Records] 47):

> *The great mountain must crumble.*
> *The strong beam must break,*
> *And the wise man wither away like a plant.*

If man loses himself in the world and its diversions, his anxiety may be a brief fleeting fear. But man is a thinking being. When he reflects on the finite and limited character of his existence, he is overcome by fear, which is, as Heidegger says, "more primordial than man himself." When the fear becomes conscious of itself, it becomes anguish. The tragedy of the soul is added to the contemplation of the world as mortal.

The consciousness of the finiteness and mortality of all our achievements makes us ask whether there is anything beyond and behind the world process. If there were not a Beyond, we should have been satisfied with the world process. The suffering individual cries out in the words of the Upaniṣad—

Lead me from the unreal to the real,
Lead me from darkness to light,
Lead me from death to eternal life.

It is the presence of the infinite that makes us dissatisfied with the finite. We are reminded of the word of God that Pascal believed he had heard: "You would not seek me if you had not already found me." Compare the confession in Romans, "We do not know how to pray as we ought but the Spirit himself intercedes for us with sighs too deaf for words."[2] The suffering is the result of the conflict in us. Man belongs to two worlds, the spiritual and the natural. He is Being and non-being (*sad-asad-ātmaka*).

Existence is essentially a process in time. It is perched on a razor's edge, as it were, which divides being from non-being. Human being is involved in non-being. We were not; we will not be. What is the nature of being? What is the mystery of non-being which surrounds and conditions existence as we know it? Being needs non-being for its manifestation. St. Augustine, in the first chapter of his *Confessions,* asks what his longing for God means. Does it mean that he has found God or has not found God? If he had not found God, he would not know of God, since it is God who gives him the yearning for God. If he had found God and knew him fully, he would be incapable of yearning, since he would be fulfilled and so would not have to struggle and suffer.

Karl Barth in *The Epistle to the Romans* has a notable passage relating to the inner, invisible conflict: "Men suffer, because, bearing within them . . . an invisible world, they find this unobservable, inner world met by the tangible, foreign, other, outer world, desperately visible, dislocated, its fragments jostling one another, yet mightily powerful, and strangely menacing and hostile."[3] Life is a perpetual drama between the visible and the invisible.

III. Reasoned Faith

The problem of meaninglessness cannot be solved by religious faith alone. Faith has to be sustained by metaphysical knowledge. We have to think out the metaphysical presuppositions and attain personal experience of the religious a priori from which all living faith starts. We need intellectual effort and spiritual apprehension, metaphysics and religion. Only reasoned faith can give coherence to life and thought.

The idea suggested by the scriptures requires to be clarified by the use of reason. The worlds of reason and religion do not turn in different orbits. Indian thought is firm in its conviction that religious propositions should be grounded in reason.

The second *sūtra* makes out that God is the world ground, the source from which the world proceeds, by which it is maintained and ended (*janmādy asya yataḥ*). How does it happen that there is something rather than nothing? Being is already there without reason or justification. It is not exhausted by any or all of its appearances, though it is there in each one of its appearances. The world with its order, design, and evidence of purpose cannot be traced to non-intelligent matter. Materialism is the theory which regards all the facts of the universe as explicable in terms of matter and motion. It explains all psychical processes by physical and chemical changes in the nervous system.

Though there are a few Christian theologians, e.g., Karl Barth, who protest against the intrusion of reason into the realm of religious faith, the main tendency in Catholic and many Protestant forms of Christianity is, however, to use reason for the defense of faith. In his Epilogue to *My Life and Thought,* Dr. Schweitzer writes: "Christianity cannot take the place of thinking, but it has to be founded on it. . . . I know that I myself owe it to thinking that I was able to retain my faith in religion and Christianity."[4]

The *Brahma-sūtra* (I.1.2) takes its stand on the *Taittirīya-upaniṣad,* which distinguishes matter, life, mind, intelligence, and spirit in the world process. In the world, to use Leibniz' words, "There is nothing fallow, nothing sterile, nothing dead." There are no sharp cleavages. The gradation from one order of being to another is so imperceptible that it is impossible to draw the line that shall distinctly mark the boundaries of each. Everything in Nature is linked together. All beings are connected by a chain of which we perceive some parts as continuous and others escape our attention.

We cannot account for this cosmic process if we do not assume the Divine Reality which sustains and inspires the process. Even as we admit a mystery behind the cosmic process, we recognize a mystery behind the flux of mental states.

Existentialism is not a phenomenon of modern times. It is one of the basic types of thought which appear in the history of philosophy whenever we stress the difference between the individual being of man and the being of objects in Nature. There is a difference between the being of self and the being of things. Man not only *is* but he *knows* that he is. His being is open to himself. Knowledge is confined to the world of objects, but the self is comprehended from within. There is objective knowledge as well as subjective comprehension.

Metaphysical thinking, which bases itself on experience, holds that Nature is grasped with the concept of necessity and the nature of the self by that of freedom. Without this concept, our understanding of man's nature will be deficient and distorted. While both man and Nature are the creation of God, the being of man is made in the image of God[5] and is therefore quite distinct from the being of Nature. Man is not a *res cogitans,* which, though distinct from *res extensa,* is still a *res,* an objective concept and not the personal "I." We cannot understand man scientifically, as if he were only an unusually complicated object of Nature. An objective account depersonalizes man and reduces him to a heterogeneous mass of fragments, which are studied by the different sciences. There is the biological man, the social man, the political man, and also the individual man, who feels pain and joy, bears responsibility, does good or evil, and is conscious of his alienation from himself when he ceases to be subject and becomes an object.[6]

IV. Religion as Experience

A philosopher's loyalty to reason does not commit him to the proposition that the nature of ultimate reality can be apprehended only as an object of reason. Many philosophers in both the East and the West have reached the conclusion that reality is supra-rational, that it is not in its ultimate nature accessible to conceptual understanding, that religious insights are also genuine revelations of ultimate reality.

The third *sūtra, śāstra-yonityāt,* may mean that the Supreme is the source of scriptures, or that we obtain the knowledge of reality from scripture. All philosophy starts from experience and returns to experience. Religion is not the mere affirmation of propositions. It is not simply an exercise of intelligence. It is the response of the whole man. It claims total allegiance though it may not always command it. The real is not an idea or a hypothesis. It should become an experienced fact. A non-discursive immediate cognition of the real (*aprokṣānubhūti lokottarajñāna*) is possible. This is not a mere glimpse into reality but a steady communion with it. As Boehme says, it is "the country which is no mere vision but a home." In spiritual experience we pass from time to eternity. This does not mean an extinction of the limited ego; it is liberation into the cosmic and transcendent consciousness.

The Śāstras, or scriptures, are the records of the experiences of the seers who have grappled with the problem of reality. Their claim to acceptance does not rest on the logical validity of a set of propositions about God or the historical validity of the reports about the activities of God. Such statements may be shaken by scientific or historical discoveries. The experience may be gained by anyone who is willing to undergo a certain discipline and put forth effort.

Those who have the experience are the pioneers in the world of spirit. They walk by sight, not by faith. Authentic religion is based on the consciousness of being in direct relationship with the Supreme. This experience transcends all forms, all images, and all concepts. The union is effected in the central self, which is the root of intellect and will alike. All religious utterances are vain attempts to deal justly with the meaning of the experience which has been attained.

The Buddha is called the Lord of mysteries (*guhya-pati*). He stresses enlightenment (*bodhi*). In all its forms Buddhism insists on intuitive insight. The Zen discipline asks us to cut through the complexities of conceptual thought to reach a radical transformation of being and consciousness.

V. Samanvaya *or Reconciliation*

The fourth *sūtra* (*tat tu samanvayāt*) deals with the reconciliation of the different reports of the seers about the nature of reality as recorded in the scriptures. Science leads to a reverent acceptance of mystery. Religion tells us that we can have a personal experience of the ultimate mystery. Philosophy of religion is based primarily on the data gained by religious men rather than on the rational concepts of abstract philosophers. We try to create out of the experience something that will save the memory of it. St. Augustine says, "We believe we know the inner mysteries, but we are still in the outer court." Whitehead tells us, "Words do not convey it except feebly; we are aware of having been in communication with infinitude and we know that no finite form we can give can convey it." Our descriptions are all partial truths and not whole truths. What is implicit in the scriptural statements is exhibited in a connected system of thought.

There are two forms of the supreme reality, *nirguṇa* and *saguṇa*, qualityless and qualitied. When, in *sūtra* I.i.2, we lead up to the Supreme from the observed data, the Supreme is conceived to be the Cosmic Lord, creator, governor, and guide of the universe. When we experience the Supreme, it is understood to be transcendent to the world, lifted above all its categories, is described only in negative terms. A great deal of zeal, passion, and ingenuity has been spent on the attempt to resolve the problems to which silence or adoration would seem to be the most adequate response. The nature of the Absolute is manifested by the comment of silence.[7] The Supreme is conceived in a twofold way, according to Śaṁkara.[8]

In the *Mahā-upaniṣad, Brahman* is described as void, as trivial, as unmanifested, unseen, inconceivable, and qualityless.[9] The Buddha says: "Verily, there is a realm where there is neither the solid nor the fluid, neither heat nor motion, neither this world nor any other world, neither sun nor moon. This I call neither arising nor passing away, neither standing still nor being born nor dying. This is the end of all."[10] St. Augustine, steeped in Neo-Platonism, defined the Absolute in negative terms. "God is not even to be called ineffable, for to say this is to make an assertion about him." The real is an unconditioned transcendent and cannot be grasped by a language without symbols.[11]

Organized religions strive to inspire the common man with a faith in the existence of God as revealed in or by the founder of a religious system. They also prescribe a discipline by which one can reach the Supreme. The Indian thinker wishes us to remember that God is above all religious systems. He is without end or limit, though theologians attempt to set limits to him.

The way in which we describe the Supreme is determined by the presupposition of our age, our tradition, and our personal upbringing. Time consecrates, and what is gray with age becomes sacred to us. In this way the gods and goddesses of the people of India were identified with the Supreme. The insistence throughout has been on the inward vision and transformation.

The significant limitation of the competence of reason to understand reality is not inconsistent with a rational investigation of the nature of experience. When F. H. Bradley said in a jesting mood that "metaphysics is the finding of bad reasons for what we believe by instinct," he suggested that our deepest convictions required to be vindicated by reason. It is the only way by which we can have a sure foundation for our beliefs. The revelations, though self-certifying to the experiencer, may be only subjective wish-fulfillments, objects projected by the individual. As for the deities to whom offerings are made, some Mīmāṁsakas contend that they are of the nature of words only and are cognized through words or are mental projections.[12] Mutually contradictory experiences are accompanied by strong subjective convictions. Hobbes is right in his observation that for a man to say that God "hath spoken to him in a dream is no more than to say that he dreamed that God spake to him."[13] The authenticity of an experience has to be judged by rational considerations.

Many people all over the world have clung with passionate intensity to beliefs in fiendish demons which never existed save in their imagination. It is by the employment of reason that we can repudiate such beliefs. Professor H. de Wolf writes about "the worship of such fiendish deities," "There has been no lack of existential faith in them. In obedience to their supposed commands thousands have fasted, burned themselves, cast themselves from precipices, endured shame, fought fanatically, and offered their own children as bloody sacrifices. Will we condemn the use of reason by which great multitudes have learned that such gods did not exist, and hence have been freed from their tyranny?"[14] Though reason may not be adequate as an organ for the apprehension of the Divine, it is useful as a critic of claims to such apprehension.

By the use of reason, Indian religious thought strives to rid religion of obscurantism and lifts faith above superstition. If we practice diabolisms and condemn others, it is like Satan rebuking sin. The mythologic beliefs and dogmas form the content of a closed, static religion. The intuitive vision of reality, which transcends the objective and formal elements, gives life and meaning to them.

In an ancient Upaniṣad, it is said that we should attain an insight into reality by hearing (*śravaṇa*), reflection (*manana*), and meditation (*nididhyāsana*). The first gives us scriptural teaching, the second a rational approach, and the third the way to assimilate the truth heard and reflected on into our being. These three are considered in the first three *sūtras* of the *Brahma-sūtra*. The reconciliation of authority, logic, and life is suggested in the fourth *sūtra*.

Notes

1. G. Hegel, *Lectures on the Philosophy of History,* translated from the 3rd German ed. by J. Sibree (London: H. G. Bohn, 1861).
2. Romans 8:26.
3. Edwyn C. Hoskyns, trans. (6th ed.; London: Oxford University Press, 1933), p. 306.
4. Albert Schweitzer, *Out of My Life and Thought,* an autobiography translated by C. T. Campion. Postscript by Everett Skillings (New York: Henry Holt & Co., 1949).
5. Genesis 1:26.
6. But I have that within which passeth show;
   These but the trappings and the suits of woe (Hamlet Act I, scene 2).
7. *mauna-vyākhyā-prakaṭita-para-brahma-tattvam.* (*Dakṣiṇāmūrtistotra*).
8. *dvi-rūpam hi brahmāvagamyate: nāma-rūpa-vikāra-bhedopādhiviśiṣṭam, tad viparītaṁ sarvopādhivarjitam.*
9. *eṣa hy eva śūnya eṣa hy eva tuccha eṣa hy evāvyakto 'dṛṣyo 'cintyo nirguṇaś ca.*
10. *Udāna,* 80. In F. L. Woodward, trans., *The Minor Anthologies of the Pali Canon,* Part II (London: Oxford University Press, 1935).
11. Professor Paul Tillich in his article on "The Religious Symbol" in *Daedalus,* LXXXVII (Summer, 1958), 14–15, observes: "The divine beings and the Supreme Being, God, are representations of that which is ultimately referred to in the religious act. They are representations, for the unconditioned transcendent surpasses every possible conception of a being, including even the conception of a Supreme Being. In so far as any such being is assumed as existent, it is again annihilated in the religious act. In this annihilation, in this atheism immanent in the religious act, the profoundest aspect of the religious act is manifest." Shelley said in "Queen Mab" that "There is no God" but added a note: "This negation must be understood solely to affect a creative deity. The hypothesis of a prevading Spirit co-eternal with the universe remains unshaken." *The Poetical Works of Percy Bysshe Shelley,* Vol. I, Ernest Rhys, ed., *Lyrics & Shorter Poems* (1st ed.; London: J. M. Dent & Sons, Ltd.; New York: E. P. Dutton & Co., 1907; reprint, 1930), pp. 96, 126 (Everyman ed., Vol. I).
12. *śabdātmakā eva devatā śabdabodhyā vā manaḥ-kalpita-rūpā vā devatāḥ svīkāryāḥ. Mīmāṁsā-sūtra,* II.i.22.
13. *Leviathan,* Everyman ed. (New York: E. P. Dutton & Co., 1950), p. 200.
14. *The Religious Revolt Against Reason* (New York: Harper & Brothers, 1949), p. 115.

P. T. RAJU

Religion and Spiritual Values in Indian Thought[1]

I. Introduction

THIS ESSAY is devoted to a discussion of the question whether Indian religion permits and contributes to the full development and realization of what are called spiritual values. But what are spiritual values? For any religion that is not denominational and that considers itself to be a way of life and every man a wayfarer (*mārga-yāmin*) all values of life—ethical (including the social and political), intellectual, and aesthetic—are spiritual, provided they are recognized and realized as oriented toward the innermost spirit. Then the distinction between spiritual and secular values is one of significance knowingly accepted and striven for. If religious life is the same as spiritual life—as Indian religion understands it—then, on the one hand, all values that are apparently secular must contain reference or directedness to the spirit, and, on the other hand, the spirit must support and encourage their pursuit and realization. The present paper discusses how and how far Indian religion and its thought satisfy both of these requirements.

II. Nature of Indian Religion

Indian religion does not mean a fixed set of dogmas, doctrines, creeds, and rituals. There are several Indian religions, the old Aryan *Dharma*, Brāhmaṇism, the religions of the Vedānta, Jainism, Buddhism, Śaivism, Vaiṣṇavism, Śaktism, Sikhism, and the modern Brāhmo Samāj (Brāhma Samāja) and Ārya Samāj (Ārya Samāja). They have both common and differing features. Many of their doctrines and rituals are different. All except Buddhism and Jainism owe allegiance to the Vedas in some form or another. Even Jainism and Buddhism originated in the atmosphere of Vedic thought.

Second, the word "religion" is an English word. Etymologically it means that which binds a man back or holds him onto the source from which he derived his being. This meaning can apply to every philosophy and practice, even undiluted materialism, in which man has to go back to his material origins. Somewhat corresponding to this word is the Sanskrit word "*yoga*,"[2] meaning that which unites and therefore that which unites man to the divine spirit. But the English word is usually translated by the Sanskrit word "*dharma*" (*dhamma* in Pali), which etymologically means that which supports. In this sense, the word is philosophically understood as law—natural, ethical, and legal. Natural law sustains Nature; the other laws sustain man and society. At the human level, the word carries the meaning of duty. But religion, which contains creeds and ritual, obedience to which is required of all its followers, is also called *dharma*.

Third, Indian religions have retained some of the most primitive forms of worship, giving them a symbolic value, and yet have developed the highest forms of religious thought and spiritual philosophy, culminating in the non-dualism (*advaita*)—often called monism—of Śaṁkara. Śaṁkara's monism is not only a philosophy but also a religion.

Fourth, according to the Indian tradition, it is not necessary for a philosophy to accept the reality of God in order to be called spiritual. Even if Śaṁkara's *Brahman*, the Mādhyamika's *Śūnya* (Void), and the Vijñānavādin's *Ālaya-vijñāna* (unperishing consciousness) are said to correspond to God in some way, the main Sāṁkhya, the early Mīmāṁsā, Jainism, and the other schools of Buddhism argued against the reality of God—yet they are great religious philosophies. Not even belief in the *ātman* (self) is an essential requirement: most of the Buddhists reject the reality of the *ātman* also. Yet, taking all these philosophies together, if we ask: What is their common characteristic that entitles them to being called religious?—the answer is: The conviction about the inwardness of man's conscious being. The inward, as I pointed out elsewhere,[3] is not the same as the inner. For all these philosophies, there is something deeply inward to man, and it is called *Ātman* (Self), *Śūnya* (Void), the *Brahman* (Absolute), Īśvara (God), etc. Man's conscious being has two directions, the inward and the outward. Each direction has a limit. The inward limit is called by the above names; the outward is called matter, whatever be the definition given to it by scientists. Indian philosophers could go only so far as to say that it consists of five elements: earth, water, fire, air, and ether. But the understanding of man with two directions of conscious being is not alien and unacceptable to Western religion and philosophy.

Fifth, none of the Indian religions is a revealed religion. A revealed religion is one for which the divine truth is revealed to a single founder; others must know it only through him. The Indian religions are reflective. The Buddha and Mahāvīra are the founders of Buddhism and Jainism, respectively; but they do not claim that the truth was revealed to them alone; everyone who cares to go through the necessary discipline and reflects on his experiences can reach the truth. This reflective nature of Indian religions prevents the conflict between science and religion. There has been no development of dogmatics and theology in India.

Sixth, none of the Indian religions is a tribal religion. Yahveh is said to have been originally a local divinity,[4] worshipped by a tribe; he later became the God of Israel, and still later the universal God. It is characteristic of tribal religion to insist upon a particular social and ethical code, which was originally the code of the tribe. A reflective religion does not insist upon a single code, but allows every group to follow its own code. Buddhist reflectiveness emancipated its spirituality from all social codes, and it could therefore suit itself to the social forms of India, Tibet, Mongolia, China, Japan, and the countries of Southeast Asia. Even tribal religion becomes reflective after a time. But, so far as the Vedic religious ideas are concerned, they developed out of Nature and Nature-gods, Nature including both man and the material world. It is said that Indra (who later became the god of clouds and the thunderbolt) was originally a tribal god. But he was turned into a Nature-god. Nature-religions, when they develop, do not involve a social code to impose upon their converts. Max Müller calls Indian religion psychological religion; Hocking calls it reflective religion. If Nature means everything that exists, then we may call Indian religion natural religion, as Nature includes spirit, mind, and matter.

Seventh, it is said that some religions are universal, and others are particularist. Christianity and Islam are called universal, because they accept converts; Judaism and Hinduism are called particularist, because they do not accept converts.[5] But there is another principle of distinction which is important. If inward spirituality is the essential meaning of religion, then every religion in which every man can realize God through his own inwardness should be called universal, and every religion which holds that such realization is possible only through faith in its own founder should be called particularist.[6] Conversion means conferring communal membership; it does not mean the conferring of, or initiation into, inwardness. Truth, whether scientific or religious, is open to all; it is not the monopoly of an individual or group. In this sense, Hinduism is a universal religion.

III. The Growth of Indian Religion and Its Thought

It has already been said that all the Hindu religions grew out of Vedic thought. The Vedas themselves contain four parts, of which the second part, the Brāhmaṇas, and the fourth part, the Upaniṣads, are considered to be primary by the Mīmāṁsakas and the Vedāntins, respectively. The former uphold the religion of Brāhmaṇism, which is the religion of sacrifices; and the latter uphold the Vedāntic religion, which is the religion of self-realization. Sacrifice is activity, but self-realization is meditation on one's self. Activity must conform to the injunctions of the Brāhmaṇas (ritual texts); and the idea of this conforming developed into that of duty. Thus, not only the ritualistic activities of sacrifice but also other activities, such as the social, became duties. And duty was defined as action according to Vedic injunctions. On this idea of duty was raised the superstructure of the Mīmāṁsā religion and philosophy, which was first propounded by Jaimini. It is a system of rigorous ethical activism, accepting a pluralistic world—a world of a plurality of atoms and a plurality of selves as agents of action. Sacrifices are addressed to different gods, who were at first regarded as capable of bestowing rewards and punishments but later as mental creations, when ethical action was raised to the level of the Supreme and was considered to be capable of bringing the fruit without outside help. The original meaning of *karma* is action, not fate; and the Mīmāṁsā is a philosophy of *karma.*

The growth of the Vedāntic religion may also be briefly indicated. Western scholars usually interpret Vedic religion as the growth from polytheism (animatism and animism), through henotheism and monotheism, to monism (religion of the impersonal *Brahman*). But this description belongs to an outward point of view. The truth of this growth lies in the transformation of outward polytheism into inward monism. The early Aryans in India realized that the physical elements and psychical activities are correlated.[7] Earth is the correlate of smell, water of taste, fire of sight, air of touch, and ether of sound. The presiding deities of the elements (which polytheism accepted) became the presiding deities of the senses also. Then it was thought that the same deity must have polarized itself into the sense and the corresponding element. Next, the Supreme Deity controlling the activities of these gods was considered to be the Supreme *Ātman* controlling the senses. Similarly, the organs of action such as the hands and feet and the internal organs such as the mind and speech were each assigned a deity, and the organs themselves were considered to be transformations of the deities. In religious language, man was considered to be the vehicle of the subjective poles of the deities, and man's field of action the field of action of the deities for their enjoyment. His action and enjoyment were in essence the action and enjoyment of the deities.[8]

The Vedas thus gave rise to two kinds of religion and philosophy, the Mīmāṁsā giving all importance to active life and upholding a pluralistic philosophy and the Vedānta giving all importance to meditative life and upholding, on the whole, a monistic philosophy. There has been no proper reconciliation of the two,[9] though as Vedic philosophies they are equally important and orthodox. It is also important to remember that the early Mīmāṁsā denied the reality of God, but not of the *ātman*. Some of the essential and relevant features of these two major Hindu religions and philosophies may be noted.

Mīmāṁsā religion and philosophy: This is also called Brāhmaṇism, since it is based on the Brāhmaṇa texts of the Veda. For it, only those sentences of the Veda which enjoin action are primary; the rest are secondary. For instance, the sentence "The *ātman* has to be realized" is not of primary validity, as it does not lead to any action. *Dharma* (right action) is more important than *mokṣa* (salvation, liberation). The Vedas are eternal, and the world is without beginning and end. So, God as creator is not necessary. Actions performed by man control the universe and its processes. There is a universal, single, unitary activity (*karma*), of which the different kinds of action are forms.[10]

How does *dharma* (right action) work? How does it produce its results? *Dharma,* or duty, is action.[11] Action may or may not produce its results immediately. Then how is it connected with the results? How are the results related to the agent? According to the

Mīmāṁsā, ethical and religious action, when it is completed, does not die out but assumes a subtle latent form called *apūrva*[12] (extraordinary) and resides in the *ātman* of the agent. From there it works with or without his knowledge. Thus, action becomes an unconscious force or will, producing results for the agent when proper conditions appear, and controlling his destinies and those of the universe. External action, then, is not only the result of will, but also produces it and modifies it. Thus, man becomes the master of his destiny through his own action, and consciously or unconsciously chooses what he will be through ethical action. If, as J. H. Muirhead says, will is self which is directed toward action,[13] then the Mīmāṁsā conception of the *ātman* is essentially that of the will. Action is meant and is necessary for producing the right kind of will, and will can produce results. Then what are called merit and demerit are not adjectival attributes of the *ātman* but its dynamic potencies.

The Mīmāṁsā understanding of action has two important aspects. On the one hand, action produces a chain of effects in the objective world; and, on the other hand, it adds new potencies to the will of the agent and transforms it. The latter aspect points to the spiritual significance of ethical action. Furthermore, the Mīmāṁsā view implies the truth of the correlation through action between our outward existence and our inward. Without this correlation, our inward life may become imaginary, fanciful, and isolated, not necessarily connected with, or based upon, the realities of the world. The modern man may not accept the Mīmāṁsā doctrine of sacrifices, but the underlying doctrine of action seems to be important for ethical and religious philosophies of action and has much in common with pragmatism.[14]

As mentioned earlier, by postulating a unitary eternal *karma* (action) in place of God, the Mīmāṁsā not only dispenses with God as the bestower of the rewards of ethical action, but also rejects the reality of minor gods, saying that they are only mental creations. Action, by becoming a kind of unconscious will with latent potencies, spontaneously produces the required forms in the external world in which the agent of action enjoys its fruit. The question as to how a non-intelligent principle such as action can have the discriminative power of apportioning fruit according to the type of action done by the agent is not answered by the Mīmāṁsakas satisfactorily. Some of the later Mīmāṁsakas and those

Vedāntins who hold that action is necessary for salvation postulate a supremely intelligent God for the purpose. But the Nairuktas, whose philosophy is regarded as subsidiary to the Mīmāṁsā, maintain that action is the essential nature of the *ātman,* which is conscious, and that, therefore, action, as the *ātman,* can produce the results intelligently. But the Mīmāṁsakas do not seem to accept this view of the Nairuktas.

Vedāntic religion and philosophy: Though some scholars believe that the Vedas should be interpreted as presenting one philosophy and one religion, it is difficult to show that the classical Mīmāṁsā is the same as the classical Vedānta. The usual interpretation that the two are meant for two different levels of intellectual maturity is unsatisfactory, because, when any metaphysical system claims to be true, it claims to be the absolute truth. But neither of these two systems admits that it is only relatively true. And, if both are true for particular intellectual levels, then man, the possessor of intellect, must be ultimately real. But then it is the Mīmāṁsā, not the Vedānta, that confers ultimate reality on man. For the Mīmāṁsā, *dharma,* or ethical action, and enjoyment are the highest ideals of man's life. *Mokṣa,* liberation, is meant for the tired soul and is not even commendable, since it is only a neutral state of no pain and no pleasure.[15] Of course, man may choose whatever ideal he likes.

An absolute opposite of the activism of the Mīmāṁsā is the Advaita Vedānta of Śaṁkara, who teaches that salvation (liberation) is the highest aim of life and that it can be achieved through renunciation of action and through the inward realization of one's identity with the Supreme Spirit (the *Brahman*). Right action (*dharma*) and the religion of sacrifices have only an instrumental value, that of purifying the mind.[16] One cannot know the truth through action, but only through reflection.[17]

Śaṁkara's contention that one cannot know the truth through action is contested by many. At least so far as empirical truth goes, action confirms cognition, which is as weak as action in giving certainty. Each confirms the other. The Naiyāyikas, the Buddhist Vijñānavādins, and Rāmānuja hold that empirical truth is known through action; that is, a cognition is true if its object is known to serve the purpose for which it is meant.[18] From the modern point of view, we may say that without action we may be living in our private subjective world of imagination and dream, but in action we live in the world of reality. The truth in Śaṁkara's view is that we cannot know our inward reality through actions pertaining to outward reality.

Śaṁkara does not discuss how right action (*dharma*) purifies the mind. Rāmānuja also holds this view, insisting in addition that one should lead a life of action until death.[19] But what is meant by purification of the mind? If action is successful when it is in accordance with reality and the object cognized is a true object, then purification of the mind must mean bringing it into accord with reality. A "true" object, which is the same for all minds, means that the perceiving subject is similar and therefore universal in all agents. This implication, in its turn, means, particularly in ethics, the ridding of the mind of egoistic impulses and ideas. As long as there is the danger of man's falling into egoistic particularity, he has to perform right actions. Rāmānuja thinks that this danger exists up to death; but Śaṁkara thinks otherwise. Rāmānuja defends the utility of the Mīmāṁsā doctrine of right action as leading to the right knowledge of the *Brahman,* and says that right knowledge leads to the love of the Lord. But Śaṁkara rejects this view as self-contradictory.[20]

Rāmānuja occupies a middle position between the Mīmāṁsā and the Advaita in reconciling right action (*dharma*) with liberation (*mokṣa*). The ideal of life presented by the Mīmāṁsā is made a necessary instrument to the ideal of the Vedānta. But Śaṁkara treats it as a dispensable instrument.

The *Bṛhadāraṇyaka,* the earliest of the Upaniṣads, reinterprets sacrifice as the sacrifice of outward reality by the sacrificer. Renunciation of outwardness is necessary for gaining inwardness. Here, the modern objection will be that inwardness is a fluid, amorphous expanse, the distinctions in which are hard to define. The individual is not a defined part of the inward-outward continuum, but a creative part with an independence and privacy of his own, and he may mistake his imaginative projections for actualities of inwardness. He has to keep his mind in exact tune with actuality, whether inward or outward, in order to know the truth as it is. Inwardness has its own objectivity, that is, independence of the subject's privacy, as outwardness has its own independence of the subject. Just as material objects are common to our outward cognitions, God, or the Divine Spirit, is common to our inward knowledge. When we rightly perceive an external object, our mind is in tune with external objectivity; similarly, our mind has to be in tune with inward objectivity, if it is to see spiritual reality. Mind is pure when it becomes one with reason and transcends its egoistic particularity. This is the reason Pythagoras thought that mathematics leads us near to God. The *Logos* as Reason is the first evolute of God for the Greeks. The Sāṁkhya and the Vedāntic schools maintain the *Mahat*[21] (the Great, Reason, *Mahān Ātmā, buddhi*) is close to the spirit. Reason transcends the ego and lifts man to the level of cosmic universality. But more effective than cognitive reason in lifting man above his egoistic particularity is ethical action, in which man not only knows what is true but also does what is good. Man's selfish interest in the external world is through his ego. Selfless action is ethical action that lifts man to a universal standpoint without at the same time depriving him of his actuality and without turning his existence into an imaginary and false dream. Selfless action is action according to universal *dharma,* the law of the universe controlling human destiny.

The philosophy of action according to the Bhagavad-gītā. It is selfless action that is called "desireless action" by the *Bhagavad-gītā. Niṣkāma-karma* has been variously misunderstood as desireless action, motiveless action, disinterested action, and so forth. There have been classical interpretations of this type, particularly by the Advaitins, who extol desirelessness (*ataraxia*), the killing of all desires, under the influence of the ideas propagated by monastic Buddhism and Jainism. But this negative form of desirelessness is not really advocated by the *Bhagavad-gītā.* Kṛṣṇa exhorts Arjuna not to have anything to do with non-action.[22] The lower *karma* (action), that is, the egoistic *karma,* is far removed from reason (*buddhi*), and so one should take refuge in reason.[23] One who acts according to the dictates of reason, the *Logos,* is not touched by the merits or demerits of his action.[24] Reason is higher than the ego (*ahaṁkāra*), according to both the Sāṁkhya and the Vedānta; and, when actions are performed by man after he has risen to the universality of reason, they become non-egoistic and he is not touched by their merit or demerit. Such actions are called "desireless actions" because they are not motivated by egoistic desires but by desires in tune with the processes and dispensations of the Cosmic Person (Virāṭ), or the *Logos,* the World Reason. Kṛṣṇa does not ask Arjuna to kill all desires; on the contrary, he says that he himself is desire which is not opposed to *dharma,*[25] the universal ethical order or law. Thereby Kṛṣṇa asks Arjuna to attune his desires with the processes of the universal ethical order, which he later revealed to Arjuna by showing his Cosmic Person. In fact, the universe is created out of the desire of the Supreme Spirit,[26] and works according to that desire. That desire is *dharma.* Man is not to kill all desire, but to channel desire according to the laws of the universal spirit by lifting himself to the level of Reason or universality.

Buddhism and Jainism: Before the rise of Buddhism and Jainism, right action was understood in terms of the Mīmāṁsā principle as action according to the injunctions of the Veda. The injunctions are contained in the Brāhmaṇas, which treat performance of sacrifices as a duty. The ethical inward transformation which the performance of action produced was lost sight of; and the popular mind attached all importance to external action and its pomp and paraphernalia. It was thought that the wider the scale of sacrifice, the better would be the result. The Upaniṣadic teaching of inwardness and self-realization was already current, but did not appeal much to the popular mind, which cared little for the bloodshed in the sacrifices. The Buddha and Mahāvīra developed the idea that religion was meant for spiritual realization, which is inward, that external acts of worship and sacrifice were by themselves meaningless as religion, and that true ethics did not lie in literal obedience to the Vedic injunctions but in those forms of discipline and self-control which enabled man to reach his inward depths. In preaching their views, they had to turn against the Upaniṣads also, since they were part of the Vedas, which preached the religion of sacrifices. The Buddha was not really opposed to the spiritual teachings of the Upaniṣads, but only to the sacrificial religion. For instance, it is said in the *Dhammapada* that a true *brāhmaṇa* is one of high ethical and spiritual qualities, but not one who was at that time merely following the Brāhmaṇas. Thus, Buddhism and Jainism were reform movements within the *Ārya Dharma* (the Aryan religion or way), as it was called, though later they came to be regarded as separate religions. It is relevant to note that, like the early Mīmāṁsā, neither Buddhism nor Jainism accepted the reality of God, and both gave all importance to man's own effort and exertion. Furthermore, the brunt of opposition to the Mīmāṁsā seems to have been borne by the Buddha, who enunciated a new philosophy of *dharma* as opposed to that of the Mīmāṁsā.[27] *Dharma,* the Buddha maintains, is not literal obedience to the Vedic commands, but the law of ethical and spiritual discipline, and the bearing of this law is inward, not outward. Again, the Mīmāṁsakas maintain that man cannot understand how the performance of ethical actions produces results through the agent, because they are produced by an unseen potency (*apūrva*, will). But the Buddha said that *dharma*, the law of ethical action, falls within man's experience and can be realized in experience. Thus, the word "*dharma*" was given a new meaning: at first, it meant action and its potency; now it means ethical and spiritual inwardness. The law of this inwardness and discipline is not a command from a book, but a law of the nature of man's inwardness itself.

The Upaniṣads do not speak of the *ātman* as the *dharma* of man. But the Buddha, had he propounded the reality of the *ātman*, would have called it *dharma*. *Dharma* in Buddhism is not only the law and nature of man's inward being, but also the inward being itself. The Mīmāṁsakas and many Vedāntins reject the idea that self-realization is a *dharma* (right action), because it is no action at all. But the Buddhists will accept it, if we substitute *vijñāna* (consciousness) or *śūnya* (void) for the *ātman*. It was perhaps by following Buddhism that the Vaiśeṣikas regarded self-realization as a *dharma* (duty) and *vidhi* (injunction). Later, the word "*dharma*" came to acquire the meanings of ethics, religion, law, and Nature—and many other meanings besides, which are not relevant here.

The chief ways of God-realization. In the Upaniṣads, man was understood, not only horizontally, as one of the objects of the world, but also vertically, as consisting of several layers of reality—matter, life, mind (*manas*), reason (*buddhi*), and spirit (*ātman*),[28] and his goal and destiny were not to be found on the horizontal level but in the vertical. The teachings of the Buddha resulted in placing almost exclusive emphasis on the vertical in India. With Bosanquet, Indian philosophers would agree in saying that the world is the vale of soul-making, but would add that it is also the vale of soul-finding.[29] But a way for discovering the soul has itself to be found. Hence, the idea of the way (*mārga*) and of man as the wayfarer entered India's religious thought. The goal is the inward spiritual essence of man, however it may be called by the different schools. But the Buddha's insistence that it can be realized by analysis of man's conscious existence (existential self-analysis) gave rise to the doctrine of *jñāna-mārga*, the way of knowledge. This seems to have been adopted *mutatis mutandis* by the Vedāntins. But the orthodox schools did not give up the way preached by the Mīmāṁsā, and called it *karma-mārga,* the way of self-realization through action.

Although, for the early Mīmāṁsā, self-realization was not the primary goal of man, after the idea of salvation later entered its thought, its followers held that action, if non-egoistic, would lead to salvation. We have already explained the meaning of non-egoistic action. The ordinary man, who cannot understand this philosophical import of ethical action, is asked to surrender himself and his actions to God and to act without desires of a selfish nature. This is the way of action, the religion of the Mīmāṁsā reinterpreted in the light of theism.

But neither the way of knowledge nor the way of action satisfies man's needs for love, confidence, and faith. Man is not only an intellectual and active being but also an emotional creature. If he is to treat the Supreme Being as the source of his intellect and as the goal of his action, he is to treat it as the object of his love also. Surrender is easier through love than through knowledge and obedience. The Supreme Being is of the nature of intense bliss, and can satisfy emotional needs also. Besides the Brāhmaṇical and the Upaniṣadic religious thought, there were Śaivism, Vaiṣṇavism, and Śāktism, which teach that the Supreme Spirit is like father and mother, always ready to forgive and love. Thus, another way was made open to man, the way of love or devotion (*bhakti-mārga*). Rāmānuja says that *dharma* (right action) leads to *jñāna* (knowledge), and knowledge leads to *bhakti* (love, devotion). Śaṁkara says that love of the Lord leads to knowledge. The main characteristic of all the three ways is the transition from outwardness to inwardness.

The wayfarer and his opportunities. Man's opportunities to obtain salvation are not limited to one life. Birth and death are not the limits of existence. Man can have several lives for obtaining salvation; and, if he does not care for salvation, he can choose an infinite number of lives, one after another, for enjoyment through ethical action. The doctrine of reincarnation is accepted by all schools, except the Cārvāka, which can hardly be called religious. It is difficult, however, to prove or disprove the theory of reincarnation.

Again, all schools, except the Cārvāka, believe that the nature of future birth is determined by past and present ethical action. Patañjali says that it determines one's caste or race (i.e., the family in which his birth takes place), his facilities for enjoyment, and the duration of his life.

The doctrine of *karma* has been wrongly interpreted as fatalism. Indian writers divide *karma* into three kinds. It has been mentioned above that *karma* (action) assumes a potential form immediately after the action is completed. This potency also is called *karma* and is of three kinds: the whole accumulated potency of *karma*, the potency that has started to bear fruit, and the potency that has not yet begun fructifying. The latter two are parts of the first. The second cannot be thwarted, but the third can be prevented by performing a stronger *karma* of the opposite type or by complete renunciation of all *karma* and self-realization. It is difficult to verify these ideas thoroughly. However, the doctrine of *karma* and that of reincarnation have acted as ethical checks on the conduct of man, and the latter doctrine offers endless opportunities and hope for salvation.

The problem of evil: The question whether human nature is essentially evil or good did not attract the attention of the classical Indian thinkers as much as it attracted that of the classical Chinese thinkers. But the question whether the world itself is inherently good or evil occupied the minds of the Indians. Only the Buddhists say that the world is misery, but the others say that it contains misery along with pleasure. Again, whereas the Christian thinkers were obsessed by the doctrine of original sin, the Indians were obsessed by the doctrine of original ignorance. Even Rāmānuja is concerned about ignorance and says that *karma* (both right and wrong action) is ignorance, probably meaning that we have to perform ethically right *karma* only so long as we are ignorant of the essential nature of ourselves and of the Lord. Ignorance is the cause of evil. And evil is real for those schools for which the world is real; and even for the other schools it is real as long as the world is real. One can rise above evil through self-realization. The Mīmāṁsā alone says that one can rise above evil through right action.

IV. Ātman and Its Realization

Ātman-realization is called self-realization, because the word "*ātman*" is generally translated by the word "self." According to the Mīmāṁsā and the Nyāya-Vaiśeṣika, this realization is not very covetable because the pure *ātman* is only existence and has neither consciousness nor bliss, which the *ātman* obtains incidentally when reason comes into contact with it. But the *ātman* is detached from reason in the liberated state. According to the Sāṁkhya and the Yoga, the *ātman* is both existence and consciousness, but not bliss; it obtains bliss only so long as it is connected with reason (*buddhi*). According to the Vedānta, the *ātman* is existence, consciousness, and bliss (*sat, cit,* and *ānanda*). Most of the Buddhist schools reject the reality of the *ātman,* and differ in describing the essential nature of man's conscious being. For all, it is a state of pure non-disturbance (*nirvāṇa*). Some Buddhists, the Vijñānavādins, hold that it is *vijñāna* (consciousness). But that it is bliss also is not asserted. In this section, we shall present mainly the view of the Vedāntins.

Realization of the *ātman* is often understood as mysticism; but mysticism is a blanket term that means many things, irrational, vague, and mysterious. The *Bṛhadāraṇyaka-upaniṣad* says that the *ātman* has to be heard about from a teacher, then reflected upon, and meditated upon by oneself, and then perceived directly.[30] According to Rāmānuja, it is the I-consciousness itself (*ahaṁdhī*); but, according to Śaṁkara, it is the support of I-consciousness and transcends it. Meditation is recommended in order to retain the experience of the pure *ātman* once it is obtained.[31]

The "I" is the knower, and cannot be the object known.[32] The physical body, senses, mind, and reason are objects of consciousness, and therefore cannot be the "I." The I-consciousness transcends everything that can be made its object. Here Rāmānuja says that the I-consciousness itself (*ahaṁdhī*) it the *ātman,* and is different from the ego (*ahaṁkāra*),[33] which is derivative and identifies itself with the physical body, etc., and appropriates to itself all actions, their merits and demerits, and suffers and enjoys. The *ātman* is essentially an onlooker, but, through identification with the ego, becomes involved in the activities of the ego. Śaṁkara often speaks of the "I" as the perceiver, but when giving a technical explanation he treats it as the knowing consciousness without the "I" (*aham*). For him, the I-consciousness (*ahaṁdhī*) and the ego (*ahaṁkāra*) are the same. The *ātman* is pure self-consciousness. The "I" is the result of gradual contraction of unlimited consciousness into a center of experience. The subject-object polarization develops through this contraction. This contraction should not be imagined spatially. It is the development of a projective focus, the development of pure self-consciousness into a knower-consciousness, the projection in the outward direction out of pure existential inward self-contained consciousness. The ego is part of the inner sense (*antaḥ-karaṇa*) and is lower than reason, which also is a part. The word "*ātman*" is translated as "self" in order to distinguish it from the ego. But there is continuity of the consciousness of the latter into the former.

According to Śaṁkara, the *ātman* is the same as the Supreme Spirit. But, according to Rāmānuja, the Supreme Spirit is the *Ātman* within our *ātmans*. Now, the Western thinker may find it difficult to understand Śaṁkara's view that pure consciousness, which is the Supreme Spirit, can be creative, can be a dynamic force. Even in understanding Rāmānuja's view, this difficulty may be felt, for, in the above analysis, the *ātman* is shown as the consciousness which transcends the body, senses, mind, and reason. In Western thought, consciousness, except for the existentialists, is a pale light not integrally related to the existing world and thus deprived of existence. The Advaita Vedāntins also treat conscious processes (*vṛttis*) in this way. But they treat the *ātman* as consciousness that is existent. And existence is not necessarily material existence. How, then, are we to understand that the realization of the *ātman* does not deprive us of existence, and that it is the highest goal of life? According to Śaṁkara, the consciousness that is the *ātman* and is not directed toward the objects of the world is one with the whole reality, subjective and objective. Reality understood inwardly is the Supreme Spirit and understood outwardly it is the physical universe. According to Rāmānuja, the *ātman*, though atomic (*aṇu*) and different from the Supreme Spirit, can be identical with God, matter, and other spirits through its attribute-consciousness (*dharma-bhūta-jñāna*). But this identity is not existential identity, although the existential consciousness of the atomic *ātman* and its attribute-consciousness are both existent (*sat*). Śaṁkara does not hold that the *ātman* has attribute-consciousness in its essential being; this is only its projective power. The existence of both is the same. Like Marcel, he would distinguish between "to be" and "to have." What I am is different from what I have. I have the attribute-consciousness, but I am not the attribute-consciousness, and I project it out of myself as I project mental images out of myself. For Śaṁkara his attribute-consciousness has no existence of its own apart from the existential consciousness of the *ātman*, at the highest stage of realization. But, for Rāmānuja, it has its own existence.

In general, Western philosophy—and even Western psychology

—studies only what the Vedāntins call attribute-consciousness, not existential consciousness. Hence the difficulty for Western philosophers. Now, the peculiarity of the *ātman* (existential consciousness) is that it can identify itself with some of the objects of its own consciousness. Though the physical body is an object of my consciousness, and therefore different from the subject of that consciousness, I say, "I am so many feet tall." I identify myself with my mind and say, "I am happy," and so on. Through this kind of identification with objects which I have before me, my *ātman* alienates itself from its original nature, is diffused through existential *diaspora*, spread out through senses and mind. But its original nature can be realized by reversing this process, by dis-identification, by dis-alienation. And the several kinds of *yoga* are prescribed for this purpose.

V. *Supreme Realization in Buddhism and Jainism*

The general principle underlying the *yoga* of all the Indian religious schools is the same: it is retraversing the process of identification and alienation. According to Buddhism, the psycho-physical individual is an aggregate of five aggregates: matter, feelings, ideas, instincts (*vāsanas, saṁskāras*), and consciousness; or twelve bases (*āyatanas*) of being: the five senses and their objects, and mind and its objects. When man analyzes himself into these elements, he finds there is no remainder. And that state is *śūnya* (void) and *nirvāṇa* (non-disturbance).

Jainism, unlike Buddhism, believes in the reality of the *ātman*, which it calls *jīva*. The spirit is bound by its *karma* (action) and becomes finite. Salvation lies in weeding out *karma*—understood by Jainism as consisting of particles—from the spirit, when it becomes pure and perfect in knowledge. Such a spirit becomes omniscient. All spirits are independent of each other and form a plurality. Salvation is not transformation of outwardness but giving up outwardness altogether. In this belief, Jainism is at one with the Nyāya-Vaiśeṣika and the Sāṁkhya. The difference is that for both the Sāṁkhya and Jainism the spirit in its pure state is consciousness, whereas for the Nyāya-Vaiśeṣika it is not conscious.

VI. *Religion and Ethical Values*[34]

For all Indian systems, except for the early Mīmāṁsā and the Cārvāka, ethical discipline is geared to salvation, and it is difficult to separate completely ethical from spiritual discipline. Yet, their moral teachings, except those of the Cārvāka, are as rigorous as those of any. The Cārvāka is no religion; and its ethics is individualistic, hedonistic, and opportunistic. The Mīmāṁsā ethics is more or less like the Jewish, a set of commands issued by the Veda. Practically every virtue upheld by Western writers is upheld by the Indians also; but the supporting reasons are different. Ethics is not developed with the problems of social organization in view, as it was by the Greeks, or by a study of social relationships, as by the Chinese. The Mīmāṁsā developed ethics for the happiest life of man in terms of the invisible potentiality of action. Only the ethical codes (Dharma-śāstras) have social organization in view in terms of castes and stages of life (*āśramas*). But the codes cannot be called systems of ethics; they are only lists of guiding principles or, rather, laws and rules codified for ready use in social life and courts of justice.

The Mīmāṁsā and the ethical codes. We have already mentioned the Mīmāṁsā concept of *dharma.* It has two main interpretations, given by the two leading Mīmāṁsakas, Kumārila and Prabhākara. According to Kumārila, *dharma* is action enjoined by the Veda; and it enters the *ātman* as a latent force, called *apūrva,* before producing its fruit. According to Prabhākara, *dharma* is the potency produced by action, not the action itself. For both, however, there is, first, action and then the latent force produced in the *ātman.* This force is really a kind of unconscious will. But the Mīmāṁsā is interested mainly in the production of the will that produces otherworldly fruit,[35] and does not discuss the forms of activity in the social context. This task is left to the ethical codes (Dharma-śāstras). And, according to the times and conditions, the authors of these codes observed the customs and practices of the different groups living in the country, codified them, and gave the laws. All the authors accepted the Mīmāṁsā concept of *dharma,* but they extended the concept to this-worldly activity also.

But, by the time the ethical codes were written, the ideas of the Supreme Spirit and of salvation entered the Mīmāṁsā. God was introduced as the intelligent agent who apportions the fruits of actions according to merit and demerit. It is also said that the latent potency which action assumes does not reside in the *ātman* but in the Supreme Spirit, as Rāmānuja maintained. But some of the Mīmāṁsakas still continue to hold that the potency resides in the *ātman.* If one performs his duties according to his caste and stage of life, and surrenders himself and his activities to God, one obtains salvation. The idea of the fourth stage of life (*āśrama*), namely, that of renunciation, was also introduced by the codes. But the question was not raised as to how the life of renunciation and the way of action can be reconciled. In fact, Manu calls his work *Karma-yoga-śāstra* (science of the way of action). But the codes remained codifications of the laws of conduct for the different castes and stages of life.

As the codes accept the Mīmāṁsā concept of *dharma,* they involve the ethics of the will.[36] Law is not meant merely to put a check on man's liberty of action, but to exhort him to produce a will, the potency of the *ātman,* its power to produce and enjoy the fruit. Will is not mere wish or intention, but must result in action. The peculiarity of the Mīmāṁsā conception is that will and action are invariably related. Without action, the will cannot be produced; and, without the will, the fruit cannot be obtained. The violation of a positive law is a violation of *dharma,* like the violation of a Vedic injunction. The Indian writers did not draw a line between the "ought" and the "should." The "ought" is a "should," if one wants a particular result such as heaven. It is a "should" to refrain from evil, if one wants to avoid hell. But man has freedom of choice.

Ethical values in the Bhagavad-gītā: The *Bhagavad-gītā* is a reconciliation of the ideal of the early Mīmāṁsā with that of the Vedānta by expounding the doctrine of selfless action, called *karma-yoga.* It discredits the pure Mīmāṁsā theory of action and the idea of life in heaven, and says that action according to reason, whether the result be pain or pleasure, is the only right way. True reason is always steadfast and unwavering; those who do not attain that level are infirm and wavering.[37] Firmness in being one with reason is the main virtue. In order to obtain it, selfish desires, lust, anger, etc., have to be given up, because in steadiness there is no disturbance or agitation. When one's reason is destroyed, one is destroyed. When one's reason becomes steadfast, one can enter one's pure *ātman* in what is called *samādhi* (concentrated or collected consciousness).

Ethical discipline in the Vedānta. For the Vedānta, the highest ideal of life is salvation. To attain it, Śaṁkara says that one must develop the following four virtues: (1) discrimination between the eternal and the transient; (2) renunciation of all enjoyment here and hereafter; (3) the six qualities of (a) tranquillity, (b) restraint of the senses from their objects, (c) withdrawing the mind from outer objects; (d) endurance of all pains without complaint; (e) faith in what is rationally understood from the teacher and the scriptures; and (f) keeping the mind always directed toward the *Brahman;* and (4) passionate desire for liberation by understanding the true nature of the ego, mind, and the senses and their objects.[38] The performance of other duties is only a means for purifying the mind.

For Śaṁkara, the way of knowledge is the highest. But, for Rāmānuja, the way of love or devotion is the highest. He defines love as the continuity of knowledge without effort.[39] This is possible only in passionate love and desire for communion. Hence, knowledge is only a means to love. Rāmānuja insists that one should lead a life of action until death, after which one obtains salvation; and the life of action should be according to the Mīmāṁsā and the codes. Love or devotion (*bhakti*), defined as continuity of knowledge, is difficult to practice; and therefore self-surrender to God is also preached.[40] In Rāmānuja's philosophy, the doctrines of grace and of God's love for his devotees play an important part. Self-surrender is explained by the followers of Śaṁkara as non-egoistic activity. The ethical discipline of the other orthodox schools is more or less the same as that of the Vedānta. That the early Mīmāṁsā is an exception has already been mentioned.

Ethical discipline in Buddhism and Jainism. The Buddha preached the Noble Eightfold Path as the ethical discipline necessary for spiritual realization. The eightfold way consists of right views, right intention, right speech, right action, right livelihood, right effort, right mindfulness, and right meditation. In the Mahāyāna literature, the ideal man is conceived to be the *bodhi-sattva.* This word may be etymologically rendered as the person whose being is knowledge. It is interesting to note that the *Bhagavad-gītā* calls the ideal man the *sthita-prajñā,* which may be translated as the person whose reason is firmly settled. Literally, the words come to mean the same, because *prajñā* is a synonym of *buddhi* or *bodhi.*[41] The *Bhagavad-gītā* describes its ideal man as one "who is steadfast in his reason, is without selfish desires, unagitated by pains and unattached to pleasures, without fear and anger; he neither hates nor favors any. He controls his senses and does not allow them to run after pleasures. . . ." The Mahāyāna describes its ideal man as one who possesses the six main virtues: charity, morality (character, *śīla*), patience, energy, meditative power, and knowledge. All virtues are precipitated into these six; and, of the six, again, knowledge is regarded as the highest.[42]

The ethical discipline of Jainism is the severest of all schools. Its main point is that salvation can be had only be weeding out all *karma* particles from the soul (*jīva*), at which time it regains its pure state. This can be achieved through faith in Jaina teachings, true knowledge, and character.[43] Of all the Indian schools, Jainism attaches the greatest importance to *ahiṁsā* (non-injury) and vegetarianism. The highest character is that which has developed complete indifference to the objects of the world.[44]

VII. Religion and Intellectual Values

Because of the reflective nature of all Indian religions, there has been no conflict between science and religion in the cultural history of India. True, the Vedāntins and the Buddhists maintain that reason cannot give certainty of the spirit.[45] But that is because the rational methods used for studying objective Nature cannot be applied to the inward reality of man. The methods for studying the latter have to be different. But, though different, whether it is reasoning about the objective world or reflection on one's inner being, the work has to be performed by the same mind. That which does the work is *buddhi,* or reason.[46] It is not a function of mind. From the time of the Upaniṣads, the different levels of man's inward being have been demarcated by Indian thinkers, and the stages are not regarded as functions of mind but as levels of inward being, mind itself being the lowest level. In the classification of these stages, there is no unanimity,[47] but, on the whole, the levels are three: mind (*manas*), ego (*ahaṁkāra*), and reason (*buddhi*). The function of mind is to analyze and synthesize the impressions and carry them to the ego, and also to cognize pains and pleasures and convey them to the ego. The ego appropriates them in saying, "I see, I enjoy." Reason is beyond the ego, deeper and higher. It interrelates the several results from a universal point of view, not from the point of view of the particular ego. But the ego and reason have a continuity of being. The ego rises to the level of reason in the process and loses its particularity. Reason is always objective, universal, and cosmic in its processes and nature. It commits no mistakes when it is pure and does not get involved in egocentricity.[48] When the ego intrudes into the universality of reason, the latter commits mistakes. Indian philosophers would accept the Pythagorean contention[49] that reason in man is nearer the Supreme Spirit than mind or senses, and the Heraclitean view[50] that the *Logos* is common to all.

It is necessary to keep these psychological distinctions in view in order to appreciate how Indian spirituality incorporates intellectual values. If intellectual values are values achieved by the intellect or reason in the form of scientific discoveries in the objective world, Indian philosophy is not opposed to them, though it will add that they are not the highest in life, but only instrumental. Yet, understanding the true nature of the world is necessary in order to know what the highest values are. If "intellectual values" mean that the attitude of man to the world and to himself is to be rational, then Indian philosophy will support them and say that man should raise his ego to the universality of reason. The highest intellectual value, from the standpoint of religion, is reason itself, and the highest intellectual attainment is to become one with reason, which is a higher state of the self than the ego. Man's reason is really part of the Cosmic Reason, and the two are essentially continuous and one. In no other philosophical tradition is the idea of truth more admired than in the Indian. Gandhi said that God is Truth, with a capital T.

But the highest truth for Indian thinkers is not reason or the *Logos,* but something still higher, namely, the *Brahman.* The Greeks generally accept the *Logos* as the highest, although there are indications in Plato's thought that there is something still higher. One synonym for *buddhi* (reason) often used by the Upaniṣads is *vijñāna,* which also means mundane science and arts.[51] *Jñāna* is knowledge for salvation, and *vijñāna* is knowledge about sciences and arts. This distinction corresponds to the distinction made in the Upaniṣads between higher and lower knowledge. What is meant by calling the realization of truth a spiritual value? If one realizes that the object in front of him is a fly, is this attainment of truth a spiritual value? Has it even moral significance in the context of the development of one's personality? What is spiritually valuable in this context is that aspect of man's personality which is characterized by his readiness for and susceptibility to truth or the receptivity to universality and objectivity. It is the purity of reason, its readiness to be above ego-involvements. It is the development of this aspect of personality that is a spiritual value. Thus, reason, as part of the *Logos* present in us, is itself the value. It is a value, not only for intellectual work, but also for ethical uplift, as the *Bhagavad-gītā* teaches.

VIII. Religion and Aesthetic Values

For an understanding of the doctrine of the beautiful in Indian thought, as for understanding the doctrines of the true and the good, the clue lies in the conception of *buddhi* (reason).[52] Aesthesis (*rasa*), or aesthetic pleasure, like truth and goodness, belongs to *buddhi.* The Sāṁkhya attributes to *buddhi* the qualities of determination (certainty, assertion, will), *dharma* (virtue), knowledge, dispassion, and power.[53] But these qualities belong to it when it is pure.[54] When it is impure, the opposite qualities belong to it.[55] Impurity means ego-involvement. Generally, when the word is used it is understood in its pure state. Thus truth and goodness are its attributes. Now, when the Sāṁkhya explains aesthetic pleasure, it again attributes it to *buddhi* (reason). In fact, all orthodox schools attribute it to *buddhi,* however it it conceived. According to the Sāṁkhya and the Yoga, aesthetic pleasure cannot belong to the *ātman,* which is only existential consciousness, but not bliss (*ānanda, rasa*); it belongs to *buddhi* only. According to the Nyāya and the Vaiśeṣika, the *ātman* is only existence but not consciousness or bliss; *buddhi* has no substantial status, but is an adventitious quality which the *ātman* acquires when mind (*manas*) comes into contact with it. However, it is the *buddhi* that contains aesthetic pleasure and conveys it to the *ātman.* But the Advaitins say that the *ātman* is essentially bliss also and is aesthetic (*rasa*); and the aesthetic pleasure experienced in the world is a reflection of the bliss aspect of the *ātman* in pure *buddhi* (reason). This is the view of practically all the Vedāntins. Taking all these views together, we may say that the general tendency of Indian thought is to assign what we generally call aesthetic value to reason itself. The Vedāntic schools have more religious significance than the others.[56] The common point in their arguments comes to this: The experience of aesthetic pleasure belongs to *buddhi,* or reason, freed from ego-involvements, that is, with egoistic motives held back. But when I say, "I experience that pleasure," my ego connects that experience to itself as it connects to itself the experiences of dream and deep sleep. I am able to do this because my ego is continuous and essentially identical with reason (*buddhi*). And there are no ego-involvements in the experience of aesthetic pleasure, because, as Kant says, there is no urge in the ego at that time to appropriate the object and to work on it in a possessive activity, but only to appropriate the pleasure derived from it. Of course, the desire to have that pleasure exists.

Abhinavagupta (tenth century), Bhoja (eleventh century), and Jagannātha (seventeenth century) are the foremost exponents of aesthetics in India, although Bharata was the founder of the theory first associated with dance. All explain aesthetic pleasure in terms of sentiments.[57] Whether the aesthetic activity is painting, music, dance, or drama, it is due to the working out of a sentiment such as love, dread, anger, etc. In actual life, when the sentiments arise in our mind, they result in action toward the object, and there is ego-involvement. In the aesthetic situation, however, they do not result in the usual action, but in representation in color or sound, in movements in dance, or in the working out of a dramatic plot. Aesthetic activity, like play, is a creative activity, which, when completed, satisfies the mind. Then, *buddhi* (reason) assumes the state of equanimity, or harmony (*samatā*). According to the Sāṁkhya, this emotional equanimity is itself aesthetic pleasure; according to the Vedānta, this equanimity, because it becomes pure (*sāttvika*), reflects the bliss aspect of the *ātman* and becomes pleasure. In music, the different notes combined properly in different forms called tunes (*rāgas*) stir up different emotional components and, when the last note is reached, the stirrings readjust themselves into a placid state, which is aesthetic pleasure. In this state, particularity is submerged, and the ego rises above itself. The higher stage is *buddhi* (reason) in its pure (*sāttvika*) aspect. Thus man can lift himself above the ego and nearer the Divine, not only in the realization of truth and goodness, but also of the beautiful. If so, God can be realized by systematic aesthetic cultivation.

God-realization through aesthetic cultivation has been developed into a *yoga*. The philosophy of music, for instance, is based on a study of the Sound *Brahman* (the Word, *Nāda-Brahman*), which is called an evolute of the Supreme *Brahman*. The Sound *Brahman* is not the origin of speech only but also of music. One who practices music in the right way finally obtains communion with the *Brahman*. Tyāgarāja is said to have made music his path of God-realization. This is the reason for the depth and perfection which music reached in India and also for the importance of music in temples. All fine arts are spiritual disciplines in India, although many who study them do so for secular reasons.

Abhinavagupta maintains that all sentiments have their source in the sentiment of peace (*śānti*), rise out of it like waves out of the ocean, and enter it again. Peace is a positive sentiment or emotion, not the absence of emotions. It is the harmony of all, a state in which *buddhi* (reason) becomes completely pure and aesthetic pleasure is intense and undisturbed. Images of the Buddha, for instance, produce this state in us. Bhoja maintains that the highest form of aesthetic pleasure is love (*śṛṅgāra*), and all the others are only its forms. He defines love as the purest form of the *ātman* at its peak. Only Bhavabhūti, perhaps under the influence of Buddhism, says that compassion (pity, tenderness, *karuṇā*) is the highest aesthetic pleasure; the others are its forms appearing under different conditions. But this view has not been worked out either by him or by others.

Clearly, then, Indian religion and philosophy not only encouraged the realization of aesthetic values but also made them important ingredients of spiritual discipline. And what should strike any student of Indian thought is that the *Logos* is not only rational and ethical but also aesthetic.[58] The realization of each of these aspects leads to the same goal, although, as far as mundane life is concerned, they remain separate. Thus there has been no hostility of religion toward the values of truth, beauty, and goodness, because they have been made spiritual values, though instrumental, in the literal sense of the term. But, when their spiritual significance is forgotten and man pursues them for other purposes, they become secular values. Even then, when pursuing them he is unknowingly pursuing spiritual values. And all three are aspects of reason, which belongs to man's inward being, is cosmic in its nature and reference, and is above the subjectivity of the ego.

IX. Conclusion

So far, a general description of the nature of Indian religious thought and its attitude to the other spiritual values has been given. Many schools have been referred to incidentally; many Vedāntic schools have been omitted; and, even of the two Vedāntic philosophies of Śaṁkara and Rāmānuja, many details have been left out for want of space. One must have seen that the Mīmāṁsā religion supplied the real counterpart of the Vedānta by advocating ethical activism as the highest philosophy. Together, the Mīmāṁsā and the Vedānta have guided the life of Indians for centuries. After the rise and spread of Jainism and Buddhism, the philosophies of salvation became dominant, and the activistic philosophy and religion of the Veda was left, comparatively, in the background. Also, the political conditions from about A.D. 1100 until India attained her independence contributed to the neglect of activism. But it is not dead, since it is an undeniable aspect of India's Vedic culture, as can be seen by any student of Indian thought and culture, if he approaches the subject without contrary preconceptions. Half of the Veda cannot be denied as non-existent.

It is wrong to think that Indian thought, particularly the Vedānta, leads to totalitarian philosophies, in which the individual is submerged in the *Brahman*, and that Eastern despotism is due to this outlook. One may as well say that any philosophy for which God is the Supreme Controller of the universe leads to autocracy and despotism in political thought and that only a philosophy like that of Leibniz, for which God is merely a monad among monads and gets the position of God by election, can support democracy. But no application of religious philosophy to political thought was made in India. Only those philosophies and cultures which have not been able to recognize the peculiarity and reality of inwardness would attempt to apply the concepts of the Absolute, God, Supreme Controller, etc., to outward society and the objective world. Even supposing that Śaṁkara's philosophy is true, then, since everyone is essentially the *Brahman*, there can be no difference between the despot and his subjects. If the despot wishes to "absorb" (rule, suppress) his subjects, then every one of his subjects, since he is the same as the *Brahman*, can have the same wish. Then the result will be either a war of all against all or equality and democracy. Śaṁkara, however, was not interested in this deduction. He knew, of course, that his philosophy confers sacredness and dignity on the individual, because the essential core of each individual is the *Brahman*. He knew also that the recognition of inwardness is the same as the recognition of the freedom of the individual.

But the recognition of inwardness—and the interpretation of intellectual, ethical, and aesthetic values with reference to inward transformation—is not the same as preaching absorption in subjectivity. If man's essential nature is intimately connected with the objective world—some Western philosophers have explained this relation as the relation between the microcosm and the macrocosm —then man's true inwardness can be realized only through proper correlation with outwardness. None can have aesthetic pleasure without seeing the aesthetic object; none can be good without ethical activity in the objective realm; and none can know truth without knowing the objects as they are. And, ultimately, what are these values for? They are for the inward transformation of man. They are not meant for the dissipation of man in external objectivity. If dissipated in objectivity, man's soul is wasted and lost. Like Christ, Indian philosophers would ask: Of what use will it be if a man conquers the world and loses his soul? But man's true spirit can be realized only through activity, intellectual, ethical, and aesthetic.

The contribution of Indian religious thought, then, is the recognition and explication of the inwardness of man, of its freedom, dignity, sacredness, and importance. It is certainly true that India has not produced great ethical systems and political philosophies. The only attempts are that of the Mīmāṁsā and the ethical codes. Social ethics and political thought were not regarded as important by the classical philosophers. This, indeed, has to be admitted and may be traced to the classical philosophers' deeper interest in the inward reality than in the outward.

But, it is difficult to accept the view of Dr. Haas,[59] for example, that, although the Eastern mind is engrossed in subjectivity and the Western is diffused in objectivity and each is reaching a danger point, they cannot be synthesized. Very few will admit that China is at present engrossed in subjectivity. Even taking India, the Mīmāṁsā—therefore, half of the Veda—was not engrossed in subjectivity but in the conquest of objectivity through ethical action. This school had no idea of scientific and technological conquest, but a philosophy that belonged to a period twelve centuries ago can hardly be expected to think of science and technology. However, even leaving out the Mīmāṁsā, as this paper might have shown, this subjectivity is not a closed, windowless subjectivity, but a subjectivity that has not cared so far to look through the windows with microscopes and telescopes. Similarly, one may say that the Western mind has not been lost in objectivity, but it tends to forget itself. Truth is never lost, but may be undiscovered or forgotten. It can therefore be discovered or recovered. Neither man's inwardness nor his outwardness can ever be lost. "Losing one's soul" is a metaphorical phrase. Man's inwardness and outwardness are the two directions of his very being; he can never lose either. The shock of reality will awaken him to each. But, instead of being roused by a devastating shock, the Eastern mind may be awakened by a friendly touch of the Western mind and vice versa. Each is a complement of the other, and each can enter into a synthesis of the two. Mutual understanding leads to assimilation of each other's values, and this assimilation is synthesis, not enforced by an external agent but spontaneously developed by life's becoming conscious of what it has missed.

Then, if the contemporary demand, voiced by Radhakrishnan, that a spiritual view should be sustained by sound social institutions is true, then social institutions cannot be considered to be sound if they do not make possible the realization of the spiritual ideal. And society can make this possible by offering the individual scope for the development of his spiritual qualities and activities—intellectual, ethical, and aesthetic. These presuppose the inwardness, freedom, dignity, and sacredness of the individual. Freedom, dignity, and sacredness are due to his inwardness, without which the physical body is nothing but dirt and filth. There is, in every living body, a skeleton which frightens us, but does not endear us to itself; the human form is divine because the inward spiritual qualities are expressed through it. It is the expression of these qualities that makes social life worth living. Indian religious thought did not have the necessity, at the time when it was formulated, to devote itself to the problems of social organization and the study of social relationships, which have become intimately connected with economic and political problems, the forms of which are fast changing on account of scientific and technological progress. But, whatever be the changes, man should not be lost in them by losing his inwardness and its freedom; and this inwardness should not disenable him for reacting appropriately to the changing complexities of outward existence. Here, East and West have much to learn from each other. True inwardness is not privacy, or mere subjectivity, or loneliness. Whitehead said that religion is what man does in his loneliness; but Hocking said that religion is not private. True inwardness, as this paper might have shown, is the sacrifice of privacy and subjectivity.

QUESTION: You are speaking of some inwardness as objective. How can inwardness be objective? The objective is the external world.

ANSWER: There is inwardness that is private to each individual and inwardness that is public to all. We call the latter reason, although it is found in each man. We may remember what the Kantians and the Hegelians say in this connection, namely, that it is reason that confers objectivity even on the objects perceived externally to us. This view is in accord with Conant's view that a true object is the one fitted into a conceptual scheme, which is rational and which, therefore, belongs to reason. Reason is the public property of all rational beings and is, therefore, objective in its essence. Yet, it is continuous with the subject, or the ego, and belongs to a higher level. For instance, Plato and Aristotle call it the highest part of the soul and treat it as immortal. We may leave out the question of immortality, but we have to recognize that it is higher than the ego. What is merely private to any individual cannot be fitted into a conceptual scheme which belongs to all. The private is what is merely subjective. What is public is truly objective. As reason is public, we may call it objective.

I do not know how to improve upon these words. Even the word "real" has ambiguity. Are illusions real? This is an ambiguous question. It may mean: Are there illusions? Or, can the objects seen in illusions be fitted into the conceptual scheme of the physical world?

NOTE: Dr. Werkmeister suggested that the word "mysticism" should not be used as representing Indian religion, for "mysticism" means everything from witchcraft, necromancy, medieval alchemy, and self-hypnosis to inward realization. I do not know what other single word there is in English for better representing Indian religion. Perhaps "inward realization" is a more suitable phrase. One can see by reading Bradley's ethics that even "self-realization" becomes an ambiguous word to express the Indian spiritual ideal. One may like to use the term "*ātman*-realization"; but the reality of the *ātman* is not accepted by Buddhists. In Western literature, the word "mysticism" is used in both a respectful and a disrespectful sense. In the disrespectful sense, we may agree that it is, as Dr. Hu says, psycho-pathological. But, if reason belongs to the inward being of man, just on that ground it cannot be called pathological. Reason, on the contrary, confers sanity. On the other hand, if one denies the reality of the inward being of man on the basis of what one considers to be science, we may call him "scientio-pathological." The words "scientism" and "historicism" are already current in depreciatory meanings also. As there is the "naturalistic fallacy" (G. E. Moore's term), there can also be the "scientific fallacy," the fallacy committed by some scientists who think that with the help of the method of a particular science everything in the universe can be explained and that whatever cannot be so explained has no reality. And, to make matters worse, "science," although etymologically it means knowledge, has come to mean particularly the physical sciences.

Notes

1. My paper, "The Concept of the Spiritual in Indian Thought," *Philosophy East and West,* IV, No. 3 (October, 1954), may be used as a basic supplementary paper. An acquaintance with the ideas presented there is recommended. It would also be useful if the reader were acquainted with my "Activism in Indian Thought" (Anniversary Address, Bhandarkar Oriental Research Institute, Poona, September 17, 1958, published in the *Annals of the Bhandarkar Oriental Research Institute,* XXXI, Parts III–IV, October, 1958), which deals with the thought of the Brāhmaṇical religion, the Mīmāṁsā. The activism of the Mīmāṁsā and the inward realization of the Vedānta are the two primary opposites in Vedic thought.
2. In its narrower meaning, which is given by Patañjali, *yoga* is the stopping of the functioning of mind. In its wider meaning, it means all forms of activity leading to communion with the Divine Spirit. In its widest meaning, it is skillfulness in action (*yogaḥ karmasu kausálam*), as the *Bhagavad-gītā* explains (II.50).
3. "The Concept of the Spiritual in Indian Thought," *op. cit.,* p. 210.
4. A. J. Toynbee, *A Study of History,* abridged by D. C. Somerwell (New York: Oxford University Press, 1951), p. 501.
5. The Ārya Samāj, a modern reform movement, is converting non-Hindus.
6. See the author's *India's Culture and Her Problems* (Jaipur: University of Rajputana, 1951), p. 33.
7. Among Greek philosophers, Democritus held a similar view.
8. See *Aitareya Upaniṣad,* I and II, for an account of creation according to this correlation.
9. See the author's "Activism in Indian Thought."
10. See *ibid.*
11. This is Kumārila's view, generally accepted by most of the Mīmāṁsakas; but Prabhākara's view is that *dharma* is the potential merit produced by action.
12. According to Kumārila. According to Prabhākara, as *dharma* itself is *apūrva,* it is produced by action.
13. *Elements of Ethics* (London: John Murray, 1910), p. 55.
14. Prabhākara's view that the meaning of a word is understood only

when associated with action is practically that of the pragmatists.

15. See my "Activism in Indian Thought."
16. Śaṁkara, *Vivekacūḍāmaṇi,* 10, 11 (Bombay: Lakshmi Venkateswar Press, 1949).
17. *Vastusiddhirvicāreṇa na kiñcit karmakoṭibhih.*
18. The Vijñānavādins say that all cognitions are false, whereas Rāmānuja says that all cognitions are true. But both say that, in our mundane experience, the cognition which leads to expected results in action is true, otherwise false. This means that action enables us to know truth.
19. Rāmānuja, *Śrī-bhāṣya,* I.i.1. See M. Raṅgāchārya and M. V. Varadarāja Aiyaṅgār, trans., *The Vedānta-sūtras with the Śrī-Bhāshya of Rāmānujāchārya* (Madras: The Brahmavādin Press, 1899), Vol. I, p. 22.
20. *Ibid.*, p. 10. For the controversy, see pp. 8–26.
21. As the Sāṁkhya does not accept the Supreme Spirit, it treats the individual's reason itself as cosmic. But the Vedānta calls the individual's reason, "*buddhi,*" and Cosmic Reason, "*Mahat,*" or "*Mahān Ātmā.*" See the *Kaṭha-upaniṣad* I.ii.10 and 11.
22. *Bhagavad-gītā,* II.47.
23. *Ibid.*, II.49.
24. *Ibid.*, II.50.
25. *Ibid.*, VII.11.
26. See *Bṛhadāraṇyaka-upaniṣad,* I.ii.4 f.
27. The significance of the *Dhammapada* can be estimated in this context in delineating the growth of Indian religion. This paper does not present Buddhism in any detail.
28. These levels are different for Buddhism and are understood by it as *skandhas,* aggregates.
29. The English word "soul" does not really correspond to *ātman,* but to what the Indian writers call *jīva.* The *jīva* is the psycho-ethical individual, but the *ātman* transcends it. Indian religion is really in search of the *ātman.* But I use the word "soul-finding" in a very general sense to correspond to Bosanquet's word "soul-making."
30. II.iv.5. But the *Upaniṣad* immediately asks: How can one know the knower? (II.iv.14.)
31. Rāmānuja, *Śrī-bhāṣya,* I.i.1. See *op. cit.*, Vol. I, p. 18.
32. Śaṁkara, *Vākyavṛtti,* and *Ātmajñānopadeśavidhi,* I.2–6. See Swami Jagadananda, ed. (Madras: Sri Ramakrishna Math, 1953). Cf. Gabriel Marcel's view that being cannot be made objective. *Journal Métaphysique:* Bernard Wall, trans., *Metaphysical Journal* (Chicago: Henry Regnery Company, 1952), p. viii.
33. Rāmānuja, *Śrī-bhāṣya,* I.i.1. See *op. cit.*, Vol. I, p. 94.
34. As another chapter in this volume treats the ethics of India, I do not discuss ethical values in any detail, but very briefly present the

relation of Indian religion to ethical values in order to preserve the unity of the presentation of the relation of religion to spiritual values.

35. It is interesting to note that, whereas this will has cosmic significance for the Mīmāṁsā in that it controls the processes of the cosmos to suit its workings, reason has cosmic significance for the Sāṁkhya and the Vedānta, which assign conative qualities also to it.
36. See my "Activism in Indian Thought."
37. II.41.
38. *Vivekacūḍāmaṇi, op. cit.*, pp. 18 ff.
39. For instance, a girl in love remembers her paramour continuously and without effort.
40. Cp. *prapatti* (self-surrender). See Śrīnivāsācārya, *Yatīndramatadīpikā,* Swami Adidevananda, ed. and trans. (Madras: Sri Ramakrishna Math, 1949), pp. 94 ff.
41. See the lexicon, *Amarakośa.*
42. See Prajñākaramati's *Bodhicaryāvatāra-pañcikā* and also the author's *Idealistic Thought of India* (Cambridge, Mass.: Harvard University Press, 1953), p. 230. Further details are not given, as other chapters in this volume deal with Buddhism.
43. Mādhava Ācārya, *Sarva-darśana-saṁgraha* (Poona: Anandasrama Press, 1928), pp. 25 ff.
44. S. Radhakrishnan, *Indian Philosophy* (London: George Allen & Unwin Ltd., 1928), Vol. I, p. 325.
45. See Asaṅga, *Mahāyāna-sūtrālaṅkāra* (Paris: Honoré Champion, 1907), p. 5: *Bālāśrayo matah tarka tasyāto viṣayo na tat* (Logic is the refuge of children, and so this, i.e., *paramārtha,* spiritual truth, cannot be the object of logic).
46. H. H. Price saw some similarity between the Indian conception of the Self (*Ātman*) and Kant's conception of the transcendental ego (*The Hibbert Journal,* LIII, No. 3 [April, 1955], 228). But closer examination shows that the transcendental ego corresponds to the *Mahat* of the Sāṁkhya and the *Mahān-Ātmā* of the *Kaṭha-upaniṣad,* and is more or less the *Logos* of the Greeks. This may be treated as the Pure Reason of the *Critique of Pure Reason,* but Kant seems to be somewhat hesitant to identify this Pure Reason with the Practical Reason of the *Critique of Practical Reason* and the Aesthetic Reason of the *Critique of Judgment.* The *Sattva* (*Mahat, Mahān Ātmā*) of the Sāṁkhya and the Vedānta performs all the three functions; it is above the ego, but below the *Ātman.*

    It may also be noted here that the modern existentialists' hostility to reason deprived them of the use of the *Logos* and prevented them from seeing its existential nature. The result is that they have generally tended to be shut up in subjectivity, and are unable to explain how reason has validity even for the objective world.
47. See the author's "The Nature of Mind and its Activities," in *The*

Cultural Heritage of India (Calcutta: The Ramakrishna Mission Institute of Culture, 1953), Vol. III, pp. 507 ff.

48. For this reason the *Kaṭha-upaniṣad* differentiates between the individual's reason and Cosmic Reason (between *buddhi* and *Mahān-Ātmā*). The Sāṁkhya uses the word *"mahat"* for the individual's reason.
49. The Pythagoreans believed that mathematics takes man near God.
50. Georg Misch, *The Dawn of Philosophy*, R. F. C. Hull, trans. (Cambridge, Mass.: Harvard University Press, 1951), pp. 258–259. It is interesting to note that Heraclitus identified the *Logos* with fire, and the Indian philosophers treated the god of fire as the deity of speech. The speech which directly issues from the god of Fire is said never to be false.
51. See *Amarakośa*. Buddhist scholars usually translate the word *"vijñāna"* as consciousness, mind, etc., and Indian scholars translate the word *"buddhi"* as intellect, intelligence, and understanding. If we study the words, which are synonyms, in their contexts and connotations, we find that they have the significance of reason and *Logos* in Greek philosophy. It is better to translate the words by "reason," which has many shades of meaning in Western thought as in the Indian, than by intellect, intelligence, or understanding.
52. For a detailed account, see K. C. Pandey, *Indian Aesthetics* (Banaras: Chowkhamba Sanskrit Series, 1950), and P. N. Srinivasacari; *The Philosophy of the Beautiful* (Madras: Thompson and Co., 1942).
53. Har Dutt Sharma, ed. and trans., *Sāṁkhya-kārikā*, XXIII (Poona: Oriental Book Agency, 1933).
54. *Sāttvika.*
55. *Tāmasika.*
56. Buddhism and Jainism do not seem to have devoted much thought to aesthetics. There are important differences between the orthodox schools, but they are not discussed here for want of space. Not even all the Vedāntic schools can be presented here. Only the general trend is given.
57. "Sentiment" is the English word used for *"bhāva."* But some of the *bhāvas* listed by Indian writers are emotions.
58. Even the science of language or linguistics is traced to the *Logos* as the Word, *Nāda-Brahman*. The more one studies and thinks about the concepts of Indian thought, the more does one realize the importance of the role of *sattva* (*mahat, Mahān-Ātmā, buddhi, Nāda-Brahman*) for interpreting Indian spiritual values and culture. It is a mistake to think that these concepts are only speculative. They are primarily existential concepts of man's inward being, and secondarily concepts of constructive philosophy. If this feature is ignored, the spirit of Indian thought, particularly that of the Vedānta, the

Sāṁkhya-Yoga, and Buddhism, and also the truth of these schools as religions, will be missed. The quarrels between the schools are not so important for the modern man as the correlation of their concepts. The first and primary task of the modern student of Indian philosophy who seeks the importance of philosophy for life should be to correlate the concepts of the Indian schools after a critical study. If he wants to do comparative philosophy, he should then correlate them with the concepts of Western philosophy. The tendency of Western interpreters is to treat them as concepts of speculative metaphysics, which is a purely outward approach. The Western man also has his inwardness over which he should reflect when interpreting Indian concepts.

59. W. S. Haas, *The Destiny of Mind: East and West* (London: Faber and Faber, Ltd., 1956). The strength of inwardness can be used for outward conquest, as evidenced by the adoption of Zen Buddhism by the *samurai* of Japan. See Joachim Wach, *Sociology of Religion* (London: Kegan Paul, Trench, Trübner and Co., Ltd., 1947), pp. 261–262.

SWAMI NIKHILANANDA

The Realistic Aspect of Indian Spirituality

A WIDESPREAD VIEW persists among Western scholars that the spiritual perspective of Indian[1] philosophy[2] is incompatible with ethical practice and the ordinary values of life. In this view, Hinduism is, by and large, an otherworldly doctrine concerned with the salvation of the individual and leaves the great mass of humanity to its fate. This attitude, it is often alleged, accounts for India's poverty, illiteracy, and general backwardness. If the world is unreal, as the followers of non-dualism contend, why bother about it?

It will be my endeavor, in this paper, to show that Indian thinkers, including the non-dualists, are not indifferent to the world; that, on the contrary, they take the world to be very real in a certain important sense; that they do not repudiate moral values, but, rather, point out that the fulfillment of social obligations is indispensable for the attainment of spiritual experience. To be sure, Indian leaders have often shown indifference to the welfare of the many; but this attitude is due either to their ignorance of the basic truths of Hinduism or to the distortion of these truths prompted by expediency and opportunism.

Indian culture has been molded in a special fashion by religion and philosophy. From time out of mind, spirituality has formed the backbone of India. It has left an indelible impression, not only upon her social structure, but also upon her many cultural achievements. Loyalty to certain spiritual concepts, moreover, has preserved Indian society during the many centuries of foreign domination. During the darkest period of Indian history, great thinkers, saints, and prophets never failed to exhort the people to perform their social duties, face misfortune calmly, cultivate patience, and keep faith in the ultimate triumph of righteousness and truth. The cause of India's downfall was not her spirituality; on the contrary, spirituality has preserved the country's vitality up to modern times[3]—a fact amply demonstrated in recent years by her heroic struggle for political freedom and her strenuous efforts, along democratic lines, to rebuild the nation after centuries of stagnation.

India has not always been a land of poverty. When India was spiritually great, she was also materially prosperous and culturally creative. It was her fabulous wealth that invited foreign invaders, from Alexander to the English. The foundation of the edifice of the new India must rest on her past attainments; but she must keep her windows open for fresh air from outside to prevent inner stagnation. If India abandons her traditional spiritual heritage and takes exclusively to politics, science, and technology to build her future, she will be courting disaster: this is the lesson of India's past. But the spiritual truths of Hinduism must be reformulated with the help of science, technology, and a modern philosophy to suit the conditions of our age.

Two Ways of Life

Indian thinkers have always recognized two *dharmas,* or ways of life. One of these is "characterized by activity and the other by renunciation. This two-fold *dharma* is the cause of the stability of the world order and also the means by which men attain prosperity and the highest good."[4] By means of activity one enjoys material happiness here and hereafter, and renunciation leads to the highest good. The desire for happiness is universal and persistent. At a certain stage of evolution, a man feels an equally irresistible urge for liberation of the spirit from all forms of attachment. Both the desire for worldly happiness and the desire for the highest good are legitimate desires, and they are always present.[5] The means to their fulfillment are the warp and the woof of the fabric of Indian thought. Both are accepted as valid in the Vedas, the Upaniṣads, the *Mahābhārata*, the *Rāmāyaṇa,* and the *Manu-smṛti* (*Code of Manu*). The *Bhagavad-gītā* centers around a war fought for the preserving of the social order. Desire for the contemplative life, which is cherished at a certain stage of spiritual growth, arises only after a man has gone through all the material enjoyments provided by society. One cannot experience inner tranquillity without having first led an active life.[6] Very few, indeed, seek perfection, which is unattainable without inner peace. "Among thousands of men, one strives for perfection; and of those who strive and succeed, one perchance knows Me in truth."[7] The majority of men are satisfied with a worldly life. For them, religion and philosophy are designed to awaken their desire for higher ideals and show them the means to their realization. For the enlightened, they are redundant: "The Vedas cease to be Vedas."[8]

According to the Vedic philosophers, material pleasures can be meaningfully enjoyed through gratifying the gods and discharging one's duties toward one's fellow men and sub-human creatures. The gods, in the Vedic tradition, are the controllers of such natural phenomena as rain, sunshine, and wind, and also of the activities of the mind and the sense-organs. Furthermore, they are jealous custodians of social welfare, obstructing the liberation of those mortals who seek liberation without fulfilling their social duties. Yama, the god of death, imparted the knowledge of self to Naciketas after the latter had discharged his duties to his father.[9] The *Muṇḍaka-upaniṣad* states that the god of fire severely punishes the man who performs the Agnihotra sacrifice without showing hospitality to guests.[10] According to Kauṭilya's *Artha-śāstra,* Varuṇa, the god of justice, punishes the king who neglects his kingly duties.[11] Agni, the god of fire in the Agnihotra sacrifice, keeps an eye upon the husband and wife to see that they perform properly their family duties. The Vedas regard the universe as a seamless garment in which all living beings have their appropriate places. Their interdependence is emphasized, the welfare of one being determined by the welfare of all. The Hindu scheme of life is not competitive but co-operative. It is by the ceaseless co-operative activity of both inanimate Nature and living beings that the wheel of creation is kept moving. "From food all creatures are born; from rain food is produced; from sacrifice comes rain; sacrifice is born of action. Know that action arises from the Vedas, and the Vedas from the Imperishable."[12] He who does not recognize this all-pervading co-operative spirit lives in vain.[13]

The Hindu scriptures speak of four kinds of spiritual discipline, called *yajña* (sacrifice). The sacrifice for the propitiation of the ancient seers, who are the creators of the spiritual culture, consists in daily recitation of the scriptures and the imparting of their instruction to pupils. By means of this sacrifice, the culture of the race is preserved and developed. Next comes the sacrifice for the propitiation of the manes, who wield power over men and are interested in their welfare. They are propitiated by the regular offering of food and drink. There is also the sacrifice for one's fellow human beings, who, when in distress, should be helped by the gift of food, drink, and clothing. "He who cooks only for himself verily eats sin."[14] Another part of this sacrifice consists in digging wells, building roads, and planting fruit trees for the benefit of one's fellow men.

An embodied person receives various favors from the gods, the seers, and the manes. They are called his debts (*ṛṇas*), which must be paid off before he is qualified for liberation. The debt to the gods is to be paid through offering oblations in the sacrificial fire, to the seers through scriptural study, and to the manes through the procreation of children.[15]

Social Values in the Vedas

The Vedic seers were exhilarated by the beauty and sublimity of Nature and composed moving songs in praise of the earth, the sun, fire, the dawn, and the wind.[16] They reflected deeply on the moral principles behind the universe and sang hymns in honor of the cosmic order, ethical laws, and social virtues.[17] Vedic philosophers never denied the physical world and the pleasures it offers. "This [the physical universe] is real."[18] "If a man wishes to live a hundred years, he should live performing action."[19]

The following quotations will show how keenly interested the Hindus in Vedic times were in marriage, procreation, morality, and other worldly concerns.

About marriage: "I take your hand in mine for a happy future, that you may reach old age with me as your husband."[20] "Be not parted; dwell here; reach the full term of human life. With sons and grandsons, sport and play, rejoice in your abode."[21] "I am this man, that woman are you; I am the psalm, you are the verse; I am the heavens, you are the earth. So will we dwell together here, parents of children yet to come."[22]

About procreation: "This woman has come like a fertile cornfield. There sow, O man, the seed of future harvest. She from her teeming side shall bear you children and feed them from the fountain of her bosom."[23]

About liberality: "They seek the fleet steed for the bounteous giver; the maid adorns herself and waits to meet him. His home is adorned and made splendid like a god-made lake with lotus blossoms."[24] "Let the rich satisfy the poor, and keep in view the long pathway. Riches come now to one, now to another, and like the wheels of cars are ever turning."[25]

About hospitality: "Now that man who eats before the guests eats up the sacrifice and the merit of the house. He devours the milk and the sap and the vigor and prosperity and the progeny and the cattle and the fame and reputation, the glory and understanding of the house. . . . When the guests have eaten he should eat. This is the rule for the success of sacrifice and the preservation of its continuity."[26]

About concord in council: "Walk together, speak together, let your minds be all alike. May the purpose be common, common the assembly, common the mind; so be your thoughts united. . . . May your decision be unanimous, your minds being of one accord. May the thoughts of all be united so that there may be a happy agreement among us all."[27]

About longevity: "May we see a hundred years. May we live a hundred years. May we know a hundred years. May we progress a hundred years. May we prosper a hundred years. May we be a hundred years; may we assert our existence a hundred years; yea, even more than a hundred years."[28]

About health and vigor:

Power art Thou, give me power;
Might art Thou, give me might;
Strength art Thou, give me strength;
Life art Thou, give me life;
Eye art Thou, give me eyes;
Ear art Thou, give me hearing;
Shield art Thou, shield me well.[29]

"May I have voice in my mouth, breath in my nostrils, sight in my eyes, hearing in my ears, hair that hath not turned grey, teeth free from yellowness, and much strength in my arms. May I have power in my thighs, swiftness in my legs, steadfastness in my feet. May all my limbs be uninjured and my soul unimpaired."[30]

About the home: "I, full of strength, enlightened and happy, come home rejoicing in my spirit—home where joy and cheerfulness abide. May joy be ours, felicity and blessing."[31]

About being a householder: "Agni, may I become a good householder. Agni, mayest Thou become a good householder. O Agni, may our household matters be smoothly managed for a hundred years, not like a one-ox cart."[32]

About general prosperity: "O Lord, may there be born in the kingdom *brāhmaṇas* distinguished for the knowledge of *Brahman;* heroic *kṣatriyas,* skilled marksmen, piercing with shafts mighty warriors; cows giving abundant milk, good at carrying weight; swift horses; and industrious women. May the clouds send rain according to our desire; may our fruit-trees ripen; may we secure and preserve property."[33]

About the welfare of the king: "Let him be the lord of endless treasures; let him as king be master of the people. Grant him great power and strength; let his enemies be deprived of strength and vigor."[34]

About battles and the attitude toward enemies, etc.: "May Indra aid us when our flags are out; may our arms be victorious. May our brave warriors come home with flying colors. O Lord, protect us in the din of battle."[35] "Confusing the minds of our enemies, seize their bodies; depart, O panic. Attack them, confound them. Let our foes abide in utter darkness."[36] "We do not hate the conquered enemy; may we enjoy peace and security."[37] Whoso with an ungodly mind tries to injure us, proud of his might among princes, let not his deadly blow reach us. May we humble the wrath of the proud miscreant."[38]

From these quotations it will be apparent that the Indo-Aryans of Vedic times lived a full and happy life and regarded the world as real. They communed with the gods and pursued the path of justice and truthfulness and discharged their social responsibilities. It was not a purely materialistic happiness that they sought, however; for them, worldly enjoyment was a means to a higher end, as will be presently shown. The sacrificial part of the Vedas is not devoid of philosophical speculation about ultimate reality. Mention is made of the non-dual *Brahman.*[39] The disciplines of continence,[40] self-control, and inner purification[41] are described, and knowledge and wisdom[42] extolled.

The Upaniṣads and Social Values

The Upaniṣads form the concluding part of the Vedas and embody their essence; hence, they are called Vedānta. Here the philosophical inquiries of the Vedic seers reach their full depth. They raise the question: "Who am I?" and answer it with the statement: "That thou art."[43] When a man experiences his oneness with God and the universe, his philosophical thinking cannot go any farther. It should be stated here that the Vedas are made up of both the Mantra and the Brāhmaṇa sections, which apply to the two stages in man's evolution. The Mantra, or sacrificial part, is meant for those who still desire material happiness here and hereafter. The Upaniṣads, the philosophical part contained in the Brāhmaṇas, are for those who, weary of material happiness, seek the highest good or liberation.

The aim of the Upaniṣads is to establish the existence of *Brahman,* Absolute reality; they have been interpreted in different ways by different schools of Indian philosophy. In the opinion of non-dualists such as Gauḍapāda and Śaṁkara, *Brahman* is one and without a second; besides it, nothing else exists. It is to be realized by the method of negation. Here it may be noted that the followers of non-dualism in India are numerically fewer than those of the qualified non-dualistic and dualistic schools. These schools affirm the reality of living beings and the universe as parts of *Brahman* or as independent of it, respectively. According to non-dualists, as long as a man regards the physical universe and the individual ego as real, he should regard himself as separate from or part of reality. Many non-dualists, at the beginning of their spiritual life, worship, pray, and perform their social duties like dualists.

The Upaniṣads do not deny the reality of the world. They allow it an empirical reality (*vyāvahārika-sattva*). As long as a man is conscious of multiplicity, he must deal with it as real. He must accept social values and ethical laws. The householder must be hospitable to guests; otherwise, his "hopes and expectations, the reward of his intercourse with pious people, the merit of his kindly speech, the good results of his sacrifices and beneficial deeds, and his cattle and children are destroyed."[44] Unless he gratifies his father and propitiates the gods, he cannot attain knowledge of *Brahman.*[45] The *Bṛhadāraṇyaka-upaniṣad* narrates the story of the Creator's exhorting the gods, men, and the demons (*asuras*) to cultivate, respectively, the virtues of self-control, charity, and compassion.[46] According to Śaṁkara, the "gods" represent here those men who are endowed with many noble and refined qualities but are lacking in self-control. Those men who are particularly greedy are here called "men." And the "demons" among men are those who are cruel and given to injuring others. Hence, the instruction imparted here applies to men alone.

In King Aśvapati's description of the state of his kingdom, in the *Chāndogya Upaniṣad*, are reflected the high standards of society in Upaniṣadic times: "In my kingdom there is no thief, no miser, no wine-bibber, no man without a sacrificial fire, no ignorant person, no adulterer, much less an adulteress."[47]

Again, that the importance of moral conduct is clearly recognized can be seen in the advice of a teacher to his students who have finished their education and are about to embrace the householder's life, as recorded in the *Taittirīya-upaniṣad:*

Speak the truth. Practice *dharma.* Do not neglect the study of the Vedas. Having brought to the teacher the gift desired by him, [enter the householder's life and see that] the line of progeny is not cut off. Do not swerve from the truth. Do not swerve from *dharma.* Do not neglect [personal] welfare [health and longevity]. . . . Do not neglect your duties to the gods and the Manes. Treat your mother as God. Treat your father as God. Treat your teacher as God. Whatever deeds are faultless, these are to be performed—not others. Whatever good works have been performed by us, these should be performed by you—not others. . . . Now, if there arises in your mind any doubt concerning any act, or any doubt concerning any conduct, you should conduct yourself in such matters as *brāhmaṇas* would conduct themselves—*brāhmaṇas* who are competent to judge, who [of their own accord] are devoted [to good deeds] and are not urged [to their performance] by others, and who are not too severe, but are lovers of *dharma.* . . . This is the rule. This is the teaching. This is the secret wisdom of the Vedas. This is the command. This you should observe. This alone should be observed.[48]

The Indo-Aryans longed for sons endowed with noble qualities. The rituals of birth have been vividly described in the Upaniṣads.[49] A typical prayer for wealth, cattle, prosperity, and longevity is the following: "Bring me, without delay, fortune which will always provide me with clothes and cattle, food and drink. . . . May I become famous among men. May I become richer than the rich."[50] The desire for wealth, children, grandchildren, cattle, gold, long life, and happiness both here and hereafter is widely expressed in all the principal Upaniṣads. All the teachers of the major Upaniṣads were householders. Yājñavalkya renounced the world only after having entered into two marriages.

Social Values in the Secondary Scriptures

We come, next, to the secondary scriptures of the Hindus, called the Smṛtis, among which may be listed the *Rāmāyaṇa,* the

Mahābhārata, the various Purāṇas, the *Code of Manu,* the Tantra treatises, and the *Artha-śāstra* of Kauṭilya. They are based chiefly on the Vedic tradition. In contrast to the Śruti, or Vedas, the truths of which were discovered by the seers through their spiritual insight, the Smṛtis are ascribed to human authorship. They give a popular interpretation of the philosophic truths of the Upaniṣads and show how these may be applied in the life of the individual and of society. The Smṛtis change from time to time, according to the needs of the age, but they show the way to liberation. One interesting feature of Hinduism is that, though it is based upon certain immutable and universal philosophical truths, it recognizes that these must be adapted to peculiar social conditions of time and place. And this latter task falls to the Smṛtis.

The *Rāmāyaṇa,* India's earliest epic poem, describes the penetration of Indian culture into the south and the gradual assimilation of the non-Aryans by the Aryans. In its pages are expressed the Indian ideals of filial piety, the chastity of women, friendship, loyalty, kingly duties, and the courtesy to which inferiors are entitled from their superiors.

The *Mahābhārata* is a "miscellany of history and mythology, politics and law, philosophy and theology."[51] Both the *Rāmāyaṇa* and the *Mahābhārata* give the picture of a happy and prosperous society. In the *Mahābhārata,* one observes the gradual assimilation of different backward tribes into the Aryan family. The *Bhagavad-gītā,* which is part of this great work, is designated as a Mokṣa-śāstra, a treatise showing the way to liberation. Arjuna, the hero of this poem, is faced with a moral dilemma. The stability and the ethical values of society are threatened, and can be preserved only by a war. Arjuna seeks an escape through the easy life of retirement from the world, but Kṛṣṇa characterizes his attitude as "lowness of spirit, unbecoming an Aryan, dishonorable, unmanly, and an obstacle to the attaining of heaven."[52] Since all attempts for a just and peaceful settlement with the wicked enemies have failed, he urges Arjuna to fight. According to the *Bhagavad-gītā,* there is no conflict between spiritual enlightenment and the performance of social duties in a spirit of non-attachment. "Verily, by action alone men like Janaka attained perfection. Further, you should perform action with a view to guiding people along the right path."[53] An enlightened man, no doubt, is above duty. There is nothing in the three worlds he has not gained and nothing that he has to gain. Yet, he works, for, if he does not engage, unwearied, in action, men in every way will imitate his example. If he ceases to work, the world will perish.[54] Arjuna heeds Kṛṣṇa's advice, plunges into the war, witnesses, without being distracted, the death of his near and dear ones, and on the battlefield itself obtains a rare exalted spiritual experience.[55]

For many centuries the *Bhagavad-gītā* has inspired the lives of countless Hindus, whether monks or householders, recluses or social workers. In our own times, Mahatma Gandhi drew inspiration for his unceasing labors from this book. The method of non-violence and non-resistance to evil prescribed by Gandhi to win India's political freedom is not in accordance with the teachings of the Hindu scriptures such as the *Rāmāyaṇa,* the *Mahābhārata,* the *Bhagavad-gītā,* the *Candi,* and the *Code of Manu.* In Hindu society, the *kṣatriyas,* or the military people, occupy the second position. Śaṁkara says in his Commentary on the *Bhagavad-gītā*[56] that the lack of co-operation between the *brāhmaṇas* and the *kṣatriyas* destroys the *yoga,* or the spiritual culture. According to the last verse of the *Bhagavad-gītā,* one sees good fortune, triumph, welfare, and firm morality where "Kṛṣṇa, the lord of *yoga,* and Arjuna, the wielder of the bow," co-operate with each other.[57] Righteous war, according to Indian thinkers, is justified when all reasonable efforts for peaceful settlement fail. Gandhi's advocacy of non-violence was his personal religious creed, not accepted by many even among his intimate followers. The latter approved of non-violence as an expediency dictated by the existing political condition of the country.

Another important part of the *Mahābhārata* is the section on Peace (*Śānti-parva*), which contains the instruction given on the battlefield by Bhīṣma, an elder statesman and military general, to the princes who participated in the war.[58] The teachings cover the duties of householders, kings, and monks, and also the rules of conduct to be observed as expediencies in times of crisis. Among the general ethical laws are mentioned truthfulness, justice, compassion, amiability, patience, and procreation of offspring with one's wife. Bhīṣma does not give any categorical definition of good and evil, righteousness and unrighteousness, the concepts of which vary according to time and place. A general principle seems to emphasize harmlessness to all creatures as good or virtuous, and injury to them as evil. But one meets with difficulty in the practical applications of this principle. Forgiveness is not extolled as the highest virtue under all circumstances. One need not always speak the truth. Under certain circumstances, "it is better to speak what is beneficial than what is true."[59] Though upholding the Law of *Karma,* Bhīṣma also stresses the virtue of self-effort. Destiny and exertion equally operate; yet exertion is superior, for "destiny is ascertained from what is begun with exertion."[60] The Law of *Karma* is often misinterpreted as fatalism. In reality, it is nothing but the law of cause and effect. "As one sows, so one reaps." The effect need not be confined to the present life alone; it is seen in a future life, too. The Law of *Karma,* according to Indian thinkers, supplies a man with a blueprint of life, as it were, at the time of his birth. His habits and attitudes are explained according to impressions left by his actions done in his previous life. What does he know of life who knows only one life? The Law of *Karma* teaches a man to regard his present misfortune as the result of his own past, and, at the same time, exhorts him to act now in such a way that he will avoid suffering in the future. Destiny (*adṛṣṭa*) is nothing but the accumulated impressions of a man's action in the past life, of which he is not aware in the present life. Bhīṣma condemns the renunciation of ascetics if it is not accompanied by knowledge: "Emancipation does not consist in poverty, nor is bondage to be found in affluence. One attains emancipation through knowledge alone, whether one is indigent or affluent."[61] He warns seekers of the highest good against worldly pleasures: "The desire for wealth can never be fraught with happiness. When acquired, great is the anxiety that the acquirer feels. If lost after acquisition, that is felt as death. Lastly, respecting acquisition itself there is uncertainty."[62]

The *Code of Manu* deals with the conduct of the individual as a member of society, which ultimately leads him to the attainment of the highest good. According to Manu, the purpose of the caste system is to encourage social harmony for the common good. A special feature of this work is the respect shown to women, though their dependence upon men is not overlooked. ("Where women are worshipped, the gods are pleased.")

Kauṭilya, who lived about three hundred years before Christ, is the author of the famous *Artha-śāstra,* a treatise on politics and diplomacy. Among other topics dealt with in this work are the duties of government superintendents, the conduct of courtiers, war and invasion, espionage, the plan of a treaty, the life of a saintly king, law, marriage, the source of authority of sovereign states, and the nature of political alliances.

The *Mahā-nirvāṇa-tantra,* a scripture esteemed especially by the followers of Tāntrika mysticism, discusses at length the duties of the householder. Some of its ideas are given below:

A householder should be devoted to God; yet he must work constantly, performing all his duties; he must give up the fruits of action to God. The great duty of a householder is to earn a living, but he must take care that he does not do this by telling lies or by cheating or by robbing others; and he must remember that his life is for the service of God and the poor. . . . Knowing that his mother and father are the visible representatives of God, the householder always and by all possible means must please them. . . . Equally important is his duty to his wife, and he must always maintain her as if she were his own mother. Even when he is in the greatest difficulties and troubles, he must not renounce his wife if she is chaste and devoted to him. . . . To his enemies the householder must be a hero. When threatened by them he must resist. He must not sit down in the corner and weep, and talk nonsense and nonresistance. If he does not show himself a hero to his enemies, he has not done his duty. And to his friends and relatives he must be as gentle as a lamb. . . . It is the duty of the householder not to pay reverence to the wicked, because, if he reverences them, he patronizes the wicked. And it will be a great mistake if he disregards those who are worthy of respect—the good people. . . . A householder must struggle hard to acquire two things: first, knowledge, and second, wealth. This is his duty, and if he does not do his duty he is nobody. A householder who does not struggle to acquire wealth is immoral. If he is lazy and content to lead an idle life, he is immoral, because upon him depend hundreds of other people. If he gets riches, hundreds of others will be supported. The householder is the center of life and society. It is a kind of worship for him to acquire and spend wealth nobly. The householder who struggles to become rich by good means and for good purposes is practically doing the same thing for the attainment of salvation as the anchorite does in his cell when he prays; for in them we see only different aspects of the same virtue of self-surrender and self-sacrifice prompted by the feeling of devotion to God and to human beings who are His manifestations.

If the householder dies in battle, fighting for his country and religion, he comes to the same goal that the *yogī* attains through meditation.[63]

The Dark Age in India

A great change came over India when she lost her political freedom in the eleventh century. Muslim power was established in

Delhi and gradually spread throughout the country. The new rulers brought with them a different outlook on life which profoundly disturbed the old concepts. During the seven hundred years of Muslim domination, Hindu society lost its creativeness and became conservative. Instead of producing original ideas, scholars preoccupied themselves with giving subtle interpretations to the ancient texts. The caste system became stratified, and social customs grew rigid. All this, however, brought about one good result: an almost impenetrable wall was thus erected around Hindu society, which foreign influence could not pierce. At the same time, it prevented fresh ideas from coming from the outside. But, even during the period of alien rule, Hinduism produced great religious leaders such as Rāmānuja, Kabir, the Mārhattā saints, and Chaitanya of Bengal, who tried to improve the condition of the masses, especially the untouchables. What one sees in India today does not reflect the dynamic Indian culture of a thousand years ago, but the continuation of many of the rigid social and religious practices prevalent during the long period of foreign domination.

During the British rule of one hundred and ninety years, India remained culturally sterile. But the introduction of English education brought educated Indians into contact with the rational, aggressive, and dynamic West. Through the notable efforts of Western Orientalists and British historians and archaeologists, the Indians again learned to value their past cultural achievements, though it is a fact that many of those who received English education became thoroughly Westernized in outlook. Christian missionaries also aroused the dormant social consciousness of the Indians. Thus there took place a new cultural revival with significant political and social implications.

Social Values in Modern India

The Brāhmo Samāj, established in 1828, was founded by Raja Ram-Mohan (or Rāmmohan) Roy (1744–1833). A religious liberal, he drew ideas from Christianity, Buddhism, and Islam; but the main source of his inspiration remained the Vedas. The ethics of Christianity moved him deeply. The Brāhmo movement declared the supremacy of reason, advocated the ideals of the French Revolution, abolished the caste system among its members, sanctioned the remarriage of Hindu widows, stood for the emancipation of women, and agitated for the abolition of early marriages. Though a religious movement, the Brāhmo Samāj, under the influence of Western culture, advocated mainly social reform. Its influence was confined, however, to a comparatively small number of intellectuals.

The Ārya Samāj, founded by Swami Dayananda (1824–1883), stood for Hindu orthodoxy and asserted the supremacy of the Vedas, especially the Vedic sacrifices. Its influence spread among the common people in northern India. Like the Brāhmo Samāj, it advocated social reform. Both these movements were natural reactions against the stagnation which had all but paralyzed India during its thousand years of foreign rule.

The Ramakrishna Mission

The non-dualistic traditions of the Upaniṣads were revived in modern times by Ramakrishna and Vivekananda. The Ramakrishna Mission, founded in 1897 by Swami Vivekananda (1863–1902), has blended India's traditional spiritual disciplines with philanthropic activities, which are carried out through institutions organized on more or less Western lines. Vivekananda stated in the rules and regulations of the Ramakrishna Mission that his ideal was to turn the Belur Math, the headquarters of the organization, into a finished university where the traditional spiritual culture of India and the physical sciences of the modern West would be studied side by side.

Ramakrishna (1836–1886), unlike the leaders of the Brāhmo Samāj and Ārya Samāj, who were essentially social reformers, was a man of God. Diagnosing the cause of the human malady as spiritual, he exhorted people to realize God—dwelling in all living beings as their inner spirit—as the only reality. According to his teaching, when a man knows God he rids himself of ego, which is the cause of greed, lust, anger, and the other vices. He did not explain away the world as unreal, as do some extreme non-dualists, but described it as a manifestation of God's creative power called *māyā*. He did not regard *māyā* as a sinister force, but gave it a spiritual status. For him, human relationships find true meaning only through the knowledge of men's relationship with the Godhead. Ramakrishna realized the divinity of the soul and thus pointed out where the true spiritual basis of individual freedom and democracy lies. By his experience of the oneness of existence and the solidarity of mankind, he showed the real foundation of ethics. Further, he realized that religions, in their essence, are not antagonistic but complementary. His spiritual experiences have great social implications. He dedicated his body, mind, and soul to the service of others.

Ramakrishna asked his foremost disciple, Swami Vivekananda, to see God, not merely with eyes closed, but with eyes open as well. The most effective way of worshipping God, he taught him, is to minister to the needs of people by bringing education to the illiterate, food to the hungry, and medicine to the sick. Needy people, however, should be served not as objects of pity but with respect as living images of God. Vivekananda said later: "You may invent an image through which to worship God, but a living image already exists—the living man. You may build a temple in which to worship God, and that may be good, but a better one, a much higher one, already exists—the human body."[64]

A social worker, according to Vivekananda, must fulfill three conditions: he must intensely feel the suffering of others, he must know the remedy for it, and he must be totally unselfish. Vivekananda felt deeply for the unfortunate masses of India: "The great national sin of India is the neglect of the masses, and that is one of the causes of our downfall. No amount of politics will be of any avail until the masses in India are once more well educated and well cared for. They pay for our education, they build our temples, but in return they get our kicks. They are practically our slaves. If we want to regenerate India, we must work for them." "Him I call a *mahātmā* (noble soul) whose heart bleeds for the poor; otherwise he is a *durātmā* (wicked soul)."[65] He strongly emphasized that "the national ideals of India are renunciation and service. Intensify her in those channels and the rest will take care of itself."[66] The monks of the Ramakrishna Mission take the twin vows of self-realization and service to humanity. To them, work is worship. Their lives alternate between meditation and social service. They are taught to feel the presence of the same God in the market place as in the cloister, in the laboratory as in the temple.

It is often said that Indian thinkers, on account of their preoccupation with transcendental reality, neglect the visible universe. Even in ancient times, Indians made considerable progress in the positive sciences. They cultivated, among other things, knowledge of astronomy, chemistry, metallurgy, mathematics (including algebra), medicine and surgery, and logic and grammar.[67]

In the *Chāndogya Upaniṣad,* Nārada describes to his teacher,

Sanatkumāra, the variety of subjects he has studied before seeking the knowledge of the self. He lists them as follows:

The *Ṛg-veda,* the *Yajur-veda,* the *Sāma-veda,* the *Atharva-veda* as the fourth [Veda], the epics and ancient lore as the fifth, grammar, the rules of sacrifice by which the Manes are gratified, the science of numbers, the science of portents, the science of time, logic, ethics, etymology, the science of pronunciation, ceremonials and prosody, the science of elemental spirits, the science of weapons, astronomy, the science of serpents, and the fine arts.[68]

Then Nārada adds: "But, venerable sir, with all this I know words only; I do not know the self. I have heard from men like you that he who knows the self overcomes sorrow. I am one afflicted with sorrow. Do you, venerable sir, help me to cross over to the other side of sorrow."[69] Evidently, even in Vedic times Indian thinkers cultivated the knowledge of both the physical sciences and the science of the soul.

Justification of Social Values

In the foregoing pages I have tried to show that Indian thinkers have not been really otherworldly in their outlook, but, on the contrary, have taken a keen interest in the nature of the universe according to the information available in their times and also in moral and social values. In what follows I shall attempt to show that India's idealism is not in conflict with its realism.

Indian philosophers have investigated the nature of reality from two standpoints: the relative (*vyāvahārika*) and the absolute (*paramārthika*). The relative reality of the physical world is based upon the undeniable evidence of the seers. The diversity of ego and non-ego is its very structure. Śaṁkara[70] refuted the doctrines of Buddhist nihilism and subjective idealism.[71] Again, undeniable experience of the seers reveals the fact that there is a reality which is absolute existence, knowledge, and bliss (*saccidānanda*).[72] For Śaṁkara, this reality, called *Brahman,* is non-dual, eternal, immutable, relationless, and the unattached source of the creation, preservation, and dissolution of the universe.

That both the Absolute and the relative can be real, though under different conditions, has been illustrated by the examples of the desert and the mirage, waking and dreaming, the rope and the illusory snake superimposed upon it through ignorance. But they are not experienced as real from the same point of view. When you see the desert, you do not see the mirage. When you see the non-dual *Brahman*, you do not see the phenomenal universe. The universe is called *māyā*. *Māyā* is the power inherent in *Brahman* which accounts for the appearance of the universe. Owing to it, the appearance is taken for reality. But this apparent reality does not in any way affect the true nature of *Brahman:* the mirage does not moisten a grain of sand in the desert. At first, *māyā* hides the nature of reality; next it projects multiplicity. *Māyā* is neither real nor unreal. It is not unreal, because, under certain conditions, the effect, namely, multiplicity, is perceived to exist. It is not real, because multiplicity disappears when one achieves knowledge of *Brahman.* According to Śaṁkara, the ultimate goal of the Upaniṣads is to prove that whatever exists is the non-dual *Brahman*. The Upaniṣads have condemned duality, but never non-duality. "By mind alone is *Brahman* to be realized; then one does not see in it any multiplicity whatsoever. He goes from death to death who sees multiplicity in it. This, verily, is that."[73] "Duality does not exist for one who knows reality." *Brahman* is "one without a second." *Brahman*, as absolute reality, always exists, even when the world is taken to be real, just as the desert alone really exists even when one sees the mirage. The reality of the sense-perceived universe is empirical. Social values cannot be denied by those who regard themselves as part of the relative world.

To the enlightened all that exists is *Brahman*.[74] Non-dualism is not illusionism (*māyā-vāda*); it is an experience which sees the sole reality of *Brahman* (*Brahmāstitva-vāda*). But dualism regards the universe of multiplicity as real; so, also, are the pairs of opposites such as ego and non-ego, pleasure and pain, good and evil, virtue and vice. Therefore, one cannot deny his relationships with others or his social obligations. He must pray, worship, work, and reap the fruit of action. For him the Personal God is real as the controller of his destiny and the universe. But, when the universe disappears in *Brahman*, the Personal God, heaven, and earth merge into it, too.

Indian thinkers admit the inherent perfection of the soul, though this perfection may be distorted (according to the dualists) or hidden (according to the non-dualists) by the power of *māyā*. They also believe that every soul will eventually attain perfection. But, as this cannot be attained in one life, they postulate the doctrine of rebirth—which is governed by the Law of *Karma*. Birth, growth, decay, and death apply to the body and not to the soul.

The very divine nature of the soul, hidden or distorted though it may be, makes it seek absolute existence, knowledge, and bliss. Man wants to be, to know, and to enjoy bliss. He seeks the fulfillment of these three basic desires on earth and in heaven. To that end, he performs selfless action, propitiates God, or pursues knowledge. He assumes numberless bodies, but nowhere does he discover absolute existence, knowledge, and bliss. The knowledge that is acquired through the senses and the mind has a beginning and an end. There is no abiding happiness in the finite. In creation nothing exists forever. The cause produces the effect, and in time the latter disappears. Absolute existence cannot be realized in the phenomenal world, in which one experiences constant birth and death. "Frail indeed are those rafts of sacrifices"[75] to take one across the ocean of interminable births and deaths called *saṁsāra*. "Having enjoyed the vast heavenly world, they come back to the world of mortals when their merit is exhausted. Thus abiding by the injunctions of the three Vedas and desiring desires, they are subject to death and rebirth."[76]

Let a *brāhmaṇa,* after having examined all these worlds, acquire freedom from desires. Nothing that is eternal can be produced by that which is non-eternal. In order that he may understand what is eternal, let him, fuel in hand, approach a teacher who is well versed in the Vedas and always devoted to *Brahman*. To that pupil who has duly approached him, whose mind is completely serene, and whose senses are controlled, the wise teacher should rightly impart the knowledge of *Brahman*, through which one knows the immutable and all-pervading spirit.[77]

Practice of Yoga

Now the pupil begins in earnest the practice of spiritual discipline, which is known by the general name of *yoga*. For the active man, the discipline of action is prescribed.[78] Through selfless action the pupil acquires serenity of mind, remaining unruffled in pain and pleasure, success and failure. He discharges his social obligations, regarding himself as God's instrument, or always remaining conscious that the sense-organs perform the action, the spirit remaining a serene witness. He sees "action in non-action, and non-action in action,"[79] but never gives up action. "May you never be attached to non-action."[80]

The emotional man is asked to follow the discipline of the love of God, a love that knows no fear, a love that seeks no reward, a love that is cultivated for love's sake.[81] A dualist generally practices this discipline. He regards himself as an instrument in God's hands, and wholeheartedly serves both God and living beings, whom he regards as God's creatures. Chaitanya, a great dualist saint of the sixteenth century, exhorted his followers to cultivate taste for God's name, to show compassion to living beings, and to honor holy men, for realization of God. "By that devotion alone he knows me, knows what, in truth, I am and who I am. Then having known me in truth, he forthwith enters into me."[82]

The discipline of concentration is recommended for the introspective.[83] Its goal is the isolation of the soul from the body through *samādhi*, or deep meditation. Though a follower of this path confines himself to a minimum of social action, yet he is told that one of the means of controlling the restless mind is to show friendship toward the happy, compassion toward the unhappy, and gladness toward the good.[84]

The discipline of knowledge is meant for philosophic minds. Its followers—the non-dualistic monks—pursue the negative path of renunciation and give up exclusive or restricted attachment to all physical objects. These monks control all desires which spring from finite existence. "When all the desires that dwell in the heart are got rid of, then does the mortal [man] become immortal and attain *Brahman* in this body."[85] The Upainṣads are emphatic that immortality cannot be attained without the total renunciation of attachment to the world, whose three chief pillars are offspring, wealth, and heaven. "The knowers of *Brahman* of olden times, it is said, did not wish for offspring [because they thought]: 'What shall we do with offspring—we who have attained this self, this world?' They gave up, it is said, their desire for sons, for wealth, and for the worlds, and led the life of [religious] mendicants."[86] "This self is dearer than a son, dearer than wealth, dearer than everything else [because] it is the innermost."[87] According to the *Muṇḍaka-upaniṣad*, renunciation must be accompanied by monastic vows.[88] Śaṁkara upholds this view; but, in the Purāṇas, mention is made of householders, such as the Emperor Janaka, a butcher, and a housewife, who attained to the knowledge of *Brahman* through the performance of their respective worldly duties. However, the practice of total non-attachment, both in action and in thought, is absolutely necessary prior to the direct knowledge of *Brahman.* Therefore, it is easier for monks to follow this discipline.

Hindu Ethics[89]

Now I propose to discuss Hindu ethics, both in its personal and in its social aspects. According to Hindu philosophers, ethics is the steel-frame foundation of the spiritual life and the practice of *yoga.*

Ethical disciplines in Hinduism are derived from certain spiritual concepts. They are not justified on purely utilitarian or biological grounds. Indian thinkers have discussed ethics from both the social or objective and the personal or subjective standpoints, with emphasis on the latter, in consonance with the Hindu metaphysical view that the ultimate goal of life is liberation. The excellence of a culture, according to Indian thinkers, is to be judged, not by the material prosperity or creature-comforts it provides for the society or the individual, however important they may be, but by its upholding of the principle of plain living and high thinking. A man profits very little if he gains the whole world, but loses his soul, as the Bible says.

Social ethics centers around the Hindu concept of *dharma.* Generally translated as "duty," "righteousness," or "religion," *dharma* means much more than what is connoted by any of these terms. The sanction of duty often comes from the outside. Many people take religion as a set of dogmas laid down in scriptures, through which a devotee can approach God, who is external to him. But, according to Indian philosophy, *dharma* is the law of inner growth, by which the embodied soul is supported in the present state of his evolution and also shown the way for his future development and ultimate liberation.

Dharma, formed by a man's past actions and thoughts, determines his attitude toward the outer world and governs his mental and physical reaction in a given situation. It constitutes his righteousness, his code of honor. Hindu thinkers recognize certain universal *dharmas,* such as truthfulness, non-injury to others, and compassion. There are also specific *dharmas,* relative to particular castes, stages in life, and circumstances. As already stated, nothing is absolutely good or evil in the ever-changing phenomenal world; evil may be defined as what is less good. One cannot stipulate what is absolutely good or evil for all men, or even for an individual, for all times or circumstances. The attempt to do so—and to judge all people by a single concept of *dharma* and to impose it upon all without paying attention to relative circumstances—has been a cause of much of the injustice and cruelty committed upon humanity. If one wants to give a comprehensive definition of *dharma,* one may say that what helps a man in establishing kinship with his fellow creatures is good, and its reverse is evil.

Social ethics, whose immediate purpose is the promotion of social welfare, has been enjoined upon householders who are conscious of their social responsibilities. Such people form the bulk of society. Through the observance of social ethics, an ideal society is created which affords individuals opportunities to realize their highest spiritual potentialities. The discharge of social duties in a large measure preserved Hindu society from utter collapse during the period of foreign domination. Their neglect, on the other hand, undermined its vitality.

The Hindu caste system is intimately connected with the social aspect of ethics. It has served various purposes. As long as its original meaning was followed, the caste system promoted harmony and co-operation between the divergent members of society. It eliminated friction and competition, and saved the weak from exploitation by the strong. It has helped Hindu society to absorb alien peoples according to their merits and aptitudes. Through it, men recognized renunciation, self-control, service, and sacrifice as cardinal virtues. The present state of the caste system of India is deplorable. Its true spirit has been practically forgotten; people are clinging merely to the outer forms.

The *brāhmaṇas* are priests and teachers. They are men of knowledge and science, thought and learning, self-control and austerity, uprightness and forbearance.[90] The *kṣatriyas,* who are fighters, are endowed with the qualities of heroism and high spirit, boldness and fortitude, firmness and dexterity, generosity and rulership.[91] According to Śaṁkara and the *Bhagavad-gītā,* through co-operation between the spiritual and the royal power, the spiritual culture is preserved and social welfare assured.[92] The *vaiśyas,* who are farmers and traders, are men of desires, possessions, and acquisitive enterprise.[93] The main duty of the *śūdras,* the laborers, is action in the form of service to the higher castes.[94] They are men of little intelligence, who cannot be educated beyond certain restricted limits, who are incapable of dealing with abstract ideas, and who are capable of only manual work. Men are not born equal, though all men should be regarded as equal before law and given equal opportunities to develop their latent powers. These four types exist in every organized society. It is Nature, and not the Vedas or Manu, that is responsible for divisions in society. The *Bhagavad-gītā* says that in the beginning the positions in the castes were determined by men's action and merit.[95] Each of the four castes has its own hygiene, its own domain of labor, its own sentiment of perfection, and its own special superiority. The rules regarding the castes sum up the social experience and sagacity of long centuries of Hindu thinkers. Regarding the caste system, Mahatma Gandhi said, "It is a law of spiritual economics and has nothing to do with superiority and inferiority."

The hierarchy in the caste system as originally formulated was determined by the degree of voluntary renunciation and poverty, self-control, and intellectual and spiritual attainment. The higher the position of a man in the caste system, the greater is his obligation to the members of the lower castes. *Noblesse oblige.* It is obligations that are the crux of the caste system, and not rights. Whatever right a person demands must be derived from the fulfillment of his obligations. Through the caste system India indicated the supremacy of spirituality and intellect over military power, wealth, and labor. In time, everything becomes corrupt. People of upper castes enjoyed power for a long time and became selfish and greedy. They demanded rights and privileges without fulfilling their obligations. Caste laws became rigid and stratified. Contact with the West, which prizes equality, democracy, freedom, and social justice, has revealed to thoughtful Indians many drawbacks in their caste system. Since India's attainment of freedom, laws have been enacted removing caste inequities. But there is no room for the caste system in a secular and industrialized society, which is controlled primarily by the power of machines, wealth, and labor. If India gives up the principles of the caste system and denies the supremacy of intellect and spirituality, she will surely lose her spiritual backbone. The leaders of society in free and democratic India must be endowed with the spiritual qualities of self-abnegation, understanding, justice, and compassion. These new *brāhmaṇas* may be drawn from all sections of society.

Untouchability is a blot upon Hindu society. It was originally introduced to protect the spiritual culture of the Indo-Aryans from contamination by contact with primitive people, who were uncouth and of low mental development. It also served the purpose of saving the aborigines from annihilation. The social and spiritual standards of the Aryans were not imposed upon them by force. On the other hand, efforts were made to assimilate these people gradually through education. But during the dark days of Hindu society the process of assimilation stopped, and great injury was done to these unfortunate people. Now free India is making atonement for her past sins. Laws have been passed removing discriminatory treatment toward the untouchables.

Apart from the caste laws, a man's *dharma* is formulated according to his stage in life. Hinduism speaks of four stages with their respective ideals, all of which are legitimate. During the student stage a man must study in order to acquire knowledge, lead an austere life, conserve energy, and protect himself from defilement of body and mind. During the second stage he marries. Marriage is obligatory for all except those who suffer from a dangerous ailment which may be transmitted to children, and also for those who at an early age forsake the world at the call of God. It may be mentioned here also that, in certain important religious sects, for instance, the one founded by Rāmānuja, a man is not entitled to the monastic life unless he has passed through the stage of a householder. Children endow marriage with social obligations; and family life provides the householder with a training ground for the practice of unselfishness. During the third stage he retires into a forest or a solitary place to contemplate the deepest problems of existence. During the fourth stage, when a householder renounces the world and becomes a *sannyāsin* (monk), a well-disciplined life attains its fullest development. For him, the call of the infinite becomes irresistible. He rises above narrow responsibilities of family or society, and regards himself as a citizen of the world. He becomes a living demonstration of the reality of God and the ultimate unreality of material existence. He acts as a teacher and monitor of mankind. According to Hindu injunction, a man should give up individuality for the sake of the family, the family for the sake of the country, the country for the sake of the world, and everything for the liberation of the self.[96] Through the discipline of the four stages, a man learns progressive non-attachment. Today, for all practical purposes, one sees in Hindu society only the two stages of the householders and the monks. Unfortunately, in modern times many monks do not lead the life expected of them. They renounce the world in order to escape the hard realities of life and to find means of sustenance from credulous people who respect the holy garb of the *sannyāsin*. Genuine monks can come only out of the householders who lead ideal lives. At any time they are few and far between. A healthy society, in the Indian tradition, should have at the top a few genuine monks, devoted to the life of renunciation and service, who are living examples of non-attachment and serenity.

Affirmative Attitude Toward Life

The affirmative attitude of Hinduism toward life has also been emphasized by the four ideals or values which an intelligent and normal person should aspire to realize. First, *dharma*, or duty, which has already been discussed. This is the basis of society, where people must live together in harmony. Second, *artha*, or wealth, which is absolutely necessary in the present state of human evolution for preserving the physical body, promoting human welfare, and creating the leisure without which no culture can be built. Third, *kāma*, or the enjoyment of sense pleasures which cover a vast area, from the enjoyment of conjugal love to the appreciation of art, music, and literature. Life becomes drab and gray unless one cultivates aesthetic sensitivity. Both wealth and sense pleasures should be pursued according to *dharma;* otherwise, they will turn into greed and sensuality. The fourth ideal, equally forceful and legitimate, is the attainment of *mokṣa*, or spiritual freedom. How can a man enjoy peace, even though he performs his worldly duties, possesses wealth, and enjoys sense pleasures, if he is a slave of passion, anger, and greed?

In the *Kaṭha-upaniṣad*, when Naciketas is offered material pleasures to be enjoyed on earth or in heaven, he says: "These endure only till tomorrow. Furthermore, they exhaust the vigor of the sense-organs. Even the longest life is short indeed. Keep your horses, dances, and songs for yourself."[97] And in the *Bṛhadāraṇyaka-upaniṣad* Yājñavalkya teaches Maitreyī that one can never expect to attain immortality through wealth.[98] Even when all the desires for individual happiness and social welfare are fulfilled, still he wants to know how to suppress inner restlessness. Suffering is due to man's estrangement from the universal life. The individual is like a bone dislocated from its socket or a wheel separated from its axle. The result is constant friction accompanied by pain. The fourth ideal shows a man the way to liberation. But the three other ideals are not to be neglected. Their rightful fulfillment prepares the way for the realization of the fourth. Now we come to the disciplines of personal ethics, which have a direct bearing upon liberation.

Personal Ethics

The chief disciplines of personal ethics are austerity, control of the body and mind, non-attachment, chastity, reverence, forbearance, and concentration. Their main purpose is the purification of the individual's mind, and has no direct bearing upon social welfare. These disciplines are more or less common to all the major religions.

A few words may be said here as to why the Hindu philosophers emphasize personal ethics more than social ethics. First, if the individuals who constitute society are righteous, the welfare of society will be easy to achieve. Unfortunately, India has often overlooked the fact that a good society is also necessary to create good individuals. Second, the general moral tone in ancient Hindu society was high; everyone was expected to follow his own *dharma,* which asks him to help those who are in distress. The country was prosperous, and people were hospitable. Therefore, no special need was felt for organized charity. Third, the peculiar physical and cultural climate of India inclined Hindu minds more to an introspective than to an active life. Fourth, the Hindus regarded spiritual help as of more enduring value than physical help. A spiritual man can remain unruffled in pain and suffering, which are inevitable to a certain extent in our embodied existence. Finally, Indian thinkers have not accepted the modern idea of progress in the sense that evil and good are two completely different entities, of which one can be gradually eliminated and the other increased until in the end good alone will remain. The idea of progress applies to the individual and not to the world at large; it is the individual who attains liberation. The idea of world progress has been a rather recent development in the West, especially since the growth of science and technology. According to Hindu thinkers, "pain and pleasure constantly rotate like a wheel." The sum total of happiness and unhappiness remains constant. The cosmic process resembles the surface of the ocean, where every crest is followed by a trough. It may take many a century for the rise of the wave to reach the crest before it begins to fall. If a man takes a short-range view of existence and confines his view only to the rise, he may speak of some sort of progress, which idea also rests on faith and not on historical evidence. The Vedas speak of the *kalpa* (aeon or world-duration). Each *kalpa* contains its golden age (*satya*), silver age (*tretā*), bronze age (*dvāpara*), and iron age (*kali*). The world process is sustained by the rotation of the *kalpas.* We live in a changing world, but it need not be a progressive world. Every age, in spite of its many drawbacks and superstitions, has shown sincere seekers the way to the highest goal. Indian philosophers, without encouraging the illusion of a perfect society to be created by human effort and intelligence, have urged people to do good to others as a part of their spiritual discipline. That is the essence of *karma-yoga* (action as a spiritual discipline to purify the mind) as taught in the *Bhagavad-gītā.* Though neither good nor evil in the relative world is the ultimate truth, yet we come nearer to truth by doing good than by doing evil or remaining indifferent to both. The world is a moral gymnasium where through constant exercise we go beyond evil and finally beyond good also. Doing good to others has an instrumental but not an ultimate value.

Social ethics should be encouraged in modern India. Times have changed. The old concept of *dharma* has lost its hold upon the people.

Duty and Freedom

An ethical person works from a sense of duty which generally implies compulsion or necessity. Duty often creates unpleasantness and friction. When stretched too far it can become a disease. Furthermore, if a man wishes to attain perfection, which is inherent in the soul, he should not always look outside. But ethical duties can be performed through love. This love does not mean sentimentality, but springs, for the dualist, from the consciousness that all living beings are children of God, and, for the non-dualist, from the perception of the oneness of existence. Love greases the wheel of duty and makes it run without friction. Thus duty paves the way to freedom.

A non-dualist can look upon ethical practices from both ascetic, or negative, and affirmative standpoints. The negative discipline consists in suppressing the craving of the ego or the I-consciousness, which separates a man from others. This separation is responsible for attachment to friends or aversion for enemies and indifference to the rest. A man yields to selfishness, which must be suppressed for the realization of a higher life. There lies the efficacy of ascetic disciplines. On the other hand, the affirmative ethical discipline of the non-dualist is based upon the recognition of *Brahman* as the self in all. He must always remain aware of this oneness and show his awareness by his action and thought. He must cultivate a feeling of kindliness for all. Broadly speaking, the ascetic discipline shrinks the ego, and the affirmative expands it. The final result is the same: the destruction of the finite ego that feels attachment or aversion, or remains indifferent.

The enlightened person goes beyond ethical thought. No more does he consciously practice ethical disciplines. But by no means can he perform an unethical act. Ethical virtues adorn him like jewels. However, when an enlightened person acts as a teacher he practices ethical disciplines to set an example for his pupils. According to Indian thinkers, ethics is not an end in itself, but a means to attain a higher state beyond the strife and struggle of the relative world.

The Ultimate Goal of Life

What is the goal of life? It is the realization of freedom (*mokṣa*), also called perfection, enlightenment, or immortality. This is not a new acquisition, but the discovery of the true nature of the self, which was hidden by *māyā,* or cosmic ignorance. It is the highest state of understanding. The Vedic seers always sought this understanding. "May he awaken our understanding."[99] The enlightened man is free from doubt,[100] and always dwells in the self.[101] As he sees the Lord equally existent everywhere, he does not injure the self by the self and therefore attains the highest goal.[102] He gets rid of selfish desires.[103] It is not a case of escapism. He attains to reality, light, and immortality. The enlightened man enters into a new realm of consciousness; the chrysalis emerges as the butterfly. He is like the one who, having been blind, is now restored to eyesight; who, having been sick, is now made whole; who, having been asleep, is now awake. He has attained absolute existence, knowledge, and bliss (*saccidānanda*), and has realized in its fullness a man's desire to exist, to know, and to be happy.

How does an enlightened man live and act?[104] It is difficult for one who has not attained enlightenment to understand. But certainly he does not lead a life of quietism or inactivity. He devotes himself to the welfare of all.[105] Śaṁkara, the paragon of Indian nondualists, was active every moment of his life—writing commentaries on the scriptures, establishing monasteries, and instructing people about the supreme wisdom. An enlightened man lives, works, and dies under the spell of the soul's immortality, non-duality, and divinity. After transcending his human limitations, he embraces again the whole of humanity. He returns to the world and sees it as the manifestation of *Brahman.* "With every state of mind he experiences *samādhi* [communion with *Brahman*]."[106]

The enlightened man, as long as he dwells in the body, cherishes desires to promote human welfare. He exhorts the worldly minded to perform their social duties. In cases of emergency, he himself undertakes those duties. Śaṁkara, by his strong support of the caste system and the four stages of life (*varṇāśrama-dharma*) encourages social duties. In modern India many *sannyāsins* engage themselves in various kinds of humanitarian activities. Śaṁkara said somewhere that a man should first realize that he is *Brahman* and then regard all as the manifestation of the same *Brahman.*

Outwardly active or inactive, an enlightened person constantly seeks and works for the welfare of humanity:

> May I be able to look upon all beings with the eye of a friend. May we look upon one another with the eye of a friend.[107]
>
> May the world be peaceful. May the wicked become gentle. May all creatures think of their mutual welfare. May their minds be engaged in what is auspicious. And may our hearts be immersed in selfless love of the Lord.[108]
>
> O Lord, I do not want any kingdom, nor heavenly pleasure, nor even escape from rebirth. But I do desire that the affliction of all beings tormented by the miseries of life may cease forever.
>
> May all be freed from danger. May all realize what is good. May all be animated by noble thoughts. May all rejoice everywhere.
>
> May all be happy. May all be free from disease. May all realize what is good. May none be subject to misery.
>
> O glorious Lord, urge even a miser to charity, and soften the heart of the niggard.[109]

In the short space of this paper I have tried to show that the religious and philosophical thought of India, from the earliest times, has harmonized realism with idealism. It is not otherworldly or antisocial in the usual sense of these words. Indian thinkers have come to grips with reality, the meaning of which changes at different levels of the evolution of the soul. They have reflected upon man's real problems of life from his first wandering into the realm of phenomena to his final liberation. Their teaching seems to be: first idealize the real, then realize the ideal.

Notes

1. The word "Indian" in this paper is generally used to signify "Hindu" because, despite the fact that during the past thousand years non-Hindu elements also entered into the thought-current of India, Indian culture has been largely created and influenced by Hindu philosophical and religious concepts.
2. In the Hindu tradition there has been no sharp division between religion and philosophy. The former is the emotional and practical approach to reality, the latter is the intellectual. Both intellect and emotion, reason and faith, play important parts in the attainment of the knowledge of reality.
3. *Bhagavad-gītā,* XVIII.78.
4. *Ibid., Śaṁkarācārya's* introduction to his Commentary.
5. *Kaṭha-upaniṣad,* I.ii.2.
6. *Bhagavad-gītā,* III.4.
7. *Ibid.,* VII.3.
8. *Ibid.,* II.46; VI.44.
9. *Kaṭha-upaniṣad,* I.i.10–11.
10. *Ibid.,* I.ii.3.
11. R. Shamasastry, trans., *Kauṭilya's Arthaśāstra* (Mysore: Wesleyan Mission Press, 1909), p. 307.
12. *Bhagavad-gītā,* III.14–15.
13. *Ibid.,* III.16.
14. *Ibid.,* III.13.
15. *Manu-saṁhitā (Manu-smṛti),* VI.35.
16. Sarvepalli Radhakrishnan and Charles A. Moore, eds., *A Source Book in Indian Philosophy* (Princeton: Princeton University Press, 1957), pp. 5 ff.
17. *Ibid.,* pp. 25 ff.
18. *Muṇḍaka-upaniṣad,* I.ii.1.
19. *Īśa-upaniṣad,* II.
20. *Ṛg-veda,* X.lxxxv.36.
21. *Ibid.,* X.lxxxv.42.
22. *Atharva-veda,* XIV.ii.71.
23. *Ibid.,* XIV.ii.14.
24. *Ṛg-veda,* X.cvii.10.
25. *Ibid.,* X.cxvii.5.
26. *Atharva-veda,* IX.vi.31–38.
27. *Ṛg-veda,* X.cxci.2–4.
28. *Atharva-veda,* XIX.lxvii.
29. *Ibid.,* II.xvii.
30. *Ibid.,* XIX.lx.
31. *Yajur-veda,* III.41–43.

32. *Ibid.*, II.27. (The phrase "one-ox cart" refers to a situation created by disagreement between husband and wife.)
33. *Ibid.*, XXII.22; see also *Ṛg-veda*, I.xcvi.8; II.xxi.6; III.xvi.5; IX.xcvii.50.
34 *Atharva-veda*, IV.xxii.3.
35. *Ṛg-veda*, X.ciii.11.
36. *Yajur-veda*, XVII.44.
37. *Atharva-veda*, XIX.xiv.
38. *Ṛg-veda*, II.xxiii.12.
39. *Ibid.*, I.clxiv.46; VI.xlvii.18; X.cxxxii.3; *Atharva-veda*, XIII.iv.14–21; XIII.iv.22–24.
40. *Atharva-veda*, XI.v.1; XI.v.10; XI.v.17.
41. *Ṛg-veda*, I.lxxxix.8; *Yajur-veda*, XXXIV.iv.6.
42. *Ṛg-veda*, I.clxiv.37; *Atharva-veda*, X.ii.28–30; *Yajur-veda*, XL.6.
43. *Chāndogya Upaniṣad*, VI.vii.7.
44. *Kaṭha-upaniṣad*, I.i.8.
45. *Ibid.*, I.i.10–13.
46. *Bṛhadāraṇyaka-upaniṣad*, V.ii.1–3.
47. *Chāndogya Upaniṣad*, V.xi.5.
48. *Taittirīya-upaniṣad*, I.xi.1–4.
49. *Bṛhadāraṇyaka-upaniṣad*, VI.iv.l ff.
50. *Taittirīya-upaniṣad*, I.iv.2–3.
51. Sarvepalli Radhakrishnan and Charles A. Moore, *op. cit.*, p. 99.
52. *Bhagavad-gītā*, II.2–3.
53. *Ibid.*, III.20.
54. *Ibid.*, III.21–24.
55. *Ibid.*, XI.
56. *Ibid.*, IV.2.
57. *Ibid.*, XVIII.78.
58. All the information regarding the *Mahābhārata*, the *Rāmāyaṇa*, the *Code of Manu*, and Kauṭilya's *Artha-śāstra* is based on *A Source Book in Indian Philosophy*. The quotations from these works are also taken from that book.
59. *Mahābhārata*, Śānti-parva, 329.13.
60. *Ibid.*, Śānti-parva, 58.14–15.
61. *Ibid.*, Śānti-parva, 321.46–52.
62. *Ibid.*, Śānti-parva, 177.26–28.
63. Swami Vivekananda, *Karma-Yoga* (New York: Ramakrishna-Vivekananda Center, 1955), pp. 20 ff.
64. Swami Nikhilananda, ed., *The Complete Works of Swami Vivekananda*, Vol. II (Mayavati Memorial ed.; Mayavati: Prabuddha Bharata Office, 1919), p. 311.
65. *Ibid.*, Vol. V, p. 45.
66. *Ibid.*, Vol. V, p. 157.

67. S. Radhakrishnan, *Indian Philosophy,* Vol. I (London: George Allen & Unwin Ltd., 1923), pp. 29–30.
68. *Chāndogya Upaniṣad,* VII.i.2; see also *Muṇḍaka-upaniṣad,* I.i.5.
69. *Chāndogya Upaniṣad,* VII.i.3.
70. Śaṁkarācārya is usually called Śaṁkara.
71. Commentary on *Bṛhadāraṇyaka-upaniṣad,* IV.iii.7.
72. *Taittirīya-upaniṣad,* II.i.1; II.v.1; III.vi.1.
73. *Kaṭha-upaniṣad,* II.i.11.
74. *Chāndogya-upaniṣad,* III.xiv.1.
75. *Muṇḍaka Upaniṣad,* I.ii.7.
76. *Bhagavad-gītā,* IX.21.
77. *Muṇḍaka-upaniṣad,* I.ii.12–13.
78. Swami Nikhilananda, *Hinduism: Its Meaning for the Liberation of the Spirit* (New York: Harper & Brothers, 1958), pp. 94 ff.
79. *Bhagavad-gītā,* IV.18.
80. *Ibid.,* II.47.
81. Swami Nikhilananda, *Hinduism: Its Meaning for the Liberation of the Spirit,* pp. 105 ff.
82. *Bhagavad-gītā,* XVIII.55.
83. Swami Nikhilananda, *Hinduism: Its Meaning for the Liberation of the Spirit,* pp. 130 ff.
84. Patañjali, *Yoga-sūtra,* I.33.
85. *Bṛhadāraṇyaka-upaniṣad,* IV.iv.7.
86. *Ibid.,* IV.iv.22.
87. *Ibid.,* I.iv.8.
88. *Muṇḍaka-upaniṣad,* III.ii.4.
89. Swami Nikhilananda, *The Upanishads,* Vol. II (New York: Harper & Brothers, 1952), pp. 1 ff.
90. *Bhagavad-gītā,* XVIII.42.
91. *Ibid.,* XVIII.43.
92. Śaṁkarācārya's Commentary on *Bhagavad-gītā,* IV.1; *Bhagavad-gītā,* XVIII.78.
93. *Bhagavad-gītā,* XVIII.44.
94. *Ibid.,* XVIII.44.
95. *Ibid.,* IV.13.
96. *Mahābhārata,* Ādi-parva, 115.38–39.
97. *Kaṭha-upaniṣad,* I.i.26.
98. *Bṛhadāraṇyaka-upaniṣad,* II.iv.1–3.
99. *Ibid.,* VI.iii.6.
100. *Muṇḍaka-upaniṣad,* II.ii.8.
101. *Bhagavad-gītā,* XV.5–6.
102. *Ibid.,* XIII.28.
103. *Kaṭha-upaniṣad,* II.iii.14.
104. *Bhagavad-gītā,* II.54–72.

105. *Ibid.*, XII.3–4.
106. *Ibid.*, II.70.
107. *Yajur-veda-saṁhitā,* XXXVI.18.
108. *Bhāgavata,* V.xviii.9.
109. *Ṛg-veda,* VI.liii.3.

C. P. RAMASWAMI AIYAR

The Philosophical Basis of Indian Legal and Social Systems

Early Theories

IN THE EXAMINATION of the philosophical basis of the legal and political systems of various major cultures, it is inevitable that the right apperception of Indian ideals should be of fundamental importance. A study of the sources of Indian philosophical theories as applied to politics and the law may therefore be of some assistance, not only to the student and philosopher, but also to the man of affairs who is grappling with the crucial problems of the present-day world. I have essayed to take a bird's-eye view of such theories and to furnish an *aperçu* of the Indian doctrines relating to political and social evolution.

It is very true, in the words of the poet, that each age is a dream that is dying or one that is coming to birth. Is it not also manifest that the ideas and ideals of each country as they progress from age to age have and indeed ought to have something indigenous in them, and that in politics and philosophy, as well as in literature and the arts, nothing that is not evolved from within and is not in harmony with inherited as well as individual traditions will be characteristic or essentially fit to live? Today we are producing and putting to practical use new constitutions. New thoughts are thundering at our doors and while we shall do well, as throughout our history, ever to be tolerant and hospitable to fresh views, nevertheless, we must also be alive to the need for assimilating them with our own culture and we may imitate the wise gardener when, for improving the yield, he skillfully inserts a graft. A great French critic, Henri Taine, declared: *"Quand on veut comprendre un art, il faut regarder l'âme du public auquel il s'adressait."* Although this was said of art, it is equally true of a nation's philosophy and politics that they are outward expressions of national culture and sentiment and that they use the symbols best understood in the country of origin. They bespeak an acquaintance with national life and thought. Our political ideas are a function of our intellectual and civic life, and it may not be out of place to remember that during many millenniums we have had a succession of thinkers who, like the medieval Churchmen in Europe, were founders and partakers of what may accurately be called a university tradition and an educational system which in India as in Europe until recent times was based on, and culminated in, religious training but included also in its scope an attempt at universal research born of catholic sympathies and curiosity.

It has been our good fortune to be brought into touch with the currents of Western thought and speculation, and Indians have been under their influence for nearly a century in our universities. Owing to our natural anxiety to utilize the new opportunities which have come to us, we have perhaps overlooked, if we have not disdained, our past traditions and history. There is a great danger of our not securing the full benefit of the newer culture for lack of proper assimilation. Should it not be our aim to build, on the foundations of our own accumulated lore and inherited stock of capacities and temperament, a stately and enduring structure with the full aid of Western learning and science and thus to develop our own soul? Especially is this process called for in the study and practice of politics, an art and a science more intimately connected with national aptitudes and national outlook than almost any other. What is in the bone cannot be eliminated and, as pointed out recently by a discerning thinker, the author of *The Dangerous Sea,* one realizes with a shock the cyclic character of life and of ideas. The French proverb *"Plus ça change plus c'est la même chose"* ("The more it changes, the more essentially it remains the same") is not a mere piece of blasé cynicism. The whole history of the French Revolution, its rise and fall, and the dictatorship which followed it, as the author of *The Dangerous Sea* indicates, constitute really a transplanted chapter of Roman history. The Fascists, the Spartacists, and the Nazi revolution of our own times have also had their prototypes in the past. The curious student may also discover analogies between certain developments of communism at the present moment and similar phenomena which were observed by the compilers of the Purāṇas, not to mention incidents in the history of the later Roman Empire and the Middle Ages. It was in these so-called dark ages that there arose the idea of a league of nations fulfilling the functions which were part of the program of the Holy Roman Empire and which were elaborated by medieval theorists, both regal and private, who strove to bring about an effective policing of the nations.

No nation building its future political or social habitation can afford to ignore its past racial culture or the lessons of its history. My endeavor, therefore, has been to try to find out how far in the various departments of political and socio-economic theory we can get guidance from our own heritage of speculation and action. I was stimulated to perform this task after I read the scholarly analysis of the social and political life in the Vijayanagara empire (1336–1565), which we owe to the research of Dr. B. A. Saletore, and, later, it became necessary for me to deal with one aspect of the subject in its practical application when I was endeavoring, as head of the administration of His Highness the Mahārāja of Travancore and for reasons connected with the formulation and carrying out of His Highness' historic Temple Entry Proclamation, to discover the sources and methods of legislation in the old days. I then saw that the monarch who, in *The Code of Manu,* is described as embodying in himself the four ages was understood by the medieval philosopher Śukra to be the maker of the age, so that if customs, usages, and movements are not assimilated to the needs of the times the fault is said to lie with the king himself. Sukra avers that "the king is the maker of the age as the promulgator of duties and sins. He is the cause of the setting on foot of the customs and usages and hence is the cause or maker of the times." The same principle of politics and social legislation was enunciated by Bhīṣma in the Śānti-parva thus: "Whether it is the king that makes the age or the age that makes the king is a question about which you should not entertain any doubt. The truth is that the king makes the age." As Dr. Saletore aptly observes in the book to which I have already alluded, national regeneration was regarded by the great kings of the Vijayanagara dynasty as achievable only when the ruler created the proper environment, both political and cultural. It is evident that other rulers, of whom there are records in our sacred and secular literature and from whose achievements we can construct a fairly coherent political philosophy, have adopted the same view—a view which may be made suitable to modern times and conditions.

Beginning with the times prior to recorded history, we find as an indisputable fact that the evolution of what are termed *Kēraḷa-ācāras* is a conclusive proof of the flexibility of ancient lawgivers and pristine laws. It is incontestable that there are laws, customs, and observances prevalent among the Nambudris on the west coast of India which are not followed by the *brāhmaṇas* of other parts of India and which furnish clear evidence that the Hindu *ācāras*, or laws, have been modified to suit special or local conditions. The form of marriage known as *sarva-sva-dānam*, which is not recognized by the widespread code of the *Mitākṣara* (commentary on the *Yājñavalkya-smṛti*), the adoption of a son in the *dvāmuṣyāyana* form as the son of two fathers (the natural and the adopted), the difference in the custom regarding the marriage of girls, the absence of any rigid insistence on the early marriage of women under penalty of forfeiture of caste—obviously a later innovation in Hindu law forced on the people on account of foreign invasions and the insecurity of the times—the possibility of a woman's remaining unmarried to the end of her days, the modification of the rule that every male should marry within his own caste in order to lead a *gṛhastha* (householder) life, the importance given in worship and ritual to Tantras as distinguished from the Mantras—all these and many other differences in social usages, etiquette, and practices relating to daily life, which taken together distinguish the *ācāras* of Paraśurāma's country, indicate that there was no crystallization of social or even religious law and practice and that there was abundant scope for changes to meet altered situations and conditions. This policy was not confined to prehistoric ages, but was followed even later, as was triumphantly demonstrated by what is historically known regarding Rāmānuja's teaching and that of the Teṅkalai saints, who brought about the adoption of Tamil as a concurrent sacred language with Sanskrit, their remodeling of the society of their days by virtue of a process of religious fusion and the consequent and inevitable unification of sects and communities.

The basic idea of *dharma* underlay alike the ethical, social, and political ideas of Indian lawgivers. Wherever there was doubt or controversy, the practice of right-minded Aryans was the touchstone and determining factor. In the "Śikṣā Vallī" of the *Taittirīya-upaniṣad* (11th Anuvāka) occurs the well-known passage: "Those *brāhmaṇas* in thy neighborhood who are of sober judgment, who are meek and set upon the performance of their duties, as they act in any matter, so also do thou act therein."

As a logical result, it was ordained that, the higher the station or caste, the more serious the offense when a moral law is broken. Manu[1] says that a king should be fined a thousand times as much as a common man for the same offense. The *Mahābhārata*[2] lays down that the greater the men, the weightier should be their punishment.

It must be admitted, however, that the later developments and the hardening of the caste system led to conditions and regulations analogous to those present in other countries where a small racial or religious aristocracy is surrounded by a large number of so-called inferior races.

The pristine lawgivers began, as in the case of the Egyptians and the Hebrews, to consolidate and compile lists of domestic and social observances and rules; their task gradually expanded; more general rules were enacted; and lawbooks came into existence.

The source of legal power was the king, and, as will be pointed out later, he was regarded as embodying the wish of the people, by whom, according to many Hindu sources, he was originally elected "to avoid confusion and anarchy." The law and order to be maintained constituted the *dharma,* or right order, of the world, which was generally equated with ancient divine rules and age-long usages (*prayoga*). Such usage was held to stand next to the Vedic texts in authority.[3] The real lawgiver or law-creator was thus not the king but right usage, of which the enforcement was vested in the king.

The elimination of conflict and strife and the avoidance of interference with a man's right to happiness and peace undisturbed by a neighbor's violence were the objectives of this polity. It is noticeable that there has always existed in India, side by side with the elaboration of ritual and propitiatory ceremonies, the realization that *dharma* transcends sacred or ritual observances. "He who has performed all the sacred observances and has not the following qualities comes not to a union with Brahmā. These qualities are compassion, patience, freedom from turmoil and avarice and envy, purity, active endeavor, and thought."[4]

Righteousness (*dharma*), which has to be promulgated and enforced by the king, implies and connotes a comprehensive code of behavior and attitude necessary to maintain peace and order.

The importance of "natural law" and of conscience is recognized by way of guidance in matters of doubt where the Vedas, usage and custom, and divine commands do not furnish any help.

Hindu thinkers proceeded by a logical method and also relied upon traditions and past history in their investigation of the essentials of a state. Their theories regarding the evolution of the state from the non-state are most instructive, the explanation being found by them in the doctrine of what is called *matsya-nyāya* (the doctrine of the fish). Hooker in his *Ecclesiastical Polity* and the *Leviathan* of Hobbes were anticipated by Indian philosophers who declared that the state of Nature is a state of war and the right of might. It is seen that the same theory or doctrine also flourished in China. The *Mahābhārata*, in the Śānti-parva,[5] declares that, if there were no rule to regulate life and to punish the guilty, the strong would devour the weak, like fishes in water. This theory of the state of Nature had an important bearing on the doctrine of Indian political philosophy. This doctrine of the fish was also termed in later literature the logic of *sundopa-sunda* (two destructive demons). This state is further described in the *Mahābhārata* as the greatest of evils, and the following description may be noted: "The one is deprived of his loot by two and the two are robbed of theirs by several combined."

The doctrine of *daṇḍa* (law) and its sanction arose out of a contemplation of this *matsya-nyāya* (the doctrine of the fish, or of Nature) and the means to overcome its results. The philosophical theory of the state which evolved was that its exists because it can restrain and compel. If control be eliminated from organized social life, *samūha* (the state as an entity) vanishes.

The doctrine of *dharma* and the doctrine of property (*mamatva*) are then envisaged as essential factors in the theory of the state. Manu makes it clear[6] that *dharma* is created by the state and the sanction of the state. A people can have no *dharma*, according to Indian philosophy, when, through loss of freedom, revolution, or anarchy, the state and its life come to an end. *Dharma* is a very elastic term; it comprises all the attributes of law as analyzed by Western jurists as well as the concept of natural justice as perceived by a regulated conscience. *Dharma* is obeyed as such because of the coercive might of the state, and the Dharma-śāstras of India (the legal textbooks), such as those of Manu, Yājñavalkya, Nārada, Bṛhaspati, and others, acquire the validity of statutes on the recognition of their authenticity and authority by the state.

In Europe, law has sometimes been regarded as the embodiment of eternal justice, as part of the natural heritage of man, and as embodying natural reason. Another school of thought is that law is that which is brought into existence by the fiat of a lawmaker—in other words, that law is obeyed, not merely because it is just or good, but because it has been laid down by the state. In this way arises the distinction between positive law and ethics. The ethical conception of law was the first to be expounded by Indian lawgivers and philosophers. In the *Bṛhadāraṇyaka-upaniṣad,*[7] law is equated with truth, and Brahmā, in order to enforce his strength, is said to have created law "than which nothing is higher." It declares, "Therefore even a weak man rules the stronger with the help of the law." In the Āpastamba *Dharma-sūtra,*[8] law is what is approved in all countries by men of the Aryan society. In the *Manu-saṁhitā,*[9] law is defined as what is practiced and cherished by the virtuous and the learned. Vasiṣṭha[10] holds that law is the practice of the Śiṣṭas, that is, disciplined persons. The well-known definition of Yājñavalkya contained in the opening verse is that law is the practice and conduct of good men (*sadācāra*). Later on, theories were supplemented by the concept of positive law, and there is a long catena of Indian lawgivers, including Nārada, Śukra, and Jaimini, who hold that, the performance of duty for its own sake having fallen into disuse in the course of human history, positive law (*vyavahāra*) was introduced and the king became the superintendent of the law, the wielder of the power to punish (*daṇḍadhara*). Kauṭilya lays down that *dharma*, or law, is *rājñām ājñā*—the command of the ruler. Having laid this down, Śukra insists that on this account the greatest amount of publicity should be given to the laws by the king, who should have them inscribed in all public places, bearing the king's signature and date.[11] This interpretation gives rise to the theory adumbrated in the *Śukra-nīti*[12] that the king is the maker of the age and the promulgator of the principles of virtue and vice. The philosophical basis of this concept of law is also illustrated by Jaimini in his definition of *dharma*, which says, "*Dharma* brings about its object as the result of command."

It cannot be forgotten that, side by side with these definitions of *dharma* and the emphasis laid on the coercive powers of rulers and kings, there came into existence definitely radical ideas about the authority of the people and the logic of resistance. Śukra[13] states that the ruler is a servant of the people, getting his revenue as remuneration. His sovereignty is conferred only for the protection of the people. Bodhāyana[14] proceeds so far as to declare that the king, like every other public servant, is liable to fines for violation of the law. In fact, it may be rightly claimed that arbitrary monarchy has no place in Indian philosophical thought. It is, in fact, laid down that the monarch who follows his own will soon gets estranged from his kingdom and alienated from his subjects.[15]

It follows from this doctrine that Hindu political philosophers have not ignored the possibility of active resistance to tyranny or misrule. The *Mahābhārata*[16] says that the king who is not a protector and leader can be destroyed by the people, and the *Śukra-nīti-sāra*[17] emphasizes that, if the king is an enemy of virtue, morality, and strength, the people should expel him as the cause of disaster for the state.

Whether as a result of such revolutions or otherwise, republics have been known to exist in India from very early times and are mentioned not only in Buddhist and Jaina records but also by Greek and Roman writers. The *Aitareya-brāhmaṇa*[18] states as a fact that among the Uttara Kurus the whole community exercised rulership. In the Śānti-parva of the *Mahābhārata,*[19] there is a description of a state in which the rule of equality is observed among all people. The men in charge of the executive government of such republics were, however, called *rājās,* or kings. During and soon after the lifetime of the Buddha, the Śākyas and the Videhas were numbered among the republics, the Videhas being originally monarchical and later having abolished the monarchical system and joined the Vaiśālis to form a confederacy. It is stated that the business of the Vajjian republic was carried out in a common hall by representatives of the people. The Buddha, in fact, in more than one of his dialogues refers to such a political development. In the *Mahā-nibbāna-suttanta,* the Buddha is reported to have stated, "So long as the Vajjian clans meet often for discussion, so long may they be expected not to decline but to prosper," and when the king of Magadha sought to destroy the republican state, the Buddha declared that the Vajjians should not be allowed to be overcome by the king of Magadha.

These types of government as well as the *sabhā* (council) form of administration seem to have existed side by side for a long time, and the council system grew out of the village and tribal organizations (the so-called village communities), but it seems gradually to have disappeared in India before the Mauryan Empire (326–185 B.C.) assumed its predominant character. But, all through the pre-British history of India, rural communities existed as more or less self-sufficing units of local government, neighboring villages having also united to build halls of assembly and construct rest-houses, reservoirs, and irrigation works. Metcalfe's report on the "rural communes" of India is worth quoting in this connection: "They seem to last where nothing else lasts. Dynasty after dynasty tumbles down. Revolution succeeds revolution, but the village communities remain the same."[20] No one who ignores this basic ideal of Hindu life can build securely for the future.

The political evolution of the India of the *Ṛg-veda*, according to Radha Kumud Mookerji, may be traced in the following ascending series of groups, viz., the family (*kula*), the village (*grāma*), the clan (*viś*), the people (*jana*), and the country (*rāṣṭra*).[21] A family was composed of several members living under a common head. An aggregate of several families made up a village. The *viś* was a larger formation, implying settlement, while "*jana*" was an even more comprehensive term, embracing as it did the entire population occupying a particular area which subsequently converted it into a *rāṣṭra*. Society in those days had to keep itself in constant readiness for combat, not only to quell external aggression but also internal dissension, and the origin of the *rājanya* (*kṣatriya*) class has to be traced to this circumstance. The invocation of the blessings of unseen powers through an adept agency became a necessary incident of that arrangement, and this gave rise to the *brāhmaṇas* as a distinct class. The bulk of the Aryan community not included in either of these categories was known as the *viś* or *vaiśyas*, while the exigencies of conquest led to the absorption into the Aryan fold of numerous non-Aryans who eventually became *śūdras* (laborers).

Later Theories

The *Mahābhārata* narrates the following story on the origin of kingship: In ancient days men were ruined in consequence of the prevalence of anarchy. They devoured one another as stronger fish devour the weaker ones. A few men then assembled and agreed among thmselves that the babbler, the cruel, the voluptuous, and the greedy among them should be renounced. That arrangement worked for some time. But then, seeing that it was no longer satisfactory, they approached Brahmā with a prayer to grant them a king. Brahmā thereupon induced Manu to take up the kingship. The people agreed to pay certain taxes and prayed that in return the king should destroy their enemies to enable them to lead peaceful lives.[22] Bhīṣma, who relates this incident to Yudhiṣṭhira, gives a slightly different version of the same story in a previous chapter. He says that in the *kṛta-yuga* (golden age) there were no sovereignty, no king, no punishment, and no punisher, and that all men protected one another, actuated by a sense of righteousness. They soon found, however, that this work was too much for them and they gradually became a prey to confusion (*moha*), greed (*lobha*), desire (*kāma*), and lust (*rāga*). When such confusion set in and righteousness perished, men sought the help of Brahmā, who thereupon composed a stupendous treatise on the *puruṣārthas* (the right objectives of man's existence), of which the works of Bṛhaspati, Śukra, etc., were but abridgments. The Devas then prayed for a king to rule over men and Viṣṇu created Virajas. Virajas, however, did not relish the kingship conferred on him, and Anaṅga, his great-grandson, became the first king of Bhāratavarṣa.[23] Both these stories show, as does the passage cited from the *Aitareya-brāhmaṇa,* that the Aryans had no ruler in the olden days and that kingship with them was regarded as a comparatively late institution. There are certain passages in the Vedas pointing to the king's divine origin, and this had become an accepted belief by the time Manu's *Dharma-śāstra* (*Manu-smṛti*) was composed. Manu states that when men were without a king and dispersed through fear in all directions the Lord created a king for the protection of all of them and that the essence of the *dikpālas* (protectors of the corners) was used for his creation.[24]

There is, however, no doubt that this was in reality a merely metaphorical description of the paramountcy of the monarch designed to enforce obedience from the subject. In a striking passage Kauṭilya says that the vulgar opponents of a king may be silenced by the argument that the duties of Indra (the rewarder) and Yama (the punisher) are blended in him and that whoever disregards him will be visited with divine punishment.[25]

The Buddhist *Dīgha-nikāya* also says that mankind was righteous at the beginning and that, as sinfulness gradually crept into human society, men selected one who was the most handsome, gracious, and powerful among them and made him king. He was called *mahā-sammata* (great knowledge) because he was selected by the great.

Śukra, who also propounds the theory of the divine origin of kings, is careful to explain at the same time that they resemble Indra and other gods only in the performance of certain functions.[26]

Although the early rulers were elected, kingship in course of time became hereditary. Ordinarily, the crown descended from father to the eldest son; but, if that son was a minor, if a younger son had to be preferred to an elder, if an heir-apparent had to be ordained, or if an interregnum had to be avoided by the appointment of a temporary ruler, the express consent of the people was imperative. The same was the case in the event of a king's desire to abdicate.

There were several ways in which the king's possible leaning toward the exercise of unbridled authority was kept in check. In the first place, the right to oust an unrighteous king was emphasized, although seldom exercised in practice, in India. In the Anuśāsana-parva of the *Mahābhārata,* it is stated that a king who tells his people he is their protector, but who does not, or is unable to, protect them, should be killed by his subjects like a rabid dog.[27] In the Śānti-parva we come across a passage to the effect that a king who follows the advice of bad ministers and becomes a destroyer of righteousness deserves to be killed by his subjects with all his dependents.[28] The appellation *Naradeva,* a god among men, is applied only to virtuous kings. Śukra, in his *Nīti-sāra,* stated that, while a virtuous king is a part of the gods, a vicious king is a part of the devils.[29] Manu says that a king who does not afford protection but receives his tax will soon sink into hell and that he takes upon himself all the foulness of all his people.[30]

The most common name used for a king in Sanskrit is *rājan.* The *Mahābhārata* says that, seeing Pṛthu, his subjects exclaimed, "We love him," and on account of their loving attachment he was called *rājan.*[31] Kālidāsa expresses the same idea in the *Raghuvaṁśa* when he states that Raghu's appellation of *rājan* became possessed of meaning when he made himself lovable to his subjects.[32] If a king without doing violence to the dictates of righteousness does what is good for all his subjects he stands as firm as a rock,[33] and everybody thinks of him: "He is mine." Manu says that he should behave toward his subjects as a father treats his children.[34] Kālidāsa expands this idea in the *Raghuvaṁśa* when he says that Dilīpa was the real father of his people because he led them along the path of righteousness, protecting and feeding them. It is also stated in the *Mahābhārata* that he is the best of kings in whose realm every subject moves fearlessly as a son in the house of his father.[35] From the constant comparison instituted between the king and a father in ancient works, some scholars have come to the hasty and unwarranted conclusion that his position was that of a benevolent despot. This is by no means correct. The actual conception was that the king should live for his subjects and not for himself. It is stated in the *Mārkaṇḍeya-*

purāṇa that the prince was entitled to enjoy himself only up to the moment when the sacred *abhiṣeka* (bath) water fell on his head.[36] How the king should conduct himself thereafter is well explained in the *Mahābhārata* by the observation that, just as a mother who, not even caring for the objects which she likes best, seeks the well-being of her child alone, so the king should sacrifice what he loves best to secure the well-being of his subjects.[37] The same idea is repeated in the *Agni-purāṇa*.[38] In the *Mahābhārata* it is stated that everywhere all the people from *brāhmaṇas* to peasants were more attached to King Yudhiṣṭhira than to their own parents.[39] Kauṭilya says, "In the happiness of his subjects lies the king's happiness, in their welfare his welfare; whatever pleases himself he shall not consider as good, but whatever pleases his subjects he shall consider as good."[40] Kauṭilya also says, "The religious vow of a king is his readiness for action; the discharge of his duties is the performance of his sacrifice; and equal treatment of all is his offer of fee and ablution at consecration."[41] Somadeva also points out that the sacrifice to be performed by a king is the protection of his subjects and not the killing of animals (which is incidental to ordinary sacrifices).[42]

"*Paripālanam,*" all-round protection, is an expression embracing a very wide meaning. It is not merely the preservation of law and order. It is the administration of the state in such a degree of perfection as to enable the king and every one of his subjects to pursue undisturbed the paths of *dharma*, *artha* (wealth), and *kāma* (desire). The king himself is to be the exemplar of his subjects, since whatever *dharma* is respected by him will be respected everywhere and since the subjects will generally like to move only along the path trod by him.[43] Righteousness should therefore be first practiced by him before he enforces it on his subjects. The king, according to the *Mahābhārata*, was created in order that righteousness might emanate from him and that, if he were devoid of it, he should be called a *vṛṣala*.[44] One becomes a king to advance the cause of *dharma* and not to act capriciously. All creatures depend on *dharma*, and *dharma* depends on the king. He is therefore the true king who maintains *dharma*.[45] The question "What is *dharma*?" has been clearly answered in Chapter 109 of the Śānti-parva. *Dharma* is what is conducive to the advancement of everybody, what prevents injury to everybody, and what is capable of upholding everybody. It need not be precisely what is stated in the Vedas, because everything has not been ordained in them.

In order that the subjects might carry on their occupations peacefully and earn a sufficient competence for pursuing the other two *puruṣārthas* included in the *tri-varga,* (morality, pleasure, and material welfare), it was imperative that the tax imposed on them should not be heavy. In the *Mahābhārata* it is observed: "A king should milk his kingdom like a bee collecting honey from trees. He should act like the cowherd, who takes milk from a cow without injuring her udder and without starving the calf. He should, like the leech, take blood mildly. He should treat his subjects like a tigress carrying her cubs, touching them with her teeth but never biting them. He should behave like a mouse, which, although it has sharp and pointed teeth, nibbles at the feet of sleeping animals in such a manner as to keep them unaware of it."[46]

The protection of subjects necessarily involves, as a correlative, the punishment of the wicked. A king should be neither too lenient nor too severe, but should administer such punishment as may be deemed fit and proper. Kauṭilya says, "Whosoever imposes severe punishment becomes repulsive to the people, while he who imposes mild punishment becomes contemptible. But whoever imposes punishment as deserved will be respected."[47] In the *Mahābhārata* it is stated: "Although the most impregnable fortress of a king is the love of his subjects and it is therefore essential that he should be merciful, if he is always forgiving, the lowest of men may guide him as a mahout guides an elephant. Nor should he be ferocious. He should be like the vernal sun, neither too hot nor too cold."[48]

The activities of the state covered a very wide range. As observed by Dr. Beni Prasad:

> While there was much which had been fashioned by other associations and on which the State could only set its *imprimatur,* the seal of its force, there was much else which it essayed to perform by means of its own resources. From time to time it elected to propagate *dharma,* to inculcate and enforce morality, to maintain or improve the social order, to encourage learning, education, and art, to subsidise various academies, to regulate industry and commerce, to foster agriculture, to relieve the distress from famine and other calamities, to establish hospitals, rest-houses, charity halls, etc. All this it essayed to do in addition to its primary functions of defence, order and justice.[49]

The seven constituent elements of the state were the king, the ministers, allies, treasure, territory, fortress, and army. The ministers formed an important and indispensable part of this constitution. The *Mahābhārata* says that it is impossible for a king to look after all his duties and that hence he should devolve his duties on his ministers.[50] Kauṭilya also points out: "Sovereignty is possible only with assistance. A single wheel can never move. Hence a king should employ ministers and hear their opinion."[51]

Even in Vedic days, there were gradations among the kings, importing some kind of paramountcy, or a feudal integration. This feudalism was more or less of the federal type. The "*maṇḍala*" was a circle of states, generally twelve in number, some of which did not have full sovereign powers. In this connection, some observations made by Dr. Beni Prasad as a result of his close study of ancient Hindu states are worthy of quotation. He says: "The State in ancient India was not unitary in the strict sense of the term. It was saturated through and through with the principles of what for convenience may be called federalism and feudalism. . . . They are only meant to imply that as a general rule a Hindu kingdom comprised a number of feudatories who enjoyed varying degrees of autonomy, that they might have themselves subfeudatories of a similar status under them and so to the third, fourth, or fifth degree. A big empire was partly a series of alliances, partly a series of relationships of suzerainty and vassalage and partly an area of directly administered territory. The high-sounding 'Digvijayas' could only lead to such a result on a large or small scale. The tie which held an empire together was not very strong. Under every regime, suzerain or feudal, the village was the ultimate unit of society. . . . Finally there were a number of associations and corporations, religious, economic, and social, which enjoyed a fair degree of autonomy. Sovereignty *de facto* was diffused among all these organisations and influences which supported them."[52]

Dr. Radha Kumud Mookerji points out: "The administration of the Mauryan empire was possible because it did not cherish the ambition of setting up a centralised government consciously legislating for and controlling the life of every part of that vast whole, but aimed only at an elastic system of federalism or corporation, in which were incorporated along with the central government at the metropolis, as parts of the same system, the indigenous local administrations. The essence of this imperial system was thus a recognition of local autonomy at the expense of the authority of the central government, which was physically unfit to assert itself except by its enforced affiliation to the pre-existing system of local Government."[53] There are also passages in the ancient texts leading to the inference that our ancestors were not for the wholesale destruction of alien nations. Kāmandaka says that peace may be concluded by Aryan kings even with non-Aryan, because by such alliance an Arya can never become a non-Arya even in times of calamity.[54]

The village was the unit of ancient Hindu society, since agriculture was the main occupation followed by the people. The desertion of villages in favor of town life was viewed with disfavor by *smṛti-kāras* (lawgivers). "Let him avoid going into towns,"[55] says Āpastamba, while Bodhāyana says, "It is impossible for one to attain salvation who lives in a town covered with dust."[56] While towns were enclosed by high walls, villages had no such artificial enclosure. Rules were laid down by Kauṭilya for the formation of new villages. He states: "Either by inducing foreigners to immigrate or by causing thickly populated centers of his own kingdom to send forth the excess population, the king may construct villages either on new sites or on old ruins. Villages consisting each of not less than a hundred families and of not more than five hundred families of agriculturists, mainly of the *śūdra* caste, with boundaries extending as far as a *krośa* (2,250 yards) or two and capable of protecting each other, shall be formed."[57] R. K. Mookerji correctly remarks, "India presents the rare and remarkable phenomenon of the State and the society coexisting apart from, and in some degree of independence of, each other as distinct and separate units or entities, or independent centres of national, popular, and collective life and activity."[58]

I have now completed a rapid and necessarily imperfect survey of some of the political ideas and theories that were evolved and obtained currency at various periods of Indian history. To summarize, they point to a continued tradition of a strong central government where the king was a real factor to be reckoned with and not a *roi fainéant.* His authority and powers were exercised, however, after constant consultation with a ministry and through heads of departments whose jurisdiction was extensive and who, under wise kings, were always encouraged to speak their minds. Kingship was mainly hereditary but sometimes elective. The pulse of the public was felt, not only through the espionage system of those days, but also by means of assemblies which, especially in the south of India, flourished in great abundance and with much vigor. Provincial, or, rather, local, autonomy was, however, the main feature of Hindu India, and the essence of government lay in the formation and functioning of village groups, taxing themselves, expending their revenues on works of public utility, and governing themselves. Political speculation was active and the theory of a compact with the king, the idea that taxation is the return for good administration and protection, the formulation of the need for a cabinet system of government with *dharma* or *vox populi* as the ultimate sanction—these were some of the conspicuous features of Indian polity. The resort to popular opinion was in the nature of a referendum.

The old dispensation was outwardly and, in later theory and practice, actually unfettered and autocratic; but, nevertheless, by reason of the grant of complete local freedom and the practice of what, in effect, was a form of welfare state, the king acted as being ever in the great taskmaster's eye—the taskmaster being what was indifferently called *dharma* or the voice of the people, which latter, when it expressed itself, was clear and unequivocal. Popular gatherings, if the *Atharva-veda* furnishes an accurate picture, were full of life but at the same time animated by a lively desire to achieve concord.[59] The greatest contribution to posterity made by the Hindu tradition was the broad-mindedness, sympathy, and tolerance of different viewpoints exhibited almost alone in India amongst the civilized communities of earlier days. When Egypt persecuted the Jews, when racial and communal conflicts disfigured the history of Babylon and Nineveh, when, later on, we see that the slave states in Greece and Rome formed the basis of those marvelous cultures, and when in the medieval ages the baiting of Jews alternated with the baiting of Roman Catholics by Protestants and vice versa, we had the spectacle in India of unfailing hospitality to foreign religions and foreign cultures. It would be unfair and inaccurate not to mention that the Buddhists and Jainas suffered some pains and penalties especially in the south of India; but what country can show anything like the treatment of the Parsees, who, flying from oppression in their own country of Persia, asked for and obtained succor of the wise west-coast king, to whose protection and active encouragement of their faith and tradition the Parsees ultimately owe their dominant position in the India of today? What country can furnish a parallel to what happened in Travancore under the rule of extremely conservative and religious-minded monarchs? From the days when Christian congregations were split into innumerable and warring factions owing to the Arian controversy at the Council of Nicaea and the question of images, the Cera kings of Travancore gave a wholehearted welcome to the followers of the Eastern Church whose Patriarch of Antioch even now boasts of a larger following in Malabar than perhaps anywhere else in the world? What king outside of India has surpassed the monarchs of Travancore and Malabar who conferred sacerdotal honors, presents, lands, and dignities on the ministers, bishops, and archbishops of the Christian Church with the result that today the largest Christian population in India is found in the State of Travancore? What ruler in the world's checkered history has enunciated in more moving and powerful language than is found in the Edicts of Aśoka the Great the principles of tolerance and comprehension of differing creeds and ideals co-existing with a spiritual urge toward the consolidation and regeneration of the ruler's own faith?

Such have been the marks and the characteristics of Indian civilization not only at its peak points but through the centuries until recently, and it is not too much to say that the Proclamation of His Highness the Mahārāja of Travancore has an authentic Hindu background and lineage. Can this instinct of universality, this understanding of all points of view, and the feeling that the realization of the Supreme must connote a sympathy with, and a reconciliation of, many forms of thought and belief, be better expressed than in the words of Tāyumānavar in his Hymn to Pārvatī: "The light and bliss of supreme knowledge that envelops and absorbs all forms of belief as the ocean absorbs all rivers"?

In Rock Edict 12, Emperor Aśoka declares that he does reverence to men of all sects, whether ascetics or householders, and he adds that he who does reverence to his own sect while disparaging the sects of others wholly from attachment to his own, with intent to enhance the splendor of his own sect, in reality, by such conduct inflicts the severest injury on his own sect; and he ends the Edict with these ever memorable words: "Concord is the supreme good" (*samavāya eva sādhuḥ*).

This is the idea that underlies the United Nations Organization; it has uniformly characterized the philosophies that have been evolved in India, which have been always based on non-violence (*ahiṁsā*) and compassion (*dayā*), as well as on fearlessness (*abhaya*), and on the recognition of the conformity and unity of all existence.

Notes

1. VIII.336.
2. XII, Śānti-parva, 368.
3. Āpastamba, *Dharma-sūtra,* I.xiii.11.
4. Bodhāyana, *Dharma-sūtra.*
5. Chaps. 67, 68.
6. VII.14.
7. I.iv.14.
8. I.vii.20.
9. II.1.
10. I.v.6.
11. II.606, 607, 608.
12. IV.1.
13. I.375, 376; IV.2.
14. I.10,18.
15. *Śukra,* II.5–8.
16. XIII.61,32.
17. II.549, 552.
18. VII.314.
19. 106, 30, 32.
20. See J. William Kaye, ed., *Selections from the Papers of Lord Metcalfe* (London: Smith, Elder and Company, 1855).
21. R. K. Mookerji, *Hindu Civilisation* (New York: Longmans Green & Co., 1936), p. 78.
22. *Mahābhārata,* Śānti-parva, 67.
23. *Ibid.,* p. 59.
24. VII.
25. *Artha-śāstra* (Trivandrum, ed., 1924–1925), Vol. I, pp. 63–64.
26. *Śukra-nīti-sāra,* I.73–77.
27. 61.
28. Chap. 92.
29. I.70.
30. VIII.307–308.
31. Śānti-parva, 29.
32. Chap. 4.
33. *Mahābhārata,* Śānti-parva, 120.
34. VII. 80.
35. Śānti-parva, 57.
36. Chap. 130.
37. Śānti-parva, 56.
38. Chap. 222.
39. Sabhā-parva, 13.
40. *Artha-śāstra,* Vol. I, p. 97.

41. *Ibid.*
42. *Nītī-vākyāmṛta,* Pandhit Pannālāla Sonī, ed. (Bombay: Maniscandra Digambara Jaina Granthamālā Samiti, 1922), p. 273.
43. *Mahābhārata,* Śānti-parva, 75.
44. *Ibid.,* 90. *Vṛṣla:* A man of one of the three highest classes who has lost his caste by the omission of prescribed duties.
45. *Ibid.*
46. *Ibid.,* 88.
47. *Artha-śāstra,* Vol. I, p. 33.
48. Śānti-parva, 56.
49. *The State in Ancient India* (Allahabad: India Press, 1928), p. 505.
50. Śānti-parva, 93.
51. *Artha-śāstra,* Vol. I, p. 40.
52. *Op. cit.,* pp. 504–505.
53. *Local Government in Ancient India* (Oxford: Oxford University Press, 1919), p. 10.
54. *Śukra-nīti-sāra,* 9.
55. Āpastamba, *Dharma-sūtra,* R. Halasyanatha Sastry, ed., Sanskrit Series (Mysore: Government Oriental Series, 1895), chap. 1, p. 32.
56. Bodhāyana, *Dharma-sūtra,* R. Sharma Sastri, ed., Sanskrit Series, No. 34 (Mysore: Government Oriental Library, 1907), chap. 2, p. 3.
57. *Artha-śāstra, op. cit.,* Vol. I, p. 109.
58. *Local Government in Ancient India,* p. 3.
59. III.xxx.5–6.

DHIRENDRA MOHAN DATTA

Some Philosophical Aspects of Indian Political, Legal, and Economic Thought

I. The Philosophical Background

THE BASIC philosophical concepts guiding Indian political, economic, and legal thought can be traced, partly in germinal forms, in the Vedic literature (the four Vedas, the Brāhmaṇas, and the Upaniṣads) and partly in the later-developed systems of philosophy, Vedic and anti-Vedic, numbering about a dozen. During at least 2,000 years before the Christian era, there must have been a struggle among the conflicting ideas of the different schools, and the ones that survived and were harmonious got practically adopted by society and social thinkers. The literature on social philosophy, including political, legal, and economic thought, began to evolve and took definite shape before the Christian era. Social philosophy is to be found chiefly in some parts of the voluminous Great Epic (the *Mahābhārata*), in the many works called the Dharma-śāstras (Sūtras and Smṛtis), of which Manu's is the most important, in the eighteen Purāṇas, and in the more technical later works on polity called the Nīti-śāstras (the science of statecraft), of which the *Śukra-nīti-sāra* is the most elaborate and in the allied works called Artha-śāstras, of which Kauṭilya's is the most exhaustive one available now.[1]

THE MORAL CONCEPTION OF NATURE

With the exception of the materialists, all schools of Indian thought, including the Buddhists and the Jainas, have a moral conception of Nature.[2] They hold that all natural phenomena are guided by inviolable laws that ensure the conservation of moral values, so that human actions, good and bad, can give rise to appropriate effects, within man and in the outer world in this life or hereafter. Nature helps and ensures the reaping of the fruits of human actions. Action (*karma*) includes, not only the gross overt act, but also its subtler causal states in mind and speech. Early in the *Ṛg-veda*[3] we find the concept of *Ṛta*, the inviolable, eternal law which makes for order, regularity, and harmony in the universe, the law which even the gods obey, and in accordance with which the god Varuṇa metes out justice to man. It should be noted that *Ṛta* combines here the idea of a positive, natural law and that of a moral principle.

This moral conception of Nature generates in the Indian mind a deep confidence in cosmic justice. We find it reflected in the oft-quoted maxims: "Truth alone prevails, not falsehood";[4] "The righteous side will have the victory";[5] "*Dharma* kills if it is killed; *dharma* protects if it is protected";[6] "The entire world rests on *dharma*."[7] *Dharma*, which has among its many senses the meaning of morality, is etymologically explained as the principle of preservation—that which holds together and preserves the people. "By unrighteousness man prospers, gains what appears desirable, conquers enemies, but perishes at the root," says Tagore, following Manu (4.174). This unity of moral outlook, in spite of the diversity of metaphysical theories, supplies the common background to Indian culture.

HUMAN LIFE A RARE OPPORTUNITY

Counterbalancing the possible defeatist attitude springing from the thought of life's transitoriness there is the common belief that, though the present life is momentary, the individual has a beginningless existence continuing through successive lives; his action in his preceding lives determines the quality of the succeeding one. It is foolish, therefore, not to utilize the present life for improving the individual's future possibilities.

Human life is regarded, therefore, as a great opportunity. "Rare is human birth," says the *Bhāgavata*.[8] "The human status is hard to attain," says the Buddha.[9] In the evolutionary scale of living beings (*jīvas*), the status of man is the highest and is obtained after a long series of incarnations.

DHARMA AS MAN'S DIFFERENTIA

The differentia of man is not the mere intellect, which lower animals also possess to some degree. The oft-quoted verse runs: "Hunger, sleep, fear, sex are common to all animals, human and sub-human. It is the additional attribute of *dharma* (morality) that differentiates man from the beast. Devoid of *dharma*, man is like a beast."

It is necessary to understand the meaning of "*dharma*," which has many senses, as does the English "good" or "law." These are brought under one principle by Bhīṣma in the *Mahābhārata* (Śānti-parva, 258), which anticipates Kant's moral maxim. This basic principle of *dharma* is put positively and negatively thus: "What you desire for yourself, you should desire for others" and "What you do not like others to do to you, you should not do to others." Bhīṣma shows that falsehood, cruelty, theft, and other vices would be suicidal in practice—making the doer the victim of his own bad action, and would make society, the state, or any corporate existence impossible. So, *dharma* comes to be regarded as the principle of preservation as well. Though one in the abstract, *dharma* expresses itself in many new forms in different spheres of life.

The *Mahābhārata*[10] holds that the essence of *dharma* is self-control (*dama*). The human self is often described figuratively as the occupant of the body, its chariot:[11] the sensory-motor organs are the horses, the sensuous mind (*manas*) is its rein, reason (*buddhi*) is the driver. Self-control thus comes to mean the rational control of the body, the senses, and the mind, guiding it along the desirable path. *Dharma* supplies the principles for good guidance. The irrational impulses of the body, senses, and senseward mind express themselves in the life of animal propensities (*pravṛtti*)—hunger, sex, fear, etc. It is the rational guidance of *dharma* that tames them and harnesses them and saves them from running riot and from conflicts of selfish desires which may lead to ruin.

THE INDIVIDUAL

Emphasis on the importance of the individual is common to all the Indian systems of philosophy. It is worthy of special note that even those who believe in God as the creator do not hold that the individual soul is created by God. God creates only the material objects, including the human body. But the soul is co-eternal with God.

For the Sāṁkhya, the individual soul, though ignorantly identified with the finite body, is essentially pure, infinite consciousness. For the Advaitin (the Vedāntin of the school of Śaṁkara), the individual soul is nothing but *Brahman* itself illusorily identified with the finite body. For the Jaina, every individual soul has the potentiality for infinite knowledge, faith, power, and bliss. Even the Buddhist, who does not believe in a soul as such, believes in the potential *buddha*hood of every individual. For theists in general, the individual can attain spiritual freedom and God. And, for all, it is by using the opportunities of this life that the individual can realize its high destiny.

Every individual, every living being, thus comes to be regarded as a sacred center of potential value, deserving of respect and possessing freedom for unhampered progress toward its goal. Non-injury to life (*ahiṁsā*) is universally enjoined, therefore, by all these schools of thought as a fundamental virtue. The individual's right to life and freedom of development is recognized as a fundamental right. It results in the universal maxim: Treat everyone as yourself (*ātmavat*). From *ahiṁsā* also follow logically the other virtues (or duties toward every individual), such as truthfulness (*satya*), non-stealing (*asteya*), kindness (*karuṇā*), friendliness (*maitrī*), forbearance (*upekṣā*), etc. As all these may be logically deduced from respect for life, *ahiṁsā* is often described[12] as the supreme virtue (*parama-dharma*). The altruistic virtues and duties lay the secure foundation for a harmonious society in which individuals can respect and help one another and work out their respective spiritual destinies.

INDIVIDUAL AND SOCIETY

We should briefly consider here the Indian conception of the relation between the individual and society. Is the individual the basic and independent unit and society a mere collection of individuals? Is society the primary reality, of which individuals are mere parts? Or are they both equally real and organically related? It is difficult to bring all Indian views under one type. But perhaps they are in some respects nearer to the organic view, with some reservation. For a rough description, we can call the general Indian trend spiritual individualism through social organicism.

Insofar as the individual is a self, it is a distinct reality; its spiritual freedom is the ultimate end to which its entire life's activities should be directed. But insofar as the self is embodied, and all its activities are through the body, subtle and gross, and the body is an inseparable member and product of the world of Nature, out of which the bodies of other selves also have evolved, there is an indissoluble natural bond between the embodied individual and all other such individuals forming the social corpus. In this naturalistic, empirical perspective, the evolution of the world of objects and human society is conceived in the *Ṛg-veda*[13] as taking place out of the body of the Supreme Person (*puruṣa*), the four castes being differentiated as his mouth, arms, thighs, and feet. The Person, however, also transcends the manifested form. In the later theistic literature and also in the Smṛtis and Purāṇas, we find the analogy of the Cosmic Egg (*Brahmāṇḍa*), out of which the world evolves by internal organic differentiation. Judged in this naturalist perspective, human society is a part of the cosmic organism, the phenomenal manifestation of God, and the individual human being is a part of the social organism.

The empirical bond of the individual to Nature and other beings finds recognition in various ways. Nature (*prakṛti*) comes to be regarded by some theists as the mother, the consort of the Supreme Self or God, who is the father of all beings, and so the entire universe is conceived as one's own country. Again, in the five daily rounds of duties for the householder is recognized the multiple duty of the individual to his parents, from whom the body derives its existence; to the sages, who conserve and propagate the cultural heritage; to the deities that govern Nature; to the stranger-guest as a man; and to lower animals as fellow beings.[14] The individual can advance only by gradual steps through the hard disciplines of the life of a student, a householder, a retired spiritual aspirant, and, finally (for a *brāhmaṇa*), a life of renunciation.[15] Manu repeatedly warns that one who tries to rush to the last stage of life without discharging the prior obligations to family and society goes down.[16] The individual requires maintenance, protection, and help even for spiritual realization, and therefore the economic, political, and legal organizations of society are deemed necessary.

THE INTEGRAL OUTLOOK AND THE GOLDEN MEAN

All through Indian thought one comes across an integral outlook—a serious concern for the self's ultimate end (*sādhya*) combined with a realistic appreciation of the graduated series of means (*sādhana*) by the proper cultivation of which alone the ultimate end can be attained. This is so important for a correct appreciation of Indian thought and culture that we should dwell a little upon it. In education, we find this outlook reflected in the attempt of the Upaniṣadic teacher not to reveal the ultimate truth all at once, but through graduated steps in strict relation to the present fitness of the student. *Brahman,* or *Ātman,* is revealed first as the body, then vitality, then sense-mind, then pure reason, and then bliss. The real, present, physical, mental, moral nature (*sva-bhāva*) of the individual determines his particular aptitude or right to know and do (*adhikāra*); it also determines his own sphere of duty (*sva-dharma*).[17] The fourfold division of society into the sage, the warrior, the trader, and the laborer is a natural division based on the recognition of quality (*guṇa*) and *karma* (action),[18] so far as the justifiable ideal behind it is concerned. Each class has its own well-defined duties in accordance with its own nature. But at the same time all have also universal duties (*sādhāraṇa-dharmas*) and virtues to cultivate, because of their common human nature and obligations. "Each one can achieve the highest end by holding to one's duty."[19] The preaching of an indiscriminate equality of rights and duties is considered an unrealistic confusion of thought leading to social chaos.

The *Īśa-upaniṣad* realizes the great harm and imbalance that one-sided concern for the knowledge (*vidyā*) of transcendent *Brahman* can cause to the necessary life of duty, and to the lower empirical knowledge (*avidyā*), on which normal life depends. So, it gives a stern warning against one-sided otherworldliness as well as to *one-sided* worldiness, and balances the transcendent with the immanent aspects of *Brahman.* "Into a blind darkness enter those who follow after ignorance, they as if into a greater darkness who devote themselves to knowledge alone" (verse 9). "Doing verily works in this world one should wish to live a hundred years" (verse 2). "That moves and that moves not; That is far and at the same time near; That is within all this and That also is outside all this. But he who sees everywhere the Self in all existences and all existences in the Self shrinks not thereafter from aught" (verses 5–6).[20]

This golden mean, based on an integral view reconciling the eternal with the transitory, knowledge with action, the individual's spiritual freedom with an active life in society, is taught again in the *Gītā,* in the *Mahābhārata,* and also in the Dharma-śāstras.

It is by re-emphasizing this integral view that the leaders of the modern Indian social and political renascense try to arouse the people to the spiritual ideal and moral life. Tagore, Gandhi,

Aurobindo, Vinoba—all go back again and again to the *Īśa-upaniṣad* for inspiration. B. G. Tilak, Gandhi, Aurobindo, and Vinoba all write commentaries to interpret the *Gītā* in their respective lights—but all in support of a harmonious life of knowledge, devotion, and action.

UNITY IN DIVERSITY

Most of the modern Indian social and political leaders constantly emphasize the Indian spirit of unity in diversity in their attempts to understand and reconcile the ideas and interests of the divergent racial, religious, and linguistic groups that compose the population of India and the world. What are the philosophical roots of this attitude in classical Indian thought? We can find in the Vedas and the Upaniṣads the idea that the same reality manifests itself in various forms (just as the sun's one white light is diffused into many colors), that the same reality is called by the names of different gods, that differences are only matters of names and forms, whereas the underlying reality is the same, that all are destined to find their way back into the same reality (just as rivers running in different courses and directions become one in the sea). These monistic ideas developed along different lines in the many schools of the Vedānta, which can be broadly divided into two: the Advaita (pure monism) of the Śaṁkara school and the non-Advaita schools of theistic Vedānta. The first, which is more known to Western scholars (and even today thought by some as *the* philosophy of India), regards the reality (*Brahman*) underlying all phenomena (including what is sometimes called the "undifferentiated aesthetic continuum"[21]) as devoid of all distinctions and assignable predicates. The perceived world of diverse objects is only an appearance. Yet, this phenomenal world is not groundless; it is grounded in *Brahman,* and enjoys a lower status of practical (*vyāvahārika*) reality, which is, however, higher than the status of illusory objects of everyday life, and higher than the utterly unreal (like the son of a barren mother). In spite of their uncompromising monism, therefore, even Advaitins allow degrees of reality and value, and think in terms of identity-in-difference in respect to all phenomena, including social ones. Identity is the ultimate truth, but differences are its appearances; and to be able to realize identity through diversity is a necessary and valuable step toward the ultimate truth. It is nearer the truth than the naïve contentment of resting in sheer diversity. The theistic Vedāntins (who command the largest following among the masses) hold, on the other hand, that the diverse manifestations of reality are also real. *Brahman* possesses eternally diverse elements which become manifest in creation. Unity in diversity is, therefore, true even of the ultimate.

Among the pluralists, we may mention the early Buddhists and the Jainas. In a sense, the early Buddhists, who consider everything as unique, and admit no common positive universal, are the most uncomprising particularists. But the later Buddhist thinkers of the Mahāyāna school approach in many respects the Absolutist Advaita point of view and try to understand all phenomena as the appearance (*saṁvṛti*) of an underlying indescribable Absolute (*Paramārtha*). The Jainas not only believe in many ultimate reals, but also discover the innumerable real aspects of each real. They develop, therefore, in epistemology a realistic relativism, with a scheme of seven different kinds of possible logical judgments at the same time in respect of the same thing viewed in different aspects. This logic of the manifold truth[22] (*an-ekānta-vāda* and *syād-vāda*) exposes the weakness of every cocksure dogmatism that tries to monopolize truth. It is a pluralistic way of understanding and appreciating the possibility of divergent true views and lays the foundation of practical social philosophy that tries to accommodate different views and interests. Gandhi—and following him now Vinoba—advocates this Jaina logic in practical politics.[23] Nehru's foreign policy of *Pañca-śīla* (five rules of mutual good conduct), or peaceful co-existence, can be thought to stem from this pluralistic, realistic, relativist logic.

On the whole, then, we find that there is sufficient philosophical support, both from the monists and from the pluralists, for the spirit of reconciliation and synthesis that we find in Indian social and political thought.

II. Philosophy as Embodied in Indian Politics, Law, and Economics

We can now try to understand how the foregoing ideas influenced Indian political, legal, and economic philosophy. The very first thing that strikes one is the fact that *dharma* is taken as the only sound basis of personal life, as well as of all social institutions and organizations. A good state and good government can therefore be based only on the principles of *dharma*. Even the more secular works on politics and economics, such as the *Artha-śāstra* of Kauṭilya and the *Śukra-nīti-sāra,* generally recognize the soundness of this view despite their occasional deviation from high moral standards.

ORIGIN OF THE STATE

We have seen previously that man, the embodied self, is conceived of as possessing potentiality for infinite perfection, but as hampered by his ignorance, passions, and immoral tendencies generated by his own past actions. As he is, he is both good and bad.[24] It is the duty of the ideal state to create conditions and opportunities that will gradually help man overcome his ignorance, selfishness, and immoral tendencies, so that a harmonious community may evolve in which every individual can advance toward the supreme goal of spiritual freedom—freedom from ignorance and selfishness and all the vices and sufferings that follow therefrom.

Man without society, or society without a state, is never contemplated as a historical possibility or as a desirable ideal. We find occasional hypothetical speculation as to what would have been the fate of individuals if the state did not exist. Manu (7.20) surmises that "if the king did not vigilantly inflict punishment on the guilty, the stronger would have roasted the weaker like fish," for, he frankly says, "an absolutely pure man is rare in this world." Similarly, in the *Mahābhārata* (Śānti-parva, 15.30), Arjuna says: "If there were no scepter in the world, people would have perished. The stronger would have devoured the weaker just as fish do in water." This analogy of the fish (*matsya-nyāya*) has been generally employed by all political thinkers in describing the probable fate of a hypothetical stateless state of men. In the *Mahābhārata* (Sānti-parva, 59) there is the mythical account of a kingless society in the golden age, and a subsequent degradation of the people leading to the necessity of their entrusting the protection of the land to a king, selected, at their request, by God. Similar mythical accounts are found in Buddhist and Jaina works in slightly altered forms. All these would point to a kind of social contract theory.[25] But such a theory is not seriously advocated.

THE SCEPTER (DAṆḌA)

In Indian political literature, the figure of the scepter (*daṇḍa*) has come to stand, by a kind of metonymy, for the state—with its awe-inspiring and irresistible authority that rules by law and punishment. So, like the word *"dharma," "daṇḍa"* has various associated meanings, e.g., political authority, rule of law, punishment, etc.

Political philosophy itself is sometimes called "the principles of the scepter" (*daṇḍa-nīti*). The scepter is idealized by Manu (7.14) as an original creation of God, out of *Brahman's* radiant energy, it being nothing but *dharma* itself, the child of God and the protector of all beings. It is the prototype of all earthly political authorities. In a similar manner, Manu (7.3) speaks of the ideal king, the prototype of all kings, as being created by God to protect all beings from fear resulting from anarchy.

The royalists have sometimes wrongly interpreted such statements as supporting the divine origin of kings, and for inculcating implicit loyalty to particular rulers. But that such an interpretation is unsound is evident from the fact that Manu (7.26–31) and other thinkers[26] repeatedly point out that only the righteous ruler is worthy of the scepter, which itself destroys an unrighteous king, and the *Mahābhārata* even holds that a tyrant should be destroyed, as King Veṇa was in olden times. Moreover, according to most authorities,[27] the king or the state is not even recognized as the owner of the country. Revenue was paid by the people, in kind or cash in lieu of the protection and welfare services rendered by the state. Manu would almost support the principle: No protection, no taxation.[28]

THE THREE VALUES OF THE STATE: MORAL, HEDONIC, ECONOMIC

The political literature of India generally speaks of the threefold human value (*tri-varga*)—*dharma* (morality), *artha* (wealth), and *kāma* (enjoyment)—and omits the last one, *mokṣa* (liberation), which, along with the first three, constitutes the fourfold traditional value (*catur-varga*) of Indian philosophy. Even the *Mahābhārata* (Śānti-parva 15.3) and Manu (2.224) speak of the threefold value and omit spiritual freedom (*mokṣa*), the highest end. We can think of two reasons for this secular attitude: (1) Though liberation is recognized as the ultimate goal, it does not enter directly into the immediate objects of social and political organization. (2) The concept of spiritual freedom—and of the path leading to it—differs from school to school, and political philosophy need not necessarily be affiliated to any one of these. The reasonable object of a liberal political philosophy is to lay down the broadest principles, free from conflict with morality (*dharmā-viruddha*), on which can be founded an ideal corporate life conducive to the free pursuit of the higher spiritual goals in accordance with the aptitude and choice of the individual concerned. While it is dangerous for the state to allow the violation of the essential laws of morality, the state need not interfere with the individual's spiritual life.

We find in India a peculiar blend of a strict demand for social morality and conformity and a wide latitude for freedom of thought and choice in ultimate matters. And it is here that we can find also the ancient pattern of a secular, but morally grounded, state, free from religious sectarianism—the ideal of Aśoka[29] and Gandhi[30] and professed by the present Indian Constitution.

ONE-SIDED ECONOMICS, HEDONISM, AND ASCETICISM RECONCILED

Some materialist economists in ancient India, as in the West, claimed that all values ultimately depend on wealth. Their case was passionately advocated by Arjuna, the great fighter, in the *Mahābhārata*. His long lecture is summed up thus: "Performance of duty (*dharma*), enjoyment of pleasures (*kāma*), and even the attainment of heaven depends on wealth, on which life itself depends" (Śānti-parva, 8.17). Interpreting wealth (*artha*) in the widest sense of all objects, including the earth, which constitute the means of subsistence, Kauṭilya also thinks of "wealth" as the foundation of human existence and the basis of the other two goals. The other extreme side is revealed in the ascetic disgust for wealth expressed in the *Yoga-bhāṣya* (II.30) and in the *Mahābhārata* by Bhīṣma. The earning of money, its preservation, its loss, its expenditure, are said to be sources of suffering. So, wealth is a great evil.

Manu (2.224) rejects, however, the different views that *dharma* alone, or that *dharma* and wealth, or that wealth and enjoyment are the most important values. He holds that all three, harmoniously cultivated, jointly constitute the threefold end of human life. This is the balanced golden mean of Indian social thought, which rejects both one-sided hedonism and one-sided asceticism. It represents the most influential current of social thought, too.

THE STATE AND SOCIETY

The state is primarily a product of society, and, therefore, it reflects the ideas and beliefs that dominate the society of a particular place and time. The early Indian state accepted for the most part the established notions of the four classes and the four stages of life, and their respective duties, privileges, and obligations. The state had among its obligations the protection of the established social order and the helping of every individual in the performance of the duties of his caste and stage of life. The four classes were assigned different kinds of work. This also involved an economic organization based on the division of labor. The classes were not originally very rigid and were not hereditary, but were based more on the quality and work of the individual. The Dharma-śāstras and even the Artha-śāstras expect the state to maintain the social order. The state had to recognize and maintain whatever inequalities of opportunity were prevalent in society.

But it should be remembered that, though the higher castes enjoyed higher social prestige, in the ideal state this prestige had to be earned by a higher standard of knowledge and conduct, and a greater sacrifice of material advantages and creature comforts. That the sole criterion of birth is unsound is realized by political thinkers such as Śukra (1.38), who advocates the assignment of duties in accordance with merit and work (*guṇa-karma*). Moreover, Śukra holds that, instead of submitting to the trends of the age, the king, as the head of the state, should take the initiative in ushering in a new era, and should introduce new practices. In this, Śukra was only making a new application of Manu's idea that the king should be the maker of his age.[31] Whether it is to be a golden, silver, copper, or iron age depends on his initiative.

THE CONSTITUTION AND MULTIPLE FUNCTIONS OF THE STATE

Though there are stray references to different kinds of state (*gaṇa,* people's state; *saṅgha,* community state; *rāṣṭra,* territorial state; and *rājya,* kingdom) in Indian literature, the works on politics discuss only the constitution and functions of monarchical states. In Vedic literature, we come across terms suggesting different kinds of states such as monarchy (*rājya*), diarchy (*dvairājya*), empire (*sāmrājya*), and self-rule (*svārājya*). There is an ambiguous term, "*vairājya,*" which may mean either "kingless state" or "good state." Two northern states (Uttara Kurus and Uttara Madras) are said to have been kingless republics. There were also later some federal republics, such as the Yaudheyas and the Licchavi Mallas. But monarchy was always the general and dominant pattern.[32]

Kingdoms varied widely, however, from small village and city-states to far-flung empires covering major parts of India. "The Mauryan empire covered a territory certainly as wide as India and Pakistan"[33] (during *ca.* 324–232 B.C.). It supplied the background for Kauṭilya's work. A cursory glance at the contents of his book, and of the more elaborate work of Śukra, gives us detailed knowledge of the aims, constitution, and functions of the state, of which we have only broad outlines in the Dharma-śāstras. Among the subjects discussed are: the basic sciences and arts; the ends of life; the duties of the different classes; the duties and the training of civil and military officers; the training and management of soldiers, spies, ambassadors, horses, elephants, navy; the science and art of diplomacy, warfare, strategy; constructions of forts, tunnels, bridges, roads; arms and ammunitions; peace, treaty, fair and unfair expedients; raising of revenues from rents, taxes, mines, forests; seizing of enemy property; administration of justice through laws; removal of "thorns"; provision of welfare services for health; mental and moral education; irrigation, traffic, building of temples; celebration of festivities, etc.

THE CONSTITUENTS OF THE STATE

The seven essential elements constituting a monarchical state are described by Manu (9.294) in order of importance as: the king, the ministers and other officials, the fortified capital, the territory of the kingdom, the treasury, the forces of the scepter (army, cavalry, etc.), and the allies of the state. Though the king is regarded as the most important and supreme seat of authority, political thinkers constantly remind us that, however able he may be, the king should be helped by the counsel of good ministers in the daily administration of the state, in the administration of justice, in conducting wars, in negotiations for peace and treaties, etc. In a large state, as envisaged by Kauṭilya and Śukra, there were a legion of administrative departments with thousands of officers, composing a large hierarchy of delegated authority, and with a vigilant supervisory and co-ordinating staff.

But it would appear that the kingdom was a federation of different parts, down to the villages, which were more or less autonomous units internally ruled by the village elders. Allegiance to the center consisted primarily of the willingness to pay land revenues and taxes for different kinds of professional incomes and to cooperate with the state in the maintenance of peace and order and in the defense against foreign attacks. Villages were grouped in hierarchies of tens, twenties, hundreds, and thousands; and there were chiefs and officers appointed by the state for each of such units.[34]

THE KING AND HIS OFFICERS

The foundation of an ethical state required a long process of careful training of princes, the heirs apparent, and the selection of honest and efficient officials. The king's cabinet consisted of from three to seven ministers, the royal priest, and a chief judge.

All political philosophers require the king and the high officials to have a sound training in the different Vedas (including their subsidiary disciplines), sciences, arts, logic, and philosophy. The reason the works on polity are so encyclopedic is perhaps to be sought in the fact that they were meant for the education of the young princes, and were used as manuals by administrators. It is of special interest for us to note that a high place is given by all to logic (*anvīkṣikī*), which, along with philosophy, is eulogized in the famous couplet of Kauṭilya thus: "The light to all branches of knowledge, the means to all activities, the eternal basis of all virtues."[35] Logic, with epistemology, is specially discussed in relation to the administration of law. Among the philosophies, the Sāṁkhya, the Yoga, and the Vedānta are often mentioned as aids to the administrator's equanimity, detachment, and steadfast devotion to the ultimate goal of life.

Along with intellectual education, great stress is laid on enthusiasm, moral discipline, control of the senses, speech, thought, and action. Control of passions—such as anger, jealousy, greed, egoism—is also thought necessary. Addiction to vicious hobbies is strongly condemned.

The net result of this all-round intellectual and moral culture is called *vinaya,* which connotes both discipline and genuine humility. Kings are advised to wait daily upon the learned and experienced for acquiring this quality. Again and again, the *Mahābhārata,* the lawgivers, and political philosophers cite a black list of mythical and historical rulers who lost their kingdoms owing to the lack of this quality and another list of worthy persons who rose to be great kings by virtue of it.[36]

The ceremony of the coronation of the young prince by the old king (retiring for spiritual pursuit) also gives us some glimpses of the philosophy of kingship.[37] The new king takes the solemn pledge of serving the *Brahman* manifested as the earth (*Bhauma-Brahman*), in the presence of the subjects, who are described as Viṣṇu, the God manifest as the people. The scepter that the king assumes is regarded as an earthly emblem of the righteous rule of Varuṇa, the god of justice, over the world of Nature and living beings. The ideal king of the *Artha-śāstra* (15.19) is described thus: "In the happiness of his subjects lies his happiness; in their welfare his welfare; whatever pleases him he shall not consider as good, but whatever pleases his subjects he shall consider as good."

Needless to say, such ideals were extremely difficult of practical attainment. We hear of many kings who fell far short. Against tyrants, political thinkers provide checks such as mass migration by subjects deserting the king's territory, or the deposition of a bad king and the installation of his good son with the consent of the subjects. Along with such checks of visible consequences, there is the moral check of invisible consequences often cited as a warning; for example, a king who fails in his duty but takes his remuneration, namely, one-sixth of the land's proceeds, is warned that he will suffer for one-sixth of the vices of the subjects. Moreover, as we shall see later, the king has to atone for the miscarriage of justice, by starvation and privation.

We have not found in any of these ancient treatises, however, any instances of a positive moral check such as Gandhi's methods of *Satyāgraha,* non-violent non-co-operation, non-payment of unjust taxes and levies, and civil disobedience of immoral laws. These Gandhian experiments, developed under Eastern and Western influences, try to avoid the two extremes of passive resignation to the automatic law of *dharma,* on the one hand, and violent revolution and destruction of the tyrant, on the other. While Gandhi believed in the inviolable course of the moral truth, the inexorable law of *dharma,* he also believed in the truth of the moral effort of the individual, which can bring about desirable changes in accordance with that supreme moral law itself. The attempt to remove an evil by a wrong act of violence forgets the evil consequences which would also inevitably follow the bad attempt, if the moral law is inexorable. Gandhi's method therefore gives full recognition to the law of *dharma.* It follows the precept of the Buddha that evil cannot be conquered by evil; evil can be conquered only by good.[38] Gandhi also urges: "Conquer hate by love, untruth by truth, violence by self-suffering."[39]

THE ETHICS OF ADMINISTRATION AND FOREIGN RELATIONS

The philosophy of internal administration is inspired by lofty ideas. But, in practical dealings, it is always remembered that human nature is both good and bad, that men are not all of the same nature and do not deserve the same kind of treatment. So, absolute trust and absolute distrust are both to be avoided, says the *Mahābhārata* (Śānti-parva 181.8–12), which recommends the golden mean and constant vigilance. Equity and justice—rather than indiscriminate equality—constitute, therefore, the aim of political behavior. Says Manu, "The king should be righteous in his own state, severe in punishing the enemy, candid to friends and allies, and lenient to the gentle *brāhmaṇa*" (7.32). The same idea is clearer in Śukra's work (2.282): "The king should behave in three different ways: like the [pleasant] autumn moon to the learned, like the [scorching] summer sun to the enemy, like the [moderate] spring sun to his subjects."

While such internal policies are morally justifiable, foreign policies leave much to be desired. Four possible expedients are broadly distinguished: (1) Peace or conciliation by negotiation (*sāman*), (2) placating by giving (*dāna*), (3) fomenting dissension (*bheda*), and (4) punishment by attack (*daṇḍa*). These expedients (*upāyas*) are to be applied in accordance with one's own and the enemy's strength and weakness. Of these four, peace and punishment are better for the kingdom, says Manu (7.109). When war breaks out, any of the six kinds of alternative strategies (*ṣaḍguṇas*) can be judiciously resorted to, namely, peace-treaty, declaration of war, invasion, remaining in one's own country for self-defense and yet inflicting loss on the enemy, division of the forces to wage guerrilla warfare, or seeking asylum in a friendly country.

An elaborate diplomatic theory of the balance of power is developed by political thinkers who use their psychological and logical acumen in analyzing and naming technically about ten different kinds of relation that can possibly exist between an ambitious king, residing in a power zone (*maṇḍala*), and sixty or more different ways of tackling the enemy, the ally, the neutral, and so on.[40] The basic principle is to build power on common hatred, distrust, greed, and fear.

RIGHTEOUS AND UNRIGHTEOUS WAR

If the cause is right and the means adopted is fair, war is called righteous. Righteous war (*dharma-yuddha*) is justified by the *Mahābhārata*, the *Gītā*, and the works on *dharma*, e.g., Manu's.[41] It is regarded as the duty of the warrior caste; and battle fought without fear is commended as leading to the most desirable ends, fame here and heaven hereafter. An ethical code of personal chivalry and fearlessness is formulated. It forbids all unfair means and intrigue. Manu lays down, for example, that in a righteous battle no one should use secret weapons or poisonous and incendiary weapons; no one should kill a fighter who is unprepared, unarmed, begs pardon, surrenders himself, has lost his armor, is naked or unconscious, is a mere observer or a noncombatant companion of the enemy, or has turned back from the battle. One who kills such a man takes the burden of all his sins. An emissary, even if discourteous, is never to be killed.

Such a battle is confined to the battlefield, and to the conventional hours of the day; and striking is allowed only on particular parts of the body. Convention entitles the victor to the rightful ownership of the property of the defeated. But war does not much disturb the civil population of their peaceful occupations. Megasthenes and Hsüan-tsang were surprised to observe these good points during their sojourn in India.[42]

In addition to the righteous warfare described above, political thinkers, such as Kauṭilya,[43] describe the methods of unrighteous warfare (*kūtā-yuddha*), in which treachery, secret assassination, poisoning, and all kinds of satanic methods are employed to achieve victory. They remind us of the last two great wars of this century.

ŚUKRA'S AND ARJUNA'S REALISTIC VIEW OF THE STATE, WEALTH, AND WAR

The large gap between the ethics of internal administration and the ethics of international relations, particularly during war, rankles in the conscience of Śukra, who poses a hypothetical imperative: If you want success and if the state is to survive and prosper, you must fight when necessary, and also practice deceit and appropriate the wealth of the defeated enemy. He cynically observes: "Stealing is bad for a thief, but plundering is good for a king. We need not try to unravel the mystery of *dharma*. What is condemned by many is bad, what is praised by many is good (*dharma*)."[44]

This frank defense of the violation of the rules of inter-personal morality in war is an appeal to conventional morality, in which the modern world still believes. In ancient India, where the defense and protection of the country were left to the warrior class (*kṣatriyas*), for whom the fear of facing a fight was a sin and dying in bed meant hell. Elaborate rational justification of such a class morality is found in the *Mahābhārata* (Śānti-parva, 15), mostly in the words of its greatest military leader, Arjuna, who presents together a philosophy of the state, wealth, and non-violence, which are interconnected. We give here the substance of his arguments:

Life is an undeniable value. But life and the realization of all its values, including spiritual freedom, depend on wealth, the means of subsistence. In the struggle for existence, the stronger try to oust the weaker. This is the universal law of Nature, too, as can be seen among animals. This can be prevented by a strong organization like the state, headed by a king and backed by soldiers capable of fighting back intruders who are threatening the life and property of the subjects and capable of punishing and restraining the subjects themselves from encroaching upon one another's rights. If violence—the application of force and even killing—is necessary for such a sacred purpose, it is right. Absolute non-violence is both impossible and suicidal. It is impossible because even the ascetic who retires to the forest kills every day visible and invisible living beings in treading on the ground, drinking water, eating fruit, and even in breathing the air and moving the eyelids. So, living means taking life. Total abstinence from violence is suicidal also because, if the shepherd hesitates to kill the wolf, he helps the destruction of the flock and himself. So, injury to life for the protection of life is permitted by classical texts. Such virtuous and dutiful violence (*sādhu-hiṁsā*) is really a kind of non-violence (*ahiṁsā*), properly understood. If life, property, and spirituality are to be preserved, the state must resort to violence to prevent violence, if it is necessary.

The foregoing summary of Arjuna's arguments also sums up the main stream of religious and moral thought in India. This realistic golden mean of social, political, and international morality recognizes that harmlessness, truthfulness, and other universal virtues which should be practiced in thought, speech, and action can be practiced and reached only by degrees, in accordance with the capacity of the individual; and the possibility of practicing them in political and international fields is increasingly more difficult than in inter-personal behavior. Manu (8.350–351) permits, for self-defense, the killing of even "one's teacher, an old man, a child, a learned *brāhmaṇa*." He also holds that killing, if necessary for carrying out the injunctions of the Vedas, should not be regarded as a sin (5.44). He also permits (8.104) the speaking of untruth if necessary for saving any life, and thus allows "pious perjury." Though he also allows war, and advises the king to fight and adopt various strategies, he places first peaceful, amicable interstate relations (*sāman*).

THE HIGHER IDEAL

The highest practical effort for moral relations within the state and with other states was made, however, in the third century B.C., by the greatest emperor of India, Aśoka, (third century B.C.),[45] whose earlier experience of unrighteous war, causing untold suffering to the people, roused him to the truth of the noble teachings of Gautama, the Buddha. He not only established many kinds of welfare services for the people, and even hospitals for men and animals, but also abjured all intentions of war, even though he was the strongest. He realized the superiority of peaceful relations with other states, and concluded treaties for mutual non-aggression. He sent out good-will missions with medicines for men and animals, and ethical emissaries (*dharma-mahā-mātras*) to distant lands (as far away as Greece) to preach the universal human virtues and toleration of the faith of others as the best service to one's own.[46] It should not be forgotten, however, that even Aśoka had his army and that he had founded his empire on bloodshed and devastation. But the ideal of moral conquest (*dharma-vijaya*), rather than territorial conquest, which he conceived and subsequently tried to practice, has left a blazing trail for humanity's uphill struggle toward an ethical state and ethical international relations.

More than 2,000 years after Aśoka, Gandhi tried to relive his ideal of Truth and non-violence, and even took a step forward, by mass practice of morality, in political struggles.[47] He was influenced mainly by the Sermon on the Mount as interpreted by Tolstoi, the Friends, and Henry David Thoreau; the teachings of the Buddha and the Jainas; the philosophy of the *Gītā;* and the ideas of Ruskin. He interpreted the war in the *Gītā,* not as a historical fact, but as an allegory for the inner battle with desires and other evil forces which every individual spirit, like Arjuna, should overcome, as a spiritual duty, in order to attain God. He did not believe, therefore, that the *Gītā* teaches violence. He also thought, as did Tilak, Aurobindo, and Vivekananda, that liberation can be attained through work without attachment. He believed that selfless service to God's creatures is the best way of realizing God. So, politics became a religion for him. He differed, however, from all those ancient and modern Indian thinkers who regarded violence and untruth as justifiable by the good political ends which they might serve. He was aware that, as long as one is in the body, perfect non-violence is difficult to observe. Injury to life may be caused unknowingly, as Arjuna pointed out. But we are morally responsible only for our consciously performed actions. Moreover, the difficulty of attaining a high ideal does not justify its lowering, but demands, rather, the intensification of moral effort, which itself is more ennobling and important than success. "Full effort is full victory."

The modern age of democracy, Gandhi thought, has made the founding of the state on force and immoral principles an anachronism. Democracy is the way of social and political life which tries to raise every individual to a higher sense of moral dignity, responsibility, and freedom. Violence and untruth are precisely the denial of these higher principles. Only a state enjoying "moral authority" can advance democracy.

With a keen moral consciousness, Gandhi sees theft and violence in an economic organization of society which deprives the laborer of the rightful fruit of his labor and impairs thereby the economic basis of his life. He sees violence also in a society which denies equality of status and opportunity to any class of its members.

But, like Aśoka, Gandhi also has only blazed for humanity again a trail in the limited sphere of liberation from foreign domination. It has only dimly lighted the path of Western democracy, which free India has adopted.

III. The Indian Philosophy of Law

DHARMA—AS THE LAW OF THE STATE

One of the various later developments of the Vedic concept of *Ṛta,* the principle of cosmic order and harmony, is *dharma,* which is the principle of preservation and harmony in the human world. *Dharma* expresses itself in personal life as virtues and duties, and in political life as the laws of the state—just laws which restrain evil propensities and promote virtuous life. The king has to take the vow of protecting and maintaining the people with *dharma* on earth, as Varuṇa rules with *Ṛta* from heaven. *Dharma* as law is above the king, just as *Ṛta* is above the gods. The king obeys the law, *dharma,* and inspires virtue and loyalty in the people by his own example.

Dr. Fritz Berolzheimer[48] holds that the Vedic idea of *Ṛta* and the concept of *dharma* influenced the legal and ethical theories of the Greeks and Romans. He holds: "What Augustine sets forth as

Pax appears to have been a possession of all cultures. We may recall that, to the Vedic Aryans, the central philosophic conception of organized nature was 'rita,' which included the natural and human order. A closely related conception was dharma. The Greeks emphasizing the creative energy made of 'rita' [*phūsis*] and of the 'Dharma' [*Thémis*]. The Romans, through the Greeks, derived from *rita,* their central conception *ratum, ratio, 'naturalis ratio'* and Augustine christianized *rita* into Pax."[49]

Whatever be the historical value of this view, there is, no doubt, a striking similarity between the Indian moral conception of Nature and the Greek concept, particularly of the Stoics, that Nature and men are both governed by a common moral law. Zeller thinks that the Stoics "may be said to be the real creators of the moral theory of the world."[50] But the *Ṛg-veda,* which conceives the moral law of *Ṛta,* is much earlier than the Stoics. The Indian conception of the evolution of law from the moral law governing the universe bears a striking resemblance to the evolution of law in ancient Greece and Rome from the Stoic conception of the law of Nature. Roman Natural Law (*ius naturale*) is the ideal law, to which the laws of the state should try to conform. In Western legal literature, "natural" thus comes to mean "ethical," "reasonable," "equitable," and "natural law" becomes, for some, an ideal basis for international law as well.

THE MANY SOURCES OF INDIAN LAW

Dharma, morality, in the abstract, or, as expressed in basic moral precepts, is too general for judging the rightness of specific kinds of human relations and actions which the individual and the State should know how to deal with justly. Consistent with morality, there are different kinds of practices, customs, conventions, and contracts, in respect of familial, social, economic, and other relations among members of the state, in different places, times, and classes. The individual and the state must recognize these as the specific embodiments of *dharma,* conducive to social stability and welfare.

Manu recognizes four chief sources of law: (1) The Vedas (which include the Brāhmaṇas and the Upaniṣads), (2) the Smṛtis (works on *dharma* like those of Manu himself, Yājñavalkya, and others), which expound the teachings of the Vedas, (3) the practice of the virtuous, and (4) the satisfaction of the self.[51] Of these four, the Vedas enjoy the highest authority, since they are believed to contain eternal truths directly perceived by the purest sages, the seers. In order to understand the Vedas, where they are obscure or silent, it is recommended that light should be sought from the Smṛtis, and also the *Mahābhārata,* the Purāṇas, etc., all of which follow the Vedic tradition. But, in cases of doubt still unresolved, light should be sought from the conduct of the virtuous, how they behave under the circumstances. Approved and good customs prevalent among a class, a guild, a family, in a particular region, and in a particular age thus come to be recognized by the state as laws in dealing with cases relating to them. (These compare with customary and conventional laws in the West.)

The interpretation of the texts, the resolution of conflicts between authorities, and decisions of what is just and right, when no light is available from the other sources, ultimately depend on the reason of the judge himself, and what satisfies him will have to be the law in application. Manu[52] lays great stress in different contexts on the satisfaction of the self, the inner self (*antar-ātman*), as a criterion for right decision. In the Vedāntic background of Manu, the inner self means the self as detached from its ordinary selfish identification with the outer body, the senses, and the lower sensuous mind, the self which judges things with the higher mind, the pure reason (*sāttvika-buddhi*).[53] Through pure reason the self can have integral comprehension of the worth of a thing in the widest of perspectives in relation to the cosmos. Its decision would therefore be in accord with the cosmic *Ṛta.*

THE TURNING BUT STEADY WHEEL OF LAW

It is seen thus that, though the Indian conception of law initially starts with an ethical monotone of *dharma,* it gradually assumes a variety of forms and taps a variety of sources to cover the various manifestations of *dharma* in the scriptures, customs, conduct, and the individual's reason. This makes Indian law a unity in diversity, rooted in the idea of *dharma,* yet progressively accommodative, and comparable to a steadily moving wheel. This idea can be seen in the following extract from a dialogue between Janaka, the model of India's philosopher-king, and *dharma,* disguised as a *brāhmaṇa,* India's traditional wise man: "You [Janaka] are the person to turn the *wheel* [or *dharma* as law], the nave of which is the *Brahman,* the spoke, the understanding, and which does not turn back, and which is checked by the quality of goodness as its circumference."[54]

In addition to the earlier works, a vast literature—in the form of commentaries and digests and manuals—appeared in medieval times. Some of these specially recognized regional customs and conventions. So, the corpus of law was further expanded. But there was not much positive law enacted by the state, except the occasional edicts (*śāsanas*) of kings, e.g., Aśoka's, as revealed by inscriptions. The British rulers enacted laws based partly on Roman and English principles and partly on Indian ones. Recently, free India has modified and codified the Hindu laws of marriage, divorce, succession, etc., which had for so long been left to the interpretation of the Dharma-śāstras by lawyers and judges.

ADMINISTRATION OF JUSTICE

In a large state there were many courts of justice, higher and lower. Many legal disputes and slight offenses were dealt with by village elders, professional guilds, and regional courts established by the king. Major offenses and appeals were dealt with by the king, assisted by from three to seven judges, among whom was the royal priest. The king, as well as his officers, was required to have unimpeachable character, good knowledge of the three Vedas, the other law books, and the subsidiary disciplines, particularly logic. The priest was expected to be able to guide the court on all points of law and custom and to be absolutely upright. Though the ultimate judgment was passed by the king, the entire court, called the *sabhā*, had to contribute to the decision by ascertaining the facts, examining the evidence, and weighing the arguments in the light of relevant laws. They were all morally responsible for the decision. Manu says (8.18) that, if any injustice is done to the complainant, "one-fourth of the resulting sin goes to the respondent, one-fourth to the witness, one-fourth to the judges, and one-fourth to the king." The court is called "The house of *dharma*" (*dharmādhikaraṇa*), and the judges "men of *dharma*" (*dharma-stha*).

JUSTICE AND LOGIC

It is of philosophical importance that the judicial process (*vyavahāra*) is conceived in terms of the Indian method of philosophical discussion aiming at truth, as described by the Nyāya. Kātyāyana defines "*vyavahāra*" as "judgment aiming at the removal of doubts raised by the conflicting statements of the complainant and the defendant."[55] When we see how the Indian law books discuss the process of ascertaining truth by adopting all the technical terms of logic[56] (*hetu,* reason; *liṅga,* middle term; *pakṣa,* minor term; *pakṣābhāsa,* fallacious minor; *pramāṇa,* valid source of knowledge; *yukti,* reasoning; *anumāna,* inference; *tarka,* hypothetical reasoning) and epistemology, we understand why so much stress is laid on the king's and the judge's knowledge of logic. The picture of the king's court of justice gives us a concrete background against which we can place, and understand the utility of, Gautama's (author of the *Nyāya-sūtra*) methodology of debate, in which also two contending parties are conceived as presenting opposite points of view in a council presided over by learned and impartial judges, who declare defeat or victory for the proponent after weighing all arguments for and against him, supporting the decision with all relevant sources of knowledge. This would explain why justice itself is called *nyāya* (logic) and why the judicial process is called *vyavahāra* (application), and the king is asked to wield the scepter with reasoning.[57]

CASES FOR DECISION

Cases for judicial decision are analyzed by Manu (8.4–7) into eighteen kinds, which give us a rough idea of the field of legal rights and legal action. They are: non-payment of debt, entrusted wealth, illegal sale, co-operative business, resumption of gifts, non-payment of remuneration, violation of contract, disputes between buyers and sellers, disputes between owners and tenders of flocks, boundary disputes, harshness in speech, and in physical handling, theft, audacious violent aggression defying the people and the scepter (e.g., robbery, arson, homicide), immoral sex-relation, conjugal disputes, division of inherited wealth, and gambling. These branch off into a hundred others, as Kātyāyana observes.

It is interesting to note that for failing to punish a culprit Vaśiṣṭha prescribes that the king shall fast one night, and the priest, his legal adviser, for three nights.[58] This shows that moral responsibility is in direct proportion to the prestige and position enjoyed in the system. Kauṭilya follows Yājñavalkya in holding that in fining an innocent person the king should atone for the sin by offering thirty times that fine to Varuṇa (the god of justice) and the priest by hard penance.[59]

FORMS OF PUNISHMENT

Forms of punishment varied from mild admonition, censure, fine, branding and parading in public places, mutilation of limbs and organs, fetters, imprisonment, exile, and confiscation of property, to death. In addition, some forms of expiation through repentance, austerity, and rituals are prescribed under certain conditions. Some of the forms of punishment, such as mutilation of limbs, appear to us too harsh, and even barbarous. That shows how our humane sentiments have developed; and it marks the unmistakable progress of man in civilized life. Historians of India point out by comparing the recorded impressions of the Greek envoy, Megasthenes, of the third century B.C., and those of the Chinese pilgrim, Fa-hsien, about seven hundred years later, that the harsher forms of punishment were gradually replaced by fines, imprisonment, etc. We may remember that as late as the beginning of the nineteenth century more than a hundred kinds of offenses were punishable by death in England, and even in 1832 a child was hanged there for stealing a box of paints worth twopence.[60] How incredible it sounds. How incredibly fast our moral sentiments have developed.

As early as the *Mahābhārata*[61] we hear the protest against the unreasonableness of capital punishment. The sentiment and reasoning against capital punishment gather force in Śukra, who points out (4.1.92–108) that this bad practice violates the Vedic injunction against taking any life; it should be replaced by imprisonment for life, if necessary, and a natural criminal should be transported to an island, or fettered and made to repair the public roads. Brutality in punishment was gradually replaced. Fa-hsien reports that he did not find any capital punishment in India (A.D. 399–400), but fining was there, and mutilation in cases of treason.

EQUITY IN LAW

Were all individuals equal in the eyes of law? Manu tells us (8.335): The king should spare neither his father, nor his teacher, nor friend, nor mother, nor son, nor priest, if he or she violates the law. But in the very next stanza (8.326) he says: "Where an ordinary man is fined one coin, a king should be fined a thousand coins." Śukra (4.5.282) prescribes deterrent punishment for judges violating their duties. Again, not to speak of a child under five who is totally exempted from punishment, an old man above eighty, a boy below sixteen, and all women are given half-punishment compared to male adults. Women are exempted by Kātyāyana (487) from capital punishment; they suffer excision of a limb, instead. *Brāhmaṇas* are exempted from physical mutilation and death by most authorities, though branding, fining, imprisonment, and exile are permitted. But, in case of theft, a *śūdra* (laborer) is punished the least, a trader above him is punished twice as much, a warrior four times, and a *brāhmaṇa* eight times. Again, a *brāhmaṇa,* but not the lower castes, is punished for drinking. Also, crimes against higher classes and against women are more severely punished than those against lower classes and against men. Crimes against lower animals are recognized and punished (Manu, 11.131 ff.).

Legal authorities try to reduce these apparent inequalities to a principle of equitable relativity. Manu (8.126) says punishment should be inflicted after examining the circumstances, place, and time, as well as the worth and offense of the culprit. Yājñavalkya (1.368) puts it more clearly: A culprit should be punished after considering the offense, place, time, strength, age, work, and economic condition. This list obviously does not cover all points of special treatment noted above, but the points mentioned would be found acceptable to modern conscience, though the leniency shown to hereditary higher castes would be objected to, as was the case with Śukra (1.38) and others in India, so that legal privileges of caste gradually disappeared. Discrimination against backward classes in public places and in civil life has now been prohibited by legal enactment. The underlying spirit behind ancient Indian law was to protect and promote a social system in which wisdom and goodness—the ultimate means to spiritual freedom—would receive the highest regard. But the spirit of the law became corrupted in practice.

THE OBJECTIVES OF PUNISHMENT

If we analyze the implied and explicit purposes of punishment, we find that punishment was conceived, first, as a deterrent measure calculated to strike fear into the hearts of the criminally minded and to check their immoral and anti-social passions. This purpose was served particularly by disproportionately severe punishment and by branding, parading, and publicizing punishment. The second object was the prevention of the possibility of the culprit's repeating the crime. So, the culprit was imprisoned, fettered, killed, or exiled. Retribution may be said to be the third motive of punishment in two different senses: retaliation and making the wrongdoer suffer the fruits of his own *karma.* The first is particularly noticed in the mutilation of that very limb by which the wrong was done (e.g., cutting off fingers or hand of a thief, the tongue of a defamer). Punishments, fourthly, are conceived to be an educative, and, therefore, a reformative process also. Śukra points out that, consistent with the Vedic teaching of non-injury to life, a culprit should be educated (*śikṣayet*) and made to work. He takes a very modern socio-psychological view when he says (4.1.110), "Such persons were corrupted by bad company. The king should punish them and always educate them back onto the right path." But punishment was thought to be, not only reformative, but also purificatory in a moral sense. This is more evident in the fact that punishment also included different forms of repentance, confession, prayer, penitential starvation, and long periods of penance (e.g., a *brāhmaṇa,* while spared capital punishment, had to live even as long as twelve years in the forest in austerity and celibacy to atone for murder).

It will also be seen that violation of law was regarded primarily as a crime against society and its guardian, the king, who was thought responsible for all preventable natural calamities and human vices threatening society.[62] Compensation for personal damages, torts, was also provided for, but even in such cases fines were payable to the state also.

LEGAL RIGHTS

It has struck modern scholars that Indian social thinkers consider human relations in terms of duties rather than rights. This peculiar attitude follows perhaps from an emphasis on "what I should do for others" rather than on "what others should do for me." But, when duties are well defined and performed, rights are also determined, respected, and fulfilled thereby. The laws of the state, in punishing the violation of duties toward others, also safeguard their rights. The duties of the king or the state to the people define the rights of the people. The necessity of a clear definition of political rights arises when the state is brought into existence after dispute, negotiation, and contract. But, as we saw, the state in ancient India was based neither on contract nor on enacted laws.

ECONOMIC JUSTICE, RIGHTS, AND DUTIES

The conception of proprietary rights in respect of wealth is found, however, as early as the Vedic period; and there are even terms to distinguish between ownership (*svatva, svāmitva*) and mere possession (*bhoga*). The right to life, as recognized in the duty of non-injury to life, led logically to the recognition of the right to wealth as the means to the maintenance of life. Manu says that there are seven righteous sources of ownership, namely, inheritance, finding (unowned things), purchase, labor, victory (for the warrior), investment for increase (in case of the trader), and acceptance of gift (in the case of the *brāhmaṇa*). Others add a few more. The king is not generally regarded as the owner of the lands.

The *Bhāgavata* (17.14) raises the concept of ownership to a high plane: all wealth is God's; his creatures have a right to as much as will support life; one who claims more is a thief and deserves punishment. A similar idea is traceable in the *Īśa-upaniṣad.* Vinoba is utilizing this idea in his movement for voluntary gifts and the sharing of land (*bhūdāna*), by which process he has collected more than five million acres of land (including about five thousand whole villages now communally shared).

While advocating the right of everyone to the God-given natural resources, Gandhi insisted that this right has to be earned by everyone by performing the duty of spending the God-given physical powers for producing the necessities of life out of the natural resources. Economic justice, the equitable distribution of wealth, cannot be enforced by state laws unless society is morally aroused to the sense of duty and fraternal love.

IV. Conclusion

India has now outwardly adopted from the West political democracy, industrial organization, and part of its legal system. But to understand why India still shows some strange inclinations and conflicting moods we must know the contending and indecisive forces inwardly active, for example, the cold, utilitarian realism of Kauṭilya and Śukra; the high idealism of Yudhiṣṭhira, Aśoka, and Gandhi; and the golden mean of Manu and Arjuna. It is hoped that this short account will throw some light on these divergent forces, and their general philosophical background, which still dominate Indian thought and action.

QUESTION: What would Gandhi do if India were attacked?

ANSWER: Let Gandhi answer: "India must not submit to any aggressor or invader and must resist him."[63] "There are two ways of defense. The best and the most effective is not to defend at all, but to remain at one's post risking every danger. The next best but equally honourable method is to strike bravely in self-defense and put one's life in the most dangerous position. If we bear malice and hatred in our bosom and pretend not to retaliate, it must recoil upon us and lead to our destruction."[64] "I would rather have India resort to arms in order to defend her honour than that she should, in a cowardly manner, become or remain a helpless witness to her own dishonour."[65]

Gandhi thinks that violence springs from inner weakness, fear, and malice; it leads to more violence and demoralizes both parties. The meeting of violence by non-violence or love (the way of the Buddha, Mahāvīra, and Christ) ennobles both parties, quenches enmity, and, though it needs long moral training and entails great sacrifice, it is the best way consistent with the spiritual dignity and destiny of man, who must rise above the brute.[66]

Notes

1. For an exhaustive survey of the vast literature of polity, law, and economics, see P. V. Kane, *History of Dharmaśāstra,* Vol. III (Bombay: Bhandarkar Oriental Research Institute, 1946). Indian chronology is uncertain. Some tentative dates are: Vedic period, 2500–600 B.C.; Epic period, 600 B.C.–A.D. 200; Dharma-śāstras, same period; Kauṭilya's *Artha-śāstra,* between 321 and 296 B.C. (See S. Radhakrishnan and C. A. Moore, eds., *A Source Book in Indian Philosophy* (Princeton: Princeton University Press, 1957), pp. 193–223. Śukra, *Śukranītisāra,* Jivānanda Vidyāsāgara, ed. (Calcutta: Narayana Press, n.d.), is placed by different scholars from pre-Christian times to several centuries after Christ.
2. D. M. Datta, "The Moral Conception of Nature in Indian Philosophy," *International Journal of Ethics,* XLVI, No. 2 (January, 1936).
3. *Ṛgveda* (Ajmer: Vaidika Yantrālaya, 1900), I.lxviii.2; I.cv.12; I.cxxxvi.2 *et passim.* (The numerals refer successively to *maṇḍala,* hymn, and stanza.) See Kane, *op. cit.,* pp. 244–245.
4. The motto now adopted by the Indian Government.
5. P. Tarkaratna, ed., *Mahābhārata* (Calcutta: Bangabasi Press edition, 1909), Salya-parva, 63.60. (The numerals refer successively to chapter and stanza.)
6. *Manusmṛti* (hereafter *Manu*), V. L. Paṇśīkara, Amendator (Bombay: Nirṇayasāgara Press edition, 1920), 8.15.
7. *Mahānārāyaṇa-upaniṣad,* XXII.1 (in *A Compilation of 120 Upaniṣads;* Bombay: Nirṇayasāgara, 1948). N. R. Acarya and R. L. Mitra, eds., *Taittirīya Āraṇyaka* (Calcutta: Asiatic Society of Bengal, 1872).
8. P. Tarkaratna, ed., *Śrīmadbhāgavatam* (Calcutta: Bangabasi Press

edition, 1920), 11.2.29. (Numerals refer successively to part, chapter, and stanza.)

9. *Dhammapada*, S. Radhakrishnan, ed. and trans. (London: Oxford University Press, 1950), XIV.4.
10. Śānti-parva, 60.9.
11. *Kaṭha-upaniṣad*, III.3.
12. *Mahābhārata*, Anuśāsana-parva, 116.38.
13. "Puruṣa-sūkta." See Radhakrishnan and Moore, eds., *A Source Book*, p. 31.
14. *Manu*, 3.70.
15. *Ibid.*, 7.97.
16. *Ibid.*, 6.35; 6.37.
17. *Gītā*, II.31; II.33 *et passim*. See also Sri Aurobindo, *Essays on the Gītā* (Calcutta: Arya Publishing House, 1945), 2nd series, chap. XX.
18. *Gītā*, IV.13.
19. *Ibid.*, XVIII.45.
20. Sri Aurobindo's translation in his *Isha Upanishad* (Calcutta: Arya Publishing House, 1945).
21. By F. S. C. Northrop, in his *The Meeting of East and West* (New York: The Macmillan Co., 1946), pp. 335 *et passim*.
22. See K. C. Bhattacharyya, "The Jaina Theory of *Anekāntavāda*," in his *Studies in Philosophy*, Vol. 1 (Calcutta: Progressive Publishers, 1956).
23. See N. K. Bose, *Selections from Gandhi* (Ahmedabad: Navajivan Publishing House, 1948), pp. 4, 20; *Young India*, January 21, 1926; *Bhūdāna-Yajña* (Banaras), November 15, 1957.
24. *Manu*, 12.10.
25. See A. S. Altekar, *State and Government in Ancient India* (Delhi: Motilal Banarasidas, 1958), chap. II.
26. *Mahābhārata*, Śānti-parva, 59.94; *Śukra*, 2.274–275.
27. See U. N. Ghoshal, *Agrarian System in Ancient India* (Calcutta: University of Calcutta, 1930), Lecture V.
28. *Manu*, 8.304–309.
29. See Aśoka's Rock Edicts XII, XIII, *et passim*, in D. C. Sircar, ed., *Inscriptions of Aśoka* (Delhi: Government of India Publication, 1957).
30. Bose, *Selections*, p. 224: "Here religion does not mean sectarianism. It means belief in an ordered moral Government of the Universe." Also, Gandhi, *An Autobiography* (Ahmedabad: Navajivan Publishing House, 1948), p. 5: ". . . the essence of religion is morality."
31. *Manu*, 9.30 ff.
32. See U. N. Ghoshal, *History of Hindu Public Life* (Calcutta: R. Ghoshal, n.d.), pp. 86–87; and Altekar, *op. cit.*, chap. II.
33. Altekar, *op. cit.*, p. 320.

34. See *Manu,* 7.115 ff.; and Kane, *op. cit.,* pp. 153 ff.
35. Kauṭilya, *Arthaśāstra,* R. Shamasastry, trans. (2nd ed.; Mysore: Wesleyan Mission Press, 1923), I.i.2.
36. *Manu,* 7.40–42; *Arthaśāstra,* T. G. Śastrī, ed., I.i.2; *Mahābhārata,* Śānti-parva, 18.8; *Yājñavalkya-smṛti* (Trivandram: Government Press, 1922), I.304–306.
37. See Caṇḍeśvara, *Rājanīti-ratnākara,* K. P. Jayaswal, ed. (Patna: Bihar and Orissa Research Society, 1924), chap. XVI.
38. *Dhammapada,* XVII.3; I.5.
39. See Bose, *Selections,* p. 184.
40. See Kane, *op. cit.,* chap. IX.
41. *Manu,* 7.88–95.
42. See Altekar, *op. cit.,* p. 298.
43. *Artha-śāstra,* X, XIV.
44. *Śukra,* 5.32–35.
45. See H. G. Wells, *The Outline of History* (New York: Garden City Books, 1949), pp. 402–404.
46. See Aśoka's Rock Edicts XII, XIII, *et passim, op. cit.,* pp. 50–55.
47. Bose, *Selections,* p. xi.
48. Author of *The World's Legal Philosophies.* In the Introduction to the English translation of this German work, Sir John Macdonell says that it enables us to "ascend to a height from which we can see law as an ever-present part of an ever-flowing stream." (Boston: The Boston Book Company, 1912.)
49. Quoted by R. B. Pal in *The Hindu Philosophy of Law* (Calcutta: Bishwabhandar Press, n.d.), pp. 1–2.
50. Eduard Zeller, *Philosophie der Griechen* [Stoics, etc.]. English translation by Oswald J. Reichel (London: Longmans, Green & Co., 1870), p. 178.
51. *Manu,* 2.6; 2.12.
52. *Ibid.,* 2.6; 2.12; 4.161; 8.84; 11.233.
53. *Ibid.,* 12.27.
54. Quoted by R. B. Pal in *The History of Hindu Law* (Calcutta: University of Calcutta, 1958), p. 194.
55. Quoted by Kullūka on *Manu,* 8.1.
56. *Śukra,* 4.5.128 ff; *Arthaśāstra,* III.i, Shamasastry, *op. cit.,* p. 150; Kane, *op. cit.,* pp. 304, 354–355.
57. *Mahābhārata,* Śānti-parva, 24.34.
58. *Ibid.,* 36.17.
59. *Arthaśāstra,* Shamasastry, *op. cit.,* p. 307; *Rājanīti-ratnākara,* p. 73.
60. Kane, *op. cit.,* pp. 390–391.
61. *Mahābhārata,* Śānti-parva, 266.
62. See Kane, *op. cit.,* p. 387, and P. N. Sen, *Hindu Jurisprudence* (Calcutta: University of Calcutta, 1918). See Lecture XII, for refutation

of Sir Henry Maine's theory that ancient law recognized only torts, not public crimes.

63. See Bose, *Selections,* p. 173.
64. *Ibid.,* p. 154.
65. *Ibid.,* p. 155.
66. *Ibid.,* chap. XI.

KALIDAS BHATTACHARYYA

The Status of the Individual in Indian Metaphysics

I. Introduction

REGARDING THE Indian attitude toward the individual, Westerners hold certain views which are not wholly correct. They are:

(1) In Indian metaphysics there is no place for a plurality of individuals. Plurality of individuals is ultimately an illusion: the ultimate reality is one ineffable Absolute (called *Brahman*).

(2) This metaphysics has so influenced the general Indian mind that in formulating the ideal of life it has ignored what concerns, or should concern, individuals as individuals. The ultimate aim of life, for the Indians, is complete merging in the Absolute.

(3) It is because of this neglect of the individual that the Indians could never develop systematic ethics and social philosophy, and the only spiritual religion they have developed is a mystical form of pantheism which, according to many Westerners, is no religion at all and borders dangerously on a life which is thoroughly irreligious and irresponsible.

(4) Even where they have admitted individuals, as, for example, on the empirical (*vyāvahārika*) plane, they have systematically deprived them of freedom of will. Westerners hold that the Indian doctrine of *karma* is a direct denial of freedom of individuals.

Of these four views, the last one is wholly incorrect, and the first, second, and the third are correct only insofar as they represent the standpoint of the Advaiṭa Vedānta. But the Advaita Vedānta is only one of the Indian systems of philosophy. There are other systems, such as the Nyāya, the Vaiśeṣika, the Sāṁkhya, the Yoga, the Mīmāṁsā, and the non-Advaita Vedāntic systems, none of which is of less significance to Indian life in general than the Advaita. There are also lesser philosophers, such as the Śaivas, Śāktas, and Grammarians. Add to the list the three great heterodox systems (Buddhism, Jainism, and the philosophy of the Cārvākas), and we have all kinds of Indian views of the individual. Except for a few Śaivas and Grammarians and the philosophers of one or two schools of Buddhism, none denied plurality of selves, none recommended the liquidation of individuals, and none spoke of the Absolute as the only reality or preached pantheism of the Advaita brand.

In fact, there is no *one* Indian view of the status of the individual. There are many views, each upheld by substantial Indian thinkers and by a large section of the Indian people. The Cārvāka system apart—which somehow could not stand repeated onslaught by every other system—if there is anything common to the different Indian views of the individual, it is (1) that every individual has a spiritual side, (2) that his spiritual side is, from the valuational point of view, more essential than his material side, (3) that its autonomy has to be fully realized, and (4) that this realization is possible through progressive detachment (*vairāgya*) from the less essential sides of his being. Detachment from these has not always meant their dismissal.

II. Individuals as Free Agents

To show now that the last one of the four views of the Indian attitude on the individual is wholly incorrect:

By the word "individual" we mean throughout this paper a human being who is not entirely an item of Nature, accepting unquestioningly what Nature offers and submitting blindly to its forces, but one who often resists it and initiates new actions, one, in other words, who is as much above Nature as in it. This over-natural status of man is called "freedom."[*][1] We are told that in this sense of the word "freedom" Indians have never admitted free individuals. Their Law of *Karma*, we are told, is a direct disavowal of such freedom.

[*] Because of continued serious illness, the author was unable to supply the full documentation he had intended to provide.—*Editor's note.*

This, however, is entirely wrong.[2] Movements made by an individual have been classified by Indians into three groups—*tāmasika, rājasika,* and *sāttvika. Tāmasika* movements are those over which the individual, whose movements they are, has no control, the individual remaining in a state of stupor, as it were. These movements are absolutely unfree. Movements which are blindly biological belong to this group. *Rājasika* movements are those of which the individual is conscious, though unreflectively, as *his* actions—actions, viz., for which he is prepared to take full responsibility, but which are still not free, because they proceed through, and are determined by, emotions and sentiments, the keynote of which is positive attachment (*rāga*) or repulsion (*dveṣa*). These unfree movements are as much biological and blind as the *tāmasika* ones, and yet they are claimed by the individual as *his* actions only because he can, and often does, follow, though unreflectively, quite a large number of subtle varieties of attachment and repulsion, which animals and men-in-stupor cannot. There is an important reason, again, why the individual is prepared to take responsibility for these actions. It is always possible for the individual, though this requires a good amount of effort, not to yield entirely to the operating attachments and repulsions, but either to keep his actions confined within his mind, preventing them from maturing into physical actions, or to channelize them into moral contexts, maintaining all through an over-all control over them.

So far, this over-all control is only possible. As and when, however, it becomes actual, the actions that result have risen to the level called *sāttvika.* The guiding principle at this level is detachment (*vairāgya*), which, however, admits of degree. Short of absolute detachment, it leads to actions which are socio-moral (*dharma*) at the lower stage and spiritual (*ādhyātmika*) at a higher. At the moral level, noted in the last paragraph, actions proceeding through attachment and repulsion are only channelized, and in more austere forms of *dharma* attempts are made to render these two motive forces more and more inoperative. Attempts at channelizing ordinary actions or preventing them from maturing into physical movements, practiced again and again, lead in their turn to the accumulation of corresponding dispositions which, as they grow stronger and stronger, sap, in proportion, the life-force of the germs of action that could mature through attachment and repulsion. This entire course of progressive sapping constitutes the spiritual life of the individual, and, with sapping concluded, he reaches a stage which is the last doorway to liberation (*mukti*). Activities prior to that liberation, beginning with the first actual control, are *sāttvika;* and, when liberation is attained, one finds oneself in a new dimension altogether, beyond all *tamas, rajas,* and *sattva.* Through all stages, *sāttvika* actions are free in the sense that one so acting has so far detached himself from Nature.

This account is given explicitly in the Sāṁkhya, and, somehow or other, with minor variations here and there, it has also been accepted in most other systems.[3]

Also, the Law of *Karma,* properly understood, is *not* against freedom of action. It is true that, according to this law, my present life is somehow determined by the merits and demerits of what I did in my previous life, that life, again, by the merits and demerits of what I had done in a life still previous, and so on ad infinitum, but this does not mean that everything of a particular life is determined. It has been explicitly stated that only three things in my life are determined. They are (1) the bodily and mental make-up and social position at the time of birth in that particular life (*jāti*), (2) the span of that life (*āyuḥ*), and (3) particular experiences with all the hedonic tones that they have in that life and all that is necessary as objects or direct or indirect causes of those experiences (*bhoga*). Among these direct and indirect causes are included my physiological movements and actions which proceed through attachment and repulsion but not actions at the moral and spiritual levels. Moral and spiritual actions have been excepted on the following grounds:

(1) We are definitely told that with the results yielded in a particular life the merits and demerits of actions done in the previous life get exhausted, and these results as experiences with appropriate hedonic tones are meant as rewards or punishments. It follows that, if the results as experiences in the present life could in their turn yield further results with hedonic tones—whether in this life or in the next—that would be the grossest form of injustice. It would amount to rewarding or punishing an individual for all eternity. That would also go against the accepted theory that merits or demerits of actions get exhausted in their results.

(2) It would also speak against all possibility of betterment of the individual, and equally against all conscious effort for liberation (*mukti*), unless, of course, the betterment and the effort in question are results of good actions in the life preceding the

present one. But, then, even in the case of the latter alternative, the goodness of these previous actions has to be explained, and, should one say that it, too, is similarly the result of good actions done in a life preceding the previous one, it would follow that an individual once good in one life is good in all lives, and similarly with individuals who are bad; and that, in turn, would mean that bad individuals could never become good and the good never bad—a thesis which no Indian system would ever allow. Perhaps it would also follow that a bad soul should continually grow worse than before—a doctrine more severe than that of eternal damnation and never acceptable to Indians. It would also follow that, if as a result of non-meritorious actions an individual is born in the next life as a tree or a sub-human animal, he would lose all chance as much of betterment as of worsening, for the actions (movements) of these latter, as not proceeding through attachment and repulsion, could never acquire merit or demerit—they are completely amoral.

(3) If the Law of *Karma* is understood as a theory of complete determination, this would go against the very spirit of scriptural or, for the matter of that, any, prescription or prohibition. It one is bound to do what one does, why should there be prescription or prohibition?

So, Indians never meant that everything of the present life is determined by what one did in the preceding life. Add to this the fact that they have distinguished moral and spiritual actions from actions that are biological, and it will follow that there is nothing against these actions' being considered free. To repeat: Spiritual actions, which proceed from detachment (*vairāgya*), have maximum freedom, because there is no submission to attachment and repulsion; moral actions as channelizing, according to prescriptions and prohibitions, normal biological activities are free in the sense that in their case there is no blind submission; and actions which proceed consciously through attachment and repulsion and are consequently accompanied by an I-feeling are free only in the sense that in their case there is always a possibility of not having submitted to them.

III. Plurality of Individuals

It is only in one Indian system, viz., the Advaita Vedānta, along with a few sub-schools of Śaiva philosophy and the philosophy of Grammar, that the plurality of individuals has been denied an ultimate status. All other schools and sub-schools have recognized plurality as an ultimate truth. Most of these schools and sub-schools have taken this for granted; only a few have come forward to meet the Advaita thesis on logical grounds.

The Advaita Vedāntist has denied the ultimate status of individual persons principally on three grounds. They are:

(1) The individual as we ordinarily understand him is a complex consisting of a body, a mind (*ahaṁkāra* = ego),[4] and a self. Of these three constituents, the self is the most important; it is the essence of the individual. Normally, this essence remains fused—one might even say confused—with the mind and the body, but, since in itself it is an autonomous essence, the individual, whose ultimate duty is to realize himself, will have to distinguish this essence. He will have to dissociate it from the mind and the body, which are only accidents. This dissociation of the self has been understood by the Advaita Vedāntist in an extreme sense. He understands it as the severance of all its relations with the mind and the body, even of the slightest relation called "reference," and from this he concludes, a little too easily, that therefore this dissociate self cannot be many, for it is only the bodies and minds (*ahaṁkāras*) that are many, and, if the dissociate self—the self-in-itself—has no need of even referring to these, there is no reason why it should be many. To admit plurality of selves over and above that of minds and bodies would unnecessarily multiply entities.

(2) Often, again, the Advaita Vedāntist has denied the plurality of selves on the *ipsi dixit* of the Vedic texts, specifically, the Upaniṣads.

(3) Later Advaita thinkers have attacked the very concept of plurality (difference). They have pointed out inconsistencies in that concept.

The Advaita Vedāntist thus holds that ultimately there is only one self, and, as the self is the essence of the individual, all individuals must be essentially one. This one essence—the Absolute, or *Brahman* as it is called—is in no need of even referring to minds and bodies. It follows that the many individuals we normally are in this world are due only to illusory identification of this Absolute with different mind-body complexes.

However, other Indian systems[5] have rejected this Advaita

doctrine. They have not indeed denied that the self constitutes the essence of the individual or that it is the duty of the individual to realize his self as the autonomous essence. What they have refused to do is to interpret this autonomy as rejection of all its relations, even the relation of reference, to the mind and the body.

The Sāṁkhya, the Yoga, and a number of Śaiva thinkers hold that the self, even in its full autonomy, constantly refers to—in the language of Indian philosophy, reveals or witnesses—mental states and, through these, as the occasion arises, objects that are non-mental. Mere reference (revealing or witnessing) need not affect the freedom of the self. One may keep oneself aloof from certain things and just witness their behavior. The self as just witnessing the mind and its states is what is actually found in self-consciousness. As the self, while witnessing the mind and its states, can yet retain its autonomy, there is no need to reject this witnessing. The autonomy of the self need not, therefore, transcend its witnessing or reference function. The free self as just witnessing the mind and its states is called in the Sāṁkhya and the Yoga, and even in the Advaita Vedānta, *sākṣin* (witness) or *sākṣi-puruṣa* (witness-self); and, since it thus refers, of its own nature, to a particular mind (ego), which reference it has no need to transcend or abjure, it follows that the self as witness is particular. Since, again, no witness can refer in this way to another particular mind (ego), it follows, further, that selves, even as autonomous, are many.

Free reference of the witness to the particular mind corresponding to it may indeed imply that it might not have exercised that reference and is, therefore, capable of withdrawing it. But this may well be an impotent capability, just wishful thinking, not capable enough to mature into actuality. One may be reminded here of Kant's Ideas of Reason. A possible need not be a possible actual. The Advaitist has not shown that this possible withdrawal of reference is a possibility of actual withdrawal.

The Advaita has indeed attributed this reference at the witness stage to the last vestige of nescience (*ajñāna*). But what exactly is meant here by "last vestige" and how it can possibly disappear have never been clearly stated in Advaita texts. The Advaitists have only expressed their conviction, that it should disappear.

We may note in this connection that the doctrine of *jīvan-mukti* (liberation in one's lifetime), to which the Advaitist, along with many others, has subscribed, is not very consistent with his denial of individuality. The Advaitist admits that some individuals may realize their autonomous essences and, therefore, their complete identity with the Absolute, even in their lifetime, still retaining their minds (and bodies). These are the *jīvan-muktas.* If, now, these *jīvan-muktas,* who have retained their minds (and bodies), can yet be completely free (liberated), it is difficult to believe that they have ceased to be individuals. If their activities were merely biological, and nothing more, we could somehow imagine them as wholly identical with *Brahman,* for it is not difficult to conceive that these activities are not appropriated by the self. But the Advaitist has, as a matter of fact, attributed to them actions which are also moral and spiritual.

The plurality of individuals was denied only by the Advaita, not even by other schools of the Vedānta. The Rāmānujists and Madhvas, for example, have resolutely held that even pure selves are many. They have replied to all the Advaita charges against the concept of difference and interpreted the so-called monistic scriptural texts along different lines; and, as regards the autonomy of the self, they have distinguished it from the body only, the mind (*ahaṁkāra* = ego) and the self being the same thing in their systems. This is equally the view of Nyāya-Vaiśeṣika thinkers and the Mīmāṁsakas.

That there are many individual selves in addition to many bodies is for all these thinkers an obvious truth to start with,[6] and, if the Advaitist has argued against this obvious truth, they have offered counterarguments. Their main point is that, even if the ultimate realization of the self amounts to severance of all connection with the body[7] that the individual had, even then the distinctive individuality of the self need not disappear. Appeal to the law of parsimony would be useless here, for parsimony is relevant only in the context of hypotheses, not with regard to obvious facts.

Some hold even that at no stage is there complete freedom from the body. Even God, for them, has an eternal body made of a pure stuff, and so has the self that at liberation severs connection with the gross (and subtle) body.

With the exception of the Rāmānujists, these philosophers are all deists, holding that God is one of the many selves, though infinitely superior to others in many respects. They understand God in such a way that his infinity is not in any way jeopardized by the independence of others.

The Rāmānujists and Vedāntists of a few other schools, on the other hand, have preferred theism. The Rāmānujists hold that the individual selves, distinct from one another and from God, are all still adjectival to God, and believe that God and all these adjectival selves have formed one grand unity. Of this grand unity, God forms the central part—he is the substantive to which these selves, and the world, too, cling as adjectives. The Rāmānujists warn, however, that the relation between God, on the one hand, and the individual selves and the world, on the other, is no form of identity-in-difference. Much along the lines of the Nyāya-Vaiśeṣika, they hold that, if two things are identical, they cannot be different at the same time, and vice versa, though they admit at the same time that this does not preclude the possibility of these factors' forming a unity. In the case, for example, of a man with a stick in his hand, the man and the stick, though each a distinct thing, have formed a unity, viz., the man-with-the-stick. Such unities may sometimes be very close (*apṛthak-siddhi* = inseparability), as in the case of a blue flower, where the flower and the blue color, each distinct from the other, form such a close system that it is impossible to divorce one of them from the other. The example of loose unity (*pṛthak-siddhi* = separability) is the man-with-the-stick. The unity that God and the individual selves have formed is a close one, according to the Rāmānujists. Often, indeed, Rāmānuja has compared the relation between God and individual selves with that between a master and his servants or that between a king and his subjects, or that between the soul and the body, etc., almost suggesting that the unity formed need not be a close one. But this is only a loose way of speaking. What he means is perhaps that God, the substantival part of the unity, could remain without reference to individual selves but never does remain so, his remaining alone being a mere possibility that never, even from the metaphysical point of view, can mature into actuality. With the Advaitist, on the other hand, this possibility indicates actual metaphysical transcendence.

The Vedāntists of some other schools, viz., the Bhāskarites and Nimbārkists, have argued, however, in favor of identity-in-difference. The notion of identity-in-difference has always troubled the Indian mind. Nyāya-Vaiśeṣika thinkers and the Rāmānujists have openly denounced it as self-contradictory, and those who have favored the concept have always had to defend their case. They have defended it in one of the three following ways:

(1) Logic cannot denounce what is, after all, a patent fact. Is not identity-in-difference evident in the cases of substance and

its characters, material cause (stuff) and its effects (modes), parts and their whole, etc.

If the Nyāya-Vaiśeṣika has, in such cases, proposed to replace identity-in-difference by what it calls inherence (*samavāya*), this is not merely a gratuitous complication of the issue; it involves another difficulty, viz., that the relation of this *inherence* with that to which something stands in that inherence relation goes unexplained. Rāmānuja's attempt to replace identity-in-difference by what he calls "unity of differents" is no less defective, for he, too, has faltered over clear cases like the relation between a substance and its attributes and could bypass the difficulty only by postulating the hasty notion of close unity (*apṛthak-siddhi*).

(2) Others, less defiant of the Law of Contradiction, have defended identity-in-difference by holding that the two things between which this relation holds are identical in one way (i.e., from one point of view) and different in another (i.e., from another point of view).

(3) The third way of defending identity-in-difference is to argue that, though ultimately (from the *pāramārthika*—ultimate—point of view) identity-in-difference is untenable (because self-contradictory), we in our daily life put up with it, which means that it has provisional, pragmatic (*vyāvahārika*) value.

The first of these three defenses was offered by the Bhāskarites and Nimbārkists, and, to some extent, by the Sāṁkhya. The second way of defense was advocated by the Mīmāṁsakas, and, again, sometimes by the Sāṁkhya. The third was the way of many Advaita thinkers.

The problem of plurality or non-plurality of individuals and their relation to God or the Absolute is one that concerns only the essence of individuals, i.e., their selves. So long, however, as individuals are understood as body-self or body-mind-self complexes, there is no denial anywhere in Indian philosophy of their plurality and difference from God. Except in metaphysics, again, which concerns the essence of the individual, Indians have not generally underrated the status of the body and the mind. Full compliments are paid to these in *artha-śāstra* (economics and politics), *daṇḍa-nīti* (science of government), *āyur-veda* (medicine), *kāma-śāstra* (science of living and enjoyment), and different other *vidyās* (sciences and arts); and, though the philosophical ideal is always regarded as the highest for the individual, so much so that other ideals have been subordinated to it and placed in proper perspective, in actual life the average Indian has not been nearly so unbalancedly otherwordly as he is believed to be by people in the West. Regarding the philosophical ideal, again, there have been, as we have already seen and shall see more fully later, all kinds of views, of which the Advaita view is just one, and the average Indian's life has not been less influenced by any of these other views than by the Advaita. One must not forget also that materialism, which had for ages been dominant in India in some form or other, has always been a problem for all other Indian thinkers. As we have already said, there has never been *one* Indian view of the status of the individual, except in the sense stated on page one. The systems that have influenced Indian life most are Śaivism, Śāktism, and Vaiṣṇavism in their different forms, and they were mostly for the plurality of individuals and some significant difference somewhere between them and God (or the Absolute).[8]

IV. Doctrine of Inaction and Its Refutation[9]

The only school of Indian philosophy that has preached inaction as the ultimate goal of life is the Advaita Vedānta, and undoubtedly this doctrine has had some influence on Indian life in general. But there are two points to be noted in this connection. First, no other system has preached this doctrine, and in the whole field of philosophical literature it has more often been opposed than supported. Second, even as the Advaita preaches it, there is always the prefatory warning that this inaction is only for those who have attained liberation. Until that liberation is attained, every man is called upon to perform moral and spiritual action, and it is clearly said in the Advaita that performance of such actions is a necessary prerequisite for earning the right (*adhikāra*) to inaction, so that the common charge against the Advaita that it has left no scope for morality and religion is so far unfounded.

If, in spite of all this, the doctrine of inaction has sometimes appealed to the lay Hindu public, this can be traced, in most cases, to political debacles. One cannot also deny altogether that, to some extent, the Advaita philosophy itself was responsible for that. It often extended the scope of inaction by prescribing it even for those who are on the path to liberation, not actually liberated. The esoteric exercises (*sādhana*) which they are to practice have often been designated as cognitive (*jñāna-sādhana*), as opposed to the performance of moral actions and the worship of God (*karma-sādhana*). If others have argued that *sādhana* itself cannot but be an action, the Advaita has gone the length of saying that it is only a pseudo-action (*bidhicchāyā*), i.e., something which is really of the nature of cognition, though spoken of (perhaps necessarily) in terms of action. The Advaita idea is that the individual on the way to liberation is only to seek discovery of the Absolute, and discovery, or seeking discovery, is a cognitive affair.

Liberation is freedom from all bondage. The Advaita holds that freedom proper is found only in a knowledge situation which is, or at least tends to be, free from attachment, even to the ego. Knowledge of X is not primarily *I knowing* X; it is equivalent to *X is X* or *it is X*. This is true as much of reflective knowledge as of unreflective knowledge: the I that is evident in reflection is only another X—another object or a self-evident entity; and whatever of subjective I-feeling accompanies reflection—in the form *"I know X,"* and whatever still less might accompany even unreflective knowledge—is what, as unwanted in a cognitive situation, ought to disappear, according to the Advaita Vedānta. Of action, on the other hand, the subjective I-feeling is an integral factor. Action, almost by definition, is some agent acting. Action can never be impersonal; of its very nature it is egocentric; and, unlike what is desirable in cognition, there is no question of this egocentricity's disappearance. Hence, according to the Advaita philosopher, no action is free, and action cannot, therefore, belong to the essence of the individual.

The Advaita alone has held this view. No other system has subscribed to it in this extreme form. Very few of them have, it is true, denied that liberation is a stage of cognition in that the self as the essence of the individual comes to be discovered,[10] but none has said that it is nothing else. They hold that, besides cognitive freedom, there is freedom of action also. For them, therefore, there is no denial of the things of the world, for, in the absence of such things, no action is possible. Every action is some manipulation of things in the world, and free action, as we have seen, is only that type of manipulation which, as not proceeding through attachment and repulsion, is not entirely determined by Nature. Free actions, actions, viz., which are moral and spiritual, are thus constructive and forward looking, not acts of mere withdrawal. The best representation of this view is found in the concept of action which is absolutely disinterested (*niṣkāma-karma*) in the *Bhagavad-gītā.* Śaṁkara's interpretation of this *niṣkāma-karma* as but a form of cognition does not appear to be convincing, and no other interpreter (unless he is an Advaitist) has understood it that way.

Indians speak of three approaches to liberation (*mukti*), viz., cognitive (the way of *jñāna*, knowledge), actional (the way of *karma*, i.e., action), and emotional (the way of *bhakti*, i.e., love, respect, etc.).[11]

Mukti attained in the cognitive way is only discovery (rediscovery) of the self as the essence of the individual, and beyond this discovery there is nothing else for the liberated individual to know or do. For one who attains *mukti* through *karma*, however, there is no cessation of action. He has indeed got entirely beyond the clutches of attachment and repulsion, but he continues his *niṣkāma-karmas*, i.e., his duties and spiritual activities—actions, in other words, which are for the sake of duty only and also those which are meant for the well-being of others (including God and gods). In *mukti* attained by the way of emotion, on the other hand, the purified individual (the self) is placed in proper relation to God, and, through that, to other selves—purified or not. It is only in pure cognitive *mukti* that the question of the individual's relation to other individuals loses all meaning, the discovery of the self = the Absolute being the sole end. But in *mukti* attained in other ways there inevitably arises the problem of adjusting oneself to others.

A vital weakness of Indian philosophy should here be frankly admitted. Indian philosophers who advocate *mukti* through action or emotion have not discussed as systematically as they should have the problem of the relation of the liberated individual to other individuals, liberated or not, or, in the light of this, the relations that should bind unliberated individuals to one another. Even Advaita philosophers have manifested this weakness in another way. Normally, they should not consider the relation of the liberated individual to other individuals. But sometimes, unable to avoid the problem, they have discussed whether one's own liberation only or others', too, should be the ideal of one's life.

In Indian philosophy this weakness has manifested itself in still another way. Most Indian systems[12] have, uncritically enough, combined all the three approaches. This synthetic view is called "*samuccaya-vāda*." The weakness here lies in the fact that these systems, somehow conscious of some disparity between cognition, action, and emotion, have, instead of working it out, slurred over it and allowed the three approaches to combine without further ado. For, it is more than evident—and the Advaita and, to some extent, the

Bengal Vaiṣṇavas already referred to depend upon it—that the further one proceeds along the cognitive, the actional, or the emotional paths, the further these three diverge: cognition, seeking to discover the self, looks more and more inward; action proceeds more and more outward; and emotion, unable to be at peace with either, alternates between the two. It is not without reason, therefore, that the Advaita doctrine of inaction—a necessary consequence of cognitive *mukti*—has found favor with a large section of educated Indians.

It is interesting to see, again, how with his extreme attitude even the Advaita philosopher has sometimes faltered. We have seen (page 309 f.) how incongruously he has allowed action for the *jīvan-muktas.* His God (as distinct from *Brahman*) also, who is otherwise completely free, acts. He creates, sustains, and destroys the world.

True, according to the Advaita, God, as distinct from *Brahman,* has still retained cosmic nescience (*māyā*) though as wielded by him it cannot bind him: and the *jīvan-muktas,* similarly, we are told, have *māyā* still left in them. But, so far as *māyā* does not bind a self, and, if sometimes the self can behave as even its master, why need the Advaita thinker take so much trouble to get rid of this innocuous *māyā?* The heavens would not fall if even in its fullest freedom the self could retain *māyā* and use it.

The lack of interest on the part of non-Advaita philosophers to keep *jñāna* and *karma* as apart as they really are and their hasty theory of synthesis (*samuccaya*) have done one permanent mischief. It is that the intrinsic outwardness of *karma,* due to which the freer a *karma* is the more outward and encompassing it should be, has been overlooked, not merely by philosophers, but equally by the lay public, for whom the easy theory of *samuccaya* has had a natural appeal. The result is that the lay public, as much as the philosophers in India, has taken it almost for granted that the higher and freer our *karma* becomes the more inward it grows, the highest one being meditation on the self or God or both. *Karma* intended for *mukti* has thus been largely confused with *jñāna;* and the *karmas* that proceed outward—social, political, and moral actions—are not considered as spiritual, i.e., intrinsic to *mukti* (*antaraṅga-sādhana*). The only merit these *karmas* are said to have is that they prepare us—much as measured quantities of food and water do—for undertaking spiritual work. They are taken as extrinsic, though helpful, to spiritual action or liberation—they are called *vahiraṅga-sādhana* (external discipline), as contrasted with *antaraṅga-sādhana* (internal discipline).

QUESTION: Why did you not consider the Buddhist and Jaina views of the metaphysical status of the individual?

ANSWER: Buddhism is to be considered in detail by others. I did not include Jainism because of space limit.

QUESTION: You say that the Advaita conception of the *jīvanmukta* and God as absolutely free and yet acting is self-contradictory. But there is nothing of self-contradiction here. God and the *jīvanmuktas* are egoless individuals that are not yet wholly the Absolute (*Brahman*).

ANSWER: This is a possible interpretation. But the idea never occurred to me.

QUESTION: Is not your use of the term "Absolute" on different occasions in your paper ambiguous?

ANSWER: I believe I have throughout used the term "Absolute" in one sense, viz., in the Advaita sense of *Brahman*. If I have used it in any other sense, it was unintentional. I have always meant that the Absolute is in an important sense different from God, though I have pointed out that with Indian philosophers God, even falling short of the Hegelian Absolute, is omnipotent, omniscent, etc.

QUESTION: You say that there are different views of the status of the individual in the different systems of Indian philosophy and that none of these systems is of less importance in the general Indian life than the Advaita Vedānta. But why, then, is it so widely held in the West that the Advaita Vedānta is the quintessence of philosophic speculation in India?

ANSWER: Four things are responsible for this wrong impression. They are:

1. Modern Indian monks of the Advaita school and some modern Indian philosophical writers have somehow popularized this wrong notion. Of course, the Advaita Vedānta is one of the finest systems of philosophy, but in India there are other systems also, not all of them less important than the Advaita Vedānta.

2. It is often believed, even by many Indians, that the spiritual

side of man is the monopoly of the Advaita Vedānta. They have not noted that, except for the Cārvāka, every other system has studied the spiritual side, and in many of these other systems this spiritual side is the dominant topic throughout.

3. Historically, it is Śaṁkara who completely broke the dominance of Buddhism in India and from his time Buddhism has practically ceased to be a living system in India. Śaṁkara is practically the father of systematic Advaita Vedānta. Naturally, the general mass of the Indian people were persuaded to believe that the only dominant system after the disappearance of Buddhism was the Advaita Vedānta. Add to this another historical fact: Madhusūdana Sarasvatī, in his many works, particularly in the *Advaita-siddhi,* almost successfully (for the time being) refuted all the charges that had been brought against the Advaita Vedānta by the dualist Madhvas, the Vaiśeṣikas, and others. This certainly lent support to the then popular view that the most dominant, if not the only working, system in India was the Advaita Vedānta. But we, in the twentieth century, cannot ignore the fact that, except for Buddhism (and probably also the Sāṁkhya), other systems were then continuing as before and continued for some centuries after that, and there were always large sections of the people attaching themselves to these schools.

4. All the orthodox Indian systems claim descent from the Upaniṣads, and the Upaniṣads are called "*Vedānta.*" This naturally confused the Western mind, which thought that therefore all Indian systems are Vedāntic. There was another confusion, even in the minds of Western-educated Indians, viz., that the Advaita was the only form of Vedānta. It is time now to tell the Westerners in unambiguous terms (a) that the Upaniṣads, *technically* called "*Vedānta,*" need not be Vedānta in the sense in which other Vedāntic systems are, and (b) that, even inside the Vedāntic fold, there are various (at least six major) sub-schools, often sharply opposed to one another. We should also tell Westerners (a) that, though some major Upaniṣads definitely speak in the Advaita strain, there are other Upaniṣads (and some of them are equally major) which speak either in a full-dualist or half-dualist trend, and (b) that the regular systems of philosophy other than the Advaita Vedānta have interpreted even the apparently monistic statements in the Upaniṣads in their own ways quite as much as the Advaita Vedāntists have interpreted their apparent dualistic (pluralistic) statements in their own way.

QUESTION: The concept of freedom of will has undergone many changes and different formulations in the West. Has there been any such thing in India?

ANSWER: No. The problem of freedom of will has never been systematically discussed in Indian philosophy.

QUESTION: Free will cannot keep itself detached from Nature. It requires involvement. How, then, can you say that freedom is detachment from Nature?

ANSWER: There are both detachment and involvement. There is involvement insofar as free will is, after all, will or action, and there can be no action unless one manipulates a given situation and thus gets involved in it. However, the manipulation is free: a free individual does not manipulate the situation as a sub-human animal does. Behind the entire manipulation there is an attitude of detachment, i.e., the manipulation is not for any personal gain or loss, but just because it is duty.

QUESTION: Is there any emotional involvement in free manipulation?

ANSWER: No, except for one type of emotion, viz., respect for morality or spirit (as in Kant).

QUESTION: *Sāttvika* action is, after all, a part of Nature. How, then, can it be free or over-natural?

ANSWER: It is natural insofar as there is manipulation of items of Nature, but it is over-natural in that it is still free, and between this naturality and over-naturality there is no contradiction. Indeed, over-naturality is some sort of shadow (symbolic representation) in Nature, of the ultimate freedom, which is *mokṣa.*

Or, much as Kant, in his *Religion Within the Limits of Reason,* spoke of a diabolical tendency of the Practical Reason (which in itself is good) to act wrongly, we, in the same way (though in the reverse direction) may speak of an over-natural tendency in Nature (which in itself is only Nature).

QUESTION: Though in his *Critique of Practical Reason* Kant spoke of the Categorical Imperative as detachment from Nature, in his *Perpetual Peace* he regarded good action as the very movement of Nature.

ANSWER: Yes, but when I referred to Kant in my paper I had in mind the Kant of the Second Critique; and, further, I have not altogether denied that there is a movement in Nature toward the good.

QUESTION: What would be the difficulty if the idea of *cognitive liberation* could be rejected altogether in favor of that type of liberation in which the liberated individual goes on acting and acting for the good of the world? At least, that is the dominant Chinese view.

ANSWER: Yes, that is the dominant Chinese view. It is also the dominant Western view. Some Indians, too, have held this view. Yet, the very idea of cognitive freedom is an expression of the typical Indian attitude. While Chinese and Westerners are generally in the attitude of assertion, speaking, motion, and action, the general Indian preference is for provisional submission in listening to others and for seeking peace and stability. These are guaranteed most in cognitive liberation, and few Indian philosophers are against cognitive freedom; only, many of them have *added* action and emotion at the stage of liberation. Submission and listening have not, however, meant blind submission and lethargy in speaking out. They have always prescribed rigorous ratiocination after listening, and, after that, seeing things for oneself. It is in ratiocination and seeing for oneself that there are the elements of assertion and speaking.

QUESTION: Wisdom in the East consists in merging oneself in the great ineffable distinctionless Absolute, whereas Western wisdom lies in differentiating all that can be differentiated. Is this not correct?

ANSWER: I do not agree. I do not like to say anything positively regarding the Western attitude, but what you are saying regarding the Eastern attitude (and by "Eastern" you obviously mean "Indian") is true only of the attitude of the Advaita Vedāntist. But, even there, the Advaita Vedāntist is never against differentiation in the daily work-a-day life, indeed at any stage prior to liberation, though certainly unity is considered as of more importance than the distinct entities. No other Indian system of philosophy has spoken for elimination of distinctions even at the highest stage, and none has attached more importance to unity than to the distinct entities.

QUESTION: How was it possible for India to keep so many different views in peaceful co-existence?

ANSWER: These different views—sometimes exactly opposite to one another—have generally for ages continued in peaceful co-existence (though this does not mean that clashes or syntheses have not taken place). It is the peculiar genius of the Hindus that made this possible. Hindus form a loose family in which the only tie is that they recognize they belong to one grand family. The entire Hindu people is like a big oak tree with its many branches and roots, with birds and reptiles and insects having permanent residence there or just coming there occasionally and perching or crawling over the trunk and branches, and even with travelers taking shelter in its expansive shade—all a loose but a very living unity. Thus, a large number of groups belong to the Hindu fold; and, though the rules for living may be rigid for each group, there are no strict rules—or only a handful—to bind the different groups together. The most living principle that cements them is simply the consciousness that they belong to the grand Hindu fold. This is as much true of the socio-political life of the Hindus through all ages as of their systems of philosophy.

QUESTION: You have distinguished among the knowledge-way, the action-way, and the emotion-way to liberation. You have said that the more one goes up a way the more it is found that it diverges from the other two ways. But why?

ANSWER: I have stated in my paper that, as the knowledge-way means discovery (or rediscovery) of the self, it is necessarily in the inward direction—toward the self—and that the action-way as manipulating things of Nature is necessarily in an outward direction, etc. This is the type of divergence I meant.

QUESTION: But is the knowledge-way necessarily an inward attitude? What, for example, would be the case with knowledge of this table before me?

ANSWER: Knowledge of this table is certainly not an inward attitude; it is clearly an outward attitude.

QUESTION: Do you hold, then, that knowledge may be inward in some cases and outward in other cases? If so, what would be the feature common to the two types of knowledge? And how would you distinguish between knowledge and will?

ANSWER: Yes, knowledge may be inward or outward, as the case may be. The common feature of knowledge, is twofold: (1) In knowledge there is always the desired elimination of egocentricity, which elimination is neither possible nor desirable in will, and (2) knowledge is distinguishment—whatever is known is distinguished in itself and from other things.

Notes

1. It is because of this over-natural status that man can, in theoretical pursuit, question why Nature behaves as it does and can certify or reject what it offers and thus build science and philosophy.
2. This is mainly the Sāṁkhya doctrine. We find it discussed in the *Gītā,* in Vyāsa's Commentary on the *Yoga-sūtra,* and also in the subcommentaries on Vyāsa's Commentary.
3. Except in the Cārvāka system, which is frankly materialistic, and also in the Nyāya and the Vaiśeṣika, which never took an interest in these details.
4. The self is distinguished from the mind on the ground that it can keep itself dissociated from certain states and affairs which clearly belong to the mind. For example, one may very deliberately keep oneself undisturbed by insults and worries even while these, as mental affairs, are actually taking place in the mind, quite as much as one may calmly tolerate physical torture.
5. With the exception of a few Śaivas and Grammarians.
6. The famous Sāṁkhya argument to which others have also subscribed, viz., that, if there were only one self for all individuals (*jīvas*), then with the birth or death of one individual other individuals would also be born or die, or that, if one individual were deaf or lame, others, too, would have the same lot, is either pointing to the simple truth that, like individuals, their selves, too, are many, or arguing to its plurality from the *sākṣin*hood of the selves.
7. Severance not as in death. For, according to Indians, death is not the end of the self's journey. There are repeated births and deaths. Hence, severance of all connections means such absolute severance as is calculated to prevent further birth. Again, most Indian thinkers hold that, though an individual is completely liberated, he, even after death, remains with a subtle body which, in complete liberation, is almost a permanent appendage around which different grosser and grosser elements accumulate to form grosser and grosser bodies.
8. Kashmir Śaivism, however, developed along Advaita lines. Indian life was largely influenced by Buddhism also (and probably by Jainism, too), and, though later Buddhism practically disappeared

from India, many Buddhist concepts have, in disguise, continued in the Yoga, Śaivism, and Śaktism, and, some add, in the Advaita Vedānta also.

9. This section is in answer to the third objection by Westerners to the Indian view of the individual cited on page 299 of this volume.
10. A few schools of Bengal Vaiṣṇavism deny even this. They have denounced cognition as having anything to do with liberation and have relied mainly on sublimated emotion and, secondarily, on good action.
11. The monism of the Advaita Vedānta can be understood only from the point of view of jñāna-mārga, and not from the point of view of *karma-mārga* or *bhakti-mārga*. In order to explain this, I here discuss the three *mārgas* and show how those who acknowledge *karma-mārga* or *bhakti-mārga* with or without *jñāna-mārga* have been compelled to vote for plurality.
12. With the exception of the Advaita Vedānta and the extreme Vaiṣṇava systems in Bengal already referred to.

T. R. V. MURTI

The World and the Individual in Indian Religious Thought

Introduction

AS A PRELIMINARY DEFINITION we may take the individual as a free being, exercising choice and doing actions purposefully, and as one who has attained some measure of awareness of his situation. Whether this person is ultimately free, whether his individuality or personality is real, and what his destiny is and whether it is bound up with that of other individuals are precisely the questions for which we seek an answer in this discussion. The human world may be understood as the community (reciprocity) of such "free" beings, or individuals. But among men there are different grades or types of spiritual temperament. Indian thought—especially the Vedānta and Mahāyāna Buddhism—expressly recognizes these empirical differences and provides for their spiritual needs.

I. The Religious Problem

There is no religious problem for man unless, in his reflective mood, he reviews his position and is conscious of his peril. No religious problem is involved in efforts to overcome the hardships imposed by adverse Nature or in making adjustments with fellow men. Both of these could be solved without recourse to any total or transcendental effort. The religious situation emerges only when man reviews his existence as a whole. It is an awareness of the deeper aspects of life, of the root problem, and extends over his entire existence. The religious solution, like the problem, aims at a final and total solution of all problems. It is man's ultimate concern (*parama-puruṣārtha*). This statement of the religious problem would be acceptable to Buddhism and Jainism and some forms of Hinduism which do not find a place for a personal God and, therefore, cannot consider the aim of religious endeavor as the establishment of an intimate relationship with God.

We are led to this review of our existence by a deep and sustained sense of frustration. This is suffering, and it takes the form principally of disease, decay, and death. The Buddha describes suffering graphically: "Birth is ill; decay is ill; sickness is ill; death is ill; to be conjoined to things which we dislike, to be separated from things which we like—that is also sorrow."[1] If all our desires were completely and instantaneously satisfied as they arose in our mind, or, in the alternative, if our nature were completely in accord with the environment, no frustration could arise, and no suffering would result. But the very nature of the individual, or the ego, engenders suffering. As an ego, its essence consists in self-centeredness, and its pursuits and impulses are selfish. And yet, the ego has to depend on other selves and on the entire creation. A kind of implicit and inherent disharmony seems to be built into the very essence of the individual self.

Suffering, unlike enjoyment, which lulls us into a sense of security, engenders reflection. Man becomes aware of himself when he becomes aware of his deep involvement. To be conscious of suffering is to be conscious of an alternative to the present state in which we happen to find ourselves. Without the contrast between what is and what might have been, between the actual state and the possible, there could be no sense of grievance; hence no suffering. If everything that happens to us were thought to be completely inevitable and inexorable, there could be no grievance. We feel that things can be helped; they could have been otherwise; we could have done better. Thus, in all suffering, man is conscious, however implicitly, of freedom, of the non-inevitability of the present situation and of his ability to help it.

If, on the other hand, we enjoyed freedom so completely as to dominate all situations and if our will could prevail absolutely over all and always, there would be no suffering. This, then, is the inherent dialectic of suffering. Man is free, but not completely free. Suffering discloses the inherent freedom of man. And, although it is freedom in involvement, it is pregnant with possibilities. There is a demand to realize freedom fully and in final form, as *mokṣa* or *nirvāṇa*.

The germ of spirituality is implicit in suffering (*duḥkha*). Buddhism and all the systems of Indian philosophy (excluding the Cārvāka) show their keen spiritual insight in beginning with the truth of suffering (*duḥkha-satya*). To all of them, not only the actual states of painful feeling, but phenomenal existence in its entirety (*saṁsāra*) is suffering.[2] A state of unpleasant feeling is but a sample of what could befall us at all times. The awareness is not complete unless it is extended before and after this life. Its inexorability, given the causes and conditions which engender it, must be realized. Much of our pleasure is pain in the making; pleasures make us hanker after them and thus create anxiety. Frustration in this pursuit brings anger, bitterness, and conflict. Moreover, one's pleasures are by way of encroaching upon others. We seem to take for granted our right to happiness, even though it may be at the expense of others. Again, our shortsightedness and distraction in the immediate present prevent us from appraising our existence in all its comprehension and depth.[3]

Excepting the materialists (Cārvākas), every section of Indian thought without question believes and accepts the Law of *Karma*—the exercise of free will and the responsibility for its consequence and the continuous chain of birth, death, and rebirth. The doctrine of rebirth seems to be a necessary implication of the more basic doctrine of the souls (*jīvas,* individuals) as being uncreated, their existing beginninglessly and not perishing with the body. What was the mode of their existence before the actual physical birth and what will it be after the death of the body? What other more plausible explanation could we offer for the inequalities of beings than the doctrine of *karma* and rebirth, which is consistent with free will and the conservation of moral values? The Semitic religions, which assert the creation of finite souls by a personal God, not only do not seem to feel the need for the doctrine of rebirth, but are even opposed to it. The acceptance of the Law of *Karma* and rebirth means a more universal perspective. Unlike the Semitic religions, Indian religions are not necessarily committed to a theism and a personal deity. Absolute dependence on God, even for the existence of the soul, determines that the highest and perhaps the only form of spirituality is the loving personal relationship of trust of and surrender to God.

The existentialist philosophers of the present day pointedly bring out the predicament of man, his anxiety and deep distress, caused by the thought of the inevitability of passing away into nothingness. Many of their analyses and the phraseology used could be matched by passages from Buddhist and Hindu texts. What the existentialist philosophers fail to present, however, is a clear and sure way out of this anxiety and distress. Indian religious thought is most re-assuring in this respect. It definitely and most emphatically asserts that man can overcome his predicament and that he can attain freedom and the fullness of his being. It is also singularly rich in indicating some well-tried paths or types of spiritual life by which freedom can be attained.

It is common ground in Indian thought that the adoption of secular means and methods do not lead to freedom or salvation. It may be held that, if we could conquer Nature and fully exploit her resources, we might satisfy all our wants, and as soon as they arise. The modern man in the atomic age with his immense faith in technology is prone to think that the solution lies this way. But wants may still outstrip our ability to satisfy them; a leap-frog race may result. The root problem is left untouched. Technology cannot provide the wisdom and the good will necessary to make a wholesome use of our power. Control over Nature without control over oneself (self-restraint) can lead only to rivalry, domination, conflict, and suicidal warfare. The human problem is basically spiritual; it lies in self-control and self-education.

Still another ill-advised way out of the difficulty is that of succumbing to the existential situation and, in utter despair, to seek extinction of one's being. To succumb to instincts and to consider ourselves as sharing the destruction of the body are a species of spiritual suicide.

A third way to end suffering is what may be called purely ethical discipline by the practice of a strict regimen to control the passions calculated to stop the flow of phenomenal life. The Hīnayāna ideal of the *arhat* (Buddhist perfected man) and the self-mortification of the Jaina could be cited as instances of this. The ethical discipline in both of these is very impressive in vigor and intensity. The ego is disarmed, suppressed, and made inoperative; but it is not put to any active good use. Negatively, there is the cessation of suffering; this is not accompanied by any positive fulfillment. The *arhat* or the *kevalin* (one who has attained isolation from material adjuncts in Jainism) seems to be bent only upon achieving his own salvation. There is even a lurking fear that the world would enmesh him again if he tarried here too long. Does not the very insistence on getting away smack of selfishness, and is it not therefore unspiritual? An essential mark of the spiritual is the identification of one's good with the good of all. It may well be that the egoistic tendencies are not entirely eliminated. The Mahāyāna makes pointed criticism of this.

We have, finally, the solution of suffering offered by the Vedānta and Mahāyāna Buddhism, which understand freedom as the attainment of a positive state of fullness and complete identification with all beings. It is both a negative process and a positive attainment. It is negative insofar as the "I" is dissociated from its accidental limitations by the removal of ignorance; but this results in a positive and transcendent realization of one's true nature as the Absolute.

The theistic schools of Śaivism and Vaiṣṇavism conceive the highest goal of human attainment as an intimate and inalienable relationship with God and not as complete identity.

In the kindling of spiritual life and the way to the highest attainment, the guidance of God, or revelation, is considered necessary. Otherwise, as there are several possibilities, and, if man were to rely on his unaided reason, he might go astray. It is said in the Vedānta that the *Ātman* is attained by him to whom it chooses to reveal itself; even the inclination toward the Advaita is itself the grace of God. Śaivism explicitly states, "It is through God's grace that we adore his feet," and that is a descent of grace (*śakti-pāta*). It is the deity that chooses to reveal himself to man and takes possession of him. He comes to us in the form of the *guru* (spiritual preceptor and guide).

In the context of freedom and spiritual discipline, the entire range of Indian thought can be classified under three heads:

(1) There were those who did not accept freedom or autonomy of spirit in any form. The Cārvākas denied the existence of the individual self apart from the physical body and ridiculed the very notion of salvation. As a piece of Nature and constituted by a conglomeration of natural ingredients, consciousness or man can have no value other than gross bodily pleasures. The question of freedom does not arise. The Ājīvakas (materialists or naturalists), although they accepted the *jīvas,* conceived the world process and the entire progress of the soul as an automatic and inevitable process; they advocated a most rigorous form of determinism (*niyati-vāda*). Everyone is bound to reach his destiny in the fullness of time. They advocated, according to Buddhism and Jainism, a thoroughgoing fatalism and denied the Law of *Karma.* Both the

Buddha and the Jaina Mahāvīra call this doctrine a species of non-activism and condemn it as pernicious and inimical to the spiritual life.[4]

(2) There were philosophers and religious men, such as the Buddha and Mahāvīra, who accepted what we might call immanent freedom as felt and exercised in human involvement. Every man's suffering is evidence of this freedom. The Buddha took his stand, like Kant, on the moral act, the immanent freedom implicit in man's endeavor to better his condition. The emphasis is on self-effort and the right exercise of one's volition.

The fundament in Buddhism and Jainism is the autonomy of the Moral Law (*karma*)—the freedom which we feel and exercise in our actions, in our involvement, and which determines what we are and what we would be. The Moral Law is moral, i.e., it is not a natural or mechanistic operation of brute necessity. Nor is it the dictate of an inscrutable and capricious Person—God. The Moral Law is impersonal; it has absolute authority, no matter whether it is fulfilled frequently or seldom or not at all; its authority is innate and underived. The Moral Law is perfectly autonomous.

This was not an altogether new idea discovered by the Buddha or Mahāvīra. The Ṛg-vedic hymns speak of *Ṛta* and *Satya,* the Order and Truth of the universe; the deities Indra, Agni, and Varuṇa are invariably spoken of as upholders of the moral order (*dhṛta-vrata, satya-dharma, dharmasya-goptā*). It is not, as in the Semitic religions, God's fiat which makes anything moral or good. There is an innate propriety (*dharma*) in things, and the deities only reveal and uphold this order; they do not create the order. The impersonality of the Law of *Karma* was first developed as a cosmic principle by the Mīmāṁsakas, who were the first to deny a personal God. Unfortunately, the *karma* or *dharma* they understood and were interested in was ritualistic *karma,* the performance of what the *Bhagavad-gītā* would term "*dravya-yajña*" (sacrifice with substance-oblations) and not duty or moral *karma.* And it was with the latter that the Buddha and Mahāvīra were concerned.

Taking his stand on the autonomy of the Moral Law, the Buddha was led to deny two opposed standpoints: one was naturalism (*sva-bhāva-vāda*) or nihilism (*uccheda-vāda*), which totally denied, as is done by the Cārvāka and the Ājīvika, the Moral Law (free act and its result, *karma* and *karma-phala*), and reduced man to a fortuitous conglomeration of natural forces; the other opposed standpoint was that of eternalism (*śāśvata-vāda*), which stood for the transcendent freedom of God (and even of an unchanging soul or *ātman*), who is above the Moral Law (*karma*). The Buddha characterizes both *uccheda-vāda* and *śaśvata-vāda* as specimens of inactivism (*akriya-vāda*).

Salvation or, rather, freedom is freedom from moral evil, from passions and their defilement (*saṁskāra*); spiritual discipline is the path of purification (*viśuddhi-mārga;* Pāli: *visuddhi-magga*), and this is achieved through self-effort and self-regeneration. There is no place for outside help or divine guidance. Salvation is strictly a sustained and heroic act on the part of the individual man himself. It is not an act of God or co-operation between man and God. Buddhism, at least early Buddhism, is a moral religion, a universal religion without God, a perfection of self-discipline and self-analysis. As the spiritual discipline is a catharsis or eradication of passions, the Ultimate is described negatively as *Nirvāṇa.*

The position of earlier Buddhism was considerably modified in the Mahāyāna. To all intents and purposes, the Buddha becomes a divine person—the free phenomenalization of the impersonal Absolute. The personality of the Buddha and the awareness of his unique position ushered in this revolution in Buddhism.

(3) The third class is represented by the Hindu (Brāhmaṇical) systems, which in some form or other accepted a free, transcendent Being (God) besides the finite selves. It is not that this free being achieved his freedom after destroying his previous bondage. He is eternally free (*sadaiva-muktaḥ*) and transcendent (*sadaiva-Īśvaraḥ*).

If for Buddhism the fundament is the moral consciousness, and the spiritual urge is for purifying the mind of its passions, the fundament of Hinduism is God-consciousness; and the goal is exaltation or deification. The Vedas, which are the fountain source of all forms of Hinduism, are intoxicated with the idea of God, of a transcendent Being, ever free and ever the Lord. The Vedic seers had an unusually quick and open sensitiveness to the transcendent being. They try to grasp him now as Agni, now as Indra, now as Varuṇa, Viṣṇu, or Rudra, and in a hundred other ways. These are predicates or characteristics of the Godhead rather than substantive entities in their own right, as has been wrongly contended. The Vedic seers had an almost overwhelming sense of the infinite impinging on man. Religion, for them, was not the labored suppression of passions, of control and regimen, as in Buddhism, but a relationship with the transcendent through prayer and devotion. This *en rapport* relationship with God is what distinguishes Hinduism from earlier Buddhism. And this consciousness has never left it at any stage of its long history. Newer deities emerge; rather, the old ones are given new names (e.g., Rudra is called Śiva; Viṣṇu is Nārāyaṇa or Vāsudeva) and are worshipped in newer forms; but the pattern remains the same. This may be theism, but it is not a theism of the Semitic type. The difference between God and man (creatures) is not absolute.

The deity is not discovered by man by his self-effort; it is the deity that freely chooses to reveal itself. Man just receives and realizes it. He is saved by this relationship, by his sense of kinship and identity with the transcendent spirit. Practice of moral virtues and concentration of mind have value as enabling one to perceive this inherent identity, just as a spotless mirror is able to entertain the image without distortion. The purity of the mirror is not, however, the source of the image; it is merely ancillary to the reflection. As realizing an already existing fact, spiritual attainment for Hinduism is symbolic, not labored and literal, as in earlier Buddhism.

It might be thought that the atheistic Mīmāṁsā and the Sāṁkhya do not conform to the pattern of a pure, transcendent Being. But, since in both of these the Veda (the Eternal Word) is accepted as the infallible and omniscient source of truth, the conformity is essentially present.

It is interesting to note, however, that in the Hindu and the non-Hindu (Buddhist and Jaina) traditions, both the impersonal spirit and a personal God find a place. This is the basic dialectic in Indian religious thought. There is no doubt that this obtains in other religions also. This problem will engage us toward the end of the paper.

II. Religious Life

The religious or spiritual life in Indian thought is conceived in terms of self-control and self-regeneration. We may speak of it as a new dimension of being, much as St. Paul said, "I do not live, Christ liveth in me." This is a re-discovery or regaining of what one had lost unconsciously in ignorance.[5] It is not a new acquisition; for, if it were so, there could be no finality; the accumulation of merit could mount higher and higher, there being no conceivable limit to its amount. And, conditioned as it would be by certain specific circumstances, the state of freedom would be transitory; it might even cease to be. It would also admit of degrees. This is not how *mokṣa* is understood in the Indian religions. It is eternal, does not admit of gradation, and is unconditioned. In its attainment, there may be epistemic novelty or emergence, but ontologically nothing new is engendered. Therefore, Śaṁkara always speaks of *mokṣa* as no effect and as the nature of *Brahman.*[6] Nāgārjuna says, "*Nirvāṇa* is what is not abandoned or acquired, what is not annihilation or eternality, what is not destroyed or created."[7]

Freedom is not a conferment of something which one did not possess; it is release from delusion and suffering. God does not confer freedom; he may and does show us the way to achieve freedom. That is his grace. Freedom is therefore not exactly the same as the salvation of the Semitic religions.

The essence of self-control is the bringing about of a change in oneself, in one's mentality, and not in the environment. To control the external world, including the world of fellow human beings, is the way of worldly men. This is bound, sooner or later, to raise antagonism and strife. And this is precisely what we wish to avoid. Philosophical knowledge or wisdom (*prajñā*) does not transform the world, but only our attitude. It certainly means a radical change in our mental make-up.

The path of freedom is one of purification and disassociation from the not-self, from the false or superficial aspects of the self. Cognitively, it is a case of enlightenment or insight into the nature of things. We may call it a negative process, since it is a case of divestification of the encumbrances with which we have cluttered ourselves on life's journey. It is not negative in result. For what we are left with is not nothing, but our real being in its innate immediacy. Also, the path's being characterized in negative phraseology does not mean that we are to be inactive or that it is easy of accomplishment.

There are two fundamental presuppositions underlying this position. One is that all our troubles are due to ignorance, primarily ignorance of oneself. This is not merely privation of right knowledge, but a positive wrong idea. I wrongly take myself as the body or the mental states or even the intellect, and, owing to this wrong identification, I gratuitously share the misfortunes of the body. With its injury or death, I consider myself to be undergoing these misfortunes. This wrong identification is not a conscious, deliberate process. No one can consciously fall into illusion. One does not say,

"Lo, I am falling into illusion" or "Let me commit this error." He may get out of it consciously and also know when he gets out of it. We can consciously disassociate or disavow our connection with the body, but not vice versa. Nor is it that the self (the "I") and the body started their career as separate and independent entities and at some particular time were joined together. The Indian view is that we can begin only with their togetherness, their fusion or confusion. All accounts depicting a point of time when they were apart, etc., are merely expressions to bring out the essential purity and uniqueness of the self. It is a demand to disassociate it from the body. Although we cannot assign any conceivable beginning to this incongruous relationship, it is not inseparable. We can undo this wrong identification. We can educate and correct ourselves. Any attempt to refute this position would itself presuppose correction, i.e., the removal of my wrong views by the opponent. In fact, only wrong views are removed.

It is common ground in all the Indian systems that ignorance (*avidyā, ajñāna*) is the cause of suffering. The nature of ignorance, or wrong knowledge, differs somewhat in the various systems, depending upon their different metaphysical standpoints. In the Sāṁkhya, it is wrong identification of the self (*puruṣa*) with the object (*prakṛti*) in its various modifications beginning with the intellect; in the Advaita Vedānta, it is considering the self as finite and limited, whereas it is really the infinite *Brahman;* in Jainism, it is the intrusion of karmic matter into the soul (*jīva*); in earlier Buddhism, it is the substance-idea itself, wrongly taking things (which are really changing and perishing) as permanent and identical and clinging to them; in the Mādhyamika, it is indulging in philosophical speculation, in the setting forth of views of the real.

The second presupposition, which is almost a consequence of the first, is that in the make-up of the self there are several layers or aspects. To a superficial view, the individual is the "body-mind-I" complex, and in the ordinary course of life the distinction among these elements is seldom made. It is only when we become reflective and begin to raise questions about our true nature that the distinction can be made. Spiritual discipline has for its objective the progressive realization of the pure self as distinct from the body. The body itself is understood in a much wider sense, to include not only the physical body but also the sense-organs, the mental states, the intellect, the psychical dispositions, etc., which constitute the inner body, as it were. It is stripping the "I" of all its external trappings and accidental accretions. The point to be reached is a foundational consciousness that is unconditional, self-evident, and immediate (*svayaṁ-prakāśā*). It is that to which everything is presented, but is itself no presentation, that which knows all, but is itself no object. The self should not be confused with the contents and states which it enjoys and manipulates. If we have to give an account of it, we can describe it only as what it is not, for any positive description of it would be possible only if it could be made an object of observation, which from the nature of the case it is not. We "know" it only as we withdraw ourselves from the body with which we happen to be identified, in this transition.

That such a foundational self is there and can be reached by the right kind of discipline is taught by the Vedānta. The Sāṁkhya view is not very different. Mahāyāna Buddhism implicitly affirms the existence of a deep underlying reality behind all empirical manifestations in its conception of *śūnyatā* (the indeterminate, the void), or *vijñapti-mātratā* (consciousness only), or *tathātā* (thatness), or *dharmatā* (noumenal reality). Its spiritual discipline differs considerably from that of the Vedānta or the Sāṁkhya, but the ultimate goal is remarkably similar.

We have been talking of the spirit and the spiritual; some definition of it may be attempted. In all religions, especially in the Indian religions, spirituality implies the giving up of narrow, selfish, ego-centeredness and the attainment of the universal. In its extreme form, this would take the form of complete identity with all beings, as in the case of the Advaita Vedānta and the Mahāyāna. The good of one is the good of all. The spiritual person does not divide himself from others. Nor is he divided in himself. His personality is integrated, as there is no conflict—or cross-purposes—in his inner make-up. The secular man does not react to a situation in a total way; in him, there are surface motives and deeper drives, often in disharmony. In the spiritual, the means and the end coincide. In the moral or social sphere, we do certain acts, e.g., acts of charity and kindness, for some otherworldly benefits or for social solidarity which may benefit us undirectly. Nor do moral acts carry with them their own sanctity. Their observance is commanded by external authority, fear of God, or the approval of society. The spiritual person is good, he is chaste or charitable, not because he desires to gain anything in this or the other world. It is his nature to be so; his goodness is motiveless. The spiritual act is not a means to an end; it is the end itself. It therefore carries within itself the criterion of its validity and efficacy.

Some account, or at least a general indication, of the lines of approach to the ultimate reality may be given. What strikes one in this regard is the diversity of the paths advocated, and some of them represent daring experiments with the psyche. There is an explicit recognition, not only of the obvious surface differences among individuals, but also of the diversity in their deeper psychical levels, or their spiritual temperaments. Individuality is not mere plurality, the colorless stereotyped repetition of entities, but the recognition of many distinct types. Within the basic types, there are sub-types, and these shade off into personal variations and versions. Indian religious thought is explicitly aware of the different modes of spiritual progression as depending upon basic types—*prasthāna-bheda* (differences in modes of practice) and *gotra-bheda* (differences of family relationships). Either they all lead to the same result or they meet at some penultimate point where the others are merged into one mode.

All would enjoin, as a prerequisite of the spiritual life, the practice of moral virtues and concentration of mind (*śīla* and *samādhi* in Buddhism).[8] It is customary to speak of the three paths of knowledge (*jñāna*), of action (*karma*), and of devotion (*bhakti*), as leading to *mokṣa*. In actual practice, these three are not exclusive. It is not that in the path of knowledge there is no place for an active good life or for a feeling of devotion to God. These latter would be required in the preparatory stage, to purify the intellect of its passions and prejudices and to make it one-pointed. But it is the knowledge or the insight into the real that will engender freedom, or is freedom itself. The cognitive urge to know the ultimate truth is the spearhead behind which other psychic factors work. And this spearhead gives the predominant tone to the entire discipline—not that the other factors are absent. There is a psychological reason why this should be so and not otherwise. As spiritual attainment is the satisfaction of the entire man and not merely of a part of him, if the urge for active altruism or the feeling of surrender to God is repressed, there will result a split in the personality of the individual; there will be no integration of personality, which is a distinctive mark of the spiritual. It is possible, however, to organize the various factors with differing emphases. Each such organization would be a distinct and integrated unit, and not a medley of discordant notes.

And this would be in confirmity with the demand that the spiritual path chosen should be suited to the individual's particular spiritual temperament. One master idea or sentiment will so fully and utterly grip the mind as to bring about a catalytic reaction in the entire personality—for instance, in the Advaita Vedānta the knowledge, "I am *Brahman*" (*aham brāhmasmi*) (i.e., I am not this body, or these mental states, or the puny creature that I have been taking myself to be) is of this nature. The thought or the conviction that I am *Brahman* makes for the individual's regeneration. This is not a mere idea or a reasoned conviction lacking metaphysical foundation, but we are not at the moment concerned with that aspect of it. When this conviction or realization sways the mind and possesses it, one no longer sorrows after the body or is drawn into the pettiness of secular life. Friendliness, charity, non-violence, and other virtues follow easily, and are not labored and restricted. The picture drawn here is *mutatis mutandis* true of other modes of religious thought also.

III. Individual, God, and Absolute

What is the state of final attainment, the goal? Is it a kind of ineffable absorption into the abyss of the Absolute (*Brahman* or *Nirvāṇa*), or is it a form of God-realization? This is bound up with the question, as to whether there is separate and individual salvation from time to time or universal salvation. The question is discussed in all seriousness and implication both in Mahāyāna Buddhism and the Advaita Vedānta, where it takes the pointed form of "freedom of one or of all" (*eka-mukti* or *sarva-mukti*).

Mahāyāna Buddhism has clearly given the answer in its doctrine of the Buddha and the *bodhi-sattva* (one whose essence is perfect wisdom). Even while entering the path of spiritual discipline for enlightenment, the *bodhi-sattva* makes the Great Vows. The chief one of these is that the merit and the knowledge that he would acquire would be for all beings, high and low, and not for himself.[9] "He shuns retiring into the final state of *nirvāṇa,* though fully entitled to it, preferring, by his own free choice, to toil for even the lowest of beings for ages. He is actuated by this motiveless altruism from the very start of his career. It is not that the *bodhi-sattva* cannot achieve his own freedom without achieving the freedom of all. This would involve a vicious circle: he cannot free others without first freeing himself, and he cannot free himself without freeing others. No, his freedom is full and complete by itself; but he condescends to raise others to his level. This is a free phenomenalizing act of grace and compassion. A deeply religious element is introduced into Buddhism, which would have otherwise remained an exalted moral naturalism. The Buddha, which the *bodhisattvas* follow and eventually become, is a Person, the Highest Person. In the Buddha, we have the conception of a person without any trace of ego. There is activity without attachment."[10] In the *Mahā-vagga* of the *Vinaya-piṭaka* we have a very moving account of how Gautama the Buddha was sorely tempted, after his enlightenment, to pass away into final release, but was persuaded by Brahmā, the Great God (actually his innate religious consciousness), to accept the ministry.[11] Free, egoless personality must be accepted. It is not that as one achieves freedom one is absorbed into the Absolute wholly and at once. Though free, one has still enough of the phenomenal in oneself to feel kinship with fellow beings and to help them out of worldly life. Freedom does not repel personality; nor does all personality mean bondage. There can be a free person, and the Buddha is such a person.

In the Advaita Vedānta, too, the position is not different. It is definitely accepted that, as long as other individuals remain to be liberated, the freed self realizes his union, perhaps even his oneness, with God (Īśvara), rather than become merged in the Absolute (*Brahman*). The reason for this is that, as long as other individual souls are struggling in this world, there will continue to be the distinction between God (Īśvara) and the finite selves (*jīvas*); there is no Pure Being (*Brahman*) as such apart from its varied manifestations. God will continue to perform his function as long as there are any souls needing to realize their identity with *Brahman*. How and when will there be the state in which all the souls shall have been freed is an apocalyptic question that cannot be easily answered. The possibility of such a happy event as the total release of all souls is not ruled out. The question regarding the nature of the interim release of individual souls is fully discussed in the *Brahma-sūtra* and by Śaṁkara in his Commentary thereon.[12] It is stated with cogent arguments that identity with the Lord (*Īśvara-bhāvāpatti*) is the nature of liberation of individual souls.

In the state of union with God (Īśvara), the individual, for all practical purposes, is God; he is no longer an ego, having transcended his petty and private status. Like God, he is also an egoless personality. He freely identifies himself with others and enters into their being. Of this state it is said in the Upaniṣads, "He attains all his desires; he becomes one-, two-, threefold, aye, manifold." "He goes along disporting himself . . . [and so on]."[13] It is stated that even such freed souls are sent on cosmic errands (*ādhikārika-puruṣas*)[14] and actively participate in the maintenance of the cosmic order. From the nature of the case, these statements are not capable of rational explanation.

The factors which generally constitute the empirical individual and which mark him off from other individuals, e.g., the physical body, mental traits, and dispositions, aspirations and achievements, may not be present in this state. But it cannot be denied that some form of personality is present. The desire to help others and the capacity to participate actively in the cosmic good are present and may constitute the basis of personality.

It may well be asked: Why should we accept both the Absolute (*Brahman*) and God (Īśvara), impersonal and personal spirit? Could not either of them do as well? The basic dialectic in Indian religious thought, as stated earlier, is between personal God and impersonal spirit. This assertion is not made on a priori grounds but because we find it exemplified quite pointedly in the orthodox Hindu as well as in the Buddhist tradition. There is no doubt that this obtains in other religions also. Tillich speaks of the "tension between Being and God," or of "the God beyond God." Either the personal appears first, as in Hinduism, or the impersonal, as in Buddhism and Jainism. Very soon the other dialectic aspect discloses itself and has to be reckoned with. A synthesis is called for.

To explain. The personal God or gods of the Vedic hymns are the first intimations of the holy or the numinous in Hindu religious consciousness. From the personal God, there is the movement toward the unity underlying this, the Godhead behind these manifestations, *That One* (*tad ekam*), for which the gods really stand. This position is explicitly reached in the Upanisads and is formulated as the philosophy of the Vedānta. In Buddhism (and this is largely true of Jainism, too), the impersonal as the Moral Order (*Dharma*) and the ideal of *Nirvāṇa* is the prius; the personal is even repudiated and the stand is anti-theistic. However, the inner dynamism of the spiritual life led, as explicitly admitted by the Mahāyāna, to God in the person of the Buddha. It is not that the Mahāyānists deified the human Buddha, but that the Buddha's divinity became clear to them as a new insight. In fact, the human form of the Buddha prevented his being recognized as divine. The Buddha performs the divine functions of grace and revelation, though not the cosmic functions of creation and sustenance of the world. *Dharma* or *Nirvāṇa,* being impersonal and completely transcendent, could not reveal or declare itself to man. It requires the appropriate organism, a teacher endowed with the necessary qualities; just as geometrical truths cannot reveal themselves—they require to be taught by a teacher. If *Nirvāṇa* itself could come down, as it were, and disclose itself, then we could be persuaded of its authenticity. And yet, only a person can perform this function. Paradoxically, the Buddha had therefore to be at once identical with *Nirvāṇa* (so as to enable him to have direct and intimate knowledge of *Nirvāṇa*) and also be different from it, as only a person (accepting and operating under human conditions and using human forms of communication) could reveal and declare the truth of *Nirvāṇa.* Impelled by this dialectic of religious consciousness, "the Buddhas were subjected to a six-fold process: they were multiplied, immortalised, deified, spiritualised, universalized, and unified," as Dr. Har Dayal so happily states.[15]

The problem of Absolute and God is really the problem of ultimacy and concreteness, their relation and balance. How preserve both without reducing one or the other to insignificance? God's nature is not exhausted in his relationship to man or in the performance of cosmic functions; he has a non-relational, transcendent nature of his own; he is something *in himself*. This is the Absolute. The theistic religions generally slur over this distinction. God as the "Wholly Other" has to be sharply distinguished from the creatures over whom he dominates. Here God is one term of the relation of difference. But God is also the being of all things, that in which they move and have their being. In the latter sense, as the foundational and only Being, God cannot be distinguished from anything, as there is no other besides him. The Advaita Vedānta rightly understands God in this aspect as the *"Great It,"* as *Brahman,* the Great Being without a second. Even the relation of "I and Thou" is itself possible because of the Being underlying the opposites; it is the common platform on which both of them stand equally. Therefore, the Absolute cannot be denied. It stands for the principle of ultimacy, the original and inexhaustible source of being and power. It is Being without any touch or threat of non-being. As Being without any other facing it, it is the whole or universal being. Not lacking anything, as full being, it is termed bliss on that account. As the only being without divisions, without even the division of subject and object, it does not stand in need of being evidenced. Although not evidenced, it is immediate and self-evident.

There are two prevalent misconceptions regarding Being (*Brahman*). One is to take it as a particular existent, conditioned and limited. The other, which is more pernicious, is to understand Being as a conception, as a generalized idea or abstraction. Hegel is guilty of this. He created a phantom so that he could the more easily knock it down. He used what might be called the de-ontological argument, the ontological argument in reverse. For he reduces the Ontic Being to an idea or a descriptive character. It is less of a mistake to identify Being with any particular existent (God or man), for here at least we have a concrete experience of Being. This is why the Upaniṣads speak of it as "*neti, neti,*" and Śaṁkara understands *Brahman* as *nirguṇa* (without qualities), because it is the fullness of Being, and not a system or bundle of ideas.

If the Absolute cannot be denied, God also cannot be denied. For it is he who reveals to us the nature of *Brahman.* The truth, being impersonal, needs to be declared and proclaimed as truth by a person. *Tathātā* (the thatness of things) requires a *tathāgata* (one who has realized thatness) to reveal it to us. The two facets, then, are present in Hinduism and Buddhism, in any mature religion. They cannot be left unrelated; nor can they be related coordinately, as this would make for opposition. As they have to be synthesized or related in a whole, the only alternative left is to take one as higher, the other as lower—higher in the sense of providing the ground or sustenance for the other. If I may venture to coin a term for this situation, I would call it "Synthesis in Depth," to distinguish it from synthesis in comprehension, in extensity and inclusiveness. The Hegelian synthesis is of the latter kind. Depth-synthesis is the acceptance of two levels of Being, the impersonal and the personal spirit. No doubt, these are spatial metaphors, but they may help to bring out more picturesquely the relationship between the two.

Depth-synthesis also implies a mechanism or device by which the impersonal spirit can become the personal God, without loss, without being transformed or diminished. It is the logic of a one-sided relation. It may well be that all relation is one-sided. It is a connection between two terms, one and only one of which has a transcendent existence (i.e., is not exhausted in the relational context), while the other is confined to the relational context.[16] *Māyā,* or *avidyā,* is the principle of this mediation. It is a device to reconcile God's transcendence with his immanence—what he is in himself and the manner in which he chooses to reveal himself to finite beings. It is not the principle of utter rejection or negation of God or the world in the Absolute, but the insistence on the transcendence of the Godhead and the inapplicability of empirical characteristics to it. *Māyā* is not an explanation, much less a derivation of the lower from the higher (we may leave this jugglery to Hegel). The mystery remains. In fact, "*māyā*" is the most expressive term for the mystery of such so-called derivation. It affirms, however, that they are not unrelated or independent entities. The correct formula is that the lower is neither identical with nor different from the higher, the absolute (*tattvānyatvābhyām-anirvacanīya*). A sort of hierarchy is implied between *Brahman* and Īśvara (as between *Dharmatā* or *Śūnyatā* and the Buddha), without either of them being unreal or redundant.

In a way, *Brahman* and Īśvara (*Dharmatā* and the Buddha) typify the two ways in which we can understand freedom—freedom as "free *from*" and freedom as "free to do." Free Being (*Brahman* or *Śūnyatā* or *Dharmatā*) is free from empirical determination and limitations. Īśvara or the Buddha is a free agent, free to act; his will or act, being always in accord with the truth (*satya-kāma* and *satya-samkalpa*), is never impeded (*apratihata-śaktiḥ*). In both the traditions, it is well-understood that it is only through the mediation of Īśvara or the Buddha that we can realize our free nature as *Brahman* or *Dharmatā*, and that the liberated individual first realizes his identity or union with Īśvara or the Buddha.

QUESTION: You observe, almost in the beginning of your paper, that "there is no religious problem unless man is conscious of his peril." I have also been saying that every religion is a kind of answer to the problem of evil. But, conceivably, religion could arise in some way other than from suffering; as, for instance, in a feeling of ecstatic wonder or sublimity with regard to the world. Perhaps, we make too much of sin-consciousness. You make the observation that "the Vedic seers had an unusually quick and open sensitiveness to the transcendent being and that religion was not the labored suppression of passions, of regimen and control, but the *en rapport* relationship with the transcendent through prayer and devotion." Would you agree that we could have religion without suffering and sin-consciousness?

ANSWER: I largely agree with you. In Buddhism and Jainism

the fundament is the moral consciousness and suffering is emphasized. In the Vedic religion, the religious attitude as kinship with God is prominent. Even in this *en rapport* relation there is the consciousness of a lack of imperfection in the background. The distinction eventually turns out to be one of relative emphasis on one or the other—on exaltedness or suffering.

QUESTION: Regarding freedom, you say that in "the state of union with God, the individual for all practical purposes is God; he is no more an ego." What sort of personality does an individual have in that state?

ANSWER: Although no longer self-centered and egoistic in his pursuits and outlook, the freed individual still has a personality insofar as he unceasingly and intelligently strives for the good of others and participates in the cosmic order. He is not a mere principle. The term "ego-less personality" is not an inconsistent expression, nor is that state an incongruous one. All enlightened sages, like the Buddha, freed of their ignorance and selfishness, are concrete examples of this. They are actively free. And this freedom may be distinguished from the freedom of Pure Being (*Brahman*), which is a state of absorption and a self-completeness. Personality could significantly be attributed to one who is actively free.

Notes

1. *Saṁyutta-nikāya,* Part II (*Nidāna-vagga*), XV.3 ("Assu-sutta"), L. Feer, ed. (London: Pali Text Society edition, 1888), pp. 179–180.
2. The Buddha gives a graphic description of this fact of suffering: "What do you think, O monks! Which may be more, the flow of tears you have shed on this long way, running again and again to new birth and new death, united to the disliked, separated from the liked, complaining and weeping, or the water of the four great oceans? . . . But how is this possible? Without beginning or end, O monks, is this round of rebirth. There cannot be discerned the first beginning of beings, who, sunk in ignorance and bound by thirst, are incessantly transmigrating and again and again run to a new birth. And thus, O monks, through a long time you have experienced suffering, pain and misery, and enlarged the burying ground; truly long enough to be disgusted with every kind of existence, long enough to turn away from every kind of existence, long enough to deliver yourself from it." *Saṁyutta-nikāya,* II.xv.13. Quoted in Grimm, *The Doctrine of the Buddha,* (Berlin: Akademie-Verlag, 1958), pp. 100–101.

Jaigīṣavya (*Yoga-sūtra-bhāṣya,* III.18) gives expression to *duḥkha-satya* in identical terms: *daśasu mahasargeṣu bhavyatvād anabhibhūtena buddhisattvena mayā naraka-tiryagbhavam duḥkham sampaśyatā devamanuṣyeṣu punah punar utpadyamanena yat kincid anubhūtam tat sarvam duḥkham eva pratyavaimi.*

3. *Duḥkha* is usually considered in the threefold way: *duḥkha-duḥkhatā* (the actual pain); *tāpa-duḥkhatā* (longing, desire); and the *saṁskāra-duḥkhatā*—the root causes, *kleśas* (passions), e.g., attachment, aversion, etc. In short, phenomenonal existence, or all the five *upādāna-skandhas,* are pain.
4. Madhva's doctrine of predestination comes perilously close to this point of view.
5. The Christian doctrine of the Fall and Redemption may be taken in some sense as the religious counterpart of this conception.
6. Śaṁkara's *Bhāṣya* on *Brahma-sūtra,* I.i.4.
7. *Mādhyamika-kārikā,* XXV.5–6, Louis de La Vallée-Poussin, ed. Bibliotheca Buddhica, Vol. IV. (St. Petersburgh, Bibliotheca Buddhica, 1913), pp. 521, 527.
8. Śaṁkara (*Brahma-sūtra-bhāṣya,* I.i.1), for instance, lays down four conditions as necessary prerequisites for undertaking *Brahma-jijñāsā* (*Brahma*-knowledge): discrimination between the true and the false (literally the eternal and the ephemeral), detachment from secular pursuits of this world and from heavenly pleasures; practice of the moral virtues of control and contentment, and an intense desire for freedom. The *Yoga-sūtra* enjoins the observance of restraints (*yama*)—non-violence, truthfulness, non-covetousness, continence, non-acquisition—and the practice of moral virtues (*niyama*)—contentment, purity, penance, reading of scriptures, and devotion to God—as the first steps to the higher reaches of *yoga* discipline.
9. See *Aṣṭa-sāhaṣrikā-prajñā-pāramitā,* R. L. Mitra, ed. (Calcutta: Bibliotheca Indian edn., 1888), p. 293. See also *Śikṣā-samuccaya* (St. Petersburgh: Bibliotheca of Śantideva, Cecil Bendell, ed., Bibliotheca Buddhica, 1897–1902), Vol. I, p. 14.
10. Quoted from T. R. V. Murti, *The Central Philosophy of Buddhism* (London: George Allen & Unwin Ltd., 1960), pp. 263–264.
11. The *Mahā-vagga* of the *Vinaya-piṭaka,* Sec. I. Söderblom, in his *The Living God,* comments on this, saying that only the Buddha or Christ could be subjected to this unique kind of temptation. (Jesus is reported to have uttered: "Let this cup pass from me, Father. Thy will be done.")
12. *Brahma-sūtra,* IV.iv.5, 7, and the Commentary of Śaṁkara thereon; see also the *Siddhāntaleśa-saṁgraha,* (Benares: Chowkhamba edn., 1916), pp. 512–542. Consult the Symposium on *eka-mukti* and *sarva-mukti* in the *Proceedings of the Indian Philosophical Congress,* Mysore Session, 1932.

13. *Chāndogya Upaniṣad,* VII.xxvi.2; VIII.xii.3.
14. See *Brahma-sūtra,* IV.iv.17–18.
15. Har Dayal, *The Bodhisattva Doctrine in Buddhist Sanskrit Literature* (London: Kegan Paul, Trench, Trübner, & Co., Ltd., 1932), p. 28.
16. For a somewhat fuller discussion of the concept of relation in the Advaita Vedānta, reference may be made to the writer's paper, "The Two Definitions of Brahman in the Advaita," in the *Professor K. C. Bhattacharyya Memorial Volume* (Amalner: Indian Institute of Philosophy, 1958), pp. 136 ff.

SURAMA DASGUPTA

The Individual in Indian Ethics

THE OVER-ALL PROBLEM here is the status of the individual. One aspect of that problem is the status of the individual in ethical thought and action. For our purposes, this special problem is constituted by two major considerations, first, the individual's right of conscience as opposed to social duties and obligations, and other related problems, and, second, the relation of morality to the ultimate spiritual end that the individual strives to achieve.

In India, all such discussions have been intimately related to the consideration of the nature of man from the philosophical point of view. Since most philosophy in India became religion and had tremendous significance for practical life, ethical problems could not be dissociated from these. Yet, Hindu thinkers were not concerned with the ultimate goal alone, but drew up a practical scheme of social life and its obligations, keeping in view the final end to be achieved. Buddhism and Jainism, being monastic orders of religion, were not concerned with life in society, but, since man lives with his fellow beings, all these systems stressed the moral values of man in every sphere of life.

I

The Hindu systems, whatever differences there might be about the ultimate nature of the soul or self, all agreed that the knowledge of the self was the highest good, and that a moral life was essential for this spiritual enlightenment. Man has a dual nature: one, his spiritual and immortal essence, the other, his empirical life and character. This led to the twofold idea of the good, that of an individual's life in society, in which there is a conflict of good and evil, and the other as the complete or the wholly good, as represented by the concept of enlightenment about the nature of the self, which meant liberation from wrong perspectives and false values and passions associated with these. The latter was called the highest good (*śreyas*).[1]

The literature which discuss the legal and social duties is known as the Dharma-śāstras. They cover a wide period of Indian history, ranging from the third or fourth century B.C. to the eleventh or twelfth century A.D.—in some cases even later than that. The *Mahābhārata,* the Great Epic, is supposed to be of very ancient origin in spite of later interpolations, and so is the other epic, the *Rāmāyaṇa.* In all these texts and even in the *Caraka-saṁhitā,* a recondite book on medical science, social values in consonance with the highest good were discussed.

The Smṛtis (traditional texts) offered a plan of life according to different professions, depending on the caste system and also according to the different stages of life, such as those of the student and the householder, the stage of retirement and study, and the final stage of meditation on philosophical truths.[2] One was considered preparatory for the other, and hence life in society was to be led in consonance with the final goal to be attained. A scholar, a king, a businessman—all had to pass through all these stages, and therefore moral discipline and the observance of respective duties were emphasized.[3] In a general manner, both standards of the good, that of social duties and the other based on the spiritual nature of man, were helpful to a person in his social life. The belief that man is essentially pure and free from all impurities of passions helped him to do his duty well as a good and efficient member of society, and this in its turn contributed to his progress toward his spiritual destiny.

The *Mahābhārata* and the Smṛtis took up the practical problems of life in detail and tried to offer solutions, bearing in mind the good of society and the spiritual ideal of the individual. There cannot be any fixed or rigid standard of duties for all times, because life is complex and ever moving. What appears to be good or right in one context may not be so in another; at most, some general maxims and principles can be laid down. The *Mahābhārata* holds a realistic attitude toward life. It gives three standards of moral actions: (1) the advancement of society, maintenance of social order, and preservation of traditions and customs, (2) the realization of the self, which is the highest good, and (3) the standard of conduct to guide people in abnormal times, i.e., in times of war or political upsets or similar unusual situations.[4]

For the good of society, it was held, as it is also in the *Gītā*, that, provided the heart is clean and pure and free from all passions and small self-seeking motives, whatever one does, as one's duty, has moral value. It has been repeatedly asserted in the *Gītā* by Kṛṣṇa that morality proceeds from the inner spirit of man. If one has achieved equanimity of mind by conquering the evil in him, he will be doing the right in doing his duty. Virtues and duties in a society have to be determined in the proper context of the situation. For instance, truthfulness and non-injury are universally valid principles of moral action,[5] but in specific situations these are modified. For the sake of giving encouragement to a patient the physician is certainly justified in holding out hope of health and normal life. But a true statment which has a correspondence with facts but has been uttered in a spirit of malice to hurt others does not have the dignity of moral value.

A utilitarian view is expressed in the *Mahābhārata* when it says that a man can give up his own interest for the sake of his family, give up that of the family for the sake of the community, and give up that also for the good of the greater number of people; but it adds that he may give up everything for finding out the spiritual truth of the self.[6]

In the case of conflict between a general maxim and a particular, man in society should attend to the latter, since maintenance of society depends on that. For instance, it is a universally accepted principle that one should not cause hurt to others; but a king or a government has to do this for the maintenance of law and order.[7]

Non-injury to others has been acclaimed in India as a great virtue, but, for the protection of the weak, for the sake of a right cause, or in self-defense, one should fight the aggressor, and in times of war, the enemy.[8]

The case of Arjuna in the *Gītā* has been discussed as an instance of the way in which an individual's right of conscience was denied in a situation of emergency, that is, that of war. Taken out of context, this instance has led to oversimplification of the problem of the individual's right of judgment in conflict with social duties.

The story in the *Mahābhārata* is that on the day before the war was to start Arjuna assured his eldest brother that, though their army was smaller and the enemy had reputed leaders like his great grand-uncle Bhīṣma and a teacher like Droṇa, he was confident that he and his brothers would be victorious because theirs was the cause of righteousness and justice, and he himself and his brothers were excellent warriors. Then, at the time when the war was about to begin, and Arjuna saw his relatives on the other side, which he knew very well would be the case, his emotions became uppermost, and he declined to fight. He was not a conscientious objector to war, as has been contended sometimes; he had loved his career as a warrior all his life and had shown exceptional talent and ability in this respect, and on the present occasion he was the leader of his army. But at the critical moment he wished to withdraw. It was not a crisis of conscience; it was a conflict of his sense of the right against his emotions such as may have been felt by many a soldier on the battlefield. Nowhere in the world when a country is at war are people in the army allowed to withdraw and desert it. In this context, Kṛṣṇa reminded Arjuna of the spiritual truth about man and of his duties as a warrior, and Arjuna declared that his confusion was removed and his understanding was clearer.

Life is full of complex situations, and, however elastic and wide the rules of guidance may be, the individual is bound occasionally to face a dilemma, a conflict of different social duties, or a conflict of these with his own good sense or conscience, whatever we may call it. In the *Manu-saṁhitā* and also in the *Mahābhārata*, a warning was repeatedly given to the individual that he should be very clear in his mind as to where his duty lies. The *Manu-saṁhitā* says there are four sources of morality (*dharma*): the Vedas (the scriptures), the Smṛti literature based on these, the conduct of good and wise persons, and the individual's own judgment.[9] In whatever he does, the individual should have the satisfaction that he is doing the right (*ātmanastuṣṭireva-ca*). At all times and in all our duties we have to employ ourselves with enthusiasm and sincerity; otherwise, social life becomes insipid and dull and loses its force. That is why the awakening of intellect (*buddhi-samprajanana*) has been greatly emphasized. In the "Gāyatrī-mantra," a Vedic hymn recited in daily prayers, one prays that one's intellect may ever be alert and enlivened so that one's understanding may become clearer. In times of crisis and confusion due to an abnormal situation, it is the individual who has to decide his course of action. His own conscience is his sole guide. There is a long section in the *Mahābhārata*[10] where Yudhiṣṭhira, the eldest of the Pāṇḍu brothers, repeatedly asks Bhīṣma, the leader of the family, how one can make a proper decision in a difficult situation. Bhīṣma answers that doubts and confusions are essential[11] for a man of character—it is through such conflicts and the overcoming of them that he can grow and attain the good. Thus, Viśvāmitra, a *kṣatriya* (warrior) scholar of great repute, who had become a *brāhmaṇa,* violated the rules of conduct prescribed by society for a *brāhmaṇa* and went to a butcher and begged prohibited food for himself, because he thought this was the right thing to do. Bhīṣma said, "In times of doubt, O, son of Kunti, one has to decide by using one's own good sense."[12] The *Caraka-saṁhitā* has mentioned that care should always be taken to avoid errors of personal judgment.[13]

Bhīṣma himself had given up his claim to the throne in favor of his step-brothers, and, in addition, took the vow of celibacy to ensure the legal rights of their descendants.[14] This was against the social practice at the time; in this action he did not follow any pattern or type of norm laid down by society, but acted according to his own values. Instances like this, in which the individual makes a special contribution of his own over and above the accepted standards followed by average men in society, are not rare.

The theory of *karma* attributes full responsibility for one's actions to the individual himself. He is also responsible for the actions of others if he induces or forces them to do a particular act. So, in spite of social injunctions, the individual has to be careful about the moral nature of his actions. Society has tried to help the average man by mapping out for him a scheme of life and duties, but it is on the individual himself that his *karma* depends, and results will accrue to him accordingly. So, from every point of view, the social good or the personal, the final responsibility for actions rests on the individual alone.

The concept of conscience has been discussed in various ways in Western thought. It is a faculty of discriminating right from wrong, good from evil. In Sanskrit, there is no one particular word to denote this, though there are expressions which would convey similar notions. Moral values are expressed by words like "*dharma*" (good) and "*adharma*" (bad), and "*puṇya*" (merit) and "*pāpa*" (demerit). The concept of intellect (*buddhi*) that helps man to distinguish these may be taken as similar to conscience.

The spiritual good (*śreyas*) is different from the social good.

In social life, man is tied by obligations which may be quite customary, based on traditions or on a broader perspective of human relationships. But there is also the consideration of the individual man himself and the aspirations that he wishes to achieve. This spiritual ideal is inherent in man. We have a similar idea in Bergson when he says, ". . . the two moralities [are that of] pressure [that is, of society] and aspiration . . . they are no longer to be found in a pure state. The first has handed to the second something of its compulsive force; the second has diffused over the other something of its perfume."[15] "Immanent in the former is the representation of a society which aims only at self-preservation. . . . The morality of aspiration, on the contrary, implicitly contains the feeling of progress."[16] Similarly, it can be said from the Indian point of view that, in spite of the moral obligations laid down by society, the higher nature of man is considered to be of greater significance.

In all systems of ethics, the possibility of confusing conscience with other inclinations and impulses of man's nature has been discussed, and care has been taken to avoid this perplexity of conscience. In India, the individual has been warned over and over again about this confusion and has been asked to bear in mind this dual perspective of values, so that he can see, through the various entanglements of his social and self-seeking interests, the right course of action. That is why two sets of duties were drawn up to help the average man in society: one, virtues which have universal validity, love, charity, compassion, benevolence, forgiveness, and the like, and the other, the specific duties of man according to his profession and stage in life.

From the above discussion it is now clear that no special preference has been given to ones' loyalty to personal ties like that of family or group or community. The highest loyalty is to one's moral values. Thus, in the story of two brothers, Śaṅkha and Likhita, when the latter committed a theft, the former, the elder one, sent him to the king to confess his guilt and receive punishment, because this was the right course of conduct.[17] We are reminded in this connection of Gāndhārī, the queen mother of Duryodhana (Arjuna's cousin and opponent), who pleaded with the king, her husband, to banish her own son, who was evil in character and was in the wrong. And when, in spite of her protestations, the war was started and her son came for her blessings, she said only one thing, "Wherever there is righteousness, victory will be there."[18]

Consideration of the individual's rights and duties changed

the pattern and social standards in different times. In very early times, men and women were free to choose a career in quest of knowledge, in which case they could remain single and dedicate themselves to study and meditation, or they could marry and follow a normal course of life. But in the Smṛtis, marriage (householder stage) and the other stages (*āśramas*) in their due order were emphasized, with occasional exceptions. In later times, those who chose to renounce worldly life for knowledge could do so. Śaṁkara himself is an illustration of this. He revived Hinduism in an atmosphere dominated by Buddhist influence, but he did not accept the householder's life.

The conflict of the individual and society also expressed itself in different forms of marriage and marital rights, which underwent various changes. Though Hindu marriage was considered sacramental and, therefore, indissoluble, divorce was known to take place in the time of Kauṭilya (fourth century B.C.) and also in the days of some of the later Smṛtis. Among other grounds, mutual incompatibility was admitted for the annulment of a marriage.[19] Eight different forms of marriage were accepted for meeting the requirements of various situations.[20]

Caste duties also underwent various phases of change. In very early times, different professions and duties were assigned to people so that social structure could be maintained with efficiency. These were hereditary, and people born in a particular caste were supposed to acquire aptitude and skill for them. But this went against the individual's right of choosing his vocation and reactions against caste set in. Viśvāmitra, a *kṣatriya* by birth, became a *brāhmaṇa* by undergoing severe penances and struggle. As individuals started choosing their own career, both because of their choice and also for economic reasons, the division of society into four principal castes and sub-castes became useless, and the system began disintegrating. Besides, since intercaste marriage was prevalent from very early times, this had led to an intermixture of castes. In the *Mahābhārata,* Yudhiṣṭhira said that a *brāhmaṇa* was no longer known by birth but by the special behavior that the individual displayed.[21] In the *Chāndogya Upaniṣad,* the story of Satyakāma shows that he was accepted as a *brāhmaṇa* because he was so truthful in that he did not hesitate to state the fact that he was born out of wedlock and did not know his father's lineage.[22] We may also mention that the Śaiva and Vaiṣṇava sects did not have caste distinctions as a rule, though these are Hindu systems of thought. Reformative sects of Hinduism, such as the Ārya Samāj, the Brāhmo Samāj, and others, as well as Buddhism and Jainism, did not have caste distinctions.

In its history of three thousand years or more, Hindu society passed through various phases of beliefs and practices which, though contrary to one another, were all absorbed, making a vast mosaic structure of the co-existence of different beliefs.

Coming to Buddhism, we find that its emphasis has been on solving the problem of human misery, and, since this could be done only by a proper perspective on things and through moral effort and great love and compassion for fellow beings, it became a religion of love. On the one hand, it asserted the impermanence of all things and denied a permanent soul; on the other, it held a very noble and lofty ideal of human character. Buddhism, being a monastic order (though it had its followers among the householders), did not encounter complicated social problems. But, since man lives in relation with his fellow beings, it had to deal with the moral values of human life. Great emphasis was laid on the building up of one's character. It carried the problem of conflict with one's environment to the conflict within oneself. It therefore stressed the necessity of solving the conflicts within a man himself. The evil proceeds, not from outside, but from within.[23] A man has to conquer the evil impulses of his nature, hatred, animosity, and intolerance, and has to understand others on an analogy with his own self and to extend to them the same kindness and love that he has for himself.[24] He is responsible for building up his own character and also for helping others.

King Aśoka (third century B.C.), who is said to have been a Buddhist, erected Rock Edicts giving simple moral instructions to his people. He reiterated the necessity of promoting the essentials of all religions. He said, "One should not criticize other sects and praise one's own, but one should try to appreciate the points of view of other religions and realize the defects of his own."[25] The Buddhist texts are never tired of discussing the virtues of universal friendliness and compassion, the equality of all beings, and the ideal of peace for all. The worst enemy of man is man himself; unless he can destroy all passions and evil thoughts, he can never attain peace, nor can he give it to others. Buddhism is a philosophy which, without the assumption of God or soul, has given much to the world by way of lofty ideals and thought. In the *Dhammapada* and the *Visuddhi-magga*, as also elsewhere, there are very detailed and inspiring discussions about moral virtues. Details as to how one can control anger and hatred and encourage good will and sympathy for others have been worked out in a well-reasoned manner.

In both Hīnayāna and Mahāyāna Buddhism, service for the good of others is emphasized. No individual, if he wishes to develop his personality, can ever exclude others. His personality becomes an all-embracing one because he expands in kindness and sympathy and becomes a part of others and makes them a part of himself. The *bodhi-sattvas* (beings whose essence is perfect wisdom) of the Mahāyāna school, who hold emancipation of all beings as the ultimate end, pray that their own emancipation might be postponed until and unless all beings have achieved enlightenment and peace.[26] The *bodhi-sattva* resolves that he may be able to be of any service that others may ask of him; even for those who have done him a bad turn he wishes that they may all attain enlightenment.

These principles are noble and lofty, but, still, in the task of character-building there are bound to be confusions; and the Buddha emphasized again and again the need of using one's own judgment. He said to Ānanda, ". . . be ye lamps unto yourselves. Be ye a refuge to yourselves. Betake yourselves to no external refuge. Hold fast to the Truth as a lamp. Hold fast as a refuge to the Truth. Look not for refuge to anyone beside yourselves."[27] Again, he says, "And whosoever, Ānanda, either now or after I am dead, shall be a lamp unto themselves, shall betake themselves to no external refuge, shall not look for refuge to anyone besides themselves—it is they, Ānanda, among my *bhikkhus* (monks), who shall reach the very upmost height, but they must be anxious to learn."[28] He says, again, that, of all losses, loss of character and loss of sound opinions are the worst.[29]

It is clear from the discussions brought up so far in this paper that an individual is free to challenge the socially accepted moral schemes of life, and follow his own judgment. This has been true, not only in the case of social reformers like Vidyāsāgara and Mahatma Gandhi in recent times, but also of many other less well-known personalities who have done the same thing. Hinduism and Buddhism—and Jainism, too—all aim at developing man's personality in such a way that his better nature will be able to assert itself in life. A character in which various tendencies and impulses are fully integrated in the light of moral values was thought indispensably necessary for attaining any proper philosophical perspective—and ultimate emancipation.

II

I now turn to the question raised at the beginning of this paper about the relation of morality to the ultimate goal of life, which an ethical individual strives to achieve. It has been often asked, "Is morality—or the individual moral being—negated in the ultimate goal, since this has been sometimes described as a transcendental state of awareness, beyond good and evil?" It is necessary, therefore, to explain the concept of immortality, the nature of the spiritual goal, and also how this can be attained through the moral process.

The immortality of the individual man is not mere continuance of existence, but an experience of the spiritual nature of man. It is not taken as a further projection of the life in society with its values and conflicts, a repetitive existence involving moral struggle. Though the *karma* theory, or the theory of heaven and hell, implies such a continuation of human life, yet, everywhere in Indian thought this repetition of man's struggle in society and in himself as that of good against evil is supposed to end completely with the realization of the spiritual nature of man. Morality implies conflict, in human nature, of good and evil or right and wrong. There is an oscillation between the two aspects of the dual nature of man, the higher and the lower. A moral man is one in whom the right perspective and good emotions dominate and can keep the evil in check. In a spiritual man the evil has been overcome completely, and goodness has become spontaneous. This is what is meant by the concept of the saint (*sthitadhī*) in the *Gītā*—and what Kant implies as "holy will" as distinguished from a moral will. Though moral values and the spiritual nature of man are distinct from each other, they are not necessarily found in their separateness; the latter extends and transforms the former.

Throughout man's psychic history he finds that his appetitive tendency, however valuable it may appear for his self-preservation and however strongly it may be grounded throughout his biological history, subordinates itself to the superior claims of his higher social self. The history of humanity, so far as it is superior to that of beasts, is manifested by the continual assertion of the claims of the higher social self over the original strength of the primary appetitive demands and values. This social value consists in the consideration that is extended to others, but there emerges a still higher sense of values. These are in a sense anti-biological and repudiate the instruction that Nature has been giving throughout her animal history.

To love my enemy as myself, to follow the advice that one should turn his left cheek to anyone who may smite on the right, is in flagrant contradiction to the formula of evolution involved in the struggle for existence and the survival of the fittest. Yet, it is by carrying out demands of this type, however imperfectly it may have been done, that the progress of humanity has been possible, and that charity, fellow-feeling, love, and forgiveness have been extended far beyond the expectations of society and have succeeded in welding humanity together as it is today. To distinguish the social ideal from the spiritual we may say that the former may have variations and sometimes be limited in its use and content, but, in the latter, human virtues such as love, compassion, and forgiveness become limitless. To do to others as you would be done by is a social or moral virtue, but to forgive your enemies when you are hurt and to pray that they may attain a correct perspective of values and attain good in the end shows an ideal of love and compassion far beyond the sense of right and wrong or fairness and justice in society.

In the Upaniṣads there is the concept of the five sheaths of the self, which are unfolded one after another, leading to the ultimate truth as the highest goal. These are: the physical (relating to matter), the biological (relating to life), the mental, the conceptual or intellectual (i.e., the higher level of knowledge), and, last, infinite knowledge and wisdom, purity and joy.[30] All these sheaths, or different levels of existence, are infinite in themselves, one leading to the other. Though all of these are contained in the self, the highest manifestation is in the infinite joy of self-realization in its purity and fullness emerging from the other levels as their continuation. It has been said that none of these levels should be thought derogatory. Each is vastly important and leads to the unfolding of the other, and in their mutual association they lead to another order of truth until they come to the highest as infinite knowledge and joy. These concepts may be compared to the emergence of different orders of value-sense that operate in each man. It can be imagined that each level will have its own values, which in their interaction make way to the superior one and eventually find their culmination in the highest.

I wish to clarify and elaborate this idea further, and will refer in places to certain passages from the book *Religion and Rational Outlook*, by the late Professor S. N. Dasgupta.

The personality of man may be briefly viewed under two aspects, the spiritual nature of man and the other, comprising his biological nature and his social self, as it were, surcharged with social beliefs, aspirations, fears, apprehensions, ideals, and the like. The individual self is a part of a larger social self. "The existence, ideally, of the entire human society and, more definitely and concretely, the family, the immediate environment and the nation within us manifests itself in directing our social self on the lines on which the society has proceeded and developed."[31] In the self that works or behaves as a person the differences of the so-called biological and social selves are so integrated that there is usually no hostility between them. It is only when there is an inner conflict that the two selves appear to manifest their opposing characteristics, and the demands of the social self are felt as a norm which should guide the biological or the appetitive self. "We value our biological pleasure and the self-preservative instinct, but the unity that holds together the psychical elements which form the complex social self is wider and bigger than the unity established by the appetitive self." "We thus find the rule that the more uniting the wider and the later emergent the force of unification, is, the greater is its transcendence over, and superiority to, the earlier and narrower uniting agencies."[32] We may have a series of value-senses, the economico-appetitive, the economico-social, and the spiritual or religious or supramoral. With the emergence of mind, we have found a sense of values manifested in morals and in love of truth and beauty.

The spiritual life is an awakening in which norms of our moral life are extended in a unity which, within itself, holds man and the universe together. The individual is a totality of different selves and different senses of values. The spiritual unity of all life opens up new dimensions of value, a new order of experience. This may be described as the unity of all beings and objective Nature in one Truth, as the Upaniṣads and Śaṁkara Vedānta put it; it may be the union of God and man, as theistic systems call it; it may be the awareness of man himself in his purity, as the Sāṁkhya calls it. This experience is of a different order and is, in most systems of Indian thought, associated with joy. The conflict that an individual experiences in society is dissolved with the realization of man's spiritual nature.

"The exhilaration [that comes out of this experience] of his soul, which shines as a mystic light, regulates his conduct and other experiences, his relationship with his environment, and is in intimate unity with the universe as well as his ultimate dissociation from it. At this stage the sense of joy that suffuses him does not tax him as does a moral ideal, by projecting obligatory courses and demanding submission, but it makes morality easy and spontaneous. The joy that runs through the veins and nerves deluges, as it were, all other considerations and plunges the individual into such a stream of mystical ecstasy that the complexity of the universe loses all its mystery, all doubts are resolved, and the whole personality of the individual is transformed into cheerfulness and blessedness. In its true nature there is practically no form of this intuition or immersion and we may call it by any name we please, such as the realisation of the good or of God or participation in God's love."[33] It is for this that Maitreyī said, "What shall I do with what the whole world can give me, if I do not get immortality?"[34] The Upaniṣads, in referring to this state, say, "The knots of the heart are torn asunder, and all doubts are dissolved."[35] Thus, on the spiritual level life is spontaneous, and the oscillations of moral life have vanished.[36] It is also said in the Upaniṣads that evil does not overcome him, but he overcomes all evils. Evil does not burn him, for he burns all evil. Free from evil, free from blemish, free from doubt, he becomes a true man.[37] Evil and suffering melt away in an intuitive perception which breaks open the bonds of the finite and the infinite. This is the realization of the immortal in every individual man. From this point of view, morality is not negated in the ultimate state, but has found its culmination in helping man to pass through his struggles of life, leading him to a goal which shines in its purity and fullness.

Coming to the problem of the continuation of individual personality in the ultimate stage, the answer from the theistic systems is in the affirmative. The Upaniṣads, Śaṁkara Vedānta, and the Sāṁkhya-Yoga indicate that the final awareness is an intuitive vision of truth, in which notions of duality and of the "ego" disappear. But all these systems admit two phases of liberation: one here, on this earth, when a man attains enlightenment in this life (*jīvan-mukti*), and another, in its continuation beyond this (*videha-mukti*). In the former, the liberated man has attained a personality which is different in its nature and content from worldly experience. He lives here in this world and helps others to attain their spiritual end. His existence is illuminated through and through by the glow of his spiritual nature, in which truth is no longer an abstraction, but a reality. Faith in the highest possibilities of man has now become a conviction, and he is no longer affected by the social life, but stands over and above it. He lives to instruct others, to help them in their development toward this ultimate truth. The *yogī* retains his enlightened mind[38] out of compassion for others. The *bodhi-sattvas* offer their services to humanity. So do the holy men described in the *Gītā* and other Indian philosophical texts. The wisdom (*prajñā*) achieved by men in their mystical states, which defies all attempts to express it, forms the core of their existence. Yet, it does not destroy their personality, but makes it richer with kindness, love, and compassion. It may be that these mystical states (*samādhi*) are unrelated to worldly experience; but their effect on men is of tremendous significance, for they become freed from all impurities and struggles and live here on earth a life of immortality in the sense of purity and holiness which extends beyond death. The enlightened man thus attains an existence which is freed from the narrow, confined sense of the ego or the self in ordinary experience, and is extended to all beings and the world. This is the spiritual immortality that it is the destiny of man to attain. Since it is possible to realize this immortality in its spiritual loftiness and glory even in this life, this solves the ethical inquiry about the ultimate good, which is not a mere abstraction, but which shines in all its fullness and beauty through man's being, his character, and his aspirations.

QUESTION: Does the situation of Arjuna in the *Gītā* come under abnormal times, as stated in the paper?

ANSWER: The war is an abnormal situation. But it is normally the duty of *kṣatriyas* to take part in a war for the sake of a justified cause, as it was in this case. Arjuna himself was aware of this. The standard referred to in the *Mahābhārata* for abnormal times stands for a situation in which our normal conditions of the state, the country, or society have been disturbed owing to a political upset, or this kind of unusual distress. But the war in the *Mahābhārata* took place between two well-organized governments, and there was some established code of behavior which could be followed by both parties. Arjuna's conflict in the present instance was not of different ideals of conduct. It was the conflict of his own sense of the right with his emotions which he felt for his kinsmen. Kṛṣṇa made him aware of this and reminded him of his duty as a *kṣatriya*, and of the spiritual end that an individual has to achieve through his duties and self-knowledge.

QUESTION: Can it be said that the theory of *karma* started from the time of the Upaniṣads?

ANSWER: Yes. The idea of *karma* and its consequences is mentioned in the Upaniṣads but not in a systematic and well-developed form. The Upaniṣads contain philosophical speculations but do not present them in a systematic manner. Both philosophical and ethical ideas, therefore, are collected from the Upaniṣads, and are synthesized into different streams of thought by the philosophers of later periods.

QUESTION: In the *Gītā* it is said that man is a product of Nature (*prakṛti*) and therefore is not a free individual. If man is not free to act, then he cannot be responsible for his actions.

ANSWER: The *Gītā* and the *Brahma-sūtra* are the two philosophical texts based on Upaniṣadic statements, but the former is not as systematic as the latter. The *Gītā* therefore makes statements, which sometimes appear to be contradictory but can be reconciled when we try to interpret them together. There are verses which describe the empirical nature of man, how there is an interplay of the three constituents (*guṇas*) of Nature which urge a man to act in a determinate manner. At the same time, almost immediately after this statement, there are other verses which emphasize the need of self-control in man so that he can transcend his empirical nature. Thus, the presupposition that man is essentially free in the midst of the opposite tendencies of his nature is very clearly stated and emphasized. A man is free in his spiritual nature and has to have free control over the inclinations and impulses which proceed from his psychophysical existence.

QUESTION: If the moral process leads to spiritual enlightenment, how is it that the moral struggle ends completely in the ultimate state?

There cannot be any sharp dichotomy between end and means, particularly with reference to a moral act and a moral means. The means by which a moral end can be achieved becomes the process of the realization of the end at each step; otherwise, the means and the end would stand completely isolated and wide apart. A moral man, through his conflicts, his successes, and his failures, is getting an insight into, an intuited touch of, the reality of the spiritual end, and that is how he can eventually overcome the conflict completely and be established in the final enlightenment, from which there is no more backsliding.

QUESTION: Does this mean that the same act may be performed by a moral man who has to make a decision in favor of his "good will" and check the evil impulses of his nature and also by a spiritual man who has attained enlightenment and that it therefore can be accomplished by him in a spontaneous and easy manner, without any conflict whatsoever?

ANSWER: Yes, the spiritual man will naturally and spontaneously do the right act, while a moral man may be doing the same act, but passes through an oscillation of his will in reaching the final decision.

QUESTION: Does an individual have the right to challenge the accepted norms of conduct laid down by society?

ANSWER: Every individual has the right to challenge any pattern or ideal of conduct presented by society. No society can ever be big enough to suppress an individual's freedom of opinion in moral life. Individuals all over the world have stood up for their own convictions, have challenged the state or society, as the case may be, have even courted death, imprisonment, and punishment, and have stood triumphant in the end, thereby correcting society and introducing reforms and new ideals.

QUESTION: Is it characteristic of Buddhism to maintain that an individual can actually overcome evil in himself through discipline? Another way of expressing this is to ask whether there is any moral process that can lead to actual perfection, or whether every moral process, just because it is to be carried through by the very self that needs the perfection that is to be the outcome, must remain incomplete and imperfect?

As a corollary of the last point, how far was it characteristic of Indian moral philosophy to hold that the "I" that is aware of the good or what ought to be done is thereby above or beyond the actual imperfections of the actual self whose conduct is being appraised and to whom commands are addressed?

ANSWER: In all systems of Indian thought (including Buddhism) it is held that an individual can achieve the spiritual end as self-realization or knowledge of the ultimate truth through the moral process. Whatever differences there may be as to the ultimately true nature of the self, it has been admitted by all the systems that a realization of this is possible through moral excellence, which helps the individual to overcome his lack of knowledge and the evil tendencies of his character. The "I" that knows is also the "I" that is above false perspective and false values; the empirical "self," whose conduct is appraised or to whom the commands are issued, has to correct and develop itself in the light of this truth and can eventually achieve enlightenment and perfection, and there is no further dichotomy between these two. In the theistic systems, the individual shares the divine nature of God in his enlightened and perfected self, which has completely overcome his imperfections and ignorance. In other systems, the ultimate state is an awareness in which this duality of the higher and lower selves, and their conflict, have ultimately been dissolved into a state of purity, and this is associated with joy.

Notes

1. *Kaṭha-upaniṣad,* II.1.
2. *Manu-saṁhitā,* I.88–91.
3. *Mahābhārata,* Śānti-parva, 60–64.
4. *Mahābhārata,* Rājadharma-parva, 15.49; also Āpaddharma-parva, 141.
5. *Yoga-darśana,* II.31.
6. *Mahābhārata,* Udyoga-parva, 37.17.
7. *Mahābhārata,* Rājadharma-parva, 15.14, 20–23.
8. *Ibid.,* 14 and 15.
9. *Manu-saṁhitā,* II.1, 6, 12.
10. *Mahābhārata,* Āpaddharma-parva, 140–143.
11. *Ibid.*
12. *Ibid.*
13. *Caraka-saṁhitā,* IV.i.100.
14. *Mahābhārata,* Ādi-parva; Sambhava-parva, 101.
15. *Two Sources of Morality and Religion.* R. Ashley Audry and Cloudesley Bereton, trans., with the assistance of W. H. Carter. (New York: Henry Holt and Company, 1935), pp. 42–43.
16. *Ibid.,* p. 43.
17. *Mahābhārata,* Śānti-parva, 23.
18. *Ibid.,* 76.
19. *Arthaśāstra,* R. Shamasastry, trans. (Mysore: Mysore Printing and Publishing House, 1961), Book III, p. 126.
20. *Manu-saṁhitā,* III.21–34.
21. *Mahābhārata,* Ājagara-parva, 180.

22. *Chāndogya Upaniṣad,* IV.4.
23. *Visuddhi-magga,* IX; *Dhammapada,* I.1–5.
24. *Visuddhi-magga,* IX.
25. *Rock Edict of Aśoka,* Corpus Inscriptionum Indicarum, Vol. I, Girnar Rock Edict No. XII.
26. Śāntideva, *Bodhicaryāvatāra-pañjikā,* Buddhist Sanskrit Texts, No. 12 (Darbhanga: Mithila Institute, 1960), III. 5–18; *Śikṣā-samuccaya,* compiled by Śāntideva. C. Bendall, ed. (St. Petersbourg: Imperial Academy of Sciences. 1897–1902), p. 2.
27. *Dialogues of the Buddha,* T. W. and C. A. F. Rhys Davids, trans. (4th ed.; London: Luzak and Company, Ltd., for the Pāli Text Society, 1959), Part II, D.ii.100.
28. *Ibid.,* 101.
29. *Ibid.,* Part III, D.iii.234.
30. *Taittirīya-upaniṣad,* III.
31. *Religion and Rational Outlook* (Allahabad: Allahabad Law Journal Press, 1954), p. 279.
32. *Ibid.,* p. 280.
33. *Ibid.,* p. 288.
34. *Bṛhadāraṇyaka-upaniṣad,* IV.v.3.
35. *Muṇḍaka-upaniṣad,* II.8.
36. *Bṛhadāraṇyaka-upaniṣad,* IV.iv.22–25.
37. *Ibid.*
38. *Yoga-darśana* (*Vyāsa-bhāṣya* and Commentary by Nāgeśa), IV.4; IV.30–31.

S. K. SAKSENA

The Individual in Social Thought and Practice in India

WHEN AN INDIVIDUAL is given the same freedom which any other individual may claim for himself he is treated as an individual and is given the rights of individuality. Another way to make the same point is by the use of the concept of ends and means. If an individual is treated as an end in himself—in terms of equality of freedom and status—and never as a means to another individual's purposes, he is then considered a genuine individual.

But this kind of individualism is a purely abstract and atomistic individualism, on which alone no society can be based, and practically all social philosophies recognize this fact, in India as elsewhere. Expressions of pure individuality are always suspect in all societies. All sane societies put a limit to individualism in the interests of social welfare and other values which alone make individualism respectable through the ages. One fact about India stands out prominently. It is this highest regard for such over-individual ends through which alone an individual is supposed to live his life in society and be a significant individual. But this does not mean that the rights of an individual are thereby disregarded.

It has been superficially assumed by some observers that the Indian* social set-up itself is anti-individualistic, that in Indian

* What has been said here pertains primarily, but certainly not exclusively, to Hindu society. The Buddhist in India, from the time of the Budda himself, protested against all kinds of class or birth distinctions and gave full dignity and status to all individuals, but, later, Buddhism almost disappeared from the country of its origin. When the Muslims came to India in about the twelfth century A.D., though they adopted in practice the Hindu social evils of

social thought and structure there is too much authoritarianism, that not all men are regarded as individuals having equal rights in themselves, that the right of underprivileged persons to improve their individual social status is denied to them. In spite of the fact that such anti-individualistic practices have existed at times in India, the whole spirit of Indian social thought and structure originating from the most ancient times of the Vedas up to the present time has accorded due regard to individuals as individuals. All efforts of social theorists have been directed in India, not only toward the betterment of the individual, but also toward the opportunity of every individual ultimately and finally to attain his social destination. Society exists for the sake of the individual, and the social heroes in India have always revolted against discriminating practices. India has always tried to accord social equality to all individuals, though with little success during its dark ages.

Indian tradition has always been tied in intellectual and emotional admiration only to individuals who created and molded the society. The heroes in the Indian social mind are all individuals—sages and saints—and not schools or "isms" or ideologies. The Indian mind traditionally does not bother about ideologies or "isms" as such. It allows them all to co-exist and has a genuine tolerance toward all ideological diversities. Rāma, Kṛṣṇa, the Buddha, hundreds of medieval saints, and such reformers in recent times as Tagore, Gandhi, Ram Mohan Roy, Ramakrishna, Aurobindo Ghosh, and Nehru are all prized as individuals. What is adored in social Hinduism or in any social period is not a historical social process as such, but a particular individual who has brought about social betterment. Not the adoring of the age of Gandhi, but Gandhi himself.

It may be worth noting also that the recent linguistic wrangle among the different zones of India and even the traditional style of personal names are other interesting signs of individualism.

Early Period

The history of the early Indian period reads like that of a perfectly modern and individualistic society wherein the standards

---

caste hierarchies in daily life, they were by their religion not supposed to have any social distinctions between man and man. Thus, what pertains socially to Hindu society is true of the entire Indian social structure, in thought and practice.

of equality and of the freedom of the individual as an individual irrespective of any kind of discrimination are firmly established in theory and in practice. No differential treatment existed. Women had the same freedom and equality as men; there was absolutely no seclusion. Women sometimes had more education than men and had a prominent position in religious and social gatherings. Monogamy was the rule of life. Neither prohibition on remarriage of widows nor the evil of *satī* (the practice in which the wife immolates herself on the funeral pyre of her husband) was known. This was a time in India when, according to Davies, "There was no woman question at Athens because all women were as mere vegetables, and there was no woman question at Sparta because both men and women there were little better than animals. Whereas in India, boys and girls underwent a ceremony of *upanayana,* or initiation, into education together."[1] Even much later we have the names of great women participating with men in religious and philosophical debates. It is well known that women were among the great Upaniṣadic philosophers. Men and women performed sacrifices together. There is no doubt in the minds of scholars and historians about the extreme liberality of attitudes toward all, including even fallen women and women captured in war. To die in defense of women was regarded as the surest way to heaven. Megasthenes, the great Greek historian, who was in India in about 300 B.C., has left a lifelike picture of the Indian people. The Greek ambassador observed with admiration "the absence of slavery in India."[2] This is perhaps an exaggeration, because there was slavery of a kind in India during that period, although it was of an altogether different kind from that prevalent in other parts of the world during the same period.

There is positive evidence of equality among the different races that came to India from the outside in early times. The characteristics of the early Indians to absorb different social elements into a unity has been so predominant as to become one of the chief points of Indian culture. That there were marital relationships between these outsiders and Indians is also well known. All this on the basis of recognition of the equality of all as individuals.

The Indian theory of *varṇa,* or classification of society into four classes, was in perfect conformity with contemporary ideas of freedom and the status of the individual and social justice, and was and remains democratic with regard to the individual's status and his relation to society. It is supposed to be of divine origin, but this is not to be taken literally. It has purely ideological and functional bases and is universal inasmuch as society must have classes of individuals according to their qualifications, interests, and abilities to engage themselves toward the progress of society and toward their own fulfillment, religious or secular. This does not mean that the classification was static or immobile or that an individual, if he was endowed with ability and knowledge, could not attain to whatever classification he aspired to.

In India they recognized the learned as the highest class, because only the wise can lead or lay down and perpetuate the faith for the people. They were called *brāhmaṇas,* who are supposed to give us the ideals and faith to live by. The *kṣatriyas,* were second—they were the political and military leaders, who were supposed to defend the policies and ends of the social order. Third was the class of the wealth producers and distributors, called *vaiśyas.* The last class was that of the manual workers, craftsmen, and artisans, the *śūdras.* This classification was not based on heredity; birth had nothing to do with it. In their ideological functions there is to be found no fifth class, according to the *Mahābhārata* and the much-maligned Manu also.[3] One's *varṇa* is determined completely by one's actions, pursuits, and ideals. By man's own nature he falls into these four types, the *varṇas.*

While the first three classes are said to be twice-born, the fourth is said to be once-born, and therefore inferior. This means only that the members of the fourth class have not had the education and do not have the skill of the other three classes. There are persons who are only biologically born, but not born a second time by the training of education and culture. The qualities which are predominant in each one of the four classes are not exclusive of one another. The *Gītā* says that the four classes were established on the basis of "*guṇa,*" which means ability, and "*karma,*" which means actions or vocations.[4] The most sacred *Bhāgavata-purāṇa,* which is well known even by the illiterate, says, "I consider *śvapaca* (literally, a dog), that is to say, the lowest class, whose mind, speech, activity, purpose, and life are fixed on the lotus feet of Viṣṇu (God), to be better than a learned *brāhmaṇa.*"[5] "A person should be identified by the class whose characteristics he possesses, even though that class is not his own by birth."[6] We read further, "By devotion a *śūdra* may attain the highest status."[7]

It is interesting to note that not only was Suta, the narrator of the *Bhāgavata-purāṇa,* himself born of the lowest class, but so were numerous spiritual and moral personalities who are regarded as teachers of the highest truths, such as Nārada, Prahlāda, etc. They were all men of low-class origin, a fact not very often stressed. Numerous lower-class men and women, such as hunters, and even *caṇḍālas* (lowest in the social scale), have attained the abode of Viṣṇu. The *Bhāgavata,* which is the most representative of all the Purāṇas, does not at all depict the viewpoint of the later-established orthodox social or economic group. According to the *Bhāgavata,* the devotees of Viṣṇu should be free from all pride in their birth and should recognize no distinction between themselves and others. The main point of the teaching of the *Bhāgavata-purāṇa* is the absence of qualifications based on birth, etc.

The primary objective in the whole of India's extensive devotional literature is to refute the idea that a person's social status or class membership is of any significance at all. It is well known that the *gopīs,* the cowherd girls of the Kṛṣṇa *līlā* (play), are the primary examples of true devotion, despite their low-class status. The most singularly condemned in the *Bhāgavata-purāṇa* are the twice-born members of the three upper classes. In the Rāmāyaṇa, Rāma, the divine incarnation, ate berries previously tasted by Śabri, a woman of the lowest class (*bhīlinī*).[8] What is central is that the *Bhāgavata* does not acknowledge the superiority of even *brāhmaṇas* on the basis of their birth alone. The famous story of Satyakāma Jābāla in the *Chāndogya Upaniṣad* is refreshingly pertinent in this connection.[9] In the *Mahābhārata,* great warriors like Droṇa and Aśvatthāma, etc., were all *brāhmaṇas.* In Vedic times, the *brāhmaṇas* were all agriculturalists. As a social practice, old persons—men and women—and the blind had precedence over kings and *brāhmaṇas.*

Dakṣa says, "One who desires happiness should look on another just as he looks upon himself."[10] Devala says that "the quintessence of *dharma* is that one should not do to others what would be disliked by oneself."[11] The same is repeated in the *Āpastamba-smṛti,* and in other Smṛtis, too. Mitākṣara remarks that *ahiṁsā,* non-hurting, and other qualities are the *dharmas* (duties) common to all, even the *caṇḍālas.*[12] The *Mahābhārata* says that "for protecting a family one individual may be abandoned; for protecting a town, the family may be abandoned; for protecting the society, the town may be abandoned; and for protecting the true self, even the world may be abandoned."[13] The great empire-builders of India, the Nandas, the Mauryas, and the Guptas, were all low-born. The Gupta emperors married *licchavis* (lower-classed dynasty).

Young girls had a decisive voice in the selection of their husbands. On festive occasions and at tournaments girls appeared in all their gaiety. In the Vedic period, women did not suffer from any special disabilities. In the *Mahābhārata,* Śvetaketu's father says, "The women of all classes on earth are free."[14] A single standard for both men and women prevailed. Women were so sacred in India that even the common soldiery left them unmolested in the midst of slaughter and devastation. Wrote Dubois, "A Hindu woman can go anywhere alone, even in the most crowded places, and she need never fear the impertinent looks and jokes of idle loungers. . . . A house inhabited solely by women is a sanctuary which the most shameless libertine would not dream of violating."[15]

The refrain of the prayer in the *Mahābhārata* is not for the *brāhmaṇas* or for any special class of individuals. We read, "May all beings be happy, may all attain bliss. . . ."[16] This emphasis on "*sarva,*" meaning "all," without distinction of caste, class, or creed, is typical of the Vedic and the Epic literature or period. The *Āpastamba* declares that "there is nothing higher than the soul" and the *Śatapatha-brāhmaṇa* says, "None among souls is, on the whole, greater than any other soul."[17] Numerous quotations from other sacred literature can be adduced in support of similar social sentiments. When Nārada, a household name in Hindu society, lists the thirty features of the *sāmānya-dharma* (the duties of all the people), he specifically states that these are for all men. That is to say, that are not the *dharmas* of any particular group or class or caste of people, but are *sarva-dharma,* i.e., for all men. The *Manusmṛti,* the Śānti-parva of the *Mahābhārata,* and the *Bhāgavata-purāṇa* abound in similar sentiments.[18]

Socially, in the Indian spirit all people have been regarded as different and separate individuals living their lives as different entities, responsible for their thoughts and practices, and expected to rely on their own efforts toward their betterment and ultimate liberation from bondage. The Indian doctrine of *karma* has had trememdous social effects on the Indian mind. Because of this law, an Indian regards himself as completely responsible for all his deeds. In fact, the Law of *Karma* is the greatest contribution of the Indian mind in having formulated a truly individualistic attitude *vis-à-vis* society. It is the most powerful social element of individualism in Hinduism and also in Buddhism. Everyone is exclusively and completely responsible for his or her actions and their consequences.

No individual is saved or condemned by any force outside himself—in some schools, not even by God. The Law of *Karma* is an affirmation, in the strongest terms, of the principle of personal individuality and responsibility.

But, in spite of all this, the existence of slavery of some kind admits of no doubt. Emperor Aśoka (third century B.C.), when proclaiming his law of piety enjoined that the law of piety consist in kind treatment of slaves and hired servants.[19] In the *Arthā-śāstra,* Kauṭilya gives important kindly provisions about slaves.[20] Manu speaks of different kinds of slaves.[21] Malcolm writes that male slaves were "generally treated more like adopted children than menials."[22]

Medieval Period

Such is the story of the status and dignity of the individual in India in relation to society for about two thousand years of its early history—in the basic and classical texts and in the life of the times. Then came a long period of what is known as India's Medieval Period. India lost its political status and unity. There was no one central authority to legislate for the Indian population as a whole. The country stood divided and separated into hundreds of local or regional kingdoms, all competing and vying with each other to keep their own powers intact. India lost its original spirit of freedom and free enterprise, its earlier outlook; it felt oppressed and driven to mere existence. All efforts centered on preserving its identity, allying all social customs and behavior completely to their religions which remained the only common bond among the Indians.

Then the caste (as distinct from the *varṇa*) system of India became rigid. Enslaved Hindus, with no education or freedom of the spirit, found it easier to take up and grow in the profession of their fathers and forefathers. To try to do anything new, or to seek new careers, would have been not only too hazardous but practically impossible. All those professions which continued as hereditary became *jātis,* castes, and each caste took to social relationships between its own group in inter-dining and inter-marrying. There came to exist some 3,000 castes based on occupation for livelihood.

Along with this, it was natural that ideas of hierarchy were introduced. The *brāhmaṇas,* being responsible for religious ceremonies and the reciting of the sacred *mantras* (hymns), and being the only literate men, were still at the top, and at the bottom came the practitioners of the dirty work of cleaning the latrines or dealing with the skins of dead animals, etc. Since personal cleanliness was a surviving heritage, it gave rise to ideas of pollution and untouchability. The learned kept reading and studying ancient texts and copying manuscripts even in this age, but the people at large were practically living animals under their own religious beliefs, devoid of all spirit of dignity and of free inquiry and criticism.

The caste system, all sorts of discrimination, restrictions on widow marriage, forced *satī,* slavery, early marriage, etc., spread on grounds of sheer survival. These are not the social thoughts and practices of civilized India in its period of glory; they are the survivals of a dead India in itself unfree and slave.

Contemporary India

The new India wants to eradicate these evils as quickly as possible. They do not represent the living India, which has come to breathe its own air again only recently, though India had always been looking backward to its earlier period, the "*Sat-Yuga,*" the period of truth, justice, and freedom. As India became a political unity and free once more after centuries of political slavery, her freedom of spirit revived. The evils of India are not her representative or characteristic theories of the status of the individual in society, but abominations attempted in its own defense at a critical period for its own preservation. They have to be rooted out from Indian society in spite of the place they found in the Hindu Dharmaśāstras, which give only the record of a time and do not prescribe eternal truths or facts. Even orthodox smṛti writers like Manu recognized that a time may come when their rules might become obsolete, and therefore declared that, if any rules framed by them are found to be not conducive to the welfare of society or against the spirit of the age, they should be unhesitatingly abrogated or modified.[23] As the famous Indian poet Kālidāsa says, "Nothing is good simply because it is ancient, and nothing is faulty merely because it is new."[24] The same sentiment is expressed in the Śāntiparva of the *Mahābhārata* also. The modern challenge to caste is by no means the first challenge caste has encountered. The evils of caste have dogged India for centuries, to be sure, but they and the entire institution itself have been under repeated challenge and criticism. Over the centuries, long before the arrival of the British, new reform movements within India repeatedly attacked the caste system.

A religion on the defensive has to be reactionary, and consequently the growth of Hindu feeling at the time did not create conditions suitable for a reorganization of social life. The situation is different today. The Hindu feeling which has developed now is primarily secular and not religious. Today, there is no danger to Hinduism, and the urge for reorganization for society and the individual is there. It is an uprising of the lower classes and the unpriviledged groups. The transfer of political power has provided the masses with the power to destory social institutions based on privilege and on heredity. Social problems are being tackled from the point of view of a reawakened social conscience. The desire of the Indians to take their place with the progressive nations of the world, which is one of the major motivating forces in India today, has an urgency. It may be asked, if the variety of anti-individual customs which until now constituted the social structure of Hinduism have been destroyed or replaced, what will be left that will be characteristically or traditionally Hindu? The answer is that, except for the *varṇas* and the *āśramas* (stages of life), other social institutions of Hinduism are in no way integrally connected with the inner spirit of Hindu religion. No Hindu would argue that, if the joint family ceases to exist in the very near future or castes cease to operate as an institution, Hindu religious thought would be affected. (Incidentally, only 14 per cent of families in India are of the joint type, and so the view that the joint family greatly lessens or denies the significance of the individual does not apply seriously to India as it apparently does to the Chinese and Japanese traditions and cultures.)

For a proper appreciation of Hinduism, with its basic principles of equality of opportunity and for "*loka-saṁgraha*," the common good, and for the perfection of man, it is necessary that it should not be confused with or infused by the social order of medieval times. The challenge of "modernism" that Indian society faces today is something which it never had to face before. It is the authority of the national state armed with legislative powers and motivated by a desire to bring Indian institutions in step with new ideas that is new today. Once this movement starts, it cannot stop. During the present transitional period, many Indians seem to live simultaneously in two worlds, the traditional, static, caste-bound, family-centered, and the new, Westernized, modernized, rationalistic world of dynamic individualism and social progress. This is probably inevitable, and it is not altogether bad, so long as the quite visible changes toward individualism inherent in industrialism and modernism hasten to destroy all remnants of social injustice.

To some, the economic planning of contemporary India indicates or implies an anti-individualistic program which is often interpreted as socialism. This is not an accurate picture even of contemporary India and surely not true to the Indian tradition in its economic life. Economic freedom in the sense of free and equal opportunity for all has been the essence of the Indian way of life throughout history, except during the Medieval Period. No one has been prevented from making his or her livelihood or seeking economic welfare and even accumulating money—almost in any way one pleases, provided, the books say, this is achieved without violating the rules of morality (*dharma*). There were no anti-individualistic curbs on the economic activities of the householder except *dharma*. As a matter of fact, the householder was praised as most important by Manu as being the supporter of society as a whole.[25] True, what did not exist in the earlier centuries—and to a certain extent recently—were the actual opportunities for attainment of financial security and economic accumulation. But the freedom for such opportunties was always recognized.

After the coming of freedom, India introduced a number of agricultural and land reforms for the betterment of the people as a whole. Landlordism, in which the great mass of individuals had practically no economic status, was abolished. Also, a new movement for the consolidation of scattered and small holdings of individual farmers has been established. Also, the Government has aided in providing mechanical tools, irrigation projects, and improved techniques. But little of this is actual socialism—the economic system of India is only partly socialistic—but, rather, development in the direction of social welfare for all the people. The so-called socialistic program of India's economic life does not deny individual opportunity, individual wealth, or individualistic economic justice, and is not in any way connected with any political ideology of an anti-individualistic nature.

The reforms that have been made have been directed against those who were without any sense of social welfare or social responsibility, and do not have any destructive effect whatsoever upon the opportunity, the freedom of choice, or the right of economic pursuit by individuals. There has been some socialization or nationalization of industries which are vital to the country as a whole, but this has been indispensable in view of the unscrupulous attitudes and practices of many of the big industrialists and manufacturers and in the interest of social and economic justice for all.

These reforms have been based largely upon practical concerns. Neither these economic nor any other alleged social monistic tendencies really find their bases in any alleged philosophical monism, such as the Advaita Vedānta, which is, after all, only one philosophical point of view, the most extreme of all, and not typical even of Indian metaphysics, or any other Indian philosophical schools, as some are inclined to think.

Conclusion

We have given, in the foregoing pages, a brief survey of the social ideas and practices of the Indians spreading over a three-age period of about three thousand years. Our conclusions are three:

First, India has a glorious tradition of respect, freedom, and dignity of the individual, and the individual in relation to society—as glorious as any country has today. This ancient tradition of India was, of course, never purely individualistic. This was because of the religious and moral teachings of the Hindus and Buddhists that the highest destiny of the individual lies in the perfection of his individuality in a way which inevitably takes him outside his narrow egoism and brings him fulfillment in relation to the society in which he lives. That is one reason why Hindu social structure provided for deep sanctity of social institutions such as the family, the school, the four *varṇas,* and the four stages of life.

Second, in Indian society the main concepts which governed the individual were those of his duties and obligations toward other individuals or something extra-individual. This is the reason they did not give a prominent place to the *rights* of the individual. Rights are there, but rights always carry obligations, and, if the concept of one's obligation is kept in the forefront of one's mind, society should be deemed (other things being equal) as giving a praiseworthy place to the individual and his relation to society. In terms of Indian thinking, no individual can be completely perfected if the core of his being lies merely in his insistence on his own rights. The rights of an individual are the minimum he should have and should not be deprived of. But no individual should be content with merely the miminum. He should rise above his rights and perfect himself by concentrating on his duties and obligations. The Indian emphasizes his qualifications or abilities rather than his rights. After all, it is one's qualifications (*adhikāras*) that determine his rights. Without qualifications there are no rights. If an individual fails to perform his duties, he is deprived of his qualifications and rights.

Third, ever since India obtained the authority of legislating for itself as a nation, it has, in keeping with its past tradition, passed legislation against the practice of all obsolete and anti-individualistic practices between individuals and between society and the individual. Thus it has once again shown its ancient tradition of respect, dignity, and equality of all men. There are numerous working factors, such as the spread of education of both sexes, increasing industrial and economic opportunities, equality of the sexes, the example of socially advanced countries, and the urge of individuals and groups which have been discriminated against to catch up with the lapses of centuries—it is these factors that make the Indian people hopeful that medieval undemocratic social practices will become a relic of history much sooner than has been achieved in any country in the past.

There are some modern writers who emphasize the inevitable cultural lag, the distance between the democratic laws enacted in present-day India and the actual social practices, and the fact that in practice India is still tied to its traditional discrimination. Such a cultural lag is probably inevitable, but this feeling only shows our impatience and does not take into account the reality of the situation, the centuries for which the individual has been neglected. In fact, nobody can foresee or foretell how long it will take India to become factually and in social practice completely democratic, giving every individual perfect equality and opportunity to make himself into whatever kind of individual he wants to be under the law. But the writing on the walls of the time can be easily read. The modern Indian democratic ideal in society is no gift obtained from Western people alone, whose own ideas of democracy and freedom and universal individuality are quite new. India's contact with the West is certainly one of the main causes of the acceleration of the speed of reform. But the reforms are in the spirit and tradition of Indian society itself.

It is only now, quite late in her long history, that India has come to have an idea of the whole Indian community as such, the nationhood of the Indian people, secular and humanitarian, and, as such, divorced from religion, and has come to think of the status of the individual and the whole community in a secular fashion.

Today, even the poor, the illiterate, and the low-caste have all become conscious of their human rights, as well as duties. And so, now—at long last—the original Indian spirit of the dignity and freedom of the individual shows signs of significant revival.

QUESTION: Do we have enough historical factual data to justify the explanations you have given?

ANSWER: I do not know how to answer the question for the simple reason that it does not indicate any specific instance of factual or historical inaccuracy in the paper. After all, everything said in the paper has been supported by quotations from either authoritative texts or authoritative historians. Of course, quantitatively, many more references in support of all that I have said or maintained could have been given, but there was neither space nor time for such elaboration. I feel that the information in the paper is quite adequate under the circumstances.

QUESTION: The Buddha was critical of the caste system and therefore did it not exist essentially in its later objectionable form prior to the Middle Ages?

ANSWER: This may be true, but the question does not challenge the statement made in the paper that the Vedic and earlier periods in Indian history were much more liberal and individualistic than its later degeneration in the medieval period, in which caste distinctions came to be based entirely on birth rather than on qualifications or profession. Distinctions of some kinds are bound to exist in all societies and at all times, and the Buddha, looking at the society of his time, must have criticized all distinctions from an exclusively moral standpoint. My point was and is simply that caste distinctions as they existed in the medieval period, or even in the British period, never existed in earlier India, a statement for which numerous references have already been given from the *Gītā*, the Epics, and even the Purāṇas and the Dharma-śāstras.

QUESTION: Do you not confuse the social philosophy and the religious philosophy of India—for example, do not the Dharma-śāstras essentially ignore the spiritual goal of man, whereas you relate it intimately to social philosophy?

ANSWER: Such terms as "*mokṣa*," "*mukti*," and "*niḥśreyas-siddhi*" (the attainment of the highest) are to be found in almost all basic texts. And, although it would be correct to say that the social goals in India had nothing to do with the individual's spiritual goal, almost all individuals in India are conscious of the idea of their own *mokṣa,* at least in the later stages of life. The religious goal of life had a primacy even in the secular spheres of life. The separation of life into autonomous compartments of the political, legal, economic, and social spheres is a purely contemporary phenomenon in India.

QUESTION: Your justification of duties as prior to the rights of the individual seems to be open to question. Would you elaborate a bit?

ANSWER: The point is simple enough. A society in which all individuals are conscious only of their individual rights and do their duties exclusively for fear of losing their rights would not be a strictly ethical society, nor would the behavior of the individual be strictly ethical. We can still imagine a society wherein all individuals are prompted and motivated in action solely by regard for their ethical duties in all circumstances. The Indians thus based their social structure on duties and obligations rather than on rights. The social end in both cases may be the same, but the difference lies in the Indian emphasis on the ethical motivation.

Notes

1. J. L. Davies, *A Short History of Women* (New York: Viking Press, 1927), p. 172. Quoted in A. S. Altekar, *The Position of Women in Hindu Society* (Benares: The Cultural Publishing House, 1938), p. 407.
2. J. W. McCrindle, *Ancient India as Described by Megasthenes and Arrian* (Calcutta: Thacker, Spink & Co., 1877), p. 71. Quoted in P. V. Kane, *History of Dharmaśāstra,* 4 vols. (Poona: Bhandarkar Oriental Research Institute, 1941), Vol. II, Pt. 1, p. 183.
3. *Manu-smṛti,* X.4.
4. *Bhagavad-gītā,* IX.13.
5. *Bhāgavata-purāṇa,* VII.9–10.
6. *Ibid.,* VII.11–35.
7. *Ibid.,* VII.23–32.
8. The *Rāmāyaṇa,* Āraṇyaka-kāṇḍa, 31–33.
9. *Chāndogya Upaniṣad,* IV.iv.1–5. Jābāla went to learn *Brahma-vidyā* (knowledge of *Brahman*) from a *guru* who asked him the name of his father. He said he did not know but would ask his mother. His mother told him that she herself did not know because in her youth she slept with many young men. He told this to the *ṛṣi,* whereupon

the latter said that he was fully entitled to the highest wisdom because few men and women dare tell the full truth.

10. Dakṣa, *Dakṣa-śāstra,* III.22:

    yathaivātmāparas
    tadvad draṣṭavyaḥ sukham icchatā
    sukha duḥkhāni tulyāni yathātmani tathā pare.

    Quoted in Kane, *op. cit.,* pp. 5 *n,* 7 *n.*
11. Devala: "*ātmanaḥ pratikūlāni pareṣāṁ na samācaret.*" Quoted in Kane, *op. cit.,* p. 7 *n.*
12. Mitākṣara on *Yajur-veda,* I.1.
13. *Mahābhārata,* I.115.36:

    tyajed ekaṁ kulasyārthe grāmasyārthe kulaṁ tyajet
    grāmaṁ jana padasyārthe ātmārthe prithivīṁ tyajet.

    Quoted in S. Radhakrishnan, *Religion and Society* (London: George Allen & Unwin Ltd., 1947), p. 59 *n.*
14. *Mahābhārata,* I.122.44.
15. Abbé Dubois, *Hindu Manners, Customs and Ceremonies* (Oxford: Clarendon Press, 1877), p. 340.
16. *Mahābhārata:*

    sarve ca sukhinaḥ santu, sarve santu nirāmayāḥ
    sarve bhadrāṇi paśyantu mā kaścid duḥkhabhāg bhavet.

    Quoted in S. Radhakrishnan, *Religion and Society,* p. 91 *n.*
17. S. Radhakrishnan (*Religion and Society,* p. 62) says, "Apastamba declares that there is nothing higher than the possession of the soul." (*Dharma-sūtra,* I.vii.2.)
18. *Manu-smṛti,* X.63: "*Ahiṁsā satyam asteyaṁ śaucham indriya-nigrahaḥ etaṁ sāmāsikaṁ dharmaṁ cāturvaiṇeya abravīn Manuḥ.*" Also, *Mahābhārata,* Śānti-parva, 72. 8–12.
19. Aśoka, 9th Rock Edict, in the *Corpus Inscriptionum Indicarum,* Vol. I.
20. Kauṭilya, *Artha-śāstra,* III.13.
21. *Manu-smṛti,* VIII.415, and Kane, *op. cit.,* pp. 183–185.
22. Sir John Malcolm, *Memoir of Central India* (London: Kingsbury, Parbury, & Allen, 1923), Vol. II, p. 202.
23. *Manu-smṛti,* IV.176. Also, *Mahābhārata,* Śānti-parva, 160–161.
24. Kālidāsa, *Mālvikāgnimitra,* I.2.
25. *Manu-smṛti,* VI.89–90; III.77–78.

TARA CHAND

The Individual in the Legal and Political Thought and Institutions of India

I PROPOSE to deal in this paper with the thought and institutions of India during the three stages of the development of her history—ancient, medieval, and modern. The span of time covered by the paper is long. But it has to be remembered that Indian thought and institutions emerged thousands of years ago and possess an unbroken continuity. The situation of today is indissolubly linked with that of yesterday and the day before. No understanding of contemporary India is possible, therefore, without a knowledge of the past.

Let me begin with the broad features of Indian life as they manifested themselves in the first stage of development in ancient India.

How did the Indian thinker define the individual and visualize the relation between man and society? The individual (*jīvātman*), according to Indian philosophy, is a union of nature and spirit. *Jīva,* literally "that which breathes," or the biological organism, in some mysterious inexplicable way (*anirvacanīya*) becomes associated with *ātman* (the spirit). The first represents the element of finiteness, the second infinitude, and their coming together produces the ensouled body, the individuation of the infinite. Dialectically, body and spirit—non-being and being—become synthesized in the individual.

The spirit is in essence self-conscious, self-illuminating, the knowing subject, the organizer of experience, and therefore the principle of order. The body, on the other hand, becomes conscious by the light of the spirit; it is the object, the chaos of experience, which seeks to be organized and rendered meaningful. Spirit is knowledge (*vidyā*); body is nescience (*avidyā*). One is the real, unchangeable, not bound by the categories of time, space, and causation—the unmoved mover. The other is relative, ever changing, ever becoming, ever moving, conditioned.

The life of the individual is a confluence of two different principles that make it a continuum of inner conflicts, and man's natural endeavor is to resolve and transcend them. This may be achieved through the perfection (*saṁsiddhi*) of the individual and the welfare of the world (*loka-saṁgraha*). The two together contribute to the realization of the individual's freedom. They are the values whose pursuit is most worth while, for in them is enshrined the supreme good of man. The search for other goods is secondary. The identity of perfection with world welfare is important. Equally important is the view that the pilgrimage of man's life is divided into four stages (*āśramas*)—studentship and celibacy, marriage and householding, seclusion and withdrawal, and renunciation and world welfare. Kālidāsa bears witness that the *āśrama* principle was followed by the kingly descendants of Raghu (the ancestor of Rāma).[1]

The individual's perfection is a continuous, life-long process in which all stages are of equal value. The *āśrama-dharma* (duty) reinforces the teaching of the *Bhagavad-gītā* and places action and renunciation on the same level. The same truth is indicated in the doctrine of the *puruṣārthas*—the four objects of life's striving. They are *dharma* (performance of the duties of the social order), *artha* (gaining of wealth), *kāma* (gratification of biological impulses and enjoyment of pleasures not opposed to *dharma*), and *mokṣa* (liberation or beatitude). Life is a devotion to all its fundamental urges, but beatitude is supreme, although attainable only by the select few. Among the other three, the *Mahābhārata*[2] regards *dharma* as the best, *artha* as middling, and *kāma* as the lowest, and subordinate to the other two.

Laws and institutions make full provision for the functioning of the individual so conceived. Society is a whole of interdependent parts, with certain necessary vocations which answer to the needs of the individual—of the spirit and of the body.

Indian legal and political theory takes society for granted, coexistent with man, natural. It does not, therefore, speculate about its origins. Man's needs are primordial, and so is his society. Nor is theory concerned with the question whether society exists for the individual or the individual for society. As both are oriented toward the same end—the realization of the great objects of human endeavor—there can be no incongruity in their claims. Society, however, is a structure which has parts and functions. Society is a community of communities, and not a mere conglomeration of isolated individuals. The parts of society are the factors which perform the necessary functions of social life; namely, knowledge, security, wealth, and service. They are the four *varṇas* (classes), viz., *brāhmaṇa, kṣatriya, vaiśya,* and *śūdra.* The communities which constitute society are family, caste (*jāti*), and subcastes. They determine the status and occupation of the individual, and his relationships.

Society's organization and functioning are so devised as to enable the individual to fulfill his function as an individual—a free spirit associated with the whole apparatus of mental, biological, and rational substructures. This plan contemplates the maximum automatization of the activities of the inferior part so that the maximum opportunity may be available for the consummation of the free self.

Let us examine the Hindu social organization in order to see how far it fulfills this purpose. In the hierarchy of groups which form the social pyramid, the family comes first. The constitution and principles of the family are described in the Smṛtis, or law books.[3] The joint and undivided family was the normal unit of Hindu society. It consisted of the male members descended lineally from a common male ancestor, together with their mothers, wives, and unmarried daughters, down to the seventh generation. The joint family for the purposes of holding property shrank into the coparcenary, which consisted of the persons who by birth were entitled to an interest in the property of the holder for the time being. The coparcenary commenced with a common ancestor and included the holder of the property and the male descendants down to the third generation. Thus, the family of coparceners was a legal entity, a corporate body, in which ownership, possession, and enjoyment of property were in common, but the share of each fluctuated with births and deaths in the family. The father (great-grandfather or grandfather) was the manager (*kartṛ*) of the property, empowered to dispose of it by mortgage, sale, or gift in times of distress, in the education of children, in marriage, and in performance of religious rites of the members of the family, who had the right of maintenance, but no right of disposal.

The individual was thus merged in a group which was founded upon birth, and which was perpetual but purely legal. The family was the basic association of the social system established by Nature and recognized by law. It rested upon two fundamental instincts—preservation of man and progagation of species. It relieved the individual from any anxiety regarding his livelihood. It dispensed with the need for orphanages, poor houses, old-age pensions, and life insurance. To this association may be appropriately applied the phrase of Burke, "partnership of the past, the present and the future."

The second group in the social hierarchy was the caste and the subcaste. In the social philosophies of Aristotle and his follower, Hegel, an intermediate association is recognized between the family and the state. This, according to Aristotle, was the union of families for discharging the function corresponding to the animal part of the individual.[4] Broadly, it is responsible for the economic activities of society, Hegel gives the name "Civil Society" to it. It is comprised of the agricultural, industrial, commercial, and ruling classes.

The intermediate association of the Hindu system occupies a position which is somewhat similar. It mediates between family and society. According to Hindu law, the social system (*samāja*) is made up of four classes (*varṇas*). Each class consists of a multiplicity of castes and subcastes (*jātis*). Each caste (*jāti*) comprises a number of families, and a number of castes are grouped together under one or the other class. Some castes, however, are regarded as outside the four classes. They are the untouchables.

The confluence of castes constitutes society.

In the Vedic age, the system of class and caste was fluid. But, in later times, caste regulations became inflexible and their guiding principle was heredity. The functional inflexibility of caste was somewhat modified, however, in practice; for example, not all *brāhmaṇas* were devoted to learning, and many took to other occupations, including agriculture, which was frowned upon by the Smṛti writers; many *kṣatriyas* also followed professions other than the military. Some of these deviations were sanctioned by the law books.

By and large, the caste was an inward-looking institution which defined the duties of its own members. But, apart from determining the status of the individual, it prescribed few obligations of the castes *inter se* and toward society as a whole. It is true that co-operation between *brāhmaṇa* and *kṣatriya* was considered necessary for success, and *kṣatriyas* were enjoined to protect the *brāhmaṇas* and *dharma,* but the fact remains that the *vaiśyas* were required to live apart from the two higher classes and to render obedience to them, and the *śūdras* had mostly obligations and few rights.

This was the result of the specialization of functions which the system enforced. Thus, a *brāhmaṇa* was required to study and teach, but the teaching was confined to *brāhmaṇas* principally and to *kṣatriyas* secondarily. The *vaiśyas* were legally entitled to education, but a large majority of them were deprived of it in practice. The *śūdras* were even legally excluded. Then, again, the *kṣatriyas* alone were expected to bear arms and to fight. The others were exempted from this duty.

As probably more than 80 per cent of Hindu society consisted of *vaiśyas* and *śūdras*—these castes which were regarded culturally and socially inferior and were debarred from participation in defense—it lacked the inner cohesive strength needed to resist aggression, as was demonstrated again and again in history.

Caste placed strict limitations upon the liberty of the individual, and constrained him to unalterable conformity with what is called *jāti-dharma,* the rule of the caste. As caste was autonomous in enforcing this rule, and as it possessed judicial authority, including punishment of breaches of its regulations, a large part of a man's life was taken out of the sphere of the individual as well as of the state.

Family and caste covered a large sector of the life of the individual and provided strong and unyielding bonds of social solidarity. Beyond the ground occupied by them, the larger association, the social organism, had little more to offer. But there remained one basic need of society and the individual which was so urgent and so vital as to require the creation of an institution possessed of capability equal to the demand. It was the state (*rājya*).

The state in India was unique in both funcion and structure. It was not the *Polis* of Greece, not the *Imperium* of Rome. It had some resemblance to the *Regnum* of medieval Europe, but nothing in common with the modern sovereign state, autocratic or democratic. It was not an independent institution endowed with absolute power.

The state, in the abstract, was not discussed by Hindu writers on polity, for they were concerned with social order and concrete government (*rājya* or *rājan*). Not *Staatrecht* but *Sittlichkeit* was the subject of their study.

The *rājan,* or prince, was an instrument of society, an upholder and protector of social law (*dharma*). But he had no authority either to make or to modify law, for *dharma* was divine, ancient, revealed in words heard from God (Śruti) and preserved in memory (Smṛti). After *dharma*, custom, usage, or the tradition of the people, or the wisdom of ancestors, was binding upon king and society. Conscience was the guide in judging. Thus, the function of legislation was wholly denied to the state.

The second important division of the powers of the state is the organization of the judiciary and the dispensation of justice. This power, too, was hedged in by many limitations. The *Artha-śāstra* of Kauṭilya (fourth century B.C.) speaks of a court presided over by the king and assisted by learned *brāhmaṇas*. This court was, in all likelihood, the highest judicial authority for the administration of criminal laws. This may be inferred from the fact that the king was the bearer of *daṇḍa*, the power to punish. But whether there were other subordinate criminal courts similarly constituted or not is difficult to say. The probability is that officers entrusted with executive and military functions were charged with apprehending and punishing crime, and, therefore, there was no regular hierarchy of courts and criminal justice.

In the villages, the caste *pañcāyats* (committees of representatives) dealt with petty offenses.

It is difficult to say whether the government established any civil courts. The inscriptions on copper plates of the twelfth century give titles of state dignitaries. We find among them mention of such officers as *Dharmādhikaraṇika* (judicial officer) and *mahā-dharmādhyakṣa* (supreme judicial officer), who were obviously concerned with *dharma*, or the law. But it is impossible to say exactly what their duties were. The probability is that civil laws and customary laws were administered by arbiters chosen by the parties, or by *pañcāyats*, or by learned *brāhmaṇas*, who possessed the reputation of knowing the Dharma-śāstras.

This leaves to the ruler real and unlimited authority only in the executive branch of government. In a society in which legislation was virtually non-existent and justice largely private, where the concept of man-made law was inconceivable and crime was considered more a sin than a violation of social order, the whole emphasis of political theory was on the aspect of the force of the state. It is not surprising, therefore, that the wielder of the force—the *rājan*, or prince—should have been endowed with superlative authority. High-sounding titles were conferred upon him, e.g.,

Mahārāja (great king), *Samrāṭ* (emperor), *Mahārājādhirāja* (over-lord of kings), *Parama-bhaṭṭāraka* (the Supreme Lord or Master), *Parameśvara* (the Supreme Lord), etc.

The origin of his authority was curiously both divine and contractual—in its nature divine and in its form contractual. Says Manu: "The Lord created a king for the protection of the whole creation, taking [for that purpose] eternal particles of Indra, of the wind, of Yama, of the sun, of fire, of Varuṇa, of the moon, and of the Lord of Wealth."[5]

Manu also holds that kingship was set up for the protection of the people and their laws in exchange for a sixth part of their produce. Kālidāsa[6] echoed this sentiment when he wrote, "In order to advance the welfare of the subjects, he [the king] took from them the tax of one sixth; in the same way as the sun takes up water in order to give it back a thousandfold."

Āryadeva, a Buddhist monk, chided a king in these words: "What is thy pride worth, O king, who art a [mere] servant in the *gaṇa* [multitude, i.e., body politic] and receiveth the sixth part as wages?"[7]

This account of the origin of Lordship suggests what ought to be the duties of the king. They are all instrumental and not originating functions and are comprehended in the word "protection"—(1) protection of *dharma,* i.e., maintenance of the *varṇāśrama* (division of classes and stages) system; (2) protection of people from natural and man-made calamities; (3) protection of culture, education, literature, art, music, painting, dance, etc.; (4) protection of economic activities, e.g., control of commerce, banking, professions, occupations, and labor, the promotion of state trading and agriculture, famine relief, provision of roads, inns, etc. Thus there was hardly any aspect of the people's life which was considered beyond state protection and control.

What about the relation of the state and the individual? Considering how almost every aspect of life, almost all potentialities, capabilities, and needs were provided for in minute detail by the various branches of *dharma, kula-dharma* (family law), *varṇa-* and *jāti-dharma* (class and caste law) and *rāja-dharma* (law of the state), precious little seems to have been left for the exercise of the freedom of the individual.

Against this conclusion, however, a caveat must be entered. The state of Hindu theory is not at all a replica of its Hegelian counterpart. It is not to be regarded as the end but as the means, the instrument. The purposes and objectives of life were formulated, not by the state, but by society and its God-made law. The state's function is to see that they are fulfilled, that the necessary conditions are maintained and fostered. Therefore, the individual obeys the state because it is a necessary aid to the realization of the supreme end of life, that is, self-realization.

The Hindu state is not Hegel's objective mind, which comprehends all of man's capacities for feeling, willing, and knowing. It is simply an important and essential part of society and has to function as such. But there are other limitations upon the state. Not only does society transcend the state; the *brāhmaṇa* is only partially within the ambit of the state; he, too, stands somewhat above it, for the state is identified with the *kṣatriya* class.

But there was a more serious delimitation which was inherent in its very structure. The state was composed of units, viz., the villages. Now, each village (*grāma*) was an almost autonomous republic. The village was a self-sufficient, isolated economic unit, and at the same time a political unit. It not only controlled the agricultural and industrial activities of the villager; it also made arrangements for peace and order, for which it had its own police and judiciary. It looked after education, culture, entertainment, fairs, and festivals. Each village had its own deities (*grāma-devatā*). The village *pañcāyat* was the instrument of village administration. When invaders came, the state toppled, but the village continued almost unconcerned. It paid to the state its share of the produce, but it scarcely minded as to who wielded the lordship or held the state scepter.

In another way the relationship of the state to the individual was circumscribed. The individual as such, as a separate atomic unit, had few dealings with the state, for he was a member of one group or the other—family, caste, guild, village—and it was through them only that the state impinged upon him.

Obviously, such a state is neither sovereign nor autocratic. The description "Oriental despotism" does not apply to it. The individual is hardly a citizen, for he is primarily a member of a hierarchy of associations, socially of a family, caste, *samāja*, politically of a village, economically of a subcaste and a guild.

But there is one capacity of the individual which is not exhausted in these associations and institutions. The individual is the bearer of a precious principle. He is essentially a sharer in and is identical with what is timeless, extentless, uncaused. His involvement in society provides for his temporal existence in order that he may be released from the pressures of the world and find opportunity to attend to the needs of his real self.

The family, caste, village look after his creature needs and comforts, but the individual alone and by himself traverses the path which leads to true freedom. Neither the ties of the family, nor the restrictions of caste, nor the regulations of village and state can obstruct him in following this path. This flight of the alone to the alone takes place in an empyrean where there are no clouds.

The legal and political theories and institutions of the Hindus followed logically from the metaphysics which defined the concepts of man, Nature, and reality. It may be said that this metaphysics made too sharp a distinction between the two aspects of man, spiritual and temporal, and tended to attach too mean a value to the temporal, with the result that the Hindus had to pay dearly for the shortcomings of their philosophy and the defects of their institutions which embodied it. Nevertheless it must be admitted that the truths that these theories and institutions contain have a value for humanity, and this is becoming recognized more and more by both the East and West.

Hindu polity and its legal system failed to meet fully the challenge of history. When, in the eleventh century, the Central Asian Turks, who had received Islamic religion and culture through Iran, penetrated into India, they met with little resistance and were able to overthrow many Hindu principalities easily. By the fourteenth century, their dominion had spread over a greater part of the country as far south as the Kaveri River. But in another hundred years the impulse to conquest was exhausted, and the fifteenth century saw India divided again into numerous kingdoms, many under Muslim rulers but some still under the sway of the Hindus, particularly in the south. Then the Mughals, who were Turks by race, invaded India under the command of Babur, a descendant of the two great conquerors of Central Asia, Timur and Genghis Khan (Chingīz Khān). His successors built up an empire whose wealth and magnificence Shakespeare and Milton extolled. Their decline in the eighteenth century opened the gates for the influx of Western adventurers—Portuguese, British, Dutch, and French.

For six hundred years, Muslims and Hindus lived together, or, rather, the Muslimized tribes from Central Asia and Afghanistan settled down in India, made it their home, and lived among the peoples whose religion and culture were indigenous. The rulers brought with them their own legal, social, and political systems. These systems bore the deep impress of Islamic canonical laws and principles evolved by the early Muslim theologians. But they retained some features of their original culture and acquired some as a result of their residence in India. The Muslim divines, however, who were the custodians of their conscience, were strict traditionalists, and they sought to approximate their practice to Islamic theory. But India was far from the centers of Islamic civilization, and the milieu in which the Indian Musalmans lived was so different from that of the Muslims of the homeland that deviations were inevitable.

The *sharīʿat* (law) of Islām, like the *dharma* of the Hindu, was all-embracing, seeking to regulate the life of the individual and the community in every aspect—religious, social, economic, and political. But encounter with the realities of India obliged the Muslims to effect compromises. While the majority of the *Sunnīs* (sects of Muslims who constitute the majority of Muslims in India) followed one of the codes compiled by the four Imāms (religious leaders), and the *shīʿahs* (a minor sect of Muslims in India) had their own jurisprudence, many converts from the Hindu fold either retained their personal laws or adapted their customary laws to the requirements of their adopted religion.

The Muslims, in turn, adopted many elements of Indian culture. Among the most important was language. While the educated among them continued to study Arabic and Persian, the spoken language of both the educated and the uneducated became the language of the region of their residence.

So far as religion was concerned, they continued to profess the dogmas and doctrines of Islām and to perform the rites and ceremonies prescribed, but the mysticism of the Hindus deeply affected their religious attitudes. Muslim *ṣūfīs* and Hindu *yogīs* came very near one another, with the result that many Muslims became latitudinarians. On the other hand, the Hindus developed *bhakti*, devotional movements, which bore the impress of Muslim thought and practice. Among the uneducated Muslims many followed Hindu rites and ceremonies and shared Hindu modes of worship and superstitions. The uneducated Hindus reciprocated.

In social life, the exchanges were striking. The division into hereditary castes, which was the mark of the Hindu social system, affected the Muslim society and the distinction of high (*ashrāf*) and low (*ajlāf*), and the specialization of occupations based on birth became established among them. Although the divisions among the Muslims never became as rigid as they were among the Hindus, yet, surprisingly, the Muslims recognized the four-class system of the Hindus.

But the greatest departure from the *sharī'at* appeared in the Muslim polity. From the time of the early Turkish sultans the complete eclipse of Muslim rule in India in the nineteenth century, there was almost continuous complaint and protest by Muslim jurists against the non-conformity of the sultans and emperors with the political principles of Islamic law.[8] In the circumstances of India, it could not have been otherwise. The laws of Islām were developed in lands where the religion of the overwhelming majority of inhabitants was Islām. In India, the conditions were just the reverse, and, naturally, practice could hardly follow the law.

Now, the *sharī'at* in Islam had the same position as *dharma* in Hinduism. It provided the standards of morality and right. It was for the divinely instituted community of the Muslims the divinely given law. Although the state was expected to enforce it through the courts, the learned jurists (*'ulamā'*) were its real custodians. It was their self-imposed responsibility to guide the community on all matters comprised in the *sharī'at,* both those that concerned the spiritual (*'ibādat*) duties and also those that affected social or human (*mu'āmalat*) welfare. The supreme object of both the *sharī'at* and *dharma* was to establish conditions in which the individual could live as enjoined by God for the salvation of his soul.

As the *brāhmaṇa* scholar (*paṇḍit*) was expected to lead a dedicated life independent of the favors of the ruler, so was it expected of the Muslim scholar that he would remain aloof from the patronage of the powerful and the wealthy. Exceptions were provided by self-seeking individuals who were ready to play to the whims and fancies of princes.

Yet, as the *sharī'at* differed from state-made law in its origin, substance, and sanctions, the rulers found it irksome, if not actually politically dangerous, to give effect to it. There was always some tension, therefore, between the wielders of temporal and spiritual authority.

But, in spite of deviations, whether dictated by political expediency or necessitated by sociological situations, that is, whether deliberate or unintended, the *sharī'at* constituted an unalterable standard to which all Muslims were expected to conform. Thus, the *sharī'at* was instrumental in holding the whole world of Islām together in loyalty to one divine law. The modern conflict in the Muslim world between the concepts of Pan-Islamic society and Muslim nationality finds its battleground in the *sharīʿat.*

From the point of view of the individual, the grasp of the *sharīʿat* is as close and its scope as comprehensive as that of *dharma.* No aspect of human life and no detail of conduct, however insignificant, is beyond its purview. Yet, the *sharīʿat* leaves more room for the play of the individual's personality than does *dharma.* For instance, in Islamic law, the family is not so well knit, and property is not so collectivized, as in Hinduism. Again, the individual in Muslim society is master of his conduct—although only to a limited degree—and possesses a certain measure of freedom (*ikhtiyār*). He is not irrevocably bound to the wheel of *karma,* nor destined to an unlimited series of births and deaths until he has earned his release by exhausting his action through devotion or through vision of the ineffable.

Again, although Islām believes in the equality of men, commands mutual deliberation and consultation in determining the community's affairs, in actual practice, until recent times, the individual was almost completely excluded from politics. Legislation, as in the Hindu system, remained altogether beyond the authority of the state and became completely stereotyped. During the early days, the principle of consensus (*ijmāʿ*) had allowed some scope for innovation (*ijtihād*), but since the ninth century the door has remained closed, and *taqlīd* (tradition) has so dominated the *sharīʿat* as to leave no room for any departure from the rigid code. In the domain of justice, though crime was under the jurisdiction of the state, the state-appointed judicial officers functioned almost exclusively in the towns, leaving the great majority living in the villages largely to their own devices. Much of the civil adjudication was in the hands of the people themselves or with the learned jurists selected by the parties to the dispute. In this manner the state was mainly the instrument of executive authority. Notwithstanding law, the executive authority was exalted to dizzy heights, and epithets similar to those used by the Hindus were conferred upon it. The monarch was the shadow of God (*ẓill-e-allāh*).

In India, the *sharīʿat,* or Islamic law, was applicable, however, to Muslims alone, with the result that non-Muslims were left to be governed by their own laws. Thus it happened that throughout the period of the rule of Muslim monarchs the Hindus continued to live under the regime of ancient Hindu law (*dharma-śāstra*) as propounded by lawgivers like Manu and interpreted by later commentators. But in different parts of India, different interpretations of the Smṛtis were accepted. These differences, however, did not radically affect the general character of the law.

In the middle ages, therefore, two legal systems existed side by side, the *sharīʿat* and the *dharma-śāstra*. Both were upheld or recognized by the state. Both were equally sacred in the eyes of their respective followers. But their assimilation was rendered impossible, because they were both regarded as divine, and this fact has been responsible for the sharp division in India between the Hindu and the Muslim communities. This division retarded also the growth of national consciousness and the unity of India. For, so long as the sanctity of the two systems remained intact, even the fusion of the other elements of the two cultures—art, music, language, and literature—could not bring about the merger of the two.

In spite of this legal dichotomy, however, there was a substantial unity of outlook between the two systems concerning the position of the individual. Under both cultures the individual was divested of freedom in temporal matters in order to safeguard freedom in matters which were considered of supreme value, i.e., in spiritualities. So long as nothing obstructed the realization of the highest aims of life, it did not matter if the individual allowed society to direct and control his entire earthly conduct. To gain spiritual freedom, the individual could afford to sacrifice temporal freedom.

This situation was completely changed when the West, with a different philosophy of life, with different social and political norms, and a different conception of the individual, intruded upon the East and brought to bear upon its society the full weight of modern civilization. During the first stages of the conflict between the East and the West the verdict of history seemed to condemn the East lock, stock, and barrel. So much so that some Western observers began to hear the tocsin of its death and the rumbling of the tumbrels for the removal of its cadaver. But the doomed patient refused to oblige.

For the last two hundred years a strange drama has been played on the Indian stage. The drama is unique, and its issue is still in doubt. Two forces are contending to possess the soul of the people. Which will gain the victory? It is hard to tell. Maybe the two will be reconciled in a synthesis which transcends both.

Meanwhile, the battle is on, and the ground is strewn with *membra disjecta*—the moribund bodies of Indian polities, the wrecked organs of Indian economy, and the headless trunk of Indian society. During the battle a fierce attack was launched upon the whole of Indian culture—its laws, its social institutions, its religion and philosophy, its way of life, its art, and its literature. The Christian missionary, the British schoolmaster, and the government official joined forces to demolish the edifice of heathendom, to civilize the barbarian, and to raise a new structure of civilization *à l'Occident*.

But, out of the general devastation and as a result of the new economy, the new administrative system, and Western education there sprang up a new social class—the middle class—which assumed the lead of Indian society. This class was composed of several groups, of which the more important were three: (1) the agrarian group consisting of big and small renters, landholders, and village moneylenders, (2) the urban business groups, which included merchants, bankers, contractors, etc., and (3) the professionals, some of whom followed independent professions such as law, medicine, teaching, engineering, etc., and others who provided personnel for governmental, semi-governmental, and private services. These groups were not rigid or self-contained; ingress into and egress from them were easy. They were eager to acquire modern education without which admission into professions was impossible.

But the middle class was not large in numbers; in fact, it was like an island in the ocean—the ocean of ancient tradition, blind conformity, custom and status, which supplied it with sustenance and the sap of life.

The middle class faced the challenge of the West. The ingredients of this challenge were a critical and rational approach to the problems of thought and life, an objective scientific attitude toward Nature and the universe, a self-authorized morality, a legal system of human origin and of earthly sanctions, and a political order deriving its authority from the will of the people, a society bound together with ties of secular interests—above all, an individual who is free to think, to act, and to associate, who owes attachment to his territorial group and loyalty to his territorial state, and who identifies his supreme end with the rational good and disregards the good which transcends reason.

The operative conditions in which the middle class lived and the ideas which it imbibed from Western education and from direct contact with Western people and their culture inevitably affected its intellectual make-up, attitude of mind, and system of values.

The British-devised legal and political setup fostered and stabilized these changes. Under this system, the status of the individual has been transformed. In the first place, property has become individualized. In pre-British days, no one possessed absolute and exclusive rights in land. The peasant had a hereditary right to cultivate, but he shared the produce with some middleman—landholder—and the state, and his rights of alienation by sale, mortgage, or gift were strictly limited. The landholder was similarly bound. He could not evict the tenant so long as he did not default in payment. He was only a mediatory between the cultivator and the state, which could deprive him of his share and transfer it to others. But the state, too, was not the owner.

The British abolished the old system and created three classes of owners of land: (1) in Bengal and some other territories, landlords who possessed absolute rights, (2) in Bombay and Madras, peasants who cultivated the land, and (3) in the Panjab village, jointholders who were made responsible for collection and payment of government revenue. This was a vast and far-reaching revolution. Land became a marketable commodity and the landowner the holder of a commodity which he could sell. Property had acquired movement, and the village community as a collective unit was broken up.

Under British rule, an entirely new economy had thus come to be established. The old Indian economy dominated by a self-subsistent agrarian system was replaced by an economy in which production was geared to foreign demand, to the world market, in which barter was giving way to exchange through the medium of money; and in which the dominance of agriculture was modified by the growth of trade. Population was multiplying; urbanization was increasing. Communal property in land had become individual property. Thus, the sea of humanity became agitated by the fresh winds that blew.

The new administrative order reinforced the economic change. The system of direct taxation, the introduction of election and representative institutions—municipal and district boards, legislative councils, etc.—the establishment of direct relationships between the government and the individual and the disregard of all intermediary groups such as the *pañcāyats*, the recognition of individual rights and obligations, converted society from a community of communities to an amorphic congeries of isolated and atomic individuals. Status gave place to contract. Natural and traditional fellowship yielded to artificial law-based partnerships and associations.

The family system began to disintegrate under the new laws of marriage and inheritance. In 1856, the Hindu Widows Remarriage Act legalized the marriage of Hindu widows. In 1872, the Special Marriage Act, with its amendment of 1923, permitted the solemnization of purely civil marriages without the accompaniment of religious rites. In 1954, the Special Marriages Act provided a special form of civil marriage and gave recognition to marriages of persons belonging to different faiths. The Hindu Marriage Act XXV, passed in 1955, insists upon monogamous marriages, lays down the minimum ages for the bride and bridegroom, and provides for the dissolution of marriages.

The Act has effected fundamental changes in the sacramental laws of the Hindus. "The religious character of the institution has been blurred in the modern notions of matrimony based upon the Western culture and social outlook."[9] It has also done away with all the restrictions against intercaste and intercommunal marriages and has abolished once and for all the polygamous connections sanctioned by the Śāstras.

The Hindu Marriages Disabilities Removal Act of 1946 made marriages between subdivisions of a caste valid, and the Acts of 1954 and 1955 opened the door for intercaste and interreligious marriages.

The Indian Succession Act of 1865,[10] as amended by the Act of 1925, the Hindu Inheritance (Removal of Disabilities) Act of 1928, and the Hindu Succession Act of 1956 have made deep inroads into the ancient Śāstric laws and the old ideas relating to family relations and women's status in society.

The first official attack on the caste system was made in 1850, when the Caste Disabilities Removal Act secured to the convert the right of inheritance on change of religion, setting aside the provision of Hindu law which penalized the renunciation of religion or exclusion from caste.

Marriages between castes, prohibited by Hindu lawgivers, had been held legally valid by the Bombay High Court, even before the Acts of 1954 and 1955.[11] Thus, the rigors of caste in the vital matter of matrimony were mitigated.

The Constitution of India has struck further blows. It declares, in Section 17, that untouchability is abolished, and its practice in any form is forbidden. The enforcement of any disability arising out of untouchability is an offense punishable in accordance with law. Section 19 of the Constitution gives to everyone the right to practice any profession, or to carry on any occupation, trade, or business, and Section 16 guarantees equality of opportunity for all citizens in matters relating to employment or appointment to any office under the state, and abolishes all discrimination based on religion, race, or caste in the matter of state employment.

All these new laws and constitutional provisions have had the effect of legally dissolving all caste barriers which had divided individual from individual and group from group. The trends of social evolution under a modern system of government have been wholly contrary to the traditional order. A new social system is gradually supplanting the old, and a new individual is emerging in succession to the traditional one. In the new world he finds his temporal and natural potentialities released from old bonds, and material and worldly interests besiege his mind to the progressive exclusion of traditional interests which appear remote, unreal, and mystical.

The direct, intuitive vision of reality which gave him certainty, stability, and finality is receding and becoming dim, and the second-hand, indirect knowledge based upon senses and subject to change both in its formal and empirical content is invading and possessing his intellect.

The Indian seems embarked upon fulfilling Macaulay's prophetic description made over a century and a quarter ago. He foresaw "a class of persons Indian in blood and color, but English in tastes, in opinions, in morals and in intellect"[12] replace the generation living in his times.

But this surely cannot be. The past will not be wiped out so easily. The values cherished in India through the ages are too precious to be denied, especially now that the world—even the Western world—is beginning to recognize their relevance to man's life and destiny. Carlyle, a hundred years ago, drew attention to these values. He wrote, "This earthly life and its riches and possessions, and good and evil hap, are not intrinsically a reality at all, but are a shadow of realities eternal, infinite; that this Time world as an image, fearfully emblematic, plays and flickers in the ground still mirror of Eternity; and man's little life has Duties that are great, that are alone great, and go up to Heaven and down to Hell."[13]

Jacques Maritain says: "We know well enough how emphatic the East is about its calling to the contemplative life and how proud of it; while the West with no less pride,—a pride which is beginning to suffer much,—boasts that it has chosen action. . . . We see . . . that activism and pragmatism, the rejection of contemplative values, the dethronement of Wisdom, are the West's greatest woe. It seems as if to-day the West sought a remedy in the frantic exaggeration of this evil. . . . The West has here much to learn from the East and from its fidelity to the primacy of contemplative values."[14]

Northrop writes, ". . . for the first time in history, not merely in war but also in the issues of peace, the East and the West are in a single world movement, as much Oriental as Occidental in character. The East and West are meeting and merging. The epoch which Kipling so aptly described but about which he so falsely prophesied is over. The time is here when we must understand the Orient if we would understand ourselves, and when we must learn how to combine Oriental and Occidental values if further tragedy, bitterness, and bloodshed are not to ensue."[15]

How is India responding to this need of East-West understanding? It is doing so through the concepts of the new individual and the new society. They are taking concrete shape in India's new institutions, laws, and politics. The new individual has taken to his bosom the freedoms of the West. He has discovered through experience that an exclusive devotion to the transcendent values of the self and relative evasion of the claims of the other is a boomerang which jeopardizes the realization of both. The two builders of this New India joined together to raise the edifice of the new society, in which the elements of the two cultures are mingled. Gandhi told the individual to discipline himself through the exercise of the five old *yogī* virtues—non-violence (*ahiṁsā*), truth (*satya*), honesty (*asteya*), abstinence (*brahmacarya*), and non-covetousness (*aparigraha*). He prescribed for him, for the disciplined individual, the aim of life to be the service of mankind, or, more concretely, of God, who lives among the poor and humble (*daridra-nārāyaṇa*). Thus, ancient discipline finds fulfillment in modern aims.

Nehru, the radical rationalist who had discarded much of past dogma and tradition, declares, "I do not wish to cut myself off from the past completely. I am proud of that great inheritance that has been, and is, ours, and I am conscious that I, too, like all of us, am a link in that unbroken chain which goes back to the dawn of history in the immemorial past of India. That chain I would not break, for I treasure it and seek inspiration from it."[16]

Nehru gave form to the Gandhian ideal and worked for the establishment of a society free from want, hunger, disease, and ignorance; a society based on equality and liberty; a society which offers security for the needs of the body; but a society which provides at the same time opportunities for the realization of the highest capacity of the individual. Thus, Indian laws and Indian institutions, in Independent India, are seeking to translate the dream of Gandhi and Nehru into the life and conduct of New India, and in them the old teaching of the *Bhagavad-gītā* comes to life again: "But a man of disciplined mind, who moves among the objects of sense, with the senses under control and free from attachment and aversion, attains purity of spirit. And in the purity of spirit, there is produced for him an end of all sorrows; the intelligence of such a man of pure spirit is soon established in the peace of the self."[17]

Notes

1. Kālidāsa, *Raghuvaṁśa,* Canto I.
2. *Mahābhārata,* Śānti-parva, 167, 8–9.
3. P. V. Kane, *History of Dharmaśāstra,* 4 vols. (Poona: Bhandarkar Oriental Research Institute, 1930), Vol. III, chap. 28. N. R. Raghavachariar, *Hindu Law: Precedents and Principles* (Madras: Law Journal Office, 1960), chap. 8; Sir Henry Mayne, *Treatise on Hindu Law and Usage,* N. C. Aiyar, ed. (11th ed.; Madras: Higgenbotham's Ltd., 1953), chap. 8.
4. Vide Aristotle's *Politics,* Book I.
5. *History and Culture of the Indian People,* R. C. Majumdar, ed. (Bombay: Bharatiya Vidya Bhavan, 1953), Vol. II, p. 305.
6. Kālidāsa, *op. cit.,* Canto I, verse 18.
7. R. C. Majumdar, ed., *op. cit.,* Vol. II, p. 305.
8. For earlier differences between the Caliphs and the jurists see the lives of Abū Ḥanīfah and Ibn Hanbal.
9. Raghavachariar, *op. cit.,* pp. 878 ff.
10. Mayne, *op. cit.,* p. 73.
11. Bai Gulab v. Jivanlal (1922). 46 Bombay, 871, Natha V. Mehta Chhotal (1931) 55 Bombay 1. Mayne, *op. cit.,* p. 163. See D. F.

Mulla, *Principles of Hindu Law* (12th ed.; Bombay: N. M. Tripathi, Private Ltd., 1959), p. 610, notes b, c).
12. T. B. Macaulay, *Minute on Education,* February 2, 1835.
13. Thomas Carlyle, *Sartor Resartus.*
14. Jacques Maritain, *Scholasticism and Politics,* translation edited by Mortimer J. Adler (New York: The Macmillan Company, 1941), pp. 170, 190.
15. F. S. C. Northrop, *The Meeting of East and West* (New York: The Macmillan Company, 1947), p. 4.
16. Extracts from the Will and Testament of Jawaharlal Nehru.
17. *Bhagavad-gītā,* II.64, 65.

P. T. RAJU *Extracted from "Indian Epistemology and the World and the Individual"*

AS SAID EARLIER, not all of the conference papers presented by Indians are included in this volume. "Indian Epistemology and the World and the Individual," by P. T. Raju is one of these. This is an important aspect of Indian philosophy, little known and almost completely ignored by non-Indians.

The reason for including this extract is to indicate to Westerners the *genuine importance* in Indian philosophy of epistemology, semantics, logic, and grammar.

Indian epistemology is generally divided into three topics: (1) The distinct means (*pramāṇas*) of obtaining valid knowledge; (2) the nature of validity (*prāmāṇya*); and (3) the nature and status of the object of illusion (*khyāti*).

Semantics was from the beginning of the systems a part of epistemology, for the word was recognized as a distinct means of valid knowledge by almost all the schools and classified under the means of knowledge . . . . verbal knowledge is a distinct kind of knowledge. . . . In addition, the Veda was orally transmitted and was considered to be sacrosanct. How can the words of the Veda contain the mystery of the universe? Hence, also, the philosophical interest in the word. In the third place, grammar was prescribed as an indispensable subsidiary study to the Veda; it must therefore lead to what the Veda teaches, namely, knowledge of the most important reality. Then, the philosophy of grammar must be almost as important as the philosophy of the Veda and has to support it. Hence the importance of the philosophy of grammar. But, as the philosophy of the Veda is differently understood by the different schools, they developed different philosophies of grammar also. Thus the interest in the nature of language, grammar, and semantics was very intense from the very beginning.

Right from the time of Gautama (*ca.* 400 B.C.), the founder of the Nyāya [the logical system of the famous Six Systems of Hindu Philosophy], or perhaps even from an earlier time, it has been recognized that the knowable (*prameya*) is dependent upon the means of knowledge (*pramāṇa*), i.e., metaphysics is dependent on epistemology. But, *first,* as is often done in the West, we can so interpret the same epistemological processes and criteria as to fit a particular metaphysics. The schools need not accept the same metaphysics even when they accept the same sources of knowledge. *Second,* Indian thought did not start in the Upaniṣads with epistemology, but with a kind of ontology, to which at least nominally all the orthodox schools owe allegiance. *Third,* even if a school accepts a number of ways of knowing, that does not mean that whatever is known through those ways is also accepted as unmistakably true. This distinction is often overlooked, but it is important. The question is about the ways by which our consciousness can reveal Being or beings . . . . if every one of them is a means of valid knowledge, how can invalidity come in? And what is, then, the nature of invalid knowledge? *Fourth,* if we have several sources of valid knowledge, what are we to do when there is conflict between any two or three? Śaṁkara says that in such cases perception has to be ignored and inference is to be accepted. Rāmānuja says that both have to be accepted and somehow reconciled. In any case, Indian philosophers maintain that with the help of the different sources of knowledge we have to build up our knowledge.

The question of the validity of knowledge occurred to the Indian thinkers in a peculiar way. They knew that every one of the ways of knowing may misfire: illusions and hallucinations of perception are false; fallacious inference cannot give truth; postulation has to stand the test of modal negation (*tarka*); and so on. They knew also that whatever is contradicted cannot be valid. . . .

The Nairukta philosophy of language: Yāska, the author of *Nirukta,* the earliest lexicon in the world, refers to the view of Śākaṭāyana, who maintained that all nouns are derived from verbal roots. Yāska accepts this view because it agrees with his philosophy that the *Ātman* is the ultimate reality and that it is activity itself. This understanding of the *Ātman* is in accord with the etymological meaning of the word "*Brahman*," which is derived from the verbal root "*bṛh*," meaning "to grow," "to expand. . . ." The *Brahman* is the ever-growing, the ever-expanding. . . . Being is activity itself. "To be" is a verb and represents an act. Then the primary part of the sentence is the verb. . . . The most basic of all verbs is the root "*as*" (to be). What we have to note is that "to be" is an act, and the "is" is not a mere copula. In the Nairukta philosophy, Being is the same as becoming. . . .

The first peculiarity of Bhartṛhari's [the greatest of the Grammarians] semantic theory is that there is no cognition without a corresponding verbal sentence. . . .

Bhartṛhari's philosophy of language is based, of course, upon the grammatical structure of Sanskrit. . . . Furthermore, Sanskrit has its own peculiarities, particularly the compounds. The schools differed from one another in interpreting them. Not even the Grammarians are unanimous. . . .

For the Advaita of Śaṁkara, all knowledge is meant ultimately to reveal the primary Being itself, although in the pragmatic world we are interested in secondary beings and ignore Being. For both the Nairuktas and the Grammarian Bhartṛhari, also, the ultimate purpose of knowledge is to reveal primary Being itself, however differently it is understood. Both base their philosophies on language, not merely on logic. Their methodology is etymology and analysis of grammar, respectively. . . .

All the schools, including the Advaita and Mahāyāna Buddhism, affirm that this world satisfies also the pragmatic criterion of truth, although many schools of the Vedānta and of Buddhism say that this world is only that which satisfies the pragmatic criterion. For they say that this world is only a world of action. But the others maintain that this is a world that exists in its own right also. Here we see the interpenetration of epistemology and metaphysics.

Who's Who

SIR C. P. RAMASWAMI AIYAR.

K.C.S.I., K.C.I.E., Retired Dewan (Prime Minister) of Travancore State, India. Former member of the Madras and Central Cabinets in India. Former Vice Chancellor, Travancore University. Indian representative to the League of Nations, 1926–1927. Law and Commerce Member, Government of India, 1931, 1932, 1942.

B.A., Madras University; LL.B., Law College, Madras; LL.D. (Honorary), Travancore University.

Member, Second East-West Philosophers' Conference, 1949.

President Indian Philosophical Congress, 1946.

Major publications: *Pen-Portraits, Essays and Addresses;* and *Phases of Religion and Culture.*

Died, 1966.

KALIDAS BHATTACHARYYA

Director, Centre of Advanced Study in Philosophy; Professor and Head of the Department of Philosophy, Viśva-Bharati.

B.A., 1932, M.A., 1934, Ph.D., 1945, Calcutta University.

Prefessor of Indian Philosophy, Government Sanskrit College, Calcutta, 1954–1956; Principal, Vidya-Bhavana (College of Post-Graduate Teaching and Research); Viśva-Bharati, 1961–1964. (Now, 1967, Vice Chancellor, Viśva-Bharati.)

Honorary Professor, World Academy of Sanskrit, Bharatiya Vidya-Bhavan, Bombay, 1954–1956; Khudiram Basu Lecturer in Philosophy, University of Calcutta, 1962; Buddha Jayanti Lecturer, Indian Philosophical Congress, Waltair, 1960.

President, Section of Logic and Metaphysics, Poona Session of the Indian Philosophical Congress, 1951; Delegate, Entriens, International Institute of Philosophy, Paris; Member, Board of Studies in Philosophy in the Universities of Calcutta, Gorakhpur, Mysore, Banaras, Saugar, Andhra; Member, Council of Cultural Relations, New Delhi, 1961; Member, Philosophy Review Committee, University Grants Commission, India, 1961; General Secretary, Indian Philosophical Congress, 1961–1964; Honorary Fellow, Indian Academy of Philosophy, Calcutta; Member, American Philosophical Association, Eastern Division; Member, Rabindra Bharati University, Calcutta.

Member, Fourth East-West Philosophers' Conference, 1964.

Author of *Alternative Standpoints in Philosophy; Object, Content and Relation; The Concept of Cause in India and the West; The Indian Concepts of Knowledge and Self; Language, Logic and Philosophy;* and many articles in professional journals. Editor of *Recent Indian Philosophy* (Selected Papers from the Proceedings of the Indian Philosophical Congress, 1925–1934) and *Rabindranath Tagore Birth Centenary Celebrations,* Vol. III (Proceedings of the Indian Philosophical Congress, 36th Session). Editor or member of the editorial boards of *Indian Philosophical Quarterly; Journal of the Academy of Philosophy; Bharat Kosa; Rabindra Centenary Publication,* Vol. III; *K. C. Bhattacharrya Memorial Volume; Visva-Bharati Quarterly; Visva-Bharati Journal of Philosophy.*

TARA CHAND

Honorary Professor, Indian School of International Studies.

Educated at Meerut College, Meerut; Muir Central College, Allahabad; and Queen's College, Oxford.

Member, Indian Parliament; Chairman, History of the Freedom Movement in India, New Delhi.

Kayastha Pathshala College: Professor of History, 1913–1918; Principal, 1925–1945. Allahabad University: Professor of Politics, 1945–1947; Vice Chancellor, 1947–1948. Secretary, Hindustani Academy.

Secretary and Educational Advisor to the Government of India,

1948–1951; President, Indian History Congress; Indian Ambassador to Iran, 1951–1956.

Member, Fourth East-West Philosophers' Conference, 1964.

Publications: *A Short History of the Indian People from the Earliest Times to the Present Day; History of the Freedom Movement in India; Influence of Islam on Indian Culture; Growth of Islamic Thought in India; State and Society in the Mughal Age;* Editor, *Sirr-i-Akbar* and *Gulzar-i-Hall.*

MRS. S. DASGUPTA

Reader in the Department of Philosophy, University of Lucknow, 1950.

M.A., 1930, and Ph.D., 1941, Calcutta University; Ph.D., Cambridge University, 1948.

Lecturer in a Degree College of Calcutta University, 1933–1945; Advanced Research Scholar, Research Department, Government Sanskrit College, 1931–1941.

Awarded the Government Shastri title from the Government Sanskrit College, 1939, and a Ghosh Travelling Fellowship, 1945.

Whitney Fulbright Professor to the University of Nebraska and the University of New Mexico, 1957–1958. Taught at Wellesley College, 1961–1962.

Member: American Philosophical Association, Eastern Division; Council for the Marathi Encyclopaedia of Philosophy, Poona; Sanskrit Literary Association, Lucknow; University Women's Federation, Lucknow Branch.

Member, Fourth East-West Philosophers' Conference, 1964.

Author of *Development of Moral Philosophy in India.* Collaborated with the late Professor S.N. Dasgupta in the writing of the last three volumes of his five-volume *A History of Indian Philosophy* and edited some of his posthumous publications: *Religion and Rational Outlook; Fundamentals of Indian Art; A History of Indian Philosophy,* Vol. 5; *History of the Religions of the World* (in press); (in Hindi) *Aesthetics.*

DHIRENDRA MOHAN DATTA

Retired Professor of Philosophy, Patna University. Now at Santiniketan, since 1953.

Ph.D., Calcutta University.

Received training for social work in Mahatma Gandhi's Ashram at Sabarmati, Bombay, and did social work in Mymensing villages, 1921–1924.

Formerly Basu Mallik Professor of Indian Philosophy at Bengal National Council of Education, Calcutta; Professor of Philosophy, Patna College, Patna University; Visiting Professor at the University of Wisconsin and the University of Minnesota.

General President, Indian Philosophical Congress, 1952.

Member, East-West Philosophers' Conferences, 1949 and 1959.

Publications: *Six Ways of Knowing; Introduction to Indian Philosophy* (with S. C. Chatterjee); *The Chief Currents of Contemporary Philosophy;* and *The Philosophy of Mahatma Gandhi.*

T. M. P. MAHADEVAN

University Professor of Philosophy, University of Madras.

B.A., Presidency and Pachaiyappa's colleges, Madras, 1933; University research scholar, 1933–1935; Ph.D., University of Madras, 1937.

Professor of Philosophy, Pachaiyappa's College, Madras, 1937–1943; Head of the Department of Philosophy, University of Madras, 1943–.

In 1948–1949, lectured on Indian Philosophy at Cornell University and other American universities; gave the Foerster Foundation Lecture at the University of California (Berkeley); participated in the Goethe Bicentennial Convocation at Aspen, Colorado.

General President of the Thirtieth Session of the Indian Philosophical Congress, 1955.

Program Member, East-West Philosophers' Conferences, University of Hawaii, 1949 and 1959.

Among his publications are: *The Philosophy of Advaita; Outlines of Hinduism; Guaḍapāda: A Study in Early Advaita; Time and the Timeless; The Idea of God in Śaiva Siddhānta.*

GUNAPALA PIYASENA MALALASEKERA

High Commissioner for Ceylon in London. Emeritus Professor, University of Ceylon.

College, Panadura, Ceylon, 1918; M.A., Ph.D., D.Litt., University of London. D.Phil., (Honorary) Moscow University.

Vice-Principal, Ananda College, Colombo, 1921–1923; Principal, Nalanda Vidyalaya, Colombo, 1925–1927. Professor of Pali and Buddhist Civilization, University of Ceylon, from its inception to the time of appointment as the Ambassador for Ceylon to the U.S.S.R. in 1957.

Dean of the Faculty of Oriental Studies, University of Ceylon, for nine years.

Formerly Ambassador to Czechoslovakia and Poland, Minister of Ceylon to Romania; High Commissioner for Ceylon in Canada. Permanent Representative of Ceylon to the United Nations; Deputy Chairman, Ceylon Delegation to the United Nations Assembly sessions and to the General Assembly; Leader of the Ceylon Delegation to UNESCO, 1960.

President: All Ceylon Buddhist Congress, 1939–1958; Ceylon Society of Arts, 1955–1959; World Fellowship of Buddhists, 1950–1958; Indian Philosophical Congress, 1957.

Lectured widely in Europe, Asia, and the United States and participated in many East-West Symposia of UNESCO.

Panel Member, East-West Philosophers' Conferences, 1949 and 1964.

Among his publications are: *The Pali Literature of Ceylon; The Buddha and His Teachings; Commentary on the Mahāvamsa; The Extended Mahāvaṁsā;* many articles in scholarly journals. Editor-in-chief, *Encyclopaedia of Buddhism;* Editor of several Sinhalese translations in the field.

SWAMI NIKHILANANDA

Leader, Ramakrishna-Vivekananda Center, New York.

Spent four years at University of Calcutta. Joined the Ramakrishna Order in 1921. Came to America in 1931. Founded the Ramakrishna-Vivekananda Center of New York in 1933.

Taught a special course on Indian thought at Columbia University; Member, Seminar on Inter-religious Relations, Columbia University; frequent lecturer at universities, churches, and other cultural organizations.

Delegate to Second and Third East-West Philosophers' Conferences, 1949 and 1959.

Among his works are *The Gospel of Sri Ramakrishna; The Bhagavad Gītā; The Upanishads* (4 vols.); *Self-Knowledge; Vedāntasāra; Hinduism: Ātma-Vidyā and Its Meaning for the Liberation of the Spirit.*

SARVEPALLI RADHAKRISHNAN

President of India

Educated at Madras Christian College.

Professor of Philosophy, Presidency College, 1909–1917, and Mysore University, 1918–1921; Professor of Mental and Moral Science, Calcutta University. Vice Chancellor, Andhra University; Spalding Professor of Eastern Religions and Ethics, Oxford University; Vice Chancellor, Banaras Hindu University; President, Indian Philosophical Congress, 1927; Chancellor, Delhi University.

Upton Lecturer, Oxford University; Haskell Lecturer, University of Chicago, 1926; and Hibbert Lecturer, Oxford University, 1929.

Member, League of Nations International Committee on Intellectual Co-operation; Leader of Indian Delegation to UNESCO, 1946–1952; Chairman, UNESCO Executive Board; President of UNESCO, 1948–1949. Ambassador to U.S.S.R., 1949–1952. Vice President of India, 1952–1962. President of India, 1962–.

Panel Member for East-West Philosophers' Conference 1959; Honorary Member, 1964.

Major publications include: *Indian Philosophy* (2 vols.); *Philosophy of Rabindranath Tagore; Hindu View of Life; Reign of Religion in Contemporary Philosophy; An Idealist View of Life; East and West in Religion; Kalki or the Future of Civilization; Religion and Society; Eastern Religions and Western Thought; India and China; The Bhagavadgītā; The Dhammapada; The Principal Upanishads; The Brahma Sutra.*

P. T. RAJU

Retired Professor of Philosophy and Psychology, University of Rajasthan; Professor of Philosophy and Indian Studies, The College of Wooster.

B.A., Allahabad University, 1928; M.A., 1931, Ph.D., 1935, Calcutta University; Sampūrṇa Madhyama, Śāstri, Banaras Sanskrit College.

Tata Visiting Professor of Philosophy, The Asia Institute, New York, 1949; Visiting Professor of Philosophy, University of California (Berkeley), 1950; Visiting Professor for Comparative Philosophy, University of Illinois, 1952–1953; Merton Guest-Professor, University of Mainz, 1961–1962; Visiting Professor of Philosophy, University of

Southern California, 1962; Gillespie Visiting Professor, The College of Wooster, 1962–1964.

Sir Hari Singh Foundation Lectures, Saugar University, 1956; Woodward Lecture, Yale University, 1950; Century Fund Lecture, Northwestern University, 1953; has also lectured at many European and American universities.

General President, All-India Philosophical Conference, 1958; General President, Indian Philosophical Congress, 1960.

Dean of the Faculty of Arts, University of Rajasthan, 1950–1953; Member, Committee on Gandhian Life and Philosophy, Ministry of Education, India, until 1962. Participant in several international conferences.

Member: American Philosophical Association (Eastern and Western Divisions), American Oriental Society, Metaphysical Society of America, Association for Asian Studies, American Academy of Political and Social Science.

Awarded the Order of Merit, "Padma Bhūshan," by the President of India, 1958, "for contributions to East-West understanding at the philosophical level."

Panel Member, East-West Philosophers' Conferences, 1949, 1959, 1964.

Author of nearly 150 articles in Indian, European, and American journals and the following books: *Thought and Reality: Hegelianism and Advaita; Idealistic Thought of India; Introduction to Comparative Philosophy; Indian Idealism and Modern Challenges;* Co-editor: *Comparative Studies in Philosophy* and *The Concept of Man: A Study in Comparative Philosophy.*

S. K. SAKSENA

Professor of Philosophy, University of Hawaii.

B.A., 1925; M.A., 1927, Allahabad University; Ph.D., University of London, 1939.

Taught at the University of Agra and Delhi University; 1928–1947; Head of the Department of Philosophy, University of Saugar, 1954–1960.

Deputy Director (Editorial), Publications Division, Ministry of Information and Broadcasting of the Government of India, 1947–1954.

Visiting Professor of Indian Philosophy and Culture, University of Hawaii, 1950–1952. Lectured widely in Europe, Japan, and the United States.

Panel Member, East-West Philosophers' Conferences, 1959 and 1964.

Author of *Nature of Consciousness in Hindu Philosophy,* articles in learned journals, and chapters in many symposium volumes. Member, Board of Editors, *Philosophy East and West;* formerly co-editor, *Indian Philosophical Quarterly.*

Index

PREPARED BY BARBARA FORRYAN

abhaya, fearlessness, 264
abheda, non-different, 167
Abhi-dharmaka, philosophy, 112
Abhinavagupta, 54, 205, 206
abhiṣeka, sacred bath water, 259
Absolute, 231, 324; abyss of, 332; appears as relative, 145; *Brahman,* 148, 184, 299, 304, 313, 334–4; dissolution of personality in, 68; distinctionless, 316; and God, problem of, 335; or God, 308–9; Hegelian, 313; identity with, 158, 306; *māyā* an element of, 55; nature of, 180; *paramārtha,* 168, 274; self =, 311; Spirit is non-dual, 167; is within us, 52; without attributes, *see nirguṇa*
absolutism/Absolutism (-ist, -istic), 6, 13; Advaita, 274; in Indian spiritual tradition, 10; systems, 51; trend, of Upaniṣads, 7, 51; —, of Vedāntic schools, 52; varieties of, 53
absorption, total, *see samādhi*
Abū Ḥanīfah, 392
ācāras: or laws, Hindu, 251; of Paraśurāma's country, 251
action, 50, 234, 301; Chain of Causation by, 97; cognition, and emotion, 193–4, 200–1, 311–2, 318; desireless/disinterested/*niṣkāma-karma,* 166, 191, 310; *dharma*/ethical/right, *see dharma;* discipline of, 233; is essential nature of *ātman,* 189; freedom of, 302; or *kamma,* 79; *karma, see karma;* Mīmāṁsā theory of, 188, 200; non-egoistic/selfless/*karma-yoga,* 191, 194, 200, 233; originates from ideation, 98; physical manifestation of delusion, 97; pseudo-*bidhicchāyā,* 310; social, political, moral, 312; spiritual, *ādhyātmika,* 301, 303, 313 (*see also* liberation); three standards of moral, 342–3; way of, *see* way of action; world of, 108
action-influence, 95, 96, 99, 104
activism (-ist system), 5, 50, 391; of Mīmāṁsā, 186, 189, 211; neglect of, 207
activity, 48, 79, 217; non-egoistic, 201; (*rajas*), 49; without attachment, 333

actuality(-ies), 67, 73
adaptation, insight of (*anuloma-ñāṇa*), 82
adharma (rest), 45; bad, 345
adhikāra: Indian doctrine of, 33; qualifications, 370; right, to inaction, 309; —, to know and do, 272
ādhyātmika, spiritual actions, 301
Adidevananda, Swami, 213
Adler, Mortimer J., *see* Maritain
administration: ethics of, 281*f;* of justice, 289*f*
adoption, 251
adṛṣṭa, destiny, 226
Advaita Vedānta, school of Śaṁkara/Advaitins, 41, 45, 52–5, 65, 121, 123–4, 128–30, 167, 171–2, 189–91, 197, 204, 206–7, 270, 299, 303*ff*, 329–35, 340, 352–3, 369; modern monks of, 313; non-dualism, 119, 145, 184; pure monism, 119, 273; *see also* Śaṁkara
aesthesis: *rasa,* 204; belongs to *buddhi,* 204
aesthetic(s), 204–6; sensitivity, 239
Afghanistan, 382
aggregate(s): of five aggregates (*skandhas*), 46–7, 71, 212; —, individual is, 198; five (*khandhā*), 71, 81
Agni, god of fire, 218, 220, 325, 326; is deity of speech, 214
Agnihotra sacrifice, 218
Agni-purāṇa, 259
agreement: method of, in presence (*anvaya*)/in absence (*vyatireka*), 125
agriculture(-al), 164, 262, 377, 388; classes, 377; and land reforms, 368
aham: ego, 138; I, 196; same as *ātman,* 46
ahaṁdhī, I-consciousness, 196
ahaṁkāra (ego), *see* ego
ahiṁsā, non-hurt/non-injury/non-violence, *yogī* virtue, 15, 35, 202, 235, 264, 270, 284–6, 293, 295, 332, 339, 343, 391; Gandhi's method of, 225
aim, *see* goal
air, 48, 108, 185; is correlate of touch, 187
Aitareya-brāhmaṇa, 255, 257
Aitareya-upaniṣad, 211
Ājīvakas/Ājīvikas, materialists or naturalists, 324–5
ajlāf, low, 383
ajñāna, see avijjā
ālaya-vijñāna: eighth faculty, 97; ideation-store, 97–9; receptacle-consciousness, 47–8, 184
alchemy, medieval, 210
Alexander the Great, invasions of, 63, 217
Allāh, 150
almsgiving, 154
Altekar, A. S., *The Position of Women in Hindu Society,* 372; *State and Government in Ancient India,* 296–7
Amarakośa, 213–4
analysis: as "dissolution," 70; doctrine of (*vibhajja-vāda*), 70; of "I" or "personality" (*sakkāya*), 71; of man, 25; philosophy of mere, 39; of world is analysis of personality, 47
ānanda/ānandam, see bliss
Ānanda, 349
Anaṅga, first king of Bhāratavarṣa, 257
anarchy, 256
an-ārya(*s*), ignoble, 90
anātma-vāda, Buddhist theory of, 35
an-ātman/anātman, see selflessness

anattā, doctrine of soullessness/ non-substantial/"no-soul," 72, 74–5, 79–80
ancestors, wisdom of, 379
Aṅguttara-nikāya, 85; *for translation, see* Woodward, *Gradual Sayings*
anicca, see impermanence
animal(s): crimes against lower, 292; not capable of distress, 175; propensities, *pravṛtti*, 269; sacrifice of, *see* sacrifice
animatism, 186
animism(-ists), 66, 186
anitya, see impermanence
Annals of the Bhandarkar Oriental Research Institute, 211
annihilation, 109, 110; *nibbāna* is, of lust for life, 84
annihilationists, 67; or materialists, 69 (*see also* materialists); *uccheda-vādino*, 69
annulment of marriage, 347; *see also* divorce
antaḥ-karaṇa: inner sense, 197; —, mind as, or *manas*, 122
antar-ātman, inner self, 288
aṇu, atomic, 197
anusayā, 80
anvaya, method of agreement in presence, 125
anxiety, 322–3; consciousness of death is cause of, 175
aparigraha, non-covetousness, *yogī* virtue, 391
Āpastamba, 262, 265, 373; *Dharma-sūtra*, 254; —, ed. R. Halasvanatha Sastry, 266
Āpastamba-smṛti, 363–4
apavarga, freedom, 158
appearance, *saṁvṛti*, 274
apūrva: dharma is, 211; doctrine, 50; extraordinary, 188; unseen/ imperceptible/latent force, 50, 199; will, 193
argument, 132, 134; five-membered, *see pañcāvayava-nyāya;* Four Bases of, 113; indirect hypothetical, *see tarka;* methods/categories of, 89
arhat/arhant, see saint
Arian controversy, 263
Aristotle, 210; social philosophies of, 377; *Politics*, 392
Arjuna, 170, 191, 192, 224, 275, 277, 283–6, 343–4, 346, 354; golden mean of, 294; wielder of bow, 225
art(s), 100, 239, 380, 386; fine, are spiritual disciplines in India, 206
artha, see wealth
artha-śāstra, economics and politics, 308
Artha-śāstra(s), 6, 12, 14, 267, 278, 281; *see also under individual authors*, e.g., Kauṭilya
ārya(s)/Arya, 262; Eightfold Path of noble, 116; noble, 90; *-pudgala*, noble person, 90
Āryadeva, 380
Ārya Dharma, 183; Aryan religion or way, 192
Ārya Samāj, *viii*, 183, 211, 229, 348; *see also* Dayananda
Aryan(s), 161, 257, 262; assimilation of backward tribes/non-Aryans by, 224; community/society, 254, 256; early, of India, 42, 186; practice of right-minded, 251; social and spiritual standards of, 238; Vedic, 287; *see also* Indo-Aryans; non-Aryans
Aryan *Dharma, see Arya Dharma*
āsana, posture, 142
Asaṅga, *Mahāyana-sūtrālaṅkāra*, 213
Asaṅga-Vasubandhu, 89
asat/a-sat/non-being, 42; -kārya-vāda, theory of non-existent ef-

fect, 49; no being without, 47; *see also non-ens*

ascetic(s)/forest-dweller/*vāna-prastha,* third stage in life, 164–5, 264; discipline, 241; —, shrinks ego, 242; renunciation of, 226; stage of seclusion and withdrawal, 375; *see also* stages in life

asceticism, 7, 277

ashrāf, high, 383

Asia(n): Southeast, 185; tradition, *vi*

Aśoka the Great, Emperor, 264, 277, 285–6, 294, 348, 365; law of piety, 365; (Rock) Edicts of, 264, 289, 296, 297, 348, 358, 373; D. C. Sircar, ed., *Inscriptions of Aśoka,* 296

āśramas, see stages of life

āśrama-dharma, see stages in life

assemblies, 262

asteya, honesty/non-stealing, *yogī* virtue, 270, 391

astronomy, 230–1

asukha, painful, world is, 175

asuras, see demons

Aśvapati, King, 223

Aśvatthāma, 363

Atharva-veda, 231, 244–5, 263; charms and sorceries of, 88

atheism/-ists/-istic, 67, 102, 137, 182

Athens, 361

ātman/Ātman: action is essential nature of, 189; "All this is from," 41; atomic (*aṇu*), 197; attribute-consciousness of, 197; *Brahman* as, 74, 89, 168, 272; or consciousness, 138, 150; —, and existence, 196; is denied, 112; ego (*aham*), 46, 196; is existential consciousness, 198, 204; immortality of, 86, 89; Mīmāṁsā conception of, 188; pure, is only existence, 196; or *puruṣa,* mind as knower, 122; -realization, 195, 197, 210; realization of pure state of, 45; salvation is return to original unconscious state of, 48; self/person, 35, 42; —, belief in, 184; soul, *viii,* 28, 74, 168, 199, 324, 326; —, is unconscious, 48; spirit, *jīva* associated with, 374; Supreme, 187; — Spirit, 197; is ultimate reality, 43; universal Self, 88; *see also attā*

ātmavat, 270

atoms, 108

atomic: *aṇu,* 197; age, 323; *ātman,* 197; individuals, 389; theory, 48

atomistic: individualism, 359; view of man, 25

attā, synonymous with ego, self, 75; *see also ātman*

attachment, 303; *rāga,* 301; and repulsion, clutches of, 311; *see also* detachment; non-attachment

attribute-consciousness (*dharma-bhūta-jñāna*), 197–8

Audry, R. Ashley, *see* Bergson

Augustine, Saint, 175, 179, 180, 286–7; *Confessions,* 176

Aurobindo, 38, 273, 285

Aurobindo Ghosh, *see* Ghosh, Aurobindo

Aurobindo, Sri, *see* Sri

austerity, 240

authoritarianism, 360

authority, 119, 133; logic, and life, reconciliation of, 181

autonomy of self, 305–6

Avataṁsaka, school of totalism, 103

*avijjā/avidyā/ajñanā/*metaphysical ignorance/blindness/nescience, 32, 76–7, 88, 92, 109, 159, 167, 305, 336; body is, 375; is cause of suffering, 329; lower empirical knowledge, 272; is root of all imperfections, 167; *see also māyā*

āyatana(s), 71, 72; doctrine of fields, 47; six organs of sense, 92, 94; twelve bases of being, 198
āyatanāni, or bases of cognition, 71
āyuḥ, span of life, 302
āyur-veda, medicine, 308

Babur, 382
Babylon, 263
Bādarāyaṇa, 43, 52; systematized Vedānta, 44; Vedāntins, followers of, 46; *Brahma-sūtra,* 52; *see Brahma-sūtra* and *see also* Bādarāyaṇa
Baladeva, 51
Barth, Karl, 177; *The Epistle to the Romans,* trans. Edwyn C. Hoskyns, 176, 182
Barua, B. M., *A History of Pre-Buddhistic Indian Philosophy,* 64
battles, 221
Bauddha, *see* Buddhist
beautiful, doctrine of, 204; *see also* aesthesis; aesthetic pleasure
becoming, 46; of all things, 99; being, a mere process of, 84; —, is stage of dynamic, 104; blooming, 103; is ceasing (*bhaṅgañāṇa*), 82; negation of, 117; negative views of, 102; process of, 82, 96; —, is grasping, 84; theory of, 87; world of, 106, 109
being/Being, 177; and becoming, *see* becoming; *Brahman,* 336; —, freedom of pure, 338; elements of, 73; formation of, *Bhava,* 92, 94; Free, 337; living, has no permanent center, 105; no, without non-being, 47; and non-being (*sad-asad-ātmaka*), man is, 176; —, synthesized, 374; reality of, 86; *sat,* 12, 42, 88, 89, 169; state of, is causal wave, 113; world of, 109; *see also* immediacy
belief(s): -formation(s), 20, 23, 28; Indian religions, 37; philosophical, 23; —, systems of, 36
Belur Math, 229
Bendell/Bendall, Cecil, *see Śikṣā-samuccaya*
Bengal, 388; Vaiṣṇavas(-ism), 312, 318–9
Bereton, Cloudesley, *see* Bergson
Bergson, Henri, 106, 346; *Two Sources of Morality and Religion,* trans. R. Ashley Audry and Cloudesley Bereton, 357
Berolzheimer, Dr. Fritz, 286; *The World's Legal Philosophies,* 297
Bhagavad-gītā, 6, 10, 17, 19, 24, 28, 40, 56, 143, 151, 155, 156, 163, 164, 170, 172, 191, 201, 204, 211, 212, 217, 224–5, 236–7, 241, 244, 246–7, 271–3, 282, 296, 310, 318, 325, 343, 350, 354–5, 362, 371–2, 375, 392–3; ethical values in, 200; philosophy of, 285; Śaṁkara's Commentary, *see* Śaṁkara; *see also* Sri Aurobindo
Bhagavan Das, 55
Bhāgavata-pūraṇa, 163, 247, 268, 294, 362–4, 372
bhakti: devotional movements, 383; love, devotion, 194, 201; way of, *see* way of love; *see also bhakti-yoga*
bhakti-mārga, way of love or devotion, *see* way of love
Bhakti-sūtra, see Nārada
bhakti-yoga, 146; path of religious devotion, 136; unwavering devotion to God, 166–7
Bharata, 205
Bhāratavarṣa, Anaṅga, first king of, 257
Bhāskara, 51, 54

Bhāskarites, 307–8
Bhāṭṭa(s), 121; realists, 130; school of Mīmāṁsā/Mīmāṁsakas, 119, 130
Bhattacharyya, Professor K. C., *Memorial Volume,* 340; "Studies in Philosophy," 296
Bhauma-Brahman, Brahman manifested as earth, 280
bhāva, sentiment, 214
Bhava, formation of being/existence, 92, 94
Bhavabhūti, 206
bheda, fomenting dissension, 282
bhikkhus, monks, 349
bhilinī, lowest class, 363
Bhīṣma, 225, 226, 250, 256, 269, 277, 344–5
bhoga, experiences, 302
Bhoja, 205, 206
bhūdāna, sharing of land, 294
birth(s) 46, 92; and death, 94–5; —, are "corollary of action" (*karma*), 104; distinctions, 359; *Jāti,* 92; rituals of, 223; successive/future/repeated, *see* rebirth; *saṁsāra*
black, 162
blindness, 109; a continuation of death, 93; is crystallization of actions (*karma*), 95; *see also avijjā*
bliss/Bliss/Joy, 52, 87, 158–9; *ānanda(m),* 88, 158, 169, 196, 204; attainment of supreme, 68; *Nirvāṇa* as, 109; *rasa,* 204; *saccidānanda,* absolute existence, consciousness/knowledge and, 169, 231, 233, 242; —, *Brahman* defined as, 87, 169; sheath of, 157; Supreme Being is of nature of, 194; "taste of," 146; of well-being (*sukha*), 83
Bodhāyana, 254, 262; *Dharma-sūtra,* 265
bodhi/Bodhi: (Perfect) Enlightenment, 90, 108, 111, 115, 153, 179; *prajñā* is synonym of, 201; tree, 115; *see also buddhi*
bodhi/Bodhi-sattva(s), 333, 354; ideal of, is Sixfold Perfection, 115; is ideal man, 201; (one whose essence is perfect wisdom), 111, 332, 349
Bodhidharma, 89
body: is eternal enemy of spirit, 69; fettering of soul to, 123; human, 49; —, is temple of God, 230; identification with, 124; and mind, control/discipline of (*sīla*), 83, 240; is nescience (*avidyā*), 375; physical, 57; *pudgala,* 45; and self, fusion of, 329; and spirit synthesized, 374
Boehme, Jakob, 179
Bombay High Court, 390
Bosanquet, B., 193, 212
Bose, N. K., *Selections from Gandhi,* 296–8
Bradley, F. H., 22, 27, 180–1, ethics of, 210
Brahmā, 254, 256, 257; the Great God, 333; union with, 252
brahma-jijñāsā, 175; *Brahma-*knowledge, 339
Brāhma Samāja, *see* Brāhmo Samāj
Brahma-sūtra, 40, 41, 43, 52, 175, 177, 181, 333, 339–40, 355; Commentaries, 18, 54; Śaṁkara's Commentary, see Śaṁkara; Vijñānabhikṣu's Commentary, 53, 65; *see also* Bādarāyaṇa
Brahma-vidyā, knowledge of *Brahman,* 372
brahmacārya: celibacy/abstinence, *yogī* virtue, 375, 391; studentship, *see* studentship
Brahmajāla-sutta of *Dīgha-nikāya,* 68

Brahman, 51–7, 147–50, 167–9, 180, 201, 233, 270, 274, 276, 306, 337; Absolute, *see* Absolute; as *ātman*, 74, 89, 168, 272; Being, 336; is bliss/*saccidānanda*, *see* bliss; is everything (nothing other than), 55, 169; experience/intuition/knowledge of, 157, 167, 222, 234–5; God as distinct from, 312; god personified, 104; "I am," 332; is infinite/eternal, 74, 86, 329; and individual, 52, 207; *mokṣa* as nature of, 328; *Nāda*, Word, 205; *Nirguṇa*, *see Nirguṇa;* non-dual, 147, 167,169, 221, 232; *Saguṇa*, *see Saguṇa; samādhi*, communion with, 243; of Śaṁkara, 184, 336; self identical with, 42, 146–7, 242; soul absorbed into, 52, 149; Sound, 205; Supreme (Spirit), 189, 205; transcendent, 272; is ultimate/highest/supreme/Absolute reality, 42–3, 51, 145–6, 150, 169, 203, 222, 232; (universal self) is denied, 112; Upaniṣadic conception of, 54, 168; world is (is manifestation of), 54–5, 168, 243

brāhmaṇa(s) (priest-teachers/learned men), first/highest class/caste, *viii*, 34, 161–3, 223, 225, 236, 251, 259, 271, 282, 288, 291–4, 347, 362–5, 376–81; leader (*purohita*) of community, 163; new, 237; *paṇḍit*, 384

Brāhmaṇa(s) (ritual texts of Veda), *viii*, 186–7, 221–2, 233, 256, 267, 287

Brahmāṇḍa, Cosmic Egg, 271

Brāhmaṇism, *viii*, 183, 187, 326; contrast with Buddhism, 87; a philosophy of "Thatness," (*Tattva*), 86; is religion of sacrifices, 186

Brahmāstitva-vāda, sole reality of *Brahman*, 232

Brāhmo Samāj/Brāhma Samāja, *viii*, 183, 228–9, 348; *see also* Roy

breath(-ing), regulation/control of, *prāṇāyama*, 140, 142

Bṛhadāraṇyaka-upaniṣad, 18, 40, 42, 43, 56, 64, 150, 154, 157, 169, 171, 190, 196, 212, 222, 239, 245–6, 254, 358; Śaṁkara's Commentary on, 246

Bṛhaspati: priest of gods, 45, 253; works of, 257

British, 291, 382, 388; education, introduction of, 228; historians and archaeologists, 228; invasions, 217; period/rule, 228, 289, 371; schoolmaster, 387

Buddha, 17, 24, 43–4, 46, 67*ff*, 81, 88–90, 108, 110, 115, 150, 153, 175, 180, 185, 192–3, 201, 255, 268, 295, 321, 325, 332, 338, 349, 359–60; critical of caste system, 371; has *Dharma*-body, 108; disciples of, 107; Highest Person, 333; human form of, 334; images of, 206; Lord of mysteries (*guhya-pati*), 179; *nirvāṇa/Nirvāṇa* of, 112; —, is death of, 107; —, his use of term, 158; —, is ideal body of, 108; perfect enlightenment of, 102; radical pluralism of, 74; *Dialogues of the Buddha*, trans. T. W. and C. A. F. Rhys Davids, 85, 358; *Suttas* (Discourses) attributed to, 67; *see also* "Thus-come"

*buddha*hood, *viii;* potential, of every individual, 270

*buddha*nature, *viii*, 103, 108; potential, of enlightenment, 101

buddhi: intellect, 138, 345; intelligence, 49; *Mahat*, Great One,

Reason, 191; *Prajñā* is synonym of, 201; reason, *see* reason; *see also bodhi*
Buddhism (-ist) /Bauddha, 7, 13, 17, 30, 35, 50, 54–5, 67, 70–5, 85*ff*, 95–8, 106, 115, 119–20, 126, 183, 185, 192, 201–2, 214–5, 228, 257, 263, 267, 270, 300, 313, 318, 321, 324, 331, 336–7, 348, 356, 369; is atheistic, 102; contrast with Brāhmanism, 87*ff*; denies existence of soul, 96, 98; dominance of, in India, 314; early, *vi*, 55, 274, 326–7; (four major) schools of, 6, 42, 45, 47, 55 (*see also under individual schools*, e.g., Mahāyāna, Theravāda, Yogācāra); fundamental principles of, 87, 91*ff;* idealistic, 47, 130; individualism in, 364; influence, 347; method of five steps, 125; monastic, 191, 341, 348; nihilistic, 130, 231; origins of, in Veda/Upaniṣads, 44, 184; is pansophism, 115; philosophy, *vi*, 26, 44, 46; realism, 87; rebirth in, *see* rebirth; religion of, 333, 348; rise and spread of, 207; texts, 323; tradition, 334; Vedāntic interpreters of, 158; Zen, *see* Zen; *see also* Gautama
Burke, Edmund, 377
businessman, 342

Caliphs, 392
caloricity (*tejo*), 70
Campion, C. T., *see* Schweitzer, A.
caṇḍālas, lowest in social scale, 363
Caṇḍeśvara, *Rājanīti-ratnākara,* ed. K. P. Jayaswal, 297
Candi, 225
capital punishment, 291
capitalization, use of, *vii–viii,* 86
Caraka-saṁhitā, textbook of medical science, 342, 345, 357
Carlyle, Thomas, 390–1; *Sartor Resartus,* 393
Cārvāka (s), school of materialists, 6–8, 13, 44, 55, 119, 153, 198–9, 300, 314, 318, 322–5; positivists, 154
caste (s) /class, 194, 199–200, 235, 377, 381; barriers, 390; classification/ division of society into four (*varṇa*), 155, 161–3, 237, 271–2, 277–8, 347, 361–2, 367, 369, 376–7, 384 (*see also brāhmaṇas; kṣatriyas; śūdras; vaiśyas*); confluence of, 377; community of one (*saṅgha*), 90; Disabilities Removal Act, 389; distinctions, 359; duties of, 163, 278–9, 347 (*see also* stages in life); evils/drawbacks/restrictions of, 237, 366, 382; forfeiture of, 251; hereditary, 383; hierarchies, 237, 360; inflexibility of, 161; *jāti* (*s*), 365, 376–7 (*see also jāti-dharma*); legal privileges of, 292; low-, 371; lower, 292; lowest (*bhīlinī*), 363 (*see also caṇḍālas*); modern challenge to, 366; *pañcāyats, see pañcāyats;* primarily character, 163; sub-, 347, 376–7; system, 6, 88, 160*ff*, 228, 236, 243, 252, 342, 366; —, Buddha critical of, 371; —, distinct from *varṇa* in medieval period, 365; —, fluid and functional, 164; —, purpose of, 226; *varṇāśrama, see* stages in life
category (-ies), metaphysical, 48, 50, 53, 57, 76, 89
cattle tending, 164
catur-varga, fourfold traditional value, 276
causal wave, *see* wave
causality: law of, 78; theory of,

modern physical science, 95; views of, 52
causation theory/law, 78, 91*ff*, 95, 97–101, 104, 108, 160; *hetu-paccaya,* 78; twelve-linked chain/Twelve stages of (*pratītya-samutpāda*), 46, 91*ff*, 97–8; 115 (*see also under individual links;* wheel of life)
causes, doctrine of plurality of, 160
Central Asian Turks, 382
Cera, kings of Travancore, 263
chain, continuous, of birth, death, and rebirth, *see* rebirth; *saṁsāra*
Chaitanya of Bengal, dualist saint, 228, 234
Chalmers, Lord, trans. *Further Dialogues of the Buddha* (*Majjhima-nikāya*), 85
chance (*yadṛcchā*), 43
Chāndogya Upaniṣad, 64, 131, 153, 163, 171, 223, 230, 245–6, 340, 347, 358, 363, 372; *see also* Jābāla
change, theory of pure, without substratum, 102
character: informs conduct, 159; *guṇa, see guṇa*
charity, 148, 163, 202, 222, 240, 332; organized, 240
chastity, 148, 240; of body and thought, 146
Chatterjee, Satischandra C., *An Introduction to Indian Philosophy* (with Dhirendra Mohan Datta), 18; *The Nyāya Theory of Knowledge,* 134
chemistry, 230
Chi, 89
China, *vi,* 11, 89, 173, 185, 208, 253; Western knowledge of, 10; *see also* Confucianism
Chinese, 199; social emphasis of, 31; thinkers, classical, 195; traditions and cultures, 367; view of liberation, 316
Christ, 150, 208, 226, 295, 327, 339
Christian, 137; Church, 264; congregations, 263; doctrine of Fall and Redemption, 339; era, 7; missionaries, 228, 387; mysticism, 63; theology(-ians), 63, 177
Christianity, 177; ethics of, 228; a universal religion, 185
Circle: time is, 93; waving, 105; wheel of life is, *see* wheel
cit: consciousness, 169; —, *ātman* is, 196; -move, 90; Thinking/Thought/all-knowing/knowledge, 88, 89
city-states, 278
civilization: birth of new, 173; dissolution of, 100; our present, 38
clan, *viś,* 256; *see also vaiśyas*
class(es): industrial, 377; new commercial, 377; *see also* caste
cleaving, *upādāna,* 92, 94
code(s), 199*f:* ethical, 208 (*see also Dharma-śāstras*); of Manu, *see Manu-smṛti*
cognition(s), 41, 212; action confirms, 189; —, and emotion, 193–4, 200–1, 311–2; 318; or "conception" (*viññāṇa*), *see* conception; free from, doubt (*saṁśaya*), 119; —, error (*bhrama*), 119; immediate, of real, 179; of individuality of objects (*saṁkalpa*), 150; in general (*jñāna*), 118; valid (*pramā*), 118–20; *see also* knowledge
cognitive: exercises (*jñāna-sādhara*), 309; faculties (*indriya*) six, 71
coherence, problem of, 41

cohesion, elementary quality of (*āpo*), 70
color, *varṇa, see varṇa*
commentaries, period of, 7
commentators, period of, 7
commercial classes, 377
communes, rural, *see* village-community
communion: desire for, 201; with Divine Spirit, 211; with nature, 165
communism, 249
community: *brāhmaṇa* is leader of, 163; state, *saṅgha*, 278; *see also* village
compassion, 148, 163, 222, 225, 234, 235, 252; *dayā*, 264; have (*dayadhvam*), 157; *karuṇā*, 206
complexes, see *saṅkhārā*
Comte, Auguste, 69
Conant, T. J., 210
concentration, 136*ff*, 240; *dhāraṇā*, 143; discipline/rules/method of, 90, 140, 234; higher, 140; obstacles, 141; *samādhi, see samādhi; see also* meditation
conception, *viññāṇa* (cognition), 80, 92, 93
concord, 264; in council, 220
confidence, man's need for, 194
Confucian(-ism), 59; is determinism, 104; humanism, 63
Confucius, *Shih chi* (Historical Records), 175
confusion, *moha*, 257
Conger, Professor George P., 9, 86; "An Outline of Indian Philosophy," 17
conscience, 345–6, 379; concept of, in Western thought, 345; social, 367
conscientious objector, 344
conscious processes (*vṛttis*), 197
consciousness, 46–50, 71–2, 76, 94, 109, 115, 121, 141, 147–8, 179, 196, 198, 324; or *ātman*, 138, 150, 196; attribute-, *see* attribute; (*cit*), 169, 196; concentrated, *see samādhi;* existential, 198; foundational, 330; I, -*see* I-consciousness; immediate, 123–4; kinetic, *see* kinetic; receptacle-, *see* receptacle; rise of national, 161; unperishing, *ālaya-vijñāna*, 48, 184; *vijñāna*, 47–8, 193
consecration of king, 259
consensus, principle of, *ijmā*, 385
constitution(s)/Constitution, *vii*, 260; Indian, 277, 390
contemplation, 5, 82, 157, 165; meditative (*nididhyāsana*), 168
contemporary: India, 366*f;* —, economic planning of, 368; world, *vi*
continence, disciplines of, 221
contradiction: law(s) of, 133, 308; *vyāghāta*, 125
conversion, 186
coparcenary, 376
coronation, 280
Corpus Inscriptionum Indicarum, 358
correspondence, theory of, 41
cosmic/Cosmic: form, *viśva-rūpa*, 170; ignorance/nescience, *see māyā;* justice, 268; order and harmony, *see Ṛta;* Person (*virāṭ*), 191–2; philosophy, *see* world philosophy; principle, 325; process, *see* world process; Reason, *see* reason; universality, 191
Cosmic Egg, *Brahmāṇḍa*, 271
cosmos, 168
council: *sabhā*, 255; system, 255
Council of Nicaea, 263
country, *rāṣṭra*, 256
court(s): civil, 379; criminal, 379; "house of *dharma*," 289; of jus-

tice, 289–90; king's, of justice, *see* king; *sabhā*, 289
Cowell, E. B., ed. and trans. Udayana, *Kusumāñjali*, 135; *see also* Mādhava Ācārya
craving, 46; has ceased, 84; which produces rebirth, 81; (*taṇhā*), grasping prompted by, 82
creation: account of, 211; "continuous," 79; and dissolution, processes of, 48; is only perception, 121; wheel of, 218; world of, 108; of world, 49
Creator, 222
Culla-vagga, 171
culture(-al), 381; India, 38, 387; lag, 370; penetration of Indian, into south, 224; revival of, 228; spiritual, of race, 163; synthesis of, 59
cycle(s): of changing manifestations, 105; of life/repeated births, *see* rebirth; *saṁsāra; see also* round

Daedalus, 182
Dahlke, Paul, *Buddhism*, 85
Dakṣa, 363; *Dakṣa-śāstra*, 373
dama, self-control, 269
damnation, doctrine of eternal, 303
dāmyata, "cultivate self-control," 157
dāna, placating by giving, 282
dance, 205, 380
daṇḍa: law, doctrine of, 253, 275; punishment, 275, 282, 379; scepter, 275
daṇḍadhara, wielder of power to punish, king is, 254, 379
daṇḍa-nīti, science of government, 308
The Dangerous Sea, 249
Dark Age(s), 250; in India, 227, 360
darśana (integral vision), 26
darśana-mārga, way-of-life-view, 110
Darśanas, 12
Dasgupta, Professor Surendranath N., *A History of Indian Philosophy*, 17–8; *Religion and Rational Outlook*, 351–2, 358
Dasyus, 161
datta, "be generous," 157
Datta, Dhirendra Mohan: *An Introduction to Indian Philosophy*, (with Satischandra Chatterjee), 18; "The Moral Conception of Nature in Indian Philosophy," 295; *The Six Ways of Knowing*, 134–5
Davids, Mrs. Rhys, *see* Woodward, *Kindred Sayings*
Davids, T. W. Rhys, trans. *Dialogues of the Buddha*, 85, 358; and W. Stede, *Pali-English Dictionary*, 85
Davies, J. L., 361; *A Short History of Women*, 372
dayā, compassion, 264
dayadhvam, "have compassion," 157
Dayal, Dr. Har, 335; *The Bodhisattva Doctrine in Buddhist Sanskrit Literature*, 340
Dayananda, Swami, founded Ārya Samāj, 229
death, 46, 79, 149, 175, 233, 321; birth and, *see* birth; Blindness a continuation of, 93, 95; of Buddha called *nirvāṇa*, 107; doctrine of freedom from pain and, 31; *Jarāmaraṇa*, 92; life and, *see* life; rebirth and, *see* rebirth; unreality, darkness and, is world of *māyā*, 169
debts, *ṛṇas*, 219
defilement, 73
deists, 306
deities, *see* gods

Delhi, 228
deliverance, *nibbāna* as, 84
delusion, 328; Action the physical manifestation of, 97; is illness of the mind, 97; originates from mind-action/ideation, 98; *see also* mind, disorder of
democracy, 207, 229, 286, 294; Western, 286
Democritus, 211
demons: *asuras,* 222; fiendish, 181; logic of two destructive (*sun-dopa-sunda*), 253
dependence: mutual, 133; self-, 133
Descartes, René, "continuous creation," 79
desire(s)/craving, 154, 217–8; action without, 166; for individual happiness and social welfare, 239; *kāma,* 150, 257, 259; selfish, 200, 269; of Supreme Spirit is *dharma,* 192; *taṇhā,* 82, 92, 94; three basic, 233; work, enjoyment and, round of, 166
desirelessness, *ataraxia,* 191
despotism, Eastern, 207
destiny, *adṛṣṭa,* 226
destruction, theory of world's/world-systems' periodic, 89, 90
detachment, *vairāgya,* 300–1, 303; *see also* non-attachment
determinism, 80; Confucianism is, 104; in Western schools of thought, 104; *niyati-vāda,* 324
deva(s)/*Deva,* 95, 98, 102, 257; higher grade of living beings, 102
Devala, 363, 373
devotion, *bhakti, see bhakti*
Dewey, J., 58
dhamma(-ā), see dharma
Dhammapada, Book of Religious Verse, 84–5, 105, 192, 212, 297, 348, 358; —, ed. and trans. S. Radhakrishnan, 296
dhāraṇā, concentration, 143
Dharma, Aryan, *see Arya Dharma*
dharma/dhamma (-*ā*), 72–8, 187–93, 199–200, 211, 223, 235–41, 251–4, 259–60, 274, 276, 283, 287–8, 335, 345, 363, 378–80, 383–4; branches of (*jāti-, rāja-,* etc.) 380; duty, *see* duty; element(s) of existence, 72–3, 76, 114; ethical/right action/morality, 50, 108, 153–6, 187–94, 252, 268, 276, 325, 334, 368; four sources of, 344; law, 47, 51, 184, 235, 254, 281; —, of state/social, 239, 286*f*, 375, 379 (*see also* stages in life, law of); as man's differentia, 269; is man's inner nature/being, 156, 193; is religion, 184; socio-moral actions, 301; *Thémis* derived from, 287; two ways of life: action/movement and contemplation/renunciation, 5, 45, 217; ultimate sanction, 263; virtues, 132, 204; *-viruddha,* conflict with morality, 276
Dharma-body, Buddha has, 108
Dharma-dhātu, principle- or law-element, 99–100, 103–4, 108–9
Dharma-kāya, ideal body, 103–4
Dharma-nature, 103
Dharma-śāstra(*s*), treatises on *dharma*/ethics/law, 5, 12, 14, 56, 156, 179, 199, 253, 272, 278–9, 282, 289, 342, 366, 371, 379, 385, 389; of Manu, *see* Manu; and sharī'at, 385–6; *see also* Kane; Smṛtis; Sūtras; *and individual authors*
Dharma-sūtra: Āpastamba, 254; Bodhāyana, 265
dharma-vijaya, moral conquest, 285

Dharmakīrti, 119; *Nyāya-bindu,* with Commentary of Dharmottarācharya, 134
dharmatā, 337; noumenal reality, 330
dhātu (element), eighteen, 72, 75; *see also Dharma-dhātu*
dhṛ (root), 156
Dhruva, A. B., "Presidential Address," 17
dhyāna, see jhāna
diabolisms, 181
dialectic(s) (-al), 27; ladder, 110; methods of, 110, 114; —, of school of Negativism, 106
diarchy (*dvairājya*), 278
difference, double method of, 126
differentiation, 316; indetermination in world of, 105
Dīgha-nikāya, 68, 85; Buddhist, 257
Dignāga/Diṅnāga, 89
dignity, 209
Digvijayas, 261
dikpālas, protectors of the corners, 257
Dilīpa, 258
discipline, 164, 167, 179–80, 185, 221, 233–4; of action, 233; ascetic, 241–2; ethical/spiritual/moral, 115, 144, 157, 192, 198, 201, 206, 229, 240–2, 323–4, 326, 329–30, 332, 342; —, in Buddhism and Jainism, 201*f;* —, four kinds of (*yajña*), 218*f;* —, in Vedānta, 200*f;* —, is *yoga,* 233; external, *bahir-aṅga-sādhana,* 313; of four stages in life, 238; internal, *antar-aṅga-sādhana,* 313; *vinaya,* 280; Zen, 179; *see also* self-discipline
discrimination, class, in India, 370, 390
discussion, philosophical, 132–4, 289
dissolution, creation and, processes of, 48
distractions, 146
diversity, unity in, 273
divinity of soul, 229, 243
divorce/dissolution of marriage: Hindu laws of, 289, 347; 1955 Act, 389; *see also* annulment
dogmatists, 66
doubt, 141; removal of, 132; *saṁśaya,* 119, 132; *vicikitsā,* 150
drama, 205
dravya-yajña, sacrifice with substance-oblations, 325; *see also* sacrifice
dream, 132, 204
Droṇa, 344, 363
dualism/-ists/-istic systems, 6, 67, 222, 234, 241; evolutionary/-al, 7, 89; philosophical, of Madhva, *see* Madhva; pluralism, and *śūnya* synthesized, 54; of *prakṛti* and *puruṣa,* 53; of Sāṁkhya, 43, 53, 74; of Yoga, 43
duality, 232
Dubois, Abbé, 364; *Hindu Manners, Customs and Ceremonies,* 373
dukkha/duḥkha: suffering, 70, 81, 88, 322, 339; *-satya,* truth of, 322, 339
dullness, *see tamas*
durātmā, wicked soul, 230
Duryodhana, cousin of Arjuna, 346
Dutch, 382
duty(-ies): of castes/classes and stages of life, *see* caste; stages in life; defined as action according to Vedic injunctions, 186; *dharma,* 187, 277; —, first ideal, 239; and freedom, 241*f;* God is principle of, 51; *'ibādat,* spiritual, 384; *sādhāraṇa-dharmas,* universal, 272; *sāmānya-dharma,* of all people,

364; *sarva-dharma,* for all men, 364; *sva-dharma,* sphere of, 272
dvāpara, bronze age, 241
dveṣa, repulsion, 301

earth, 48, 108, 185; is correlate of smell, 187
East: philosophical and cultural traditions of, *vi;* and West, conflict between, 386; —, philosophical synthesis, 59; —, relative terms, 173; —, understanding, need of, 391
East-West Philosophers' Conferences, *v*
Eastern: Church, 264; despotism, 207; mind, 209; —, engrossed in subjectivity, 208
economists, materialist, 277
ecstasy, 146; of communion, 148
edicts of kings, *śāsanas,* 289
Edicts of Aśoka, *see* Aśoka
education, 238, 272, 380–1; of children, 376; of illiterate, 230; introduction of English/Western, 228, 387–8; spread of, 370
effect/Effect: common, 96; Individual, 96; theory of existent, *sat-kārya-vāda,* 49; theory of non-existent (*asat-kārya-vāda*), 49
ego, 141, 150, 203, 305, 321; *aham,* 138; —, same as *ātman,* 46; *ahaṁkāra,* 49, 191, 196, 202, 304, 306; —, reason transcends, 191; *attā* synonymous with, 75; is cause of vices, 229; empirical, 37, 46, 57; is identical with reason (*buddhi*), 205; and non-ego, diversity of, 231; is part of inner sense (*antaḥ-karaṇa*), 197; reason is beyond, 202; transcendental, 213
ego-involvement, 205; impurity means, 204
egoity, transformed into non-egoity, 37
egotism, 143; individualizing center of (*manas*), 97
Egypt, 263
Egyptians, 252
eighteenth century: national outlook in, 59; revolutions of, 22
Eightfold Path, *see* Noble
element(s): *bhūtāni,* 43; *dhammā,* *see dharma; dhātu,* eighteen, 72; five, 108; —, of matter, 150; —, subtle (*tan-mātras*), 49; flow of evanescent, 78; four, 44; gross, 49; *guṇas,* 138; mental and physical in *santāna,* 75
emancipation: gateway to (*vimokkha-mukha*), 83; *mokṣa, see mokṣa;* or *mukti, see mukti;* spiritual, *see mokṣa;* of women, 228
embodied person, 219
Emerson, Ralph Waldo, 160
emissaries, ethical, 285
emotion(s): cognition, action and, 193–4, 200–1, 311–2, 318; method of sublimating, 166; way of, *see* way of love
empire, *sāmrājya,* 278
empirical: self/nature of man, 355, 357; usage, *see vyavahāra;* values, 5, 15; *see also* morality; pleasure; material welfare
empiricism, 6, 63
energism(-ists), 66, 76
energy: concept of, in *Vedānta, see śakti;* latent, 105; world of, 108
enjoyment, *kāma, see kāma*
enlightened person, 242–3
enlightenment: basis of, 99; Buddha/Gautama attained, 98, 102, 333; in continuation beyond life (*videha-mukti*), 353; "ignorant will identical with," 106; *mokṣa, see mokṣa;* about

nature of self, 342; perfect (*Bodhi*), 90, 108, 111, 115, 153, 179; potential of, 101; spiritual, 224, 355; in this life (*jīvan-mukti*), 305, 353
ens, 112, 113; realistic (*sat*) is common-sense faith, 112; school, Ideal of is realism, 114
entertainment, 381
epic/Epic(s), 231, 371; literature, 364; period, 5, 295, 364
Epicureans(-ism), 45, 69
epistemological: approach of modern Western philosophy, 52; papers, *vi;* theories, 118*ff*
epistemology, 14, 174, 280, 290; integral quality of Indian, 26; integralist, 29, 30; lack of integralist, 24
equality: of men, 385; of opportunity, 367, 390; among races, 361; of rights and duties, 272; of sexes, 370; social, 360, 392; of women, 361
equanimity, emotional, is aesthetic pleasure, 205
error: is appearance of unreal as real, 130; theories of, 130
Essays in East-West Philosophy, v
eternal, spiritual principle, 69
eternalism(-ists) 66, 69; *śāśvata-vāda*, 326; *sassata-vādino*, 68
eternity: of *prakṛti*, 89; of voice, theory of, 88, 89
ether, 48, 185; is correlate of sound, 187
ethics, 14–5, 61–3, 156, 199, 231; Cārvāka, 199; disciplines of personal, 240; Hindu, 235*f;* Jewish, 199; metaphysics of, 56; Mīmāṁsā, 199; real foundation of, 229; social, 63, 208, 240–1; true, 192; of will, 200
ethical: action, *see* action; *dharma;* codes, *see Dharma-śāstras;* discipline, *see* discipline; laws, 222, 225; philosophy, papers in, *vi;* values in *Bhagavad-gītā*, 200
"ethicism," 6
Euclid, geometrical proof of, 127
evil, 235, 353; and good, 240, 350; ignorance is cause of, 195; problem of, 195, 337
evolution: concept of, 60; prius of, 158; of soul, 243; two stages in men's, 222
exercises, *sādhana*, 309
exertion, 226
existence: absolute, knowledge and bliss, 169, 231, 233, 242; analysis of man's conscious, 193; *Bhava*, 92, 94; Buddha's view of human, 90; conditional, 97; dependent, *see paṭicca-samuppāda;* "depending upon series of causes," 96; phenomenal, in its entirety, *see Saṁsāra;* —, is pain, 339; a process in time, 176; pure *ātman* is only, 195–6; series/waves of, *see* rebirth; single moment of, 77; totality of all, 100; ultimate unreality of material, 238; *see also sat*
existent: effect, theory of, *see* effect; *sat, see sat*
existential: concepts of man's inward being, 214; consciousness, *ātman*, 198; *diaspora*, 198; nature of *Logos*, 213; self-analysis, 193
Existentialism(-ists), 177, 197, 213, 322–3
experience(s): *bhoga*, 302; direct (*pratīti* or *anubhava*), 132; immediate, 167; plenary, 169; rational investigation of nature of, 180; two orders of, 145
experts, "outside," *vii*
extended substance, *see* substance

extension, elementary quality of (*paṭhavi*), 70
external world, relation with human being, 71
extinction: antithesis of falling, 103; *nirvāṇa* is, 115; non-conditioned *Nirvāṇa*, 114

Fa-hsien, 291
fairs, village, 381
faith: existential, 181; man's need for, 194; reasoned, 177; religious, 176; *śraddhā*, 150
fallacies: fifty-four, 89; thirty-three, 89
family(-ies), 164, 256, 369, 376–8, 381; aggregate of several/joint/kula, 256, 367, 376; institution of, 165; life, 238; system, disintegration of, 389; ties of, 382
farmers, 368
Fascists, 249
fasting, 69
fatalism, 226, 324
fate (*niyati*), 43
father: king and, 258; manager (*kartṛ*) of property, 376
fear, 175; *bhī*, 150
fearlessness, *abhaya*, 264
federalism, 261
feeling(s), 46, 198; aggregate of, *see* aggregate; or "receptions" (*vedanā*),.70; *see also* emotions
Feer, L., ed. *Saṁyutta-nikāya*, 338
festivals, 381
feudalism, 261
Fichte, J. G., 61
fideists, 66
fields, doctrine of, *see āyatanas*
fire, 48, 108, 185; blown out, 107; is correlate of sight, 187; god of, *see* Agni; *Logos* identified with, 214
fish, doctrine of, *matsya-nyāya*, 253, 275
five: fields of senses/objects, 47; organs of action, 49; sense-organs, 49; -step method, *see pañcāvayava-nyāya;* subtle elements, 49; *yogī* virtues, *see yogī*
flamelessness, 102
flux, *see santāna*
forbearance, 240; *upekṣā*, 270
force, 66; *see also śakti*
foreign: domination/rule, 216, 228–9, 236; —, liberation from, 286; invaders, 217, 251, 381; policy, Nehru's, 274; relations, 281*f*
forest, 238
forest-dweller, *see* ascetic
forest-hermitages, 165
formalists, 108
formalistic, view of Buddha, 110
foundational, consciousness/self, 330
four: elementary qualities of matter, 70; -fold division of society, *see* castes; groups of mental elements, 70; human ends, *see puruṣārthas;* ideals or values, 239; positive categories, 50; stages in life, *see* stages
Four Noble Truths (*ārya-satyas*), 46, 116
free: action (*kiriyā-vādī*), 80; will, *see* will
freedom(s), 209, 321, 323–4, 338; of action, 302; is detachment from Nature, 315; duty and, 241; from care, 83; in human nature, 160; *ikhtiyār*, 385; immanent, 325; Indian philosophical theories of, 36; lies in being without will, 80; "of one or of all," 332; perfect, *Nirvāṇa, see nirvāṇa;* spiritual, see *mokṣa;* state of, 328; temporal, 386; true spiritual basis of individual,

229; of West, 391; of will, *see* will
French, 382; Revolution, 228, 249
friendliness, *maitrī*, 270
Friends, Society of, 285
friendship, with good (*kalyāṇamittatā*), 81
Fuller, Professor B. A. G., 11; *A History of Philosophy*, 17

gaṇa, people's state, 278
Gāndhārī, queen mother of Duryodhana, 346
Gandhi, Mahatma, 38, 39, 161, 203, 225, 237, 272–4, 277, 285–6, 294–5, 349, 360, 391; ideal of, 392; his method of *Satyāgraha*, non-violent non-co-operation, 281; *An Autobiography*, 296; *Bhūdāna-Yajña*, 296; *Young India*, 172, 296; *see also* Bose, N. K.
gārhastha, *see* householder
Gauḍapāda, 171; non-dualist, 222
Gautama, Prince of Kapilavastu, the Buddha, 43, 126, 127, 131*ff*, 153, 163, 285, 333; followers of, 131; systematized Nyāya, 44, 119; *Nyāya-sūtra*, trans. S. C. Vidyābhūṣaṇa, Sacred Books of the Hindus, 64, 131, 132, 135, 290, (*see also* Vātsyāyana, commentator)
"Gāyatrī-mantra," 344
generality, 50
generation-move, 90
Genesis, Book of, 182
Genghis Khan, 382
German idealists(-ism), 61, 63
Ghosh, Aurobindo, 39, 55, 360
Ghoshal, U. N., *Agrarian System in Ancient India*, 296; *History of Hindu Public Life*, 296
Gītā, *see Bhagavad-gītā*
goal/end/aim of man, 160; final/highest/ultimate/supreme, 44–5, 166, 324, 332, 342, 350, 387; —, is liberation (*mokṣa*), 235, 242 (*see also mokṣa*); —, is realization of *ātman*, 197; —, Śaivist and Vaiṣṇavist conception of, 324; —, Sāṁkhya conception of, 158; —, is self-realization, 381; —, is ultimate truth, 351; *puruṣārtha*, *see puruṣārtha;* social, 372; spiritual, 12, 371–2; of — evolution is transcendence of *guṇas*, 162; is — perfection and freedom, 166
God, 48–53, 66, 88, 140–7, 176–7, 182, 188, 190, 199–207, 229–30, 241, 270–1, 306–12, 322, 324, 327; or Absolute, 308–9, 335; becomes man, 151; -consciousness, 326; happiness is participation in, 158; with infinite attributes, *see Saguṇa;* of Israel, 185; Īśvara, oneness with, 147, 184, 333–4; love for/of, 143–4, 167, 201, 234, 353; as only reality, 229; —, denied, 77; personal, 140, 143, 145–6, 232, 322; -realization, 136, 166, 193, 205, 234, 285, 332; *śakti*, power/potentiality of, 48, 52, 53; and soul/selves, 147, 167, 269, 307; Śruti, 379; transcendent (*sadaiva Īśvaraḥ*), 144, 326, 337; and universe, oneness with, 147, 222; worship of, *karma-sādhana*, 142, 310
god(s) deities, 187, 219, 221; *devas, see deva;* of fire and speech, *see* Agni; jealous custodians of social welfare, 218; mental projections/creations, 181, 186, 188; *Ṛta* is above, 286; of village, *grāma-devatā*, 381;

see also under names of individual gods
Golden Mean, 114, 271, 272, 277, 282, 284; doctrine of, 68; of Manu and Arjuna, 294
good: evil and, 240, 350; highest, *śreyas,* 154, 342, 345; men (*sadācāra*), 254; twofold idea of, 342
goodness, *dharma, see dharma*
gopīs, cowherd girls, 363
Gorgias, 68
Gośāla, M., *see* Maskarin Gośāla
Gough, A. E., *see* Mādhava Ācārya
government, executive branch of, 379
grace, 335; descent of, *śakti-pāta,* 324; doctrine of, 201
grāma, see village
grammar, 230–1
Grammarians/philosophy of Grammar, 300, 304, 318
grasping, 46, 81–4; gives life its nutrition (*āhāra*), 82; personality/individuality a process of, 75, 77; (*upādāna*), 71
Great Epic, *see Mahābhārata*
Great Recluse, doctrine of, 70
Great Vows, 332
Greece, 56, 174, 263, 285; *Polis* of, 378; *see also* Greeks; Parmenidean school; Plato
greed, *lobha,* 257
Greek(s), 161, 199, 203, 213, 286–7; Bactrian, 162; philosophy, 211, 214; writers, 255
gṛhastha, householder, *see* householder
Grimm, J. and W., *The Doctrine of the Buddha,* 338
guide, inner, *antar-yāmin,* 151
guild, 381
guṇa(*s*): ability, 362; character, 162; elements, 138; goal of spiritual evolution is transcendence of, 162; *-karma,* 278; quality, 272; three fundamental types/constituents/attributes of nature, 49, 162, 355
Guptas, 363
guru, 377; spiritual preceptor and guide, 324

Haas, Dr. W. S., 208; *The Destiny of Mind: East and West,* 215
Hamlet, 182
happiness: domestic, 155; everlasting, *mokṣa,* 154–5 (*see also mokṣa*); infinite, 166; and unhappiness, total of, remains constant, 240
Harivarman, Nihilistic school of, 112
harmony, *samatā,* 205
Hartmann, E. von, "Essences" of, 32
health, 220
hearing, *śravaṇa,* 181
heaven: and hell, theory of, 350; life in, 200
Hebrews, 252
hedonism, 277
Hegel, Georg W. F./Hegelian(s), 56, 210, 336–7; Absolute, 32, 313; absolute idealism of, 68; "Civil Society" of, 377; metaphysics of, 22; objective mind of, 381; social philosophies of, 377; state, 380; synthesis, 336; *Lectures on the Philosophy of History,* trans. J. Sibree, 174, 182
Heidegger, M., 175
henotheism, 186
Heraclitus, 203, 214
Herbart, J. F., psychological determinism of, 79
heredity, 377
hermitages, 165
hierarchy: ideas of, 365; social, 377
Himalayas, 161

Hīnayāna (Theravāda):
Buddhism, 349; ideal of *arhat* (Buddhist perfected man), 323; schools, 47
Hindu(s)/-ism, *passim*, 6, 13, 35, 109, 216, 347; ethics, 235*f;* marriage, 347; philosophy, orthodox schools of, 5, 44; philosophy (-ers), theory of, 26, 30, 136, 150; polity, 382; psychologists, 150; scheme of life, 218; scriptures/texts, 223, 225, 323; Six Systems of, 7, 13, 88; social structure, 369; society/state, 161, 228, 240, 381; —, four classes in, *see* caste; spiritual truths, 217; tradition, *vi*
Hiriyanna, Professor Mysore, 4, 8; *Outlines of Indian Philosophy*, 17
historicism, 210
Hobbes, Thomas, 69, 181; *Leviathan*, 182, 253
Hocking, W. E., 185, 209
Holy Roman Empire, 250
home, 220
Hooker, R., *Ecclesiastical Polity*, 253
Hoskyns, Edwyn C., *see* Barth, K.
hospitality, 220
householder(s), *gārhastha/gṛhastha* (second stage in life), 164–6, 220, 222–3, 234, 236, 238–9, 251, 264, 271, 347, 368, 375; duties of, 225, 227; *see also* marriage; stages in life
Hsüan-tsang, 89, 283
Hui-k'o, 89
Hull, R. F. C., *see* Misch, G.
human nature, *see* nature
humanism: Confucian, 63; Islamic, 63; Sino-European kingship in, 63
humility, 148
Huns, 162
hunters, 363
Husserl, E., 32
Huxley, T. H., 64
hymns: Ṛg-vedic, 325; Vedic (*mantras*), 219, 222, 251, 334, 344, 365
hyphenation, *vii*

"I," 71, 73, 324, 329, 356; *aham*, 196; identified with action, 74; misconceived, 84
I-consciousness, 138, 241; *ahaṁdhī*, 196
I-feeling, 303, 310
'ibādat, spiritual duties, 384
Ibn Hanbal, 392
idea(s), 198; or "perceptions" (*saññā*), 70
ideal(s): -body, 110; four, 239, (*see also dharma; artha; kāma; mokṣa*); Indian, 224; —, are renunciation and service, 230; spiritual, 44
idealism, 6, 15, 63, 114; absolute, of Hegel, 68; in Buddhist philosophy, 46–7; of Mahāyāna schools, 47; metaphysical, of Śaṁkara, 121; objective, 68–9; pluralistic, 47; practical, 8; and realism, distinctions between, 53; —, synthesis of, 15, 231, 243; speculations of, 69; subjective, 68, 231; —, of Yogācāra Buddhists, 121; of Vijñaptimātra school, 102
idealists, 51, 66, 108; German, 61, 63
ideation: all things have their origin in, 101; chain of causation by, 98–9; theory, Buddhist, 97; world of, 108
ideation-store, *see ālaya-vijñāna*
identification: reciprocal/mutual, 106; wrong, 328–9
identity: of essence (*tādātmya*), 126; -in-difference, 307–8;

mysticism of, 88; or non-difference, doctrine of, 168; is ultimate truth, 273; with all beings, 330; with the Lord (*Īśvara-bhāvāpatti*), 333; with Supreme Spirit (*Brahman*), 189
ignorance, 46, 272, 327–8, 338; destroyed by insight, 82; doctrine of original, 195; human suffering rooted in, 118; life begotten of, 82; metaphysical (*avidyā/ajñāna*), *see avijjā*; —, (*māyā*), *see māyā*; removal of, 324; is root of all imperfections/evil, 167, 195; world of, 111
ignorant will "identical with perfect enlightenment," 106
illiteracy of India, 216
illiterate, 230, 371
illumined: person(s), 148–51; soul, 149; teacher, 147
illusion of name and form, 148
illusionism, 232
Imām(s), religious leaders, 383
immeasurable meditations, four, 89
immeasurability, meditative doctrine of (*apramāṇa*), 90
immediacy, 28; as basic character of Absolute Consciousness, 123; (being), and mediacy (concepts), correlation of, 60; of knowledge, 26, 28; spiritual, 57
immortality, 234; of *ātman*, 86, 89; concept of, 350; *mokṣa*, 242; of soul, 149, 243; spiritual, 354
Imperium of Rome, 378
impermanence/transiency/*anitya/anicca*, 79, 82, 102; Buddha proposed, 88; theory of, 103; world is, 175
imprisonment, 291
Impurity means ego-involvement, 204
inaction, Advaita doctrine of, 309*f*
inactivism, *akriyā-vāda*, 326; *see also* non-activism
inactivity, *see tamas*
Inada, Professor Kenneth K., *ix*
incarnation(s), 268; theories, 110
inclusion, possible (*saṁbhava*), 119
indetermination: principle of, 104; —, of matter and mind, 106; in world of differentiation, 105
indeterminism (*śūnya-vāda*), 121
Indian: languages, 4; mind, cultural tradition of, 38; —, intellectual curiosity of, 5; philosophy(-ies), *see* philosophy; political and economic backwardness, 32; thought, 4*ff*, —, status of individual in, *vi*; tradition, religious aspects of, 4; *see also* Hindus
individual(s), 269*f*, 374*ff*; is "body-mind-I" complex, 329; and *Brahman*, difference between, 52; Buddhist term for, is *santāna* (stream), 75; empirical, 334; freed from finitude, 167; in Indian metaphysics, 299*ff*; *jīva*, *see jīva*; *jīvātma*, 374; liberty of, 378; perfection (*saṁsiddhi*), 375; plurality of, 303*ff*; self is essence of, 304–5; selves, relation between God and, 307; and society/state, relation between, 270, 347*f*, 380*f*; (ultimate) status of, *vi*, 304
individualism, 360, 368; atomistic, 359; in Buddhism, 364; dynamic, 367; spiritual, 270
individuality: not mere plurality, 331; a process of grasping, 75, 77
Indo-Aryan(s), 223; philosophers, 150; spiritual culture of, 237; of Vedic times, 221; *see also* Aryans
Indra, 221, 325–6, 380; god of clouds and thunderbolt, 185; the rewarder, 257

induction, 123
industrial classes, 377
industrialism, 368
inference, 28–9, 119, 133; *anumāna,* 125*f;* demonstrative form of, 126; psychological process of, 126; theory of, 131
infinite: presence of, 176; "sense for," 13
inherence, 48, 76; (*samavāya*), 50, 308
initiation, *upanayana,* 361
injunction, *vidhi,* 193
inner: nature of man, 38; self, transformation of, 15, 38
innovation, *ijtihād,* 385
inseparability, *apṛthak-siddhi,* 307
insight: of adaptation (*anuloma-ñāṇa*), 82; fullness of, 115, 117; higher, 115; ignorance destroyed by, 82; intuitive, 179; —, is knowledge that liberates, 167; into nature of things, 328; of non-self, 84; into the real, 331; into reality of the spiritual, 355; religious, 178; supreme (*paññā*), 76, 83
instincts, 198; and propensities, 46
integral(-ist): epistemology, 24–30; and unitary character of knowledge and action, 36; view/outlook, 271–2; vision (*darśana*), 26
integrated individual, 29
integration: of consciousnes, 115; of personality, 331; of values, 59
intellect, 90, 141, 150, 329, 331; (*buddhi*), 138, 345
intellection-move, 90
intelligence, 138; *dhī,* 150; *mahat* or *buddhi,* 49
introspection, 129, 132, 140
introspective, 234; life, 240
intuition, 34; of *Brahman,* 167; of Indian philosophical tradition, 10; validity of, 13; in Western philosophy, 11
intuitionism, 6; dualistic meditative, 89; schools of, 116
intuitive: insight, *see* insight; vision of reality, 181
invalidity, 120
invasion/invaders, *see* foreign
inward: being of man, *see* man; realization, 210, 211
inwardness, 190, 209–10; of categories, 57; man's true, 208; reality of, 207; strength of, 215; Upaniṣadic teaching of, 192–4; of Western man, 215
Iran, 382
irrationalism, 6
Īśa-upaniṣad, 28, 40, 244, 272–3, 294
Islam, 228; humanism of, 63; a universal religion, 185
Islamic: canonical laws, 383; conception that matter is habit of Allah, 65; law, political principles of, 384; religion and culture, 382
isolation, *see kaivalya*
Israel, God of, *see* Jehovah
Īśvara: God, 184, 337; —, oneness with, 333
Īśvarakṛṣṇa, *Sāṁkhya-kārikā,* ed. and trans. Suryanarayana Sastri, 135

Jābāla, Satyakāma, 163, 363, 372
Jagadananda, Swami, ed. Śaṁkara's works, 212
Jagannātha, 205
Jaigīṣavya, *Yoga-sūtra-bhāṣya,* 339
Jaimini, 50, 186, 254; systematized Mīmāṁsā, 44; Mīmāṁsakas, followers of, 46; *Mīmāṁsā-sūtra,* 65, 182; —, commentary by Śabara, 128; —, ed. and trans.

M. L. Sandal, Sacred Books of the Hindus, 135
Jaina(s), 42, 121, 123, 263, 267, 270, 274, 327; followers of Mahāvīra, 44, 325; (naïve) realists, 6, 45; records, 255; self-mortification of, 323; theories/teaching of, 26, 45, 74, 285
Jaini, J. L., *see* Umāsvāti
Jainism, 13, 30, 183, 185, 191–2, 198, 214, 300, 313, 318, 321, 324, 329, 334, 337, 348–9; concept of salvation, 55; ethical discipline in, 201; monastic order of religion, 341; originated in atmosphere of Vedic thought, 184; rise and spread of, 207; *see also kevalin*
jana, people, 256
Janaka, King/Emperor, 154, 224, 234, 288
Japan, *vi*, 11, 173 ,185; *samurai* of, 215
Japanese traditions and cultures, 367
jāti(s), 302; castes, 365, 376–7 (*see also* caste)
jāti-dharma, law/rule of caste, 378, 380
jealousy, 143
Jehovah, 150, 185
Jew(s), 137; baiting of, 263
Jewish ethics, 199
jhāna/dhyāna: (method of) meditation, 116, 143; trances/musings, 83
jijñāsā, desire to know, 132
jīva(s), 198, 324; associated with *ātman* (spirit), 374; one individual, 51–2, 318; as individual, and Nature, 51; infinity of self, 123; living beings, 268; is psycho-ethical individual, 212; soul, 202, 212, 322, 329; "that which breathes," 374
jīvan-mukta(s), 306, 312; Advaita conception of, 313; person endowed with knowledge of *Brahman*, 148
jīvan-mukti, liberation/enlightenment in one's lifetime, 305, 353
jīvātman, individual, 374
jñāna, 312; cognition in general, 118; knowledge, 167, 194; is — for salvation, 203; —, way to liberation, *see* way of knowledge; *see also vidyā*
Jñāna-kāṇḍa, 89
jñāna-mārga, way of knowledge, *see* way of knowledge
jñāna-sādhana, cognitive exercises, 309
jñāna-yoga, path of philosophical discrimination, 136; way of self-knowledge, 166–7
Joy, *see* bliss
Judaism, a particularist religion, 185
judge(s): chief, 280; "men of *dharma*," 289
judicial process, *see vyavahāra*
judiciary: organization of, 379*f;* village, 381
jurists, 392; Muslim, 384; *ulamā*, 384
justice: administration of, 289*f;* called *nyāya* (logic), 290; cosmic, 268; court(s) of, 289–90; dispensation of, 379*f;* economic, 293*f; see also* Varuṇa, god of justice

Kabīr, 228
kaivalya: aloneness, 158; isolation, 141
kāla (time), 43
kali, iron age, 241
Kālī, 150

Kālidāsa, 154, 258, 366, 373, 375, 380; *Raghuvaṁśa,* 171, 258, 392
kalpa: aeon or world-duration, 240; world process sustained by rotation of, 241
kāma: desire, 150, 257, 259; enjoyment of sense pleasures, 239, 276–7, 375; pleasure, 153–5
kāma-śāstra, science of living and enjoyment, 308
Kamalaśīla, pluralistic idealism of, 47
Kāmandaka, 262
kamma(-ā), see *karma*
kāmya, mind, 35
Kaṇāda, 43, 119; systematized Vaiśeṣika, 44, 119; *Vaiśeṣika-sūtra,* Hans Nandalal Sinha, Sacred Books of the Hindus, 64–5
Kane, P. V., *History of Dharma-śāstra,* 295–7, 372–3, 392
Kaniṣka, King, 111
Kant, Immanuel, 35, 44, 157, 205, 213, 325; Categorical Imperative, 315; "holy will" of, 350; Ideas of Reason, 305; moral maxim of, 269; Second Critique, 316; "Transcendental Ego" of, 32; *Critique of Judgment,* 213; *Critique of Practical Reason,* 213, 315; *Critique of Pure Reason,* 213; *Perpetual Peace,* 315; *Religion Within the Limits of Reason,* 315
Kantians, 210
Kapila, 43; systematized Sāṁkhya, 44
Kapilavastu, 98–9; *see also* Gautama
karma/kamma(-ā), viii, 13, 17, 50–1, 74–80, 292, 302, 312; action, 45, 50, 79, 95, 186, 268, 272; —, way of, *see* way of action; birth and death are "corollary of action," 104; blindness is crystallization of, 95; (Indian) doctrine of, 34, 195, 299; kind of work, 162; Law of, 80, 159–60, 226, 233, 300, 302–3, 322, 324, 364–5; lower/egoistic (action), 191; means actions or vocations, 362; means "deed" and "result of deed," 159; Mīmāṁsā a philosophy of, 186; Moral Law, 325–6; potency of, 195; renunciation of, 195; as sacrifice, 50; salvation lies in weeding out, 198, 202; special force of (*patti/prāpti*), 76; theory of, 345, 350, 355; unitary eternal, 188; universal, single, unitary activity, 187; wheel of, 385
Karma-kāṇḍa, action, 89
karma-mārga, way of self-realization through action, *see* way of action
karma-phala, result of free act, 325
karma-sādhana, worship of God, 310
karma-santati, continuity of impulse, 80
karma-yoga: action as spiritual discipline, 241; doctrine of selfless action, 200; path of selfless work, 166; *-śāstra,* 200
karmic matter, 329
kartṛ, manager of property, 376
karuṇā: compassion, 206; kindness, 270
Kashmir, school of Śaivism, 54, 318
Kaṭha-upaniṣad, 18, 40, 154, 157, 160, 171, 212–4, 239, 244–6, 296, 357
Kātyāyana, 289–91
Kauṭilya, 6, 254, 257, 259–62, 277, 279–80, 283, 290, 347; realism of, 294; *Artha-śāstra* (*Treatise on Political Economy*), 131, 218,

224, 226, 245, 267, 274, 295, 297, 365, 373, 379; —, trans. R. Shamasastry, 244, 291, 357; —, ed. Trivandrum, 265
Kaveri River, 382
Kaye, J. William, ed. *Selections from Papers of Lord Metcalfe*, 265
Keith, A. B., *Indian Logic and Atomism*, 64
Kēraḷa-ācāras, 251
kevalin, has attained isolation from material adjuncts in Jainism, 323
khaṇa (*-ā*), point-instants: bare point-instants, 77; law of co-ordination between, 78; reality consists of, 77
khandha (*-ā*), 72, 85; -complex, a living being is, 79; five aggregates or groups, 71; grasping of "aggregates," 81; is *nāma* and *rūpa*, 79
kindness, *karuṇā*, 270
kinetic consciousness (*pravṛtti-vijñāna*), 47
king(s)/monarch, 254, 256–64, 275, 278, 280–4, 286, 289, 293, 342–3, 363; bearer of *daṇḍa*, power to punish, 254, 379; court of justice of, 290, 379; divine origin of, 257, 276, 380; duties of, 225, 380; and father, 258; ideal, 276; knowledge of logic of, 290; makes the age, 250; *rājan/rājās*, 255, 258, 378*f;* is shadow of God, *ẓill-e-allāh*, 385; welfare of, 221
kingship, 380; became hereditary, 257; mainly hereditary, sometimes elective, 262; origin of, 256; philosophy of, 280
Kipling, Rudyard, 391
knower-consciousness, 196
knowledge, 118*ff*, 139–40; categories of, 153; *cit, see cit;* discipline of, 234; great (*mahā-sammata*), 257; immediate/immediacy of, 26, 119, 124; instinctive, intuitive (*pratibhā*), 119; integralist theory of, 26, 28, 36; *jñāna, see jñāna;* leads to *bhakti* (love, devotion), 194; mediate, 27, 119, 167; metaphysical, 176; object of, 121*f;* path/way of, *see* way; philosophical, *see* philosophic; *prajñā, see prajñā;* rational, 25, 27, (*see also* reason); scientific, 19, 20, 23, 27; secular and sacred/lower and higher/*avidyā* and *vidyā*, 165, 203, 272, 375, (*see also avijjā; jñāna*); by/from similarity (*upamāna*), 119, 127–8; source of valid (*pramāṇa*), 118, 290; theological, 20, 23, 27; theory of, 118; three steps of search for, 16; two/three/four/six sources of, 89; unitary theory of, 27, 36; *see also* cognition
krośa (2,250 yards), 262
Kṛṣṇa, 150, 155, 170, 191, 224, 343–4, 354, 360; *līla* (play), 363; lord of *yoga*, 225
kṛta-yuga, golden age, 256
kṣatriya (*s*), warrior-kings/political and military leaders/men of action: second class/caste of society; 161–3; 225, 236, 272, 282–3, 292, 294, 347, 362, 376–8, 381; duty of, 354; is guardian of society, 163; or *rājanya* class, origin of, 256
kula, see family
kula-dharma, family law, 380
Kullūka, 297
Kumārila, 50, 199, 211
Kunti, son of, 345
Kuṣāṇas, 162

labor, division of, 278

laborer(s), 272; *śūdras, see śūdras*
landlordism, 368
language(s), 386; Arabic, 383; Indian, 4; Persian, 383; science of, 214
latitudinarians, 383
law(s): *ācāras, see ācāras; daṇḍa,* doctrine of, 253, 275; *dharma, see dharma;* formal statute, *vii;* inviolable, eternal, 268; natural, sustains Nature, 184; positive, *vyavahāra,* 254; sources of Indian, 287*f*
Law-body, 103
lawbooks, 252
lawgiver(s), 280; Indian, 251; not the king but right usage, 252; *smṛti-kāras,* 262
league of nations, 250
learning, Buddha teaches threefold, 115
legal: rights, 293; theory, 374*ff*
Leibniz, Gottfried Wilhelm, 177, 207; psychological determinism of, 79
levels of man's inward being, 202
liberality, 219
liberation, 151, 219, 224, 285, 306, 309, 310, 313; attainment of (*niḥśreyasa*), 153; Buddhist method of, 50; Chinese view of, 316; cognitive, 316; into cosmic and transcendent consciousness, 179; desire for, 201; final, 243; highest goal or, 222; of individuals souls, 333; *mokṣa, see mokṣa; mukti,* 302, 311; in one's lifetime, *jīvan-mukti,* 305; of self, 68, 238; of spirit, 217; of two phases of, 353; is ultimate goal of life, 235; from wrong perspective, 342
liberty of individual, 378
Licchavi, Mallas, 278
licchavis, lower-classed dynasty, 363
life, 79–84; conceptualized, 59; (and death), ocean of/waves of/ wheel of, *see saṁsāra; saṁsāra-cakra;* is drama between visible and invisible, 176; lust for, 81; —, *nibbāna* is annihilation of, 84; and man, unitary vision of, 37; and matter, relationship between, 60; is product (*vipāka*) of *kamma,* 79; is probity and power, 38; reconciliation of authority, logic and, 181; sheath of, 157; span of, *āyuḥ,* 302; stages in individual's, *see* stages in life
life-culture, 117; *see also* way-of-life-culture
life-flux, 90; see also *saṁsāra*
life-ideal, realization of, 115–7
life-principle, 102; search for, 101
life-view, application of, to practical life, 115
Likhita, 346
linguistics, 214
literature, 239, 386
lobha, greed, 257
Locke, John, 122
logic, 73, 152, 213, 230–1, 289; *ānvīkṣikī,* 280; of manifold truth, 274; reconciliation of authority, life and, 181; of *sundopa-sunda* (two destructive demons), 253; systematization of, 89; terms of, 290; *see also* Nyāya
logical positivism, 39
Logos, 203, 205, 213–4; existential nature of, 213; identified with fire, 214; is rational, ethical, aesthetic, 206; as Reason, 191; World Reason, 191
loka-saṁgraha: common good, 367; welfare of world, 375
longevity, 220
Lotus school, phenomenological, 103

"Lotus Store," 100
love, 241; *bhakti*, 194, 201; is continuity of knowledge without effort, 201; for God, 167; man's need for, 194; *śṛṅgāra*, is highest form of aesthetic pleasure, 206; way of, *bhakti-mārga*, *see* way of love
loyalty, highest, 346
lust, *rāga*, 257

Macaulay, T. B., 390; *Minute on Education*, 393
Macdonell, Sir John, Introduction to Berolzheimer, *The World's Legal Philosophies*, 297
macrocosm, 208
Mādhava Ācārya, *Sarvadarśana-saṁgraha*, trans. E. B. Cowell and A. E. Gough, 64, 213
Madhusūdana Sarasvatī, *Advaita-siddhi*, 314
Madhva(s), 51–3, 306; doctrine of predestination, 339; philosophical dualism of, 52, 314
Mādhyamika(s), 47, 102, 329; indeterminism of, 121; Nāgārjuna's philosophy of "middle view," 113–4; *Śūnya* (Void) of, 184, synonymous with "Highest Truth," 114; system/school, 17, 89
Mādhyamika-kārikā, 64–5; ed. Louis de la Vallée-Poussin, 339
Madras, 388
Magadha, king of, 255
Mahā-nibbāna-suttanta, 255
Mahā-nirvāṇa-tantra, 226–7
Mahā-puruṣa (Great Person), 88
mahā-sammata, great knowledge, 257
Mahā-upaniṣad, 180
Mahā-vagga of *Vinaya-piṭaka*, 33, 339
Mahābhārata, Great Epic, 5, 56, 131, 154, 163–4, 171–2, 217, 224–5, 245–6, 252–3, 255–6, 258–60, 265–7, 269, 272, 275–7, 280, 282–3, 288, 291, 296–7, 342–5, 347, 354, 357, 362–4, 366, 373, 375, 392; ed. P. Tarkaratna, 295–6; *see also Śānti-parva*
Mahadevan, T. M. P., *The Upaniṣads*, 171
Mahānārāyaṇa-upaniṣad, 295
Mahān-Ātmā, 213–4; (Cosmic) Reason, 191, 212
Mahārāja, great king, 380
mahat, 213–4; or *buddhi* (intelligence), 49, 191; Cosmic Reason, 212; "the great," 49; Great, Reason, *Mahān Ātmā*, 191
mahātmā (noble soul), 230
Mahātman (Great Self), 86, 88
Mahāvīra, 43, 185, 192, 295; *see also* Jaina
Mahāyāna, 99, 106, 202, 324, 326, 334; Buddhism, 44, 320, 324, 330, 332, 349; inclined to synthetic identification, 106; literature, 201; schools, 44, 55, 102–3, 107, 274; —, forerunners of, 107; —, idealistic and monistic, 47
Maine, Sir Henry, 297
Maitreyī, 154, 239, 353
maitrī, friendliness, 270
Majjhima-nikāya, 17, 40, 85; *for translation, see* Chalmers, *Further Dialogues of the Buddha*
Majumdar, R. C., ed. *History and Culture of the Indian People*, 392
Makkhali Gosāla, *see* Gosala, Makkhali, 80
Malabar, 264
Malalasekera, Dr. G. P., *vi, ix*

Malcolm, Sir John, 365; *Memoir of Central India,* 373
man: is Being and non-being, 176; —, temporal and spiritual, 382; being of, made in image of God, 178; biological/social/political/individual, 178; conceptualized, 59, 61; conscious being, essential nature of, 196; —, inwardness of, 184; emotional, 194, 234; ideal, 201–2; inner transformation of, 38; —, true nature of, 31, 38; integral whole, 25; inward being of, 202, 210, 214; and life, unitary vision of, 37; master of his destiny, 188; as member of society/social unit, 44, 56, 62–3; as moral agent, 61, 356; nature of, in relation to universe, 43; rational, 33, 35; his reason, part of Cosmic Reason, 203; spiritual, 356; ultimate concern of, *parama-puruṣārtha,* 44, 320–1; vehicle of subjective poles of deities, 187
manana, reflective thinking, 168, 181
manas: or *antaḥ-karaṇa, see antaḥ-karaṇa;* individualizing center of egotism, 97; mind, 47, 49, 122, 150, 193, 202, 204, 269
maṇḍala (circle), 101, 295; circle of states, 261; power zone, 282
Māṇḍūkya-kārikā, 172
manes, 219, 223
manipulation, free, 315
mantra(s), see hymns
Manu, 56, 162, 165, 252–3, 256–8, 268, 271, 275–7, 279, 282–4, 287–90, 292–3, 362, 365, 368, 380, 385; golden mean of, 294; orthodox *smṛti* writer, 366; *Dharma-śāstra, see Manu-smṛti; Karma-yoga-śāstra* (science of the way of action), 200
Manu-saṁhitā, 131, 244, 254, 344, 357
Manu-smṛti, Code of Manu, Dharma-śāstra, 171–2, 217, 224–6, 244–5, 250, 257, 267, 295–7, 364, 372–3
manual laborers, *see śūdras*
Marcel, Gabriel, 197, 212; *Journal Métaphysique,* trans. Bernard Wall, *Metaphysical Journal,* 212
mārgas, three, *see* way of action/knowledge/love
mārgayāmin, wayfarer, 183
Mārhattā, saints, 228
Maritain, Jacques, 391; *Scholasticism and Politics,* ed. Mortimer J. Adler, 393
Mārkaṇḍeya-purāṇa, 258–9
marriage(s), 155, 165, 219, 226, 376; civil, 389; dissolution of, *see* divorce; early, of women, 251, 366; —, abolition of, 288, 389; form of, *sarva-sva-dānam,* 251; Hindu laws of, 289, 347; intercaste, 347, 365, 389*f;* monogamous, 389; new laws of, 389; second (householder) stage in life, 238, 347 (*see also* householder; stages in life); of widows, *see* widows
Maskarin Gośāla, 43
material: happiness, 222; welfare, 5, 15
materialism, 177, 309; Cārvāka, *see* Cārvāka; scientific, 76; undiluted, 184
materialist(s), 67, 69, 267; Ājīvakas, 324; economists, 277
materialistic, self-indulgence, 69
mathematician, world of, 78
mathematics, 230; leads us nearer to God, 191, 214
Matrix of Thus-come, 98–9, 103; "Thusness" is (*Tathāgata-garbha*), 104; *see also* "Thusness"

Matrix of Thus Gone, 99, 103; *see also* "Thusness"
matsya-nyāya, doctrine of fish, 253, 275
matter, 69, 185, 198; concept of, 59, 61; denied reality, 77; eternal pervasive, 74; five elements of, 150, 185; four elementary qualities of, 70; is habit of Allah, 65; and life, relationship between, 60; *rūpa,* 70–1; sheath of, 157; three elements of, *guṇas,* 138; unsubstantiality of, 76
Maurer, Professor Walter H., *ix*
Mauryan Empire, 255, 261, 278
Mauryas, 363
māyā, 53, 147, 336–7; cosmic/metaphysical ignorance/nescience, 145, 242, 312 (*see also avijjā*); an element of Absolute, 55; God's creative power called, 229; or illusion, 67; as incomprehensible power of *Brahman,* 54; is indeterminable, 169; projecting power of, 145; reality and unreality of, 52; is that which is not, 169; theory of, 32–3; universe called, 232; veiling power of, 32, 145
māyā-śakti, 53–4
māyā-vāda, illusionism, 232
Mayne, Sir Henry, *Treatise on Hindu Law and Usage,* 392
McCrindle, J. W., *Ancient India as Described by Megasthenes and Arrian,* 372
Mead, Margaret, 58
Mean: golden, *see* golden; true, 103
mechanism, concept of, 60
mediacy, correlation of, and immediacy (being), 60
mediate, theories of knowledge, 27–8
medical science, 342
medicine, 230; *āyur-veda,* 308
medieval/Medieval: ages, 263; Churchmen in Europe, 249; Europe, *Regnum* of, 378; law literature, 289; Period in India, 365, 368; saints, 360; theorists, 250; times, social order of, 367; undemocratic social practices, 370; *see also* Middle Ages
meditation(s), 136*ff,* 196, 227, 230; Buddhist Yogācāra, 89; eight methods of restraint in, 89; four immeasurable, 89; higher, 115; method of (*dhyāna*), 116, 143; *nididhyāsana,* 181; on one's self, 186, 312; *see also samādhi*
meditative doctrine of immeasurability (*apramāṇa*), 90
Megasthenes, 283, 291, 361
memory, 119; a source of knowledge, 120
mental: elements, four groups of, 70; elements in *santāna,* 75; faculties (*saṅkhārā*), 75; states, 138, 143, 177; —, destroyed, 147
merit, *puṇya,* 345
Merz, J. T., *History of European Thought in the Nineteenth Century,* 64
metallurgy, 230
metaphysic(s)/-al, 14, 22, 41*ff,* 174, 181; activist system of, 50; basis for Indian theory of values, 168; of Buddhist schools, 47; define concepts of Nature, man, reality, 382; of ethics, 56; of Hegel, 22; Indian, 59, 299*ff;* —, value of, 56; Indo-European kinship in, 63; Jaina, 45; knowledge, 176; papers, *vi;* spiritual, 162; transcendental, 6
Metcalfe, Lord, 255–6; *Selections from Papers of Lord Metcalfe,* ed. J. William Kaye, 265

metempsychosis, 159*ff*
methodology, 14
microcosm, 208
middle: class, 387*f;* doctrine, 102; Path, 103, 114, 144
Middle Ages, 250, 371; *see also* medieval
Middle-Path-Ideal of Nāgārjuna, 113
"middle view," *see Mādhyamika*
Middle Way (*majjhimā-paṭipadā*), 68–9
Mill, John Stuart, 69
Milton, John, 382
Mīmāṁsā(-akas), 7, 50, 88, 120, 122, 128–9, 156, 181, 193, 208, 213, 300, 306, 325; atheistic, 327; Bhāṭṭa school of, *see* Bhāṭṭa; concept of *dharma,* 199–200; early, 184, 192, 194, 201; —, denied reality of God, 187; ethics, 199; a philosophy of *karma,* 186; a pluralistic philosophy, 187; Prabhākara school of, *see* Prabhākara; Pūrva/Prior, 50; religion, 187*ff*, 206–7; —, a system of ethical activism, 186; school of (Ritualistic) Realism, 50, 89; systematized by Jaimini, 44, 46, 186; theory of action, 200; uphold religion of *Brāhmaṇism,* 186
Mīmāṁsā-sūtra, see Jaimini
mind, 48, 137–41; body and, *see* body; conceptualized, 59; Eastern, *see* Eastern; eight faculties of, 97; function, not entity, 76; Indian, is individualistic, 164; is inner organ, 150; *kāmya,* 35; as knower (*ātman* or *puruṣa*), 122; liberation from disorder of, 108; *manas, see manas; nāma, see nāma; nāma-rūpa; niṣkāma,* 35; purification of, 190, 201, 240; sheath of, 157; subconscious, *Viññāṇa,* 92–3; unconscious, 60; Western, *see* Western
mind-action, 105
mind-stuff, 159
ministers, 261, 279–80
Misch, Georg, *The Dawn of Philosophy,* trans. R. F. C. Hull, 214
missionary(-ies), Christian, 228, 387
Mitākṣara, 363, 373; commentary on *Yājñavalkya-smṛti,* 251
modernism, 367–8
moha, confusion, 257
mokṣa, 160, 328, 331, 371–2; attainment of, 31, 239; enlightenment, 242; everlasting happiness, 155 (*see also* happiness); immortality, 242; perfection, 153, 242; release, 158–9, 167; salvation, 187; (spiritual) emancipation/freedom/liberation, 6–7, 12, 15–6, 30, 153, 158, 164, 187, 189–90, 270, 275–6, 349, 375, 386; —, goal of, 31; ultimate/supreme goal, 165, 242*f*
Mokṣa-śāstra(s), treatise showing way to liberation, 14, 224
momentary, everything is, 47
monad(s), 207
monarch, *see* king
monastery(-ies), 242
Mongols, 161
Mongolia, 185
monism/-ists/-istic, 6, 13, 51, 66, 184, 186; in Buddhist philosophy, 46; illusionistic, 8; Mahāyāna schools, 47; religion of impersonal *Brahman,* 186; of Śaṁkara school of Advaita Vedānta, 119, 273, 318, 369; scriptural texts, 306; tendencies, social, 369; of Upaniṣads, 7, 51, 74; in Veda(s), 5; Vedāntic (and non-Vedāntic), 41, 48; —, school of idealistic, pantheistic,

89; view of universe, 68; *see also* non-dualism
monks, 235; *bhikkhus,* 349; duties of, 225; genuine, 239; modern, of Advaita school, 313; non-dualistic, 234; of Ramakrishna Mission, 230; *sannyāsin,* in fourth stage in life, *see sannyāsin*
monogamy, 361
monotheism, 186; in Vedas, 5
Montague, W. P., *The Ways of Knowing,* 26, 40
Mookerji, Dr. Radha Kumud, 261–2; *Hindu Civilisation,* 265; *Local Government in Ancient India,* 266
Moore, Charles A., ed. *Essays in East-West Philosophy,* 17; ed. *The Essentials of Buddhist Philosophy, see* Takakusu, J.; ed. *Philosophy—East and West,* 17; ed. *A Source Book in Indian Philosophy, see Source Book;* (—, with Radhakrishnan), 17, 40, 244–5, 295–6
Moore, G. E., 210
moral: actions, *see* action; conduct, importance of, 223; conquest, *dharma-vijaya,* 285; discipline, *see* discipline; law, 165 (*see also karma*); order, 156; principles behind universe, 219; purification, 16; values, 216
morality, 5, 15, 60, 157, 159, 202, 219, 260; conflict with, *dharmā-viruddha,* 276; *dharma, see dharma;* discord between Nature and, 44; is foundation of spiritual life, 142; implies conflict, 350; laws of, 277; social, 80
Morris, Charles, 24; *The Open Self,* 40
mortification, 142
Motive to Live, *see saṅkhārā*
movement, principle of, *see dharma*
Mughals, 382
Muirhead, J. H., 188; *Elements of Ethics,* 211
mukti, 371; cognitive, 312; or emancipation, 17; liberation, 302, 311; *see also* enlightenment; *mokṣa*
Mulla, D. F., *Principles of Hindu Law,* 392–3
Müller, Max, 185
multiplicity, 232; perception of, 146
Mumford, Lewis, 38; *The Transformation of Man,* 40
Muṇḍaka-upaniṣad, 218, 234, 244, 246, 358
Murti, T. R. V., *The Central Philosophy of Buddhism,* 339; "The Two Definitions of Brahman in the Advaita," 340
Musalmans, Indian, 383
music, 205, 239, 380, 386; philosophy of, 205; in temples, 206
Muslim(s), 227–8, 359, 382–5
mystery: science leads to acceptance of, 179; ultimate, 179
mystic, 27; experience, 167; states, *samādhi, see samādhi*
mysticism, 6, 196, 210; Christian, 63; of Hindus, 383; of identity, 88

Naciketas, 160, 218, 239
Nāda-Brahman, Word, 214
Nāga, tribe of south India, 111
Nāgārjuna, 89, 111–4, 328; his philosophy of "middle view"/"Middle-Path-Ideal" (*mādhyamika*), 113
Nāgeśa, 358
Nairuktas, 189
Naiyāyikas, 48, 189
nāma, or mind, mental elements, 70–1
nāma-rūpa: (mind-form), 72;

(mind and matter), 46, 79; (name-form/mind-body), 92–3
Nambudris, 251
Name-form, *see nāma-rūpa*
Nandas, 363
Nārada, 153, 230–1, 253–4, 363–4; *Bhakti-sūtra,* 167
Naradeva, god among men, 258
Nārāyaṇa, Vīṣṇu is, 327
national consciousness, rise/growth of, 161, 386
nationalization of industries, 368
naturalism, 63; *sva-bhāva-vāda,* 325
naturalists, Ājīvakas, 324
"naturalistic fallacy," 210
nature/Nature, 49–52, 160, 178, 300, 323; communion with, 165; -gods/religions/worshippers, 42, 185; includes spirit, mind, and matter, 185; man's true/own, 140–1, 146, 156; mastery over, 139; moral conception of, 268, 287; and morality, discord between, 44; objective, 38; plurality of, 67; *prakṛti,* 49, 271, 355; of Principle, 103; theory of state of, 253; of things (*sva-bhāva*), 43, 272; has three attributes/types/constituents (*guṇas*), 49, 162, 355; world of individuals (*jīvas*), and, 51
Nazi revolution, 249
necessity, concept of, 178
necromancy, 210
negation/Negation, 48; Eightfold, 113–4; three items of, 87
negativism, school of, 102, 106
Nehru, Jawaharlal, 360, 391–3; his foreign policy of *Pañca-śīla,* 274
Neo-Platonism, 180; Oriental influence on, 63
nescience: *ajñāna,* 305; cosmic, *see māyā;* removal of, 32; *see also avijjā;* ignorance
neti, neti (not this, not this), 168, 336
neurosis, attainment of freedom from, 32
New Testament, *see* Romans
Newton, Sir Isaac, 137
nibbāna, see nirvāṇa
nididhyāsana, meditation, 181
nihilism(-istic), 6; Buddhist, *see* Buddhist; is Ideal of *non-ens* school, 114; school of Harivarman, 112; school, Satya-siddhi (completion of truth), 102; *uccheda-vāda,* 325
niḥśreyas-siddhi, attainment of highest, 371
Nikhilananda, Swami, ed. *The Complete Works of Swami Vivekananda,* 245; *Hinduism: Its Meaning for the Liberation of the Spirit,* 246; *The Upanishads,* 246
Nimbārka (-ists), 51, 53, 307–8
nineteenth century, 22
Nineveh, 263
nirguṇa/Nirguṇa: Brahman (Absolute without qualities/attributes), 168, 336; qualityless form of supreme reality, 180
nirodha, Final cessation (of suffering), 73, 81; *see also nibbāna, nirvāṇa*
nirvāṇa/Nirvāṇa/nibbāna, viii, 72–3, 81–7, 107–16, 171, 328, 332–5; of Buddha, 108, 112; is extinction/total negation, 114–5; —, of fire of passions/lust for life, 84, 158; *nirodha, see nirodha;* -of-No-Abode, 91, 109–10; is Perfect Enlightenment (*Bodhi*), 115; is Perfect freedom/emancipation, 86, 91, 102–4, 107*f,* 115–6, 321; is Perfect Quiescence, 110; as permanency/bliss/self/purity, 87, 109; release/deliverance, 84,

158; as salvation, 46, 73; is *Saṁsāra,* 109; state of pure non-disturbance, 196, 198; *Śūnya,* 47, 55; Ultimate as, 326; with/without residue/*upādhi* remnant, 81, 109–10; is world, 55
niṣkāma, mind, 35
niṣkāma-citta, 35
niṣkāma-karma(*s*), disinterested/desireless action, law of, 34–6, 191, 310–11
Nīti-śāstras, science of statecraft, 267; *see also under individual authors, e.g., Śukra-nīti-sāra*
Niyama: control/restraint, 141–2, (*see also yama*); practice of moral virtues, 339
niyati-vāda, determinism, 324
Noble/*ārya* Eightfold Path, 81, 111, 116, 201
nominalists, 67
non-activism, 325; *see also* inactivism
non-Aryan(s), 262; became *śūdras* (laborers), 256
non-attachment, 35–6, 139, 224, 234–5, 239–40; to material objects, 141; progressive, 238; to sense objects, 144, 149; *see also* detachment
non-being, *see asat*
non-cognition, 119, 129*f*
non-covetousness, 391
non-dual, *Brahman, see Brahman*
non-dualism/-ist(s)/-istic, 216, 229, 241; affirmative ethical discipline, 241–2; in India, followers of, 222; monks, 234; traditions of Upaniṣads, 229; Vedānta philosophy, *see* Advaita; *see also* monism
non-duality, 232; of soul, 149, 243
non-ens, 112–4; nihilistic (*a-sat*), is higher-sense truth, 112; school, nihilism is ideal of, 114; *see also asat*
non-existence, 129–30
non-injury/hurt, *see ahiṁsā*
non-resistance, 227; to evil, 225
non-soul (*ajīva*) of four kinds, 45
non-stealing, *asteya,* 270
non-violence, *see ahiṁsā*
Northrop, F. S. C., 26, 56, 391; *The Meeting of East and West,* 26, 40, 296, 393
noumenal reality, *dharmatā,* 330
noumenon, 100, 103; and phenomenon, inseparable, 116; in phenomenon, 107
novelty, 119
number, 50
nutrition (*āhāra*), grasping gives to life, 82
nyāya, logic, 290
Nyāya (School of Logic), 7, 52–3, 121–31, 153, 204, 289, 300, 318; incorporated into Vedāntā, 53; Logical Realism, 89; method, 131; pluralism of, 43, 53, 90; systematized by Gautama, 44, 119; theory, of error, 131; —, of inference, 125; —, of salvation, 55
Nyāya-sūtra, see Gautama
Nyāya-Vaiśeṣika system(s)/school(s), 31, 48–9, 122, 158, 195, 198, 306–8; categories of, 50; and external validity, 120; are pluralistic, 48; realists, 119

object(s): of cognitive faculties (*viṣaya*), 71; *prakṛti, see prakṛti;* of sense, *see* sense-objects; true nature of, 143
objectivity: reason confers, 210; Western mind diffused in, 208
obscurantism, 181
observances, sacred or ritual, 252
observation (*bhūyo-darsána*), 125

Occam's razor, 133
occasionalists, 67
occult knowledge, 139
ocean: cosmic process resembles surface of, 240; of life, *see saṁsāra*
Old Testament, *see* Genesis
Om, symbol of God, 140
omnipotence, 147
omniscience(-t), 147, 149
One: and many, 145; problem of the, 5
oneness, 242; of existence, *see* existence; of God, soul, and universe, 147, 222; of reality, 31
one-pointed(-ness): attention, 147; of mind, 141, 143
Ontic Being, 336
ontology(-ists), 66, 174
opposites, pairs of, 144, 148, 232
optimism, "ultimate," 16
organ(s): of action, five, 49; internal, 187; sense-, *see* sense-organs; transformations of the deities, 187
organicism, social, 270
organism, concept of, 60
Oriental despotism, 381
original: ignorance, doctrine of, 195; sin, doctrine of, 195
origination, doctrine of dependent (*paṭicca-samuppāda*), 78, 80
orphanages, 377
outwardness, 190, 208; transition from, to inwardness, 194
ownership: seven righteous sources of, 293–4; *svatva, svāmitva,* 293

pain: all/everything is, 46–7; and death, doctrine of freedom from, 31; and pleasure rotate like a wheel, 240
painful, *asukha*, world is, 175
painting, 205, 380
Pakistan, 278
Pal, R. B., *The Hindu Philosophy of Law*, 297; *The History of Hindu Law*, 297
Pali/Pāli, *vii, ix;* terms, *viii*, 66
Pan-Islamic society, 385
Pāñcarātra system, 54; Āgamas (sacred works), 54, 57
Pañca-śīla, five rules of mutual good conduct, 274
pañcāvayava-nyāya, five-step method of discovery and proof/five-membered argument, 126, 132
pañcāyat(s), 389; committees of representatives, 379; instrument of village administration, 381
Pandey, K. C., *Indian Aesthetics,* 214
paṇḍit, brāhmaṇa scholar, *see brāhmaṇa*
Pāṇḍu brothers, 345
Panjab village, 388
paññā: (insight), 76; supreme, 83
pansophism, Buddhism is, 115
pantheism, 54, 299–300
pāpa, demerit, 345
paradise, world identified with, 106
parama-dharma, supreme virtue, 270
parama-puruṣārtha, man's ultimate concern, 320–1
paramārtha: Absolute, 168, 274; final end, 170; spiritual truth, 213
paramārthika: absolute reality, 231; ultimate, point of view, 308
Paraśurāma, 251
pariṇāma: transformation of God's *śakti*, 53; —, of *prakṛti*, 49
paripālanam, all-round protection, 259
Parmenidean, school of greater Greece, 68
Parsees, 263
parsimony, law of, 306

Parthians, 162
particular category, 48
particularists, 274
parva, viii
Pascal, Blaise, 176
passion(s), 155; extinction of human, 107–9; *nirvāṇa* is extinction of fire of, see *nirvāṇa*
Pāśupata system, 54, 57
Patañjali, 43, 137–40, 142, 194, 211; founded/systematized Yoga/*rāja-yoga,* 31, 44, 123, 136; *Yoga-sūtra,* 246; —, ed. and trans. Ram Prasad, Sacred Books of the Hindus, 134; —, trans. J. H. Woods, *The Yoga System of Patañjali,* 65
Path(s): Eightfold, *see* Eightfold; three, *see* way
paṭicca-samuppāda, doctrine of dependent origination/existence, 78, 80
Patriarch of Antioch, 264
patti/prāpti, special force of *kamma,* 76
Paul, Saint, 327
pax, 287
peace/Peace: *sāman,* 282; *Śānti-parva,* 225 (*see also Śānti-parva*); sentiment of, *śānti,* 206
Pearce, D. F., ed. *The Nature of Metaphysics,* 40
peasant(s), 259, 388
people, *jana,* 256
perception, 28–9, 119; (*pratyakṣa*), 122*f;* requires relation of sense to objects, 130; two organs of, 150; validity of, 44; *Vedanā,* 92, 94
perfection(s), 151, 166, 224, 241; of knowledge and wisdom, 111; *mokṣa, see mokṣa;* paths to, 166; of personality, 116; *saṁsiddhi,* of individual, 375; six/sixfold, 111, 115; of soul, 29; unattainable, without inner peace, 218
Persia(-ns), 161, 174, 263
person, *see puruṣa*
personality, 46–7; dissolution of, in Absolute, 68; essential nature of, 67; free, egoless, 333, 338; "I" or (*sakkāya*), analysis of, 47, 71; perfection of, 116; process/object of grasping, 75, 82; *pudgala,* consists of five aggregates, 46; relation of knowledge to, 35
pessimism, "initial," 16
phenomenalists, 67
phenomenon: noumenon and, inseparable, 116; —, in, 107
philosophy/-ies/-er(s): *Abhidharmaka,* 112; ancient Indo-Aryan, 150; goal of, 11; Hindu, *see* Hindu; of history, 174; Indian, aim of, 157; —, major schools/periods of, 4, 171; —, of suffering, 36; —, theories of, *vi,* 1*ff,* 19–65 (*see also under individual schools*); methods of, 131*f;* political, *see* political; of religion, *see* religion; social, *vi,* 5, 14, 267*ff;* Vedic and anti-Vedic systems of, 267; Western, *see* Western
philosophic knowledge/wisdom/*prajñā,* 20*ff,* 33, 36, 328, 354; is synonym of *buddhi/bodhi,* 201; ultimate purpose of, 132
Philosophy and Culture—East and West, v
Philosophy—East and West, v, ix, 40, 211
physicists, modern, 106, 108
physical science(s), 229; Uncertainty Principle of, 106
Plato, 203, 210; his "world of ideas," 32; Oriental influence on, 63; philosophy of, 56; *Republic,* 56
pleasing, *preyas,* 154

pleasure(s), 5, 15, 260; aesthetic, *see* aesthetic; *kāma,* 153–5, 239; material, 218; pain and, rotate like a wheel, 240; of physical world, 219; worldly, 226
pluralism/-ists/-istic, 6–7, 51, 274; of Buddha, radical, 74; in Buddhist philosophy, 46; dualism, and monism, distinctions between, 53; —, and *śūnya* synthesized, 54; Hīnayāna (Theravāda) schools, 47; idealism of Śāntarakṣita and Kamalaśīla, 47; of Nyāya, 43, 48, 53; realistic, 8; universe, 169; Vaiśeṣika, 43, 48; —, school of atomic, 89; Vedāntic schools, 41; *see also* Buddhists; Jainas
plurality, 170, 318; of causes, doctrine of, 160; is expression of God's energy (*śakti*), 48; individuality not mere, 331; of individuals, 303*ff;* of Nature, 67; of selves, 300; of souls, 74; as ultimate truth, 304; world of, 169
poem, epic, *Rāmāyaṇa, see Rāmāyaṇa*
point-instants (*khaṇa*), 77–8
police, 381
Polis, 378
politics, 100, 217
political: evolution of India, 256; freedom, India's loss of, 227; — of India, struggle for, 217, 225; philosophies of India, 6, 14; speculation, 263; theory/thought, 208, 374*ff*
politicians, 23
polytheism, 186–7; transformation of outward, into inward monism, 186; in Vedas, 5
poor, 230
population, 388
Portuguese, 382
positivism, logical, 39
positivists, 67
possession, *bhoga,* 293
Posterior Mīmāṁsā, *see* Vedānta
postulation, 119, 133; *arthāpatti,* 129
posture, *āsana,* 142
potential, actualization of, 49
poverty: of India, 216; no virtue in, 154
power: knowledge is, 139; supernatural, 139
Prabhākara, 50, 121, 199, 211; school of Mīmāṁsā, 119, 130
pragmatic, *vyāvahārika,* 308
pragmatism(-ists), 188, 212, 391; theory of, 41
Prahlāda, 363
prajñā, see philosophical knowledge
Prajñā-pāramitās, 44
Prajñākaramati, 213
prakṛti, 158; eternity of, 89; Nature, 49, 271, 355; and *puruṣa,* contact of, 49; —, dualism of, 53; —, identification of, 54, 329; is *śakti* (power) of *Brahman,* 53; transformation of, 49
pramā, valid cognition, 118
pramāṇa, source of valid knowledge, 118, 290
prāṇāyama, control of breath, 142
prapatti, self-surrender, 213
prāpti, see patti
Prasad, Dr. Beni, 260–1; *The State in Ancient India,* 266
Prasad, Ram, ed. and trans. Sacred Books of the Hindus, 134–5
pratyāhāra, 142
pravṛtti, animal propensities, 269
prayer, 69, 223
prayoga, age-long usages, 252
Preceptors in ancient India, 165
predestination, doctrine of, 339
Present: Five Effects of, 92, 94; Three causes of, 92, 94–5

preservation of man, 377
preyas, pleasing, 154
Price, H. H., *The Hibbert Journal,* 213
priest, royal, 280, 289–90
priest-teacher, *brāhmaṇas,* 161
Primeval Being, 161
Principle, Nature of, 103
principle- or law-element (*Dharma-dhātu*), 103
Pringle-Pattison, A. Seth, *The Idea of Immortality,* 172
Prior Mīmāṁsā, *see* Mīmāṁsā
Proceedings of the Indian Philosophical Congress, 1932, 339
process: cosmic/world, 176–7, 324; —, resembles surface of ocean, 240; —, sustained by rotation of *kalpas,* 241
procreation, 219, 225
progress: modern idea of, 240; world, 240
progression, different modes of spiritual, 331
progressivists, 67
projections, 190; deities are mental, 181
propagation of species, 377
property, 388; father is manager of, 376; *mamatva,* doctrine of, 253
prophets, 216
prosperity, 221
protection: *paripālanam,* all-round, 259; of subjects, 260
Protestants, 263
proverb, Sanskrit, 142
Pṛthu, 258
psychoanalysis (-analyst), 32, 80
psychological discipline, system of, 31
psychologists, Hindu, 138, 150
psychology, 14–5; modern, 25; Western, 137, 197
punish, king is wielder of power to (*daṇḍadhara*), 254
punisher, *see* Yama
punishment: capital, 291; *daṇḍa,* 275, 282; forms of 290*f;* objectives of, 292; of wicked, 260
puṇya, merit, 345
Purāṇas, 224, 234, 250, 271, 288, 363, 371; eighteen, 267; *see also under individual texts,* e.g., *Bhāgavata-purāṇa*
pure: in heart, 33; *sāttvika,* 205
purification, 73, 328; discipline of inner, 221; internal and external, 141; lies in *nibbāna,* 73; of mind, *see* mind; path of, *viśuddhi-mārga,* 326
purity: *Nirvāṇa* as, 109; *sattva, see sattva*
purohita, leader of community, 163
puruṣa, 35; or *ātman,* mind as knower, 122; person, 43; —, supreme, 271; and *prakṛti, see prakṛti;* spirit, 49
"Puruṣa-sūkta," (*in Ṛg-veda*), 161
puruṣārtha (*s*), four objectives/goals of man's existence, 132, 153, 156–7, 257, 260, 375; *see also artha; dharma; kama; mokṣa*
Pūrva Mīmāṁsā, *see* Mīmāṁsā
Pythagoras, 191, 203
Pythagoreans, 214

quality (-ies), 48, 50, 60; *guṇa,* 272; substance cannot exist without, 62
quest, philosophic, 29
quiescence, perfect, 110

race (s), 194; conflicts of, 263; equality among, 361; problems of, 161
Radha Kumud Mookerji, 256
Radhakrishnan, Professor Sarvepalli, 6, 13, 39, 51, 55, 158, 160, 209; ed. and trans. *Dhamma-*

pada, 296; *Eastern Religion and Western Thought,* 59; "Gautama the Buddha," 171; *The Heart of Hindusthan,* 17; *The Hindu View of Life,* 171–2; *Indian Philosophy,* 17, 65, 213, 246; *Religion and Society,* 373; ed. *A Source Book in Indian Philosophy/Source Book* (with C. A. Moore), 17, 40, 244–5, 295–6
rāga: attachment, 301; lust, 257
rāgas, tunes, 205
Raghavachariar, N. R., *Hindu Law: Precedents and Principles,* 392
Raghavendrachar, H. N., *The Dvaita Philosophy and Its Place in the Vedānta,* 65
Raghu, 258; ancestor of Rāma, 375
rāja-dharma, law of state, 380
rāja-yoga, "kingly *yoga,*" 136*ff,* 150; consists of eight "limbs," 141*f*
rājan/rājās: prince/king, *see* king; concrete government, 378
rājanya, kṣatriya class, *see kṣatriya*
rajas: active element, 138; virility, 162
rājās, see rājan
rājasika, movements, 301
rājñām ājñā, command of ruler, 254
Raju, P. T., "Activism in Indian Thought," 211–3; "The Concept of the Spiritual in Indian Thought," 211; *Idealistic Thought of India,* 213; "India's Culture and Her Problems," 211; "The Nature of Mind and its Activities," 213; "The Western and the Indian Philosophical Traditions," 65
rājya, kingdom/monarchy/state, 278, 378
Rāma, 360, 375; divine incarnation, 363
Ramakrishna, 39, 230, 360
Ramakrishna Mission, 229; monks of, 230
Rāmānuja, 51–3, 172, 189–90, 194–7, 199, 201, 212, 228, 238, 307–8; teaching of, 251; Vedāntic philosophy of, 206; (Vedāntin) theory of error, 130; *Śrībhāṣya,* 212; *see also* Raṅgāchārya, M.
Rāmānujists, 306–7
Rāmāyaṇa, 5, 217, 223–5, 245, 342, 363, 372; India's earliest epic poem, 224
Raṅgāchārya, M., and Varadarāja Aiyaṅgār, trans. *The Vedānta-sūtras with the Śrī-Bhāshya of Rāmānujāchārya,* 212
rasa: aesthesis, 204; bliss, 204
rāṣṭra: country, 256; territorial state, 278
ratiocinative and inferential knowledge, 29
rational: knowledge, 25 (*see also* reason); and mediate theories of knowledge, 27; skepticism, 26
rationalism, 63, 67; negative, 87
realism(-ists), 32, 63; atomic, 7; Buddhist, 46, 87; critical, of Sautrāntikas, 121; direct, of Vaibhāṣikas, 121; of Hīnayāna (Theravāda) schools, 47; Ideal of *ens* school, 114; and idealism, distinctions between, 53; —, synthesis of, 15, 231, 243; Jaina, 6, 45; of Kauṭilya and Śukra, 294; logical, 7; Mīmāṁsā school of ritualistic, 50, 89; naïve, 45–6; Nyāya school of logical, 89
Realistic school (Sarvāstivāda), 102, 112
reality/Reality, 30–1, 84, 102, 119, 124, 139–45; categories of, 89; empirical (*sammuti-sacca*), 78; —,/practical/relative, *see vyāvahārika;* -in-itself/qualityless

is *Nirguṇa Brahman,* 168, 180; -in-relation-to-the-world, 168; intuitive vision of, 181, 390; knowledge of, 140, 144, 175, 244; nominal, 75; ultimate/highest/supreme/transcendental/absolute, 41–3, 139, 189, 221, 230–1; —, *Brahman* is, 42–3, 51, 145–6, 169, 273; —, *dhamma* is, 72; —, differs from scientific, 136; —, includes subject and object, 57; —, *māyā* is *śakti* of, 54; —, nature of, 177–8; —, *paramārthika,* 231; —, is plural/ground of pluralistic universe, 67, 168; —, pure, *paramattha-sacca,* 77; —, two forms of, *nirguṇa* and *saguṇa,* 180; —, *yoga* is union with, 136, 166
realization: *ātman-,* 210; direct (*sākṣāt-kāra*), of truth, 124; inward, 210–11; process of (*sādhana*), 124; spiritual, 201
reason/Reason, 24–5, 29, 134, 210; belongs to man's inward being, 206; *buddhi,* 191, 193, 196, 202–6, 212–3, 269; Cosmic, *Mahat, Mahān Ātmā,* 191, 203, 212–3; higher than/transcends ego, 191, 202, 206; *Logos* as world, 191; Pure/Practical/Aesthetic, *sāttvika-buddhi,* 35, 213, 288, 315; religious propositions grounded in, 177; sheath of, 157; supremacy of, 228; universality of, 203
reasoning: circular, 133; science of, 131
rebirth (successive/future/repeated births/existencies), 98, 194; belief in, 13; in Buddhism, 79–81; cycle/round/chain/waves/series of, 69, 108, 159, 318; —, and death, 322, 338, 385; —, and death, cessation of, 81; —, suffering and death, 83; doctrine/theory of, 17, 79, 232–3; escape from, 243; *see also* reincarnation; *saṁsāra*
receptacle-consciousness (*ālaya-vijñāna*), 47
Reciprocal Identification, principle/theory of, 106, 114
reconciliation, 274; *samanvaya,* 179*f*
red, 162
reflection, 189; *manana,* 181; philosophical, 21–3, 31; right, (*yoniso-manasikāra*), 81
reformation, moral, 124
reforms, 369–70
regress, infinite, 133
Reichel, Oswald J., *see* Zeller
reincarnation, doctrine of, 194; *see also* rebirth
relativism, 6, 67; realistic, 274
release: from wheel of life and death, 158; longing for, 168; state of, 158; *see also mokṣa; nirvāṇa*
religion(s), 100, 173–82, 183–215; called *dharma,* 184; conflict between science and, 185; Indian, approach to problem of, 173*ff;* —, is natural, 185; meant for spiritual realization, 192; organized, 180; particularist, 185–6; philosophy of, 179; — is theory of, 37; reflective nature of Indian, 185, 202; is response of whole man, 178; revealed, 185; role of, as reason with spiritual orientation, 62; sacrificial, 68; tribal, 185; universal, 185–6
religious: beliefs, Indian, 37; experiences, genuine, 137; insights, 178; institutions, 37; philosophy, 73; thought, Indian, 320*ff*
Renaissance, philosophical ideas of, 22

renunciation, 83, 200, 217, 236; of ascetics, 226; of attachment to world, 234; life of *sannyāsa,* fourth stage of life, *see sannyāsa;* national ideal of India, 230; self-, 83
republics: federal, 278; in India, 255; kingless, 278
repulsion: clutches of attachment and, 311; *dveṣa,* 301
residues, method of (*pāriśeṣya*), 133
responsibility, idea of, 80
rest, principle of (*adharma*), 45
restlessness, inner, 239
restraints(s), 15; *yama,* 141, 339
revelation, 335
reverence, 240
revolution(s), political and social, 22
Ṛg-veda, 17, 42, 64, 156, 172, 231, 244–6, 256, 268, 271, 287, 295
Ṛg-vedic: Aryans, 42; hymns, 325
Rhys, Ernest, *see* Shelley, P. B.
riddle of universe and self, 150
right(s): *adhikāra, see adhikāra;* economic, 293*f;* human/of individual, 369–71; legal, 293
righteousness, 257–9; *see also dharma*
'rita', *see Ṛta*
rites: and ceremonies, 383; Hindu, 383; of Islam, 383
ritual, vedic, 45
ṛṇas, debts, 219
Roman(s), 286–7; writers, 255
Roman Catholics, 263
Roman Empire, 250
Roman Natural Law (*ius naturale*), 287
Romans, Epistle to, 176, 182; *see also* Karl Barth
Rome, 174, 263
round of work, enjoyment, and desire, 166; *see also* cycle
Roy, Raja Ram-Mohan/Rāmmohan, 360; founder of Brahmo Samāj, 228
royalists, 276
ṛṣi, 372
Ṛta/'rita': cosmic, 288; Order and Truth of universe, 325; *phūsis* derived from, 287; principle of cosmic law and harmony, 286; *ratio* derived from, 287; (*Vedic*) concept of, 268, 286–7
Rudra, 326; called Śiva, 327
Ruggiero, G. de, 59; *Modern Philosophy,* 65
rūpa or matter, physical elements, 70–1; *see also nāma-rūpa*
rural communes, 256; *see also* village-community
Ruskin, John, 285
Russell, Bertrand, 20–1, 75; *A History of Western Philosophy,* 20, 40; *Our Knowledge of the External World,* 21, 40

Śabara, commentator on Jaimini's *Mīmāṁsā-sūtra,* 128
Śabda, testimony, 128*f*
sabhā: council, 255; court, 289
Śabri, 363
sacca, see satya
saccidānanda, see bliss
sacredness, 209
sacrifice(s), 190, 236, 361; of animals, 88, 259; —, prohibition of, 90; Brāhmaṇism is religion of, 186; *karma* as, 50; *Mīmāṁsā* doctrine of, 188; performance of, 50; —, is duty, 192; —, by king, 259; for propitiation of manes, 219, 231; religion of, 68, 189; ritualistic activities of, 186; with substance-oblations, *dravya-yajña,* 325; Vedic, 45, 50, 229; *yajña,* four kinds of, 218*f*
sadācārā, good men, 254

Saddharma-puṇḍarīka, phenomenological school, 103
ṣaḍguṇas, strategies, 282
sādhana: esoteric exercises, 309; process of realization, 124; series of means, 271; *see also* discipline
sādhana-catuṣṭaya, 33
sādhāraṇa-dharmas, universal duties, 272
sādhya, self's ultimate end, 271
sage(s), 31, 272, 360
saguṇa/Saguṇa: Brahman, endowed with attributes, 150; —, God with infinite attributes, 168; qualified form of supreme reality, 180
saint(s), 216, 360; *arhant/arhat,* 81, 84, 109; Buddhist perfected man, Hīnayāna ideal of, 323; liberated, 123; Mārhattā, 228; *sthitadhī,* 350; Teṅkalai, 251
sainthood: *arhant*-ship, 81; called *nibbāna* with residue, 81
Śaiva(s), 318, 347; philosophy, 303; sect, 54, 300; thinkers, 305
Śaivism, 183, 194, 309; Kashmir school of, 54, 318; theistic school of, 324
Śakas, 162
Śākaymuni, 110
sakkāya, "I" or "personality," 71
sākṣāt-kāra, 26; direct realization of truth, 124
Saksena, Professor S. K., *ix,* 13, 17
Sākṣi-puruṣa, witness-self, 305
sākṣin: -hood of selves, 318; witness, 305
Śākta system, 54, 300
śakti: energy/force, 50; —, concept of, in Vedānta, 53; —, of God, 48, 52–3; plurality is expression of, 48; *prakṛti* is, of *Brahman,* 53; transformation (*pariṇāma*) of God's, 53; of ultimate reality, *māyā* is, 54
śakti-pāta, descent of grace, 324
Śaktism, 183, 194, 309, 318
Śākyas, 255
Saletore, Dr. B. A., 250
salvation, 48, 194, 198, 200–3, 262, 323–4, 326, 332; ethical discipline is geared to, 198; is highest aim of life, 189; of individual, 216; *jñāna* is knowledge for, 203; lies in weeding out *karma,* 198, 202; *mokṣa,* 187; *nirvāṇa/nibbāna, see nirvāṇa;* path to, 84; philosophies of, 207; is return to original unconscious state of *ātman,* 48; of Semitic religions, 328; in Vedāntic systems, 55
Sāma-veda, 231
samādhi, 143; communion with *Brahman,* 243; deep meditation, 234; mystical states, 354; power of concentration/collected consciousness, 75–6, 200, 331; stilling of thought, 83; total absorption, 139
samāja, social system, 377, 381
sāman, peaceful interstate relations, 285
samanvaya, reconciliation, 179*f*
sāmānya-dharma, duties of all people, 364
samavāya, inherence, 50, 308
Śaṁkara/Śaṁkarācārya, 8, 10, 51–5, 155, 157, 180, 184, 190, 194, 196–7, 200–1, 222, 231–2, 234, 236, 242–3, 246, 310, 314, 328, 336, 347; *Brahman* of, 184, 336; metaphysical idealism of, 121; *Brahma-sūtra-bhāṣya,* 339; Commentary on *Brahma-sūtra,* 333; *Bṛhadāraṇyaka-upaniṣad,* 246; Commentary on *Bhagavad-gītā,* 225, 244, 246; *Upadeśa-sāhasrī,* 151; *Vākyavṛtti,* 212;

Vivekacūḍāmaṇi, 212–3; *see also* Advaita
Sāṁkhya, 43–57, 90, 119, 121, 153, 196, 198, 204–5, 212–4, 270, 280, 300, 302, 305, 308, 314, 327, 329–30, 352; believe self to be really infinite, 123; conception of final goal, 158; dualism of, 43, 53, 74; non-theistic, 7; school of, 89, 191; systematized by Kapila, 44; teaching/doctrine of, 74, 318; theory of error, 130; —, of *guṇas*, 162
Sāṁkhya-kārikā, *see* Sharma
Sāṁkhya-Yoga, 215, 353; system of, 31; theoretical philosophy of, 31
saṁnyāsa, *see sannyāsa*
sāṁsāra/saṅsāra, wheel/ocean of waves/rise and fall/flowing cycle/round, of life (and death)/transmigration of souls, 36, 70, 80, 92–3, 95–6, 99, 104–5, 108–9, 158–60, 233; *mokṣa* is release from, 158; *nibbāna* is cessation from, 73; and *Nirvaṇa* identical, 109; phenomenal existence in its entirety, 322; universe is, 87; is void, 114; *see also* rebirth
Saṁsāra-cakra, wheel of life and death, 36
saṁśaya (doubt), 119, 132
saṁsiddhi, perfection of individual, 375
saṁskāra(*s*), 198; passions and their defilement, 326; residual impressions, 159
samuccaya-vāda, synthetic view/theory, 311–2
samurai of Japan, 215
saṁvṛti, appearance, 274
Saṁyutta-nikāya, 68, 85; ed. L. Feer, 338; *see also* Woodward, *Kindred Sayings*
Sanatkumāra, 153, 231
Sandal, M. L., ed. and trans. Sacred Books of the Hindus, 135
saṅgha: "community of one caste," 90; of the noble (*āryas*), 90
Sañjaya, 43
Śaṅkha, 346
saṅkhārā, 85; an assemblage of mental faculties, 75; complexes, 70–1; motive to live (will), 92; pre-natal forces, 80
saṅkhata (conditioned) and *asaṅkhata* (unconditioned), 72
Sāṅkhya-tattva-kaumudī, trans. Ganganatha Jha, 65
sannyāsa/saṁnyāsa, monk's life of renunciation, fourth stage in life, 164–6, 200, 238–9, 271, 375; *see also* stages in life
sannyāsin/saṁnyāsin, *viii*, 35, 239, 243; is free man of spirit, 165; monk, 238; one who has renounced world, 165
Sanskrit, *vii*, *ix;* proverb, 142; terms, *viii*, 66
santāna: flux/mere flux, 73, 80; (stream), Buddhist term for individual, 75
Śāntarakṣita, pluralistic idealism of, 47
śānti, sentiment of peace, 206
Śāntideva, *see Śikṣā-samuccaya*
Śānti-parva of Mahābhārata, 225, 245, 250, 253, 255, 258–9, 265–6, 269, 275–7, 282–3, 296–7, 357, 364, 366, 373, 392
sarva means "all," 364
sarva-dharma, duties for all men, 364
sarva-dharma-anātmatā, no substance, 87
sarva-saṁskāra-anityatā, no duration, 87
sarvaṁ duḥkham, no bliss, 87

Sarvāsti-vāda, Realistic school, 102, 112
śāsanas, edicts of kings, 289
sassata-vādino, see eternalism
Śāstras, or scriptures, *see Dharma-śāstras*
śāstra-yonityāt, third *sūtra,* 178
Sastry, R. Halasyanatha, ed. Āpastamba's *Dharma-sūtra,* 266
śāvata-vāda, see eternalism
sat: being, 42, 88–9, 169; existence/existent, 49, 88; existence, *ātman* is, 196–7; -move, 90; *see also* being; *ens*
sat-kārya-vāda, theory of existent effect, 49
"*Sat-Yuga,*" period of truth, justice, and freedom, 366
Śatapatha-brāhmaṇa, 364
satī, suicide of widows, 361, 366
sattva, 138, 213–4, 302; purity, 162; transparence, 49
Sāttvika, 214; actions, 302; pure, 205; movements, 301
Sāttvika-buddhi, pure reason, 288
satya/sacca: fact/existent, 67, 75; golden age, 241; Truth of universe, 325; truth, *yogi* virtue, 391; truthfulness, 270
satya-dharma, 325
Satyāgraha, non-violent non-co-operation, 281
satya-kāma, truth, 337
Satyakāma, 163, 347
Satya-siddhi, Nihilistic school, 102
Sautrāntikas, critical realism of, 121
scepter, 280, 290; *daṇḍa,* 275*f;* forces of, 279; principles of, *daṇḍa-nīti,* 276
Schelling, F. von, 63
Schlegel, F. and C., 63
scholar, 342
Scholastic period, 7
school, 369
Schopenhauer, A., 63
Schrader, F. O., *Introduction to the Pāñcharātra,* 65
Schweitzer, Dr. Albert, *Out of My Life and Thought,* trans. C. T. Campion, 177, 182
science(s), 112, 217; discoveries of, 152; growth of, 240; leads to acceptance of mystery, 179; modern, 160; physical, 231; positive, 230; and religion, conflict between, 185; of soul, 231
scientific: "fallacy," 211; knowledge, 19–20, 23, 27; materialism, 76; philosophy, 29
scientism, 210
scientist(s), 23; object of his inquiry is external, 168
scriptural study, 219
scriptures: Śāstras, 179; secondary, of Hindus, 223; Supreme is source of, 178
Scythians, 161
Seal, Dr. B. N., 126–7; *The Positive Sciences of the Ancient Hindus,* 135
seed(s), 97–8, 104
"seedless," mind becomes, 140
seers, 179, 219, 224, 231; Vedic, 242
self/Self, 52, 73; = Absolute, 311; *Ātman/attā,* individual, 42, 75, 112, 136, 304 (*see also ātman*); —, belief in, 184; and body, identified with/fusion of, 167, 329; is *Brahman,* universal, 42, 112, 136, 146–7; is comprehended from within, 178; consummation of free, 376; five sheaths of, 157, 351; foundational, 330; infinity of (*jīva*), 123; inner, *antar-ātman,* 288; knowledge of, 153, 218, 231; liberation of thinking, 68; nature of, 50, 242, 357; *Nirvāṇa* as, 109; is primarily unconscious,

122 (*see also* 50, 52); *puruṣa*, *see puruṣa;* reality an escape from, 84; riddle of, 150; and selflessness, synthesis of, 104; is sublimated, 69; is supreme spirit, 164; ultimate end of (*sādhya*), 271; is ultimate reality, 41; *see also* individual
self-analysis, 46
self-control/restraint, 146, 150, 192, 236, 323, 327–8; cultivate (*dāmyata*), 157; *dama*, 269; disciplines of, 221; spiritual, 56; virtue of, 222
self-correction of philosophical view, 170
self-creation, 94–6, 104, 116; Buddha's system of, 90, 115; continuity of, 105; of universe, 104; world of, 109
self-cultivation, principle of, 105
self-culture, 116
self-denial, 69, 106, 117
self-dependence, 133
self-development, 38
self-discipline, 38, 115, 391; *see also* discipline
self-discovery, 38
self-education, 323
self-effort, 226
self-forgetfulness, cause of suffering, 146
self-hypnosis, 210
self-indulgence, 69
self-knowledge, 146, 354; *jñāna-yoga* is way of, 166–7
self-mortification: addiction to, 68; of Jaina, 323
self-natured body, 110
self-negation, 101; mutual identification by, 106
self-preservation, 350
self-realization, 166, 169, 192–5, 351, 356; is *dharma* and *vidhi* (injunction), 193; is meditation on one's self, 186; renunciation of, 195; is supreme god of life, 381; Vedāntic religion of, 186; vows of, 230; Way of, through action, *karma-mārga*, 194
self-regeneration, 327
self-renunciation, 83
self-restraint, *see* self-control
self-rule, *svārājya*, 278
self-surrender: to God, 201; *prapatti*, 213
self-validity, theory of, 120
selfishness, 241
selfless work/action, 191, 193, 233; doctrine of, *karma-yoga*, 166, 200
selflessness/no self/*an-ātman*, 13, 75, 88, 102; Buddha proposed, 88; theory of, 117
Semitic: religions, 322, 325; —, salvation of, 328
Sen, P. N., *Hindu Jurisprudence*, 297
sense(s), 46; cannot exist without activity, 79; -contact, 46; five (external), 122, 198; five fields of, 47; internal, 122; mind as internal, 122; related to non-existence, 130
sense-objects/objects of sense, 77, 155, 166; five, 198; non-attachment to, 144, 149
sense-organs, 136, 138–9, 218, 233, 239, 329; detachment of mind from, 142; five, 49; friction between sense-objects and, 77; six, *āyatana*, 92, 94, 96
sense-perception, 124
sentiment, *bhāva*, 214
separability, *pṛthak-siddhi*, 307
serenity, 239; inner, 144
Sermon on the Mount, 285
service, 236; life of, 239; national ideal of India, 230

Shakespeare, William, 382; Hamlet, 182
Shamasastry, R., trans. Kauṭilya's *Arthaśāstra,* 244, 297, 357
sharī'at: and *dharma-śāstra,* 385–6; law of Islam, 383–6
Sharma, Har Dutt, ed. and trans. *Sāṁkhya-kārikā,* 214
sheaths, doctrine of five, of self, 157, 351
Sheldon, Professor W. H., 13; "Main Contrasts Between Eastern and Western Philosophy," 17
Shelley, Percy Bysshe: *Lyrics and Shorter Poems,* ed. Ernest Rhys, 182; "Queen Mab," 182
shī'ahs, minor sect of Muslims in India, 383
Sibree, J., trans. Hegel's *Lectures on the Philosophy of History,* 174
Siddhānta-leśa-saṁgraha, 65
Sikhism, 183
"Śikṣā Vallī," 251
Śikṣā-samuccaya, compiled by Śāntideva, ed. Cecil Bendell, 339, 358
śīla/sīla: discipline of body and mind, 83; practice of moral virtues, 331
similarity (*sādṛśya*), 50
sin: -consciousness, 337; doctrine of original, 195
Sircar, D. C., ed. *Inscriptions of Aśoka,* 296
Śiṣṭas, disciplined persons, 254
Śiva, 150; Rudra called, 327; *śakti* of, 54
Six: -fold Perfection, 111, 115; systems of Hinduism, 7, 13, 88
skandhas, see aggregate(s)
skepticism, 6, 28; about philosophical knowledge, 23*f;* rational, 26
slave states, 263
slavery, 361, 365–6
sleep, 132
Smith, Huston, 31; "Accents of the World's Philosophies," 40
Smṛti(s), 267, 271, 287–8, 347, 363, 379, 386; law books, 376; literature based on Vedas, 344; secondary scriptures of Hindus, 223; traditional texts, 342; writers, 377; *see also under individual titles*
smṛti-kāras, languages, 262
social: classes represent groupings of *guṇas,* 162 (*see also* caste); conscience, 367; customs, 228; duties, 217, 243; ethics, 63, 240–1; institutions, 209; monistic tendencies, 369; obligations, 232–3, 238; —, fulfillment of, 216; order, 378; organization, Hindu, 376; —, problems of, 199, 209; philosophy, 267*ff;* —, papers in, *vi;* reform, 229; relationships, study of, 199, 209; system, Hindu, 383; —, new, 390; —, *samāja,* 377; values, justification of, 231*f;* —, in modern India, 228; —, in Vedas, 219*f;* welfare, 12, 236; —, gods are jealous custodians of, 218; worker, 230
socialism, 368
society(-ies): becoming industrialized, 173; classes of, 155, 160*ff;* conceptualized, 59; divisions in, 237 (*see also* castes); ethical, 372; Hindu, *see* Hindu; *kṣatriya* is guardian of, 163; man and, *see* man; relation between individual and, 270*f,* 347*f;* state and, 277; in Upaniṣadic times, 223
Socrates, 56, 132
Söderblom, I., *The Living God,* 339

Somadeva, 259; *Nītī-vākyāmṛta,* ed. P. P. Sonī, 266
Sonī, P. P., *see* Somadeva
Sophists, 68
sorcery, 7
Sorley, W. R., *Recent Tendencies in Ethics,* 64
sorrowlessness, attainment of, 153
soul(s), 45, 48, 66, 158–9; absorbed into *Brahman,* 52, 149; belief in, 7, 13; Buddhism denies existence of, 96, 98; denied reality, 77; direct experience of God, 167; divinity of, 229; doctrine of existence of, 17; essence of consciousness, 141; evolution of, 243; fettered to/isolated from body, 123, 234; -finding, 212; free, 148–9, 158, 334; God, and universe, oneness of, 147; illuminated, 145, 149; immortality of, 149, 243; inherent perfection of, 232; *jīva,* individual, 45, 202, 212, 322, 329; -making, 212; non-duality of, 149; perfection of, 29; plurality of, 74; tragedy of, 175; *see also ātman*
soullessness, 82; *see also anattā*
Sound *Brahman,* 205
Source Book, see Moore, C. A., and Radhakrishnan, S., *A Source Book in Indian Philosophy*
space, 48; (*ākāśa*), 45; is curved, 108; is one of five elements, 108; and time, 108; -time world, 108
Sparta, 361
Spartacists, 249
specialization, temptation of, 23
spirit/Spirit: Absolute, is non-dual, 167; body is eternal enemy of, 69; conceptualized, 59; Great, 58; is knowledge (*vidyā*), 375; *puruṣa,* 49; realm of, 58
spiritual: attainment, 331; culture of race, 163; goal, *see* goal; ideal, 44
spiritualism, 63
spirituality, 330; dominant in India, 9; Indian, 10; —, incorporates intellectual values, 203; inward, is essential meaning of religion, 185
śravaṇa: hearing, 181; study, 168
śreyas, (spiritual) good, 154, 342, 345
Sri Aurobindo, 11; *Essays on the Gītā,* 296; *Iśa-upaniṣad,* 296; *The Renaissance in India,* 17
Śrīkaṇṭha, 51
Śrīmadbhāgavatam, ed. P. Tarkaratna, 295
Śrīnivāsācārya/Srinivasachari/P. N. Srinivasacari, 213; *The Philosophy of the Beautiful,* 214; *The Philosophy of Bhedābheda,* 65
Śrīpati, 51
śṛngāra, love, 206
Śruti: God, 379; or Vedas, 224
stage(s) in life, four (*āśramas*), 164–6, 199, 200, 347, 367, 369, 375; and castes, law/duty of, *varṇāśrama-dharma,* 155, 164, 238, 243, 277, 380; discipline of, 238, 271; duties of, *āśrama-dharma,* 163, 278–9, 375; fourth, of meditation on philosophical truths, 342 (*see also sannyāsa*); third, of retirement and study, 342 (*see also* ascetic); *see also* householder; student
standard of living, 9
state(s): activities of, 260; administration of, 259; ancient Hindu, 261; good, 274; ideal, 275; and individual, *see* individual; origin of, 275; *rājya,* 378; seven constituent elements

of, 260, 279f; and society, 277f; three values of, 276f
Status of the Individual in East and West, v
Stcherbatsky, Thi, *The Central Conception of Buddhism,* 85
Stede, W., *see* Davids, T. W. Rhys
step(s): Buddhist method of five, (*pañca-kāraṇī*), 125; five-, method of discovery and proof, *see pañcāvayava-nyāya*
sthita-prajñā, ideal man is, 201
Stoics, 287
storing center of ideation, *see* ideation-store
stream, *santāna, see santāna*
student(ship), *brahmacarya,* first stage in life, 164–6, 238, 271, 375; *see also* stages in life
study (*śravaṇa*), 168
subconscious mind (*viññāṇa*), 92–3
subject-object polarization, 196
subjectivists, 121
subjectivity: absorption in, 207; Eastern mind engrossed in, 208
sublimating emotions, 166
submission, 316
substance, 48, 50, 66, 89; cannot exist without qualities, 62; categories of, 76; denial of, 76; (*dravya*), 45; extended (*asti-kāya*), 45; of nine kinds, 48; non-extended (*an-asti-kāya*), 45
substratum, theory of pure change without, 102
"Suchness," *see* "Thusness"
Śuddhodana, father of Buddha, 99
śūdra(*s*), manual laborers/artisans, lowest/fourth class/caste of society, 161, 163–4, 236, 262, 292, 362, 376, 378; non-Aryans became, 256
suffering, 82, 97, 115–6, 239–40, 323, 328, 337, 353; cessation of, *nirodha/nibbāna,* 81; *duḥkha/dukkha,* 70, 81, 88, 322; *duḥkha-satya,* truth of, 116, 322, engenders reflection, 321; experience of, 30; extinction of, 116; human, rooted in ignorance, 118; Indian philosophical theories of, 36; originates from mind-action/ideation, 98; is result of conflict in us, 176; round of birth, death and, 83 (*see also* rebirth); self-forgetfulness, cause of, 146; threefold, 89; unreality of, 82
ṣūfī(*s*), 27, 383
suicide: spiritual, 323; of widows, *satī,* 361, 366
Śuka, 51–2
sukha, bliss of well-being, 83
Śukra, 250, 254, 258, 278–9, 282–3, 291–3, 296; realism of, 294; works of, 257; *Śukra-nīti,* 254, 265; *Śukra-nīti-sāra,* 254–5, 258, 265–6, 267, 275, 297; —, ed. Jivānanda Vidyāsāgara, 295
sun, rays of, 53
Sunnīs, sects of Muslims, 383
śūnya, void, 47, 54, 184, 193, 198; Buddhist doctrine, synthesized with pluralism and dualism, 54; or *Nirvāṇa,* 47, 55
śūnya-vāda, indeterminism, 121
Śūnyatā (Void), 330, 337; absolute, 114
supernatural power(s), 139, 146
supposition, 133
Supreme: *Ātman,* 187; Being, 182, 194; is Cosmic Lord, 180; Deity, 187; direct relationship with, 179; *puruṣa,* 271; realization of, 264; is source of scriptures, 178; Spirit (*Brahman*), 189, 199, 203, 212; —, is *Ātman*

within our *ātmans,* 197; —, like father and mother, 194
surgery, 230
Suta, narrator of *Bhāgavata-purāṇa,* 362
Sūtra(s), 8, 267; period, 7; *see also under individual texts,* e.g., *Brahma-sūtra Suttas* (Discourses) attributed to Buddha, 67
sva-bhāva, nature of things, 43, 272
sva-bhāva-vāda, naturalism, 325
sva-dharma: each man's *dharma,* 156; sphere of duty, 272
śvapaca, lowest class, 362
svatva/svāmitva, ownership, 293
Śvetaketu, father of, 364
Śvetāśvatara-upaniṣad, 43, 172
syllogism, three/five-membered, 89
synoptic: outlook, 29; vision, 170; —, need of, 23
synthesis, 274; in depth, 336; problem of, 170; theory of, *see samuccaya*
synthetic: interpretation, 14; unity, 77, 106; view, *samuccaya-vāda,* 311

tādātmya, identity of essence, 126
Tagore, Rabindranath, 38–9, 55, 268, 272, 360
Taine, Henri, 248–9
Taittirīya Āraṇyaka, ed. N. R. Acarya and R. L. Mitra, 295
Taittirīya-upaniṣad, 18, 156–7, 172, 177, 223, 245–6, 251, 358
Takakusu, Dr. Junjirō, *v, vi, viii, ix,* 86*ff; The Essentials of Buddhist Philosophy,* ed. Wing-tsit Chan and Charles A. Moore, 86
tamas, 302; darkening element, 138; dullness, 162; inactivity, 49
Tāmasika, 214; movements, 301
Tamil: language, 251; maxim, 154
taṇhā, desire, *see* desire
Tantra(s), 251; treatises, 224
Tāntrika, mysticism, 227
Tao, or vivifying principle, 104
Taoism, 104
tarka, 133; indirect hypothetical/postulational argument, 125, 132, 290
Tathāgata, 68, 70; one who has realized thatness, 336; *see also* Buddha
Tathāgata-garbha, *see also* Thusness
Tathātā (*Tathāgata-garbha*), *see* Thusness
Tattva, "Thatness," 86
Tattvopaplavasiṁha, 44–5
tax(es), 256, 258, 260, 279; of one sixth, 380
taxation, 263, 276, 388
Tāyumānavar, Hymn to Pārvatī, 264
teacher, illumined, 147
technology, 217, 323; growth of, 240
temples, music in, 206
Teṅkalai saints, 251
testimony: a means of true knowledge, 28; *śabda,* 128*f*
That One (*tad ekam*), 334
"That thou art," 147, 222
"Thatness" (*Tattva*), 86; theory of, 88
theism, 7, 306; in Indian spiritual tradition, 10
theists, 66, 270
theistic: literature, 271; schools of Śaivism and Vaiṣṇavism, *see* Śaivism; Vaiṣṇavism; systems/religions, 335, 352–3, 357; Vedānta, non-Advaita schools of, 273
theologians, 23; Christian, 177

theological knowledge, 20, 23, 27
theology, Christian, 63
theoretical philosophy of Sāṁkhya, 31
theory, full-fledged (*vāda*), 132
Theravāda/Hīnayāna schools, 47, 102, 106
thinking, reflective (*manana*), 168
Thomas, E. J.: *History of Buddhist Thought*, 64; *The Life of Buddha*, 64
Thoreau, Henry David, 285
thought: *cit*, 88; consciousness is, 76; higher, 115
"threefold learning," 111
"Thus-come," 101; a designation of Buddha, 98; Matrix of, *see* Matrix
"Thus gone," 99, 101; Matrix of, *see* Matrix
"Thusness": causation by, 98–9; is *Dharma-dhātu* (principle- or law-element), 104; is "Matrix of Thus-come," 104; principle of, 103; *Tathātā/Tathāgata-garbha*, 87, 98–9, 101, 103, 112, 114, 116, 330, 336; ultimate state of *Nirvāṇa*, 109; universe is dynamic manifestation of, 99–100
Tibet, 185
Tilak, B. G., 273, 285
Tillich, Professor Paul, 334; "The Religious Symbol," 182
time, 48, 54; a circle, 93; (*kāla*), 43; space and, 108
time-process, 159
Timur, 382
Tirtha, Ravi, trans. Udayana, *Kusumāñjali*, 135
tolerance, India's attitude of, 14–5
Tolstoi, Count Leo, 285
totalism: principle of (*Dharma-dhātu*), 104; school of, Avataṁsaka, 103
totalitarian philosophies, 207
totality: of all existence, 100; principle of, 101
town life, 262
Toynbee, A. J., *A Study of History*, 211
trade, 164; growth of, 388
trader-craftsmen, *see vaiśyas*
tradition(s): Asian, *vi; Hindu, vi;* philosophical and cultural, of East and West, *vi; taqlīd*, 385; unbroken (*itiha*), 119
traditionalists, 66
trances, *jhāna*, 83
tranquillity, 144
transcendence, metaphysical, 307
transcendent, unconditioned, 182
transcendental ego, 213
transformation: inward of man, 207–8; (*pariṇāma*), of God's *śakti*, 53; —, of *prakṛti*, 49
transformists, 67
transcience, *see* impermanence; doctrine of (*anicca*), 79
transmigration of soul, *see saṁsāra*
transparence, *see sattva*
Travancore, 264; Cera kings of, 263; Mahārāja of, 250, 264
tretā, silver age, 241
tribes, assimilation of backward, by Aryans, 224
Trivandrum, ed. Kauṭilya's *Artha-śāstra*, 265
tri-varga, 260; threefold human value, 276
true doctrine of, 204
truth(s)/Truth: achieved by whole man, 13; all-transcending, 114; classification of, 47; common-sense (*saṁvṛti-satya*), 111–3; criteria of, 133; direct realization (*sākṣāt-kāra*) of, 124; empirical, 189; Four Noble, 46, 116; God is, 203; higher-sense (*paramārtha-satya*), 111–3; highest, 114; —, is Brahman,

203; knowledge of ultimate, 356; *satya-kāma,* 337; sacrifice, 137; of suffering, 116; theory of double, 111*f;* ultimate, 99; of world, *Nirvāṇa* is, 47
truthfulness, 235, 343; *satya,* 270
tunes, *rāgas,* 205
Turks, 382
Turkish sultans, 384
twelve-linked chain/twelve states of causation, *see* causation
Tyāgarāja, 205
tyrant, 276, 281

uccheda-vāda, nihilism, 325–6
Udāna, 85, 182
Udayana, 134; *Kusumāñjali,* ed. and trans. E. B. Cowell, 135; —, trans. Ravi Tirtha, 135
ulamā, learned jurists, 384
ultimacy, principle of, 335
Ultimate: as *Nirvāṇa,* 326; reality, *see* reality
Umāsvāti, *Tattvārthādhigamasūtra,* trans. J. L. Jaini, Sacred Books of the Jainas, 64
Uncertainty Principle of physical science, 106
unconscious mind, 60
"undifferentiated aesthetic continuum," 273
uniformity, non-causal, 126
unitary: and integral character of knowledge, 36; theory of knowledge, 27; vision of man and life, 37
United Nations Organization, 264
unity: close, *apṛthak-siddhi,* 308; in diversity, 273; of existence, 145; —, realization of, 147; illumined soul experiences, 145; of India, 386; of man and his being, 23; synthetic, 77
universal: attainment of, 330; category, 48, 50; theories about, 56
Universal Principle (*Dharma-dhātu*), causation by, 99
universality, 192; of reason, 202–3
universe: *Brahman* is ground of, 168; a co-creation, 91; a conflux of life-waves (*saṁsāra*), 87; *Dharma-dhātu* (principle-element), 108; is dynamic manifestation of Thusness, 99–100; evolution of, 153; four states of, 100; God, soul, and, oneness of, 147; infinite number of discrete elements, 77; *māyā,* 232; "One and True," 100; phenomenal, 145, 232; a plenum of fixed existents, 68; pluralistic, 168–9; riddle of, 150; a seamless garment, 218; self-creation of, 104; Supreme is guide of, 180; visible, 230
University of Hawaii, *v*
unselfishness, practice of, 238
untouchability(-ables), 237–8, 366, 377, 390
upādāna: cleaving, 92, 94; grasping, 71
upādāna-skandhas, five, 339
upādhi(s), 109–10; hidden essential conditions, 125; material and immaterial condition of being, 109
upamāna, 127–8; knowledge by/from similarity, 119, 127–8
upanayana, ceremony of initiation, 361
Upaniṣad(s)/-ic, 5, 10, 27, 31, 34, 41–5, 53–5, 86, 149, 152, 156–7, 160, 162, 175–6, 181, 186, 193, 202–3, 212, 217, 234, 267, 273, 287, 304, 334, 336, 351–3, 355; *Brahman* of, 54, 168; Buddhism is offshoot of, 44; earliest philosophical treatises of India, 131;

influence of, on German idealism and Christian theology, 63; monistic, absolutist, non-dualist trends of, 7, 51, 74, 229; social values in, 221; teaching, 16, 272; tradition, 42, 52; ultimate goal of, 232; Vedānta is name/philosophy of, 51, 314; *A Compilation of 120 Upaniṣads,* 295; *see also under individual Upaniṣads*
upāyas, expedients, 282
upekṣā, forbearance, 270
urbanization, 388
Uttara Kurus, 255, 278
Uttara Madras, 278
Uttara Mīmāṁsā, *see* Vedānta

vāda, full-fledged theory, 132
Vaibhāṣika(s), 112; direct realism of, 121; *see also Sarvāsti-vāda*
vairāgya, detachment, 300–1, 303; *see also* non-attachment
vairājya, kingless/good state, 278
Vaiśālis, 255
Vaiśeṣika(s), 7, 52, 122–3, 128, 193, 204, 300, 314, 318; concept of salvation in, 55; and Nyāya systems, *see* Nyāya; pluralism of, 43, 90; school of Atomic Pluralism, 89; systematized by Kaṇāda, 44, 119
Vaiṣṇava(s): Bengal, 312, 318–9; saint, 166; sect, 54, 347
Vaiṣṇavism, 183, 194, 309; theistic school of, 324
vaiśya(s), trader-craftsmen/wealth producers and distributors: third class/caste of society, 161–4, 272, 292, 294, 362, 376, 378; expert in economics, 164; men of feeling/desires, 162, 236; professions of, 164; or *viś,* clan, 256
Vajjian republic, 255
validity, 119*ff; *external, 120; self-, 120; of a theory, 133; *see also* cognition; invalidity
Vallabha, 51, 53
value(s): *Brahman* is supreme, 169; distinction between spiritual and secular, 183; ethical/intellectual/aesthetic, 183, 207; four, 239; —fold traditional (*catur-varga*), 276; Indian, scheme of, 160; —, spirituality incorporates intellectual, 203; integration of, 59; metaphysical basis for Indian theory of, 168; moral, 157; philosophy of, 152*ff;* spiritual, 183*ff;* three, of state, 276; —fold human (*tri-varga*), 276
vānaprastha, see ascetic
Varadarāja Aiyaṅgār, *see* Raṅgāchārya, M.
varṇa: class/caste, *see* caste; color, 161; — of one's character, 162
Varuṇa, god of justice, 218, 268, 280, 286, 290, 325–6, 380
vāsanas, 198
Vasiṣṭha, Vaśiṣṭha, 254, 290
Vāsudeva, Viṣṇu is, 327
Vasugupta, 54
Vātsyāyana, 132; Commentary on Gautama's *Nyāya-sūtra,* 131, 134–5
Vedas, *viii,* 5, 7, 10, 42, 51, 54–5, 118, 175, 184, 187, 208, 217, 228, 240, 257, 259, 273, 280, 287–8, 326, 360; activistic philosophy and religion of, 207; authority of, 43, 88; books of knowledge, 157; Eternal Word, 327; four/contain four parts, 186, 267; injunctions of (three), 233, 284; sacrifices, 50, 221; scriptures, 344; three, 289; *see also names of individual Vedas;* Vedic

Vedanā, perception, 92, 94
Vedānta/Vedāntic, 7–8, 13, 16, 31–2, 53–5, 68, 120–1, 146–8, 157–8, 166, 168, 202–5, 207, 212–4, 280, 320, 324, 330; absolutist trend of, 52; Bādarāyaṇa systematized, 44, 46; ethical discipline in, 200*f;* goal of, 146, 148; interpreters of Buddhism, 158; inward realization of, 211; monistic systems, 48, 89, 187 (*see also* Advaita); —, and pluralistic, 41; non-Advaita schools, 273, 300; non-dualistic/Advaita, *see* Advaita; philosophy of, 189*ff*, 334; is —, of Upaniṣads, 51; religions of, 183, 186, 189*ff;* Śaṁkara's monistic school of, *see* Advaita; Śaṁkara; systems/schools, 51–2, 57, 306; or Uttara/Posterior Mīmāṁsā, 51; *see also* Rāmānuja
Vedānta-paribhāṣā, 135
Vedānta-sūtras, see Raṇgāchārya, M.
Vedic: concept of *Ṛta, see Ṛta;* days/period/times, 4, 261, 293, 295, 363–4, 371, 377; hymns, *see* hymns; injunction(s)/prohibitions, 50, 291; religion, 185, 338; sacrifices, 45, 50, 229; seers/philosophers, 218, 221, 242, 326, 337; systems of philosophy, 267; teaching, purpose of, 46; texts/literature, 252, 267, 278, 304, 364 (*see also under individual texts*); thought, two primary opposites in, 211; tradition, 43, 224; *see also* Veda
vegetarianism, 202
Veṇa, King, 276
vibration, (*vāyo*), 70
videha-mukti, see enlightenment
Videhas, 255
vidhi, injunction, 193
vidyā(s): knowledge, 375; — of transcendent *Brahman,* 272; sciences and arts, 308; *see also jñāna*
Vidyābhūṣaṇa, S. C., ed. and trans. Sacred Books of the Hindus, Vol. VIII, 134
Vidyāsāgara, 349
Vijayanagara: dynasty, 250; empire, 250
vijñāna, consciousness, 47–8, 193, 214; knowledge about science and arts, 203; synonym for *buddhi,* 203
Vijñānabhikṣu, 43; Commentary on the *Brahma-sūtra,* 53, 65
Vijñānavādins, 47, 184, 189, 196, 212
vijñapti-mātratā, consciousness only, 330
Vijñaptimātra, school of idealism, 102
village(s), 279, 382; aggregate of several families, 25–6; -community, 164, 255–6, 388; deities, *grāma-devatā,* 381; *grāma,* 256, 381; *pañcāyat, see pañcāyat;* Panjab, 388; ultimate unit of (ancient Hindu) society, 261–2
vinaya: discipline, 280; humility, 280
Vinaya-piṭaka, 333, 339
viññāṇa: conception, 80, 92; subconscious mind, 92–3
Vinoba, 273–4, 294
Virajas, 257
violence, dutiful, *sādhu-hiṁsā,* 284
Virāṭ, Cosmic Person, 191
virility, *rajas, see rajas*
virtue(s), 270; cultivation of cardinal, 157, 168; *dharmas, see dharma;* four, 200; practice of moral (*śīla*), 331; of self-control,

charity, compassion, 222; six main, 202; supreme, *parama-dharma,* 270
viś, clan, 256; *see also vaiśyas*
Viṣṇu, 150, 257, 326; abode of, 363; God manifest as people, 280; lotus feet of, 362; is Nārāyaṇa or Vasudeva, 327; *śakti* of, 54
Visuddhi-magga, 348, 358
viśva-darśana, cosmic/world philosophy, 170
viśva-rūpa, cosmic form, 170
Viśvāmitra, 347
vivarta-kāraṇa, 54
Vivekananda, Swami, 229–30, 285; founded Ramakrishna Mission, 229; *The Complete Works,* ed. S. Nikhilananda, 245; *Karma-Yoga,* 245
voice, theory of eternity of, 89
void: or principle of Thusness, 103; or *sūnya, see sūnya; Śūnyatā,* 114, 330
vṛṣala/vṛṣla, 259, 266
vṛttis, conscious processes, 197
vyāghāta, contradiction, 125
Vyāsa, Commentary on *Yoga-sūtra,* 318, 358
vyatireka, method of agreement in absence, 125
vyavahāra: application, 290; empirical usage, 168; judicial process, 289–90; positive law, 254
vyāvahārika: empirical plane, 299; pragmatic, 308; relative reality, 231, 273; *-sattva,* empirical reality, 222

Wach, Joachim, *Sociology of Religion,* 215
Wall, Bernard, *see* Marcel, G.
war, 226, 344, 346; righteous, 225; —(*dharma-yuddha*), 282*f;* unrighteous (*kūtā-yuddha*), 283*f*
warrior, *see kṣatriyas*
water, 48, 108, 185; is correlate of taste, 187
wave(s): of existence/life and death, *see saṁsāra;* state of being is causal, 113
way, *mārga,* 193
way/path of action, (*karma-mārga*), 194, 200, 311, 317–9, 331; *see also dharma*
way/path of knowledge, *jñāna-mārga,* 193–4, 201, 311, 317–9, 331
way-of-life-culture (*bhāvana-mārga*), 110, 115–6; *see also* life-culture
way-of-life-ideal (*aśaikṣa-mārga*), 110
way-of-life-view (*darśana-mārga*), 110–11, 116
way/path of love/devotion/respect/emotion (*bhakti-mārga*), 194, 201, 311, 317–9, 331
wayfarer, 193–4; (*mārgayāmin*), 183; man as, 193
wealth, 165, 227, 284; *artha,* 153–5, 239, 259, 276–7; —, gaining of, 375; Lord of, 380; right to, 293; production and distribution of, 164
welfare: social or human, *mu 'āmalat,* 384; or world (*loka-saṁgraha*), 375
Wells, H. G., *The Outline of History,* 297
Werkmeister, Dr., 210
West/Western, 240, 313; adventures, 382; concept of conscience, 345; contact with, 237; conventional laws in, 288; culture, 229; dark age of, 8; democracy, 286; East and, *see* East; -educated Indians, 314; education, *see* education; freedoms of, 391; jurists, 253; learning and science, 249;

legal literature, 287; man, inwardness of, 215; mind, 9, 208–9, 314; Orientalists, 228; philosophy(-ies), *vi*, 3, 10–11, 26, 38, 48–9, 52, 56–8, 104, 118, 134, 197; —, history of, 30, 44; psychology, 137, 197; religion, 185; scholars, 156, 216, 273
wheel: of creation, 218; of *karma*, 385; of law, 288*f;* of life and death, *see saṁsāra; — -cakra;* pain and pleasure rotate like, 240; *see also* causation, twelve-linked chain of
white, 162
Whitehead, A. H., 179, 209
widows: remarriage of, 361, 389; —, restrictions on, 366
will, 321; "alone is *kamma,*" 80; *apūrva,* 193; has cosmic significance, 213; free/freedom of, 80–1, 299, 315, 322; freedom lies in being without, 80; "holy," 350; ignorant, identical with perfect enlightenment, 106; moral, 350; *saṅkhāra,* motive to live, 92–3 (*see also saṅkhārā*); is self directed toward action, 188; universal, within, 61–2
Wing-tsit Chan, ed. *The Essentials of Buddhist Philosophy, see* Takakusu, J.
wisdom, 169; of ancestors, 379; philosophical/*prajñā, see* philosophic knowledge
witchcraft, 210
witness: *sākṣin,* 305; -self, *sākṣi-puruṣa,* 305
Wolf, Professor H. de, 181; *The Religious Revolt Against Reason,* 182
womb (*yoni*), 43
women: among great Upaniṣadic philosophers, 361; captured in war, 361; crimes against, 292; education of, 361; emancipation of, 228; equality of, 361; punishment of, 291; sacred, 364; status of in society, 389; *see also* widows
Woodroffe, J. G., *The Serpent Power,* 65
Woods, J. H., *see* Patañjali
Woodward, F. L., trans. *Kindred Sayings* (*Saṁyutta-nikāya*), with Introduction by Mrs. Rhys Davids, 85; trans. *Gradual Sayings* (*Aṅguttara-nikāya*), 85; trans. *The Minor Anthologies of the Pali Canon,* 85, 182
Word, *Nāda-Brahman,* 214
work: enjoyment and desire, round of, 166; is worship, 230
world, 47–52; is *anitya,* transitory, 175; is *asukha,* painful, 175, 195; is *Brahman,* 54–5, 243; identified with paradise, 106; is *Nirvāṇa,* 47, 55; of one-all, 104; "One and True," 103; philosophy (*viśva-darśana*), 59, 170; -principle, search for, 101; process, *see* process; relative, 241; is vale of soul-making/soul-finding, 193; welfare of, *loka-saṁgraha,* 375
world-system, *kalpa,* 90
World War I, 60
worship: work is, 230; primitive forms of, 184
"wreath," 100; school, 102

Yahveh, originally a local divinity, 185
yajña, see sacrifice
Yājñavalkya, 56, 87, 154, 223, 239, 253–4, 287, 290, 292
Yājñavalkya-smṛti, 251, 297
Yajur-veda, 231, 244–5, 373
Yajur-veda-saṁhitā, 247

yama, control/restraint, 141, 339
Yama, 160, 380; god of death, 218; the punisher, 257
Yamakami, Sōger, 47–8; *Systems of Buddhistic Thought*, 64
Yaudheyas, 278
yoga/Yoga, 16, 26, 31–2, 48, 52, 89–90, 123, 136*ff*, 198, 204–5, 280, 300, 305, 318; aim of, 139; *bhakti-, see bhakti-yoga;* cognate with *yoke*, 166; concept of salvation in, 55; discipline(s) of, 139, 233, 339; dualism of, 43; *jñāna-, see jñāna-yoga;* Kṛṣṇa, lord of, 225; Patañjali systematized, 31, 44, 123; practice of, 235; *rāja-, see rāja-yoga;* is skillfulness in action (*yogaḥ karmasu kausálam*), 211; or spiritual culture, 225; that which unites, 184; theistic, 7; as union with ultimate reality, 136, 166
Yoga-bhāṣya, 277
Yoga-darśana, 357–8
Yoga-sūtra, 40, 339; Vyāsa's Commentary on, 318
Yogācāra Buddhists: meditation, Buddhist, 89; subjective idealism of, 121
yogī virtues, five old, 391; *see also ahimsā; apari-graha; asteya; brahmacarya; satya*
yogī(s), *viii*, 29, 137, 139*ff*, 227, 354, 383
yogin, viii, 29, 35, 39
Yudhiṣṭhira, King, 163, 256, 259, 294, 345, 347

Zeller, Edward, 287; *Philosophie der Griechen*, trans. Oswald J. Reichel, 297
Zen: Buddhism, 215; discipline, 179; foundation of, 89